RESEARCHES
INTO
THE NATURE AND AFFINITY
OF
ANCIENT AND HINDU MYTHOLOGY

BY

LIEUTENANT COLONEL VANS KENNEDY,

OF THE BOMBAY MILITARY ESTABLISHMENT.

GYAN

Published by

Gyan Publishing House
5, Ansari Road
Daryaganj, New Delhi-110002
Phone: 011-47034999, 9811692060
E-mail: books@gyanbooks.com

Distribution Network
gyanbooks.com
India, USA, Canada, UK, Australia, France

ISBN : 978-81-212-2640-0 (HB)
First Published, 1831

2nd Impression 2021

Printed at: Gyan Press, Delhi.

Researches
into
The Nature and Affinity of Ancient and Hindu Mythology
Author: Lieutenant Colonel Vans Kennedy

RESEARCHES

INTO

THE NATURE AND AFFINITY

OF

ANCIENT AND HINDU MYTHOLOGY.

BY

LIEUTENANT COLONEL VANS KENNEDY,

OF THE BOMBAY MILITARY ESTABLISHMENT.

Η, ετι βελτιον οιμαι, τον μεν λεγοντα αφες, ειτε χειρων ειτε αμεινων ειη· τα δε λεγομενα σκοπει, ειτε αληθη ειτε ψευδη λεγεται, προθυμως ανεγειρας την διανοιαν.

Vel potius mitte, quis sit qui loquatur, inferiorne an præstantior; quæ autem dicuntur, et vere an falso affirmentur, prompto et experrecto ingenio considera.

Jamblichus de Mysteriis, sect i. chap. 1.

LONDON:

PRINTED FOR LONGMAN, REES, ORME, BROWN, AND GREEN,

PATERNOSTER-ROW.

1831.

> Great respect is certainly due to men of learning, and a proper regard should be paid to their memory; but they forfeit much of this esteem when they misapply their talents, and put themselves to these shifts to support an hypothesis. They may smile at their reveries, and plume themselves upon their ingenuity in finding out such expedients, but no good can possibly arise from it, for the whole is a fallacy and imposition.
>
> *Bryant's Anal. of Anc. Myth.*, vol. iv. p. 189

PREFACE.

In composing my former work on the *Origin and Affinity of Languages* it naturally occurred to me that the argument which I maintained in it would have been greatly corroborated, could I have at the same time evinced that the original seat of the mythology which prevails in India at the present day was Babylonia; and that it had been thence communicated to Asia Minor, from which country the Pelasgi had, in the course of their migrations, introduced it into Thracia, Greece, Latium, and Etruria. But, when I considered this subject, it appeared to me, that it was of much too extensive a nature to admit of its being treated incidentally; and that, even for discussing it satisfactorily, the requisite materials were not available. For, though much has been written on ancient mythology, authors have been so fond of hypothesis, that it becomes impossible to ascertain from their works what is the precise nature of the information respecting it, that is really entitled to credit; while, on the contrary, so little has been published respecting the Hindu religion, and that so erroneously, that it was necessary, in order to exhibit a correct view of it, to depend solely on Sanscrit authority. Having, however, at length examined both these subjects in such a manner as will, in their discussion, prevent me, I believe, from falling into any mistakes of importance, I now venture to lay the following Researches before the public.

The affinity which appears to exist amongst the polytheisms of India, Egypt, Greece, and Italy, has already attracted considerable attention: but it will perhaps be admitted, that no correct opinion can be formed on this point, unless just notions, with respect to the principles upon which ancient mythology was founded, have been previously acquired. Unfortunately, however, all authors, whether ancient or modern, who have attempted to explain these principles, have rested their reasoning on gratuitous assumptions, and not on facts; and, in later times, it cannot but excite surprise, to observe the paucity of facts on which the most voluminous systems have been erected.* In instituting, therefore, a comparison between ancient and Hindu mythology, which of these systems ought to be preferred? or, is it not most probable that they should be all equally rejected? But I may not be a competent judge to decide on the merits of these hypotheses, because I must confess that I am one of those persons to whom this reproach of Dupuis applies with the greatest justice:—"Si les érudits à cerveau étroit trouvent notre marche trop libre, parce qu'elle n'est point pesante; nous ne chercherons point à nous justifier auprès d'eux, puisque la nature, en leur refusant le génie, les a par la même rendus incapables de le reconnoître partout où il se montre dans l'antiquité, à la hauteur de laquelle ils ne peuvent s'élever."† For I cannot but think that, however necessary imagination and genius may be in works of fiction, they are altogether misemployed in antiquarian and historical researches. I have endeavoured, therefore, in Chapters II., III., and IV. of this work, to ascertain the real grounds on which all reasoning on the subject of ancient mythology ought to depend; but the authentic materials adapted for this purpose are so scanty, that I cannot flatter myself that this attempt has been attended with much success.

The principal object, however, of these RESEARCHES is to exhibit as correct a view as possible of the Hindu religion; and, if I have not failed in attaining this object, the reader will be able to form his own opinion with respect to the affinity which exists between it and the religious systems of antiquity. But I am not certain that the manner in which I have illustrated this subject will be generally approved of; for, being convinced that, with whatever care summaries and abstracts

* For the hypotheses on this subject, prevalent amongst the ancients, I may refer to Diodorus Siculus and Cicero; and, amongst the moderns, I allude particularly to these works:—Vossius, De Origine et de Progressu Idololatriæ, 2 vols. fol.; Barrier, Mythologie, ou les Fables expliquées par l'Histoire, 3 vols. 4to; Dupuis, Origine de tous les Cultes, 3 vols. 4to; Bryant's Analysis of Ancient Mythology, and Faber's Origin of Pagan Idolatry, 3 vols. 4to, each; and Professor Creuzer's Symbolik und Mythologie, 2d edit., 6 vols. 8vo.

† Origine des Cultes, tom. i. p. 304.

may be made, they never faithfully convey the precise meaning of the original text, I have deemed it most advisable to quote at length the different passages of the Sanscrit works on which my remarks are founded. Such, also, was the only mode by which I could satisfactorily evince the justness of the grounds on which I have controverted the speculations of former writers, and the consonancy of my own statements with those opinions respecting their religion which have been entertained by the Hindus themselves from the remotest antiquity. It has hence been impossible to avoid repetition altogether; but, as the quotations are taken from different works, they may be considered as so many distinct testimonies to the point which they are adduced to elucidate.

It is now more than forty years since Sir W. Jones observed, — "Since Europeans are indebted to the Dutch for almost all they know of Arabic, and to the French for all they know of Chinese, let them now receive from our nation the first accurate knowledge of Sanscrit, and of the valuable works composed in it; but, *if they wish to form a correct idea of Indian religion and literature, let them begin with forgetting all that has been written on the subject, by ancients or moderns, before the publication of the* GITA."* But this very just remark seems to be entirely disregarded, and elaborate systems, with respect to the religion of India, continue to be founded on works, the bare perusal of which might alone evince that they were totally undeserving of being considered as competent authority. In the Beitrage, for instance, of J. G. Rhode, published at Berlin in 1819, that author enters into a discussion (in p. 73.) respecting what the book was which Holwell intended by the name *Chartah Bhade Shastah;* and yet the slightest acquaintance with the subject must have at once shown that these words should have been correctly written, *Chatur Veda Shastra*, and that the *Veda* and the *Shastra* were two distinct branches of the sacred literature of the Hindus. M. Rhode might, therefore, have spared the expression of his surprise that Mr. Colebrooke should not have noticed this pretended work in his Essay on the Vedas. But it is really

* Sir W. Jones's Works, vol. i. p. 363. The dedication to the Gita is dated 19th November, 1784.

astonishing that a person, who professes to have cultivated Oriental literature for twenty years, should not have immediately perceived that Holwell's account of the creation and the fall of the angels * must have been written by a Mohammedan; for the very expression on which M. Rhode lays so much stress, *Be, and it was*, an expression so frequently quoted by Mohammedan authors, should alone have apprized him that such an account could not have been written by a Hindu.† It seems, also, inexplicable why any attention should still be given to accounts professedly obtained through the medium of the Persian language, or of conversation with uninformed natives, when correct information, immediately derived from Sanscrit authority, is available in the unquestionably correct translations of Sir W. Jones, Mr. Colebrooke, and, in general, of Mr. Ward.

I observe, however, that the works which have been most depended upon, in speculations respecting the Hindu religion, are the Oupnekhat of Anquetil du Perron, the Systema Brahmanicum and the other writings of Fr. Paulinus a S. Bartholomeo, the Mythologie des Indous, composed from the MSS. of Colonel Polier, and the Asiatic Researches.

With respect to the Oupnekhat, it must be obvious that it is written in such a barbarous and unintelligible style, as to render impossible the deriving from it of any correct notions respecting the abstruse metaphysical discussions which are contained in the original work. It must also be evident, that no person could have properly translated a work of this kind without being acquainted with the Sanscrit language, and with the philosophy and religion of the Hindus; and yet Anquetil appears to have been not only ignorant of these indispensable requisites, but even to have possessed a very inadequate knowledge of Persian. It has hence necessarily followed, that his pretended translation differs so materially from the original, that, in

* The converting of *Mahesh-Asura* into Satan must appear somewhat ludicrous to the Sanscrit scholar.

† I observe, however, that this account of Holwell is quoted in a work recently published in Paris by M. Marlés; so that it seems destined that every erroneous opinion respecting the Hindu religion, which has been ever published, is to be perpetually reproduced.

comparing the two together, it is almost impossible to recognise that the one is intended to be a translation of the other. How far, indeed, this striking discordancy may be attributable to the Persian version, I cannot judge, as I have not a copy of it. But Sir W. Jones has remarked, — "Of this book I procured, with the assistance of Colonel Polier, a complete copy, *corrected by a learned Rajah*, named Anandaram, with whom the Colonel was very intimate; but, though the sublime and majestic features of the original were discernible in parts through the folds of the Persian drapery, yet the Sanscrit names were so barbarously written, and the additions of the translator has made the work so deformed, that I resolved to postpone a regular perusal of it till I could compare it with the Sanscrit original." *

Had, however, the Systema Brahmanicum of Fr. Paulinus corresponded with the lofty pretensions so unhesitatingly announced in the address *ad Lectorem*, it would have been presumptuous to offer to the public another work on the same subject; for that writer, among other equally modest observations, remarks, — "Ad hoc munus rite obeundum, me etiam tacente, jam intelligis, non solum linguæ Indicæ exquisitum studium, non solum jurium et consuetudinum distinctam notionem, sed etiam in recondita Gentilicæ religionis mysteria sedulam disquisitionem, in libros Indicos acre examen, atque diligentem animadversionem necessariam fuisse. . . . . Duæ itaque potissimum sunt causæ, quæ me ad hoc opus elucubrandum impulerunt. Prima: ut ex hoc classico Brahmanico codice *nugigeruli, morologi, ardeliones, arioli, linguæ Samscrdamicæ imperiti viatores Indici, Angli et Galli, aliique temerarii Indicarum rerum veteratores corrigantur, refellantur, castigentur, somnia denique eorum et ineptiæ, quibus totam repleverunt Europam, pellantur et dissipentur*." But when this wonderful work, which is to produce such remarkable effects, is examined, it exhibits the most convincing proofs

* Sir W. Jones's Works, vol. vi. p. 415. Sir William Jones has also observed, in the preface to his Translation of the Institutes of Manu, — "The Persian translation of Manu, like all others from the Sanscrit into that language, is a rude intermixture of the text, loosely rendered, with some old or new comment, and often with the crude notions of the translator; and though it expresses the general sense of the original, yet it swarms with errors, imputable partly to haste, and partly to ignorance."

of the writer's very superficial acquaintance with the Sanscrit language and literature. Of this, no more unquestionable evidence can be required, than that all the observations and arguments of Fr. Paulinus are founded on one single work, and that a COMMON VOCABULARY, which is put into the hands of every learner of Sanscrit, but which he, nevertheless, thus magnificently describes: — "Unicus et solus liber *Amarasinha* ingentem et pene infinitum veteris Indorum philosophiæ, astronomiæ, et mythologiæ acervum detegit; et hic liber, qui certe ab omnibus maximi habetur, antiquam Indorum religionem præclare describit atque explicat." * This vocabulary, however, like all other vocabularies, contains words only; and it therefore neither describes nor explains the philosophy and religion of the Hindus.

But it may be proper to adduce a few instances, from this work, of the writer's ignorance of the most common words and most common topics, which occur in the Sanscrit language and mythology. For, under the names of the different deities, he thus explains *Abjayoni*, *matrix nubium*; but it signifies *lotos-produced*, and refers to the origin of Brahma from the lotos that sprang from the navel of Vishnu. *Garudadhwaja* is explained, *quia Vishnu vehitur acquila Garuda dicta;* but *dhwaja*, which occurs in the Amara Kosha, signifies a banner. *Pashupati* is explained *bovis maritus;* and that this strange explanation should not be mistaken, it is added, *ubi notandum* pashu *bovem et vaccam significare: pashu*, however, here means a *living being*. *Kapalabhrit* (*calvam tenens*) is translated *horridis et erectis capillis;* hence evincing that the writer did not know that Shiva was thus named in consequence of bearing in his hand the head of Brahma, which he had cut off. *Tripurantika* is thus rendered, *tres urbes seu regiones inhabitans;* which betrays an ignorance of one of the most common Hindu legends, the destruction of the Tripura-Asuras by Shiva, whence he was called their *antaka* or destroyer. *Vrishadwaja* (*he whose banner is a bull*) is thus explained, *pluviam, tempestatem, fulmen, et tonitru producens.* But it seems that Fr. Paulinus did not even understand the very book which he considers to be of so much importance; for he joins these two distinct words, *Vak*, *Vani*, two names of Saraswati, and

* Systema Brahmanicum, p. 113.

signifying *speech*, and then thus explains them, *linguam seu verba regens.* It would, however, be endless to produce all the instances of Sanscrit words misunderstood, and translated at mere random, which occur in this work.

With respect, also, to the diligent and accurate enquiries into the mysteries of the Hindu religion, of which this author boasts, it is only necessary to observe, that no person could be more ignorant of them than one who asserts, as he does (p. 303.), that Shri Rama and Parasu Rama were one and the same incarnation of Vishnu; and (p. 139.) that Shri Rama was the brother of Krishna, and born from the star Rohini. Nor is it possible to understand how such a passage as the following was not sufficient to discredit entirely the authority of its writer: — "Libri, qui de his incarnationibus Indicis agunt, hoc ordine recensentur; Matsyapuranam vel Matsyakhandam, Kurmapuranam vel Kurmakhandam, Varahapuranam vel Varahakhandam, Narasinhapuranam, Ayodhyakhandam, Aranyakandam, Yudhakandam, Balakhandam. *Hi libri omnes uno libro continentur, qui Mahabharatam dicitur.*" *

The work of Madame Polier I have not been able to procure; but, judging from extracts from it, which I have read, it appears to abound in the grossest misrepresentations of Hindu mythology. But, as I have not perused it, I shall only quote the following passage, which occurs in the Symbolik und Mythologie of Professor Creuzer, illustrated by a plate, and which is thus translated by M. Guigniaut: — "Bhavani, joyeuse d'etre créé, exprimait sa joie par des sauts et des bonds; mais pendant qu'elle dansait ainsi avec beaucoup de mouvement, tout à coup s'echapperent de son sein trois œufs, d'ou sortirent les trois dieux." † But such an account of the origin of Brahma, Vishnu, and Shiva, I have never either heard in conversation, or met with in any Sanscrit work. It is also singular, that Professor Creuzer should have adopted it, when he had just before correctly observed, according to

* Systema Brahmanicum, p. 313. I need scarcely observe that the first four works here mentioned are four of the eighteen Purans, that the Bala, Ayodhya, and Aranya Khands are the first three books of the Ramayanam; and that there are no such contents in the Mahabharat. The books even of the Mahabharat are named *Parvas,* and not *Khands.*

† Religions de l'Antiquité, tom. i. p. 151. note.

M. Guigniaut's translation, "Cet être éternel, pour créer le monde à sa propre image, se révéla d'abord comme Brahma ou créateur; puis comme Vichnou, conservateur et sauveur; et enfin comme Siva, destructeur et renovateur."* The whole account, also, of Brahma's incarnations, given by Polier, rest on no authority whatever, and are therefore unentitled to the slightest degree of credit.

It must, however, appear singular, that the Asiatic Society has contributed so little to the elucidation of Hindu mythology; and that, in sixteen volumes of its Researches, the only papers which occur on this subject, with the exception of those of Lieutenant-Colonel Wilford, should be the Essay on the Gods of Greece, Italy, and India, by Sir W. Jones, and another one on the Origin of the Hindu Religion, by Mr. Paterson. But neither of these Essays is a safe guide; because the latter is much too hypothetical, and the former was written shortly after Sir W. Jones had arrived in this country, and, consequently, before he had formed correct notions respecting the Hindu religion. Yet this Essay presents a correct and elegant description of those remarkable coincidences that seem to exist between ancient and Hindu mythology, which must attract the attention of every classical scholar. But had Sir W. Jones ever resumed this subject, and more fully investigated it, he would have been convinced that these coincidences were in many instances merely apparent; for it would be as impossible to find in India the satyrs of Bacchus and the symbols of Rhea, as the castrated priests of that goddess. The remarks, however, which I am obliged to offer on the papers of Lieutenant-Colonel Wilford, would extend this Preface beyond the usual limits, and I have therefore placed them in the Appendix (A).

But the correct and learned Essays of Mr. Colebrooke are of a very dissimilar character; and it is hence much to be regretted that his attention was principally directed to the religious ceremonies and theology of the Brahmans: for I am inclined to think that, had he been better acquainted with the Purans, the view which he has given of the Hindu religion would have been very different. I am par-

* Religions de l'Antiquité, tom. i. p. 150.

ticularly at a loss to understand on what grounds these remarks have been made: — "I am myself," observes Mr. Colebrooke, "inclined to adopt an opinion supported by many learned Hindus, who consider the celebrated *Shri Bhagavata* as the work of a grammarian, supposed to have lived about six hundred years ago.* Vopadeva, the real author of the Shri Bhagavata, has endeavoured to reconcile all the sects of Hindus, by reviving the doctrine of Vyasa. He recognises all the deities, but as subordinate to the Supreme Being, or rather as attributes or manifestations of God: *a new sect has thus been formed, and is denominated from that modern Purana.*" † The composition, however, of this Puran only six hundred years ago by a grammarian of Bengal, and its having notwithstanding in such a short period obtained, without the aid of typography, general celebrity thoughout a country which comprehends an area of more than a million of square miles, are such improbable circumstances, as to require, for entitling them to the least credit, the clearest and most unquestionable evidence. The conjecture, also, respecting Vopadeva's intention, is disproved by the simple perusal of the Bhagavat; as the sole scope and object of that work are to evince that Vishnu is the Supreme Being. Nor have I ever heard of the new sect denominated from this Puran, the origin of which from this cause seems obviously impossible. Because the Bhagavat is universally acknowledged to be the principal authority on which the doctrines of the *Vaishnava* sect depend; and these doctrines are in every respect essentially the same as those contained in the Upanishads, with this only exception, that Vishnu is every where introduced in the place of Brahma or Shiva. I have been, therefore, obliged, in the course of the following work, to differ in opinion on some material points from Mr. Colebrooke; but, for the freedom of my remarks, I trust that, in the investigation of truth, no apology can be requisite: and I can with sincerity observe that, had it not been for Mr. Colebrooke's invaluable writings, it is most probable that I should have been unable to detect the errors into which I think he has fallen, and which seem necessarily to proceed from his having merely dis-

* Asiatic Researches, vol. viii. p. 467. † Ibid., vol. vii. p. 280.

cussed this subject in detached essays, and not in a connected and systematic work.

Since the publication, also, of the GITA, two English authors only, who have resided in India, have treated of the Hindu religion; Major Moor, in his Hindu Pantheon, and Mr. Ward, in his View of the History, Literature, and Religion of the Hindus. Of these works, the first, and particularly the plates, exhibit an excellent view of the external appearance of Hindu mythology, and such as conveys all the information on the subject which a person not interested in its fuller investigation can require: but there is too much justice in these remarks contained in the Edinburgh Review (vol. xvii. p. 314.):— "Mr. Moor would certainly have produced an amusing and instructive work, if he had contented himself with subjoining to each engraving a concise account of the mythological adventures, or of the character represented; with an explanation of the instruments and emblems exhibited. But, not satisfied with this merit (which we should have prized highly), he has thought it necessary to fill nearly 450 pages with extracts from the Asiatic Researches, a work of various merit and unequal claims to confidence: here we have the accuracy and erudition of Mr. Colebrooke, mixed with the often fanciful, but always ingenious, conjectures of Major Wilford; and the brilliant, but sometimes uncertain, speculations of Sir W. Jones."

But it is scarcely possible to characterise Mr. Ward's work; for it is true in substance, and yet, from its being saturated with the erroneous and prejudiced notions of the writer, it is calculated to convey a most distorted and fallacious representation of the Hindu philosophy and religion. For instance, the account of the Hindu duties contained in the first volume is quite accurate; but, by the introduction of the author's own remarks, and by his selection of such quotations only from Sanscrit works as tended to expose the abomination of idolatry, he has given a most inaccurate view of the general nature of this mythology. The mistakes, however, which he has committed in treating of the Hindu philosophy and theology, may perhaps be justly ascribed to his not being accustomed to metaphysical research and disquisition. But, notwithstanding these defects, this work contains so much valuable information, that it must be of the greatest utility to every Sanscrit scholar; and it seems, therefore, not to have met on the Continent with that attention to which it is so deservedly entitled.

It is, however, far from my intention to induce the reader to conclude, from these remarks, that all which has been published respecting the Hindu religion is erroneous. On the contrary, the accounts already given of its leading principles, and of the characters and actions of its deities, are in general sufficiently correct; nor could it well be otherwise, since the Hindu mythology is of too simple and obvious a nature, and too devoid of mysteries or symbols, to oppose any difficulty to its accurate investigation. But it is to the conclusions which have been deduced from these circumstances, and to the systems which have been erected upon them, that I object. For the accounts hitherto published consist entirely of detached extracts and isolated particulars, the bearing of which to each other has never been explained by any competent authority; and, consequently, every hypothesis formed from them must necessarily be erroneous, because it rests on an incomplete induction from well-established facts. This, however, seems to be considered of little consequence, for M. Guigniaut has actually observed: — "Nous avons fait et nous avons du, dans notre dessein, faire un emploi beaucoup plus étendu des ouvrages Allemands que des ouvrages Anglais, pour notre travail sur la religion de l' Inde. Ces derniers sont cependant d'une haute importance, bien que composés la plupart dans un point de vue étroit et dans un esprit peu philosophique. La route tracée par W. Jones, par Robertson, par le savant Maurice, a été abandonnée de bonne heure en Angleterre." * That is, in plain English, that hypothesis is preferable to fact. But I may presume that every person, who wishes to obtain information with respect to the religious opinions entertained by the Hindus, will be inclined to place greater confidence in the accounts given of them on the authority of well-informed natives and of Sanscrit works, than upon the speculations of even ingenious and learned men, who are personally

* Religions de l'Antiquité, tom. i. p. 598. note.

unacquainted with India, and with the Sanscrit language and literature.

In that part, therefore, of these RESEARCHES which relates to the Hindu religion, my remarks, however much they may differ from the opinions of former writers, rest almost entirely on the authority of Sanscrit works, particularly the *Upanishads*, the *Purans*, the *Ramayan*, and the *Mahabharat;* and the few instances in which I have availed myself of oral information, are distinctly pointed out. I have neither proposed nor attempted to support any hypothesis on this subject; and I have adduced, I believe, such a number of quotations from the Upanishads and Purans, as will render the correctness of my statements unquestionable. These quotations, also, are faithfully * translated, and the reader is thus presented with the *ipsissima verba*, which are not only employed in the discussion of Hindu mythology and theology by Sanscrit writers, but even by every well-informed Hindu at the present day, and he is thus enabled to deduce from them his own conclusions. It may, however, be proper to observe that, if the translations from the Sanscrit of the numerous passages cited in the following pages be critically examined, it is requisite that the critic should recollect that Sanscrit manuscripts still remain in precisely the same state as that in which Greek and Latin manuscripts were found on the revival of letters; and that, consequently, it is more than probable that what he may consider to be a mistranslation, an omission, or an interpolation, is merely a difference in the reading of the manuscripts which have been consulted. I must, likewise, request that Sanscrit words may be allowed to retain the signification which is given to them in this country, for in the Radices Sanscritæ of M. Rosen, under the root स्था, I observe this strange explanation of this verb when compounded with the preposition प्रति "incedere, calcare: अश्मापि याति देवत्वं महद्भिः सुप्रतिष्ठितः *Lapis quoque adipiscitur*

* By *faithfully*, however, I do not intend a perfectly literal translation; for my object has been to convey the sense, and not the verbal meaning, of the original, which I have sometimes compressed very considerably, in order to avoid the repetitions which so frequently occur in Sanscrit works of a religious character. But I have inserted nothing extraneous, and all that is given as translated is actually contained in the original.

divinitatem, a religiosis hominibus bene calcatus." And in a note, "Sic transtuli, jubente BOPPIO, originariam retinens vocis significationem. WILKINSIUS: *Even a stone, when set up and consecrated by the great, attaineth divinity.* JONESIUS: *The stone, when consecrated by holy men, acquires divine honour.* Ultimæ interpretationis patrocinium nuper suscepit BOHLENIUS; cui præterea WILSONUS adstipulatur, radici nostræ significationem tribuens; *to be erected for holy purposes, to be consecrated.*" But I can assure M. Bopp and M. Rosen that in India, as in all other countries, *the being trampled upon* is considered to be a mark of disrespect, and not respect; and that, consequently, no stone could there acquire *divinity* (!) by being *bene calcatus.* *

With respect to the reception which the present work may meet with, any remark seems unnecessary: for I may presume, that, if it at all tends to illustrate the subject discussed in it, its imperfections will be overlooked; and that correctness or elegance of composition will not be expected from one who left school before he was sixteen years of age, and who has had since but few opportunities of remedying a defective education. But I may be permitted to advert to a circumstance, which, though entirely of a personal nature, will in a great measure account for that indifference to literary pursuits with which the English residents in India are not unfrequently reproached. The late governor of Bombay, appreciating the zeal with which I had devoted myself to the study of Oriental languages and literature from my first arrival in this country, conferred upon me a civil situation †; and that I was not altogether undeserving of the patronage of Mr. Elphinstone, is perhaps sufficiently evinced by my papers in the Transactions of the Bombay Literary Society, by my former work, and by the present one; but, some months after he had resigned the government, I was deprived of this situation; and, that such was the order of the Court of Directors, was the only reason officially assigned

* This verse, also, संख्यास्ति यावती देहे हितोरोमसंभवंतोप्यपराधावै यांतिष्ठलिंगप्रति या must, according to this singular interpretation, be thus translated: *Were one's sins as numerous as the hairs of his body, they would be all expiated by* TRAMPLING UPON A LINGAM. The absurdity of which must be too evident to require remark.

† Maratha and Guzrati Translator of the Regulations of Government.

to me for its abolition.* The late Dr. Leyden, however, has very justly observed, in a letter to one of his correspondents,—"You know, when I left Scotland, I had determined, at all events, to become a furious Orientalist, *nemini secundus;* but I was not aware of the difficulty. I found the expense of native teachers would prove almost insurmountable to a mere assistant-surgeon, whose pay is seldom equal to his absolutely necessary expenses; and, besides that, it was necessary to form a library of MSS. at a most terrible expense, in every language to which I should apply, if I intended to proceed beyond a mere smattering." † These difficulties, resulting from the *res angusta domi*, must be experienced by every military man in this country who undertakes such pursuits, and by them have I too frequently found the researches which I contemplated impeded and obstructed. But the civil appointment, which I obtained in February 1822, relieved me from such embarrassments; and that I did not omit to avail myself of the facilities which it afforded, is perhaps attested by the compilation of a Maratha Dictionary; the revision, or rather composition, of a Maratha and Hindustani Grammar; and the acquisition of a competent knowledge of the Sanscrit language. Its abolition, however, has deprived me of these advantages; and necessarily compels me, though I have finished this work, as I was then engaged in it, to relinquish a favourite pursuit, and to leave the antiquities, literature, philosophy, and religion of India to be in future illustrated by those whose constitutions have not been affected by a twenty-nine years' residence in this country, nor their minds depressed, and literary ardour abated, by disappointment and discouragement.

* I have, however, understood that it was abolished in consequence of economical retrenchments. But the expense incurred by this situation was only 900*l.* per annum; and consequently, as its duties must still be performed in some manner or other, the saving effected was a mere trifle to government, though of much consequence to me.

† Dr. Leyden's Life, in Scott's Miscellaneous Works, vol. iv. p. 201.

Bombay, March 1. 1829.

*** In the following pages, in the Sanscrit proper names and words written in the Roman character, the diphthongs and vowels are to be pronounced as in Italian, and the consonants as in English, with the exception of *g*, which is always to be pronounced hard, its soft sound being represented by *j*. As a uniform mode of writing, in Roman characters, Sanscrit neuter nouns, which end in the singular in *am* and in the plural in *ani*, has not been yet adopted, it may also be proper to observe that I have in general omitted the final syllable of the singular, and that I have therefore written, for instance, *puran*, and not *purana*, which is incorrect, nor *puranam*, which would be in conformity to the Sanscrit.

CONTENTS.

RESEARCHES

INTO

THE NATURE AND AFFINITY

OF

ANCIENT AND HINDU MYTHOLOGY.

CHAPTER I.

ON THE ORIGIN OF IDOLATRY.

HUME has remarked, that "it is a matter of fact incontestable, that about seventeen hundred years ago all mankind were polytheists. The doubtful or sceptical principles of a few philosophers, or the theism, and that not entirely pure, of one or two nations, form no objection worth regarding. Behold, then, the clear testimony of history: the farther we mount up into antiquity, the more do we find mankind plunged into polytheism; no marks, no symptoms of any more perfect religion. The most ancient records of the human race still present us with that system as the popular and established creed. The north, the south, the east, the west, give their unanimous testimony to the same fact. What can be opposed to so full an evidence?" * But in opposition to this opinion it may be observed, that there are sufficient indications, both in tradition and history, to place it beyond a doubt, that all systems of religion were of a simpler and purer nature in their origin than in their subsequent progress; and

* Hume's Essays, vol. ii. p. 408.

that in all of them there are the evident traces of a primitive belief in the unity and omnipotence of one Supreme Being. * It is equally incontestable, that in all religious reformations the avowed object has been to remove all extraneous additions and innovations, and to restore the ancient faith to its pristine purity.

Had, also, polytheism been the primitive religion of mankind, it would seem most probable that it would, under all changes, have preserved some unquestionable indications of its origin, which would have obviated every difference of opinion on the subject. But, on the contrary, all systems which have been proposed for the explanation of this point, are in the highest degree contradictory and unsatisfactory; for they all rest, however they may differ in other respects, on a gratuitous assumption and a self-evident contradiction: because it is assumed that mankind remained without any knowledge of a Deity until they intuitively became acquainted with it; or until some persons of influence arose and introduced amongst them the notion of divinity, and devised the adoration of one or more celestial and immortal beings. But, in the former of these cases, if such knowledge be intuitive, there can be no reason for delaying the necessary effect of this intuition, and for supposing that man remained for any period of time after his creation without some form of religion; and, in the latter, in what manner did those, who first instructed mankind in the belief of God, themselves acquire the conviction of his existence and divine nature? Locke is of opinion, that " the existence of a God reason clearly makes

* Cudworth remarks:—" And by this time we think it is sufficiently evident that the Pagans (at least after Christianity), though they asserted many gods, they calling all understanding beings superior to men by that name, yet they acknowledged one *supreme, omnipotent, and only unmade Deity*. But because it is very possible that some may still suspect all this to have been nothing else but a refinement and interpolation of Paganism, after that Christianity had appeared upon the stage; or a kind of mangonisation of it, to render it more vendible and plausible, the better able to defend itself and bear up against the assaults of Christianity, whilst, in the mean time, the genuine doctrine of the Pagans was far otherwise: although the contrary hereunto might sufficiently appear from what hath been already declared; yet, however, for the fuller satisfaction of the more strongly prejudiced, we shall, by an historical deduction, made from the most ancient time all along downwards, demonstrate that the doctrine of the greatest Pagan polytheists, as well before Christianity as after it, was always the same—that, besides their many gods, *there was one supreme, omnipotent, and only unmade God.*" —*Intellectual System*, book i. chap. 4. sect. 15, 16.

known to us;"* and farther observes — "Though God has given us no innate ideas of himself; though he has stamped no original characters on our minds wherein we may read his being; yet, having furnished us with those faculties our minds are endowed with, he hath not left himself without a witness, since we have sense, perception, and reason, and cannot want a clear proof of him as long as we carry ourselves about us." But he admits, at the same time, that, "though this be the most obvious truth that reason discovers, and though its evidence be (if I mistake not) equal to mathematical certainty, yet it requires thought and attention, and the mind must apply itself to a regular deduction of it from some part of our intuitive knowledge, or else we shall be as uncertain and ignorant of this as of other propositions which are in themselves capable of clear demonstrations."† And, consequently, it must be self-evident that it could not be by reason and deduction that the rude and uncivilised tribes, amongst whom such a belief has prevailed, could first acquire a knowledge of the existence of a God; and that it is equally improbable that, in such a state of barbarism and ignorance, any individuals could have arisen who were capable of elaborating conceptions totally unknown to those with whom alone they were in the habit of associating.

The deification, also, of any object necessarily *presupposes* some conception, however imperfect, of a Divine Being; and the question, therefore, obviously regards not the object which may have been first selected for this purpose, but the manner in which such a conception could have originated. Yet all hypotheses respecting the origin of idolatry, except such as deduce it from the history of the Hebrews, overlook this essential question, and represent mankind as remaining for some time after their creation in a state of irreligion, until they were at length induced, by various considerations, to acknowledge the existence of a God. But, if all ideas originate from perception and reflection, it becomes impossible to understand how man could ever form the slightest notion of spirit independent of matter; or of self-existence, immutability, eternity, and the other attributes which are necessarily implied in the conception of a supreme and self-existent

* Human Understanding, book iv. chap. 11. sect. 1. † Ibid., chap. 10. sect. 1.

Being; because, arguing from his own formation, as Locke recommends, or even from a contemplation of the universe, man must necessarily conclude that, admitting the existence of spirit, it cannot subsist unless united to matter; and all that he beholds, as well as the ideas which arise in his own mind, convinces him that all which is must have had a beginning, that it is continually changing, and that it will at length cease to be. Whence, also, could man acquire, in this world of ignorance and misery, any conception of an all-good and an all-wise Being? The most learned men have attempted to answer these objections, and to demonstrate the existence of God; but the weakness of their arguments must be evident, from none of these alleged demonstrations having ever been generally admitted, and the consequent endeavours of succeeding writers to render the requisite proof more clear and conclusive.*

The hypotheses, therefore, respecting the commencement of idolatry all labour under the obvious defect of assigning inadequate reasons for its origin, or of merely describing the effects instead of explaining the cause which produced them. Eusebius, no doubt, is correct in ob-

* Lucretius, however, in the following verses, seems to think that the origin of the belief in the existence of God, so universally prevalent amongst mankind, may be easily explained:

Nunc quæ causa deûm per magnas numina genteis
Pervolgarit, et ararum compleverit urbeis,
* * * * *
Non ita difficile 'st rationem reddere verbis.
Quippe etenim jam tum divûm mortalia sæcla
Egregias animo facies vigilante videbant,
Et magis in somnis mirando corporis auctu.
Præterea, cœli rationes ordine certo,
* * * * *
Et varia annorum cernebant tempora verti;
Non poterant quibus id fieret cognoscere causis:
Ergo perfugium sibi habebant omnia divis
Tradere, et illorum nutu facere omnia flecti.
In cœloque deûm sedes, et templa locârunt,
Per cœlum volvi quia sol et luna videntur. Lib. v. v. 1160—1188.

In another place he observes:—

Quippe ita formido mortaleis continet omneis,
Quod multa in terris fieri, cœloque tuentur,
Quorum operum causas nulla ratione videre
Possunt, ac fieri divino numine rentur. Lib. i. v. 152—155.

serving that "the first and most ancient of men neither constructed temples nor erected images, as they were unacquainted with painting, carving, and sculpture, and even architecture, as it might be easily proved. Nor was there amongst them the slightest memorial of those who were afterwards called gods and heroes; neither of Jupiter, nor Saturn, nor Neptune, nor Apollo, nor Juno, nor Minerva, nor Bacchus, nor of those innumerable male and female deities, who were afterwards worshipped by the Greeks and Barbarians. Nor was there even a good or bad demon then acknowledged among mankind; but the stars of heaven alone were considered and adored as gods."* For that the worship of the sun, the planets, and the elements, was the earliest form of idolatry, is sufficiently evident from the accounts of all ancient religions which have been preserved: but the cause which led men to adopt this form still remains unexplained.

These objections apply with peculiar force to the system which has received the approbation of the most eminent ancient and modern authors; and which supposes that idolatry derived its origin from the deification of men, who had rendered themselves conspicuous by their actions and virtues.† L'Abbé Banier, indeed, judiciously concludes that some form of religion must have previously existed, for he remarks:—"Je sçais que l'ordre que je viens de mettre dans le progrés de l'idolatrie ne s'accorde pas avec Sanchoniathon, qui place l'apothéose des hommes dans les premiers temps; mais il y a beaucoup d'apparence qu'on ne se porta pas d'abord à cet excés de folie, et qu'on

* Præparatio Evangelica, lib. i. chap. 9.

Eusebius had just before quoted these words of Plato in Cratylo:—*Φαινονται μοι οἱ πρωτοι των ανθρωπων των περι την 'Ελλαδα, τουτους μονους θεους ἡγεισθαι, οὕσπερ νυν πολλοι των βαρβαρων, ἡλιον, και σεληνην, και γην, και αστρα, και ουρανον· ἁ τε ουν ορωντες παντα αει ιοντα δρομῳ και θεοντα, απο ταυτης της φυσεως της του θειν, θεους αυτους επονομασαι.*

It now appears that the nouns θεος, *deus*, and their adjectives διος, *divus*, are identical with the Sanscrit *devah* and *diwiah*, derived from the root *diw*, which, amongst other meanings, signifies *to shine*, *to be splendid*, *to move*, *to go*.

† In Cicero's Treatise de Naturâ Deorum, the general admission in his time of this opinion is clearly demonstrated; and I shall, therefore, merely quote the following passage towards the conclusion of the first book. "Quid? qui aut fortes, aut claros, aut potentes viros tradunt post mortem ad deos pervenisse, eosque esse ipsos, quos nos colere, precari, venerarique soleamus, nonne expertes sunt religionum omnium? quæ ratio maxime tractata ab Euhemero est: quem noster et interpretatus et secutus est, præter cæteros, Ennius. Ab Euhemero autem et mortes et sepulturæ demonstrantur deorum."

adora les astres, et les différentes parties de l'univers, avant de rendre aucun culte à ses semblables."* But I cannot find, either in this author or in any other writer, the slightest evidence that the principal gods of the ancients were deified men; and yet that, with respect to the Greeks, such an opinion was prevalent prior to the work of Euhemerus on this subject, seems evident from these words of Herodotus† in describing the religion of the Persians:—Αγαλματα μεν και νηους και βωμους ουκ εν νομῳ ποιευμενους ἱδρυεσθαι, αλλα και τοισι ποιευσι μωριην επιφερουσι· ὡς μεν εμοι δοκεει ὁτι ουκ ανθρωποφυεας ενομισαν τους θεους, καταπερ οἱ Ἑλληνες, ειναι.‡ It must, therefore, have originated during the four hundred years that elapsed between the times when Herodotus and Hesiod flourished, as not the slightest allusion to it occurs in the Theogony of the latter; nor does it receive any support from these verses in the Εργα και Ἡμεραι:—

Αυταρ επει κεν τουτο γενος κατα γαια καλυψεν,
Τοι μεν δαιμονες εισι Διος μεγαλȣ δια βουλας,
Εσθλοι, επιχθονιοι, φυλακες θνητων ανθρωπων·
Οἱ ῥα φυλασσουσιν τε δικας και σχετλια εργα,
Ηερα εσσαμενοι, παντῃ φοιτωντες επ' αιαν,
Πλουτοδοται· και τουτο γερας βασιληιον εσχον. § V. 121—126.

* La Myth. et les Fables expliquées par l'Histoire, tom. i. p. 181.

† Euhemerus flourished about 140 years *after* Herodotus. But Plutarch, in this passage in his Treatise de Iside et Osiride, seems to agree with Cicero in ascribing the prevalence of this opinion to the work of Euhemerus:—Μεγαλας μεν τῳ αθεῳ λεῳ κλισιαδας ανοιγοντας και εξανθρωπιζοντι τα θεια, λαμπραν δε τοις Ευημηρου του Μεσσενιου φενακισμοις παρρησιαν διδοντας, ὁς αυτος αντιγραφα συνθεις απιστου και ανυπαρκτου μυθολογιας, πασαν αθεοτητα κατασκεδαννυσι της οικουμενης, τους νομιζομενους θεους παντας ὁμαλως διαγραφων, εις ονομα στρατηγων και ναυαρχων και βασιλεων, ὡς δε παλαι γεγονοτων,

‡ Lib. i. chap. 131.

§ This passage is thus beautifully translated by Bryant, Anal. Anc. Myth., vol. iv. p. 210.

"The immortals first a *golden* race produced:
These lived when Saturn held the realms of heaven;
And pass'd their time like gods, without a care.
No toil they knew, nor felt solicitude;
Not e'en the infirmities of age. . . . .
Soon as this race was sunk beneath the grave,
Jove raised them to be demons of the air,
Spirits benign, and guardians of mankind,
Who sternly right maintain and sorely punish wrong."

For they merely intimate that this first race of men was raised to a certain degree of angelic power and dignity, but not that it was admitted to participate in the divine honours and attributes of the pre-existing gods. Nor does Homer appear to have been in any manner acquainted with this opinion*; and it may therefore be justly concluded, that it was altogether unknown to the earlier Greeks.

If, however, this hypothesis has been admitted without sufficient proof, its general reception can afford no valid argument in its favour. Its groundlessness, also, is at once evinced by the equally general prevalence of the opinion which ascribed to Egypt the origin of the gods of Greece and Italy, and thus rendered it impossible that the human genealogies subsequently attributed to them could rest on any foundation whatever. For most writers appear to have acquiesced in the justness of this conclusion of Herodotus: — "The Egyptians first invented the names of the twelve gods, which the Greeks derived from them; and they were also the first people who dedicated altars, images, and temples to the gods." † But Eusebius has observed: —

* As Homer mentions the mortal birth and subsequent apotheosis of Hercules and Bacchus, it must be evident that he could have no reason for refraining to ascribe a similar origin to the other gods, had such an opinion been prevalent in his time. But that even the deification of heroes by the Greeks had not then commenced, seems evident from his account of the *Διοσκουροι*, in the following verses:—

> *Δοιω δ' ου δυναμαι ιδεειν κοσμητορε λαων,*
> *Καστορα θ' ἱπποδαμον, και πυξ αγαθον Πολυδευκεα,*
> *Αυτοκασιγνητω, τω μοι μια γεινατο μητηρ.*
> *Η ουχ ἑσπεσθην Λακεδαιμονος εξ ερατεινης;*
> *Η δευρο μεν ἑποντο νεεσσ' ενι ποντοποροισι,*
> *Νυν δ' αυτ' ουκ εθελουσι μαχην καταδυμεναι ανδρων,*
> *Αισχεα δειδιοτες και ονειδεα πολλ', ἁ μοι εστιν;*
> *Ὡς φατο· τους δ' ηδε κατεχεν φυσιζοος αια*
> *Εν Λακεδαιμονι αυθι, φιλῃ ενι πατριδα γαιῃ.* *Il. γ.* v. 236—244.

Mr. Mitford, also, remarks that "idolatry, as far as appears from Homer, was in his time unknown to Greece; and even temples were not common, though those of Minerva at Athens, Apollo at Delphi, and Neptune at Ægæ seem to have been of some standing. Sacrifices were performed, as by the Jewish patriarchs, on altars raised in the open air; and prayers were addressed, though to many, yet to deities beyond the search of human eyes."— *History of Greece*, vol. i. p. 101.

† Lib. ii. c. 4.

Lanzi observes: — "L'origine di quegli dei sia forestiera e di paesi diversi, come ben con-

"The religious tenets of the Egyptians are thus, as we have seen, much more ancient than those of the Greeks. They, however, held that Osiris and Isis were the sun and moon; and the ether diffused through all space they named Jupiter; fire, Vulcan; the earth, Ceres; water, Oceanus, or their own river Nilus, to which also they ascribed the production of their gods; and the air, Minerva. These last five deities, air, fire, water, earth, and ether, they believe to pervade the universe, and to assume at different times the forms of men and animals; and also that mortal men have amongst them been distinguished by the names of these gods." * The substantial correctness of this account, — that is, that the deified forms of the sun, moon, ether, air, fire, water, and earth were the original gods worshipped by the Egyptians, — will receive the strongest corroboration from the same having been the first objects which were adored by the Hindus; and is alone sufficient to prove that, if idolatry first arose in Egypt, it did not originate in the deification of men.

It may also be further remarked, that had such a system ever existed, it becomes impossible to explain the cause which prevented a principle so extensively applicable, and so gratifying to the pride of man, from producing no more than the very limited number of deities which have existed in any country. The Greeks and Romans acknow-

---

jettura Banier; ma la mitologia finora descritta non è se non Greca. Or questa mitologia medesima, io trovo adotto *nella sostanza* da tutta l'Italia antica. Roma di se non lo nega, e ne ripete l'origine o da Pelasghi e dagli altri Greci che già nel Lazio abitarono; o da Romulo che in Gabio dicesi avere apprese le Greche littere; o da Numa che nato in Sabina dovea conoscere le deita recatevi da' Pelasghi. Gli antichi Etruschi lo confessano in certo modo col fatto," &c.—*Saggio di Lingua Etrusca*, tom. ii. p. 237.

I am of a different opinion on this subject, as it will appear in Chapter III., but I here merely oppose one generally received opinion to another.

* Præp. Evan., lib. iii. c. 4. See also Diod. Sic., Bib., lib. i. c. 12.

The late Mr. Payne Knight, in considering deification, has likewise observed:—"The founder of the Persian monarchy was called by a name, which in their language signified the sun; and there is no doubt that many of the ancient kings of Egypt had names of the same kind, which have helped to confound history with allegory: though the Egyptians, prior to their subjection to the Macedonians, never worshipped them, nor any heroes or canonised mortals whatever."—*Inquiry into the Symb. Lang.* &c., part viii. sect. 203.

ledged no more than thirteen principal deities*, and they appear to have been fewer amongst the other people of antiquity. But, were it admitted that the gods were originally men, who were exalted to divine honours for their virtues and beneficent actions by their grateful countrymen, it must be evident that the same cause cannot be assigned for the deification of the female possessors of Olympus; for neither tradition nor history affords the slightest grounds for supposing that a woman ever distinguished herself in such a manner as to obtain the honour of apotheosis. On the contrary, from all that is known of early times, it appears incontestable that the situation of females entirely precluded them from taking such a part in the active duties of life as might have entitled them to such a distinction. This hypothesis, consequently, is not only inadequate to explain the origin of idolatry, but it even fails in admitting of the same cause being assigned for one and the same effect; and it may, therefore, justly excite surprise that it should have been so generally considered as clear and incontrovertible. †

But notwithstanding these obvious objections, the latest writer, I believe, who has supported what may be called the Hebrew hypothesis respecting the origin of idolatry, has rested the whole of his system on this assumption, that "both the acknowledged import of the word demon, and the characters attributed to the heathen divi-

* Jupiter, Neptune, Pluto, Apollo, Vulcan, Mars, Bacchus, Juno, Ceres, Vesta, Minerva, Venus, Diana.

And yet Cicero observes:—"Quid? totum prope cœlum, ne plures persequar, nonne humano genere completum est? Si vero scrutari vetera, et ex his ea quæ scriptores Græci prodiderunt, eruere coner: ipsi illi, majorum gentium dii qui habentur, hinc a nobis profecti in cœlum reperientur."—*Tusc. Quæs.*, lib. i. c. 13.

† The only writers, that I am aware of, who have controverted this opinion, are M. de la Barre and M. Freret; for the latter has observed in a Memoir published in the 23d volume of Les Mémoires de l'Académie des Inscriptions, p. 242.:—"Je dois avertir qu'on ne trouvera ici aucune de ces explications historiques imaginées par les partisans modernes de l'Euhemerisme, qui supposent que toutes les divinités du Paganisme, sans exception, ont été des hommes élevés par l'apothéose au rang des dieux supérieurs; et qui veulent que toutes les fables soient des évènemens d'une ancienne histoire qu'ils placent comme ils peuvent, soit pour le temps, soit pour le lieu. J'ai beaucoup étudie ce système; et cet examen m'a convaincu de sa fausseté absolue: peut-être traiterai-je cette question dans un Mémoire à part." This design, I believe, M. Freret executed in his Défense de la Chronologie, but this work I have not been able to procure.

nities, prove, with sufficient plainness, that these divinities were once mere mortals, though their worship was inseparably blended with that of the heavenly bodies, and the elemental powers of nature. The chief question, therefore, is, *what* mortals were venerated after their death as the hero-gods of pagan antiquity?" * He further remarks: — "Such being the case, since the demon-gods of paganism were the mortals who lived during the golden age †; and since there was a golden age, both immediately after the creation, and immediately after the deluge, it will plainly follow, that those demon-gods were the members of the Adamitic family in the one instance, and the members of the Noetic family in the other. Eminent persons, who flourished subsequently to each golden age, might occasionally be added, and, in fact, were added; but the individuals of these two primeval families may safely be esteemed the original and genuine prototypes of the demon-gods." ‡ To enter, however, into the discussion of a hypothesis, which rests not on the slightest evidence, and which is supported by arguments that are clearly in direct opposition to all that is known of ancient mythology, must surely be unnecessary. But it may be observed, that there is nothing whatever contained in Genesis, which can in any manner tend to explain the origin of idolatry, or which is in the least degree incompatible with any system that may be proposed for this purpose: for l'Abbé Banier observes, after fully examining this point, "Ce n'est donc point dans les Livres Saints que nous pourrons apprendre la véritable époque de l'établissement de l'idolatrie, et nous n'avons dans l'antiquité aucun auteur qui mérite d'être suivi sur cette matière." §

The singular opinion, however, of Vossius on this subject deserves particular attention, in consequence of its being admitted as a valid ground of argument by all writers who have touched upon the religions of antiquity: for he states, that "the immediate descendants of Noah invented two principles of equal, or nearly equal, power,—the one of

* Faber's Origin of Pagan Idolatry, vol. i. p. 10.

† I have cited above the verses of Hesiod, on which Mr. Faber principally rests this opinion, and remarked that they admit of no such construction.

‡ Ibid.

§ La Mythologie, &c., tom. i. p. 158.

good, and the other of evil; and thence concluded, that in the same manner that they worshipped the principle of good, in order that he might confer good on them, thus ought they to venerate the principle of evil, in order that he might avert evil from them. How ancient this opinion was is proved by its having been entertained by the most ancient legislators and priests, and from its having been adopted by the philosophers of old."* But it is singular that the only authority which he cites in support of this opinion is Plutarch, who flourished about ninety years *after* the birth of Christ; and that his reasoning, with respect to the general prevalence in antiquity of this opinion, is founded entirely on the alleged existence of an individual named Zoroaster. Brucker, however, observes:—"Nor does it seem improbable that some individual (named Zoroaster) first introduced amongst the ancient Babylonians a knowledge of divine rites and astronomy; . . . . and that a Perso-Median philosopher may have subsequently assumed his name when he applied his mind to the reformation of the religion of his country. For the astronomical observations of the Chaldeans were certainly of a much greater antiquity than the period when the latter flourished; and, consequently, if Zoroaster was, according to the universal consent of antiquity, the founder of the Chaldean astronomy, he must necessarily be distinguished from the Persian philosopher." † But it is undeniable that there are no grounds whatever for attributing the invention of the peculiar religious tenets introduced amongst the Persians by the latter to any one of the other Zoroasters mentioned by ancient authors: nor is there the slightest indication in history that, previously to his time, the doctrine of two principles was known to any people of antiquity. It was most unquestionably unknown to the Egyptians ‡, the Jews, the Greeks, the Romans; and from time imme-

* De Orig. et Prog. Idol., lib. i. c. 5.

† Historia Critica Philosophiæ, tom. i. p. 123.

‡ Plutarch is the only ancient author, I believe, who ascribes this opinion to the Egyptians; but the credit due to his Treatise de Iside et Osiride may be at once appreciated, from his venturing to assert, in direct opposition to every thing known of the Greek religion, Τα δε Ἑλληνων, πασι που δηλοι, την μεν αγαθην Διος Ολυμπιου μεριδα, την [κακην] δ' αποτροπαιου Ἁδου, ποιουμενων.

Cudworth also remarks:—"From whence it may be concluded that this doctrine, *of two active principles of good and evil*, was not then looked upon as the generally received doc-

morial the Hindus have been equally unacquainted with it. The strongest proof, therefore, shows that this opinion did not begin to prevail until about five hundred years before Christ, and that it was peculiar to the Persian religion; from which it has most probably been introduced, with essential modifications, into the Christian and Mohammedan religions. In discussions, consequently, respecting the origin of idolatry, or the real nature of mythology in ancient times, it must be evident that all arguments which rest on this opinion are entirely foreign to the question, and therefore totally inadmissible.

But it is unnecessary to advert to the other hypotheses which have been proposed for the explanation of the origin of idolatry; because it cannot be denied that, previously to entering into such a discussion, it is indispensable to ascertain the manner in which man acquired the conceptions of a self-existent and supreme Being; of the soul's immateriality and immortality; and of a future state of reward and punishment. For that a belief in these important truths has prevailed amongst mankind from time immemorial cannot admit of a doubt.* But it seems equally evident that man could never have acquired a knowledge of them by means of the unassisted powers of human reason; for Locke admits that "we have the ideas of matter and thinking, but possibly shall never be able to know whether any mere

trine of the Pagans. Wherefore it seems reasonable to think that Plutarch's imputing it so universally to them, was either out of design, thereby to gain the better countenance and authority to a conceit which himself was fond of; or else because he being deeply tinctured, as it were, with the suffusion of it, every thing which he looked upon seemed to be coloured with it. And indeed, for aught we can yet learn, this Plutarchus Chæronensis, Numenius, and Atticus were the only Greek philosophers who ever in public writings positively asserted any such opinion."—*Intellectual System*, b. i. c. 4. sect. 13.

* "Ut porro firmissimum hoc afferri videtur, cur deos esse credamus, quod nulla gens tam fera, nemo omnium tam sit immanis, cujus mentem non imbuerit deorum opinio, multi de diis prava sentiunt; id enim vitioso more effici solet: omnes tamen esse vim et naturam divinam arbitrantur, nec vero id collocutio hominum, aut consensus efficit: non institutis opinio est confirmata, non legibus. Omni autem in re consensio omnium gentium, lex naturæ putanda est. . . . . Maximum vero argumentum est, naturam ipsam de immortalitate animorum tacitam judicare, quod omnibus curæ sunt, et maxime quidem, quæ post mortem futura sint. . . . . Sed nescio quomodo inhæret in mentibus quasi sæculorum quoddam augurium futurorum idque in maximis ingeniis, altissimisque animis, et existit maxime, et apparet facillime: quo quidem dempto, quis tam esset amens, qui semper in periculis et laboribus viveret?—*Cic. Tusc. Quæs.*, l. i. c. 13, 14.

material being thinks or no; it being impossible for us, by the contemplation of our own ideas, without Revelation, to discover whether Omnipotency has not given to some systems of matter fitly disposed a power to perceive and think, or else joined and fixed to matter so disposed a thinking immaterial substance."* Bishop Butler thus concludes his arguments respecting a future life:—"This credibility of a future life, which has been here insisted upon, how little soever it may satisfy our curiosity, seems to answer all the purposes of religion, in like manner as a demonstrative proof would. Indeed a proof, even a demonstrative one, of a future life, would not be a proof of religion. For, that we are to live hereafter, is just as reconcilable with the scheme of atheism, and as well to be accounted for by it, as that we are now alive, is; and therefore nothing can be more absurd than to argue from that scheme, that there can be no future state. But as religion implies a future state, any presumption against such a state, is a presumption against religion. And the foregoing observations remove all presumptions of that sort, and prove, to a very considerable degree of probability, one fundamental doctrine of religion."† And even with respect to the arguments usually employed to demonstrate the existence of God, Dr. Reid has placed among his FIRST PRINCIPLES the principle, that whatever begins to exist must have a cause which produced it; and has observed,—"I know only of three or four arguments that have been urged by philosophers, in the way of abstract reasoning, to prove that things which begin to exist must have a cause. One is offered by Mr. Hobbes, another by Dr. Samuel Clarke, another by Mr. Locke. Mr. Hume, in his Treatise of Human Nature, has examined them all and, in my opinion, has shown that they take for granted the thing to be proved; a kind of false reasoning, which men are very apt to fall into when they attempt to prove what is self-evident."‡

* Essay on the Human Understanding, book iv. chap. 3. sect. 6.

† The Analogy of Religion, &c., p. 38.

‡ Essays on the Intellectual Powers, vol. ii. p. 361.

He adds, also, in p. 380.:—"Thus, I think, it appears that the principle we have been considering, to wit, that from certain signs or indications in the effect, we may infer that there must have been intelligence, wisdom, or other intellectual or moral qualities in the cause, is a principle which we get neither by reasoning nor by experience; and therefore, if it be a true principle, it must be a first principle. There is in the human understanding a light by which we see immediately the evidence of it, when there is occasion to apply it."

I have insisted upon this point with some prolixity, because if these important truths were not discoverable by the unassisted powers of human reason*, and if they have notwithstanding been universally prevalent amongst mankind from time immemorial, it must necessarily be concluded that they were actually revealed by the Supreme Being to the first man, or the first men. On such an alleged revelation have all religions been founded; and there appears to be nothing incompatible with the divine majesty, goodness, and wisdom, in supposing that God condescended to instruct the rational beings whom he had created in a knowledge of his divine essence, the nature of the human soul, its immortality and consequent liability to a future state of retribution, and in the principal moral and religious observances which they ought to practise. That man also has been endowed with a certain degree of power over his own actions, and that human reason has the greatest proneness to error, are facts which experience has too clearly proved to allow of their being controverted. But if these postulata be once admitted, the origin of idolatry becomes immediately obvious. For the impressions made on the minds of the first men by their immediate communication with God would become fainter in each succeeding generation; and, as the human mind is scarcely capable of devotion to an invisible and incomprehensible Being, their descendants would be naturally led to adopt some sensible object, as the type of that one self-existent and eternal God whom their fathers had adored. But in this case what other object could Nature present so typical of divine excellence and supremacy, as —

> " The orb that with surpassing glory crown'd
> Look'd from his sole dominion, like the God
> Of that new world, at whose sight all the stars
> Veil'd their diminish'd heads."

* In so popular a work as Paley's Natural Theology, the illustrations, a *watch*, the *eye*, a *telescope*, *gravitation*, &c., seem to be singularly ill-chosen; for the question relates not to the powers of human reason amongst men who have attained to a high state of civilisation and mental cultivation, but amongst rude and barbarous tribes. In fact, all similar argumentation presupposes that the persons to whom it is addressed have acquired a considerable degree of observation and knowledge; and were, consequently, this work to be put into the hands of the great mass of mankind, could they either understand the premises

The sun, however, was not always visible, and the sacred fire obviously suggested itself as its adequate representative*; nor if idolatry originated in Asia or Egypt, could the inhabitants of these countries have long contemplated the serene and brilliant expanse of the heavens, without imagining that it also might be a god, and hence —

Aspice hoc sublime candens, quem invocant omnes Jovem.

The earth was the next object that impressed on the minds of men the idea of a divine nature; and the cause seems evident from all nations having, on account of its fruitfulness, represented it under the female character. The deification of sensible objects having thus commenced, its extension to the other elements is easily conceivable; and to evince that this was actually the first form of idolatry, there seems to be sufficient evidence. But the remembrance of one sole, self-existent, and supreme Being was never entirely effaced, even in the most idolatrous times; and, from the creation until the present day, a belief in the immateriality and immortality of the soul, and in a future state of reward and punishment, has continued to be the popular faith of all nations.

If, however, it be admitted that the adoration of an invisible God without some sensible medium, has been found attended with such difficulties as to have occasioned in all countries the adoption of sensible objects for facilitating devotion; it must be equally admitted

---

of the reasoning contained in it, or comprehend the validity of the conclusions? Or would it even convince those who were capable of forming a judgment on the subject?

* It is very remarkable that in the Hindu religion it appears clearly, and in other ancient religions more faintly, that the sun and fire never lost this typical character, and that as objects of adoration, they always remained distinguished from their deified impersonifications. Sir William Jones, therefore, justly remarks, in the preface to his translation of the Institutes of Menu, "that the many panegyrics on the Gayatri, the mother, as it is called, of the Veda, prove the author to have *adored* (not the visible material sun, but) that divine and incomparably greater light, to use the words of the most venerable text in the Indian scripture, *which illumines all, delights all, from which all proceed, and to which all must return, and which alone can irradiate our intellects.*" Mr. Colebrooke, also, in describing the oblation to the sun (*Asiat. Res.*, vol. v. p. 357.), observes, that it is concluded by worshipping the sun with this text: — *His rays, the efficient causes of knowledge, irradiating worlds, appear like sacrificial fires;* which sufficiently explains the origin and nature of the worship which has been so universally addressed to fire.

that the contemplation of the abstract ideas, suggested, no doubt, at first by such objects, must have also become too severe an exercise for the faculties of man. It is not, indeed, probable that, in the earlier ages of the world, mankind would have been capable of speculating on the qualities of matter and spirit; but as it was obviously inconceivable how spirit could act immediately on matter, it would naturally be concluded that the substance of those Gods, to whom energy and power were attributed, must be material.* But the only material beings in which thought and reason were discernible were themselves, and consequently, however absurd the impersonification of the heaven and the earth under a human form may appear, it seems evident that men, from their very nature, could conceive no other corporeal figure that was at all adequate to represent the notions which they entertained of deity. Reasoning, also, in a similar manner, they were equally led to ascribe to their gods the same modes of acting and thinking as prevailed amongst men †, and the immortals thus became distinguished from mortals merely by being invested with a greater degree of perfection, power, and happiness. But from these circumstances it cannot be justly concluded that the nature of these gods was ever considered by any people to be precisely the same as the human; and even the term *deification*, if it have any meaning, is alone sufficient to intimate that those who use it admit that these two natures are perfectly distinct.

* Locke observes:—" How any thought should produce a motion in body, is as remote from the nature of our ideas, as how any body should produce any thought in the mind. That it is so, if experience did not convince us, the consideration of the things themselves would never be able in the least to discover to us. These, and the like, though they have a constant and regular connexion in the ordinary course of things, yet that connexion being not discoverable in the ideas themselves, which, having no necessary dependence one on another, we can attribute their connexion to nothing else but the arbitrary determination of that all-wise Agent, who has made them to be, and to operate as they do, in a way wholly above our weak understandings to conceive."—*Essay*, &c., book iv. chap. 3. sect. 28.

† "Non enim ambrosia deos, aut nectare, aut Juventute pocula ministrante, lætari arbitror: nec Homerum audio, qui Ganymedem a diis raptum ait propter formam, ut Jovi bibere ministraret; non justa causa cur Laomedonti tanta fieret injuria. Fingebat hæc Homerus, et humana ad deos transferebat: divina mallem ad nos: quæ autem divina? vigere, sapere, invenire, meminisse. Ergo animus, ut ego dico, divinus est, ut Euripides audet dicere, deus: et quidem si deus, aut anima, aut ignis est, idem est animus hominis; nam ut illa natura cœlestis et terra vacat et humore, sic utriusque harum rerum humanus animus est expers."—*Cic. Tusc. Quæst.*, lib. i. c. 26.

Consequently, before any men received, according to this system, the honour of apotheosis, there must have been one or more pre-existing deities; and, therefore, no cause can be conceived which could have induced mankind to have believed that individuals, whose birth and life were well known, could have, after death, acquired the nature of gods.* Nor will it, perhaps, be denied that the reasons above stated are fully adequate for explaining the inducements which led mankind to impersonify the planets and elements under the human form; and that, consequently, such form can afford no ground whatever for concluding that the gods of antiquity were nothing more than deified men.

It seems, however, to be an admitted point, that the impersonification of the planets and the elements under the human figure could never have occurred to mankind; since all hypotheses concerning the origin of polytheism assume that this form of idolatry was confined to the worship of the visible objects alone. For the Abbé Foucher has remarked, with respect to the Greeks: "Ainsi que les autres nations barbares, ils n'avoient d'autres divinités que le ciel, la terre, le soleil, et les autres astres: or comme je l'ai remarqué dans le mémoire précédent, ces divinités ne se prêtent pas aux *theophanies*, parce qu'il ne peut venir dans l'esprit de qui que ce soit, qu'un homme puisse etre le ciel ou le soleil, ou qu'une femme soit la terre ou la lune, à moins qu'à la place de ces objects naturels on ne substitue les génies qui les gouvernent." † A similar opinion is thus expressed by Mr. Payne Knight: —"The primitive religion of the Greeks, like that of all other nations not enlightened by revelation, appears to have been elementary; and

* The distinction between the gods and the heroes to whom divine rites were addressed, is so clearly pointed out in the following passages, that it is surprising how a contrary opinion could ever have obtained:—Τα μεν νυν ἱστορημενα δηλοι σαφεως παλαιον θεον τον Ἡρακλεα εοντα· και δοκεουσι δε μοι οὑτοι ορθοτατα Ἑλληνων ποιεειν, οἱ διξα Ἡρακλεια ἱδρυσαμενοι εκτηνται· και τῳ μεν, ὡς αθανατῳ, Ολυμπιῳ δ᾽επωνυμιην, θυουσι· τῳ δ᾽ ἑτερῳ, ὡς ἡρωι, εναγιζουσι.—*Herod.*, lib. ii. c. 44. He also concludes the 45th chapter of the same book with these words:—Και περι μεν τουτων τοσαυτα ἡμιν ειπουσι, και παρα των θεων και παρα των ἡρωων ευμενεια ειη.

Pausanias, also, uses the same distinction:—Τῳ δε Αλεξανορι και Ευαμεριωνι (και γαρ τουτοις αγαλματα εστι), τῳ μεν ὡς ἡρωι μετα ἡλιον δυναντα εναγιζουσιν· Ευαμεριωνι δε ὡς θεῳ θυουσιν.—*Pausaniæ Corinth.* cap. xi.

† Mémoires de l'Académie des Inscriptions, tom. xxxvi. p. 330.

to have consisted in an indistinct worship of the sun, the moon, the stars, the earth, and the waters, or rather the spirits supposed to preside over these bodies, and to direct their motions and regulate their modes of existence."* But the notion of presiding spirits is undoubtedly a philosophical and not a popular opinion, as not a trace of it can be discovered in any system of polytheism with which I am acquainted; and, on the contrary, it is undeniable that Apollo was identified with the sun, Diana with the moon, and Ceres with the earth, all of whom are invariably described under the human form by both Greek and Latin authors.† When, also, rivers begot and naiads produced sons, such an effect could not possibly be ascribed to any other cause than the usual course of mortal generation. Such impersonifications, at the same time, so far from being incompatible with human belief, are evidently the natural consequences of ascribing divinity to the planets and elements. It is in the manner in which this primary idea originated that the difficulty consists; for as soon as such a conception was once formed, it indisputably appears that, in all religions, unimpeded locomotion through space, and the power of assuming, at pleasure, any corporeal form, have been considered as the

* Inquiry into the Symbolical Language, &c., part i. sect. 1.

† This fact is even admitted by Mr. Knight himself; for in the treatise above quoted, part v. sect. 129., he remarks:—"The offensive weapons of this deity (Apollo), which are the symbols of the means by which he exerted his characteristic attribute, are the bow and arrows, signifying the emission of his rays." In part vi. sect. 140.,—"Juno, Lucina, and Diana, were the same goddess, equally personifications of the moon." Sect. 142.,—"The statues of Diana are always clothed, and she had the attribute of perpetual virginity." Part ii. sect. 35.,—"The mysteries of Eleusis were under the protection of Ceres, called by the Greeks ΔΗΜΗΤΗΡ, that is, Mother Earth."

The following verses also, in the Hymn to Venus, ascribed to Homer, might have occurred to Mr. Knight:—

Τῃ δε και αυτῃ Ζευς γλυκυν ἱμερον εμβαλε θυμῳ,
Ανδρι καταθνητῳ μιχθημεναι, οφρα ταχιστα
Μηδ' αυτη βροτεης ευνης αποεργμενη ειη,
Και ποτ' επευξαμενη ειπῃ μετα πασι θεοισιν,
'Ηδυ γελοιησασα, φιλομμειδης Αφροδιτη,
'Ως ῥα θεους συνεμιξε καταθνητῃσι γυναιξιν,
Και τε καταθνητους ὑιεις τεκον αθανατοισιν,
'Ως τε θεας συνεμιξε καταθνητοις ανθρωποις.

characteristic attributes of divinity. The human figure, however, was not only the most familiar to the imaginations of men, but also the most perfect and dignified of which they could form any conception; and hence, as immensity and infinity admitted not of worship and contemplation, they were led to concentre their ideas of godhead into some one defined and conceivable object. The investing, therefore, this object, under the firm belief that deity could assume whatever corporeal form it pleased, with the human figure, must clearly be the only conclusion which could, under such circumstances, have presented itself to the human mind. It must also be evident, that in endeavouring to obviate the difficulty of adoring a supreme but invisible Being, it never could have occurred to mankind to substitute in his place the equally abstract idea of unseen spirits presiding over the planets and elements. It was a sensible object that was required to excite and command the attention, and even the planet or element was of too vague and indistinct a nature to effect this purpose completely, until it was rendered perfectly defined and conceivable by attributing to it the form, the qualities, and the passions of man.*

But since such diversity of opinion prevails with respect to the origin of idolatry, it may be presumed that an enquiry into the real principles of the Hindu religion cannot fail of exciting considerable interest. For it seems highly probable that this system has continued unchanged for a period of nearly three thousand years, and it must, therefore, be excellently adapted for determining the manner in which mankind originally acquired their notions of religion, and of deciding the much agitated question whether monotheism or polytheism first prevailed. The result, however, of this investigation will, if I be not much mistaken, clearly evince that every hypothesis on this subject, hitherto proposed, is erroneous, and that these two systems were not

* Gibbon justly remarks:—"The idea of pure and absolute spirit is a refinement of modern philosophy; the incorporeal essence, ascribed by the ancients to human souls, celestial beings, and even the deity himself, does not exclude the notion of extended space; and their imagination was satisfied with a subtle nature of air, or fire, or æther incomparably more perfect than the grossness of the material world. If we define the place, we must describe the figure, of the deity. Our experience, perhaps our vanity, represents the powers of reason and virtue under a human form."—*Decline and Fall*, &c., vol. viii. p. 268.

only coeval in origin, but that they have also coexisted from the first creation of man until the present day. Such, at least, is the conclusion which irresistibly presents itself from a consideration of the Hindu religion: because it represents the one self-existent and supreme Being as producing *ex nihilo* * the elementary atoms of this universe, and then originating from his own essence in an ineffable manner three hypostases for the purpose of creating or rather arranging and organising, of preserving, and of destroying it †; and after having thus given the first impulse to creation, and having impressed upon this system certain laws from which it never will deviate until its final dissolution, after it has endured for an inconceivable period of time, withdrawing himself from all further care of his work, and returning to that state of quiescence in which divine happiness is supposed to consist.

> Omnis enim per se divûm natura necesse 'st
> Immortali ævo summa cum pace fruatur,
> Semota ab nostris rebus, sejunctaque longe;
> Nam privata dolore omni, privata periclis,
> Ipsa suis pollens opibus, nihil indiga nostri,
> Nec bene promeritis capitur, nec tangitur ira. ‡

Amongst the Hindus, therefore, the Supreme Being never became the object of *external* worship, but his existence was most carefully

* The *words* invariably used on the occasion clearly describe a creation *ex nihilo*: but, even in the Vedas, the Hindus are decidedly pantheists, as will be fully explained in Chapter VI. Has this difference, therefore, originated in the imperfection of language, or did the ancestors of the authors of the Vedas distinguish the efficient Cause from the universe which he has formed?

† This tenet is such an essential principle of the Hindu religion, that it must have been coeval with its very origin. Yet it is so difficult to understand how this singular opinion could possibly have originated in the human mind, that it also might be with the greatest probability ascribed to an immediate revelation from God, of a much more explicit nature than the word *Elohim*, which has given rise to so much discussion.

Cudworth also remarks: — "Now since it cannot well be conceived, how such a trinity of divine hypostases should be first discovered merely by human wit and reason, though there be nothing in it (if rightly understood) that is repugnant to reason: and since there are in the ancient writings of the Old Testament certain significations of a plurality in the Deity, or of more than one hypostasis, we may reasonably conclude that which Proclus asserteth of this trinity, as it was contained in the Chaldean oracles, to be true, that it was at first θεοπαράδοτος θεολογία, a theology of divine tradition or revelation, viz. among the Hebrews first, and from them afterwards communicated to the Egyptians and other nations." — *Intellectual System*, book i. chap. iv. sect. 36.

‡ Lucretius de Rerum Natura, lib. i. v. 57—62.

inculcated, and Brahma, Vishnu, and Shiva were invariably represented as entirely dependent upon him, and equally subject to production and final dissolution as the meanest atom. The highest act of devotion, also, has immemorially been considered to be internal contemplation on the Supreme Being, with a mind completely abstracted from all other objects, and the ultimate state of beatitude to be identification with his divine essence. It will hence be evident that the belief in one sole God must have been by these means as effectually preserved as if temples and altars had been erected for his adoration; and that it must have made a much deeper impression on the minds of the Hindus, to whom it was, and still is, communicated as a sacred and mysterious truth essential for salvation, than if it had been permitted to become a topic of customary and inconsiderate discussion. But, while this has always been unquestionably the *esoteric* doctrine of the Hindu religion, the *exoteric* has presented to the people, for their veneration and worship, an infinite number of angelic and divine beings. *

On examining, however, this celestial hierarchy, which Mr. Ward has stated to consist of three hundred and thirty million *gods*†, it will be immediately observed that it remarkably confirms the origin which I have ascribed to idolatry. Because, amongst this multitude of immortals, temples and images are erected and adoration addressed only to Vishnu and Shiva, the representatives of the Supreme Being; the

* It may be proper to observe, that I have no intention of exposing the TOTAL ERRONEOUSNESS of almost every thing which has been hitherto written respecting the Hindu religion, as such a discussion would be long, tedious, and uninteresting. But I shall quote, in the course of this work, a sufficient number of passages from the Upanishads and Purans, to place it beyond a doubt, that the view which I have taken of it, is in strict conformity to the opinion which the Hindus themselves have invariably entertained on the subject. I cannot, however, avoid observing that Mr. Faber is the author who has most grossly misrepresented and perverted the accounts of it hitherto published, for the purpose of supporting a hypothesis the most absurd and untenable that ever was imagined. For the errors of Professors Goerres and Creuzer seem evidently to have proceeded from their following such very inadequate guides as Bartholomæus, Polier, and Wilford, and from that indulgence in aerial speculation to which the learned men of Germany seem so much addicted.

† Mr. Ward in several places of his work repeats this number, with the evident intention of throwing ridicule on the Hindu religion; but he knew perfectly well that for this purpose he was availing himself of the equivocal meaning of the Sanscrit word *deva*, which signifies both a *god* and an *angel*.

sun; the moon; Indra, the deified impersonification of the heaven; Agni, of fire; Vaiu, of air; Varuna, of water; and Bhumi, the goddess of the earth; the other planets also receive a certain degree of veneration. To these deities have been only added a god, who is the causer of death and the judge of the dead; Ganisha, the remover of difficulties *; Skanda, the generalissimo of the celestial armies; and Kama, god of love. The others are merely angels who are honoured with no worship, but are considered to be merely distinguished by their immortality, and their enjoying uninterrupted happiness in paradise. In this system, consequently, there is not the slightest appearance of deified men; or of the earlier distinguished characters of the Hebrew history; or of the sun's progress through the twelve signs of the zodiac; or of heaven having been indebted for its inhabitants to either symbols or allegories. The doctrine, also, of the two principles of good and evil is equally foreign to this religion; for evil is supposed to be an inherent property in matter, or in that illusion which assumes its appearance, inseparable from its existence even by the Supreme Being himself; but it is at the same time held that man is endowed with the capability of liberating himself from it, and of obtaining, by identification with the divine essence, the cessation of all worldly misery.

The extreme simplicity, therefore, of this system of polytheism, and its perfect consonancy with the principles which would lead mankind to their selection of sensible objects as *media* to facilitate devotion to an invisible God, must be hence obvious. In which case it will scarcely be denied that it affords strong presumptions, that the religions of all ancient people must in their origin have been equally simple and unsophisticated; and that a consideration of the Hindu religion may greatly assist in elucidating many a dubious point which occurs in ancient authors. But, before it can be employed for this purpose, it seems evidently indispensable to ascertain in the first place the precise nature of the information which has been preserved respecting the different mythologies of antiquity; and to extricate the subject from that mass of extraneous erudition under which it has been

* I have never, in any Sanscrit work, found him characterised as the god of wisdom.

so completely buried by many an ingenious and learned writer. This difficult task I have attempted to execute in the following three chapters; and though I can hardly flatter myself that I have altogether succeeded, it may be found that I have, at least, carefully collected together all the authorities, from which a just conclusion on the subject, according to the principles of historical evidence, can be deduced, and that I have thus enabled the reader to form his own judgment on the observations with which I have presented him.

CHAP. II.

THE MYTHOLOGY OF EGYPT.

The slightest consideration of the Egyptian religion at once evinces the extreme difficulty that there must exist in forming any correct opinion respecting it. For the earliest ancient historian now extant has made this formal declaration:—"But such accounts of divine matters as I have heard, except the mere names of the gods, I am unwilling to disclose, and shall, therefore, refrain from touching upon this subject, unless when my narrative renders it indispensable;" * and, in consequence, he mentions in more than one place of his history that religious scruples prevented his fully explaining the circumstances to which he adverts. The only other historian, anterior to the birth of Christ, who has treated at any length of the Egyptian religion, and whose work has been partially preserved, is Diodorus Siculus; but, from his having unfortunately adopted the system of Euhemerus, his account of it becomes extremely questionable.† With regard, also, to the writers who flourished *after* the birth of Christ, Mr. Payne Knight has observed: "As early as the second century of Christianity, we find that an entirely new system had been adopted by the Egyptian priesthood, partly drawn from the writings of Plato and other Greek and Oriental sophists, and partly invented amongst themselves. This they contrived to impose, in many instances, upon Plutarch, Apuleius, and

* *Τα μεν νυν θεια των απηγηματων οἷα ηκουον, ουκ ειμι προθυμος εξηγεεσθαι, εξω η τα ουνοματα αυτων μουνον· νομιζων παντας ανθρωπους ισον περι αυτων επιστασθαι· τα δ' αν επιμνησθω αυτων, ὑπο του λογου εξαναγκαζομενος επιμνησθησομαι.* — Lib. ii. cap. 3.

In another place he says, *Ει λεγοιμι, καταβαιην αν τῳ λογῳ ες τα θεια πρηγματα, τα εγω φευγω μαλιστα απηγεεσθαι.* — Lib. ii. cap. 65.

As Herodotus, therefore, merely contrasts an Egyptian with a Grecian deity, he leaves the subject in complete obscurity, as the characters and attributes of the gods of Greece are so vague and undetermined.

† The same reason renders of no use whatever the dynasties of Manetho preserved in the Armenian copy of Eusebius's Chronicon and in Syncellus.

Macrobius, as their ancient creed; and to this Jamblichus attempted to adapt their ancient allegories, and Hermapion and Horapollo their symbolical sculptures; all which they very readily explain, though their explanations are wholly inconsistent with those given to Herodotus, Diodorus, and Germanicus, which also are equally inconsistent with each other." * Nor could the conquest of the country, by the Persians, the Macedonians, and the Romans, fail to produce the greatest detriment to the Egyptian religion; for, though it might not have been persecuted, still the priesthood must have declined in power and influence, and the preservation of their sacred literature, and even of the holy institutions of their own order, must have gradually ceased to interest them.†

But, notwithstanding these strong reasons for scepticism on this subject, it cannot be controverted that, even at this day, paintings and sculptures exist which clearly attest that the notices of Egyptian mythology which occur in ancient authors cannot be altogether fictitious; and, if the recent attempts to decipher the hieroglyphics peculiar to this country be correct, it must also be admitted that these authors have recorded the names of the Egyptian deities with great accuracy. ‡ The peculiar characters and attributes, however, of these gods still remain involved in the greatest obscurity; and even in the time of Diodorus Siculus the individuality of Isis and Osiris was a subject of controversy: for he remarks that "there existed a complete diversity of opinion with respect to these deities, as the same goddess was called by some Isis, by others Ceres, by others Thesmophoron, by others the moon, by others Juno, and by others all these names were ascribed to her. Osiris, also, was considered by some to be Serapis, by others to be Dionusos (Bacchus), by others to be Pluto, by others to be Ammon, by others to be Jupiter, and by many to be Pan; but they say that Serapis is the same as the Pluto of the Greeks." § The utmost, there-

* Inquiry into the Symbolical Language, &c., part iii. sect. 65.

† Strabo remarks,—Μαλιστα γαρ δη ταυτην κατοικιαν ἱερεων γεγονεναι φασι τοπαλαιον, φιλοσοφων ανδρων, και αστρονομικων· εκλελοιπε δε και τουτο νυνι το συστημα, και ἡ ασκησις. Εκει μεν ουν ουδεις ἡμιν εδεικνυτο της τοιαυτης ασκησεως προεστως, αλλ' οἱ ἱεροποιοι μονον, και εξηγηται τοις ξενοις των περι τα ἱερα. —Lib. xvii. p. 806.

‡ See Champollion, Système Hieroglyphique, p. 84. et seq.; and Salt's Essay on Hieroglyphics, p. 33. et seq.

§ Bib. Hist., lib. i. c. 25.

fore, that is known with any degree of certainty, respecting this system of polytheism, is the names of the principal gods, and the figures by which they were represented; but their origin, their actions, and the peculiar character of each have not yet been satisfactorily ascertained.

But, if this be the case, it must necessarily follow that all the explanations of it which have been hitherto proposed rest almost entirely on gratuitous assumptions, and are therefore entitled to very little credit. It is, indeed, probable that they may be all in some degree founded in truth, but they are much too complex and elaborate to admit of its being believed that the supposed form of idolatry could possibly have originated and prevailed amongst the Egyptians, when they were still a rude and uncivilised people; because it seems unquestionable that, in the first ages of mankind, sensible objects may have given rise to metaphors and allegories, but perfectly inconceivable how allegories could have been then invented, or how they could ever produce a belief in the existence of a divine and invisible Being. Yet Plutarch, in his treatise de Iside et Osiride, gravely states as follows:—"There are persons who say that, in the same manner as among the Greeks Chronos is understood to signify time, Juno air, and the origin of Vulcan the change of air into fire; so amongst the Egyptians the Nile is held to be Osiris, that embraces Isis or the earth, and Typhon to be the sea into which the Nile is drawn by different channels, and thus becomes divided into several parts and lost." In another place of the same treatise he adds:—"As Osiris is the Nile, so is Isis the earth, but not the whole earth, only the land which is fertilised by the Nile; and from their union was produced Orus, or the conservative and nutritive atmosphere, who was said to have been brought up by Latona in the marshes near Butus, because moisture tends greatly to produce those exhalations by which heat and dryness are attempered. The margins, also, of the land in contact with the sea were called Nephthys, who was hence supposed to be married to Typhon. Whenever, therefore, the Nile overflowed and extended so far, Osiris was said to have intercourse with Nephthys; and hence Isis bore Orus in a legitimate, but Nephthys Anubis in a clandestine, manner." It appears equally improbable that any system of polytheism could have originated in the manner supposed by Jablonski, who has remarked:—"Osiridem intelleximus Egyptiis significasse auctorem temporis, et temporum moderatorem, sive solem, qui permeando zodiacum, diversas temporum in anno vicissitudines producit, et tandem ad principium, unde digressus erat, redit. Quoniam vero unus Osiris, unus idemque sol, dum cursum annuum absolvit, tum diversas temporum vicissitudines efficit, eoque naturæ rerum in mundo faciem toties vehementer immutat; ideo solem ipsum quoque, sive Osirin mutari, id est, pro diversis temporum vicissitudinibus, alium aliumque vultum habitumque induere, modo juvenem, modo virum robore florentem, modo senem, modo lætum alacremque, modo mœstum ac segnem, fingebant."*

Jablonski, at the same time, admits what cannot be controverted, that, according to ancient authors, Isis was considered to be both the moon and the earth, in the same manner as Osiris was held to be both the Nile and the sun.† But even Œdipus himself would find it impossible to discover the slightest conceivable connection between two such completely opposite ideas. Learned men, may, indeed, attempt to reconcile them; but the simple question is, whether, if they were proposed to a man living in the rude and uncultivated state in which the first men undoubtedly existed, he could possibly understand that the same object was actually the earth and the moon, or a river and the sun; and if not, it is clear that such ideas could never have originated in his own mind. In all speculations, however, respecting the origin of idolatry, this essential consideration appears to be totally overlooked; and the writer, instead of ascribing it to modes of thinking obviously inherent in the human mind, or at least therein arising without the assistance of civilisation, deduces it from a process of reasoning which is often puerile, sometimes subtle, and always inapplicable.

But Cudworth has observed:—"Having now made it undeniably manifest that the Egyptians had an acknowledgment amongst them of

* Pantheon Egyptiorum, vol. i. p. 157. Hence Jablonski's singular system which identifies the sun with Osiris, Horus, Harpocrates, Serapis, Ammon, and Hercules, at different periods of its progress through the zodiac; but religion most assuredly preceded astronomy, and the existence of one or more Divine Beings was unquestionably the subject of popular belief long before the zodiac was invented.

† Ibid., vol. ii. p. 17.

one supreme, universal, and unmade Deity, we shall conclude this whole discourse with the two following observations: first, that a great part of the Egyptian polytheism was really nothing else but the worshipping of *one and the same supreme God*, under many different names and notions; as of Hammon, Neith, Isis, Osiris, Serapis, Kneph; to which may be added Ptha, and those other names in Jamblichus, of Eicton and Emeph. And that the Pagans universally over the whole world did the like, was affirmed also by Apuleius in that fore-cited passage of his, *Numen unicum, multiformi specie, ritu vario, nomine multijugo, totus veneratur orbis;—the whole world worshippeth one only Supreme Numen in a multiform manner, under different names, and with different rites;* which different names for *one and the same Supreme God* might therefore be mistaken by some of the sottish vulgar amongst the Pagans, as well as they have been by learned men of later times, for so many distinct *unmade* and *self-existent deities*." * A similar opinion is thus expressed by Sir William Jones:—"We must not be surprised at finding, on a close examination, that the characters of all the Pagan deities, male and female, melt into each other, and at last into one or two; for it seems a well-founded opinion, that the whole crowd of gods and goddesses in ancient Rome, and modern Varanes (Benares), mean only the powers of Nature, and principally those of the SUN, expressed in a variety of ways and by a multitude of fanciful names." † But this opinion has evidently proceeded from not distinguishing between two circumstances of a perfectly different nature; for there can be no doubt but that the same God had various names, and that temples were erected, and divine rites addressed, to him in different places under some particular one only. But it appears equally unquestionable, that his other names would at the same time continue to be celebrated in all prayers and hymns in which he was invoked; for the hymns ascribed to Homer and Orpheus sufficiently attest the justness of this conclusion; and Sir William Jones must have observed that, amongst the Hindus, the litanies and laudatory addresses to the gods consist of scarcely any other topic than a simple enu-

* Intellectual System, book i. chap. 4. sect. 18.

† Sir W. Jones's Works, vol. i. p. 273.

meration of their names and epithets.* It is not, however, improbable that in migrations from one country to another, the emigrants might gradually forget that the different names denoted only one and the same God; and thus be led, as these names or rather epithets were no doubt significant, to consider them as distinct deities. But that such a consequence should ever result from this polyonomy in the country where the God had been uninterruptedly worshipped from remote antiquity, is not only improbable in itself, but clearly refuted by the evidence of the Hindu religion; and therefore, before this alleged reason can be admitted as the cause whence idolatry originated amongst any people, it must necessarily be first proved that its religion was not indigenous, but that it had been introduced by foreign emigrants.

Having premised these observations, I shall now proceed to collect together such notices of the Egyptian mythology as are preserved in ancient authors; but these are, unfortunately, much too unconnected and defective to afford any assistance in reducing it to a complete and regular system, or even in ascertaining the relation which the different deities bear to each other; for the genealogy ascribed to Osiris, Horus, Typhon, Isis, and Nephthys must evidently depend upon the authenticity of the fable relating to them, which appears so questionable as to deprive it of the requisite credit.

Yet, notwithstanding the obscurity in which the subject is involved, it seems not improbable that the Egyptians at first acknowledged only one self-existent supreme Being, manifested in three divine hypostases; and that, as in other countries, when the worship of an invisible God became too abstract for an ignorant people, occupied in the daily concerns of life, their adoration was gradually directed to the sun, the

* Sir W. Jones himself imitated this very form in the beautiful hymns to the Hindu deities which he subsequently composed; and it is sufficiently conspicuous in the odes of Pindar, of which he was so great an admirer.

Mr. Payne Knight, however, has observed in his Inquiry into the Symbolical Language, &c., that *the form of worshipping or glorifying the Deity by repeating adulatory titles was not in use in the Homeric times, though afterwards common.* But are there any other poems of those times extant except the Iliad and Odyssey? and if not, can any just conclusion respecting the form of the hymns then in use be drawn from these works alone?

planets, and the elements.* But, since it never seems to have been customary to represent the one Supreme Being by any kind of image, it would necessarily follow that the figures of Cneph, still existing in paintings and sculptures, cannot have been intended to represent him. There appears, however, to be no sufficient reason for rejecting the authority of Jamblichus on this point, who has thus written, according to the Books of Hermes:—"Before all existing things and their elements there was one God, anterior to the first [produced] God and Ruler, immovable, dwelling in the unity of his own sole-existent entity, affected by neither mental nor any other passion, the sole exemplar of deity originating from himself alone, essentially good, the first, the greatest, the fountain of all, and the base of the primary ideas of entities."† But it appears, also, that it was considered that this Supreme Being was not the actual creator of the universe, but that he had produced in some ineffable manner, from his own essence, a second divine power, by whom this great work was effected. With respect, however, to this last deity, there seems to have been some difference of opinion; for Jamblichus, after merely stating in one place that he manifested himself (εξελαμψε), adds in a following one:—"According to another arrangement, Hermes places the god Emeph as the ruler of the celestial gods, whom he describes as an intelligent

* Banier remarks:—"Je suis très persuade que l'idolatrie fut moins grossière et moins charg e de cérémonies dans ses commencemens qu'elle ne fut dans la suite, et que le peuple dont je parle (les Egyptiens) n'admit d'abord qu'un petit nombre des dieux, c'est-à-dire, les astres et les élémens. Si nous en croyons même Plutarque, il ne faut pas confondre avec le reste de l'Egypte les Thebains, dont la religion était beaucoup plus pure que celle des autres Egyptiens. *Les habitans de la Thebaide*, dit cet auteur, suivant la correction de Vossius, *sont exempts de ces superstitions, puisqu'ils ne reconnaissent aucun dieu mortel, n'admettant pour premier principe que le dieu Cneph, qui n'a point de commencement et qui n'est pas sujet à la mort.*"—*La Mythologie*, &c., tom. i. p. 456.

† Jamblichus de Mysteriis, sect. viii. c. 2.

The following passage, as translated by Cudworth, from the second chapter of the seventh section of this work is deserving of attention:—"That God, who is the cause of generation and the whole nature, and of all the powers in the elements themselves, is separate, exempt, elevated above, and expanded over, all the powers and elements in the world. For being above the world and transcending the same, immaterial and incorporeal, supernatural, unmade, indivisible, manifested wholly from himself and in himself, he ruleth over all things, and in himself containeth all things, and because he virtually comprehends all things, therefore does he impart and display the same from himself."

mind absorbed in its own contemplations. But anterior to this god he places one that is indivisible, whom he considers as the first occult power, and names Eicton; and, as he is the first intellectual principle of intellect, he is worshipped only in silence."* The authenticity, however, as an ancient Egyptian dogma, of the following part of this passage seems more questionable; as Jamblichus adds, that, besides these two gods, there is a third divine power, who, when he exerts his creative energy, is in consequence named in the Egyptian language Amoun; when he displays his skill in perfecting and harmoniously arranging, he is named Ptha; and when he dispenses blessings he is termed Osiris. "In this passage of Jamblichus," observes Cudworth, "we have plainly three divine hypostases, or universal principles subordinate, according to the Hermaick theology: first, an indivisible unity, called *Eicton;* secondly, a perfect mind converting its intellections into itself, called *Emeph;* and thirdly, the immediate principle of generation, called by several names, according to its several powers, as *Ptha, Ammon, Osiris,* and the like: so that these three names with others, according to Jamblichus, did in the Egyptian theology signify one and the same divine hypostasis. How will these three divine hypostases of the Egyptians agree with the Pythagoric or Platonic trinity of, first, το εν or τἀγαθον, *unity and goodness itself;* secondly, νους, *mind;* and thirdly, ψυχη, *soul,* I need not here declare. Only we shall call to mind what hath been already intimated, that that reason or wisdom which was the *Demiurgus* of the world, and is properly the second of the fore-mentioned hypostases, was called also amongst the Egyptians by another name, Cneph; from whom was said to have been produced or begotten the god Ptha, the third hypostasis of the Egyptian trinity; so that Cneph and Emeph are all one. Wherefore, we have here plainly an Egyptian trinity of divine hypostases subordinate, Eicton, Emeph or Cneph, and Ptha."†

The credit, however, due to this statement of Jamblichus may seem doubtful; because, had such an opinion prevailed amongst the Egyptians, it may be supposed that the three divine hypostases must have

* Jamblichus de Mysteriis, sect. viii. cap. 3.

† Intellectual System, book i. chap. 4. sect. 18.

been as obvious in their mythology as the Jupiter, Neptune, and Pluto of the Greeks, or the Brahma, Vishnu, and Shiva of the Hindus. But Cudworth remarks, that "since Orpheus, Pythagoras, and Plato, who all of them asserted a trinity of divine hypostases, unquestionably derived much of their doctrine from the Egyptians, it may reasonably be suspected that these Egyptians did the like before them." It might, therefore, be no improbable supposition, that, previously to the time of Herodotus, the worship of some one of these manifestations of the Supreme Being under three distinct forms, might have acquired such a predominance in Egypt as to render the existence and peculiar attributes of the other two powers of too little importance to attract the attention of even an inquisitive traveller. Nor can it be denied, that the accounts of the Egyptian religion given by ancient writers are obviously much too defective to admit of their silence on any point being considered as even negative proof of the non-existence of the deity or the religious tenet that may be in question; as it is clearly evinced by both Herodotus and Diodorus Siculus having omitted to mention Cneph, of whose existence as an Egyptian god there can be no doubt. It may, consequently, seem probable that the Egyptians did acknowledge that the Supreme Being had, for purposes connected with the creation and government of this universe, multiplied himself into three principal gods; but the specification of Jamblichus and Cudworth must be incorrect, as it includes the sole self-existing God, and therefore these hypostases must be sought for in some others of the Egyptian deities.

Nor can I discover any authority for this assertion of Jablonski, and he himself does not produce any proof in support of it: — "Quamvis vero ex consensu veterum in Egypto philosophorum, *Vulcanus*, sive *Pthas*, deorum omnium esset supremus et maximus, cujusque imperio omnes, ipsique adeo reliqui dei obedirent; labentibus tamen annis, honos ejus et cultus, ut videtur, frigescere ac etiam vilescere cœpit." * On the contrary, all ancient writers identify this god with *fire*, and in consequence with Hephaistos or Vulcan, as Jablonski himself admits.

* Pantheon Egypt., lib. i. c. 2. sect. 14.

But, if any credit is to be given to these authors, it must necessarily follow that, however vague and imperfect this identification may have been, it still must have rested on some grounds; and that it is highly improbable, that either their observation or their comprehension of the information which they received should have been so extremely defective, as to lead them to suppose that the god worshipped by the Egyptians as either the Supreme Being, or as one of the three divine hypostases, could possibly be the same as the blacksmith of Lemnos. According, also, to both Eusebius and Jamblichus, Ptha was the third and not the first divine power; but even this opinion seems inconsistent with any character that can justly be ascribed to *fire*, either as the material fire which is adapted to the purposes of man, or as that ethereal *calor* which pervades all nature. There seems, consequently, to be no sufficient reason for rejecting the interpretation of ancient writers, or for concluding that this god was other than a divine impersonification of fire; in which case it will no doubt appear most unlikely that he should have been one of the hypostases of the Egyptian triad, as stated by Jamblichus.

But this character seems more properly attributable to the Emeph of that author, who, as all writers concur in supposing, is the same as Cneph, Cnuph, or Chnuphis. This deity is thus described by Eusebius:—"*The Creator, whom they name Cneph, the Egyptians represent under a human figure of a dark blue colour, holding a zone and a sceptre; from whose mouth they say an egg proceeded, from which was produced another god, whom they name Ptha, but the Greeks Vulcan. This egg they interpret to signify the universe.*"* Jablonski, however, contends that Cneph and Ptha were one and the same god, for he thus concludes his remarks on the subject:—"Egyptii eundem etiam vocare consueverunt Pthan, quod dicere possis dei hujus nomen proprium; cui tamen adjunxerunt cognomen Cnuphis, ab immensa illius bonitate deductum."† But he adduces no proof in support of this opinion, which is in evident contradiction to all that is contained respecting these two deities in ancient writers. Cneph, also, is not mentioned, at least

* Eus. Præp. Evan., lib. iii. chap. 2.

† Pantheon Egypt., lib. iv. chap. 4. sect. 8.

under this name, by either Herodotus or Diodorus Siculus; but his existence as an ancient god of the Egyptians is sufficiently attested at this day, both by hieroglyphics and images exactly corresponding with those described by Eusebius.* Comparing together, therefore, the accounts of this god given by Jamblichus and Eusebius, it may be concluded, with much probability, that he is, in fact, the first divine hypostasis by whom this universe was actually created; and that he ought, consequently, to find a distinguished place in the Egyptian triad.

If, however, as Cudworth himself admits, Cneph be "that reason or wisdom which was the demiurgus of the world, and is properly the second of the forementioned hypostases," it must necessarily follow that the opinion of Jamblichus, as elsewhere adopted by Cudworth, that "the demiurgical intellect, and president of truth, as with wisdom it proceedeth to generation, and produceth into light the secret and invisible powers of the hidden reasons, is according to the Egyptian language called Hammon," must be incorrect. But, from the Greeks having universally identified this deity with Jupiter, it will be evident that he must have been one of the principal gods of Egypt; and perhaps, therefore, his real character is accurately described in these words of Diodorus Siculus:—"The ether was distinguished in the Egyptian language by a term which, being interpreted, signifies Jupiter; and, as this is the vital principle of animated beings, he was supposed to be, as it were, the father of all: thus coinciding with the Greek poets, who describe Jupiter as *the father of men and gods*."† It seems obvious that Diodorus here alludes to the opinion which is thus expressed by Balbus, in the second book of Cicero's treatise de Natura Deorum:—"Sed ipse Jupiter, id est, *juvans pater*, quem conversis casibus appellamus a *juvando Jovem*, a poetis pater divûmque hominumque dicitur: a majoribus autem nostris optimus, maximus; et quidem ante optimus, id est, beneficentissimus, quam maximus, quia majus est, certeque gratius, prodesse omnibus, quam opes magnas habere. . . . Euripides autem, ut multa præclare, sic hoc breviter,

* Salt's Essay on Hieroglyphics, p. 34.
† Bib. Hist., lib. i. chap. 12.

> Vides sublime fusum, immoderatum æthera,
> Qui tenero terram circumjectu amplectitur:
> Hunc summum habeto divum: hunc perhibeto Jovem."

Plutarch, also, in his treatise de Iside et Osiride, remarks, "Many are of opinion that the proper Egyptian name of Jupiter is Amoun (which we pronounce Ammon); and Manethos, the Sebennite, thinks that this word signifies *concealment*, or *that which is concealed.* But Hecatæus, the Abderite, says that it is the term used by the Egyptians when they call to any one; and on this account the first god, whom they consider to be invisible and concealed, they address and invoke by the name of Ammon, inviting him, as it were, to render himself manifest and visible." If, therefore, it be admitted, on the authority of Jamblichus, that this god was not, in fact, the Supreme Being, but one of the divine hypostases which had proceeded from him in some ineffable manner, and that Cneph was the creative power, it might be concluded, from the character attributed to him, that Ammon was the all-pervading and preservative energy of the one self-existent God.

But it is much more difficult to form any reasonable opinion respecting Osiris; for the whole fable concerning this god, Isis, Horus, Typhon, and Nephthys, is related by all writers as a mere historical occurrence, in which it is impossible to discover the slightest appearance of that supernatural power, by which the legends of all countries are distinguished. But it is, at the same time, equally incontrovertible that these personages were worshipped as deities in Egypt. Can it, therefore, be supposed that the Egyptians differed so entirely from all other people as to acknowledge for gods mere mortals, with whose birth, life, and death they were well acquainted, without their having performed while on earth any act which demonstrated their divine origin? The miraculous is undoubtedly indispensable for producing such a belief; and as it is entirely wanting in this fable, it must be concluded that the accounts given of it by ancient writers * have proceeded

* It seems clearly to have been known to Herodotus, as appears from these words: Λητω, εουσα των οκτω θεων των πρωτων γενομενων, οικεουσα δε εν Βουτοι πολι, ἱνα δε οἱ το χρηστηριον τουτο εστι, Απολλωνα παρα Ισιος παρακαταθηκην δεξαμενη, διεσωσε κατακρυψασα εν τῃ νυν πλωτῃ λεγομενῃ νησῳ· ὁτε δη το παν διζημενος ὁ Τυφων επηλθε, θελων εξευρειν του Οσιριδος τον παιδα. — Lib. ii. c. 156.

from some imposition of the Egyptian priests (though it is highly improbable that they would thus degrade their principal gods), or that they are altogether fictitious. In antiquity, also, the prevalent opinion represented Osiris to be the same as the sun, and yet the Greeks identified Horus, his son, with Apollo; and it is further sufficiently proved, that the sun was worshipped in Egypt under the name of PHRE. For Mr. Salt remarks:—"I shall class as fifth the god PHRE, or, as it may have been expressed, *Ph're, the sun;* though I entertain some doubt whether he was not the second, at least, of the higher order of Egyptian deities. He is generally represented by a globe, which is often encircled by the serpent, and is hieroglyphically designated by the same emblem, together with a small upright, oblong square, which together may express *phonetically Ph're.* His attributes are involved in mystery; and it seems doubtful whether he was ever represented under the semblance of any terrestrial figure, unless it be that of the hawk."* In this description, I think, will easily be recognised that faint attempt to represent the sun figuratively, in which all people have failed; as that resplendent orb too sensibly impresses on the human mind sentiments of power and glory, which it at once acknowledges must be more than human, and which nothing terrestrial, except the sacred fire, can adequately typify.†

But it cannot be contended that the Egyptians would have ever deified one and the same sensible object under two distinct forms; nor is this objection satisfactorily obviated by Jablonski, who remarks:—"Nam sol Egyptiis dicebatur ΦΡΗ, *Phre;* Osiris vero numen erat symbolicum, in quo vim, potestatem, jucundissimosque effectus solis reverebantur Egyptii, sicuti Græci et Latini, in Apolline et Phœbo. Et Osiridis nomen, quod mihi firmiter persuadeo, habitatione Israelitarum in Egypto fuit non paulo recentius."‡ For, to have rendered

* Essay on Hieroglyphics, p. 41.

† This remark of Lucian, in his tract de Syria Dea, in describing the temple at Hieropolis, deserves notice: Μονου γαρ Ηελιου και Σεληναιης ξοανα ου δεικνυουσι· ὁτευ δε εἱνεκα ὡδε νομιζουσι, εγω και τοδε εμαθον· λεγουσι τοισι μεν αλλοισι θεοισι ὁσιον εμμεναι ξοανα ποιεεσθαι, ου γαρ σφεων εμφανεα πανταισι τα ειδεα· Ηελιος δε, και Σεληναιη, παμπαν εναργεες, και σφεας παντες ὁρεουσι· κοιη αν αιτιη ξοανουργιης, τοισι εν τῳ ηερι φαινομενο ισι;

‡ Pantheon Egypt., lib. ii. cap. 1. sect. 8.

this opinion probable, he ought to have proved that the names Apollo and Phœbus were also of comparatively recent invention, and not coeval with the Greek religion: for otherwise it can never be admitted that any people would assign to their gods new names, unless the change were occasioned by some miracle of the deity, which the new name was intended to commemorate; and not merely by a wish to distinguish properties, such as the power and exhilarating effects of the sun, which must have been observed by them from the very first. At the same time the most ancient historian now extant expressly says: Οσιρις δε εστι Διονυσος κατα Ἑλλαδα γλωσσαν, — *but according to the Hellenic tongue Osiris is the same as Dionusos.** He also immediately adds: — " Although, among the Greeks, Hercules, Dionusos, and Pan are considered to be gods of very recent origin, yet amongst the Egyptians Pan was a most ancient deity and one of the original eight gods: but Hercules belonged to the second class, which consisted of twelve gods; and Dionusos to the third class, which was produced from these last." What Herodotus could possibly mean by such a succession of deities it is in vain to enquire, but it may be safely affirmed that it never existed amongst any people; and, though a new god might occasionally in some places receive the right of citizenship, still in all countries the principal gods remained the same from the very period at which the particular religion was first established. Nor does any thing occur in Herodotus which in the least evinces that he considered Dionusos to be the same as the sun; but, on the contrary, the placing of him in the third class of deities is a sufficient proof that he never could have entertained such an opinion. Consequently, the identification, by subsequent writers, of the sun with both Osiris and Dionusos, is evidently in direct opposition to the information which Herodotus received in Egypt, and leaves it more than dubious that Osiris was ever worshipped by the Egyptians as the sun.

It must, also, be self-evident that, had Osiris been a divine impersonification of the sun, it is perfectly impossible that any difference of opinion could ever have existed respecting his real character; for most assuredly nothing could have been of easier explanation, even by

* Herod., lib. ii. cap. 144.

the most ignorant Egyptian, or so easy of comprehension by the most careless foreign enquirer. What god is that? is a question which might be readily asked, and no other answer was required than merely pointing to the resplendent orb of day. How, therefore, could Osiris have been considered to be not only the sun, but also Dionusos, or Pluto, or Jupiter, or Pan, or Serapis, or Ammon, or the star Sirius? This opinion, therefore, of Cudworth cannot but appear to be the most probable:—"But much more was Osiris taken for the Supreme Deity, whose name was sometimes said to have signified, in the Egyptian language, πολυοφθαλμος, *that which had many eyes*; sometimes κρατος ενεργουν και αγαθοποιον, *an active and beneficent force*; and whose hieroglyphic was an eye and a sceptre, the former signifying power and wisdom, and the latter power and majesty (as Plutarch tells us). Who also is thus described in Apuleius:—'Deus deorum magnorum potior, et majorum summus, et summorum maximus, et maximorum regnator, Osiris;' *that god who is the chiefest of the greater gods, and the greatest of the chiefest, and which reigneth over the greatest*. . . . . The proper notion of Osiris being thus declared by Plutarch, το πρωτον και κυριωτατον των παντων ὁ τ' αγαθῳ ταὐτον εστι, *that first and highest of all beings, which is the same with good*. Agreeably whereunto Jamblichus affirmeth, αγαθων ποιητικος ων Οσιρις κεκλεται, *that god as the cause of all good* is called Osiris by the Egyptians." *

I refer so frequently to Cudworth, not only on account of his extensive erudition, but also in consequence of the view which he has taken of the polytheism of antiquity corresponding *generally*, in so remarkable a manner, with the system which still, after the lapse of ages, prevails in India; for, in the same manner that three divine hypostases were acknowledged by the Egyptians, as he contends †, so do the Hindus at this day identify Brahma, Vishnu, and Shiva, with the one self-existent and omnipotent God. But it cannot be admitted that *goodness* is such an attribute of the Supreme Being as men would ever acknowledge to

* Intellectual System, book i. chap. 4. sect. 18.

† It is to the principle, and not to the names, that I allude; for, in the uncertainty which exists respecting this religion, the gods who actually composed the Egyptian triad is a point which must necessarily be liable to doubt and to difference of opinion.

constitute a distinct hypostasis of his divine nature; or that the other two hypostases could ever have become objects of worship, had this quality, so essential for inspiring devotion, been abstracted from their attributes. Some other characteristic, therefore, is indispensable for distinguishing Osiris as one of the gods composing the Egyptian triad; and both his name, and the *phallus* by which he is distinguished, irresistibly lead the mind to assimilate this deity and his singular symbol to Ishwara or Shiva, and his well known type the *lingam;* not, however, Shiva in his destructive, but in his beneficent, character, and as he is adored by the Smàrtas at the present day in India. But that a darker shade of character than that *of the cause of all good* must have been ascribed to Osiris, seems highly probable from his having been identified with Pluto, that god whom Homer thus describes:—

"Deep in the dismal regions of the dead,
The infernal monarch rear'd his hoary head;
Leap'd from his throne, lest Neptune's arm should lay
His dark dominions open to the day,
And pour in light on Pluto's drear abodes,
Abhorr'd by men, and dreadful e'en to gods." *

Shiva, indeed, is not considered to be the infernal monarch, but he is represented as ornamented with a necklace of skulls, covered with the ashes of a funeral pile, delighting in cemeteries, and accompanied by a train of ghosts and goblins; and Osiris may perhaps have been occasionally represented in a nearly similar manner. May it not, therefore, be reasonably concluded, that, instead of being an impersonification of the sun, this deity is, in fact, one of the three principal gods into which the Egyptians believed that the Supreme Being, on willing the existence of this universe, had multiplied himself; that in the lapse of time his peculiar character and attributes had gradually become of a

* I add the original, as the translation differs so materially from it:—

Εδδεισεν δ' ὑπενερθεν αναξ ενερων, Αϊδωνευς,
Δεισας δ' εκ θρονου αλτο, και ιαχε· μη οἱ ὑπερθε
Γαιαν αναῤῥηξειε Ποσειδαων ενοσιχθων,
Οικια δε θνητοισι και αθανατοισι φανειη
Σμερδαλε', ευρωεντα, τα τε στυγεουσι θεοι περ. *Il.* υ. v. 61—65.

mixed and indeterminate nature, in the same manner as it has happened to those of Shiva in India; and that, previously to Egypt becoming known to the Greek historians, the worship of Osiris had acquired such a predominance in that country as particularly attracted the attention of foreigners, and obscured the popularity and celebrity which some of the other deities may have enjoyed in remoter antiquity?*

The singular manner in which the most learned writers have indulged in groundless hypotheses respecting the mythology of Egypt, is most strongly exemplified in the importance which has been attached to Typhon; for the notices relating to this deity which occur in ancient writers amount to nothing more than that he was the brother and murderer of Osiris. Nor does it appear that either the hieroglyphics or the figure by which he was represented have been yet ascertained, amongst the still existing inscriptions and sculptures of Egypt. Jablonski even admits: — " In genuinis gentis illius fabulis nihil reperire possum, ex quo colligas Genium hunc malum, ceu monstrum aliquod horrendum, quod de Typhœo, vidimus, pictum fictumve fuisse; et qui ex recentioribus contrarium nobis persuadere annituntur, nihil habent, quod pro tuenda sententia sua adferre queant, quam fictiones Græcorum poeticas. Quæ Herodotus, scriptorum omnium qui Typhonis Egyptii meminerunt antiquissimus, et post hunc alii, de malo hoc Genio, ex Ægyptiorum sermonibus referunt, ita comparata sunt, ut nisi ad indolem theologiæ gentis illius sollicite attendas, credere facile possis Typhonem fuisse HOMINEM, aliis prorsus similem, qui regnum Ægypti affectaverit, eoque fratrem suum Osiridem, cui et vitam eripuit, spoliaverit. † And nevertheless he gives this as his opinion: — " In ipsis primordiis idololatriæ apud Ægyptios excultæ et stabilitæ, Typhonem arbitror nomen fuisse SPIRITUS IMPROBI, cujus notitiam Ægyptii a Noachidis acceperant, vel PRINCIPII MALI, quod vetusti in Oriente theologi

* A traveller in the southern peninsula of India would unquestionably have his attention so particularly attracted to the worship of Shiva, which there predominates, that he would no doubt represent that god as being the principal deity of the Hindus. In the same manner, the English residing in Bengal have written much respecting Vishnu, and have scarcely noticed Shiva.

† Pantheon Egypt., lib. v. cap. 2. sect. 3.

Deo ac principio bono apposuere." * But it has, perhaps, been sufficiently evinced in the preceding chapter, that the doctrine of the two principles of good and evil was never known to the Egyptians; and nothing farther can be justly inferred from the fable of Isis and Osiris, than that Typhon was a cruel and ambitious man, as in it there is not ascribed to him the slightest act of supernatural power, or any thing which could denote a divine origin. The different conjectures, therefore, respecting this god, collected by Plutarch are surely deserving of no attention; and as the opinion which he also states, that Typhon was the sea, seems by far the most probable, it may be reasonably concluded that this deity was in reality considered by the Egyptians to be a divine impersonification of water †, and the god who presided over the sea.

"Quantumvis," observes Jablonski, "inter omnes constet, in toto antiquorum Ægyptiorum theologia, post Osiridem atque Isidem, celebrius nihil esse, aut frequentius occurrere, Hori, quem Osiridis Isidisque filium perhibent, nomine ac numine; negare tamen non possum, vix dari aliud ullum veteris Ægypti numen, quod mihi plus, quam quidem istud negotii facessiverit. Usque adeo, et vera nominis Hori interpretatio, et virtutis, quam in eo celebrarunt veteres Ægyptii, genuina explicatio, difficilis mihi semper visa est." ‡ The utmost, also, that is learned from Herodotus and Diodorus Siculus is, that this god was the son of Isis and Osiris, and that the Greeks considered him to be the same as Apollo. But this indisputable relationship to Isis, and the impossibility of determining in which of the characters of Apollo Horus was assimilated to him §, merely render the difficulty of ascertaining the

* Pantheon Egypt., lib. v. cap. 2. sect. 14.

† If, also, the crocodile be a symbol of Typhon, this impersonification will receive support from the vehicle of Varuna, the ocean god of the Hindus, being likewise a marine nondescript, the use of which is available equally on land as on water.

‡ Pantheon Egypt., lib. ii. cap. 4. sect. 1.

§ For Banier remarks: —"Parmi les dieux du paganisme il n'en est aucun dont les poëtes ayent publié tant de merveilles que d'Apollon, et selon eux il excella dans tous les beaux arts, tels que la poësie, la musique, et l'éloquence; et, par une hyperbole assez ordinaire en pareille occasion, on publia qu'il les avoit inventés. Il fut le dieu et le protecteur des poëtes, des musiciens, et des orateurs. Les Muses étoient aussi sous sa protection, et il présidoit à leurs concerts. Avec cela il n'y avoit aucun des dieux qui possédât

real character and attributes of this last deity the more insuperable. There appears also to be a well-founded doubt, whether the Horus of more recent times is precisely the same god as the one of remoter antiquity; for, if any credit be due to the fable of Isis and Osiris, both Diodorus Siculus and Plutarch expressly state that the elder Horus was the brother and not the son of Osiris. The latter, in particular, in speaking of the gods born on the intercalary days, says explicitly, *on the second day was Areueris born, whom some call Apollo, and some the elder Horus;* and he adds, that *the sun was the father of Osiris and Areueris;* thus completely refuting all suppositions which identify these two deities with the sun. It seems, however, that unless Horus be the same as Areueris, no trace of the existence of this latter god can be discovered in the still extant inscriptions and sculptures of Egypt; for M. Champollion remarks, "Les noms d'Horus et d'Areueris, divinités, qui ne m'ont paru former qu'un seul et même personage dans les textes hiéroglyphiques, où ils sont perpétuellement confondus."* But, as the complete extinction, not only of the worship, but of all memory of any deity, in so superstitious a country as Egypt, is quite improbable, it may be justly concluded that some mistake has occurred in the fable, and that one god only is to be recognised under the names of Areueris and Horus. It appears, at the same time, incontestable that this god was the son of Isis, and that he is distinguished by the two remarkable symbols of his father Osiris, the vau and the phallus: whence it would seem evident that he cannot be a divine impersonification of either a planet or an element; and that his real character must obviously remain undiscoverable, unless the deciphering of the hieroglyphics shall succeed in unfolding the long-concealed secrets of the Egyptian religion. †

---

comme lui l'art de connoître l'avenir; aussi fut-il celui qui eut un plus grand nombre d'oracles. A' tant de perfections on joignoit la beauté, les graces, l'art de charmer les oreilles, autant par la douceur de son éloquence, que par les accords harmonieux de sa lyre, qui enchantoit également les hommes et les dieux." — *La Mythologie, &c.* tom. ii. p. 222.

* Système Hiéroglyphique, p. 106.

† In Hindu paintings and sculptures Parwati is often represented with either Ganesha or Skanda in her lap, nor would the elephant head of the one, or the six heads of the other,

Neither the name of Serapis nor of Pluto, as applied to an Egyptian deity, occurs in Herodotus. But, in a preceding quotation, it has been seen that, according to Diodorus Siculus, this god was considered by some to be the same as Osiris, and by others to be the Pluto of the Greeks. Plutarch seems to adopt the first of these opinions; but Gibbon remarks, that "Serapis does not appear to have been one of the native gods, or monsters, who sprang from the fruitful soil of superstitious Egypt. The first of the Ptolemies had been commanded by a dream to import the mysterious stranger from the coast of Pontus, where he had been long adored by the inhabitants of Sinope; but his attributes and his reign were so imperfectly understood, that it became a subject of dispute, whether he represented the bright orb of day, or the gloomy monarch of the subterraneous regions. The Egyptians, who were obstinately devoted to the religion of their fathers, refused to admit this foreign deity within the walls of their cities; but the obsequious priests, who were seduced by the liberality of the Ptolemies, submitted, without resistance, to the power of the god of Pontus; and this fortunate usurper was introduced into the throne and bed of Osiris, the husband of Isis, and the celestial monarch of Egypt." * — Clemens Alexandrinus, also, ascribes to Serapis not only the greatest popularity, but the character of being a great demon. † The recentness, however, of this god's worship in Egypt does not seem satisfactorily established, and these words of Pausanias appear to indicate quite the contrary: — *Αιγυπτιοις δε ἱερα Σαραπιδος, επιφανεστατον μεν εστιν Αλεξανδρευσιν, αρχαιοτατον δ᾽ ει Μεμφει.* ‡ It has been likewise remarked, that these words of Tacitus, "*fuerat illic sacellum Serapidi atque Isidi antiquitus*

---

be any valid objection against identifying him with Horus, were it not that to neither of these gods are ever ascribed any of the symbols or attributes of their reputed father, Shiva. If, however, *Horus* be really an ancient Egyptian word, it coincides singularly in the accusative case *Horum* with Hărăm, a name of Shiva, or Hărim, a name of Vishnu.

* The Decline and Fall, &c., vol. v. p. 108.

† *Και τι περι ταυτα διατριβω, εξον τον αυτον μεγαλοδαιμονα ὑμιν επιδειξαι, ὁστις ην; ὁν δε κατ᾽ εξοχην προς παντων σεβασμου κατηξιωμενον ακουομεν· ταυτον αχειροποιητον ειπειν ετολμηκασιν, τον Αιγυπτιον Σαραπιν.*—*Cohor. ad Gentes*, p. 14.

‡ Pausaniæ Attica, cap. xviii.

sacratum *, would clearly evince that Serapis had been acknowledged as a god of Egypt long before the stranger deity from Pontus had been introduced into Alexandria. But, if the identification of Osiris with Shiva be admitted, the two opinions respecting Serapis may be easily reconciled; for, though neither of these gods presided over the lower regions, still, if the attributes of Osiris were similar to those of Shiva, there are certainly circumstances in the character of the latter which might lead an enquirer to conclude that he was in some manner connected with death and the regions of the dead. It may, therefore, appear probable that Serapis was an ancient and indigenous god of Egypt; and that the peculiar power which he was supposed to possess bore much resemblance to the dominion ascribed by the Greeks to Pluto, and by the Hindus to Yama.

With respect to the remaining gods of Egypt, Harpocrates, Anubis, Hermes, Papremis, and Hercules, so very little is known respecting them, and they appear to have been of such secondary importance, that they may be passed over without remark. But it is surprising that in later times the god of Mendes should have ceased to attract notice; as Herodotus represents him to have been one of the most ancient of the Egyptian deities; and Diodorus Siculus, also, observes that Pan was most particularly honoured by the Egyptians, and that his images were to be found in every temple.† The identifying, however, of this god with Pan conveys no information whatever with respect to his attributes and his real character, nor do these two authors afford any indications from which a reasonable opinion on the subject could be formed. ‡

A question now arises which, as far as I am aware, has never attracted the attention of any writer; and yet without its satisfactory

* Taciti Hist. lib. iv. c. 84. Ed. Gronovii.

† Και τον Πανα, διαφεροντως ὑπο των Αιγυπτιων τιμωμενον. τουτῳ γαρ τους εγχωριους ου μονον αγαλματα πεποιηκεναι κατα παν ἱερον, κ. τ. λ. — Lib. i. cap. 18.

‡ Even if the attributes and characters of the Grecian deities had been more clearly defined, the strange manner in which Grecian writers seem to have assimilated to them the gods of other countries, is strikingly exemplified in this passage of Lucian, in his tract de Syria Dea, in describing a statue, which he had just before stated to be that of Juno: —Ἡ δε Ἡρη σκοπεοντι τοι πολυειδεα μορφην εκφανεει. και τα μεν ξυμπαντα ατρεκεει λογῳ Ἡρη εστι· εχει δε τι και Αθηναιης, και Αφροδιτης, και Σεληναιης, και Ῥεης, και Αρτεμιδος, και Νεμεσιος, και Μοιρεων.

solution it must be evident that all systems respecting the origin of idolatry must be incomplete and inconclusive. For it seems obvious that the ascribing the distinction of sex to the divine nature is not a notion that naturally presents itself to the human mind; and that, on the contrary, the very attributes of action and power, according to the common modes of thinking, necessarily imply their exertion by a male being. The female, also, has every where been considered as a passive principle, and the mere recipient of the energy of the male. Whence, then, were mankind led to suppose that some of their principal deities were females? This question I propose; but, much as I have reflected upon it, I cannot venture to anticipate the answer which it requires. Reasoning, however, from the Hindu religion, it might be concluded that this circumstance has originated in that importance and respect which have been always attached to marriage amongst an unsophisticated people, and in an indistinct idea that the energy of the male must remain inert unless it were rendered active by a union with the passive powers of the female.* Of the operation of some such causes there are obvious traces in several systems of polytheism, as it will be evident from Isis having been considered as the wife of Osiris; Nephthys, of Typhon; Juno, of Jupiter; Proserpine, of Pluto; and in the Hindu mythology, all the female deities, except the earth †, are united in marriage to the different gods. But, if this principle be admitted, it will necessarily follow, that at the origin of idolatry the female deities were not held to be distinct divine powers, but were merely venerated as the wedded companions of their respective lords. In process of time, however, peculiar attributes may have been ascribed to some of them; but, even at this day, the only goddesses in India to whom independent powers are ascribed, are the spouses of Brahma, Vishnu, and Shiva. In endeavouring, therefore, to ascertain the real nature of polytheism in the earliest times, it would appear that the female deities could have then had no distinct character, and that, con-

* This idea frequently occurs in Sanscrit works; but it seems to be of too metaphysical a nature to have occurred to mankind at the time when idolatry commenced.

† Even the earth, however, is sometimes supposed to be united to Vishnu.

sequently, all systems respecting the origin of idolatry, which rest on a contrary supposition, must be erroneous.

But it seems to be a generally received opinion that the moon was a goddess, and the principal deity of several nations; and Mr. Faber opens his third volume on Pagan Idolatry with this portentous sentence:—"The female divinities, however apparently multiplied according to the genius of polytheism, ultimately resolve themselves into one, who is accounted the great universal mother both of gods and men; and this single deity is pronounced to be alike the moon in the firmament and the all-productive earth." I admit that sufficient authorities from ancient writers might be adduced in support of this opinion; but I contend that it bears upon its very face the strongest marks of those systematic attempts to explain the Grecian system of polytheism, which seem to have been coeval with the first Grecian historians; and that it is in direct contradiction to every principle from which idolatry could have originated: for, to give it even the appearance of plausibility, it must be shown that the aspect and influence of the moon are liable to five or six such obvious and essential changes as would have attracted the attention of the first men, and have induced them to ascribe each change to some divine power; and no person will, I may suppose, maintain so improbable an opinion. If not, can any other conceivable cause be assigned for this alleged multiplication of one and the same visible object into several deities? But there is not, at the same time, the slightest proof that the moon was ever considered by any people as a principal deity; and, until this point be first established, it must be evident that the above supposition can rest on no grounds whatever. * It also obviously assumes the point in question, and instead of clearly tracing the worship of the moon from its origin, and explaining the causes which, as it is supposed, induced mankind to adore it under the forms of several deities to whom distinct attributes were ascribed, it is, on the contrary, at once concluded that,

* That Artemis could not have been originally considered the same as the moon, seems evident from both Hesiod and Apollodorus describing the latter as the daughter of Hyperion and Thea: but even to Artemis there is no kind of pre-eminence assigned in Grecian mythology.

however varied these forms and their worship may have been, still they were all intended to represent but one and the same object, the moon. As such diversity, however, is incontestable, it must, until the contrary be proved, be held to be sufficient evidence of the actual individuality of the female deities of antiquity, and must evince the improbability of their having been all originally one and the same goddess.

This supposition, also, rests on the assumed universality of the opinion that the moon was a female deity; which assumption is demonstrably unfounded. For even Jablonski acknowledges that in the Egyptian, as well as in the German language, the moon was of the masculine gender: in the Arabic it is the same; and at this day in India the moon is a male deity. But Jablonski even admits farther:—"Verum fateri tamen cogor, me in ipsis Ægyptiorum veterum monumentis antiquis, *Lunæ* sub nomine *Ioh* cultæ, vestigia quæquam hactenus non deprehendisse;" and he had just before observed most correctly, "Nomina exercitui cœlorum, vel astris, in Ægypto imposita, primitus erant simplicia et significationis propriæ, ex communi sermonis usu depromta. *Solem* gens illa primo coluit sub nomine *Solis*, *Lunam* sub nomine *Lunæ*."* Mr. Payne Knight also remarks:—"Diana, of whom it (the deer) was a symbol, was in the original planetary and elementary worship the moon; but in the mystic religion she appears to have been a personification of the all-pervading spirit, acting through the moon upon the earth and the waters. Hence she comprehended almost every other female personification, and has innumerable titles and symbols, expressive of almost every attribute, whether of creation, preservation, or destruction."† But it cannot be denied that the last-mentioned state of any religious system incontrovertibly proves that it no longer remains in its primitive simplicity, and that it affords no evidence of that form by which it was originally distinguished. To this obvious consideration, however, writers have not adverted; and instead of producing hypotheses which, by their manifest adaptation to the modes of thinking of a rude and uncivilised people, would carry conviction with them, they have preferred adopting such views of poly-

* Pantheon Egypt., lib. iii. cap. 1. sect. 2.

† Inquiry into the Symbol., &c., part v. sect. 114.

theism as could not have possibly existed in remote antiquity, and which are evidently founded, not on the voice of popular opinion, but on the conclusions of speculative and philosophic minds.

These remarks apply with peculiar force to the opinions entertained respecting Isis, who was unquestionably the principal goddess of Egypt; but who has been described by ancient writers in such a manner as to render it difficult to form any satisfactory opinion of her real character. For, as I have before observed with regard to Osiris, had Isis been an impersonification of the moon, not the slightest doubt could ever have existed upon the subject; as the explanation of such a circumstance was so easy, and liable to no misapprehension. Herodotus, however, identifies this goddess with Ceres; and Diodorus Siculus says that she was supposed to be either Ceres, Juno, or the Moon. Plutarch remarks, "In short, it is not right to consider that Osiris and Isis are either water, or the sun, or the earth, or the heaven; or that Typhon is either fire, or drought, or the sea: but whatever is unarranged, imperfect, or monstrous, that name Typhon; and whatever is harmoniously ordered, good, and beneficial, that believe to be the work of Isis." In another part of the same treatise de Iside et Osiride, Plutarch observes, "that Isis is, in fact, the female principle of nature, the recipient of all production; the nurse and universal recipient according to Plato; and according to many she is called the *thousand-named*, on account of her mutability and capacity to receive all forms."* To the

* Ἡ γαρ Ισις εστι μεν το της φυσεως θηλυ, και δεκτικον ἁπασης γενεσεως, καθαπερ τιθηνη και πανδεχης ὑπο του Πλατωνος, ὑπο δε των πολλων μυριωνυμος κεκληται, δια το πασας ὑπο του λογου τρεπομενη μορφας δεχεσθαι και ιδεας.

The following passage from the *Lainga Puran* deserves attention; but to render it intelligible to the reader I must dispense with the variety of names and epithets which are in it ascribed to Shiva and Gauri, or Parwati:—"Shiva is the Supreme Being, and Gauri is his energy; Shiva is the male, and Gauri the female, principle of existence; Shiva is the meaning, and Gauri the voice; Shiva is the day, and Gauri the night; Shiva is the sacrificer, and Gauri the sacrifice; Shiva is the heaven, and Gauri the earth; Shiva is the sea, and Gauri the tide; Shiva is the tree, and Gauri the fruit; Shiva is Brahma, and Gauri Savitri (the wife of Brahma); Shiva is Vishnu, and Gauri Lakshoni. [In the same manner they are compared to all the other gods and goddesses, and even to the divine sages and their wives.] Shiva is every male, and Gauri every female, being; actuality is Shiva, potentiality Gauri; as multitudinous sparks issue from fire, so multitudinous forms of a twofold nature proceed from Shiva and Gauri, of which the outward form is Gauri, but the spirit Shiva; the senses

reader who is merely acquainted with Grecian mythology this description of a goddess may appear vague and indistinct, but these remarks of Sir William Jones will at once render it appropriate and definite, and sufficiently explain the real character of Isis :— "Iswara or Isa, and Isani or Isi, are unquestionably the Osiris and Isis of Egypt; for though neither a resemblance of names, nor a similarity of character, would separately prove the identity of Indian and Egyptian deities, yet when they both concur, with the addition of numberless corroborating circumstances, they seem a proof little short of demonstration. The female divinity, in the mythological system of the East, represents the active power of the male*; and that Isi means active nature appears evidently from the word *sacta*, which is derived from *sacti*, or *power*, and applied to those Hindus who direct their adoration principally to that goddess. This feminine character of PRACRITI, or *nature*, is so familiar in most languages, and even in our own, that the gravest English writers, on the most serious subjects of religion and philosophy, speak of *her* operations, as if *she* were actually an animated being; but such personifications are easily misconceived by the multitude, and have a strong tendency to polytheism. The principal operations of nature are, not the absolute annihilation and new creation of what we call *material substances*, but the temporary extinction and reproduction, or rather, in one word, the *transmutation* of forms; whence the epithet *Polymorphos* is aptly given to nature by European philosophers: hence Iswara united with Isi [and in the same manner Osiris united with Isis] represent the secondary causes, whatever they may be, of natural phenomena, and principally those of temporary destruction and regeneration." †

---

are Gauri, and the power of perception Shiva; intellection is Gauri, and the intellect is Shiva; the pedestal is Gauri, and Shiva is the lingam, the object of unceasing worship by men and gods; all things of a feminine nature are Gauri, and all of a masculine Shiva; the three worlds are but the form of Gauri, whose soul is Shiva. Thus are Shiva and Gauri the causes of all things, the preservers of this universe, and those to whom the adoration of men ought at all times to be devoutly addressed."—Part ii. chap. 11.

* Or rather the principle that gives activity to the power of the male, which, without its operation, would remain inert. Isi, consequently, cannot be considered as *active nature*, as she continues always passive until acted upon by Iswara.

† Sir W. Jones's Works, vol. vi. p. 318.

But Shiva, or Ishwara, as it will be hereafter shown, is also considered to be the Supreme Being, and Parvati his energy, by which this universe and all that it contains was produced; and at the same time they appear in popular mythology under a character in which they greatly resemble the deities of Olympus. Nor is it improbable that, in process of time, the original attributes of Osiris and Isis may have lost their primitive simplicity; and that, at the time when Grecian travellers first visited Egypt, such a variety of dissimilar qualities and powers may have been ascribed to them, as necessarily to occasion that difference of opinion respecting their real characters which occurs in ancient writers. *

The conjugal relation subsisting between Osiris and Isis seems placed beyond all doubt by the paintings and sculptures still extant in Egypt; and it appears that a similar connection between male and female deities may still be traced in one or two other instances: for Mr. Salt observes, "The second I shall describe as appearing to be, in some manner, connected with Kneeph, is Neith, one of the great goddesses representing the firmament. Her phonetic name is written in two different ways, with a waving line *n*, two feathers *e e*, and the upper half of a circle *t*; or with a vase *n*, and the upper part of a circle *t* or *θ*; these hieroglyphics being generally followed by a hieroglyphic that signifies the *firmament*, which is often found filled with stars, and is occasionally changed into one of the outstretched figures that overhang the zodiac. The hieroglyphics signifying the firmament also form a sort of canopy over every design of consequence throughout Egypt. She is also represented as a human figure with the head of a lion, and as such is the companion of Kneeph; and the goose and globe, with a feminine distinction, signifying the *daughter of the sun*, are

* I cannot conclude this point without adverting to the following passage in the third volume (p. 3.) of Faber's work on Pagan Idolatry: — "Then we are told that Devi, or the goddess, multiplies herself into the three forms of Parvati, Lachmi, and Sarasvati; and afterwards assumes as many subordinate characters as there are female divinities in the mythology of Hindustan. Yet each of these is severally, as we are assured, both the moon and the earth; and each is represented by the common symbols of the cow and the lotos." Because the first sentence is perfectly correct, but the second altogether erroneous; for the moon is in India a male deity; and though the earth is in reality but a form of Devi, yet, in appearance, she is always acknowledged to have individual existence.

then generally annexed to her phonetic name. On a mummy case in my possession, this goddess, as an outstretched figure, is represented as supported by Kneeph, who stands over a green figure recumbent, which may probably designate Egypt, or the earth." * But that any people ever deified the upper and lower firmament, as supposed by Mr. Salt, seems in the highest degree improbable; nor do I clearly understand what the sensible objects are which he intends to denote by these terms. Besides, all ancient authors, I believe, except Plutarch, identify this goddess with Minerva; and, however remote the resemblance may have been, it is most reasonable to suppose that she must have been one of the principal Egyptian deities. If, also, it be admitted that Cneph was one of the three divine hypostases, and that Neith was united to him in marriage, it would follow that she was probably distinguished by the same attributes; or, if any independent power were ascribed to her, it would be such as assimilated with these attributes. The celebrated inscription, therefore, on the temple at Sais, "*I am all that was, is, or will be, and no mortal has removed my veil,*" would be equally applicable to her as to Isis; and Jablonski has, perhaps, correctly expressed her real character in these words: — "Neitham ab Ægyptiis præsidem habitum fuisse sapientiæ, eoque potissimum Græcos deam hanc dixisse Minervam, vel eam cum Minerva sua comparasse, ambigi non potest. . . . Nec omittendum, quod Proclus in Timæum de Minerva Ægyptiorum observat. Verba Latine a me versa brevitatis studio hic appono. *Est igitur dea hæc quædam opifex, invisibilis simul*

* Essay on Hieroglyphics, p. 36.

With respect, however, to the phonetic system, I must, as a philologist, be permitted to remark, that it depends entirely upon an assumption that *Coptic was the ancient language of Egypt.* But in what manner is it proved that this language was preserved, notwithstanding the country was conquered by the Persians, the Macedonians, the Romans, and the Arabs? For the authorities quoted by M. Quatremère merely establish that, until its conquest by the Arabs, a language still continued in use which was denominated Egyptian; but that it was precisely the same as the one spoken in the time of Cambyses, or even as the present Coptic, remains not only unproved, but is also obviously unsusceptible of proof without the assistance of manuscripts. Another decipherer might, therefore, assume another language as the basis of a new phonetic system; and it would evidently require a most copious collection of hieroglyphics, and a most careful examination of them, to determine incontrovertibly that they could not be arranged into groups reducible into significant words in any other language than Coptic.

et visibilis, cui cœlum quidem sortito obtigit; sed quæ tamen generationes specierum irradiat — ideoque cumprimis virtus constituta est, quæ cuncta movet." * Nor can it fail to be considered as a most remarkable coincidence, that, after the lapse of so many ages, Sarasvati, the wedded companion of the creative power of the Hindu triad, should still be adored as the deity presiding over speech, eloquence, and wisdom.†

It would seem, also, that Ammon, the preservative power of the Egyptian triad, was, in the same manner, the lord of one of the Egyptian goddesses. For M. Champollion observes:—"Les bas reliefs Egyptiens nous montrent assez souvent à la suite d'Ammon, une déese dont les chairs sont peintes tantôt en vert, tantôt en jaune, mais dont le signe distinctif est une *grande feuille* qui s'élève au-dessus de sa coiffure. Sur le devant d'un autel soutenu par une statue de granit, qui fait partie de la riche collection d'antiquités de M. Durand, cette même déesse est figurée *donnant la main* au dieu Ammou. . . . . Le nom hiéroglyphique de la déesse écrit en lettres Coptes *sate* ou *sati*, est donc incontestablement le même que le nom ΣΑΤΗΣ ou ΣΑΤΙΣ de l'inscription de Séhrele."‡

But of this goddess no notice occurs in any ancient writer, unless she may be the one who was assimilated to the Venus of the Greeks, whose Egyptian name has not been yet satisfactorily determined: for Herodotus affords no information on this point; but Diodorus Siculus, as he mentions her among the five deities born on the intercalary days, would seem to have considered her to be the same as the Nephthys of Plutarch. This last author, however, says that Nephthys was supposed to be either Venus, or Teleutes, or Victory; but from an identification with deities of such opposite characters no reasonable conclusion can be deduced. The reasoning, also, of Jablonski, with respect to Athor and Nephthys, is singularly perplexed and unsatisfactory; for he adduces strong proofs that Athor was the Egyptian name of Venus, and yet he rejects them all on very inadequate grounds, and concludes that Athor was a deification of night. But he admits, "numen hoc

* Pantheon Egypt., lib. i. cap. iii. sect. 10.

† Brahma, also, is considered to be the author of the Vedas and of all sacred learning.

‡ Système Hieroglyphique, p. 99.

Noctis, cujus et nomen et potestatem explicuimus, per totam Ægyptum templa habuit complura, celebria, a multis frequentata, cultu ejus et laudibus personantia." * It may, however, be safely affirmed, that Night was never, amongst any people, considered as a principal goddess; and, in fact, the ascribing to her any divine *power* is quite incompatible with the common opinion of mankind. † But Jablonski seems to have been more successful in evincing that Nephthys could not have been the goddess whom the Greeks assimilated to Venus; and if it be admitted that Typhon was merely a divine impersonification of water, the following remarks of Cudworth may appear, as far as they regard the real character of this deity, to be well founded: — " Yet, as the learned Bochart hath observed, it (the word *Neptune*) may, with greater probability, be derived from the Egyptian word *Nephthus,* Plutarch telling us, ὁτι Νεφθυν καλουσι της γης τα εσχατα, και παρορια και ψαυοντα της θαλασσης· *that the Egyptians called the maritime parts of land, or such as border on the sea, Nephthus;* which conjecture may be farther confirmed from what the same Plutarch elsewhere writes, that as Isis was the wife of Osiris, so the wife of Typhon was called Nephthus. From whence one might collect, that as Isis was taken sometimes for the earth, or the goddess presiding over it, so Nephthus was the goddess of the sea." ‡

But if Nephthys be not the same as Venus, it may not seem improbable that the Egyptian goddess intended by this appellation, not indeed the *popular,* but the *celestial* § Venus of the Greeks, may have been the wedded companion of the preservative power of the Egyptian

* Pantheon Egypt., lib. i. cap. 1. sect. 15.

† The character of Night is well described in these verses of one of the hymns ascribed to Orpheus: —

Κλυθι μακαιρα θεα, κυαναυγης, αστεροφεγγης·
Ἡσυχιῃ χαιρουσα και ηρεμιῃ πολυυπνῳ,
Ευφροσυνη, τερπνη, φιλοπαννυχε, μητηρ ονειρων·
Ληθομεριμν' αγαθη τε, πονων αναπαυσιν εχουσα.

‡ Intellectual System, book i. chap. 4. sect. 18.

§ In Platonis Convivio this passage occurs: —Πως δ'ου δυο τα θεα; ἡ μεν γε που πρεσβυτερα, και αμητωρ, Ουρανου θυγατηρ, ἡν δε και ουρανιαν επονομαζομεν· ἡ δε νεωτερα, Διος και Διωνης, ἡν δε πανδημον καλουμεν. Pausanias, also, mentions the celestial Venus in several passages of his work, but such allusions are not sufficient to explain her real character.

triad. Her attributes, however, are not distinctly known; and it is not, therefore, unlikely that they are too much restricted in the beautiful lines with which Lucretius commences his poem, and that they in reality bore much resemblance to the divine qualities ascribed to Lakshmi, the beloved wife of Vishnu, in the following passage of the *Vishnu Puran**:—" Praise be to thee, O mother of all things, source of prosperity, dweller in the bosom of Vishnu! Thou art the efficient cause of existence, the fiery power which purifies this world, the manifester of twilight, night, and day! Thou art understanding, faith, and wisdom, the fount of learning, the giver of beatitude; and by thee, O goddess, is this universe filled with various forms, beautiful and unbeautiful! Deserted by thee the three worlds sink into annihilation, and supported by thee they enjoy prosperity! Blessed by thy presence, men are rendered happy by wives, children, friends, houses, and riches; by health, power, victory over enemies, and contentedness! Thou, O beloved of Vishnu, art the mother of all creation, and thy fostering care pervadeth all things movable and immovable; but without thy presence, nor wives, nor children, nor friends, nor riches, would gladden men; nor animals, nor verdure, nor fertility adorn the earth. But what tongue, even of the most learned, can adequately eulogise thy wondrous and mysterious qualities?" It will hence no doubt be admitted, that the goddess of prosperity and abundance, emphatically named the *mother* and the *mother of the universe*, is a most appropriate conjugal companion for the preservative power of the Egyptian triad; and that there is a sufficient resemblance between the Lakshmi of the Hindus and the celestial Venus of the Greeks, to render it not improbable that the Egyptian goddess, intended by the latter appellation, was actually distinguished by attributes similar to those which are at this day in India ascribed to the beloved and inseparable companion of Vishnu.

* It is a laudatory address to her by Indra, and occurs towards the conclusion of the ninth chapter, first section; in which also will be found at the commencement a description of Lakshmi, precisely similar to that of Gauri given in a preceding note; which, to be perfectly applicable, merely requires the names of Vishnu and Lakshmi to be substituted for those of Shiva and Gauri.

There still remain two Egyptian goddesses not yet adverted to, Bubastis or Diana, and Buto or Latona, who are noticed by ancient writers; but, except this identification, nothing whatever is known respecting them. It would, therefore, be useless to enter into an examination of the different opinions of modern authors as to their attributes and real character, as it would not lead to any rational conclusion on the subject.

Such are the notices relating to the Egyptian religion which occur in ancient writers, and their total inadequacy to convey any complete and satisfactory knowledge of it must be self-evident. Arguing, however, from these imperfect indications, and from the principles in which polytheism most likely originated, it may not seem improbable that in its primitive state the Egyptian bore a strong resemblance to that form of idolatry which even at this day prevails in India. It cannot, therefore, be unreasonable to conclude that the Egyptians acknowledged one supreme self-existent Being; and that this belief did not attract the attention of foreign enquirers, in consequence of its not being manifested by the erection of temples and images or any other mode of external worship. That the Egyptians held that, in all operations connected with the creation and existence of this universe, the one God, being without form and quality, acted not directly, but through the intervention of three divine powers which had proceeded from his essence in an ineffable manner, and were named Cneph, Ammon, and Osiris. That under some notion of a union of the male and female principles being indispensable for producing action, the Egyptians had assigned, as conjugal companions to these gods, the goddesses Neith, Athar or Venus, and Isis. So far the conclusion may seem to rest on admissible grounds, but the slightest inspection of the plates of Denon's Voyage en Egypte, or even of the Mensis Isiaca, will at once evince that, were this conclusion even granted, it would be of scarcely any assistance in explaining the singularly complicated system of Egyptian polytheism. Must it not, therefore, be more conducive to the promotion of real knowledge to admit this ignorance unreservedly, than to construct hypotheses on mere gratuitous assumptions, for the purpose of elucidating that which is clearly unsusceptible of elucidation?* Were these hypotheses, however, confined entirely to Egypt, they would be of little importance, but unfortunately they extend their influence to all subjects of antiquarian and historical research; and thus materially contribute to impede the rectification of error, and to prevent just views being taken of the civilisation, religion, and history of the nations of antiquity.

* Should it even be found possible to explain, by means of the phonetic system, hieroglyphical inscriptions, it cannot be supposed that these contain any information which would tend to discover the hidden meaning, which is, no doubt, concealed under the positions and figures of the Egyptian deities, their symbols, head-dresses, and all the other accessaries by which they are invariably accompanied; and, until this be ascertained, the Egyptian religion must evidently remain an enigma that admits not of solution.

CHAP. III.

THE MYTHOLOGY OF ASIA MINOR, GREECE, ETRURIA, AND LATIUM.

It cannot be disputed that, according to the prevalent opinion of antiquity, Greece was indebted for the principal part of its religion to Egypt; and, as far as I am aware, this opinion has been adopted by every modern writer who has touched upon this subject. To controvert, therefore, an admitted fact may seem presumptuous, yet it may be allowable to examine the grounds on which its existence has been so universally assumed; and, should these clearly appear to be insufficient, it must necessarily follow that the real origin of the Grecian system of polytheism has been hitherto misunderstood. Nor will it, perhaps, be denied, that, in historical researches, the only guide which can lead to the ascertainment of truth, is a strict application of those principles of evidence that induce men to give their assent to human testimony in the common affairs of life. For, in such researches, probability and certainty should be always clearly distinguished; and, though the writer may present his inferences for the consideration of the reader, he ought not to ascribe to them that importance which belongs alone to circumstances supported by the requisite proof. But it is too much the custom to found an elaborate system on authorities either questionable or inapplicable, or on conclusions deduced from a few isolated facts, too obviously tortured into a construction which was never intended by the author who may have mentioned them.

On this occasion, however, the received opinion rests principally, if not entirely, on the testimony of a single witness contained in these often-quoted words of Herodotus:—"Almost all the names of the gods have come from Egypt into Greece: for, on enquiry, I have found that they were received from Barbarians, and I think principally from Egypt; because, with the exception of those of Neptune, the Tyndaridæ, Juno, Vesta, Themis, the Graces, and the Nereids, the names of all the other gods have been known in Egypt from time immemorial. I merely repeat what the Egyptians themselves say." * It must be here particularly recollected, that this opinion relates to an occurrence which, according to the received system of chronology, must have taken place about ELEVEN HUNDRED years previously to Herodotus's visiting Egypt; and that it depends entirely on *verbal information*, and on the resemblance, the particulars of which he does not explain, which Herodotus supposed to exist between certain deities of Egypt and Greece. But so obviously liable to error are such premises, that any conclusion deduced from them must be extremely questionable. If, also, the premises themselves be obviously inconsistent and inaccurate, and the judgment of the writer be at the same time vacillating and illogical, what degree of credit can be due to any opinion which he may have formed?

But the numerous circumstances which so obviously invalidate this testimony seem to have been entirely disregarded, as not the slightest attempt has ever been made to reconcile it with the accounts given of the Grecian system of polytheism by other writers; for Herodotus expressly excludes from the number of Egyptian deities Neptune and Juno, and he nowhere identifies any one of them with Pluto. It must, however, be evident that these three deities have formed, from the time of Homer and Hesiod, so essential and constituent a part of Grecian mythology, that it is utterly improbable that they could have been introduced into it after its first establishment. Herodotus, at the same time, enters into no explanation of the causes that had occasioned the remarkable difference which is observable in the relative importance and dignity ascribed by him to the gods of Greece and Egypt; for he unequivocally admits that Isis and Osiris were the principal deities of the latter country, and yet he identifies them with Ceres and Dionusos, who most certainly never enjoyed that pre-eminence in

* Σχεδον δε και παντα τα ουνοματα των θεων εξ Αιγυπτου εληλυθε ες την Ἑλλαδα. διοτι μεν γαρ εκ των βαρβαρων ἡκει, πυνθανομενος οὑτω εὑρισκω εον. δοκεω δ' ων μαλιστα απ' Αιγυπτου απιχθαι. ὁτι γαρ δη μη Ποσειδεωνος, και Διοσκουρων, και Ἡρης, και Ἱστιης, και Θεμιος, και Χαριτων, και Νηρηιδων, των αλλων θεων Αιγυπτιοισι αιει κοτε τα ουνοματα εστι εν τῃ χωρῃ. λεγω δη τα λεγουσι αυτοι Αιγυπτιοι.—Lib. ii. cap. 50.

Greece.* The Egyptian gods, too, whom he assimilates to Pan, Dionusos, and Hercules, he describes as in every respect different from them; and he affords his reader no means of judging whether his identification of certain Egyptian deities with Jupiter, Apollo, Mars, Minerva, Venus, Latona, and Diana, is well founded or otherwise. There appears, also, to be the strongest evidence that the paintings and sculptures still extant in Egypt existed at the time when it was visited by Herodotus; and it must hence necessarily follow, that not a single god of Egypt could, in outward appearance, have then borne the slightest resemblance to any god of Greece. The names, too, he admits, were different; and, consequently, the grounds which led him to affirm that the deities of the two countries, with a few exceptions, were the same, must have rested on the knowledge which he possessed of his own religion, and on the information which he received concerning the origin, actions, and attributes of the Egyptian gods. Had he, therefore, stated the circumstances on which his opinion was founded, a judgment might be formed with respect to its justness; but as he has carefully refrained from explaining the nature of the Egyptian religion, and even from describing the figures of the gods, and their remarkable symbols, nothing appears from which it can be reasonably concluded that this opinion, invalidated as it is by various considerations, is entitled to that implicit deference which it has so universally received.†

But, even of his own religion, Herodotus clearly possessed no accurate knowledge; and his account of it is so improbable and irrational, as to destroy all confidence in his ability to draw a just conclusion from well-established premises. I must, therefore, be allowed, in order to place this point in its proper light, to quote a rather long passage from so well-known an author.—"The Pelasgi, as I heard at Dodona, at first, in worshipping the gods, sacrificed all things to them; but they did not distinguish any one of them by either name or

* I mean, of course, in its popular and most ancient mythology; for the rank assigned to these deities in the mysteries is not sufficiently ascertained.

† Josephus, also, has remarked: — *Μανεθων δ' ην το γενος ανηρ Αιγυπτιος, της Ἑλληνικης μετεσχηκως παιδειας, ὡς δηλος εστι· γεγραφε γαρ Ἑλλαδι φωνη την πατριον ἱστοριαν, εκ τε των ἱερων, ὡς φησιν αυτος, μεταφρασας, και πολλα τον Ἡροδοτον ελεγχει των Αιγυπτιακων ὑπ' αγνοιας εψευσμενον.*— *Contra Apionem*, lib. i. cap. 14.

epithet, as they never had heard any. But they called them gods, on account of their harmoniously ordering and arranging all things.* After a long time, however, they became acquainted with the names of the gods which had come from Egypt, with the exception of that of Dionusos, which they learned much later; and some time after they consulted the oracle at Dodona, respecting whether they should make use of the names introduced by the Barbarians, and the oracle advised them to adopt them. From that period the Pelasgi worshipped the gods by these names, and from the Pelasgi the Hellenes received them. But whence each of these deities derived his origin, and whether they have all eternally existed, and what their particular forms may be, these are questions which remained unknown from ancient times even until yesterday, if I may so express myself; for Hesiod and Homer, who lived not more than four hundred years before me, were the first who composed a theogony for the Greeks, and ascribed to the gods distinct epithets, and dignities, and functions, and figures. The first part of what I have just mentioned is the result of information which I received from the priests of Dodona, the latter is my own opinion." †

It will be at once obvious, that the latter part of this passage is inconsistent with the former; for, if Homer and Hesiod were the persons who first gave a fixed form to the Grecian mythology, the account given to Herodotus by the priests of Dodona must be incorrect, because, as the mere names only of the gods were introduced from Egypt into Greece, it must follow that their attributes, characters, and relations to each other, must have been previously known to the inhabitants of the latter country. It does not appear, however, to have been observed, that, according to this account, *the gods previously existed in Greece*, and that it was *their names only* which were derived from Egypt; and, consequently, the correctness of this last opinion depends simply on the probability or improbability of any people having ever worshipped a number of divine beings under the general term *gods*,

* Θεους δε προσωνομασαν σφεας απο του τοιουτου, ότι κοσμῳ θεντες τα παντα πρηγματα και πασας νομας ειχον.

† Herod., lib. ii. cap. 52, 53.

without appropriating to each of them a distinct appellation. This circumstance Mr. Mitford thus ingeniously explains: — "Herodotus, after giving an account of the origin of the names of the principal Grecian divinities, proceeds to tell us that, being at Dodona, he was there assured (apparently by the priests of the far-famed temple of Jupiter) that anciently the Pelasgian ancestors of the Grecian people sacrificed and prayed to gods to whom they gave no name or distinguishing appellation; *for*, he adds, *they had never heard of any: but they called them gods as the disposers and rulers of all things.* It is hence evident that the Pelasgians can have acknowledged but one god; for where many gods are believed, distinguishing appellations will and must be given; but the unity of the deity precludes the necessity of names." * But the prevalence of idolatry, at the period here assumed, is too unquestionable a fact to admit of its being supposed that the Pelasgi were the only people then exempt from it; and as most assuredly no instance can be adduced of gods having ever been worshipped undistinguished by any names by which they might be invoked or even spoken of, it must necessarily follow that the information given to Herodotus by the priests of Dodona is undeserving of any attention whatever.

Before, also, it can be received as an established fact that Greece was indebted to Egypt for the names of its gods, or for any part of its religion, it is indispensable to prove the particular manner in which this introduction was effected, and on this essential point all ancient authors are entirely silent. Modern writers, however, have, without any sufficient data, constructed various hypotheses for the explanation of this circumstance; but the general opinion respecting it seems to be accurately and concisely stated in these words of Mr. Mitford: — "It appears that, in a very remote period, some revolution in Egypt, whose early transactions are otherwise little known to us, compelled a large proportion of the inhabitants to seek foreign settlements. To this event Crete probably owed its early civilisation. Some of the best supported of ancient Grecian traditions relate *the establishment of Egyptian colo-*

* History of Greece, vol. i. p. 70.

nies in Greece; traditions so little accommodated to national prejudice, yet so very generally received, and so perfectly consonant to all known history, that for their most essential circumstances they seem unquestionable." * But I am not aware of a single writer who has stated in express terms that Egyptian colonies were established in Greece; though from the following passages of Diodorus Siculus and Strabo such a conclusion might perhaps be admissible. For the former has observed: — "The Egyptians say, that after this many emigrations from Egypt to different parts of the world took place; for Belus led a band of emigrants to Babylon;. . . . and those who proceeded with Danaus occupied Argos, almost the most ancient city of Greece. Egyptian emigrants, also, founded the Colchic and Jewish nations." † And Strabo says, "Pelops led people from Phrygia into the country denominated from him Peloponnesus; and also Danaus from Egypt." ‡ But all preceding authors have distinctly intimated that Danaus arrived at Argos in a single ship: and that this was the generally received tradition seems evident from this entry in the Arundel marbles: "Ep. 9. A quo navis prima ex Egypto solvens in Græciam appulit, et vocata est Pentecontorus, et Danai filiæ," &c. §; and from Apollodorus likewise adopting it, as he states, "Egyptus had by many wives fifty sons, and Danaus fifty daughters. A disagreement subsequently taking place

* History of Greece, vol. i. p. 20. In a note, Mr. Mitford, in support of this statement, refers generally to Herodotus, Plato, Aristotle, Isocrates, Strabo, Diodorus Siculus, Æschylus, and Euripides, but without citing any particular passages from their works. This mode of quotation is alone a strong presumption that these authors contain nothing which would establish the correctness of this opinion.

A remarkable instance, also, of the mistakes into which prevention will lead an author, occurs in this immediately following passage: — "Argos, according to all accounts, was an Egyptian colony;" and in support of this statement is cited Thucyd. lib. i. cap. 3. But in this chapter neither Argos nor an Egyptian colony is mentioned, nor is there even the slightest allusion made to such a subject.

† Οἱ δε ουν Αιγυπτιοι φασι και μετα ταυτα αποικιας πλειστας εξ Αιγυπτου κατα πασαν διασπαρηναι την οικουμενην. εις Βαβυλωνα μεν γαρ αγαγειν αποικους Βηλον. . . . Λεγουσι δε και τους περι τον Δαναον ὁρμηθεντας ὁμοιως εκειθεν συνοικισαι την αρχαιοτατην σχεδον των παρ' Ἑλλησι πολεων Αργος, το, τε των Κολχων εθνος εν τῳ Ποντῳ, και το των Ιουδαιων ανα μεσον Αραβιας και Συριας, οικισαι τινας ὁρμηθεντας παρ' ἑαυτων.—Lib. i. cap. 28.

‡ Πελοπος μεν εκ της Φρυγιας επαγομενου λαον εις την απ' αυτου κληθεισαν Πελοποννησον, Δαναου δε εξ Αιγυπτου.—Lib. vii. p. 321.

§ Marmora Oxon., ed. Oxon. 1676. p. 160.

between them, and Danaus fearing the sons of Egyptus, by the inspiration of Minerva, prepared the first fifty-oared vessel, and embarking with his daughters fled from Egypt."* So far, also, is Æschylus from considering Danaus to be the leader of a colony, that he describes him as a suppliant; and his daughters, in the commencement of the tragedy of the Supplicants, thus express themselves: —

> "Protector of the suppliant! gracious Jove!
> Look with an eye of pity on this train,
> Which from the gentle depths of Nile have sped
> Their naval enterprise. Those sacred fields,
> That border on the Syrian wastes, we leave,
> Not by the voice of public justice doom'd
> For blood, but willing fugitives from youths
> Too near allied, whose impious love would raise
> Perforce the nuptial bed by us abhorr'd;
> Sons of Egyptus they. Our father Danaus,
> On whose authority we build our counsels,
> And strengthen our abhorrence, plann'd these measures,
> And wrought us to this honourable toil,
> To wing our swift flight o'er the billowy main,
> And reach the shores of Argos."

And in another place: —

> "The dashing oar, the swelling sail,
> That caught the favourable gale,
> Safe from the storm, nor I complain,
> Wafted our frail bark o'er the main."†

---

* Apollodori Bib., lib. ii. cap. 1.

† I have availed myself of Potter's translation. The last four verses, however, seem so strangely translated, that I add the original: —

> Πλατα μεν ουν λινοῤῥαφης τε
> Δομος, ἅλα στεγων, δορος
> Αχειματον μ' επεμψε συν πνοαις·
> Ουδε μεμφομαι τελευτας. V. 133—136.

It hence seems very inprobable, that, in the following lines of Euripides, in Archelao (the only ones of this poet in which the name of Danaus occurs), the term ῳκισε could have been intended to signify either the establishment of a colony, or the founding of a city: —

> Δαναος, ὁ πεντεκοντα θυγατερων πατηρ,
> Νειλου λιπων καλλιστον εκ γαιης ὑδωρ·
> Ὁς εκ μελαμβροτοιο πληρουται ῥοας
> Αιθιοπιδος γης, ἡνικ' αν τακῃ χιων,
> Τεθριππου οντος ἡλιου δι' αιθερα·
> Ελθων ες Αργος ῳκισ' Ιναχου πολιν,
> Πελασγιωτας δ' ωνομασμενους το πριν
> Δαναους καλεισθαι νομον εθηκ' αν' Ἑλλαδα.

Eurip. Opera, ed. Musg. Lips. 1779, tom. ii. p. 428.

Mr. Mitford has farther stated: "With Ogyges, however, even rumour of events in Attica ceases till Cecrops became prince of the province, leading thither, according to the most received and probable accounts, a colony from Egypt." But for this assertion Mr. Mitford quotes no authority, nor can I discover any*; and, on the contrary, Apollodorus affirms, Κεκροψ αυτοχθων, συμφυες εχων σωμα ανδρος και δρακοντος, την Αττικην εβασιλευσε πρωτος.† According, also, to the received system of chronology, Cecrops flourished about the year 1556 B. C., and Danaus arrived in Greece in 1511 B. C.; and it must, therefore, be evident, that any traditions relating to such remote times must be extremely dubious. But, comparing together all the indications of such events that occur in ancient writers, it cannot be denied, that the utmost which can be justly concluded from them is, that some distinguished foreigners, with a few followers, may have migrated into Greece, and as far as individual influence extended may have contributed to its civilisation ‡; but there is not the slightest proof that Egyptian colonies had formed any establishments in that country in the sixteenth century before the Christian era.

The *modus operandi* being thus not only disproved, but it being established on the authority of Herodotus himself, that the *gods existed* in Greece previously to the introduction of *their names* § from Egypt, it

* In Wesseling's edition, however, of Diodorus Siculus, this note occurs in tom. i. p. 33.: — "A Palmerii sententia nihil admodum recedit Jo. Marsham, Canon. Chron. p. 111.: *Tres, inquit, memorat Diodorus, Petem Menesthei patrem,* CECROPEM, *et Erechtheum : desideratur Cecropis nomen ; locus enim mutilus est : sed res indicat,* τον γαρ Πετην τον πατερα Μενεσθεως του στρατευσαντος εις Τροιαν * * (*desunt nonnulla*) * * φανερως Αιγυπτιον υπαρξαντα, τυχειν υστερον Αθηνησι πολιτειας τε και βασιλειας. διφυης δ' αυτου γεγονοτος. *Ista in editis male conjuncta sunt, Peteus enim Ornei filius, Erechthei regis nepos, ab Ægeo Athenis pulsus in Phocide consenuit ; Cecrops autem et* διφυης *et rex Athenarum.* Cui et ego adstipulor," adds Wesseling.

† Bib. lib. iii. c. 14.

‡ For instance, the establishment of the Phœnician Cadmus at Thebes seems to have been a tradition so generally credited in antiquity, as to render it probable that this simple circumstance really occurred. But that he either led a colony there, or was despatched by his father in search of his sister, who had been carried away by Jupiter in the form of a bull, are events which cannot certainly command belief.

§ But it is universally admitted by ancient writers themselves, and seems fully proved by modern researches, that the names of the Egyptian and Grecian deities are totally dissimilar. Even on this point, therefore, not the slightest credit is due to the information given by Herodotus. L'Abbé Foucher, however, makes these very singular remarks: — "Il seroit à souhaiter qu'Hérodote nous eût appris comment il avoit fait cette vérification; on voit, il

must necessarily follow, that there are no grounds whatever for supposing that the deities of Homer and Hesiod differed in any respect from those which had been adored in ancient times by the Pelasgi. But Eusebius has affirmed, that "the mythology of Greece consisted of nothing but excerptions and misconstructions of more ancient systems, as it was evinced not only by the opinions of the different historians whom he had cited, but by the very nature of the theology of the Greeks; since there was nothing whatever domestic in their accounts of the gods, as these were derived entirely from the fables of foreign nations." * No authority, however, quoted by Eusebius, justifies this unqualified conclusion; nor has even Diodorus Siculus, on whom he principally relies, stated that Greece derived its religion from Egypt or from any other country. It is, at the same time, singular that, in ascribing this origin to Grecian mythology, Eusebius did not support his opinion by adducing instances of similarity or identity between it and other systems of polytheism. For it must be evident that the mere affirming that a certain god of one country was the same as a certain god of another country, conveys no information whatever; and, on the contrary, in cases of such dissimilarity as exists between the names, figures, and symbols of the deities of Greece, Egypt, and Phœnicia, this dissimilarity must be *primâ facie* strong presumption that such affirmation is unfounded. Nothing, consequently, could satisfactorily establish the alleged identity, except sufficient proof that, notwithstanding this external difference, there still was such a resemblance between the actions, attributes, and characters of the two deities com-

---

est vrai, de la conformité entre les noms E′gyptiens et Grecs de quelques-unes de ces divinités. Pan est un nom qui peut-être passé sans altération de l'E′gyptien dans le Grec: Héphaistos est probablement le dieu E′gyptien Pthas; on donne les mêmes noms à Latone et à Hercule (Léto, Hérakles), soit qu'on en parle comme de divinités Grèques ou comme de divinités E′gyptiennes; mais quel rapport entre *Amoun* et *Zeus*, *Osiris* et *Dionusos*, *Isis* et *Déméter*, *Horus* et *Apollon*, *Boubastis* et *Artémis*, *Taouth* et *Hermes? Il seroit néanmoins téméraire de donner un démenti à notre historien. Quoiqu'il sut, aussi bien que nous, que ces noms de dieux n'avoient aucune ressemblance sensible, il ne laisse pas d'assurer, après un mûr examen, que les noms des dieux étrangers sont venus aux Grecs plutôt de l'E′gypte que de toute autre nation" ! !* — Mémoires de l'Acad. des Insc., tom. xxxiv. p. 481.

* Præp. Evan., lib. ii. cap. 1.

pared together, as could leave no doubt but they were one and the same. With regard, however, to these essential circumstances, Eusebius in the Præparatio Evangelica is totally silent, nor, judging from that work, does he appear to have possessed any accurate acquaintance with the religions of Egypt and Phœnicia; and, consequently, his opinion rests on too insufficient grounds to admit of its being received as any evidence that the mythology of Greece was of a foreign, and not of a domestic, origin.

Had not, however, almost all writers, ancient and modern, united in a general conspiracy to dispossess the Pelasgi of that pre-eminence amongst the people of antiquity, to which they are so justly entitled, no doubt respecting the real origin of the Grecian system of polytheism could ever have existed: for Mr. Mitford has stated with the greatest accuracy, that "among the uncertain traditions of various hordes, who in early times overran this country *, the Pelasgian name is eminent. The name may be traced back into Asia: it is found in the islands; and the people who bore it appear to have spread far on the continent of Europe, since they are reckoned among the earliest inhabitants of Italy. It was very generally acknowledged, as the accurate and judicious Strabo assures us, that the Pelasgians were established all over Greece, and that they were the first people who became powerful there. Consonant to this, we find every mention of the Pelasgians by Herodotus and Thucydides; from the former of whom we learn, that Pelasgia was once a general name for the country. But a passage of the poet Æschylus concerning this people, for its antiquity, evident honesty, its probability, and its consistency with all other remaining evidence of best authority, appears to deserve particular notice. The Pelasgian princes, he says, extended their dominion over all the northern parts of Greece, together with Macedonia and Epirus, as far as the river Strymon eastward, and the sea beyond the Dodonean mountains westward." † Mr. Mitford farther states, that "it appears

* To the expressions, however, *hordes* and *overrunning the country* I object; as, even from Mr. Mitford's own showing, the Pelasgi could not have been a rude and barbarous people, nor the mere temporary occupants of Greece.

† History of Greece, vol. i. p. 20. And yet Mr. Mitford maintains that the Greek nation derived its origin from a mixture of the Pelasgian, and possibly some other barbarous hordes,

from a strong concurrence of circumstances recorded by ancient writers, that the early inhabitants of Asia Minor, Thrace, and Greece were the same people. . . . In the Grecian mythology we find continual references to Asiatic and Thracian stories; and even in the heroic ages, which followed the mystic, the Greeks and Asiatics appear to have communicated as kindred people. Pelops, a fugitive Asiatic prince, acquired a kingdom by marriage in Peloponnesus; and Bellerophon, a prince of Corinth, in the same manner acquired the kingdom of Lycia in Asia. Herodotus remarks, that the Lydian laws and manners, even in his time, very nearly resembled the Grecian; and the Lycians and Pamphylians were so evidently of the same race with the Greeks, that he supposed them to be emigrants from Crete, from Athens, and other parts of Greece. The inhabitants of Thrace are not distinguished by Homer for that peculiar barbarism which afterwards characterised them; apparently they were upon a level nearly in civilisation with the other people around the Ægean." * Bishop Marsh, also, remarks, " By means of the data, collected in this chapter, we may trace the Pelasgi throughout the whole of Greece, and onward through Thrace to the Hellespont. The Greek writers, as we have seen, represent either Achaia or Arcadia as the *original* seat of the Pelasgi: whence they are supposed to have migrated to Thessaly, and from Thessaly to Thrace. The question *how* the Pelasgi came to be the first inhabitants of Peloponnesus was easily resolved by making them αυτοχθονες. But as we know that Europe was peopled from Asia, either the first settlers in Peloponnesus traversed the Ægean Sea, in which case Greece might have been peopled from south to north; or the first migration from Asia Minor to Europe was across either the Hellespont

---

with colonies from Phœnicia and Egypt; that amidst continual migrations, expulsions, mixtures of various hordes, and revolutions of every kind, was formed the most perfect, copious, and harmonious language that ever existed; and that, previously to Homer and Hesiod, the religious tenets of the Greeks were totally vague, floating about partially as they happened to arise, or to be imported by foreigners, particularly Egyptians. All which circumstances are clearly incompatible with the power and predominance which Mr. Mitford himself ascribes to the Pelasgi.

* History of Greece, vol. i. p. 52, 53.

or the Thracian Bosphorus, in which case Greece was peopled from north to south. Now it is infinitely more probable that the first settlers in Thrace should have crossed the Hellespont, where the land on one side is visible from the land on the other, and that Greece should have been peopled from Thrace, than that the first settlers in Greece should have come immediately across the Ægean Sea, and have consequently embarked in Asia, without knowing that an opposite coast was *in existence*. We may, therefore, fairly presume that Thrace was the first *European* settlement of the Pelasgi, and that they gradually spread themselves southward till they had occupied the whole of Greece. Indeed, Thrace was the original seat of Grecian song, and Grecian fable. Thamyris, who is said to have challenged the Muses, was a Thracian. So was Orpheus; so was Musæus. And the mysteries of the Cabiri were celebrated in Samothrace, before the temple of Delphi existed." *

But with these indisputable facts before them, it seems most surprising that any writers could have sought for the origin of the people, language, and religion of Greece in any other country than Asia Minor. Still more singular, if possible, must it appear, that so able and learned a historian as Mr. Mitford should, after impartially stating these facts, still adhere to a preconceived opinion which they so evidently controverted; and that, instead of abandoning it, he should attempt to reconcile the manifest contradiction that existed between the *obvious* Asiatic and the *supposed* Egyptian origin of Grecian mythology, by conjecturing that, *among the early troubles of Egypt, some expelled nobles founded settlements for themselves and their followers of other classes, perhaps first in Asia Minor and Thrace, and afterward, as Danaus and Cecrops, in Greece.*† No authority, of course, is quoted in support of the alleged establishment of Egyptian settlements in Asia Minor and Thrace, nor any circumstances adduced in order to render such a supposition either probable or even plausible. But Mr. Mitford seems to have enter-

* Horæ Pelasgicæ, p. 12. To which very learned work, and, I may be permitted to add, to my own work on the *Affinity of Languages*, I beg to refer for further illustration of this point.

† History of Greece, vol. i. p. 73.

tained most extraordinary opinions with respect to the early peopling of the world; for in another place he observes, "But we find strong reason to suppose that, in the early ages, the difference of language over Asia, Africa, and Europe, as far as their inhabitants of those ages are known to us, was but a difference of dialect; and that the people of Greece, Phœnicia, and Egypt mutually understood each other." * Here clearly appears that singular prejudice in favour of Hebrew being the primitive language of mankind, which necessarily involves the conclusion that the world was peopled by the Hebrews, that has exerted such a pernicious influence over ancient history, and rendered the ascertainment of truth of far minor importance than the compelling all events related by ancient writers to accord not only with the accounts contained in the Old Testament, but also with the inferences which have been deduced from them.† Chronology and history have been thus unnecessarily perverted under some mistaken notion that such perversion strengthened the evidences of the Christian religion; and hence, in tracing the origin of the people, the languages, and religions of ancient nations, an importance is given to Phœnicia and Egypt, which rests on mere gratuitous assumptions unsupported by any proof whatever.‡

* History of Greece, vol. i. p. 93.

† Bishop Stillingfleet, in Origines Sacræ, vol. i. p. 42., openly avows this system; for he remarks: — "Far be it from me to derogate any thing even from profane histories, where they do not interfere with the sacred history of Scripture; and it is certainly the best improvement of these to make them *draw water to the sanctuary*, and to serve as smaller stars to conduct us in our way, when we cannot enjoy the benefit of the greater light of sacred history."

‡ As an instance of the strange application to ancient history of the circumstances recorded in the Old Testament, I may here quote the following passages which occur in a Mémoire of M. Gibert read at the Académie des Inscriptions on the 16th of January, 1753; but several late works prove that the same system has still many advocates: — "Je ne crois donc pas qu'on puisse raisonnablement refuser de reconnoître que le Japet aïeul de Deucalion est Japhet fils de Noé. Or il s'ensuivra de la nécessairement qu'Ocean, frère de Japet et auteur des Inachides, étoit un des frères de Japhet, soit Sem, soit Cham. . . . On sent aisément que l'origine des Pelasges, qui reconnoissoient les Inachides pour leurs auteurs et leurs chefs, doit être la même que celle des Inachides, puisqu'il est naturel que des colonies, que les Inachides amenèrent avec eux, et avec lesquelles ils s'établirent et se maintinrent au milieu des sauvages de la Grèce, fussent tirées de même pays d'où ils sortoient. Les Pélasges étoient donc, comme eux, Syriens, ou Phéniciens, ou E'gyptiens."—Tom. xxv. p. 5—6.

It must, at the same time, be admitted, that the disappearance, in ancient history, of the Pelasgi, as a distinct people, is a most unaccountable circumstance. But no writer, I believe, has ever ventured to assert that it was occasioned by their being expelled from Greece or exterminated by foreign colonists, or incorporated with them; and the common opinion ascribes it, though evidently erroneously, to some internal occurrences in Greece itself. Their existence, however, their power and predominance, are most fully attested by ancient writers; and had, consequently, their extinction been effected by violent means, it must have produced such a revolution that it is impossible to suppose that all memory of it could have become so obliterated as not to retain a place in ancient tradition. It must seem, therefore, most probable that the name alone became, in some manner, superseded, and that the Pelasgi still continued, under some other appellation, to form the principal part of the Grecian people. It is at least evident, that in no ancient writer is there any explicit account of colonists having arrived in Greece * after it had been occupied by the Pelasgi, nor of any events which could possibly have subverted their dominion. But if it be admitted, on the authority of Æschylus, Herodotus, Thucydides, and Strabo, that the Pelasgi once held the whole of Greece, it cannot seem an improbable supposition that this country may have, at one time, formed but a single kingdom †, and that it subsequently became,

* I have before quoted, from Diodorus Siculus and Strabo, the only two passages that can bear such a construction, which I can discover. But the first of these passages depends merely on the assertion of the Egyptians, and, being unsupported by any proof, cannot be considered as deserving of the slightest credit; and with regard to the other, the term λαον, used by Strabo, is too indefinite and equivocal to admit of its being understood to signify a colony.

† This is affirmed by Æschylus in these verses: —

Του γηγενους γαρ ειμ' εγω Παλαιχθονος
Ινις Πελασγος, της δε γης αρχηγετης.
Εμου δ' ανακτος ευλογως επωνυμον
Γενος Πελασγων την δε καρπουται χθονα·
Και πασαν αιαν, ἡς δι' Αλγος ερχεται,
Στρυμων τε, προς δυνοντος ἡλιου κρατω.
῾Οριζομαι δε την τε Περραιβων χθονα,
Πινδου τε τἀπεκεινα, Παιονων πελας,
Ορη τε Δωδοναια· συντεμνει δ' ὁρος
῾Υγρας θαλασσης· των δε κἀπειτα κρατω. *Supplices*, v. 253—262.

either from partition amongst the princes of the royal line, or from other causes, divided into a number of small states, which necessarily assumed distinct names, and that thus the general appellations of Pelasgia and Pelasgi fell into disuse. It is also indisputable that Greece did not receive the name of Hellas, nor its inhabitants that of Hellenes, until long after the Trojan war; and that, consequently, it could not be the Hellenes by whom the Pelasgic power was subverted: for in the poems of Homer, as Thucydides has remarked, the general name given to the Greeks is *Danai*, *Argivi*, or *Achaii*, as the name *Hellenes* was not then known. To account, therefore, for the disappearance, in ancient history, of the Pelasgic name, it cannot be indispensable that the generally received opinion of their migration or expulsion from Greece, and subsequent extinction, should be adopted. For the mere disuse of a name, when probable causes can be assigned for it, is not sufficient to prove that the nation who bore it, particularly if that nation, like the Pelasgi, were powerful and predominant, had ceased to exist as a distinct people. Until, therefore, the manner by which the Pelasgi were dispossessed of Greece, and the emigrants who replaced them, be distinctly pointed out, the only reasonable conclusion must be, that the Greeks of Homer were actually the same people who had been, in earlier times, distinguished by the name of Pelasgi.*

But if the inhabitants of Greece from the earliest times known to tradition until the Trojan war were Pelasgi, with not the slightest

* The account of the Pelasgi given by Dionysius Halicarnasseus is so inconsistent and improbable, that it cannot certainly deserve any attention; for he describes them as a Grecian people of Peloponnesian origin, who experienced the greatest misfortunes, particularly the migratory life which they were obliged to lead, and their possessing no fixed abodes. But, notwithstanding, they established themselves in Thessaly, and held it for five generations, where they enjoyed the greatest prosperity, until, in the sixth generation, they were conquered, and compelled to fly from the country in dispersed bodies, by the Curetes and Leleges, led by Deucalion the son of Prometheus and Clymene. Dionysius thus contradicts every other ancient writer, and by ascribing the expulsion of the Pelasgi to Deucalion the son of Prometheus, which event must have taken place about 1574 years B. C., completely discredits his own narrative, as the existence of the Pelasgic power in Greece, at a subsequent period, seems to admit of no doubt. On what grounds, therefore, Larcher, in his Chronologie d'Hérodote, has adopted this account I cannot understand, as he adduces no other authority than that of Dionysius, in support of it.

intermixture of foreign emigrants, except, perhaps, that occasioned by the Phrygian colony introduced by Pelops, and if the Asiatic origin of the Pelasgi cannot be controverted, it must necessarily follow that it was from Asia Minor through Thrace that Greece derived its religion, and not from Egypt, Phœnicia, or Libya. Even Mr. Mitford admits, that *in the Grecian mythology we find continual references to Asiatic and Thracian stories;* and the slightest acquaintance with Grecian writers will clearly evince that, though some of them may have expressly or inferentially ascribed the origin of the Greek philosophy and religion to Egypt, still this opinion is always delivered in general terms, and never supported by any evidence, or even by a statement of the circumstances on which it rests. The very writers, at the same time, who have originated this opinion, as Herodotus and Diodorus Siculus, relate many facts which indisputably prove the striking similarity that existed between the systems of polytheism which prevailed in Asia Minor and Greece. But if any authority be given to the poems of Homer, it must at once be admitted that, at the time when he lived, the mythologies of these two countries were precisely the same.* In tracing, however, the origin and affinity of nations, it may be assumed, as I have endeavoured to evince in a former work, that the distinct races of men now existing, had occupied *previously* to the age of Homer the countries which their descendants still inhabit; or, if changes have therein subsequently taken place, these are sufficiently indicated by history. In

* In the fourth book of the Iliad, Homer ascribes these words even to Olympian Jupiter: —

For know, of all the numerous towns that rise,
Beneath the rolling sun and starry skies,
Which gods have raised, or earth-born men enjoy,
None stands so dear to Jove as sacred Troy.
No mortals merit more distinguish'd grace
Than godlike Priam, or than Priam's race.
Still to our name their hecatombs expire,
And altars blaze with unextinguish'd fire.

And in the twentieth book, the Trojans are assisted by these deities: —

In aid of Troy Latona, Phœbus came,
Mars fiery-helm'd, and the laughter-loving dame,
Xanthus, whose streams in golden currents flow,
And the chaste huntress of the silver bow.

order, therefore, to ascertain the real nature of the religion which, in ancient times, prevailed in Asia Minor and Greece, it becomes necessary to distinguish most carefully between the account given of it by Homer and Hesiod and the innovations introduced into it in later times. For, on instituting a comparison between Grecian and Hindu mythology, it must be obvious that, as the latter had received its present form previously to the age of Homer, all subsequent innovations in the former, such as the orgies of the mother of the gods and of Bacchus, ought to be altogether excluded *; and that the comparison ought to rest entirely on the exact state in which the Grecian religion appears clearly, and without any hypothetical assumptions, in the poems of Homer and Hesiod, or in any earlier traditions that may have been preserved.

It is, however, equally evident that these poems do not afford any certain information respecting the origin of the Grecian system of polytheism, or the principles on which it was founded; and that all which has been subsequently written by ancient authors, in explanation of these circumstances, is so obviously rendered subservient to some favourite opinion or system, that its accuracy becomes extremely questionable. Yet Mr. Mitford remarks most singularly, that " the very early inhabitants of Greece had a religion far less degenerated from original purity. To this curious and interesting fact abundant testimonies remain. They occur in those poems of uncertain origin and uncertain date, but unquestionably of great antiquity, which are called the poems of Orpheus, or rather the Orphic poems; and they are found scattered among the writings of the philosophers and historians. All the Greek philosophers were aware of the recent nature of that religion which in their time was popular. † Plato, among his doubts about the

* Mr. Payne Knight has remarked: —" As there is no mention, however, of any of the mystic deities, nor of any of the rites with which they were worshipped, in any of the genuine parts either of the Iliad or Odyssey, nor any trace of the symbolic style in any of the works of art described in them, nor of allegory or enigma in the fables which adorn them, we may fairly presume that both the rites of initiation and the worship of Bacchus are of a later period, and were not generally known to the Greeks till after the composition of these poems."—*Inquiry into the Symb. Lang.*, part i. sect. 22.

† Mr. Mitford, however, in deriving it from Egypt, and ascribing its introduction to

ancient state of things, declares an opinion that, in the early ages, the sun, moon, stars, and earth had been the only objects of religious worship in Greece, as they were still in his time, he adds, in most of the barbarous nations."* But with respect to the Orphic poems, M. de la Barre has very justly observed; — "Mais l'examen leur est infiniment désavantageux; puisqu'il y découvre un mélange monstrueux d'idées philosophiques qui se croisent, et qui n'ont pas plus de rapport entre elles qu'avec la religion commune, qui ne laisse pas de s'y trouver par tout. C'est là en effet qu'Hercule est tout à la fois le premier des êtres qui a paru, né de lui-même et production de la terre, celui qui porte autour de sa tête l'Amour et la Nuit, et celui aussi dont le bras délivra la terre des scélérats qui troubloient la tranquillité publique. C'est là encore que, suivant je ne sais quelles idées, Pan est le monde entier, dont le ciel, la terre, la mer, et le feu éternel sont les membres; et que, suivant les idées Grèques, c'est un dieu qui court les forêts, qui se cache dans les antres, qui se plait à faire peur, à s'entretenir avec l'echo, à danser avec les nymphes. Pan après tout n'est devenu le monde qu'au dépens du ciel, à qui cette qualité avoit été conferée auparavant. Jupiter est représenté ici comme l'auteur de la nature, celui qui a produit la terre, la mer, et tout ce que les cieux enserrent: il est, dit-on, le commencement et la fin de toutes choses; et tout de suite on lui donne pour femme Junon, considérée simplement comme l'air. Il me paroit d'ailleurs assez plaisant de voir que Rhea soit dans un hymne fille de Protogone et mère de ciel, et que dans un autre hymne le ciel soit son père." †

But it may be contended that, notwithstanding their inconsistency and incongruity, these poems still contain indications of the real nature of the Grecian religion in its primitive state. Nor would such a supposition be inadmissible did the hymns ascribed to Orpheus exhibit the faintest outlines of the forms and characteristic features of the

---

colonies anterior to Danaus, gives it an antiquity exceeding 1511 years B.C., and consequently 1100 years before the time of Herodotus and Plato.

* History of Greece, vol. i. p. 69.

† Mémoires de l'Acad. des Ins., tom. vi. p. 28.

different deities to whom they are addressed; or the slightest exposition of the opinions which were entertained respecting them by their worshippers: but, on the contrary, not the slightest trace of those peculiar modes of thinking on religious subjects, by which men in an early state of society are distinguished, can be discovered in them; nor do they in any manner allude to that adoration of the sun, the planets, and the elements, in which idolatry most probably originated; nor do they even contain in their numerous epithets any reference to the actions and functions which were no doubt at one time ascribed to each of these deities. These poems, therefore, afford no proof of the inhabitants of Greece having been in early times less addicted to polytheism than they were in later ages; and even Cudworth has most unsuccessfully exerted his ingenuity and erudition in order to give a more spiritual character to that material religion which is described by Homer and Hesiod. Nor do the works of these poets convey any knowledge of its original nature; for, judging from the religious principles predominant in the human mind, it must be evident that the Homeric deities could never have become the objects of worship, unless far different attributes than such as appear in the Iliad had been at first ascribed to them.* The gradually forgetting the existence and omnipotence of one supreme Being is conceivable; but that

* L'Abbé Foucher very justly remarks:—"Il est vrai que les dieux d'Homère sont des êtres bien étranges. S'ils ont l'agilité, la subtilté, l'immortalité, la puissance, et les apanages qui les distinguent physiquement des mortels, ils sont le plus souvent au dessous des hommes qui se piquent de sentimens et de vertu. Divisés d'intérêt, livrés aux factions, agités par la haïne, par la jalousie, et par des passions encore plus déshonorantes; fiers et bas, dédaigneux et rampans, féroces et voluptueux. Jupiter, leur chef, ne vante que sa force, et ne parle que d'ordres absolus; il menace, il punit, et ne se fait point aimer. Si par un mouvement de ses noirs sourcils il ébranle le ciel, la terre, et les enfers, ses discours n'annoncent point la grandeur et la majesté du roi des dieux. Tyran brutal, qu'aucune loi ne retient, il ne met aucune borne à ses désirs effrénés. Les grands de son empire, ses frères ou ses enfans le craignent, mais le détestent, et ne dissimulent point, même en sa présence, ce qu'ils pensent de ses injustes caprices. Minerve elle-même n'est guère plus sage que les autres, et Vénus n'est qu'une infame prostituée. Est-il vraisemblable, dira-t-on, que les Grecs, au temps d'Homère, adorassent des dieux contre lesquels, malgré leur superiorité reconnue, les héros de l'Iliade et de l'Odyssée vomissent impunément des imprécations? Et moi je dis, il est encore moins vraisemblable qu'un beau génie, qui connoissoit si bien les décences et le prix de la vertu, eût produit de pareils dieux sur la scène, s'ils n'eussent pas été les dieux de sa nation."—*Mém. de l'Acad. des Ins.*, tom. xxxv. p. 13.

mankind should at once transfer their adoration from him to deities, in whom the excellence of the divine nature was scarcely perceptible, is utterly improbable. Nor, even on the supposition that the notion of divinity has been acquired by man through the means of his own reason, can it be credited, that human pride would have ever acknowledged as gods beings whose qualities and powers so little exceeded the capacities and energies of mere mortals. It must therefore be concluded that the poems of Homer and Hesiod, the only works now extant which contain an account of the Grecian mythology, as it existed about 900 years before Christ, are obviously inadequate to convey an accurate knowledge of its origin and the principles on which it was founded; and such other data as have been preserved are too liable to doubt, to admit of any determined and unquestionable opinion being formed from them, with respect to the real nature of this system of polytheism.

For it will no doubt be admitted that, in a discussion concerning the popular mythology of Greece, the opinions of philosophers, and the dogmas that may have been taught in the mysteries, ought not to be taken into consideration. As, however, Orpheus is the individual to whom the introduction of religion into Greece is in general attributed*, it would be desirable to ascertain both the age when he lived, and the nature of the doctrines which he inculcated: but on these points the utmost diversity of opinion exists. It nevertheless seems to be admitted that Orpheus was one of the Argonauts, and consequently flourished about thirty or forty years before the siege of Troy. In which case it must follow that, as the Pelasgi had occupied Greece long before this date, it could not have been from them that its inhabitants received the religion which prevailed in the time of Homer; nor could they have learned it from the Egyptian colonists who are supposed to have arrived in that country in the sixteenth century before

* Brucker remarks:—"Non vero suo tanto nomine per omnia ora volitavit Orpheus, sed imprimis propter insignia in Græcos merita, introductis religione, artibus, et disciplinis, quibus mores feros ad humanitatem reduxit, immortalem famam honoremque consecutus est. Quod si enim Græcos audimus, nulla fere scientia, quam Græci Orpheo non debeant, adeo ut γραμματα και σοφιαν ei tribuit epigramma vetus."—*Hist. Crit. Phil.*, vol. i. p. 377.

the Christian era. Is it, however, at all probable that Greece remained in that rude, uncivilised, and unsettled state, which is described by Thucydides, until only forty years before the siege of Troy? The poems of Homer most assuredly contain ample evidence to the contrary; and it cannot, therefore, but seem most probable that to Orpheus the Argonaut must have been ascribed the eminent merits of some more ancient poet. Since, also, the early civilisation of Asia Minor, the Asiatic descent of the Pelasgi, their temporary residence in Thrace, and their subsequent predominance in Greece, are facts which cannot be justly disputed, it must be concluded that they were not at the time of their migration rude and barbarous men, as they are in general represented, but, on the contrary, that they were fully acquainted with the arts, learning, and religion of their mother country. It is, therefore, obviously in the period of their first establishment in Thrace that Thamyras, Orpheus, and Musæus must have flourished *; though it is possible that in later ages other poets may have assumed their distinguished names.

With respect, however, to the doctrine taught by Orpheus, this subject has been so fully and carefully examined by Brucker, that farther enquiry seems unnecessary; and I shall, in consequence, avail myself of his learned researches for the purpose of explaining it. † We therefore think it most probable, observes Brucker, that the following were the opinions respecting God which were expressed by Orpheus, or rather by the Orphic theology, as no undoubted works of Orpheus have been preserved until our times: —

I. Before the creation of the world God was united with matter in such manner that in Him were contained all things that are, or have been, or shall be; and thus from all eternity did all forms remain concealed in his essence.

II. At a fixed time God separated matter from himself; and thus gods, goddesses, the sun, moon, stars, and all that is, were produced.

* Clemens Alexandrinus, Strom. lib. i. p. 139., states that Orpheus and Musæus lived in the time of Acrisius, who flourished about 200 years before the Trojan war.

† Hist. Crit. Philosophiæ, vol. i. from p. 386 to 400; but I have merely availed myself of the substance of Brucker's remarks.

III. By the laws of emanation, therefore, all things participate in the essence of God, and are the parts and members of God, and nothing is devoid of the divine nature. *

IV. As every part, therefore, of the universe participates of the divine nature, each part may be justly considered to be a god.

V. The essence of God, thus proceeding from him, and being present in all things, is the sole power which governs this world. †

VI. Hence, as all things are not only from God, but also in God, an infinity of gods must be admitted.

VII. These gods are to be worshipped, because it is impossible for human nature to comprehend the Supreme God, who is concealed, invisible, and unknowable.

VIII. No image of God ought to be formed, since he is diffused throughout the universe, and the universe, therefore, is his only proper image.

IX. Since all things have proceeded from God, they will all return unto him ; and this reunion will be the highest state of beatitude which the pious can attain.

X. But many purifications must take place before the soul can be so purified as to admit of its returning to that source from which it emanated.

If, adds Brucker, these Orphic opinions respecting the nature of God be admitted, and all Platonic παρερμηνειαι be rejected, they will appear to be wonderfully consistent ; and will thus, by affording a probable and rational exposition of the Orphic theology, reconcile the conflicting accounts given of it by ancient authors.

From the preceding remarks, the opinion entertained by Orpheus respecting the soul may be easily ascertained. For, if the soul, as well

* It will be observed that the first and latter parts of this paragraph are contradictory, if emanation mean the *separation* of the thing emanated from its source ; because, if the universe and all that it contains are merely parts and members of God, it must necessarily follow that no separation has taken place, and that, consequently, the universe remains one undivided and eternal God.

† I do not clearly understand this paragraph, as the term *essentia* seems to be employed in an unusual manner. The original is, — "Esse Dei essentiam, quæ ex eo effluxit, in omnibus rebus præsentem, eamque vim unicam et præsidem esse mundi, quæ omnia gubernat."

as all other things, emanated from God, it must necessarily follow, that it will not perish, but be again absorbed in the divine nature. It cannot, therefore, be doubted but that Orpheus considered the soul to be immortal, and capable of enjoying beatitude after death. [That the metempsychosis, also, was taught by Orpheus, seems unquestionable; as it is a necessary consequence of the doctrine which maintains the reunion, after the requisite purification, of the soul with God, its primeval source.]

It is, however, impossible, observes Brucker, to divest entirely the Orphic theogony of that allegorical veil by which it has been concealed, and to exhibit it in its original unsophisticated state: but after an attentive comparison of different authorities, the following appears to be the most probable account of it:—This universe, and all that it contains, were created by one supreme, self-existent, and eternal Being, who first originated Time, then Ether and Chaos. From the union of these two principles, Ether and Chaos, was produced an immense egg, which, being hatched by Night, opened in two parts, from the upper of which was formed the heaven, and from the lower the earth. From this egg also arose a being in the form of a dragon, having, besides its own head, that of a lion, and a god* [by whom the elements of this universe were arranged]. But, remarks Brucker, it is unnecessary to insist upon the different opinions which have been expressed respecting this *trimorphous* being; because it is evident that Orpheus held that God first produced two principles, the active and passive, or Ether and Chaos, possessing the qualities of light and darkness; and that, by their union and agitation, assisted by the energy of God, was formed the matter from which this universe was produced †; the more ethe-

* Cudworth is greatly scandalised by the production of this being; for he observes:—"And here we may take notice of the monstrosity and extravagancy of Orpheus's fancy, from what Damascius and others tell us, that he made one of his principles to be δρακοντα κεφαλας εχοντα προσπεφυκυιας ταυρου και λεοντος, εν μεσω δε θεου προσωπον, και επι ωμων πτερα: *a dragon having the heads both of a bull and a lion, and in the midst the face of a god, with wings upon his shoulders.*" —*Intellectual System*, book i. chap. 4. sect. 17.

† As the Orphic opinions on this subject are of the greatest importance, on instituting a comparison between the Greek and Hindu religions, I add Cudworth's account of them, who remarks:—"Which may be further manifested from that epitome of the Orphic doctrine, made long since by Timotheus the chronographer in his Cosmopœia, still extant

real parts of which being separated, according to the laws of motion, from the more dense, formed the heaven, and the latter subsiding formed the earth; and from the union of the heaven and earth were produced the gods. So far Brucker: but, if Orpheus acknowledged that this universe was created by God, and that all things are not only from God, but also in God, it seems highly improbable that he should have ascribed the origin of the gods to the union of the heaven and the earth; and, therefore, though Brucker has not been able to discover in ancient writers any other account of the Orphic theogony, it may be reasonably doubted whether this was the opinion which was actually entertained by Orpheus.

A remarkable account, also, of the creation has been preserved in these verses of Aristophanes:—

Χαος ην, και Νυξ, Ερεβος τε μελαν πρωτον, και Ταρταρος ευρυς·
Γη δ', ουδ' αηρ, ουδ' ουρανος ην· Ερεβους δ' εν απειροσι κολποις
Τικτει πρωτιστον ὑπηνεμιον Νυξ ἡ μελανοπτερος ωον,
Εξ οὑ περιτελλομεναις ὡραις εβλαστεν Ερως ὁ ποθεινος,
Στιλβων νωτον πτερυγοιν χρυσαιν, εικως ανεμωκεσι δινα̣ις.

---

in Cedrenus and Eusebii Chronica, and imperfectly set down by Suidas (upon the word Orpheus) as his own, or without mentioning the author's name:—Εξ *αρχης ανεδειχθη τῳ κοσμῳ ὁ αιθηρ, ὑπο του θεου δημιουργηθεις.* *First of all the Ether was made by God, and after the Ether a Chaos;* a dark and dreadful night then covering all under the whole Ether. *Σημαινων την νυκτα προτερευειν.* *Orpheus hereby signifying*, saith Timotheus, *that night was senior to day*, or that the world had a beginning. *Ειρηκως εν τῃ αυτου εκθεσει, ακαταληπτον τινα και παντων ὑπερτατον ειναι, προγενεστερον τε και δημιουργον ἁπαντων, και αυτου του αιθερος, και παντων ὑπ' αυτον τον αιθερα.* *He having declared, also, in his explication, that there was a certain incomprehensible Being, which was the highest and oldest of all things, and the maker of every thing, even of the Ether itself, and of all things under the Ether.* But the earth being then invisible by reason of the darkness, a light breaking out through the Ether, illuminated the whole creation. This light being said by him to be that highest of all Beings (before mentioned), which is called also counsel and life. *Ταυτα τα τρια ονοματα* (to use Suidas his words here) *μιαν δυναμιν απεφηνατο, και ἑν κρατος του δημιουργου παντων θεου, του παντα εκ του μη οντος παραγαγοντος εις το ειναι.* *These three names in Orpheus* (light, counsel, and life) *declaring one and the same force and power of that God, who is the maker of all, and who produceth all things out of nothing into being, whether visible or invisible.* To conclude with Timotheus, Ὁ *δε αυτος* Ορφευς *εν τῃ αυτου βιβλῳ συνεταξεν, ὁτι δια των αυτων τριων ονοματων μιας θεοτητος, τα παντα εγενετο, και* Αυτος *εστι τα παντα.* *And the same Orpheus in his book declared, that all things were made by one Godhead in three names, and that this God is all things.*—*Intellectual System*, book i. chap. 4. sect. 17.

Οὗτος δὲ Χάει πτερόεντι μιγεὶς νυχίῳ, κατὰ Τάρταρον εὐρὺν,
Ἐνεόττευσεν γένος ἡμέτερον, καὶ πρῶτον ἀνήγαγεν ἐς φῶς.
Πρότερον δ' οὐκ ἦν γένος ἀθανάτων, πρὶν Ἔρως ξυνέμιξεν ἅπαντα·
Ξυμμιγνυμένων δ' ἑτέρων ἑτέροις, γένετ' οὐρανὸς, ὠκεανός τε,
Καὶ γῆ, πάντων τε θεῶν μακάρων γένος ἄφθιτον. *Aves*, v. 695—703.

At first there was naught but chaos and night, sable darkness and the deep abyss; nor earth, nor ether, nor heaven existed then. At length the black-winged Night produced in the unbounded expanse of darkness a wondrous egg, from which, after the stated time was run, issued Love, the desired by all, resplendent, and adorned with golden wings, which he fluttered gladly o'er the deep profound. This Love uniting with nocturnal Chaos in the wide abyss produced our race, and first brought all things to light. For, until Love had exerted his power, nor gods nor men existed; but then, the elements of things combining together, were produced the heaven, the earth, the ocean, and the immortal race of the blessed gods.

This description Cudworth considers as an "atheistic creation of the world, gods and all, out of senseless and stupid matter, or dark chaos; as the only original *numen;* the perfectly inverted order of the universe." But, in adverting to the Hindu mythology, it will perhaps appear that the Love here described was intended to represent a hypostasis of the supreme Being; and that, to render this account complete, the first part of that of Orpheus ought to be added to it. Thus the belief in the creation of the universe by one self-existent God, either directly or through the medium of another divine power proceeding from himself, will remain unaffected.

In the theogony, however, of Hesiod, no mention occurs either of the mundane egg, or of a supreme Being; and whether or not he ascribed the origin of the universe to a first cause must depend entirely on the meaning given to the equivocal word γένετο. For, if it cannot here signify *was produced,* and if the construction restricts its meaning to *was* (of which I am not a sufficient judge), it must be evident that Hesiod derives the production of all things from four independent principles, Chaos, the Earth, Tartarus, and Love. But, as he invokes the muses in a preceding verse to inform him how the gods and the earth originated, it may seem more consistent with the sense of the verses quoted in the note *, to suppose that Hesiod intended to intimate that Chaos, the Earth, Tartarus, and Love, were successively created by a supreme Being, whom he has not thought it requisite to mention. Such an omission as this, however, either in these or in any other verses, is certainly not a sufficient ground for inferring that the poet denied the existence of God †; but, as Cudworth remarks, "it was a most ancient and in a manner universally received tradition amongst the Pagans, that the cosmogonia, or generation of the world, took its first beginning from a chaos; this tradition having been delivered down from Orpheus and Linus by Hesiod and Homer; acknowledged by Epicharmus; and embraced by Thales, Anaxagoras, Plato, and other philosophers who were theists." ‡ It has, however, been seen that Orpheus ascribed the origin of chaos to the supreme Being; but perhaps according to the more prevalent opinion chaos was considered to have been self-existent and uncreated. Ovid, at least, considers it as such in the following verses:—

> Ante mare et tellus, et, quod tegit omnia, cœlum,
> Unus erat toto naturæ vultus in orbe,
> Quem dixêre Chaos; rudis indigestaque moles;
> Nec quicquam, nisi pondus iners; congestaque eodem
> Non bene junctarum discordia semina rerum.

---

* Ητοι μεν πρωτιστα Χαος γενετ', αυταρ επειτα
Γαι' ευρυστερνος, παντων ἑδος ασφαλες αιει
Αθανατων, οἱ εχουσι καρη νιφοεντος Ολυμπου,
Ταρταρα τ' ηεροεντα μυχῳ χθονος ευρυοδειης,
Ηδ' Ερως. *Theogonia*, v. 116—120.

† Cudworth remarks:—"But Hesiod's Theogonia, or generation of gods, is not to be understood universally neither, but only of the inferior gods, that Ζευς, or Jupiter himself, being to be excepted out of the number of them, whom the same Hesiod, as well as Homer, makes to be the father of gods, as also king of them, in these words:—

Αυτος γαρ παντων βασιλευς και κοιρανος εστιν
Αθανατων." *Intellectual System*, book i. chap. 4. sect. 19.

The quotation does not fully support the remark; but Homer's πατηρ ανδρων τε θεων τε will be in the recollection of the reader; and the same expression occurs in Hesiod, as for instance in the 56th verse of the Εργα και 'Ημεραι:—

'Ως εφατ'· εκ δ' εγελασσε πατηρ ανδρων τε θεων τε.

‡ Intellectual System, book i. chap. 4. sect. 14.

Nullus adhuc mundo præbebat lumina Titan;
Nec nova crescendo reparabat cornua Phœbe;
Nec circumfuso pendebat in aere tellus,
Ponderibus librata suis; nec brachia longo
Margine terrarum porrexerat Amphitrite.
Quaque fuit tellus, illic et pontus et aer:
Sic erat instabilis tellus, innabilis unda,
Lucis egens aer. Nulli sua forma manebat.
Obstabatque aliis aliud: quia corpore in uno
Frigida pugnabant calidis, humentia siccis,
Mollia cum duris, sine pondere habentia pondus.
Hanc Deus, et melior litem Natura diremit.
Nam cœlo terras, et terris abscidit undas;
Et liquidum spisso secrevit ab aere cœlum.

In these circumstances antecedent to the production of the gods, the resemblance to a tradition which has been prevalent amongst all people from time immemorial is obvious. But, in whatever manner the heaven, the earth, and the sea, are supposed to have originated, the deriving, as the Greek mythology did, from their union the immortal and always existing gods is so extravagant an opinion, that it is impossible to conceive the mode of thinking or reasoning which could have suggested it. It is at the same time so incompatible with the religious sentiments inherent in the human mind, that it may justly be concluded that, from some causes now undiscoverable, the traditionary account of the further progress of the creation after the heaven and the earth were formed, had been forgotten, and that the first Grecian theogonist had supplied the deficiency in this absurd manner. The Orphic system, however, has been so imperfectly preserved, that what his doctrine on that subject really was cannot be ascertained, and the speculations of later philosophers are too questionable to admit of their being received as authority for determining the nature of the opinions which may have been prevalent in remote antiquity. Plato, also, in his Cratylus, supposes that the first inhabitants of Greece acknowledged no other gods than the sun, the moon, the earth, the heaven, and the stars; and yet in his Timæus he defends the tradition *, according to

* Could the following have been the real opinion of Plato? — Περι δε των αλλων δαιμονων ειπειν και γνωναι την γενεσιν, μειζον η καθ' ἡμας· πειστεον δε τοις ειρηκοσιν εμπροσθεν, εκγονοις μεν θεων ουσιν, ὡς εφασαν, σαφως δε που τους αυτων προγονους ειδοσιν· αδυνατον ουν θεων παισιν απιστειν,

which the Heaven and the Earth were the parents of the Ocean and Tethys, from whom were born Phorcys, Kronos, and Rhea, and from the last two Zeus and Hera, and their cognate gods. Nor do the poems of Homer and Hesiod contain any indications from which the real origin, attributes, and characters of the Grecian deities could be justly inferred; for in these poems it is obvious that not one of them is distinguished by a reference to those peculiar actions and functions by which the gods of other countries have been always characterised.

But, if the origin ascribed to the gods be so incongruous, the manner in which man was supposed to have been created is, if possible, still more ridiculous. Because, according to the popular opinion as stated by Apollodorus, it was not to the supreme Being, or to Jupiter, that mankind were indebted for their existence; but to Prometheus, one of the Titans, who formed the first man from a mixture of clay and water. On this point, however, Ovid expresses his doubts: —

> Sanctius his animal, mentisque capacius altæ
> Deerat adhuc, et quod dominari in cætera posset.
> Natus homo est. Sive hunc divino semine fecit
> Ille opifex rerum, mundi melioris origo:
> Sive recens tellus, seductaque nuper ab alto
> Æthere, cognati retinebat semina cœli.
> Quam satus Iapeto, mistam fluvialibus undis
> Finxit in effigiem moderantum cuncta deorum.

But Pausanias, about A. D. 170, saw, near the town of Panopeus in Phocis, the remains of the clay from which the whole race of man had been formed by Prometheus, the smell of which was still very like that of a human body.* This subject, however, is not, I believe, touched upon in the works of Homer, Hesiod, or the tragic poets; but a grave historian, Diodorus Siculus, thus explains the origin of things:—" At

---

καιπερ ανευ τε εικοτων και αναγκαιων αποδειξεων λεγουσιν, αλλ' ὡς οικεια φασκουσιν απαγγελλειν, επομενους τῳ νομῳ πιστευτεον.—*Plat. Opera*, tom. ix. p. 324. ed. Bipont.

* Λιθοι κεινται σφισιν επι τῃ χαραδρᾳ, μεγεθος μεν ἑκαστος ὡς φορτον αποχρωντα ἁμαξῃς ειναι, χρωμα δε εστι πηλου σφισιν, ου γεωδους, αλλ' οἱος αν χαραδρας γενοιτο η χειμαῤῥου ψαμμωδης· παρεχονται δε και οσμην εγγυτατα χρωτι ανθρωπου· ταυτα ετι λειπεσθαι του πηλου λεγουσιν, εξ οὑ και ἁπαν ὑπο του Προμεθεως το γενος πλασθηναι των ανθρωπων.—*Phocica*, cap. iv.

first the heaven and earth and the elements of all things being mingled together had but one form. Afterwards, the different substances separating from each other, the world acquired the complete arrangement which is visible in it; and the air becoming endued with continual motion, its igneous particles, on account of their levity, ascended on high; whence has originated the unceasing revolution of the sun and the other stars: but that which was slimy and watery subsided, on account of its weight, into one uniform mass, which, acquiring motion, and being continually agitated, became separated into the sea and into the earth. The last was thus soft and merely mud, but being heated by the fire of the sun it began to harden. During which process its surface, becoming fermented by the heat, produced small pustular excrescences covered with membranous pellicles; in the same manner as we observe to happen in marshy and muddy places, which, after having been subjected to cold, are suddenly heated by the sun. These excrescences becoming pregnant with animals, the embryos received nourishment from the mists of night and conformation from the heat of day. At length, having acquired their perfect growth, the membranous coverings became burnt and broken, and the embryos issued forth in all the different forms of animals. Those which possessed most heat ascended on high, and became birds; those in which the earthy particles predominated became reptiles; and those in which these were more tempered became animals [including men]; while those in which watery particles predominated became fishes, and sought the place adapted for their abode. But the earth, having been rendered completely hard by the heat of the sun, could no longer produce living things; and their different races, therefore, continued to be propagated by generation. It appears, also, that Euripides, the disciple of Anaxagoras, the natural philosopher, did not dissent from the account just given of the origin of things; for he has inserted these verses in his Menalippus. *Thus the earth and the heaven were one form. But when they separated from each other, then were generated and produced to light trees, birds, beasts, those which the sea nourishes, and the race of mortal men.*" * But were even the extreme absurdity of this description not

* Diod. Bib. Hist., lib. i. cap. vii.

taken into consideration, it must be at once obvious that it is entirely inconsistent with such opinions as could have possibly originated in those remote and pious times when polytheism first began to prevail.

With respect, therefore, to the opinions entertained by the Greeks, on the first establishment of the Grecian system of polytheism, relative to the origin of this universe and the real nature of the gods, it must be admitted that no data have been preserved in ancient authors from which any positive conclusion on the subject can be justly deduced. To enter, therefore, into any discussion of so trite a topic as the actual state of Grecian mythology, as described by Homer, Hesiod, and other writers, must be evidently unnecessary; and whether or not it can receive any illustration from that form of idolatry which still prevails in India, will be best ascertained after the nature of the Hindu religion has been fully considered.

From the poems, however, of Homer and Hesiod, a knowledge at least of the Grecian mythology, as it existed about 900 or 1000 years before the Christian era, may be derived; but neither traditions nor writings have been preserved from which any information might be obtained with respect to the religion which originally prevailed in Etruria and Latium. But, if the religion of Asia Minor were precisely the same as that of Greece, as the Iliad so incontrovertibly attests; and if those parts of Italy derived their language and civilisation from colonists who had migrated from Asia Minor; it would necessarily follow that they also received from them their system of polytheism, and that thus no difference ought to exist between the mythologies of Greece, Etruria, and Latium. It will, however, be evident that the justness of this conclusion must depend on the circumstances under which the Pelasgi occupied Greece, and the colonists from Asia Minor established themselves in Etruria and Latium, being exactly similar; and this essential point it is obvious that there is now no means of ascertaining. Yet that the language and religion of the Pelasgi were in no manner affected by their migration into Greece is fully proved by the poems of Homer; but the colonists from Asia Minor may have not been able to establish their power with the same facility in Etruria and Latium, and may have, in consequence, been obliged to reconcile the Aborigines to it by adopting some of their gods and religious rites. Gorius, however, in his Museum Etruscum, has not been able to throw much light on this subject, but his researches would seem to prove that, though the Etrurians may have worshipped some gods peculiar to themselves, their mythology was still essentially the same as that of the Greeks. The only one, indeed, of these gods who possessed any celebrity in later times was Janus, whom Ovid has thus mentioned:—

> Quem tamen esse deum te dicam, Jane biformis?
> Nam tibi par nullum Græcia nomen habet.*

An ancient tradition, also, respecting Saturn, is thus noticed by Ovid: —

> Caussa ratis superest: Thuscum rate venit in amnem
> Ante pererrato falcifer orbe deus.
> Hac ego Saturnum memini tellure receptum.
> Cœlitibus regnis ab Jove pulsus erat.
> Inde diu genti mansit Saturnia nomen:
> Dicta quoque est Latium terra, latente deo.†

From which it might be concluded that the Latin differed considerably from the Grecian theogony, but unfortunately no accounts remain of the opinions respecting the generation of the gods which were originally entertained by the Latins and Etruscans. ‡

* Fast., lib. i. v. 89.
In the same book of his Fasti, Ovid gives this singular account of Janus: —

> Me Chaos antiqui (nam res sum prisca) vocabant.
> Adspice, quam longi temporis acta canam.
> Lucidus hic aer, et, quæ tria corpora restant,
> Ignis, aqua, tellus, unus acervus erant.
> Ut semel hæc rerum recessit lite suarum,
> Inque novas abiit massa soluta domos;
> Flamma petit altum; propior locus aera cepit:
> Sederunt medio terra fretumque solo.
> Tunc ego, qui fueram globus, et sine imagine moles,
> In faciem redii dignaque membra deo. V. 103—112.

† Fast., lib. i. v. 233—238.

‡ Dionysius Halicarnasseus has remarked, in speaking of Romulus: —Τους δε παραδεδομενους περι θεων μυθας, εν οἱς βλασφημιαι τινες εισιν κατ᾽ αυτων η κατηγοριαι, πονηρους και ανωφελεις και ασχημονας ὑπολαβων ειναι, και ουχ ὅτι θεων αλλ᾽ ουδ᾽ ανθρωπων αγαθων αξιους, ἅπαντας εξεβαλε, και παρασκευασε τους ανθρωπους κρατιστα περι θεων λεγειν τε και φρονειν, μηδεν αυτοις προσαπτοντας αναξιον επιτηδευμα της μακαριας φυσεως. Ουτε γαρ Ουρανος εκτεμνομενος ὑπο των ἑαυτου παιδων

But the conclusions of the Abate Lanzi on this subject, after having most ably examined the testimony afforded by the language, medals, gems, and vases of the ancient Etruscans, are so just and important, except in one respect, that no apology can be necessary for the length of the following quotation: — "From a consideration of the vases," observes Lanzi, "it results, that the origin of the Etruscan mythology cannot have been derived from Egypt, or Phenicia, or from the Celts, but solely from Greece.* It is a fine manner of resolving the question, when, in order to reduce paganism to one uniform system, reference is made to the priests of Thebes having been in the habit of repeating the names of the twelve gods of Greece; or when too much importance is given to the discovery, still dubious, of learned men, that the Egyptian Isis, the Phenician Astarte, and the Grecian Hera, are the same deity; that it is the same idol which was named in Egypt Thaut, in Celtia Theuthat, and in Greece Erme; and that the Orus of the Egyptians was the Mitra of the Persians, the Belenus of the Gauls, and the Apollo of the Greeks. For such comparisons merely prove that polytheism was universal amongst mankind, and that each nation had some gods, as well as laws, similar to those of other nations; and perhaps a similar mode of allegorising by which the learned of all people recognised the same gods. But this does not apply to the present case. Because, in order to trace the conformity of one mythology with another, it is necessary to observe its external appearance, which alone was known to the people. Each nation, also, had a fabulous system peculiar to itself, as it has been already remarked by Clerc and others; for instance, Isis was every thing in Egypt, but in Greece

---

παρα Ῥωμαιοις λεγεται· ουτε Κρονος αφανιζων τας ἑαυτου γονας, φοβῳ τε εξ αυτων επιθεσεως· ουτε Ζευς καταλυων την Κρονου δυναστειαν, και κατακλειων εν τῳ δεσμοτηριῳ του Ταρταρου τον ἑαυτου πατερα. (*Antiq. Rom.*, lib. ii. cap. 18.) But is it to be concluded from these remarks, that such fables were prevalent in Latium previously to Romulus?

* I must, however, still contend that, if Etruria received colonies from Asia Minor, it was also from the same country that it received its mythology in the first instance. But the original identity of the Grecian and Etruscan mythologies being so very probable, it is equally probable that the Etruscans subsequently maintained that intimate religious communication with Greece which is pointed out by Lanzi; and thus there will be no real difference between his and my opinion on this subject.

Hera was surpassed in beauty by Venus, in wisdom by Minerva; in Persia Mitra was the principal god, while in Greece Apollo was a herdsman and an exile; in Egypt and elsewhere the gods were believed to be of distinct races, but in Greece a single family formed the principal object of religious worship. In Jupiter, his parents, his brothers, his sisters, and children, was there divided the province of presiding over all things natural and human; and each of them is distinguished from another by peculiar characteristics of age, symbols, names, and actions. There are besides other inferior gods, genii, and heroes, but dependent and subordinate to the first: these remained restricted to their original number; the others were multiplied to infinity, as the superstition of the simple, or the caprices of poets, suggested. This is the Grecian system; so peculiar to Greece, that Socrates was condemned as if he professed a different one. . . . .

"But the very same mythology I find adopted *in substance* by the whole of ancient Italy. Rome itself did not deny it, and derived its origin either from the Pelasgi and other Greeks who had inhabited Latium; or from Romulus, who had acquired a knowledge of Grecian literature in Gabium; or from Numa, who, being born in the country of the Sabines, must have been acquainted with the Pelasgic deities which they had received. The ancient Etruscans acknowledge it to a certain degree by their acts Nor do the few notices of them which have been preserved diverge from the same system; for, if we did not know the ties of relationship which bound them to the Greeks, it would be sufficient to reflect upon the respect which they paid to the gods of Greece, as to gods common to both people. The Etruscans sent not offerings to Belenus, or Esus, or Osiris, but to the Olympian Jupiter, and to the Delphic Apollo: they erected not temples to Isis and Astarte, but to the Argive Juno in Faleria; and to the same goddess, without that epithet, in Perugia, in Veii, and Cupra. . . . . We have seen (on the Etruscan medals, gems, and vases) many of the deities of Greece; and whoever wishes to augment the number, may add from figures in bronze and *sarcophagi* the names of Ceres, Neptune, Pluto, Proserpine, Cupid, Psyche, &c. We have found that the Greek names of the gods were better preserved by the Etruscans than by the Latins;

as, for instance, it is known that one god was named in Etruria, according to the common dialect of the Greeks, *Turmes*, i. e. Ερμης, and according to the Bœotic dialect *Camillus*, i. e. Καδμιλος. What farther, therefore, is necessary to evince that the Etruscan mythology was neither Celtic, nor Phœnician, nor Egyptian, but solely Grecian ?" *

The reason, however, assigned by Lanzi, in explanation of the total dissimilarity that exists between the Greek and Latin names of the gods, is by no means satisfactory; for he remarks, that "Spanheim (in Hymn. in Dian. v. 7.) has proved that in Greece it was considered very honourable for a deity to have many names; and on this account Diana requested as a favour from Jupiter a number of names, πολυωνυμιαν; and in Orpheus, she is invoked as πολυωνυμε δαιμων. From this custom is derived that difference which is observable in the Greek and Latin names of some of the gods: if it ought not rather to be said that the peculiar character and functions of each deity had penetrated into Italy; and that the Etruscans had from them devised and adopted names for the gods, which being taken from some different attribute, characteristic, or function, the name necessarily became different." † For the appellations of the deities constitute so inseparable a part of all mythologies, that it is inconceivable how the gods of one people could have been adopted by another without their names having been at the same time received into general use; and equally so how any colonists, who introduced their native gods into another country, could have been induced to change the sacred names invoked in their hymns and rituals into strange and barbarous appellations. The identity, however, of the Greek, Etruscan, and Latin mythologies seems unquestionable; and the cause, therefore, which has occasioned the Kronos of the Greeks to be denominated by the Latins Saturnus; Zeus, Jupiter; Poseidon, Neptunus; Hera, Juno; Aphrodite, Venus; &c., must remain one of those unaccountable anomalies and difficulties which too frequently impede all satisfactory investigation of the languages, history, and religion of ancient nations.

* Lanzi, Saggio de Lingua Etrusca, tom. ii. pp. 237—240.

† Ibid., p. 241. note.

CHAP. IV.

THE MYTHOLOGY OF THRACIA, GERMANY, AND SCANDINAVIA.

In tracing the origin of nations, it is obvious that similarity of religion would be one of the most convincing proofs of the affinity of the people amongst whom the same system of polytheism was found to prevail: but the converse of this proposition is not equally true; for many causes might conduce to alter or to change entirely the religion of their ancestors, as different tribes branched off from the parent stem, and grew up independently into populous nations. It is, at the same time, undeniable, that, in order to determine whether any similarity existed between the mythologies of any two people of antiquity, full and accurate accounts of the systems compared together are indispensable. When, therefore, no such accounts are available, it might seem that researches of this nature could never lead to any satisfactory result. But the origin of the Teutonic people is so interesting a historical problem, and so completely involved in obscurity, that no means of elucidating it, however unpromising, ought to be disregarded; and, consequently, it becomes of importance to ascertain precisely what is actually known respecting the mythologies which formerly prevailed in Thracia, Germany, and Scandinavia.

On this subject the prevailing opinion seems to be, that as Germany and Scandinavia were peopled by Scythians, it is in Scythia that the origin of the German and Scandinavian religion must be sought for. Hence, in a late work, Professor Mone expresses this opinion:—"But, in order to judge of the correctness and importance of Herodotus's accounts of the Scythians, it is necessary to illustrate the true and valuable information which he has given, by means of the language and religion of the Fins; and then, however little one may learn, it will at least evince the accuracy of Herodotus. I am, therefore, convinced that the cradle of the religion of northern Europe is to be sought for in Scythia on the banks of the Borysthenes; and if the Germans and Slavonians will recur to this country, they will find such an agreement between the popular faith of these two people and that of the Scythians as cannot be mistaken." * But Herodotus has not stated that any migrations of the western Scythians into northern Europe ever took place; nor is such a circumstance mentioned by any ancient writer. Such an event, however, is not in itself improbable, and might therefore be admitted, were it not disproved by the indisputable testimony of language; for, if Ulphilas's translation of the Gospels be written in the language of the Goths, it must necessarily follow that the Goths, Germans, and Scandinavians must have descended from the same ancestors, as the intimate affinity between their languages is self-evident.

The question, therefore, is simply, Were the Getæ and Goths the same people? and, if so, were the Getæ Scythians or not? Much has been written upon these points, but they remain still undecided; because authors, instead of admitting the plain and obvious meaning of such passages relating to them as occur in ancient writers, either pervert it in order to support some favourite hypothesis, or boldly misquote the passage itself which they adduce.† The production, therefore, of the opinions of ancient authors on this subject, expressed

* Geschichte des Heidenthums in Nordlichen Europa, vol. i. p. 113., annexed to the second edition of Creuzer's Symbolik und Mythologie.

† Of such misquotation a singular instance occurs in an article on the Vindication of the Celts, &c., contained in the second volume of the Edinburgh Review, which the writer prefaces with this remark:—"In forming our opinion as to the merits of this controversy, we have not confined our remarks to those authorities only which are cited by our author and by Mr. Pinkerton, but *have carefully consulted every ancient author who was likely to elucidate the subject in dispute.*" In page 258., however, the writer says:—"We shall lay those passages, so unaccountably overlooked by Mr. Pinkerton, before our readers:—'The Scythians, few and despised, dwelt at first near the Araxes; and afterwards, increasing in numbers, conquered many countries beyond the Tanais, even as far as Thrace.'—'It is impossible to conjecture the date of these conquests; they must, however, have been effected at a very remote period, since, according to the same author and Herodotus, Sesostris found and attacked them in their settlements beyond the Tanais, and on the borders of Thrace.'" But in neither of these passages of Diodorus Siculus, lib. ii. p. 89, 90., and lib. i. p. 35. ed. Wesseling, is the word *Thrace* to be found; and the words of Herodotus respecting Sesostris are, Ες ὁ εκ της Ασιης ες την Ευρωπην διαβας, τους τε Σκυθας κατεστρεψατο και τους Θρηικας.—Lib. ii. cap. 103. ed. Wesseling.

in their own words, may perhaps tend to its elucidation. To commence, then, with Herodotus, who distinctly says, — *Οἱ δε Γεται, προς αγνωμοσυνην τραπομενοι, αυτικα εδουλωθησαν, Θρηικων εοντες ανδρειοτατοι και δικαιοτατοι* *: and no quotation can be necessary to show that Herodotus considered the Thracians and Scythians to be distinct people. On this point Diodorus Siculus affords no information, but in Strabo occur these passages: — *Οἱ τοινυν Ἑλληνες τους Γετας Θρακας ὑπελαμβανον.* † .... *Το δε χηρους γυναικων οικειν, ουδεμιαν τοιαυτην εμφασιν ὑπεγραφει, και μαλιστα παρα τοις Θραξι, και τουτων τοις Γεταις. Ὁρα δ' ἁ λεγει Μενανδρος περι αυτων, ου πλασας, ὡς εικος, αλλ' εξ ἱστοριας λαβων·*

> *Παντες μεν οἱ Θρακες, μαλιστα δ' οἱ Γεται,*
> *Ἡμεις ἁπαντων, κ. τ. λ.* ‡

Herodotus, also, says with respect to the Thracians,—*Ουνοματα δε πολλα εχουσι κατα χωρας ἑκαστοι· νομοισι δε οὑτοι παραπλησιοισι παντες χρεωνται κατα παντα, πλην Γετεων, και Τραυσων, και των κατυπερθε Κρηστωναιων οικεοντων* §: and thus Strabo enumerates different tribes amongst them, as the Mœsi, the Daci, &c. In the same manner Pliny states, — "Thracia sequitur, inter validissimas Europæ gentes, in strategias quinquagenas divisa;" || and includes the Getæ within this country. Pomponius Mela, likewise, says, — "Una gens Thraces habitant, aliis aliisque præditi et nominibus et moribus. Quidam feri sunt et ad mortem paratissimi, Getæ utique."¶ It is, however, useless to quote any more authorities, because, if any credit be given to the concurrent testimony of ancient writers, it must be admitted that the Getæ were Thracians.

But no ancient author has ascribed to the Thracians a Scythian origin; and, on the contrary, Herodotus expressly states that *where Thracia ends Scythia begins*⸸; and Strabo, though he does not describe precisely the limits of Thracia, clearly places all the Scythians either

* Herod., lib. iv. cap. 93.

† Strab. Geog., lib. vii. p. 295.

‡ Strab. Geog., lib. vii. p. 296, 297.

§ Herod., lib. v. cap. 3.

|| Plin. Nat. Hist., lib. iv. cap. 11.

¶ De Situ Orbis, lib. ii. cap. 2.

⸸ Herod., lib. iv. cap. 99.

If Scylax, also, lived before Herodotus, it is said in the Periplus ascribed to him: *Διηκει δε ἡ Θρακη απο Στρυμωνος ποταμου μεχρι Ιστρου ποταμου του εν τῳ Ευξεινῳ Ποντῳ.* — *Μετα δε Θρακην εισι Σκυθαι εθνος.* — *Geog. Vet. Scriptores*, vol. i. p. 27. 29.

in Asia or to the north of the Borysthenes. Rennell has, therefore, very justly remarked, that it appears "that the Scythians of Herodotus were the *Sarmatæ* and *Getæ* of the Romans; and his *Massagetæ*, the *Scythians* of the same people, as well as of the Greeks in general from the time of Alexander's expedition."* If the Getæ, consequently, were Thracians, and had, subsequently to the time when Herodotus flourished, occupied the greatest part of western Scythia, it must be evident that, so far from these Scythians having been able to extend themselves over Europe, they must either have been themselves dispossessed of their country, or so incorporated amongst their conquerors as to cause their name to disappear as a distinct people. But, notwithstanding the clearest testimony of ancient writers to the Thracians being an indigenous race, several modern writers have attempted either to identify them with the Scythians, or to show that the Scythians possessed that country which was inhabited by the Getæ, Daci, and other Thracian tribes. Their arguments, however, are so vague and indefinite, and so destitute of proof, that they deserve not the slightest attention; for, in fact, they may be all reduced to this syllogism: the Getæ were Scythians; but the Getæ were also Thracians; ergo, the Thracians were likewise Scythians. The question, therefore, depends entirely on the origin of the Getæ; and to oppose, as Pinkerton does, to the authority of Herodotus, Strabo, Pliny, Pomponius Mela, and other ancient authors, nothing more than the loose manner in which the term Scythian has been incidentally applied to the Getæ or Goths by later writers, such as Trebellius Pollio, Priscus, Eunapius, Anastasius, Georgius Syncellus, Isidorus, &c., is a mode of reasoning which clearly betrays the weakness of the hypothesis in support of which it is adduced. Dr. Jamieson also, who advocates the same opinion, instead of proving its correctness by adequate authority, is obliged to rest his identification of the Getæ and Scythians on a gratuitous assumption that the Getæ and Massagetæ were originally the same people; and that as the latter were undeniably Scythians, the former

* Geog. System of Herodotus, p. 46.

must have been so too. But he does not attempt to establish this affinity by any evidence whatever. The complete failure, consequently, of every endeavour to evince in a satisfactory manner that the Getæ were Scythians, must equally prove that, as the supposed connecting link has no existence, the Thracians were no more Scythians than the Getæ.

If, therefore, the authority of ancient authors is esteemed preferable to the mere conjectures of modern writers, it must follow that, three hundred years before the Christian era, the country which extends from the confines of Macedonia, along the Hellespont, Propontis, and Euxine Sea, to the Borysthenes, and from the Hellespont and Euxine, on both sides of the Danube, to the frontiers of the Suevi, was occupied by a single race of people who were Thracians and not Scythians.* Nor can it admit of doubt, that the Thracians derived their origin from Asia Minor, and not from Scythia either western or eastern. But from this time until A. D. 250, when the Goths first invaded the Roman empire, not the slightest indication appears in history that any other people had established themselves in this country; and consequently the identity of the Getæ and Goths, as affirmed by Jornandes, cannot be disputed. Pinkerton, therefore, was most decidedly wrong, when he asserted that, "from their settlements on the Euxine, the Scythians, Getæ, or Goths, gradually extended themselves over most

* With respect to the western Scythians having been dispossessed by the Getæ of the country which they occupied in the time of Herodotus, the following passage of Strabo deserves particular attention: — Μεταξυ δε της Ποντικης θαλαττης της απο του Ιστρου επι Τυραν, και ἡ των Γετων ερημια προκειται πεδιας πασα, και ανυδρος· εν ῇ Δαρειος αποληφθεις ὁ Ὑστασπεω καθ᾽ ὃν καιρον διεβη τον Ιστρον επι τους Σκυθας, εκινδυνευσε πανστρατιᾳ διψει διαλυθηναι· συνηκε δ᾽ οψε, και αναστρεψε. Λυσιμαχος δ᾽ ὑστερον στρατευσας επι Γετας, και τον βασιλεα Δρομιχαιτην, ουκ εκινδυνευσε μονον, αλλα και ἑαλω ζωγριᾳ. — Lib. vii. p. 305.

Pausanias, Attica, cap. ix., relates this circumstance more fully; but it is sufficient for the present purpose to quote these two sentences: — Θρακων δε των παντων ουδενες πλειους εισι των ανθρωπων, ὁτι μη Κελτοι, προς αλλο εθνος ἐν αντεξεταζοντι. . . . Λυσιμαχος δε και ὑςερον προσπταισας μαχαις, και την ἁλωσιν του παιδος ουκ εν παρεργῳ ποιουμενος, συνεθετο προς Δρομιχαιτην ειρηνην, της τε αρχης της αυτου τα περαν Ιστρου παρεις τῳ Γετῃ, και θυγατερα συνοικισας αναγκῃ το πλεον.

As this event took place in 292 B. C., it will be evident that the Getæ must have occupied this part of western Scythia at least three hundred years before the Christian era.

of Europe;" but had he not unfortunately identified the Getæ with the Scythians, and had he merely considered them as forming one of the tribes of the great Thracian people, his assertion would have been unquestionably correct.* It is precisely the same with respect to the following remarks: — "*The old German and Scythic one and the same speech.* This may be proved as follows. We have a venerable monument of the Scythic or Gothic language in the Gospels translated by Ulphilas, Bishop of the Goths, in Mœsia, in the year 367. These four Gospels, the remains of a translation of the Scriptures, have been repeatedly published, since the first edition by Junius, 1665, 4to, down to that of Mr. Lye. Another fragment, containing part of the Epistle to the Romans, has been lately discovered in the library at Wolfenbuttle, and published by Knittel, Archdeacon of Wolfenbuttle. Other fragments of the Gothic language have also been found, of which see Mr. Lye's notes to his edition of the Gothic Gospels. All these remains, as being Gothic, are Scythic; for it has been fully shown that the Goths and Scythæ were but synonymous terms for one and the same people."†

But Pinkerton has farther observed: "A question remains, at what time the Scythic population reached the Rhine and north-west extremity of Scandinavia, the farthest bounds of ancient Germany. Thrace, Asia Minor, Illyricum, Greece, were certainly peopled with Scythæ at least fifteen hundred years before Christ; Italy at least one thousand. Nations that subsist by hunting and pasturage, as the barbaric Scythæ, require a prodigious extent of territory to afford means of subsistence; and their speedy progress and population we

* This erroneous opinion has detracted much from the otherwise valuable information which is contained in Pinkerton's Dissertation on the Scythians or Goths. Omit, for instance, the words *Scythæ* and *Scythic* in the following passage, p. 55., and nothing can be more correct: — "That all the Thracians were Scythæ or Getæ, and spoke the Scythic or Gothic tongue, is clear. Vopiscus says of Probus, *Thracias, atque omnes Geticos populos, aut in deditionem, aut in amicitiam, recepit.* The speech of the Mœsi was, as Ovid testifies in many passages, the Getic or Scythic. Strabo gives us the same information in direct terms (lib. vii. p. 303.): Παρα των Γετων ὁμογλοττου τοις Θραξιν εθνους· *the Getæ, a people using the same language with the Thracians:* and Strabo's Getæ extend over the whole north-west of the Danube and Euxine, even to half of Germany. Many ancients call the Getæ Thracians, and others call the Thracians Getæ."

† Dissert. on the Scythians or Goths, p. 109.

may judge of from those of the Tartars. But the German Scythæ had their way to fight against the northern Celts, a hardy race of men; and a vast region to populate; so that we may allow a very considerable period for their progress. From Herodotus, and other ancients, it is certain that the Scythians possessed Germany, nay, had driven the Celts to the farthest west of Gaul, at least five hundred years before our era."* But no ancient author has mentioned that either Scythians or Getæ had migrated into Germany and Scandinavia five hundred years before Christ; and that the Scythians had occupied Asia Minor, Thrace, and Greece, fifteen hundred years before Christ, as here supposed, must appear in the highest degree improbable, from their very name having been unknown to Homer. Were, however, this conjecture admitted, it must evidently follow that these Scythians must have been of the same origin as those whom Herodotus found inhabiting western Scythia; and it has been above fully evinced that three hundred years before Christ this country was no longer possessed by these Scythians, but, on the contrary, occupied by the Getæ, a Thracian people. Had, also, Thrace been peopled by Scythians twelve hundred years before, it is clear, from the testimony of ancient writers, that the Thracians had long become a people perfectly distinct in every respect from their alleged progenitors. The language, consequently, in which the translation of the Gospels by the Bishop of Mœsia was written, in A. D. 367, was Thracian; and Pinkerton does not even attempt to show that any affinity existed between it and the language spoken by the Scythians, when they first occupied Thracia, as he affirms, *eighteen hundred years before that date.*

I have also endeavoured to evince, in a former work, that there is every reason to believe that the languages which at present prevail in Persia, and the wide extended deserts of Tartary, are still in essentially the same state as they existed three or four thousand years ago. If, therefore, western Scythia were peopled by emigrants from Persia, as Pinkerton supposes, or from the north of the Jaxartes, as Herodotus states; and if these Scythians had subsequently occupied Thracia, Germany, and Scandinavia; some undeniable traces of affinity between the

* Dissert. on the Scythians or Goths, p. 143.

Teutonic and Persian or Tartar languages should, even at this day, be easily discoverable. But these languages differ so materially, both in words and in grammatical structure, as to place it beyond a doubt, that, if Tartary be the proper representative of ancient Scythia, Germany and Scandinavia could not possibly have been peopled by Scythians. If, however, it be argued, that there is no proof that any of the existing dialects of Tartary was the mother tongue of those Scythians who are supposed to have migrated into Europe fifteen hundred years before Christ, the objection must be admitted; but in this case to talk of a Scythic language is ridiculous, because there appears not the slightest indication, either in language, tradition, or history, of its having ever existed: for it is not denied that the earliest specimen of the Getic or Gothic language which has been preserved is Ulphilas's translation of the Gospels; since even Dr. Jamieson admits that "so few words belonging to the ancient language of the Scythian nations, except the names of persons, have been handed down to us by Greek writers; and these, which have been transmitted, are so corrupted or disguised by the Greek mode of pronunciation; that we can derive little aid from this quarter. But even here are to be traced some vestiges of radical affinity." * The few words, however, produced by Dr. Jamieson, are Phrygian and Spartan †; and that either the Phrygians or the Doric race were Scythians, he has most completely failed in proving. The argument thus returns to the real origin of the Getæ; and as this must be considered, unless the contrary be satisfactorily proved by adequate evidence, to have been Thracian and not Scythian,

* Hermes Scythicus, Diss., p. 66.

† These words are, *bedu* signifying *water* in the Phrygian language, identified with Gothic, *bada*, lavare, aqua se abluere; whence our *bath*, *bathe*, &c. Phrygian, *bek*, bread, a cognate term with Gothic, *baka*, pinsere; *quasi*, what is *baked*. Phrygian, μοιραι, the *Fates*, strongly resembling Gothic, *maer*, a virgin, or in the plural *meyar*, *quasi* the virgins. "The Spartans," adds Dr. Jamieson, "who were Pelasgi, designated their laws *rhetra*, a word said to be synonymous with *oracula*, *fata*; because Lycurgus gave forth his laws as the immediate dictates of heaven. This term has been traced to ῥεω, *dico*. But perhaps it merits observation, that as German *rat-en* is rendered *divinare*, also *constituere*; Anglo-Saxon *araed* is *prophetiza*, and *raede*, *lex*, *pactum*, *decretum*. German *recht*, Islandic *rett*, Swedish *raett*, Armoric, *rhaith*, also signify *lex*, *jus*.

The mere transcription of such etymological reasoning must throw complete discredit on the hypothesis in support of which it is adduced.

it must necessarily follow that Ulphilas's translation affords a most valuable specimen of the Thracian, but not of the Scythian, language.

It is to Thracia, therefore, and not to Scythia, that the origin of the German and Scandinavian people and religion must be ascribed. But, with regard to the latter, it is to be regretted that the system of idolatry which prevailed among the Thracians has not attracted the attention of any ancient writer. For Herodotus merely notices the subject in these few words: — "The only gods whom the Thracians worship are Mars, Bacchus, and Diana; besides which deities, their princes pay particular devotion to Mercury;" * and no information on this point can be derived from any other author. Whether, therefore, the mythology of Thracia was precisely or nearly the same as that of Germany and Scandinavia, is a question that cannot now be determined, nor can it, with any justice, be assumed that the systems prevalent in these countries were originally dissimilar. To the Pelasgic ancestors, however, of the Thracians, was Greece indisputably indebted for its religion; and it might, therefore, seem probable that the Grecian and Thracian systems of polytheism were essentially the same. But, though this may have been the case at first, it can scarcely be doubted that as the Thracians subsequently increased in numbers, and relapsed into a state of barbarism, their religion would also be affected by this change, and that, instead of receiving cultivation and improvement, it would gradually become as simple as it no doubt was at its original establishment.

It has, however, recently become the general opinion of the German literati, that their country was not peopled by the Euxine Scythians, but by a race of men who migrated into it from middle Asia at a remote period of antiquity: for Adelung, in the Introduction to the second volume of his Mithridates, gives it as his opinion that middle Asia was the ancient and abundant nursery of mankind, from which Europe received its inhabitants; and these he divides into six distinct nations; viz. Iberians, Celts, Germans, Thracians, Slaves, and Fins. †

* Herod., lib. v. cap. 7.

† Grotius, however, is of a different opinion, for he has remarked: — "Facile autem videbunt qui judicio uti volent, Mosem in antiquissimorum populorum recensione non longe

With respect, also, to Germany, Adelung observes:—"I understand this word, as others have done before me, in its most extensive signification, so as to include all the people who are allied together in origin, manners, and language, and who, in the earliest times, inhabited the country which extended from the Danube on the south to the farthest extremities of the north, and from the Rhine on the west to the Vistula on the east. They became sooner known to more civilised foreign nations through the products of their country than through themselves. For about the time of the Trojan war, and a little before the age of Homer, amber was considered as the greatest rarity, though the name of the people from whence it came was unknown. But for the truest accounts of the Germans we are indebted to Pytheas, who lived about three hundred and twenty years before Christ; at which time the *Juts* inhabited the present Danish peninsula; to the east of them, on the coast, the *Teutones* — a general name for the Germans; and next them the *Ostiæ*, and the *Cossini* or *Cotini*, or Goths. What people, however, inhabited at this time the coasts of Norway, called by him *Thule*, he does not inform us. When we consider all the people living within these limits as one whole, they immediately appear to be an original and self-formed race of men, and perfectly distinct from all the neighbouring people; though they have been, from ignorance of history and language, transformed into Celts or Scythians, or into that historical chimera, the Celto-Scythians." *

This opinion, as it will be observed, is equally adverse to the Scythian and Thracian origin of the Germans and Scandinavians; but it is

admodum ab Armenia Syriaque abiisse, quibus ex locis primum propagatum est genus humanum in eos quos ipse nominavit traduces; unde porro, procedente tempore, nonnulli in ulteriora, urgente fame, seditionibus, bellis, protrusi sunt: sicut ex Scythia per Sarmatiam in Scanziam ventum diximus, e qua Scanzia deinde Germani cæteri ortum habuere: nam Germanos omnes ejusdem ab antiquo esse originis eadem inter se et cum Scanziæ populis lingua, quamtumvis temporibus et locis nonnihil variata, demonstrat." (*Hist. Goth. Proleg.*, p. 22.) But Grotius places the Scythians in Armenia and Syria, for he had just before said (p. 8.), — "Nam ex Armenia Syriaque, ubi primos post diluvium mortales vixisse profanis etiam testimoniis, profecti Scythæ trans eas, quas nunc Sarmatarum dicimus terras, in Germaniæ septemtrionalia venere."

* Mithridates, vol. ii. p. 168.

evidently inconsistent with the manner in which it seems most probable that the world was peopled: for neither in tradition nor in history is there the slightest indication that in remote antiquity any migrations from middle Asia into Europe took place; and Adelung himself admits that the coasts of Germany did not become known to the rest of the world until three hundred and twenty years before Christ. Whatever credit, also, may be given to the voyage of Pytheas, it is undeniable that the ancients were most imperfectly acquainted with that country until the time of Cæsar, nearly three hundred years afterwards. Nor does his brief notices afford much information respecting it, though they clearly evince that it must have been but recently inhabited: for he describes the people as divided into small townships, which considered it their highest praise to extend desolation as far as possible around their respective boundaries; living in independence and paying but a voluntary obedience to their chiefs; unacquainted with property and fixed places of residence; averse from agriculture; devoting their time to hunting, rapine, and war; subsisting on milk, cheese, and flesh; and but partially clothed with skins.* One hundred and forty years afterwards this account is fully confirmed by Tacitus, which must still further prove the recentness of the peopling of Germany, as its inhabitants had not during so long a period made any progress in civilisation. "I accede," says Tacitus, "to the opinion of those who consider the Germans to be a distinct, unmixed, and self-formed race of men, unaffected by any intermarriages with other nations. Hence their bodily conformation, though amongst so great a number of people, is the same in all: for their eyes are blue and fierce; their hair reddish; their bodies large, well adapted for sudden action, but not equally patient of exertion and labour; and little accustomed to support thirst and heat, but inured to bear hunger and cold. Their country, though it slightly varies in appearance, is on the whole rendered either horrid by woods, or obnoxious by marshes; towards Gaul, moister; and towards Noricum and Pannonia, windier; sufficiently fertile; ungenial to fruit trees; productive of cattle and sheep, but of a small size, as it is not in the ex-

* Vide De Bello Gallico, lib. vi. cap. 21, 22, 23.

cellence but in the number of their cattle that they pride themselves; these are their sole and most prized wealth, for I doubt whether the gods have in their favour or their anger denied them silver and gold."* "It is sufficiently known that none of the German people inhabit towns; nor admit of their places of residence being joined together. They live separate and distinct, as a fountain, a field, or a grove induces them to fix their abode. . . . The dress of all is a cloak fastened by a clasp, or, if this be wanting, by a thorn; or, otherwise, naked, they pass whole days beside the fire."† With respect, also, to Scandinavia, Pinkerton justly observes:—"Now it can be clearly shown that Scandinavia was down to a late period, nay, is at present, almost overrun with enormous forests, where there was no room for population. Adam of Bremen, who wrote in the eleventh century, instructs us that even in Denmark, at that time, the sea-coasts alone were peopled; while the inner parts of the country were one vast forest. If such was the case in Denmark, we may guess that in Scandinavia even the shores were hardly peopled. Scandinavia is also a most mountainous region; and among a barbaric and unindustrious people, the mountains are almost unpeopled."‡

If, therefore, it appears incontrovertible that the peopling and civilisation of Germany had made scarcely any progress in the first century of the Christian era, and if even in the eleventh century Scandinavia were in the situation described by Pinkerton, it must necessarily follow that the hypotheses which ascribe the population and religion of those countries to colonies which had migrated either from middle Asia or from Euxine Scythia 1500 or 1000 years before Christ, can rest on no grounds whatever. So impressed, indeed, was Gibbon with the recentness of the period at which Germany must have been peopled, that he has observed:—"When Tacitus considered the purity of the German

* De Mor. Germ., cap. 4, 5.

† Ibid., cap. 16, 17.

In the second chapter of this most valuable tract, Tacitus expresses himself in these energetic words:—"Quis porro, præter periculum horridi et ignoti maris, Asia, aut Africa, aut Italia relicta, Germaniam peteret? informem terris, asperam cœlo, tristem cultu aspectuque, nisi si patria sit."

‡ Diss. on the Scythians or Goths, p. 23.

blood, and the forbidding aspect of the country, he was disposed to pronounce these barbarians *indigenæ*, or natives of the soil. We may allow with safety, and perhaps with truth, that ancient Germany was not originally peopled by any foreign colonies already formed into a political society, but that the name and nation received their existence from the gradual union of some wandering savages of the Hercynian woods. To assert those savages to have been the spontaneous production of the earth which they inhabited, would be a rash inference, condemned by religion, and unwarranted by reason." * It would certainly seem much more probable that Germany derived its inhabitants from the conterminous and populous country of Thracia, than that they were the spontaneous production of either the earth which they inhabited, or of the Hercynian woods. There are, also, strong grounds for believing that Europe remained uninhabited until it was peopled from western and not from middle Asia; and the gradual extension, therefore, of the Thracians from the frontiers of Macedonia along the Hellespont and Euxine to the Borysthenes, and from these limits on the south-east to the Baltic and Scandinavia on the north-west, cannot but appear in the highest degree probable. It must at least be admitted that this supposition is much more consistent with all the indications respecting the peopling of the world which have been preserved by tradition and history, and much freer from all valid objections, than any hypothesis hitherto proposed for the explanation of this subject. It is, at the same time, the sole manner in which the striking affinity between the earliest specimen of the Thracian language and the various Teutonic dialects now existing can be simply and reasonably accounted for: because, that Mœsia was a province of Thracia is undeniable; and if, consequently, the Germans and Scandinavians did not descend from the Thracians, as Adelung contends, but differed from them in origin, customs, and language, it becomes impossible to understand how the Mœso-Gothic should possess so remarkable an affinity with the Teutonic dialects. The other hypotheses, however, merely differ from the opinion which I maintain in ascribing a Scythian origin to the Thracians, which conjecture I have, perhaps, sufficiently refuted; as they all

* Decline and Fall, &c., vol. i. p. 349.

concur in deriving the population of Germany and Scandinavia from the western Scythia of Herodotus, though they vary as to the time and manner in which these migrations took place. But, as it seems much more probable that the Thracians would have commenced passing into Germany from the western and not from the eastern extremity of their country, it must be concluded that the occurrence of such migrations from the Euxine, being entirely unsupported by evidence, is a mere gratuitous assumption which rests on no grounds whatever.

If, therefore, Germany and Scandinavia were peopled from Thracia, the emigrants would, no doubt, bring with them their native religion, and thus the mythologies of these countries must have been at first precisely the same. Unfortunately, however, the system of polytheism which prevailed in Thracia is unknown, and, consequently, this means of determining the degree of affinity which existed between the Thracian and Teutonic people is not now available. But from the accounts of the German religion given by Cæsar and Tacitus, it would appear to have been that primitive system of idolatry which consisted in the adoration of the sun, the planets, and the elements. For the former states that the only objects which the Germans worshipped were such as they beheld, and from whose sensible influence they derived benefit, namely, the Sun, the Moon, and Fire*; and to these Tacitus adds Tuisto, Mercury, Mars, the Earth, Hercules, and Isis. He farther adds, that in consequence of the immensity of the gods, the Germans considered it improper to confine them within walls, or to assimilate them in any manner to the human form. They, therefore, consecrated to them groves and woods; and that secret awe which they inspire, they distinguished by the names of the gods. † The correctness of these accounts seems to be singularly confirmed by the names of the days of the week which have been preserved in English: for Sunday and Monday are obvious; Mars may have been identified with Tuisto; and

* "Deorum numero eos solos ducunt, quos cernunt, et quorum aperte opibus juvantur, Solem, et Vulcanum, et Lunam."—*De Bell. Gall.*, lib. vi. cap. 21.

† De Mor. Ger., cap. 9.

In the 39th chapter, speaking of a sacred wood amongst the Semnones, the principal tribe of the Suevi, Tacitus makes use of this expression:—"Ibi regnator omnium deus, cætera subjecta atque parentia:" from which it might be concluded that the Germans acknowledged one supreme God.

Mercury is recognised as Woden in Wednesday*; Hercules may have been supposed to be the same as Thor, whence Thursday; and some resemblance may have been perceived between Isis and Frigga, from whose name softened has originated Friday. One planet still remains, Seater, whence Saturday, which may have been omitted by Tacitus. Mannus, also, the son of Tuisto, and Herthum translated by Tacitus *terra*, are immediately recognised in the English words *man*, and *earth*.

This description, consequently, of the German religion as it existed shortly before and after the commencement of the Christian era, would seem entitled to credit; and in speculating, therefore, on the origin of idolatry, it is to be regretted that it cannot now be ascertained whether so unsophisticated a system was received from the Thracians or whether it originated amongst the Germans themselves. Unless, however, it is supposed that the latter were *autochthones*, it must be concluded that the colonists who migrated into Germany preserved their native religion; and it might hence be inferred that, at the time of these migrations, the same simple form of idolatry prevailed among the Thracians. But this subject is involved in too much uncertainty to admit of any argument being justly founded upon it, either in support or in refutation of the origin which may be ascribed to the Germans.† It cannot, however, be with any reason contended that the description of the

* Paulus Warnefridus remarks: — "Wodan sane, quem adjecta litera Godan dixerunt, ipse est, qui apud Romanos Mercurius dicitur." — *De Gest. Long.*, lib. i. cap. 9.

† On this subject Mr. Turner remarks: — "Of the sun and moon we can only state that their sun was a female deity, and their moon was of the male sex; of their Tiw [Tuisto] we know nothing but his name. Woden was the great ancestor from whom they deduced their genealogies. It has been already remarked, that the calculations from the Saxon pedigrees place Woden in the third century. Of the Saxon Woden, his wife Friga, and Thunr [Thor], we know very little, and it would not be very profitable to detail all the reveries which have been published about them. The Odin, Frigg, or Friga, and Thor of the Northmen were obviously the same characters; though we are not authorised to ascribe to the Saxon deities the apparatus and mythology which the northern Scalds of subsequent ages have transmitted to us from Denmark, Iceland, and Norway. Woden was the predominant idol of the Saxon adoration, but we can state no more of him, but so far as we describe the Odin of the Danes and Norwegians. Yet, as every people has its peculiar superstitions, it would be incorrect to apply to the more ancient Woden of the Saxons, the religious costume and creed attached to the Danish Odin. It will be better to confess our ignorance of the Saxon superstition wherever it exists, and to reserve for a separate occasion the idolatry of the latter Northmen." — *Hist. of the Anglo-Saxons*, vol. ii. p. 14.

Scythian religion given by Herodotus in any manner coincides with the accounts of the German religion given by Cæsar and Tacitus. For he enumerates as Scythian deities Jupiter, Tellus, Apollo, Venus, Urania, Hercules, Mars, and Neptune; and he states that Mars was the principal god of the Scythians, while amongst the Germans Tacitus ascribes this place to Mercury. It will, therefore, be evident that whatever opinion is proposed with respect to the origin of the ancient Germans, it must remain both unsupported and unaffected by any arguments which rest on a supposed similarity between their religion and that of any other people.

If, also, Scandinavia was peopled from Germany, which circumstance from the position of the two countries and the affinity of language seems undeniable, the Scandinavian religion must have originally been the same as the German. No accounts, however, of its primitive state now remain, but the description of a most singular system of mythology, which subsequently arose in Scandinavia, has been preserved in the two Eddas; though the manner in which it originated is involved in the most complete obscurity. For Professor Mone remarks: — " In ancient times the Scandinavians had not only one common language, but one common religion, which did not however exclude the popular fables and religious observances peculiar to different tribes. Of this common religion, and of the variations from it, sources and means of information still remain in the two Eddas, and the Sagas, to which I may add romantic and popular ballads. The older Edda consists of poems rendered metric by alliteration, and in short pieces of prose; and was, according to the general opinion, compiled by the Icelander Sæmund the wise (born A. D. 1056, died 1133), but of this circumstance no ancient evidence exists. * . . . . The younger Edda was composed by Snorri Sturlason (born A. D. 1178, assassinated 1241), and is a prosaic account of the Scandinavian mythology, in which stanzas

* Mr. Herbert remarks: — " The Edda of Sæmund is a collection of old Icelandic odes, some of which are supposed to have been written before the birth of Christ. It is said to have been compiled by the learned Sæmund, who was born in Iceland in 1056, according to some 1054, or 1057. The name of Sæmund's Edda was affixed to the manuscript in the seventeenth century by Brynolfius Svenonius, Bishop of Skalhot. The prose Edda attributed to Snorro Sturleson is founded upon these poems." — *Miscellaneous Poetry*, vol. i. p. 9.

of the older Edda are interwoven, but these do not form the groundwork of the new compilation." * Professor Mone farther observes, that "three opinions have been hitherto entertained respecting this mythology; the one, that it is nothing but the gross idolatry of a rude and wild people, the principal objects of which are war and rapine; then it is considered as a mere distortion of history by which the ancient tribes of Wani, Juts, Asi, and Alfi have been transformed into gods; and lastly the Eddas are esteemed by some to contain the most ancient and profound system of religion which has ever existed." † Another opinion on this subject is thus controverted by M. Grimm:—"It seems, at present, to be a favourite system to restrict ourselves to historic truth, and to deny every thing which admits not of proof; and hence we are required to believe that a mythology, which has originated of itself in the nature of a whole people, is nothing else than falsehood, and the mere invention of an idle imagination. But it has not been considered that it must be as difficult to invent a new mythology as a new language; and yet this opinion has been maintained by Adelung and others. For he supposes that the Edda was invented as a pleasantry in imitation of the Christian religion, intermixed with some embellishments derived without selection from the Grecian mythology. Such an opinion would not deserve notice, were it not adopted by many persons. Thus that, which could not be effected by the highest degree of cultivation and imagination, and which poets in vain attempt, was accomplished by an uninformed and uncultivated individual in the thirteenth century; who formed the idea of a new religion, and by means of an undiscovered world elaborated a new system of devotion, &c." ‡

* Geschichte des Heidenthums, &c., vol. i. p. 216. 220.

† Ibid., p. 309.

‡ Daub und Creuzer's Studien, vol. iv. p. 223.

The editors, also, of the Edda Sæmundar, Hafniæ, 1787, remark:—"Nec denique desunt, qui reliquarum hebetudinis pertæsi, re proprius inspecta, animadvertisse sibi videntur, Eddam illam vetustiorem, nam de recentioris ætate magis constat, personatam esse larvam, quæ, quo tempore religio Christiana in loca hæc borealia beneficos spargere cœpit radios, ex hoc lucis et umbræ contubernio enata, furtivis antiquitatis coloribus spurios natales occultare satagat. Hujus quæ sunt antiquissima, semipaganos esse volunt seculi a Christo nato X[mi] et XI[mi] fœtus et commenta; reliqua autem ortus esse longe

But to me it appears that there are not the slightest grounds for questioning the perfect originality of the Eddas; for the mythology therein described bears not the remotest resemblance to any religious system with which I am acquainted. It may, however, be doubted whether the Eddas present a complete and accurate description of this form of idolatry as it actually existed among the Scandinavians; but any mistakes, omissions, or additions, which may have occurred in these compilations, do not in the least detract from the evident homogeneity of the Eddic mythology. It is, therefore, to be regretted that no accounts of its origin have been preserved, and that all opinions proposed for its elucidation depend on the existence of an individual named Odin. For Mallet states:—"A celebrated tradition, confirmed by the poems of all the northern nations, by their chronicles, by institutions and customs, some of which subsist to this day, informs us, that an extraordinary person, named Odin, formerly reigned in the north; that he made great changes in the government, manners, and religion of those countries; that he enjoyed there great authority, and had even divine honours paid to him. *All these are facts, which cannot be contested.* [?] As to what regards the original of this man, the country whence he came, the time in which he lived, and the other circumstances of his life and death, they are so uncertain, that the most ingenious conjectures about them discover nothing to us but our own ignorance. Thus previously disposed to doubt, let these ancient authors I have mentioned relate the story: all their testimonies are comprised in that of Snorro, the ancient historian of Norway, and in the commentaries and explications which Torfæus has added to his narrative." *

inferioris, et ad seculum usque XII^um^ et XIII^um^ deprimendi. In hanc se sententiam inductos aiunt ipsis Odarum Eddicarum, quæ religionis dogmata, ritus, et mysteria tangunt, argumentis; horum enim plurima ex religione Christiana aut sacra Scriptura esse deprompta, licet figmentis impie turpiterque conspurcata, ac insulsis involuta fabulis. In tantis autem de Edda sententiarum divortiis litis dirimendæ partes in nos transsumere adeo non est nostrum, ut nemini sive contentum Eddæ, sive mirabundum illius studium, seu tepidum denique et suspicax ejusdem tædium, nostris laudibus aut vituperiis nec auctum eamus, nec ademptum; quin liberrimum potius de eadem sentiendi arbitrium cuivis integrum cupimus." —*Ad Lectorem*, p. vi.

* Northern Antiquities, vol. i. p. 38.

But Mallet, also, very justly remarks:—"In the second place these annals are of no great antiquity: we have none that were written before Christianity was established in the north: now, between the time of Odin, whose arrival in the north, according to Torfæus, is the first epoch of history, and that of the earliest Icelandic historian, elapsed about eleven centuries; and therefore if the compilers of the Icelandic annals found no written memoirs earlier than their own, as we have great reason to believe, then their narratives are only founded on tradition, inscriptions, or reliques of poetry. But can one give credit to traditions which must have taken in so many ages, and have been preserved by a people so ignorant?" * That such a person, therefore, as Odin ever existed no sufficient proof can be produced †; nor do the Eddas contain the slightest indication that the Odin who is celebrated in them was at first merely a mortal man. All the testimonies, also, to his existence may, as Mallet has observed, be reduced to the single evidence of Snorro; and it must, therefore, be admitted that, as there are no other accounts by which his relation could be corrected, this evidence must either be wholly received or wholly rejected. It may not, therefore, be unacceptable to the reader, if I reproduce the account of Odin given by Snorro, as I find it quoted by Sheringham. ‡

"The part of Asia which is watered on the east by the Tanais formerly possessed a metropolis named Asgard, over which presided with supreme power, a certain hero named Othin, who was, also, high-priest in that city, where sacrifices were frequently celebrated in honour and adoration of idols. Twelve senators, however, who surpassed their fellow-citizens in piety and wisdom, not only superintended the ceremonies of religion, but also administered justice. These were named *Diar*; i. e. gods or divine, and likewise *Drotner*, i. e. lords; whom all

* Northern Antiquities, vol. i. p. 51.

† In the last volume of the Decline and Fall of the Roman Empire, p. 406., Gibbon says: — "I take this opportunity of declaring, that, in the course of twelve years, I have forgotten or renounced the flight of Odin from Azoph to Sweden, which I never very seriously believed. The Goths are apparently Germans; but all beyond Cæsar and Tacitus is darkness or fable, in the antiquities of Germany."

‡ In his description of these events, Mallet has mixed up the accounts of different authors who wrote at different periods of time.

the people were bound to serve in turns, and to perform all duties which they might order. Othin was a mighty and valiant warrior, and carried his conquering arms into many countries, and subdued innumerable territories and kingdoms, and most happily conquering and triumphing he always departed victorious from every battle. The people, therefore, were persuaded that his constant success in war must be attributed to the peculiar favour of heaven : as often also, as he intrusted the conduct of a war, or any business of importance to his chiefs, he imposed his hands on their heads, as if he consecrated them ; which was considered as an auspicious omen, the certain preservative against all misfortune. Even in the midst of dangers the invoking the name of Othin was an unfailing resource, and hence was the utmost confidence placed in it in every peril.

"Othin had two brothers, the elder of whom was called Ve, and the younger Velir or Vuli. These, when Othin was engaged in travelling or in war, governed in his place and administered all affairs with the greatest care and diligence. Once when Othin had been absent longer than they expected, they divided the kingdom between them, and likewise claimed the guardianship of Othin's wife Frigga. But Othin having at length returned from his long journey, his dominion, along with his wife, was restored to him by his brothers ; and he then undertook an expedition against the Scythians called Vaner. They, however, opposed him valiantly, bravely defended their country, repeatedly rendered victory doubtful, and at last obliged him to consult his safety by a hasty retreat. From that time Othin and the Vaner harassed each other by mutual incursions, and by their plundering caused reciprocally immense loss ; until at last being wearied out, they concluded a firm and lasting peace between each other, and interchanged hostages for its observance. The Scythians gave to Othin as hostages a rich and distinguished man named Niord, with his son Froi ; and the Asiani gave to the Scythians two choice men eminent for the dignity of their forms, their valuor, their wisdom, and other qualities, the one named Heimer the most able of magistrates, and Mimer the wisest of men. In consequence of which the Scythians, in order to render the value of the hostages equal, sent to the Asiani another hero named

Quasir, whom they esteemed the wisest amongst them. Heimer immediately obtained a government among the Scythians, but he scarcely ever performed any act of importance without consulting Mimer. For he taught him the various customs, rites, laws, and institutions, which regulated the administration of affairs and of justice. But when Heimer, being deprived of his assistance, was obliged to decide in open assembly on any difficult points in dispute, he frequently said to the persons present; do you consult together, and avail yourselves of whatever opinion may appear the best, for I cannot aid you with my advice. The Scythians, then understanding that they had been deceived by the Asiani in the interchange of hostages, cut off Mimer's head, and sent it to them; which Othin embalmed, and gave it by magic charms the power of speaking, so that it revealed the most hidden secrets. Afterwards Niord and his son Froi, having participated of divinity, were received into the number of the deities of the Asiatics, as well as Freia, the daughter of Froi; who, having learnt magic from the Asiatics, particularly pleased the Scythians. Niord, however, passing his life among the Scythians, married his sister, which is permitted by their laws; but amongst the Asiatics, a marriage with one so nearly allied by blood is not considered lawful.

"Steep and lofty mountains extending from north to south divide, as by a natural boundary, Scythia from other countries, and all the people to the south of them obeyed Othin. About this time the Romans, the lords of all, having conquered innumerable kingdoms, and carrying their victorious arms far and wide, began to reduce under their dominion the most extensive states, the bravest people, the most flourishing towns, and the most celebrated cities; in consequence of which many chiefs and princes departing voluntarily from their native countries gave up their subjects to the Romans. But Othin, an eminent magician, and particularly skilled in divination, knowing that he and his posterity to the latest ages should reign in the northern part of the world, resigned the government of Asgard to his brothers Ve and Velir; and proceeded himself into Russia, thence into Saxony, which having almost entirely subdued, he entrusted its government to his sons. He likewise appointed his son Skiold to rule over Denmark, who afterwards established the royal residence and seat of government at Lethrum. When, however, Othin learned that the Swedish Gothland, over which Gylvo then reigned, was spacious, fertile, and adapted for the subsistence of a numerous people, he visited him, and having concluded a treaty with him obtained liberty to seek for new domiciles in that country. For the power of the Asiatics inspired Gylvo with fear, and he dreaded to offend them, as he perceived himself to be much inferior to them in valour and forces. He, also, contended with Othin as to their skill in magic, but Othin was always victorious.

"Othin began to inhabit the country near the river Loger, and there founded the city of Sigtuna (a town of which name existed in Sweden in the time of our ancestors), and erected there a magnificent palace, and instituted sacrifices according to the rites and ceremonies of the Asiatics. Into this country he introduced a colony as it were of deities (*deastri*), and assigned to them certain lands and temples. Thus Moal was given to Niord, Upsal to Froi, Trudvanger to Thor, Handberg to Heimer, and Broedeblik to Balder. Then Othin, proceeding with his band of idols to the northern parts of Sweden, performed unheard-of miracles by various magical arts, and established a public school for teaching magic, the use of which never before existed in this country.

"With regard to the figure and appearance of Othin. He always showed himself to his friends of a cheerful and pleasant countenance, expressive of an inclination for mirth, jests, and pleasantry; but to his enemies his countenance was fierce and terrible; the more so, as he could, like Proteus, change himself into any form that he pleased. With such eloquence, also, and persuasion could he charm his auditors, that no one could refuse belief to his words; and he frequently added a wonderful grace to his conversation, by introducing into it verses and rhythmical periods; whence he and his companions were called scalds, or poets. Besides, Othin used, by magic, to deprive his enemies of their senses, and to inspire them with the greatest terror; and when engaging with them, he, by means of incantations, so blunted their weapons, that his troops, though without defensive arms, rushed on them like wild dogs or wolves, and slaughtered them like sheep, without receiving any wound or injury. Hence this kind of fury was afterwards called the assault of the Berserkers. Othin, likewise, had such power of deceiving the eyes, that he would sometimes appear transformed into a fish, a bird, or a serpent: at others, he would recline on the ground, devoid of breathing, like one dead; and then, recovering his animation, he would affirm that he had travelled to distant countries, and relate exactly what was there occurring. By a single word he could extinguish conflagrations, quell tempests, stop inundations, and direct the winds as he pleased. He could evoke the ghosts of the dead, and enclose them in hills and mountains; whence he was called *Dronga* or *Honga Dratten*, the lord of ghosts. He had two ravens taught by him to speak in the same manner as men, who, flying to distant places, brought ample intelligence of all that was passing to their master. He opened mountains by magic arts, and thence extracted gold and silver, and discovered hidden treasures without any one pointing them out. Finally, Othin, by his *runes*, incantations, and magic arts, performed such incredible acts as procured him every where the brightest name, and caused the fame of the power and wisdom of Othin and the Asiani to be in a short time spread through every people and nation: for he so terrified his enemies, that none dared to attempt any thing against him; and so retained the fidelity of his friends and allies, that they seldom or never deserted him.

" It hence happened that the Swedes and other northern people performed solemn sacrifices to Othin and his twelve companions, and paid him that worship which is due to the Lord of heaven and earth. Their names, also, the people gave to their new-born children, calling them *Audum* and *Ovdum*, from *Othin; Thord, Thore, Torar, Steintor*, and *Haftor*, from *Thor;* which names are still in use in Norway. Othin also established various laws, of which these are most deserving of record: — He enjoined that the bodies of the dead or those slain in battle should be burned along with their most valuable ornaments and goods; the ashes to be either interred or thrown into a river; and monumental mounds to be raised in memory of the chiefs and nobles. Three times a year were solemn sacrifices to be performed; at the commencement of the winter for the year's prosperity, at the middle for fertility, and towards the end for victory. The Scythians paid to Othin, by way of tribute, a poll-tax of one denarius; and in return he was bound to protect them against their enemies, and to propagate religion and the worship of the gods. Niord married Skadi, who having left her husband was afterwards wedded to Othin, to whom she bore many sons, who were called by the common name of *Semming*. Then new Scythia, that is, Sweden, was called *Manheim*, and ancient Scythia *Gudheim*. At length his last day reached Othin in Sweden; and as he was about to expire, he directed his body to be marked with nine wounds, which were anciently called *geirs adde*. He farther ordered that they should sacrifice to him the prisoners taken in war, as this would be to him the most grateful and propitiatory offering. After his death he appeared to many persons, and particularly when any great battle was impending; to many he brought victory, and others he invited to Valhalla. His own corpse was burned, and a funeral festival and sacrifices instituted in his honour." *

Such is the earliest account of Odin which has been preserved, and its mere perusal must excite surprise that it should ever have received the slightest credit: for it has not the least resemblance to those traditionary legends and songs which might exist amongst a rude people, and, on the contrary, exhibits on its very face every mark of invention; as it may be affirmed with certainty, that no people ever degraded their

* This quotation is taken from Sheringhami de Anglorum Gentis Origine Disceptatio, cap. xii.

It is very remarkable, that in none of the more ancient authorities quoted by Sheringham, is there any mention of the following circumstances stated by Mallet; and they must, therefore, be considered as the invention of more recent writers: — "The Roman commonwealth was arrived to the highest pitch of power, and saw all the then known world subject to its laws, when an unforeseen event raised up enemies against it, from the very bosom of the forests of Scythia, and on the banks of the Tanais. Mithridates, by flying, had drawn Pompey after him into those deserts. The King of Pontus sought there for refuge, and new means of vengeance. He hoped to arm against the ambition of Rome all the barbarous nations, his neighbours, whose liberty it threatened. He succeeded in this at first; but all those people, ill-united as allies, ill-armed as soldiers, and still worse disciplined, were forced to yield to the genius of Pompey. Odin is said to have been of the number. He was obliged to withdraw himself by flight from the vengeance of the Romans; and to go seek, in countries unknown to his enemies, that safety which he could no longer find in his own. His true name was Sigge, son of Fridulph; but he assumed that of Odin, the chief god among the Scythians," &c. — *Northern Antiquities*, vol. i. p. 59.

gods into mere men, and that they have always attempted to magnify their heroes by ascribing to them the attributes of divinity. But it is not denied that Odin, Frigga, Thor, &c., existed as deities, before the Othin and his twelve companions of Snorro; and his attempting, therefore, to convert them, and the circumstances described in the Eddas, into historical personages and events, betrays, at once, that his narrative, so far from having being compiled from any authentic materials, is nothing more than the work of his own imagination. Its inconsistencies, also, and improbabilities are much too obvious to require remark. But it may be observed that the predominance of the Romans in foreign countries cannot be dated earlier than the defeat of Antiochus by Lucius Scipio, which occurred in 190 B. C.; and had, therefore, such a city as Asgard on the Tanais ever existed, or had the conquests of Odin and his subsequent victorious and triumphant migration ever taken place, it is utterly incredible that such remarkable circumstances should have escaped the notice of all ancient writers. The recent period, also, at which Scandinavia was peopled, is alone sufficient to evince that the Eddic mythology could not possibly have originated until after the Christian era.

Warton, however, has adopted and defended this gross and incredible fiction; but the arguments which he adduces in its support are singularly weak and futile, and particularly the following:—"It is notorious," says he, "that many traces of Oriental usages are found amongst all the European nations during their pagan state; and this phenomenon is rationally resolved, on the supposition that all Europe was peopled from the East. But as the resemblance which the pagan Scandinavians bore to the Eastern nations in manners, monuments, opinions, and practices, is so very perceptible and apparent, an inference arises, that their migration from the East must have happened at a period by many ages more recent, and therefore most probably about the time specified by their historians.* . . . . As the principal heroes

* Warton had just before stated,—"A few years before the birth of Christ, soon after Mithridates had been overthrown by Pompey, a nation of Asiatic Goths, who possessed that region of Asia which is now called Georgia, and is connected on the south with Persia, alarmed at the progressive encroachments of the Roman armies, retired in vast multitudes,

of their expedition into the north were honourably distinguished from the Europeans, or original Scandinavians, under the name of Asa, or Asiatics; so the verses or language of this people were denominated Asamal, or Asiatic speech. Their poetry contained not only the praises of their heroes, but their popular traditions and their religious rites; and was filled with those fictions which the most exaggerated pagan superstition would naturally implant in the wild imagination of an Asiatic people. And from this principle alone, I mean of their Asiatic origin, some critics would at once account for a certain capricious spirit of extravagance, and those bold eccentric conceptions, which so strongly distinguish the old northern poetry. *

It seems, however, highly probable that the ascribing an Asiatic origin to the Scandinavians has proceeded entirely from the misinterpretation or misapplication of the Icelandic word As, which is thus explained in the Glossary to the Edda Semundar, *deus, numen;* forsan Celtorum *Hesus, Esus.* Asamal, therefore, would signify the *speech of the gods*, and not Asiatic speech. † If, also, Asgard were situated to the south, or rather to the west of the Tanais, in which position all authorities appear to concur, Odin and his followers must have been Europeans and not Asiatics. For in the time of Herodotus (about 450 B.C.) the country to the south-west of the Tanais was occupied by Scythians, who believed that it had been possessed by their ancestors for a period of one thousand years. It has farther been above sufficiently evinced, that in this same country, as far as the Borysthenes, the Scythian name had, above three hundred years before Christ, entirely disappeared; it being then inhabited by the Getæ, a Thracian people. The state, however, of the region that extends from the Borysthenes to

---

under the conduct of their leader Odin or Woden, into the northern parts of Europe not subject to the Roman government, and settled in Denmark, Norway, Sweden, and other districts of the Scandinavian territory..... *This migration is confirmed by the concurrent testimonies of various historians*" !!

* History of English Poetry, Dissertation i.

† Gibbon, therefore, observes with his usual accuracy, that "Asgard, instead of denoting a real city of the Asiatic Sarmatia, is the fictitious appellation of the mystic abode of the gods, the Olympus of Scandinavia." — *Decline and Fall*, vol. i. p. 391. note.

the Tanais, at this period, is not exactly known, but Strabo describes it as occupied by the Roxolani, a Scythian tribe. It must hence be evident, that if any migrations from this country into Scandinavia ever took place, the emigrants must have been either European Scythians or Thracians; and their supposed Asiatic origin is thus disproved by the very authorities on which the existence of Odin, the prince and high-priest of Asgard, solely depends.

But too little is known of the manners, customs, and religion of either the Scythians or the Thracians, to admit of their being in any respect employed as evidence to determine that the Eddic mythology was not indigenous, but derived its origin from a foreign country. It is at the same time obvious, that it bears not the remotest resemblance to any religious system now existing, or of the former prevalence of which any sufficient accounts have been preserved; and if, therefore, any other people than the Scandinavians ever possessed it, not a trace of them now remains. It must hence follow that this singular mythology can receive no elucidation from foreign sources, and it would appear that the Sagas and chronicles of Scandinavia have been written at too recent a period, to convey any farther information respecting its ancient idolatry than what is contained in the Eddas.*

* That the attempt to reduce Odin and the other Scandinavian gods, and the circumstances described in the Eddas, to mere historical personages and events, is entirely the result of hypothesis, and rests not on any ancient authority whatever, is most clearly evinced in this passage which I extract from the notes to Mr. Herbert's Miscellaneous Poetry, vol. ii. p. 14. — "Suhm, in his Historie of Danmark, considers that there were three Odins. The first, son of Bior, of the nation of the Asi, who dwelt in the old Asgard at the mouth of the Tanais, and after his death was deified by his countrymen. The second, son of Heremod, a descendant of the old Odin, fled before Darius at the time of his expedition against the Scythians, built the new Asgard near the Duna, and inhabited the country between that river and the Veissel. From thence he passed over into Sweden, and waged war against all the Jotuns, who would not acknowledge him to be their god and the offspring of the Sun. Lastly came the third Odin, son of Fridlief, from old Asgard, about fifty years before Christ, stopped some time at the new Asgard, and from thence proceeded to Sweden, where he dwelt at Sigtuna, and built a temple at Upsala, which became his principal residence."

Nor should this account of Odin, which occurs in the preface to the Edda of Snorro, as translated by Goranson, be omitted: — "Ibi sita fuit urbs, quam Trojam vocamus. Trojanum vero imperium in duodecim minora divisum fuit regna, uni tamen capiti subjecta. Ibi et jam duodecim linguæ fuere primariæ. Horum unus dictus fuit Memnon, cujus

In the philosophy of the human mind, consequently, the manner in which this system originated, and its subsequent prevalence, may be interesting subjects of speculation, but they afford not the slightest assistance in tracing the affinity of nations.

In order, however, to render this conclusion the more evident, it may be necessary to advert to the theogony and cosmogony which are described in the Eddas; as their entire dissimilarity from the opinions entertained on these subjects by all other people than the Scandinavians, will be at once obvious. For, though it appears from the Edda of Snorro that they acknowledged one supreme God, the creator of heaven and earth, the origin of things is not ascribed to him, but to mere chance; and what is still more remarkable, the first beings produced are neither gods nor men, but evil genii. The rivers abounding in poison, says the Edda, called Elivages, flowed so far from their source that they became frozen; but a warm breeze having breathed over the ice, it melted into drops, from which a being was formed, who is named Ymir, and from him are descended all the families of the giants. He was not, however, a god, for he and all his descendants were wicked. Whilst he slept he fell into a sweat, and from the pit of his left arm were born a male and female. One of his feet begot upon the other a son, from whom is descended the race of the giants.

The origin of the gods is still more singular; for at the same time and in the same manner that Ymir was formed, the cow Œdumbla was produced. From her udder flowed four rivers of milk, by which Ymir was nourished; and she herself obtained her sustenance by licking the rocks covered with salt and frost. The first evening that she licked these rocks there sprang from them the hair of a man, the next

---

conjux erat filia Priami regis Trojæ. Horum filius Tros, quem nos Thorem vocamus. Qui duodecim annos natus viribus polluit maturis. Tunc terrâ duodecim pelles ursinas simul sustulit. Hic de multis simul pugilibus furiosis victoriam reportavit, nec non feris draconibusque. In septentrione mulierem fatidicam invenit, nomine Sibyllam, nobis vero Sif dictam. Prosapiam ejus nemo novit. Quarum filius vocatus fuit *Larida*, c. f. *Vingitor*, c. f. *Vingenor*, c. f. *Moda*, c. f. *Magnus*, c. f. *Sefsmeg*, c. f. *Bedvig*, c. f. *Atra*, c. f. *Iterman*, c. f. *Eremod*, c. f. *Skold*, c. f. *Bear*, c. f. *Jat*, c. f. *Gudolfur*, c. f. *Finner*, c. f. *Fridleif*, c. f. *Odinus*." —*Northern Antiquities*, vol. ii. p. 278.

day the head, and the third day the whole man, who was named Buri. His son Bör married Beizla, the daughter of the giant Bældorn, and from them were born three sons, Odin, Vile, and Ve. These rule over both heaven and earth; but Odin is the supreme God, without equal. *

The universe, however, did not yet exist; and the sons of Bör, therefore, slew Ymir, of whose flesh was formed the earth, of his blood the ocean, of his bones the mountains, of his skull the heaven, and of his brains the clouds. After this Odin and his brothers, as they were walking on the sea-shore, found two trees, an ash and an elder; to which Odin communicated life and soul; Vile, reason and motion; Ve, hearing, sight, and speech: and these trees thus became a man and woman, whom the sons of Bör named Aske (Ash) and Emle (Elder); and from these two is descended the human race. But of the production of all other things, animate and inanimate, and of the origin of the other Scandinavian deities, no account is contained in the Eddas.

With respect, also, to the state of man after death, it is, indeed, said that God hath made man, and given him a soul, which shall live after the body has perished; and then all the just and righteous shall dwell with him in a heaven named Gimle, but the wicked shall go to the infernal regions. But in the Eddas and songs no reference to this belief ever appears, and supreme felicity is placed in the obtaining access to Valhalla, the abode of Odin. No people, however, but the Scandinavians ever imagined so singular a paradise: for every day its inhabitants, as soon as they are dressed, take their arms, and entering the battle-field, fight till they cut one another to pieces: this is their amusement. But as soon as noon arrives, they all return whole and unharmed to Odin's hall, and there feast on the flesh of the boar Serimner, while they quaff ale and mead from the skulls of their enemies. The only means, also, by which these Scandinavian joys of the blest could be obtained were war, rapine, and contempt of death; and Regner Lodbrok thus characteristically concludes his death-song:—

* His father and grandfather, therefore, do not appear to have been considered as gods.

XXVIII.

"We smote with swords! where javelins fly,
Where heroes meet, and warriors die,
Fifty times and one I stood
Foremost on the field of blood.
Full young in gore I stain'd my sword,
Nor fear'd I force of adverse lord;
Nor deem'd I then that any arm,
By might or guile, could work me harm.
Me to their feast the gods now call;
The brave man wails not o'er his fall.

XXIX.

"Cease my strain! I hear a voice
From realms where martial souls rejoice.
I hear the maids of slaughter call,
Who bid me hence to Odin's hall.
High seated in their blest abodes,
I soon shall quaff the drink of gods.
The hours of life have glided by;
I fall; but smiling shall I die."*

It is needless to remark, that in the theogonies and cosmogonies of other nations, nothing so absurd can be found as the production of a monstrous being, and a miraculous cow, from the drops of melted ice; the formation of the progenitors of mankind from two trees; the originating of the grandfather of the supreme God, from a rock, in consequence of its having been licked by this cow; and the strange joys of paradise, which are held forth as rewards for savage and blood-stained warriors in a future life. The religion, consequently, which was founded on such opinions, must have been indigenous in the north of Europe; but whether the Eddic mythology was known to the Germans is a disputed point: for M. Grimm observes,—"After having considered the authenticity of the Scandinavian mythology, it may be asked, whether it has any affinity to the German. To which it must be answered, that, *on the whole*, it has not. Amongst a kindred people, however, the relation which their religions may bear to each other is an extremely dubious point: but here little can be adduced in support of the affirmation, besides the common origin of the Scandinavians and Germans, while much may be opposed to such an opinion; because it

* Herbert's Miscellaneous Poetry, vol. ii. part ii. p. 48.

is very improbable that none of the Roman authors, so remarkable for their accurate observation, not even Tacitus, should have given any intimation of the religion of Odin, had it then existed among the Germans. It is equally inconceivable that, in the case of its existence, this religion should have been so completely annihilated, that not a vestige of its temples and other monuments now remain in Germany, though, in the narrow compass of Scandinavia, and even in England, many memorials of the ancient faith still endure." * But the names of the days of the week † fully evince that the same gods were known at one time to both the Germans and the Scandinavians; and had more satisfactory accounts of the ancient German religion been preserved, it probably would appear to have differed but little from the Eddic mythology: for that, after the time of Tacitus, idols and temples became numerous in Germany, cannot admit of doubt; and experience has shown that, in its progress, idolatry invariably becomes divested of its primitive simplicity. It may, therefore, be reasonably concluded that, as Scandinavia was unquestionably peopled from Germany, the religions of these two countries were originally the same; and that, so far from Odin having introduced into them from Scythia a new form of idolatry previously reduced into one regular system, the simple worship of the sun, planets, and elements, which had there first prevailed, gradually assumed, by *indigenous* means, now undiscoverable, that peculiar character which has rendered the Edda an object of so much speculation.

* Daub und Creuzer's Studien, vol. iv. p. 228.

† I am aware that in *modern* German these names do not now coincide; but I refer to the Anglo-Saxonic and the old Teutonic language.

CHAP. V.

ON THE AUTHENTICITY AND ANTIQUITY OF THE SACRED BOOKS OF THE HINDUS.

It is undeniable that nothing in the shape of history exists, which would afford any information respecting the origin of the Hindu nation and of the Hindu religion; but it seems equally incontestable that upwards of two thousand years ago India presented to the Greeks, under Alexander the Great and his successors, the same manners, the same customs, and the same form of idolatry, which prevail in it at the present day.* Nor did these then appear to be of recent invention, but to have been the result of long established institutions. The im-

* In the following remarks of Mr. Mill, there is much more truth than in any of the other opinions which he has expressed respecting the literature, history, and religion of the Hindus: — "To the monstrous period of years which the legends of the Hindus involve, they ascribe events the most extravagant and unnatural: events not even connected in chronological series; a number of independent and incredible fictions. This people, indeed, are perfectly destitute of historical records. Their ancient literature affords not a single production to which the historical character belongs. The works in which the miraculous transactions of former times are described are poems. Most of them are books of a religious character, in which the exploits of the gods, and their commands to mortals, are repeated or revealed. In all, the actions of men and those of deities are mixed together, in a set of legends more absurd and extravagant, more transcending the bounds of nature and reason, less grateful to the imagination and taste of a cultivated and rational people, than those which the fabulous history of any other nation presents to us." [These last remarks require much qualification.]

"From the scattered hints contained in the writings of the Greeks, the conclusion has been drawn that the Hindus, at the time of Alexander's invasion, were in a state of manners, society, and knowledge, exactly the same with that in which they were discovered by the nations of modern Europe; nor is there any reason for differing widely from this opinion. It is certain that the few features of which we have any description from the Greeks, bear no inaccurate resemblance to those which are found to distinguish the people at the present day. From this resemblance, from the state of improvement in which the Indian remains, and from the stationary condition in which their institutions first, and then their manners and character, have a tendency to fix them, it is no unreasonable supposition, that they have presented a very uniform appearance during the long interval from the visit of the Greeks to that of the English." — *History of British India*, vol. i. p. 144. 146. 8vo ed.

mutability, therefore, of these institutions during so long a period, is alone a strong presumption that they must have originated in even remoter antiquity; and that the numerous works still preserved, in which they are so fully explained, must not only be authentic, but must also be of a date nearly coeval with the origin of that civil polity and that religion which they describe. To disprove, consequently, the antiquity of the sacred books of the Hindus, it is not sufficient to call their authenticity in question; but it must be farther shown that they do not contain a faithful account of those civil and religious usages by which the Hindus have been for so many ages so peculiarly distinguished. Because, if their accuracy of description be once admitted, no conceivable cause can be assigned for their supposed recent composition, or for a still more improbable conjecture that the more ancient works, having been lost or destroyed, were replaced by modern compilations.

For it must be recollected, that a remarkable characteristic of the Hindu religion is a distinct class of men, to whom not only the functions of the priesthood have been entrusted, but to whom also all learning and instruction have been restricted. But it will be evident that at the time that the Brahmans acquired this predominance, the whole system of castes must have been established, and that laws for the maintenance of the civil and religious institutions which thence resulted must have become indispensable. The princes and people, also, would require to be instructed in a knowledge of the attributes and characters of the various gods of this system of polytheism, and of the duties which they owed to them. It cannot, therefore, but seem most probable that works for these purposes would be composed at a very early period by a class of men who enjoyed perfect leisure, and whose interest it was to establish as efficiently as possible that religion on which their respectability and power solely depended. But when such works were once composed, the constant care of the same priesthood must have rendered their loss totally impossible: for nothing but the extirpation of all the Brahmans throughout the whole of India by some foreign power could have effected such a destruction; and not the slightest indication exists in history that the sacred books of the Hindus were ever exposed to such a danger. Even during the last eight hundred years, while India has been subject to so many changes and revolutions, and the Hindu religion has ceased to receive encouragement and support from native princes, the ancient manuscripts of Indian literature have been scarcely decreased in number. In the absence, therefore, of historical data, the present state of the civil and religious institutions of the Hindus incontrovertibly prove the faithfulness with which they have been described in these works; and of their antiquity and authenticity, consequently, this faithfulness must alone be considered to be as conclusive evidence as the nature of the case admits of.

Mr. Colebrooke, therefore, has most correctly observed that "the greatest part of the books received by the learned among the Hindus will assuredly be found genuine. I do not doubt that the Vedas, of which an account has been here given, will appear to be of this description. In pronouncing them to be genuine, I mean to say that they are the same compositions which, under the same title of Veda, have been revered by the Hindus for hundreds, if not thousands, of years."* But I cannot concur in the justness of the opinion expressed in the following remarks:—"Although the Rama Tapaniya be inserted in all the collections of Upanishads which I have seen, and the Gopal Tapaniya appears in some; yet I am inclined to doubt their genuineness, and to suspect that they may have been written in times modern when compared with the remainder of the Vedas. This suspicion is chiefly grounded on the opinion that the sects which now worship Rama and Krishna as incarnations of Vishnu, are comparatively new. I have not found in any other parts of the Vedas the least trace of such a worship. The real doctrine of the whole Indian scripture is the unity of the deity, in whom the universe is comprehended; and the seeming polytheism which it exhibits offers the elements and the stars and planets as gods. The three principal manifestations of the divinity with other personified attributes and energies, and most of the other gods of

* Asiatic Researches, vol. viii. p. 468.

The words *for hundreds* had better have been omitted, for the era of Vicramaditya is alone sufficient to give the Hindu religion an antiquity of 1884 years.

Hindu mythology, are indeed mentioned, or at least indicated, in the Veda. But the worship of deified heroes is no part of the system; nor are the incarnations of deities suggested in any portion of the text which I have yet seen *; though such are sometimes hinted at by the commentators." † For the objection to the authenticity of these Upanishads rests entirely upon the gratuitous assumption that Rama and Krishna were mere men, a character in which they never were considered by the Hindus. But in judging of the polytheism of any people, conclusions drawn from arguments perfectly foreign to their modes of thinking must be evidently erroneous. Neither the veneration, therefore, shown to Rama and Krishna by all Hindus, nor the worship paid to them by their peculiar sectaries, is in any sense of the term a deification of heroes, but is in both cases intended solely as an adoration of Vishnu, of whom they were incarnate portions.

But it seems to have been hitherto overlooked that the authenticity of a work is no proof of the truth of its contents.‡ The actual existence, however, of Parasu Rama, Krishna, and Buddha§, rests on no other evidence than that which at the same time attests the incarnations of Vishnu as a boar, a tortoise, a man-lion, and a fish; but if these be rejected as fabulous, on what grounds is credit to be given to the others? The events, also, related in the Purans, the Ramayan, and Mahabharat, occurred during the course of an incalculable number of years, which ends at the commencement of the present age, the Kali Yug, or nearly five thousand years ago. To attempt, therefore, to adapt these events to modern chronology can never lead to any satisfactory result, because

* Mr. Colebrooke must have here forgotten this text of the Veda, which he has quoted in the Asiatic Researches, vol. v. p. 359. — "Thrice did Vishnu step, and at three strides traversed the universe; happily was his foot placed on this dusty earth;" — which so clearly refers to the Namana Avatar; and to Vishnu's epithet of *Trivikrama*, derived from his having in that Avatar traversed the universe in three steps.

† Asiatic Researches, vol. viii. p. 473.

‡ Though no person, I may suppose, will dispute the authenticity of the Æneid, or of the Gerusalemme Liberata, yet he does not admit the truth of all that is contained in them.

§ I do not include Rama Chandra, because he occurs in the genealogies of the children of the sun.

the principles on which such a process can alone be conducted must rest entirely on gratuitous assumption and groundless conjecture.

In discussing this question, at the same time, that inveterate prejudice which insists on compelling the records of all nations to depose to the accuracy of the first eleven chapters of Genesis has exerted its usual pernicious influence; and has induced several writers to be more anxious to discover in Hindu works some forced coincidences with their preconceived opinions, than to ascertain the real nature of the information which might be derived from Sanscrit literature. Other authors again have employed it, without proper examination, as a means of impugning the correctness of modern chronology, and thus discrediting the evidences of the Christian religion. Under a similar misapprehension a writer in a popular review has made these remarks:—"It is in this spirit of credulous incredulity that it has been gravely proposed as a *serious* question, whether Moses did not borrow from the Brahmans? But we are happy to hail the dawn of reason which is beginning to appear in the minds of our Oriental literati, and it is to hasten the advancing day that we have indulged in this critique. The name of Bentley will descend with great distinction to posterity, for his intelligent criticism on the antiquity of the Brahminical books and their astronomical computations. It was a bold undertaking to be the first to break the spell of credulity which was lulling Europe into such an unphilosophical lethargy; but he will soon find himself rewarded by his success. We are satisfied that the venerated books of the Brahmans need only to be translated, in order to enable every man who can read to discover their imposture: but till those translations appear, the researches of Mr. Bentley, and those of our Sanscrit students who follow his footsteps, will be wanted to undeceive such as have been hitherto deluded."* For, if by the term *imposture* the reviewer intended to express the same opinion as results from Mr. Bentley's reasoning, that the Purans were composed *within* seven or eight hundred years ago†, and that all the Sanscrit literature is of an equally modern date, its

* Quarterly Review, vol. i. p. 65.

† "Now, since this system," remarks Mr. Bentley, "called the *Calpa* of Varaha, or of the boar, has been framed only between seven and eight hundred years, it follows indubitably

absurdity must be self-evident: because Mr. Bentley himself admits that the Hindu empire commenced 2204 years before Christ*; and it must, in consequence, appear utterly incredible that such a priesthood as that of the Brahmans should have composed no works until more than three thousand years afterwards; and that literature should only begin to flourish in India, when its northern parts were conquered by the Mohammedans, and the rest of the country was divided amongst a number of independent princes possessing little power, and no inducements to excite them to the encouragement of learning.

But this extravagant supposition is at once refuted by the mere production of the Amara Kosh; regarding the date of which work Mr. Wilson, in the preface to his Sanscrit Dictionary, has entered into a very full and satisfactory enquiry, which he thus concludes:—"As to the result of the research, I shall willingly, if convinced by worthy testimony of having erred in my conclusions, submit to correction: those conclusions, indeed, are only positive within certain limits, and, as the sum of the investigation, I have only satisfied myself with the choice of one of two alternatives; either assent to the tradition which places Amara Sinha in the time of the primitive Vicramaditya, 56 years before the Christian era; or to the inference deduced from the contiguous position of a number of persons and things, concerned more or less directly with our author's history, which designate the early part of the

---

that any work in which that *Calpa* is mentioned, cannot possibly be older than the time of its invention, *but may be considerably less.* It was not necessary that the name of Varaha Mihira should occur in the Puranas to prove them modern. For, setting Varaha and his system altogether out of the question, *yet still the names not only of the princes in whose reigns he lived, but also of several others down to the last Mahomedan conquest, with the years of each reign, are to be found in some of the Puranas;* a most certain proof that these works are not the genuine monuments of primeval times." — *Asiatic Researches*, vol. iii. p. 201.

To the assertion, however, contained in the passage printed in Italic, I must be allowed to give the most express and unqualified denial. In the same volume also, p. 241., Mr. Bentley expressly affirms "that none of the modern romances called the Puranas, at least in their present form, are older than 684 years."

* See the table of Hindu Historical Periods in Asiatic Researches, vol. viii. p. 245., and also p. 229. This opinion Mr. Bentley has altered in his last work.

fifth century as the time when Amara flourished."* But it will not be denied that the compilation of a vocabulary is sufficient proof that works then existed, for the explanation of which such an assistance had become requisite; and Mr. Wilson farther remarks, "The vocabulary of Amara Sinha, though perhaps the oldest extant, is not considered to be the first work of the kind: the author himself, in his introductory lines, mentions generally his having consulted other works; and his commentators particularise the *Tricandha* and *Utpalini Coshas*, and the works of *Vyari*, *Rabhasa*, *Catyayana*, and *Vararuchi*, as the authorities to which he alludes. Of the existence of Sanscrit literature, therefore, at the commencement of the Christian era, no reasonable doubt can be entertained; and hence even Mr. Ward, who will not be suspected of ascribing an undue antiquity to the Hindu religion, has very correctly observed, — "In the Kali Yug Vicramaditya † stands

* In another part of this preface, Mr. Wilson remarks: — "Authorities which assert the contemporary existence of Amara and Vicramaditya might be infinitely multiplied, and those are equally numerous which class him among the *nine gems*. The specification of these worthies, including the name of Amara Sinha, occurs, however, in a verse which appears, in a great measure, traditionary only, as I have not been able to trace it to any authentic source, though it is in the mouth of every Pandit, when interrogated on the subject. . . . . From the identity of some of the names contained in the above stanza, with some which occur in a work called the *Bhoja Prabandha*, a collection of literary anecdotes relating to the prince of *Dhara* named *Bhoja*; and from its being undoubtedly true that the term *Vicrama* is a title rather than a proper name, and applied in Indian history to many different princes; it has been inferred that the Vicrama mentioned in this stanza is *either Bhoja himself, or his immediate successor, whose name is said to have been Vicrama*, and that the *nine gems* flourished during the reigns of these two princes, *being first in the council of Raja Bhoja, and afterwards in that of Vicramaditya his successor.* The reign of Bhoja is placed by Mr. Bentley at the end of the tenth and beginning of the eleventh century, or from 982 to 1082; and by Major Wilford Bhoja's death is placed in the year 977, or 982 at latest. In either case, if Amara and the other writers enumerated in the verse were contemporary with Bhoja, the golden age of Hindu literature will be transferred from the century preceding the Christian era, to which it is usually referred or to the commencement of the era of Vicramaditya, to a comparatively modern period, and be not much more than eight centuries ago. *The accuracy of this conclusion, opposed as it is by the concurring and consistent traditions of the country, and by a belief that has existed unaltered and unassailed for so many centuries, cannot be unhesitatingly admitted; especially when upon investigation it appears to have been advanced upon grounds of a slight and frail texture in themselves, and which have been but loosely or partially examined.*"

† The period when Vicramaditya flourished, is thus determined by Mr. Ward: — "The era of Shalivahana is now used by the Hindus in their births, marriages, &c., ... it

highest amongst the Hindu kings as the patron of learning. Nine persons under his patronage are particularly mentioned, as having separately or unitedly composed a number of learned works. . . . . At the period when Vicramaditya lived, Magha, another king, caused to be written a poem which he called by his own name, and for each verse of which he is said to have paid a gold mohur, which amounts to 52,800 rupees. About the same period, Karnata, a king, was famed for patronising the same learned men who attained such fame at the court of Vicramaditya. A short time before this, Rukmana, a king, entertained at his court a number of learned men. Dhavaka, a poet of the same age, received from King Shriharsha 100,000 rupees for a poem called Ratnamala, &c. — *And thus the Hindu courts, filled with learned men, who could boast of works on every science then known to the world, presented, it must be confessed, a most imposing spectacle. A people who could produce works on philosophy and theology like the Vedas and the Darshanas; on civil and canon law like the Smritis; whose poets were capable of writing the Mahabharat, the Ramayana, and the Shri Bhagavata*; whose libraries contained works on philology, astronomy, medicine, the arts, &c.; and whose colleges were filled with learned men and students;* can never be placed among barbarians, though they may have been inferior to the Greeks and Romans. †

It is not, however, necessary to disprove the authenticity and antiquity

---

commenced A. D. 78;" — and "the famous Vicramaditya lost his life in a war with Shalivahana." That Vicramaditya and Shalivahana were contemporaries is the universal belief; and the difference, therefore, of 134 years that exists between the eras denominated from them, presents a chronological difficulty of no easy solution.

* Mr. Ward had better have quoted as examples the profane poems, as the *Sishupala Vaddha*, the *Naishada*, the *Raghuvamsha*, &c.; for Mr. Colebrooke has justly observed (*As. Res.*, vol. x. p. 426.), — "Indeed, the general style of the poems esteemed sacred (not excepting from this censure the *Ramayana* of Valmiki) is flat, diffuse, and no less deficient in ornament than abundant in repetitions."

† Ward's View of the Hindus, vol. iii. p. 48, et seq.

I leave it to the reader to determine whether he will adopt the opinion of Mr. Ward, who was completely master of the Sanscrit language, and intimately acquainted with the subject which he has so ably discussed; or that of Mr. Bentley, who was ignorant of the Sanscrit language, and consequently incapable of forming, from his own knowledge, any judgment whatever respecting the antiquity and authenticity of Sanscrit literature.

of Sanscrit works, in order to evince that their contents are entirely fabulous ; because neither the Vedas, the Upanishads*, nor the Purans, profess to be historical compositions : and the ascribing this character to the latter, in particular, is a most erroneous opinion ; for, with the exception of the genealogies of the princes of the solar and lunar races, the Purans contain nothing which has the slightest semblance of history. They are, in fact, solely religious works ; and were evidently intended to serve as a complement to the Vedas, by containing a full account of the legends which are merely alluded to in the Vedas ; by expatiating on the advantages to be derived from pilgrimages to holy places, and other devotional observances ; and by pointing out in a more popular manner the particular forms of worship to be addressed to different deities, and the days to be set apart as festivals, with the ceremonies appropriate to each. Besides which topics, the Purans enter, either at greater or less length, into disquisitions respecting the illusive existence of the universe, the unity and nature of God, and the most efficacious means of obtaining identification with the divine essence. It is true that each Puran contains a description of the division of time according to the Hindu system ; but the chronology of no event is fixed more precisely than by referring it generally to such a Kalpa, or Manwantara, or Yug, as the particular year is never mentioned. The attempting, therefore, to extract either chronology or history from such data, must be an operation attended with equal success as the extraction of sunbeams from cucumbers by the sages of Laputa.†

* With respect to the *Upanishads*, Mr. Colebrooke (*As. Res.*, vol. viii. p. 379.) remarks : — " The theology of the Indian scripture, comprehending the argumentative portion entitled *Vedanta*, is contained in tracts denominated *Upanishads* : some of which are portions of the *Brahmana* [a division of the Vedas] properly so called ; others are found only in a detached form ; and one is part of a *Sunhita* [division of the Vedas] itself."

† Mr. Ward, however, has observed : — " The author begs leave to refer the reader to the first volume, for a more detailed view of Hindu history, and for other observations on the subject. He cannot, however, refrain from adding his earnest wish that some Sanscrit scholar would devote his leisure to a work on this subject, drawn entirely from Hindu sources ; persuaded as he is, that the Purans, if thoroughly and judiciously examined, would afford ample materials for a succinct history of India, or supply numerous fragments of the most interesting and important nature." But without some fixed era to which they might be referred, or complete and continuous genealogies, in what manner can a number of detached and independent occurrences, undistinguished by either date or circumstance, be

It is, therefore, mortifying to find so accomplished a scholar as Sir W. Jones, and one so well acquainted, from his legal pursuits, with the principles of evidence, gravely speculating on the period when Buddha lived. It might surely have occurred to him that it was indispensable to prove in the first place the actual existence of such a character as Buddha; and yet Sir W. Jones himself observes — "Here it is clear, that whether the fourth age of the Hindus begin about one thousand years before Christ, according to Goverdhan's account of Buddha's birth, or two thousand, according to that of Radhacant, the common opinion, that 4888 years of it are now elapsed, is erroneous: and here for the present we leave Buddha, with an intention of returning to him in due time; observing only, that if the learned Indians differ so widely in their accounts of the age when their ninth *Avatar* appeared in their country, we may be assured that they have no certain chronology before him, *and may suspect the certainty of all the relations concerning even his appearance*."* But the very same evidence which attests the existence of Buddha, clearly proves that he lived at least 4930 years ago†, and consequently 754 years *before* the deluge according to the Hebrew, and 58 years according to the Samaritan, computation. On what grounds, therefore, is one part of this testimony to be admitted, and not the other? The European writers say that Buddha's living in such remote antiquity is inconsistent with the system of chronology which has been deduced from the Old Testament, and the date must therefore be rejected; but his mere existence, as it is not improbable, may be admitted. Nor would this reasoning be objectionable, were there any circumstances which connected Buddha with an

---

reduced to a regular system of chronology and history? or how can any correct opinion be formed with respect to the precise time when such events may have taken place, or even to their relative connection?

* Sir W. Jones's Works, vol. i. p. 294.

† The general opinion certainly is, that Buddha appeared just at the close of the Dwapara Yug; and this is supported by the distribution of the *Avatars* according to the number of feet on which the bull of justice is supposed to stand in each Yug. Thus four *Avatars*, the boar, the tortoise, the man-lion, and the fish, are given to the Satya Yug; three, Vamana, Parasu Rama, and Rama Chandra, to the Treta Yug; two, Krishna and Buddha, to the Dwapara Yug; and one, Kalki, to the Kali Yug.

era which could be satisfactorily fixed. But Divodasa king of Kashi, for effecting the destruction of whom he appeared, is just as little of a historical personage as Buddha himself; and the whole legend has no more the appearance of having been founded on actual occurrences*, than the change of Vishnu into a beautiful virgin for the purpose of deluding the *Asuras* and depriving them of the beverage of immortality. Without adverting, however, to this obvious uncertainty respecting the actual existence of Buddha, it has been concluded that he was a real historical character, who lived about 1000 years before Christ; and on this groundless assumption has not only the antiquity of the Hindu religion been disputed, but elaborate systems framed for the explanation of the influence which Buddhism is supposed to have exerted over the ancient religions of Asia and Europe.

But to show fully the consequences which must inevitably result from the systematic attempt to convert the religious personages which occur in the sacred books of the Hindus, into historical characters who actually existed at certain periods of time, I must be allowed to quote a long passage from from Sir W. Jones's Supplement to his Essay on Indian Chronology. " All the Brahmans agree," he observes, " that only one Parasara is named in their sacred records; that he composed the astronomical book before cited, and a law tract which is now in my possession; that he was the grandson of Vasisht'ha, another astronomer and legislator, whose works are still extant, and who was the preceptor of Rama king of Ayodhya; that he was the father of Vyasa, by whom the Vedas were arranged in the form which they now bear, and whom Crishna himself names with exalted praise in the Gita: so that, by the admission of the Pandits themselves, we find only three generations between two of the Ramas, whom they consider as incarnate portions of the divinity; and Parasara might have lived till the beginning of the Caliyuga, which the mistaken doctrine of an oscillation in the cardinal points has compelled the Hindus to place 1920 years too early. This error, added to their fanciful arrangement of the four ages, has been the sources of many absurdities; for they insist that Valmici, whom

* The reader will find this legend translated at length in Appendix B.

they cannot but allow to have been contemporary with Rama Chandra, lived in the age of Vyasa, who consulted him on the composition of the Mahabharat, and who was personally known to Balarama, the brother of Crishna. When a very learned Brahman had repeated to me an agreeable story of a conversation between Valmici and Vyasa, I expressed my surprise at an interview between two bards whose ages were separated by a period of 864,000 years; but he soon reconciled himself to so monstrous an anachronism, by observing that the longevity of the Munis was preternatural, and that no limit could be set to divine power. By the same recourse to miracles, or to prophecy, he would have answered another objection equally fatal to his chronological system: it is agreed by all, that the lawyer Yagnyawalcya was an attendant on the court of Janaca, whose daughter Sita was the constant, but unfortunate, wife of the great Rama, the hero of Valmici's poem; but that lawyer himself, at the very opening of his work, which now lies before me, names both Parasara and Vyasa among twenty authors whose tracts form the body of original Indian law. By the way, since Vasisht'ha is more than once named in the Manavisanhita, we may be certain that the laws ascribed to Menu, in whatever age they might have been first promulgated, could not have received the form in which we now see them, above three thousand years ago. The age and functions of Garga lead to consequences yet more interesting: he was confessedly the purohita, or officiating priest, of Crishna himself, who, when only a herdsman's boy at Mathura, revealed his divine character to Garga, by running to him with more than mortal benignity on his countenance, when the priest had invoked Narayan. His daughter was eminent for her piety and her learning; and the Brahmans admit, without considering the consequence of the admission, that she is thus addressed in the Veda itself: — *Yata urdhwan no va samopi,* GARGI, *esha adityo dyamurdhanan tapati, dya va bhumin tapati, bhumya subhran tapati, locan tapati, antaran tapatyanataran tapati*; or, 'That Sun, O daughter of Garga, than which nothing is higher, to which nothing is equal, enlightens the summit of the sky; with the sky enlightens the earth; with the earth enlightens the lower worlds; enlightens the breast, enlightens all besides the breast.' From these facts, which the Brahmans cannot deny; and from these concessions, which they unanimously make; we may reasonably infer that, if Vyasa were not the composer of the Vedas, he added at least something of his own to the scattered fragments of a more ancient work, or perhaps to the loose traditions which he had collected: but, whatever be the comparative antiquity of the Hindu scriptures, we may safely conclude that the Mosaic and Indian chronologies are perfectly consistent; that Menu, son of Brahma, was the Adima, or first created mortal, and consequently our Adam; that Menu, child of the sun, was preserved with seven others, in a bahitra or capacious ark, from an universal deluge, and must, therefore, be Noah; that Hiranyacasipu, the giant with a golden axe, and Vali or Bali, were impious and arrogant monarchs, and, most probably, our Nimrod and Belus; that the three Ramas, two of whom were invincible warriors, and the third not only valiant in war but the patron of agriculture and wine, which derives an epithet from his name, were different representations of the Grecian Bacchus, and either the Rama of scripture, or his colony personified, or the sun first adored by his idolatrous family; that a considerable emigration from Chaldea into Greece, Italy, and India, happened about twelve centuries before the birth of our Saviour; that Sacya, or Sisak, about two hundred years after Vyasa, either in person or by a colony from Egypt, imported into this country the mild heresy of the ancient Bauddhas; and that the dawn of true Indian history appears only three or four centuries before the Christian era, the preceding ages being clouded by allegory or fable." *

If, however, the sacred books of the Hindus evidently prove, as they undoubtedly do, that the lives of holy sages were extended to an indefinite period, it is obviously contrary to every just principle of reasoning to conclude that any particular sage lived only at the latest time that he is mentioned in any Sanscrit work. Garga's being contemporary, therefore, with Krishna, is, according to these books, no proof that he may not have existed millions of years before; and, consequently, the mention of his daughter's name in the Vedas proves nothing

* Sir W. Jones's Works, vol. i. p. 325.

with respect to the antiquity or genuineness of these sacred writings.* The argument, also, relative to the age of the laws of *Manu*, drawn from *Parasara* being the grandson of *Vasishta*, is equally futile: because *Vasishta* was one of the *Rishis* who sprang from the mind of Brahma at the commencement of the creation of the universe. But from the whole of this passage it will be evident that Sir W. Jones must have been aware that the circumstances contained in the sacred books were never intended to be described in a chronological and historical manner; and that he was induced to maintain the contrary merely from a wish to discover coincidences between the events related in them, and in the first eleven chapters of Genesis. Though the Hindus, however, believe that mankind has descended from one pair, male and female, and that *Satyavrata* was saved from a deluge which destroyed the universe; still the modes in which these occurrences are stated to have taken place in Genesis and in the Purans are totally dissimilar. Yet it must be obvious that it is not a bare isolated fact, but the circumstances with which it is accompanied, that can alone determine whether such similar points of belief as are entertained by people so totally unconnected as the Hebrews and Hindus were derived from one common origin. On what principles of reasoning, therefore, can the production of *Manu* and *Shatarupa* from Brahma's having divided himself into two parts, be identified with the formation of Adam from the earth, and of Eve from one of Adam's ribs? or the simple circumstance of *Satyavrata* and the seven *Rishis* having been miraculously preserved in a boat by Vishnu in the form of a fish, be identified with Noah and the ark; which Noah went into, and his sons, and his wife, and his sons' wives with him, because of the waters of the earth: of clean beasts, and of beasts that are not clean, and of fowls, and of every thing that creepeth upon the earth, there went in two and two unto Noah in the ark, the male and the female?

The concluding sentence, however, of the above-quoted passage is surely too extravagantly absurd to require remark. But it may be

* In the Brahma Puran, Suta mentions that, when residing at Kurukshetra, there came to visit Vyasa, the holy sages Kashyapa, Jamadagni, Bharadwaja, Gauttama, Vasishta, Jaimini, Dhaumia, Markandaya, and Valmiki.

observed, that neither *Hiranyacashipu* nor *Bali* were *mortal* monarchs, but princes of the *Asuras* or evil angels; and that the characters and actions of the three *Ramas* * have not the slightest resemblance. The identifying, at the same time, *Sacya* or *Buddha* with Sisak, must alone evince how misled by hypothesis Sir W. Jones must have been, and how totally unfounded his whole system of Indian chronology must be considered. For the existence of Sisak depends entirely on the book of Chronicles in the Old Testament, as no ancient author has mentioned such an individual among the kings of Egypt.† But were it even admitted that Sisak was the same person as Sesostris, Bryant has very correctly remarked, with respect to the account of the latter given by Diodorus Siculus:—"The detail given by the historian is very plain and precise: and we proceed very regularly and minutely in a geographical series from one conquest to another: so that the story is rendered in some degree plausible. But we may learn from Diodorus himself, that little credit is to be paid to the narration, after all the pains he may have taken to win upon our credulity. He ingenuously owns that not only the Grecian writers, but even the priests of Egypt and the bards of the same country, varied in the accounts which they gave

* Bala Rama, the brother of Krishna, is, in more than one Puran, considered as an incarnation of Vishnu: but this is not the general belief of the Hindus.

† On this point Sir Isaac Newton has made these remarks:—"Sesostris reigned over all the same nations of Libyans, Troglodytes, and Ethiopians, and came out of Egypt with a great army to conquer other kingdoms. The shepherds reigned long in the lower part of Egypt, and were expelled thence before the building of Jerusalem and the Temple, according to Manetho; and whilst they reigned in the lower part of Egypt, the upper part thereof was under other kings; and while Egypt was divided into several kingdoms, there was no room for any such king of all Egypt as Sesostris; and no historian makes him later than Sesac; and, therefore, he was one and the same king of Egypt as Sesac."—*Newtoni Opera*, vol. v. p. 54.

Bryant very justly observes:—"Sir John Marsham and Sir Isaac Newton suppose him (Sesostris) to have been the Sesac of the Scriptures, and they consequently bring his reign to the time of Rehoboam king of Judah. But the only reason for this, as far as I can perceive, seems to be, that Sesostris is represented as a great conqueror, and Sesac is presumed, from his large army, to have been so likewise. . . . . This is the whole of the history of Sesac, or Shishak; by whom no other expedition was undertaken that we know of; nor is there mention made upon record of a single battle which he fought. Yet from a notion that Sesac was a great warrior, he is made the same as Sesostris."—*Anal. of Anc. Myth.*, vol. ii. p. 363.

of this hero, and were guilty of great inconsistency. It was, therefore, his chief labour to collect what he thought most credible, and what appeared most consonant to the memorials in Egypt, which time had spared: *τα πιθανωτατα, και τοις ὑπαρχουσιν ετι κατα την χωραν σημειοις τα μαλιστα συμφωνουντα, διελθειν.* But, as these memorials consisted chiefly in hieroglyphics, I do not see how it was possible for Diodorus to understand what the bards and priests could not decipher. The adjustment of this history, had it been practicable, should have been the work of a native Egyptian, and not of a person from either Greece or Sicily."* If, therefore, the events recorded in the sacred books of India are to be identified with occurrences that have taken place in other countries, it might at least be expected that of the latter such only as are not liable to doubt would be selected for comparison.

The antiquity and genuineness of Sanscrit works have been called in question on still more extraordinary grounds by the late Lieutenant-Colonel Wilford, who has stated as follows: †—"It appears that, long before Christ, a renovation of the universe was expected all over the world, with a Saviour, a King of peace and justice. . . . . A short time before the birth of Christ, not only the Jews, but the Romans on the authority of the Sibylline books, and the decision of the sacred college of the Etrurian augurs, were all of opinion that this momentous event was at hand. This was equally the case in the East; and a miraculous star directed the holy men, who were living in anxious expectation, where to find this heavenly child. At that time the emperor of India, uneasy at these prophecies, which, he conceived, portended his ruin and the loss of his empire, sent emissaries to enquire whether such a child were really born, in order to destroy him; and this happened exactly the 3101 year of the Kali Yug, which was the first year of the Christian era. This traditionary account is known all over India, and is equally current among the learned and the ignorant. *But the Hindus fancy that these old prophecies were fulfilled in the person of Krishna.* . . . . The Hindus having once fixed the accomplishment of these prophecies to a period greatly anterior to the Christian era, *every thing in*

* Anal. of Anc. Myth., vol. ii. p. 361.

† Asiatic Researches, vol. x. p. 27 and 35.

their books was either framed, or new modelled accordingly; and particularly in the Purans, every one of which is greatly posterior to our era; though many legends, and the materials in general, certainly existed before in some other shape. Yet, as inconsistency and contradiction are the concomitants of falsehood and deceit, it may be supposed that some circumstances and particulars, tending to remove the veil which they have attempted to throw over these events, may have escaped them. *This is very probable; but as I never had the most distant idea of ever investigating this subject till very lately, I may probably have overlooked many passages of this nature, and I recollect now only two material ones.*" * It is difficult to understand what Lieutenant-Colonel Wilford intended by these passages. Because, in his Chronology of the Hindus, he places Krishna between 1300 and 1200 years before Christ; and he could, therefore, scarcely mean to maintain that all the traditionary legends and written compositions relating to Krishna, which had accumulated for twelve centuries, were entirely new modelled at the commencement of the Christian era, or, that during so long a period, during which the memory of Krishna had been preserved, nothing whatever, in the shape of either legend or composition, had ever been invented. But, before advancing an opinion so obviously improbable, Lieutenant-Colonel Wilford ought at least to have been prepared to support it by the requisite proof: for at present it rests on nothing more than bare assertion; and he has not even explained what the premises were, from which he drew such extraordinary conclusions.

A late writer, however, has adopted a similar opinion, and carried it to the extreme of absurdity, by gravely stating that "early in this period, that is to say, about the year A. D. 51, Christianity was preached in India by St. Thomas. This circumstance introduced new light into India in respect of the history and opinions of the people of the West, concerning the time of the creation, in which the Hindus found they were so far behind in point of antiquity; *their account of the creation*

* These two passages relate merely to the anticipations of Vishnu's *avatars*, which occur in discourses attributed to him in the Purans; and of such anticipations Lieutenant-Colonel Wilford could have had no difficulty in producing a great number of examples. But it would be impossible to discover the slightest similarity between these predictions and the prophecies which announced the advent of the Messiah.

going back only to the year 2352 B. C.*, which was the year of the Mosaic flood, and therefore they would be considered as a modern people in respect of the rest of the world. To avoid this imputation, and to make the world believe they were the most ancient people on the face of the earth, they resolved to change the time of the creation, and carry it back to the year 4225 B. C.; thereby making it older than the Mosaic account; and making it appear, by means of false history written on purpose, that all men sprang from them.† . . . . In fact there is no imposition too gross or absurd, that a Hindu will not employ to gain his ends, if he can effect it by that means. We see that, by means of this system of Brahma (invented in A. D. 538), and of various passages

* Sir W. Jones's opinion was very different; for he has correctly remarked, — "Such is the arrangement of infinite time which the Hindus believe to have been revealed from heaven, and which they generally understand in a literal sense. . . . . Thirty such days, or *calpas* [a calpa consists of 432,000,000 years], constitute, in their opinion, a month of Brahma; twelve such months, one of his years; and a hundred such years, his age; of which age they assert that fifty years have elapsed." — *Works*, vol. i. p. 283 and 285.

† Bentley's Hindu Astronomy, p. 79.

A person, however, who dogmatically pronounces that the whole of Sanscrit literature is spurious, ought at least to have acquired such a knowledge of the elements of Hindu mythology, as to prevent his writing such passages as these: — "All that we are informed is, that in the first part (quarter) of the *Treta Yug*, the daughters of *Dacsha* were born; and that of these, he gave twenty-seven to the moon." (*Hindu Astronomy*, p. 2.) "From the union of the daughters of *Dacsha* with the Moon, the ancient astronomers feigned the birth of four of the planets, that is to say, Mercury from *Rohini*; hence he is called *Rohineya* after his mother. *Magha* brought forth the beautiful planet Venus, hence one of the names of that planet is *Maghabhu*. The lunar mansion *Ashad'ha* brought forth the martial planet Mars, who was thence called *Ashad'habhava*; and *Purvaphalguni* brought forth Jupiter, the largest of all the planets." — *Ibid.* p. 4.

But the daughters of *Daksha* were born at the very commencement of the *Satya Yug*; *Shukra* or Venus was the son of Rhrigu, one of the ten Prajapatis; Vrihaspati or Jupiter of Angiras, one of the seven Rishis; and Mangala or Mars, the son of the earth. Nor are there any such Sanscrit words as *Maghabhu* and *Ashad'habhava*. Of Mr. Bentley's opinion, p. 17., that there are sufficient data for determining the time of the extraordinary fiction of the *war between the gods and giants*, I shall say nothing, as it speaks for itself. But, before Mr. Bentley is quoted as authority, it might be as well to show, in the first place, the grounds on which the conclusions of a person who gravely fixes, by astronomical computations, the time of an evidently fabulous occurrence that never had existence except in the imagination of a poet, ought to be implicitly received as unanswerable demonstrations of the spuriousness of Sanscrit literature. These remarks, and others that follow, may appear improper to those who adopt the maxim *de mortuis nil nisi bonum*; but, in a defence of the genuineness of the sacred books of the Hindus, they could not possibly be avoided.

like the above inserted in books with a view to support it, the real Hindu history and chronology have been completely destroyed. . . . . But to carry all this into effect many things were necessary. In the first place, it was requisite that all their ancient books on astronomy, history, &c., that could in the smallest degree affect or contradict the new order of things, should be either destroyed, new modelled, or the obnoxious passages expunged: and secondly, that others should be written or composed, having the appearance of antiquity by being fathered on ancient writers, to support, as it were, by their evidence, the existence in ancient times, and through all ages, of the new system of years thus introduced. . . . . This will account not only for the books that now exist being either entirely modern, or else new modelled to correspond with the new order of things, but also for the paucity of ancient facts and observations that have reached our time. Indeed, the few scattered and insulated fragments which have reached our time, would not have been allowed to pass, had they been supposed to be of any consequence, or could convey any idea or knowledge of ancient times. *And we may rely on it, that the moment they become known, the books in which they are contained will either be destroyed, or the facts themselves expunged; for the Brahmans of this day are fully as eager in support of this monstrous system as those that first invented it, and watch every opportunity of destroying such facts against it as may appear to have escaped the vigilance of former Brahmans.*" *

The mere transcription of such opinions must assuredly be the best means of refuting them; for their inconsistency and improbability must be self-evident: because both Lieutenant-Colonel Wilford and Mr. Bentley are obliged to admit that ancient Sanscrit works did at

* Bentley's Hindu Astronomy, p. 106.

Were such a system in actual operation, it must appear extraordinary that it should have escaped the observation of all the persons in this country, who have been engaged in the study of the Sanscrit language, and that its detection should be reserved for a person who could not have read a Sanscrit manuscript had it been presented to him. With regard, however, to the west of India, the Brahminical days of literary imposture, if they ever existed, have been long passed; for, so far from the Brahmans having for many years been able to compose in Sanscrit, very few of them have possessed any knowledge of the language beyond its mere rudiments.

one time exist, but they contend that they have been either destroyed or new modelled. These writers, however, seem to have entirely forgotten that this alleged revolution in Sanscrit literature must have been effected in a country, the area of which is upwards of one million square miles, divided into a number of independent states speaking distinct languages, and containing more than one hundred and thirty millions of inhabitants.* It is these very circumstances that depose so strongly to the great antiquity of the Hindu religion; for nothing but a long course of time could have enabled the Brahmans to extend their influence over so extensive and populous a country. But, in whatever manner this may have been originally effected, it is incontrovertible, that, *at the commencement of the Christian era*, and more particularly at a period of *one thousand years subsequent to it*, India was so situated as to render the destruction of all the Sanscrit works, then spread over so wide an extent, or the composition of new works, or the new modelling of old ones on a uniform plan, totally impracticable. The only reasons, also, assigned for this supposed change are utterly improbable. Because the power of the Brahmans, their possessing alone a knowledge of Sanscrit literature and the right of instruction, and their exercising exclusively the functions of the priesthood, are not denied; and yet it is seriously maintained that a class of men so influential, distinguished, and revered, would be induced to destroy, new model, or recompose their sacred writings and the valued works of ages, in consequence of a few obscure individuals arriving in India and preaching a new religion. The utter contempt with which, during the last two hundred years, the Brahmans have viewed the Christian missionaries, even when their countrymen possessed power and authority in the land, might surely have been sufficient to prevent any reasonable being from forming so insane an opinion.

I regret much that my ignorance of astronomy prevents my forming any opinion respecting the arguments founded on astronomical computations, which have been adduced to prove the recent period at which all existing Sanscrit works were composed or rewritten. But

* See the Introduction to Hamilton's Description of Hindustan.

to show how little reliance can be placed on them for determining the antiquity of a Sanscrit composition, I gladly avail myself of the very learned, able, and competent authority of Mr. Colebrooke, whose intimate acquaintance with Sanscrit literature must insure it every credit. "The truth is," says Mr. Colebrooke, "that the observations of Hindu astronomers were ever extremely coarse and imperfect, and their practice very inferior to their theory of astronomy. An improved theory, or the hint of it, was borrowed from the West; but they did not learn to make correct observations. They were content, in practice, with a rude approximation. *Varaha Mihira* teaches two rules, which give results widely different, for the rising of Canopus; yet he marks no preference for one above the other. The Hindu observations of this star are so discordant, that the longitude of its circle of declination differs 10°, as given in various tables. It is 90° in one, 87° in two others, and 80° in a fourth. We are not to try their rules by the test of their agreement with accurate observation at any assignable moment, and thence conclude that the rule and the correct application were contemporaneous. This has always been the point at issue between Mr. Bentley and me. He mentioned, in his first essay, that the age of an astronomical Hindu treatise can be so determined with *precision; I have always contended, that their practical astronomy has been too loose and imperfect for the application of that test, unless as an* approximation. *In one instance, by the rigorous use of his test, he would have had to pronounce that the work is of an age yet to come* (1454 *years after A. D.* 1799).—See As. Res. vol. vi. p. 570. *To avoid so monstrous an absurdity, he rejected this case, and deduced a mean from the whole of the other results varying from* 340 *to* 1105 *years.* He should have done the same with *Varaha*'s two rules for the heliacal rising of Canopus: he should have taken the mean of the two; or, what would have been more consonant with his own method of proceeding, he should have deduced the mean of all the data which any one work (Varaha's, for example) furnished, and not garbled it by selecting the case of Canopus singly, and drawing an inference from one out of two rules given. *The absurd conclusions at which Mr. Bentley has arrived by the limited and exclusive application of* *his test, and the utter confusion which ensues, sufficiently demonstrate that it is not to be safely and implicitly trusted.*" *

But, without entering into an enquiry respecting the correctness of Mr. Bentley's reasoning on astronomical grounds, I may be allowed to point out some objections to the data on which it rests that seem to me to be insuperable. For, supposing that the astronomical notices occurring in a work afford sufficient means for computing its date, it is self-evident that they do not prove that the work itself was written by the individual whose name is prefixed to it, or that the circumstances anterior to this date, which may be mentioned in it, are actually founded in truth. These points, therefore, require to be proved by other evidence of a perfectly distinct nature. But Mr. Bentley argues in this manner:—"According to the Ramayan called Valmika's, five of the planets were in their houses of exaltation, as the astrologers term it, at the birth of Rama. . . . . The facts pointed out here show that there was an eclipse of the sun at or near the beginning of Cancer, at the moon's ascending node (*Rahu* being present); and that the planets were not far distant from each other. These circumstances, therefore, point out the time to have been the second of July, in the year 940 B. C.; so that Rama was then one and twenty years old. . . . . We are, therefore, led to this important conclusion; that the beginning of Cancer and that of *Pushya* coincided when the author of the Ramayan wrote that work, and that he therefore concluded, erroneously, that they were so at the time of Rama. Now this gives us a clue to ascertain the date of the Ramayan. In the time of Rama, the beginning of Cancer, or, which is the same thing, the beginning of *Sravana*, coincided with 3° 20′ of the lunar asterism *Aslesha;* and thence to the beginning of *Pushya* is exactly 16° 40′. Now, the beginning of Cancer must fall back 16° 40′ in respect of the fixed stars before it could coincide with that of *Pushya:* the precession was found equal to 3° 20′ in 247 years and one month: therefore 16° 40′=1235 years 5 months; from which subtract 940, and *we get A. D.* 295, the time when the beginning of Cancer and that of *Pushya* coincided, and, *consequently, the period when the Ramayan was*

* Asiatic Journal for March, 1826, p. 365.

written. In thus giving the age of the Ramayan of Valmika, as it is called, I do not mean to say that the facts, on which that *romance* was founded in part, did not exist long before; on the contrary, my opinion is that they did, and probably were to be then found in histories or oral traditions brought down to his time. *The author of the Ramayan was more a poet than an astronomer, and being unacquainted with the precession, he fell into the mistake alluded to; for I do not suppose it was intentional, as that could answer no purpose.*"*

But it will, I think, be admitted, that extracting astronomical data from a *metrical romance*, written by an individual who was more a *poet than an astronomer*, which data even require conjectural correction before they can be adapted to the purpose for which they are adduced, is a totally inconclusive mode of evincing that all existing Sanscrit literature is the mere result of modern imposture. Mr. Bentley, however, does not seem to have been aware that the premises themselves, from which his conclusions were drawn, required proof. For he remarks: — "I was induced to make particular enquiries respecting the time of Krishna, who, I was satisfied, was not near so ancient as pretended. . . . . These [books] I examined, but found they were insufficient to point out the time. I therefore directed my attention towards obtaining the *Janampattra* (horoscope) of Krishna, containing the positions of the planets at his birth; which at length I was fortunate enough to meet with. . . . . These *place the time of the fiction to the year A. D.* 600, *on the 7th of August.*† But it is singular that the same person, who disputes the genuineness of all Sanscrit works, should complacently adopt an alleged horoscope of the authenticity of which there is not the slightest proof.‡ If, also, all ancient Sanscrit works have been destroyed, and those now extant have been either rewritten or

* Bentley's Hindu Astronomy, p, 14, et seq.

† Ibid., p. 110, 111.

‡ The belief in astrology throughout Asia is too well known to require remark. But, were ancient history lost, would any person in his senses think of determining the period when Alexander the Great was born, from this horoscope given by Nizami in the Sikandar Namah? Leo was rising, Sol was in Aries, Mercurius in Gemini, Luna and Venus in Taurus, Jupiter in Sagittarius, Saturnus in Libra, and Mars in the sixth house. Or, at least, would he not first enquire whether the poet had any authority for ascribing such a horoscope to Alexander?

new modelled, it must be perfectly obvious that Mr. Bentley, according to his own showing, could have no grounds whatever for the hypothesis which he has supported. Because he alleges that it was in A. D. 538, that means were adopted by the Brahmans for completely doing away their ancient history, and introducing the periods now in use; and that, consequently, all Sanscrit works in which these periods are mentioned must have been composed subsequently to that date.* But this division of time is mentioned in the Vedas, the Upanishads, the Purans, the Institutes of Menu, and I believe there is not a single Sanscrit work in which some allusion to it does not occur. In the Ramayan, in particular, it is expressly noticed, and therefore this poem must also have been written subsequently to A. D. 538; and thus Mr. Bentley formally contradicts himself by stating that it was composed in A. D. 295.

Mr. Bentley, however, gives this sketch of ancient Indian history, according to those very authorities which, as he himself asserts, have been long destroyed:—"The Hindus commence the reigns of their kings with the *Treta*, which, according to the table, began on the 28th of October, in the year 1528 B. C. common reckoning. Rama, whose birth we have already shown, from astronomical facts, to have been in the year 961 B. C., was the last prince that reigned in the *Treta*; and, from the first, named Ikswaku, down to Rama inclusive, there were about fifty-six reigns in the space or period of 627 years, which gives an average of about $11\frac{1}{6}$ years to a reign.† The *Treta* terminated in the year 901 B. C.; and as Rama was born in 961 B. C., he must, at the close of the period, have been sixty years of age, if then living. The next period, the Dwapar, began in 901 B.C. and ended in 540 B. C.; and therefore lasted about 361 years, in which space there were thirty reigns, of about twelve years to a reign. The next period, the Kali, began in 540 B. C.; therefore Yudishthira, whose time I have shown to have been 575 B. C., was, of course, but thirty-five years before the beginning of the Kali Yug. The Kali lasted from 540 B. C. to 299 B. C.; but the reigns

* See Hindu Astronomy, part ii. sect. 1.

† A duration perfectly absurd in a country where the throne was hereditary, and where contests for the sovereignty were entirely unknown.

of the kings for that particular space of time are not distinguished from those that reigned after the period terminated, for a reason that will be hereafter explained. This, however, cannot prevent us from discovering the real period to which the reigns extended, taking them at the average already found; which, taking the two periods *Treta* and Dwapar together, gives an average of about twelve years to a reign. Now the number of princes in the solar line, that reigned after the commencement of the Kali, before that time became extinct, was twenty-eight; and twenty-eight multiplied by twelve gives us 336 years for the period they reigned, which, being reckoned from the year 540 B. C., when the Kali began, will bring them down to the year 204 B. C., the very year at which the astronomical period commenced, and when the periods of the four ages were invented, as aboved stated; but what is equally remarkable is, that the whole solar line of princes, the lunar line of princes, and the line of Jarasandha, should all become then extinct at one and the same time, as if the history after this period were discontinued from some particular cause. The duration of the Kali from 540 B. C. to 299 B. C. being 241 years, the number of reigns in that period, at twelve years to a reign, would be twenty; and from the year 299 B. C. down to 204 B. C. would be the eight remaining reigns, when the whole terminated. We may, from these circumstances, plainly perceive that Vyasa, the son of Parasara, who lived 540 years before Christ, was not the author of the ancient Hindu history, much less of its division into the periods above given, though pretended so to have been. Vyasa could have given a history only to his own time, if he gave any; which, however, is very much to be doubted, as we find many other assertions of the modern Hindu not only totally void of truth, but of the slightest foundation."*

On reading this passage it becomes impossible to understand what object Mr. Bentley could have had in view in proposing his hypothesis: because he could not suppose that the average duration of reigns, so contrary to all probability, which he assumes, would be admitted; and, consequently, if from the establishment of the Hindu empire, until

* Bentley's Hindu Astronomy, p. 77.

304 B. C., 142 reigns took place, it must necessarily follow that, on ascribing to each of them the very moderate average of twenty-one years, the Hindu empire, at the first year of the Christian era, must have endured for a period of 3186 years; and that it must, therefore, have been founded 838 years *before* the deluge according to the Hebrew, and 142 years according to the Samaritan, computation. It likewise follows, that the reasoning of Mr. Bentley becomes self-contradictory; because, if the periods which he assigns to the different ages be correct, it is perfectly impossible that the number of reigns which he also gives could have taken place within such short durations of time. But setting the number of reigns aside, and supposing that his astronomical calculations are exact, Mr. Bentley admits all that can be reasonably contended for, when he places the establishment of the Hindu empire in 1528 B. C. *: and to his system, therefore, the authenticity or spuriousness of Sanscrit works could have been of no importance, the more especially as he has adopted the number of reigns that are stated in those very works which he considered to be spurious.

On this subject, however, I find the following very just remarks in the *Kala Sakalita* of Lieutenant-Colonel Warren, p. 234. :—" It will be observed that the abolition of sidereal astronomy, pronounced by the work alluded to (*Bentley's Hindu Astronomy*) to have taken place from the fifth century upwards, renders a great part of my speculations unavailing: to which I shall reply that, although agreeing in substance to a doctrine which the scholiast has so ably supported, yet I do not go with him the whole length of believing that the use of ancient or tropical astronomy was so suddenly relinquished, and the sidereal so readily adopted, as might be inferred from the precise epoch which he assigns to that event (March, A. D. 538). It required nearly two centuries to drive the Aristotelian philosophy out of the universities of Europe; and, arguing from analogy †, it is not to be supposed that a

* In a former essay, he placed it in the year 2204 B. C.; and in his last work he does not explain the grounds on which he has been induced to curtail the antiquity of the Hindu empire of no less than 675 years.

† The analogy is far from complete, because typography is unknown in India; and, without its assistance, the philosophy of Aristotle would probably have withstood all the attacks made against it.

people, of all others the most attached to its institutions, would have simultaneously adopted new theories, when the old ones were still found to answer (and were in reality better than the new), for no other purpose than *to appear the most ancient nation in the universe.* . . . . Before the epoch referred to, the sidereal astronomy (certainly the more commodious of the two) must surely have thrown out some roots in the minds of the learned men of those times, and have lurked, perhaps during several centuries, in the public opinion. Some sect of philosophers must have taught it; and some separate tribe or nation must have counted time by the same, before it became the general doctrine of India: and from the same considerations it may be believed that the ancient astronomy had left shoots which it must have taken time to extirpate. Nor can I believe that the Brahminical power (which rests entirely on opinion, great as it now is, and has been) could have proved so efficient as to have occasioned the sudden and total overthrow of the latter, in the same manner as Timur Lung and Nadir Shah subsequently annihilated their public institutions. It is, therefore, highly probable, that sidereal astronomy began to be in repute some hundreds of years before it openly superseded the tropical one; and as to the motive of its abolition, I cannot be persuaded that the specific purpose of any set of men, when effecting a change, can have been to *do away their ancient history.*"

Mr. Davis, also, had so far back as 1789 made the following very judicious observations:—"It is evident from what has been explained, that the Pandits, learned in the *Jyotish Shastra* (astronomy), have truer notions of the form of the earth and the economy of the universe than are ascribed to the Hindus in general; and that they must reject the ridiculous belief of the common Brahmans, that eclipses are occasioned by the intervention of the monster *Rahu,* with many other particulars equally unscientific and absurd. But, as this belief is founded on explicit and positive declarations contained in the Vedas and Puranas, the divine authority of which no devout Hindu can dispute, the astronomers have some of them cautiously explained such passages in those writings as disagree with the principles of their own science; and where reconciliation was impossible, have apologised, as well as they could, for propositions necessarily established in the practice of it, by observing that *certain things, as stated in other Shastras, might have been so formerly, and may be so still; but for astronomical purposes, astronomical rules must be followed.*"* The astronomical works, therefore, are of a perfectly distinct nature from the sacred books of the Hindus; and the alterations, consequently, which either the lapse of time or other causes might have rendered necessary in treatises of astronomy, could in no manner affect other compositions which required no change. Of this circumstance Mr. Bentley could not be ignorant, but he had unfortunately adopted the opinion that the term *Kalpa* and the system dependent upon it were not invented until A. D. 538; and in support of a conjecture, to which he has been unable to give even the semblance of plausibility, he has laboriously endeavoured to demonstrate the spuriousness of all existing Sanscrit literature.

That a writer is at perfect liberty to alter the opinions which he has published cannot be denied; but he ought, in common fairness, to notice the change, and to explain the reasons which had occasioned it. Mr. Colebrooke, therefore, justly remarks,—"In many instances Mr. Bentley has altered his opinions, but without the candour of acknowledging the change.† . . . . . All these positions are abandoned in Mr. Bentley's posthumous work: *Varaha Mihira* is now not the author of the *Surya Siddhanta*, nor of any other of the five *Siddhantas*. The *Pancha Siddhantica* of *Varaha Mihira* is an unseen and unheard of work, which he is disposed to think never existed. The *Calpa* of *Varaha* may not have taken its name from this astronomer; who did not flourish at the age assigned by Mr. Bentley to the *Surya Siddhanta*, but so recently as twenty-six years before the accession of the emperor Akbar, an interval of nearly five centuries. The *Jatacarnava*, which was proved by the same train of computation which deter-

* Asiatic Researches, vol. ii. 257. Sir W. Jones had also observed,—"I will only remark that, in our conversations with *Pandits*, we must never confound the system of the *Jyantishicas*, or mathematical astronomers, with that of the *Pauranicas*, or poetical fabulists; for to such a confusion alone must we impute the many mistakes of *Europeans* on the subject of *Indian* science."—*Ibid.* p. 290.

† The reader will find an instance of this in p. 127, in a quotation from an essay of Mr. Bentley's in the eighth volume of the Asiatic Researches.

mined the age of the *Surya Siddhanta*, and that of *Brahmagupta*, to have been composed 739 years before A. D. 1799, is still maintained to have been the work of *Varaha Mihira*, but written 300 years ago, instead of 750. Consequently, *all the evidence and reasoning to which Mr. Bentley had trusted, for determining the age of any astronomical work, falls to the ground.* It is of no more validity to determine the age of the *Surya Siddhanta*, than that of the *Jatacarnava; which he maintained to have been contemporary, but which he now affirms to have been 450 years distant.*"* How far such fluctuations of opinion with respect to this particular subject ought to detract from Mr. Bentley's authority, I must leave to astronomers to decide; but on all just principles of reasoning, it must be evident that the opinion of an individual who draws, at different times, conclusions so totally dissimilar, from the very same premises, can be entitled to no attention whatever.

At the same time I am convinced that the sacred books of the Hindus afford no data, from which the period when they may have been composed could be determined, even by approximation. For the events, possibly historical, that occur in them, are not related in a connected manner, nor are they referred to any fixed era, nor is there even the slightest appearance that the writer himself intended that they should be subjected to any kind of chronological computation. The occurrences, also, which are described in the Purans, took place principally in the Satya Yug †; a few happened in the Treta Yug; and in the Dwapar Yug the only important circumstance is the incarnation of Krishna, who was contemporary with the *Kurnwas* and *Pandawas*. It is likewise precisely at the end of the Dwapar Yug that the imperfect computation of time contained in the Purans closes: and, with the exception of some slight prophetical notices which are annexed to two or three of them, the Purans are totally silent with respect to all the events which have taken place in the Kali Yug; though this age is supposed to have commenced 3102 years before the Christian

* Asiatic Journal for March 1826. p. 360, 361.

† It may, perhaps, be necessary to explain that the Satya Yug comprises 1,728,000 years; the Treta 1,296,000; the Dwapar 864,000; and the Kali 432,000; and the first three ages have elapsed, and that the year A. D. 1828 answers to the 4930th year of the Kali Yug.

era. But in the traditions of India, with respect to subsequent occurrences, the first circumstance which assumes an unquestionably historical appearance is the era of Vicramaditya, which commenced 56 years before the birth of Christ; and thus a period of 3000 years remains, of which the Hindus themselves do not pretend to possess any continuous accounts either religious, traditionary, or historical. It is this chasm, consequently, which it is obviously impossible to fill up in any manner; because there are no complete and uninterrupted genealogies, or any other data by which a connection between the end of the Dwapar Yug and the era of Vicramaditya could be even plausibly established. Hence Sir W. Jones thus concludes his essay on the Chronology of the Hindus:— "On the whole we may safely close the most authentic system of Hindu chronology, that I have yet been able to procure, with the death of Chandrabija (452 years before Christ). Should any farther information be attainable, we shall, perhaps, in due time, attain it either from books or inscriptions * in the Sanscrit language; but from the materials with which we are at present supplied, we may establish as indubitable the two following propositions: that the three first ages of the Hindus are chiefly *mythological*, whether their mythology was founded on the dark enigmas of their astronomers, or on the heroic fictions of their poets; and that the *fourth*, or *historical*, age cannot be carried farther back than about 2000 years before Christ."† But the mere perusal of that essay will at once evince on what very inconclusive grounds Sir W. Jones has applied the term *historical* to the Kali Yug; and how unsuccessfully he has attempted to adapt the heroic, or rather the religious, fictions of the Hindu poets to the dates of European chronology.

But though it evidently seems impossible to determine the precise period when the sacred books of the Hindus were composed, or when the circumstances related in them actually took place; still there are other than chronological and historical considerations, from which a

* Unfortunately, this expectation is not likely to be realised, as there appear to be no inscriptions of an older date than the ninth century; or if there are, they are written in a character which cannot now be deciphered.

† Sir W. Jones's Works, vol. i. p. 309.

probable opinion can be formed with respect to the authenticity of these books, and to the antiquity of the Hindu religion. For nothing certainly can be a more convincing proof of the perfect genuineness of an immense number of works on all kinds of subjects, than an unvarying uniformity of conception, and a total absence of all foreign modes of thinking and extraneous interpolations. But this character is so incontrovertibly impressed on the whole of Sanscrit literature, that even the persons who have called in question its antiquity in its present form, are obliged to admit that ancient materials did exist, from which were composed the Sanscrit works now extant. "The Puranas," says Lieutenant-Colonel Wilford, "are certainly a modern compilation from valuable materials, which, I am afraid, no longer exist;" and Mr. Bentley remarks, — "In thus giving the age (A. D. 295) of the Ramayan of Valmika, as it is called, I do not mean to say that the facts, on which that romance was founded in part, did not exist long before; on the contrary, my opinion is that they did, and were probably to be then found in histories or oral traditions brought down to his time." Whatever, therefore, the antiquity of Sanscrit works may be, their authenticity, that is, their containing an accurate description of the manners, customs, modes of thinking, and religion of the Hindus, is not controverted. But even with respect to their literal genuineness, the reasoning of Mr. Colebrooke, in his Essay on the Vedas, seems to me so conclusive as to refute unanswerably all cavils on the subject; and I am persuaded, that the more Sanscrit literature is known, the more just will these remarks of his be found, as applicable, not only to the Vedas, but to the other sacred books of the Hindus.* "On this ground I defend the authentic text of the Indian scripture as it is now extant; and although the passages which I have so verified are few, compared with the great volume of the Vedas, yet I have sufficient grounds to argue, that no skill in the nefarious arts of forgery and falsification could be equal to the arduous task of fabricating large works, to agree with the very numerous citations pervading thousands of volumes,

* The quotations from the Purans, the Ramayan, and Mahabharat, which pervade the whole of Sanscrit literature, are, I believe, more numerous than those from the Vedas, as they are considered less sacred.

composed on diverse subjects in every branch of literature, and dispersed through the various nations of Hindus inhabiting Hindustan and the Dekhin." *

I am, however, well aware that the recent composition of Sanscrit works, and particularly of the Purans, is a prevalent opinion ; but as I have never met with it (except in the writings of Mr. Bentley) under any other shape than that of *bare assertion unsupported by the slightest argument or proof*, I am completely at a loss to understand on what grounds it could have been formed. It seems, indeed, to rest on a supposition that the Purans were intended to be geographical, chronological, and historical treatises ; and, because it is impossible to give them this character, it is hence concluded that they must be incomplete, and that they merely contain badly arranged fragments of some larger works. But I have most carefully examined sixteen † of the Purans, and a great portion of the Skanda Puran, and I cannot discover in them any other object than that of religious instruction.‡ Nor do

* Asiatic Researches, vol. viii. p. 465.

† I have not been able to procure the *Bhavyshia Puran*, nor even to obtain any account of its contents.

‡ But this statement of Mr. Colebrooke (*As. Re*., vol. vii. p. 202.) has been repeatedly quoted: — " Every Purana treats of five subjects: the creation of the universe, its progress, and the renovation of worlds; the genealogy of gods and heroes; chronology according to a fabulous system; and heroic history, containing the achievements of demigods and heroes." One, however, of these five subjects has been here omitted, and, unless the term *chronology* means the division of time according to the Hindu system, no such subject occurs in the Purans. But, though these topics are certainly treated of at greater or less length in most of the Purans, still they by no means form the principal subject of those works; for this Mr. Colebrooke has unaccountably overlooked, and yet it is the only reason which has conferred on them a sacred character, — I mean the moral and religious instruction which is inculcated in them, and to which all the legends that they contain are rendered subservient. In fact, the description of the earth and of the planetary system, and the lists of royal races that occur in them, are evidently extraneous, and not essential circumstances, as they are omitted in some Purans and very concisely discussed in others; while, on the contrary, in all the Purans, some or other of the leading principles, rites, and observances of the Hindu religion are fully dwelt upon, and illustrated either by suitable legends, or by prescribing the ceremonies to be practised and the prayers and invocations to be employed in the worship of different deities. Of the real nature, however, of the Purans, the extracts which follow will convey a sufficiently accurate idea.

This opinion, also, of Lieutenant-Colonel Wilford, seems not only to have been generally adopted, but to have been extended to other Purans than those which he mentions (*As. Res.*, vol. viii. p. 252.) : — " Other impostors," he remarks, " have had recourse to the

I perceive in them any *lacunæ*, or indications of failure or imperfectness in executing the design of their composition ; from which it might justly be inferred that they were not original works, but were compilations from other books ; for they appear to me to be precisely such compositions as would be produced by a first attempt to commit to writing the mythological legends and religious lessons which had no doubt been previously communicated by oral instruction. Hence have proceeded that total want of arrangement, that humility of style, and those constant repetitions, which are so observable in each of the Purans ; and also their having been written in the form of dialogues, in which the speaker acts the part of preceptor, and the hearer that of pupil. But it is these very circumstances, that seem to have induced some writers to suppose that the Purans were merely modern compilations, which induce me to ascribe to them a remote antiquity : because the ability of the Brahmans to produce much more perfect works cannot be disputed ; and had they therefore determined, at some modern period, to recompose the Purans, it is quite incredible that they would have allowed them to appear in their present state ; for, besides the faults of

---

Skanda, Brahmanda, and Padma Puranas, a great part of which is not at present to be found ; and for that reason, these are called the Puranas of *thieves or impostors*." But, with the exception of the Skanda, all the other seventeen Purans are to be found in an entire state, as they have always remained perfect ; and the contents of the Brahmanda and Padma Purans are too well known to admit of any falsification taking place in them. If, however, Lieutenant-Colonel Wilford merely meant that legendary stories relating to the erection and sanctity of different temples have been composed and circulated as extracts from these two Purans, the statement is correct ; but this circumstance can, obviously, in no manner affect either their completeness or authenticity. For the spuriousness of such stories is unquestionable ; and, consequently, their not being to be found in the Purans to which they are ascribed, must evince the genuineness, and not the spuriousness, of those Purans. But, with respect to the Skanda, it has long been in an incomplete state, and circulated in detached portions only ; nor are even its divisions and contents known with any degree of accuracy. In the commencement, however, of the *Suta Sanhita* of this Puran, it is said to consist of six *Sanhitas ;* the *Sanatkinnara, Suta, Shankari, Vaishnavi, Brahmi,* and *Saurani ;* of 500 *Khands ;* and of 500,000 stanzas. It will, therefore, be obvious that the circulation of such an extensive work in detached portions only, might afford every facility for composing spurious works and circulating them as extracts from this Puran ; but, as far as I can judge from internal evidence, I think that all the *Sanhitas* and *Khands* may be admitted as genuine, though the *Mahatmyams* said to be extracted from it have rather a questionable appearance.

style and composition which they contain, they exhibit a remarkable diversity in a number of important particulars, which the Brahmans would most assuredly have then so corrected, as to reduce the contents of the Purans to one uniform system. This diversity, however, is exactly what must have resulted from eighteen different persons having, probably at different times and places, collected together and committed to writing the mythological and religious opinions and legends which had been previously formed and preserved merely by tradition. The present state, therefore, of the Purans, in which the most important legends, and even the origin of the deities, are related in a discordant manner, though not in such a manner as in the least affects the perfect homogeneity of the Hindu religion, must alone be a strong presumption that they exist at the present day in precisely the same state in which they were originally composed; and that, as the Brahmans have preferred to reconcile by explanation the discordances that occur in them (which they do not deny), rather than to correct them, they must have been prevented by religious scruples from giving uniformity to their religious system; and, consequently, that there can be no grounds whatever for supposing that these works are mere modern compilations.*

But if the authenticity and genuineness of the sacred books of the Hindus cannot be contested, and if quotations from them pervade the whole of Sanscrit literature, it is merely necessary to refer to the lists of Sanscrit works contained in the fourth volume of Ward's View of the Hindus, and to advert to their being numerously dispersed over an area of more than one million of square miles, to be at once satisfied

* Mr. Colebrooke (*As. Res.*, vol. iii. p. 467.) has incautiously made this admission:— "I am myself inclined to adopt an opinion supported by many learned Hindus, who consider the celebrated *Shri Bhagavata* as the work of a grammarian supposed to have lived about six hundred years ago." For it is unquestionable that the number of the Purans have been always held to be eighteen; but in most of the Purans the names of the eighteen are enumerated, amongst which the *Bhagavat* is invariably included; and, consequently, if it were composed only 600 years ago, the others must be of an equally modern date. For the supposition of an interpolation cannot be here admitted; as it must at the same time be admitted, that not only one of the ancient Purans, but even its very name, has disappeared, a conjecture too improbable to merit attention. But Mr. Colebrooke's own reasoning in this essay is the best refutation of so erroneous an opinion.

that their composition and circulation, *without the aid of typography*, within the last 700 or 800 years, is an absolute impossibility. Whether, also, the Amara Kosh be supposed to have been written at about the commencement of the Christian era, as is the general belief, or in the fifth century, on the grounds pointed out by Mr. Wilson; that vocabulary is alone conclusive proof that the civil and religious polity, described in Sanscrit works, was at the period completely established.* But to determine the number of ages before the birth of Christ that this polity may have been first instituted, can depend only on conjecture; though, from the brief notices contained in ancient writers, it may certainly be concluded with much probability that it must have existed in the same state at least 300 years before Christ. This point Sir W. Jones has attempted to determine by philological reasoning; for he has remarked in his preface to the Institutes of Menu — "The Sanscrit of the three first *Vedas* (I need not here speak of the fourth, that of the *Manava Dharma Sastra*, and that of the *Puranas*) differ from each other in pretty exact proportion to the Latin of Numa, from whose laws entire fragments are preserved, that of Appius, which we see in the fragments of the twelve tables, and that of Cicero, or Lucretius where he has not affected an obsolete style; if the several changes, therefore, of Sanscrit and Latin took place, as we may fairly assume, in times very nearly proportional, the *Vedas* must have been written about 300 years before these Institutes, and about 600 before the *Puranas* and *Itihasas*, which, I am fully convinced were not the productions of Vyasa: so that, if the son of Parasara committed the traditional Vedas to writing in the Sanscrit of his father's time, the original of this book must have received its present form about 880 years before Christ's birth."† This argument, however, is entirely fanciful; for though the

* I purposely adopt a *vocabulary* as authority, because it will not be denied that such a work can be liable to no suspicion, as it contains nothing more than names, which would not have been inserted in it had not the objects denoted by them really existed.

It may be also observed, that the Sanscrit literature which is undoubtedly modern strongly attests the existence of a more ancient one; for, like that of Alexandria, it consists, besides mathematical and astronomical works, of nothing but grammars, vocabularies, and commentaries.

† Sir W. Jones's Works, vol. iii. p. 55.

grammatical construction of the Vedas differs from that of later writers, but very few of the words contained in them have become obsolete, and not one of those which occur in the *Manava Dharma Shastra*. In another work, also, I have perhaps sufficiently evinced that the Sanscrit language must have been completely formed about one or two centuries before the age of Homer, and that in its words and structure no change whatever is observable in any of the Sanscrit works now extant. But so long a duration of the Sanscrit language in the very same state must be considered as a very strong presumption that the civil and religious institutions, by which the Hindus are so peculiarly distinguished, must have been established at least 1100 or 1200 years before the Christian era. *

In a former work, however, I have endeavoured to evince how probable it is that neither the Brahminical literature nor the Brahminical religion were of indigenous origin in India, but that they were introduced into it by colonists who had migrated from Babylonia. If, consequently, the Brahmans belonged originally to the Chaldean priesthood, they would no doubt bring with them the sacred books in which the laws of their civil and religious institutions were contained; and hence the antiquity of the Vedas and earlier Sanscrit works need no longer be questioned, since they were the productions of those Chaldeans whose remote antiquity and whose learning are attested by the whole of ancient history. To the philological reasoning which I there employed, I may now add the remarkable similarity which exists in the signs of the zodiac that were adopted by ancient nations; for Sir W. Jones has observed,—"Now I undertake to prove, that the Indian

* No argument can be necessary to show that a language must be affected by the establishment of institutions which have a greater or lesser influence on every act which a people are in the daily habits of performing. For, were the institutions of a foreign origin, foreign terms would be introduced into the parent tongue, as is obvious in both the English and Persian languages; or, if the requisite terms were of indigenous invention, new combinations of words would become necessary to express them: and had these, therefore, originated after the language was completely formed, they would inevitably betray their newness; as is sufficiently proved by the many strange compound words that abound in German. But the Sanscrit is so wonderfully homogeneous, that the language, and the civil and religious institutions of the people speaking it, must have arrived at their complete form at precisely the same period.

zodiac was not borrowed mediately or directly from the Arabs or Greeks; and since the solar division of it in India is the same in substance with that used in Greece, we may reasonably conclude that both Greeks and Hindus received it from an older nation, who first gave names to the luminaries of heaven, and from whom both Greeks and Hindus, as their similarity in language and religion fully evinces, had a common descent."* And Bailli has remarked, — "La plus antique notion de l'astronomie chez les Grecs est celle de la sphère, inventée, dit-on, par Chiron et décrite par Musée; sphère qui, comme Newton l'a remarqué, doit être plus ancienne que le voyage des Argonautes. Tous les faits s'accordent à prouver que cette sphère est du treize ou quatorzième siècle avant l'ére chrêtienne. On peut conjecturer que cette sphère a été prise par les Argonautes mêmes dans quelque contrée de l'Asie. Eudoxe, qui avoit fait une description astronomique de cette sphère, dit que les colures coupent l'écliptique par le milieu des signes du Bélier, de la Balance, de l'Ecrevisse, et du Capricorne. Cette designation avoit pour objêt d'établir, relativement à des points fixés dans le ciel, la position des equinoxes et des solstices, qui sont des points mobiles et retrogrades. Ces points fixés ne sembloient pas pouvoir être autre chose que les étoiles et les figures des constellations. Mais cette supposition, si naturelle, étoit sujette à de grandes difficultés. . . . . Cette impossibilité prouve que ces designations n'étoient pas ce qu'elles paroissoient être; il y avoit quelque chose qu'on n'entendoit pas alors: elles se rapportent à un zodiaque qui n'étoit connu ni d'Eudoxe ni d'Hypparque, et c'est le zodiaque indien. Dès que ce zodiaque a été communiqué aux differens peuples de l'Asie, et particulièrement aux Chaldéens, il a été natural que ce peuple, qui faisoit usage d'une année tropique, ait fixé dans ce zodiaque le lieu des equinoxes et des solstices, les points où les colures coupoient ce zodiaque."† But would it not

* Sir W. Jones's Works. vol. i. p. 333.

† Astronomie Indienne, p. 262, 263.

Delambre has also remarked, — "Un zodiaque et surtout 12 signes, dont les noms et les figures ont tant de ressemblance, ne sont pas, comme l'obliquité de l'écliptique, le diametre du soleil, ou même comme la période de 19 ans, de ces choses qu'on peut déterminer en differens temps et sans se rien communiquer. Il en est de même des jours de la semaine et de leurs noms planétaires, comme au zodiaque, il leur faut une origine commune;

be more consistent with probability, and with the concurrent testimony of ancient history to the learning of the Chaldeans and to the remote period from which they had cultivated astronomy, to conclude that it was the Chaldeans who had invented the zodiac, and who had communicated this remarkable division of the heavens to other nations.*

But, with respect to Sanscrit literature in general, the justness of the following remarks, of which I gladly avail myself, as they will no doubt carry more conviction to the reader than any with which I could present him, cannot be reasonably disputed: — "It may be said, that in a country of which the actual condition is so imperfectly known, investigation should first be directed to the existing state of society, which admits of being accurately ascertained, and may lead to practical conclusions highly beneficial to the community, before we attempt to explore the obscure paths of remote antiquity, by the feeble lights afforded by a few mutilated or suspicious documents. The Indian nations, it may be contended, have no claim to any extraordinary attention, either from the philosopher or the historian: their boasted civilisation has rather been asserted than proved; neither their literature nor their arts indicate any considerable progress in the pursuits which refine and adorn mankind; and some of their customs betray a ferocity scarcely to be found amongst the most savage nations. But,

---

mais faut-il la chercher chez un peuple plus (peu?) ancien et totalement inconnu? N'est-il pas plus simple de supposer une communication entre les divers peuples de l'Asie?"— *Astronomie Ancienne*, tom. i. p. 446.

* These remarks, likewise, of Bailli, if restricted to the Chaldeans, seem highly probable: — "On voit encore que cette durée si exacte de l'année n'a dû appartenir qu'à un seul peuple dans l'antiquité et dans l'Asie: car ces déterminations astronomiques qui approchent si près de la vérité des mouvemens célestes, n'ont pu être obtenues que de deux manières; ou par des instrumens très parfaits dont il ne semble pas qu'on puisse accorder la connoissance et l'usage à des siècles reculés, ou par des siècles accumulés, par un long temps de puissance, de tranquillité, et de culture des arts et des sciences, qui n'a pas été accordé à tous les peuples. Il y a donc lieu de croire qu'il y a eu jadis dans l'Asie une masse de connoissances, qui a été fondée par un seul peuple, d'où elles se sont étendues à tous les autres par une communication plus ou moins retardée, commes nous avons aujourd'hui en Europe un grand nombre de déterminations, auxquelles differens peuples ont pu ajouter differens degrés de perfection, mais dont l'origine est commune, et dont la base se trouve chez les Grecs d'Alexandrie."— *Astronomie Indienne*, p. 273.

even admitting that it would be desirable to trace the remote revolutions which this people have undergone, the little probability of attaining any deductions which may be relied on with confidence ought to induce us to relinquish so hopeless a task. The Puranas appear to be extravagant romances, which, however amusing as poetical compositions, can furnish no addition to authentic history, whatever portion of it they may be supposed incidentally to contain. When we find gods and heroes mingling in doubtful fight; events natural and supernatural succeeding each other indifferently; a fact probably historical, followed by another evidently allegorical; — the only rational conclusion is to consider the whole of these poems as works of imagination, and to appreciate their merits by the rules applicable to similar compositions amongst other nations. But if such be the judgment we must pass on the Puranas, the Hindu compositions of a later date are not better entitled to attention, unless with respect to poetical excellence: and it probably may be affirmed, that the Hindus cannot produce a single historical composition; whilst the Mahometans of the same country have amply, and even ably, illustrated all the events subsequent to their entrance into Hindustan. To these, therefore, such as may be disposed to investigate the history of the East should consequently confine themselves: the materials are ample and authentic; the occurrences more recent, and therefore more interesting; and the subject so far from being exhausted, that such parts of it as have hitherto been treated of in European languages are rather calculated to excite, than gratify, the curiosity of the public.

" On the other hand, it may be contended with much plausibility, and we think with justice, that an indiscriminate accumulation of facts is no object with the philosopher, and only a subordinate one with the historian; that in proportion to the peculiarity and reputed antiquity of the religious and civil institutions subsisting amongst any people, it is natural to feel curiosity as to their origin; that the minute peculiarities which discriminate the nations of Europe scarcely produce any sensible modification of character, or exhibit to our observation any beings whose manner of acting and thinking is materially different from our own. In order accurately to appreciate the efficacy of religious dogmata, and of civil institutions, in modifying the character of a people or of individuals, our observation should be particularly directed to those nations who differ most widely from ourselves in those particulars. Such comparisons are not less delightful than instructive; and to this source we may trace much of the amusement and much of the knowledge we derive from a perusal of the compositions of classic antiquity. From the same cause, the manners of savage tribes have attracted and deserved the attention of philosophers; but these are in general extremely uniform, and little modified by any other circumstances than the greater or less facility of acquiring food. It is not amidst a people in such a stage of society that the influence of moral impressions can be accurately ascertained. A nation must have advanced some steps in civilisation, must have cultivated the arts, and been tinged with science, before it is susceptible of that indelible stamp which defies the efforts of time. If, therefore, the peculiarities of the Hindu institutions, opinions, and manners deservedly render them the object of philosophic research, the gradations by which such a state of society was attained must be highly interesting, and can only be discovered through the medium of such literary monuments as are still extant among them."*

The remarks in this chapter have extended to a much greater length than I at first intended; but the opinions which have been expressed respecting the antiquity or recentness of the Hindu nation, and respecting the genuineness or spuriousness, the value or worthlessness, of Sanscrit literature, are so discordant, that it became necessary to enter into a full discussion of so much agitated a question. The dispute, however, as in many other instances, has proceeded evidently on a misapprehension of the real points in issue; for it ought never to have been supposed that any person acquainted with the subject believed in the extravagant computations of time adopted by the Hindus, or with Bailli that the commencement of the Kali Yug in the year 3102 B. C. had been actually determined by astronomical observations.† But in order to refute this imaginary supposition, it is

* Edinburgh Review, vol. xv. p. 175.

† A writer in the Quarterly Review, vol. i. p. 64., pays these high compliments to the

equally absurd to contend that the whole of Sanscrit literature was invented and composed, or new modelled, 700 or 800 years ago*; and to maintain that "the sacred writings of the Brahmans have been long mentioned with those phrases of solemn wonder, which would still have misled the public, if the translations and extracts of them, which have successively appeared, had not discovered their puerility and imposture. It is therefore important that the Sanscrit books, which have been held up as so sacred and so ancient, and which some of our *learned* Orientalists obviously prefer to the Jewish historian, should be given to Europe in the languages familiar to every one; that we may not be blinded by the erroneous admiration of credulous and misjudging enthusiasts, but be enabled to criticise fairly and judge impartially for ourselves."† Of the genuineness, however, of Sanscrit literature no doubt can be reasonably entertained; and there appears to be most

---

sense and understanding of his countrymen in India:—"Yet it is amazing to see, in the dissertations and publications of most of our Asiatic gentlemen, how anxious they are to accredit more or less of these absurd antiquities. Although nothing has ever appeared in the world with the characters of wilful and wanton falsehood more grossly palpable; although the fictitious histories of Annius of Viterbo, Geoffrey of Monmouth, and Archbishop Turpin, are probable and reasonable in comparison with them, yet have the Brahminical antiquities been listened to with respect, and repeated with a credulity in the highest degree discreditable to a reasoning age. In vain had our most learned and scientific scholars, during the last two centuries, by their Herculean labours, settled the chronology of the world and of ancient history, on just and true foundations; in vain had the historiographers of the various countries of Europe at last emancipated themselves from the wild fables of ostentatious vanity, and determined the antiquities of their several nations by precise and authentic boundaries. These objects had scarcely been attained with laudable, but in some cases painful, sacrifices of national vanity, when a sudden assault was made upon our chronological repose by the phantoms of Hindustan. Even enlightened men, misled by other theories and other wishes, caught a revolutionary mania, and one of them received the fantastic apparitions with such fond credulity, that he wrote volumes to assure us that not only our history but our geography, must be subverted; and that Siberia, now the region of eternal snows, was once the scene of an equatorial summer, and the source of human civilisation!"

This critique, it must be observed, was published in February, 1809, when the Asiatic Society had pursued their valuable researches for twenty-five years, and in whose Transactions nothing whatever is contained that could in any manner justify such remarks.

* In his posthumous work Mr. Bentley has extended this period to 1300 years ago; but apparently only, for he still asserts in it (p. 104.) that, in fact, none of the Puranas are ancient, and some of them not a hundred years old!!

† Quarterly Review, vol. i. p. 68.

valid grounds for believing that Sanscrit works began to be composed at least 1100 or 1200 years before Christ. Nor will, perhaps, my conjecture that the Brahmans were Chaldeans be deemed improbable; in which case a still remoter antiquity may with justice be ascribed to the Vedas and the earlier works of the Hindus.

But it must at the same time be admitted that the sacred books of the Hindus contain neither geographical, chronological, nor historical information; that in them the use of numbers, with respect to both time and space, is extravagantly absurd; and that, in their style and want of arrangement, they are not only deficient in the beauties by which the immortal works of Greece and Rome are distinguished, but even err against all principles of refined taste and classical composition.* It remains, therefore, merely to determine whether such defects

* But the slightest conversancy with Sanscrit literature would have prevented Mr. Mill from hazarding such absurdly erroneous remarks as the following, and from thus dogmatically pronouncing condemnation in a case, with the merits of which he was totally unacquainted: — "It is incompatible with the present purpose, to speak of these poems in more than general terms. They describe a series of actions in which a number of men and gods are jointly engaged. These fictions are not only more extravagant and unnatural, less correspondent with the physical and moral laws of the universe, but are less ingenious, more monstrous, and have less of any thing that can engage the affection, awaken sympathy, or excite admiration, reverence, or terror, than the poems of any other, even the rudest, people with whom our knowledge of the globe has yet brought us acquainted. They are excessively prolix and insipid. They are often, through long passages, trifling and childish to a degree, which those acquainted with only European poetry can hardly conceive. Of the style in which they are composed, it is far from too much to say that all the vices which characterise the style of rude nations, and particularly those of Asia, they exhibit in perfection. Inflation, metaphors perpetual, and these the most violent and strained, often the most unnatural and ridiculous, obscurity, tautology, repetition, verbosity, confusion, incoherence, distinguish the Mahabharat and Ramayan. That amid the numberless effusions which a wild imagination throws forth, in its loose and thoughtless career, there should now and then be something which approaches the confines of reason and taste, is so far from surprising, that it would be truly surprising if there were not. A happy description, or here and there the vivid conception of a striking circumstance, is not sufficient; the exact observation of nature, and the symmetry of a whole, are necessary to designate the poetry of a cultivated people." — *History of British India*, vol. ii. p. 46.

In this elaborate description, the Sanscrit scholar will seek in vain for the slightest semblance of the Sanscrit style and composition; as it is entirely a fancy picture, which has no existence in reality. But the opinion of a writer, who gravely affirms that *the poetry of the Persians resembles that of the Arabians, and that both resemble that of the Hindus*, can be entitled to no attention whatever, as it betrays such a consummate ignorance of Oriental literature. The fact is that the scholars of Europe have formed their opinions respecting

may not be compensated by the novel views of human nature which they exhibit, and by the various materials for promoting the prosecution of enquiries into the philosophy of the human mind which they so amply afford; for civil and religious institutions which, in all probability, have endured unchanged for more than three thousand years; a system of polytheism which its internal evidence proves to be of the highest antiquity; and a peculiar but highly civilised state of society of which no other memorials exist, are certainly subjects not undeserving the study of the philosopher. Hence even Mr. Mill has been led into these remarks:—"The meritorious researches of the modern Europeans, who have explored the institutions, the laws, the manners, the arts, occupations, and maxims of this ancient people, have enabled philosophy to draw the picture of society, which they have presented through a long revolution of years. We cannot describe the lives of their kings, or the circumstances and results of a train of battles; but we can show how they lived together as members of the community, and of families; how they were arranged in society; what arts they practised; what tenets they believed; what manners they displayed; under what species of government they existed; and what characters, as human beings, they possessed. This is by far the most useful and important part of history; and if it be true, as an acute and eloquent historian [Hume] has remarked, *that the sudden, violent, unprepared revolutions incident to barbarians, are so much guided by caprice, and terminate so often in cruelty, that they disgust us by the uniformity of their appearance, and it is rather fortunate for letters, that they are buried in silence and oblivion,* we have perhaps but little to regret in the total absence of Hindu records." *

---

what is called the *Oriental style* from the Old Testament; and nothing can possibly be more dissimilar from Persian and Sanscrit composition than the Hebrew.

* History of British India, vol. i. p. 147.

CHAP. VI.

GENERAL REMARKS ON THE HINDU RELIGION.

THE Hindus have from time immemorial believed in the existence of one supreme Being, in the immateriality and immortality of the soul, and in a future state of reward and punishment: but, in their opinion respecting the nature of the supreme Being, they are unquestionably pantheists. Numerous passages, however, occur in Sanscrit works, and various expressions are in familiar use among the Hindus, which apparently convey the most exalted ideas of God, as perfectly distinct from the universe which he has created: but when such passages and expressions are closely examined, and compared with other descriptions of the Deity, their pantheistic tendency becomes evident.

It hence seems probable that the Hindus originally entertained correct notions respecting the nature of God; but subsequently, finding it impossible to understand how spirit could produce and act upon matter, they either identified the two together, or denied the real existence of matter. It is this latter system which now prevails in India, and which also appears to be the doctrine of the Vedas from the following verse quoted by Mr. Colebrooke:—“ Originally this [universe] was indeed soul only; nothing else whatever existed, active [or inactive].” * This system is thus beautifully described by Sir W. Jones:—

* Asiatic Researches, vol. viii. p. 408.

The same doctrine is contained in the *Upanishads*, as will be observed from the translation of the *Kaivalya Upanishad*, in p. 188. Consequently, these unquestionable facts evince not only the groundlessness of this assertion of Mr. Mill, but also the extreme want of the requisite research with which his much admired History of British India has been written:— “ The Vedanti doctrine, which has caught the fancy of some of the admirers of Sanscrit, appears to be delivered *vivâ voce*, and solely in that mode. As no passage implying it has been quoted from any Sanscrit work, it might, if it were any refinement, be suspected of being wholly modern.” (Vol. i. p. 71.) For the volume of the Asiatic Researches, in which Mr. Colebrooke's Essay on the Vedas is contained, was published in 1805;

"It will be sufficient here to premise, that the inextricable difficulties attending the *vulgar notion of material substances*, concerning which

"We know this only, that we nothing know,"

induced many of the wisest among the ancients, and some of the most enlightened among the moderns, to believe, that the whole creation was rather an *energy* than a *work*, by which the infinite Being, who is present at all times and in all places, exhibits to his creatures a set of perceptions, like a wonderful picture or piece of music, always varied, yet always uniform; so that all bodies and their qualities exist, indeed, to every wise and useful purpose, but exist only as far as they are *perceived;* a theory no less pious than sublime, and as different from any principle of atheism, as the brightest sunshine differs from the blackest midnight. This *illusive operation* of the Deity the Hindu philosophers [and all classes of Hindus] called Maya, or *deception.*" * But, although matter has only an apparent existence in the actual forms of which this universe is composed, still the perceptions which they cause proceed not from the mere volition of the Deity, but from a positive manifestation of his own divine essence under these illusive appearances. The soul also of the *percipient* has a real existence, and the great object therefore, which is prescribed to the Hindu, as the only means by which he can obtain final beatitude, is the acquisition of the knowledge that quality † (that is matter and spirit) does not exist, and that there is in reality nothing but one self-existent, infinite, and all pervading SPIRIT, of which he is himself an *undivided* part.

This system, however, is free from the inconsistencies which have

---

and in 1812 was published the translation of the *Prabod'h Chandrodaya* by Dr. Taylor, in the appendix to which is given a succinct but correct account of the Vedanta system, and also the translation of a small Sanscrit tract on the same subject, by the celebrated Shankara Acharya.

* Sir W. Jones's Works, vol. vi. p. 367.

† The reader will be aware of the difficulty of expressing correctly the metaphysical terms of a system of philosophy which has been always unknown in Europe; and will, therefore, no doubt excuse any uncouthness of phraseology in my attempts to explain it. The great point is to convey faithfully the idea intended, and in this I trust that I have succeeded.

been objected to that of Berkeley. Because the Hindus, at the same time, suppose that, in consequence of illusion, men are irresistibly impressed with a belief that the universe really exists; and that, as long as this illusion endures, they must suffer pleasure and pain, and be subject to all the cares and miseries of this life: but they contend that there are means by which man can free himself from its bonds, and thus become again identified with the supreme Spirit. Until, however, this emancipation is effected, man must necessarily act, not according to his essential nature, but according to the unavoidable influence of the illusive appearance and passions to which God has exposed him; and it is therefore for the purpose of obtaining this emancipation that all the ascetic practices of the Hindus have been devised. But that extreme degree of devout abstraction which is indispensable for attaining his object, as it consists in the complete abnegation of all action, is so difficult of observance, that the Hindu, according to the tenets of his religion, seems doomed to a continual succession of different states of being in this world; except during the intervals that he may be condemned to suffer the pains of hell, or permitted to enjoy the delights of paradise. For, aware of human frailty, the Hindu religion teaches that, although man may not be able to obtain final beatitude; still, if he be virtuous, he will receive a future reward in proportion to the purity and meritoriousness of his life; but, if otherwise, he must atone for his sins by undergoing a certain period of punishment. When, however, the appointed time for his residence either in paradise or hell has elapsed, he returns again to this world, in some state of being or other, until he becomes at length sufficiently purified to admit of identification with the supreme Being.

But the dogma of the ancient Persian, the Christian, and the Mohammedan religions, which inculcates a belief in the existence of an *evil principle* distinct from the divine essence, is altogether unknown to the Hindus. Nothing can be more erroneous, I should hope not intentionally so, than these remarks of Mr. Ward: — "The Hindu writings further teach, that it is the great Spirit which is diffused through every form of animated matter; that actions of *every kind* are his; that he is the charioteer, and the body the chariot; that it is the highest attainment of human wisdom to realise the fact, that the human soul and Brahm are one and the same. By this doctrine all accountability is destroyed and liability to punishment rendered preposterous. How often has the author heard it urged by the most sensible Hindus, that the moving cause of every action, however flagitious, is God*; that man is an instrument upon which God plays what tune he pleases! Another modification of this doctrine is fate, or unchangeable destiny, embraced without a dissentient voice by all the Hindus. Thus the Deity on his throne is insulted as the author of all crimes, and men are emboldened to rush forward in the swiftest career of iniquity."† For the doctrine of the sacred books of the Hindus, and of the Vedantikas, is, that perfection consists in complete quiescence, and that the mere volition of the supreme Being to manifest himself, being a change from this state, was necessarily evil, and consequently communicated its nature to the effects produced by this volition; and that hence it was that evil originated. This opinion may detract from the omnipotence of God, but it exempts him from being the proximate cause of every evil action. The continual wars, also, of the *Suras* and *Asuras*, on which so much has been erroneously written, have not the slightest similarity with the *Miltonic* war in heaven. For they were both children of Kashyapa, but by different mothers. The *Suras* possessed angelic qualities, and for their residence therefore was paradise assigned; but the disposition of the Asuras being evil, they were in consequence doomed to inhabit Tartarus. It was, therefore, to free themselves from it, and to enjoy the delights of paradise, that they continually waged war with the *Suras*.

It will hence be evident that the Hindus believe in the unity of God; for even the lowest amongst them have some notion of the transmigration of souls, and of final beatitude consisting in identification with one God, perfectly distinct from the deities which they are in the habit of worshipping. It seems, also, obvious that, abstractedly

* I know not with what kind of Hindus Mr. Ward conversed, but such sentiments are at total variance with the clearest principles of the Hindu religion; and, besides, the whole scope and object of Mr. Ward's work is to prove that the Hindus do not believe in God.

† View of the Hindus, vol. i. p. xci.

speaking, these tenets must be conducive to morality: for the Hindu is taught that the miseries and misfortunes of this life are the consequences of sins committed in a former state of being; and thus there is held out to him the strongest inducement to lead a virtuous and pious life, in order to avoid being exposed to even greater suffering in another birth. The doctrines, therefore, relating to practice, of the Hindu religion are undoubtedly moral; for it renders the attainment of future bliss and final beatitude dependent on the exertions of man; and, whatever opinion may be entertained of some of the devotional acts which it enjoins, it most strongly inculcates a complete abandonment of all vicious and sinful indulgences.

But what the motive was which induced the supreme Being to will the manifestation of this universe, and these different apparent states of existence, the Indian metaphysician attempts not to explain, and only infers the will from the effect. In his opinion, however, it was impossible for a being devoid of form and quality to render his power perceptible without manifesting it under a visible form. Hence from the mere volition to originate this universe arising in God atoms were produced, and from these variously agitated and combined have proceeded the illusive appearance of matter and all its infinite modifications: but the Indian philosopher or theologist fell not into the mistake of Democritus, nor supposed that any possible aggregation of atoms could produce the soul of man*: and this, therefore, the Hindu believes, is an *undivided* part of the *supreme Spirit*, though excluded in some ineffable manner from actual participation in his divine essence.

The *human soul*, however, is not of precisely the same perfect

* As Lucretius also observes in his third book:—

> Hæc eadem ratio naturam animi, atque animai
> Corpoream docet ėsse: ubi enim propellere membra;
> Conripere ex somno corpusue mutareq; voltum;
> Atque hominem totum regere, ac versare videtur;
> (Quorum nil fieri sine tactu posse videmus,
> Nec tactum porro sine corpore;) nonne fatendum 'st
> Corporea natura animum constare, animamque? V. 162—168.
>
> Nunc igitur, quoniam 'st animi natura reperta
> Mobilis egregie; perquam constare necesse 'st
> Corporibus parvis, et lævibus, atque rotundis. V. 204—206.

purity as the *supreme soul;* for when God willed to manifest himself, then was his nature in a certain degree changed from its real and original state by the production of three essential qualities, which combining together gave rise to *ahankar*, or consciousness of individual existence.* This ideal increment is considered to be a substance capable of being added to and abstracted from other substances; and received the name of *ahankar*, in consequence of the first thought, formed by God on becoming conscious, being *Aham*, I am. It is this *ahankar* which is conjoined with the human soul, and which suffers pain and joy in this world, and is subject to reward and punishment in a future state: consequently, as the supreme Being, after willing the manifestation of this universe, becomes unconscious †, or devoid of *ahankar*, this increment no longer forms a part of his essence; and it hence necessarily follows that, whatever the *human soul* suffers from being united to it, cannot affect the *supreme soul*. The former, also, is supposed to be excluded from actual union with the latter by being enclosed in a subtle vehicle, as air in a vessel; and it is not, therefore, until the walls of this vehicle are dissolved, that the *human soul* becomes again homogeneous with the *supreme soul:* as when the sides of the vessel are broken, the air contained in it immediately mixes with the circumambient atmosphere.

But Bayle has, with his usual acuteness, observed: — " Je remarquerai en passant une absurdité de ceux qui soutient le système de l'ame du monde. Ils disent que toutes les ames, et des hommes et

* Nothing is more difficult than to conceive the manner in which these qualities could originate in the supreme Being, nor have I yet found any solution of this difficulty. For Dr. Taylor has very justly observed, in the Appendix to the translation of the *Prabod'h Chandrodaya*, p. 112.; — " It must have been observed in reading the play, and the treatise of *Shankara Acharya*, that there are no attempts to establish the Vedanta doctrines by any process of reasoning. The authors announce the principles of their sect in a dogmatical authoritative style, as indubitable truths, or establish their assertions by the authority of the sacred text alone, and attribute the disbelief of them to passion and ignorance. It is in this manner that the Vedanta doctrines are generally taught; but sometimes we find an appearance of reasoning and argument." Hence when explanation is required, the answer is a quotation from some treatise of authority, which leaves the point in just the same obscurity as before, as it merely affirms without condescending to explain.

† For an explanation of these different states of the supreme Being, see the commencement of the following chapter.

des bêtes, sont des particules de l'ame du monde, qui se réunissent à leur tout par la mort du corps ; et pour nous faire entendre cela, ils comparent les animaux à des bouteilles rempliés d'eau, qui floteroit dans la mer. Si l'on cassoit ces bouteilles, leur eau se réuniroit à son tout ; c'est ce qui arrive aux ames particulieres, disent ils, quand la mort détruit les organes où elles étoient enfermées. . . . . Il est facile de voir la fausseté du parallèle. La matière des bouteilles qui flottent dans l'océan est une cloison, qui empêche que l'eau de la mer ne touche l'eau dont elles sont pleines ; mais s'il y avoit une ame du monde, elle seroit répandue dans toutes les parties de l'univers, et ainsi rien ne pourroit empêcher l'union de chaque ame avec son tout. La mort ne pourroit pas être un moyen de reunion."* It is, however, useless to oppose this objection to even a well-informed and intelligent Hindu ; for he will still maintain that the *supreme soul* is one infinite and undivided whole, and that the enclosing the *human soul* within its subtle vehicle occasions no discerption of that whole. Emanation, therefore, has been always a doctrine completely unknown to the Hindus, who held the notion of such a continual discerption of the divine essence in utter abhorrence ; and there is likewise no attribute of deity in Sanscrit of more frequent occurrence than *akhandita*, or *undivided.* The opinions, however, of the Hindus on this point will be best understood from this passage of the *Garura* Puran.†

Vishnu, addressing Narada. — " Listen, O Narada ! to the knowledge of the true nature of the soul, which consists in discriminating the non-existence of duality : for as soon as this is acquired the bonds of illusion are dissolved ; pain and joy, desire and fruition, exertion and anxiety disappear ; and man thus enlightened depends no longer on the practices of devotion. Let the tree of worldly solicitude be cut down by the axe of divine knowledge, and then is final beatitude obtained. This life is but a sleep in which dreams arise from illusion ; but, on awakening, their unreality is at once perceived : thus, when illusion is destroyed, it is known that these apparent forms exist not, and that there is in reality nothing but one omnipotent Being, without beginning

* Dictionnaire Critique ; Spinosa, remarque A.

† See, also, the second extract, in Appendix D.

and without end. The sole means, therefore, of obtaining deliverance from illusion is the knowledge that *I am Brahm*, and for this purpose the two injunctions of the Vedas *do* and *forsake** are inefficient; but the heart being thus liberated from desire, the soul will undoubtedly obtain beatitude. For, as the supreme soul pervades all, is immaterial, incorporeal, and immortal, where else can the human soul find a place? or where can that which is formed of ether, after its composition is dissolved, repair to, except to the expanse of ether? and, in like manner, the soul no longer involved in illusion attains identification with the all-glorious and undivided essence of God; that longed for recipient of all souls, the source of all understanding and intellect, the eternal and sole-existing of all apparent existences, where consciousness of individuality ceases and is absorbed in that whole which shall endure to all eternity. For, were not the soul undivided, how could man, awakening from long sleep, recollect all that had preceded it, or how could he recall to remembrance that which he had at one time forgotten, or how could each single individual be subject to such a variety of pains and joys and other affections, were not the soul one undivided whole? Thus when a knowledge of the real essence of things is acquired, the conviction follows that there is neither individuality, nor divisibility, nor beginning, nor end, nor pain, nor pleasure, as nothing exists but *Parabrahm*; and the sum, therefore, of divine knowledge is the certainty that *I am Parabrahm.* Many vessels are fashioned of clay; but the clay remains the same: many ornaments are formed of gold; but the gold suffers no change: so the *supreme Spirit* appears under many forms and appellations, but his essence still continues one and the same. In the dark the cord appears a serpent; but light rectifies the error: so, deceived by the illusion of God, man supposes that distinct substances exist; but divine knowledge dispels the illusion and convinces him that multiform as these appearances are, they are all as deceptive as the cord taken for a serpent, or the mirage of the desert, and that nothing has a real entity but one, sole, self-existent Spirit. A Brahman pos-

* *Do* refers to religious acts here enumerated, as reading the Vedas, sacrifice, visiting holy places, &c.; and *forsake* implies ascetic practices, and an abandonment of all worldly concerns.

sessed with a devil thinks *I am a Shudra;* but as soon as the devil is expelled he says, *I am a Brahman.* Thus immersed in illusion the soul thinks, *I am corporeal;* but, as soon as illusion is destroyed, it knows its own nature and is convinced that *I am Brahm.* Then enabled to discriminate between reality and unreality, it knows that duality is occasioned solely by illusion; and that husband and wife, male and female, pleasure and pain, beginning and end, are mere deceptive appearances and notions. As the pleasures enjoyed in a dream *are* and *are not,* since they cease to exist as soon as the dreamer awakes; thus the belief in two substances, produced by illusion, ceases, when it is known that duality has no real existence. By the acquisition, therefore, of this divine knowledge, that there exists nothing but one supreme, eternal, immovable, immaculate, and undivided Spirit, and that *I am that Spirit,* man is liberated from the bonds of illusion, and obtains final beatitude by identification with that all-pervading Spirit."*

From this extract, which is in exact consonance with all that is contained in the Vedas, the Upanishads †, and Purans, and of which even the lowest Hindu has some conception ‡, it will at once be obvious how very erroneous the following remarks of Mr. Ward are:— "But the enquiry returns, *what is the object of worship among the Hindus?* It is not the one God, but this compound being, the soul of the world enclosed in matter, primeval energy, the prolific and

* Garura Puran, the chapter entitled *Atmadgnyanam,* near the end.

† Mr. Colebrooke states in his Essay on the Vedas:— "The whole of the Indian theology is professedly founded on the Upanishads. Those, which have been before described, have been shown to be extracts from the Veda. The rest are also considered as appertaining to the Indian scripture: it does not, however, clearly appear whether they are detached essays, or have been extracted from a *Brahmana* of the *Atharva* Veda."

‡ Sir James Mackintosh, in a letter quoted by Mr. Dugald Stewart, has on this point very correctly observed:— "What struck me was, that speculations so refined and abstruse should, in a long course of ages, have fallen through so great a space as that which separates the genius of their original inventors from the mind of this weak and unlettered man. The names of these inventors have perished; but their ingenious and beautiful theories, blended with the most monstrous superstitions, have descended to men very little exalted above the most ignorant populace, and are adopted by them as a sort of articles of faith, without a suspicion of their philosophical origin, and without the possibility of comprehending any part of the premises from which they were deduced." — *Stewart's Elements of the Philosophy of the Human Mind,* vol. ii. p. 529.

vivifying principle dwelling in all animated existences, or, in other words, the personification of whatever the disordered imaginations of the Hindus have attributed to this god encompassing himself with delusion." In a note, he adds: — "When the following lines of Pope were read to Gopala Tarkalankaza, a learned Brahman, he started from his seat, begged for a copy of them, and declared that the author must have been a Hindu: —

> " 'All are but parts of one stupendous whole,
> *Whose body nature is, and God the soul;*
> Warms in the sun, refreshes in the breeze,
> Glows in the stars, and blossoms in the trees;
> Lives through all life, extends through all extent,
> Spreads undivided, operates unspent." '*

For, if the second of these verses were correctly translated to him, the Brahman must have considered the thought expressed in it as gross impiety; unless indeed, he belonged to the *Sankhya* school of philosophy. The *Sankhya*, however, is a philosophic system, and it has, consequently, no relation whatever to the religion of the Hindus.† Mr. Ward has also stated that *Adwyananda*, a *Sanyasi*, and the compiler of the *Vedanta Sar*, says: — "*Brahm and life are one, that which, pervading all the members of the body, gives to them life or motion, is called jiva; that which, pervading the whole universe gives life and motion to all, is Brahm; therefore these two are one. Every kind of matter is without life;*

* Ward's View of the Hindus, vol. i. p. 15.

In the first sentence of this work, Mr. Ward also, remarks equally erroneously: — "The whole system of Hindu theology is founded upon the doctrine that the divine Spirit, as the soul of the universe, becomes, in all animate beings, united to matter; that spirit is insulated or individuated by particular portions of matter, which it is continually quitting and joining itself to new portions of matter; that the human soul is, in other words, God himself."

† Mr. Colebrooke remarks: — "Though not strictly orthodox, both *Sanc'hyas* and the *Vaiseshica*, as well as the *Nyaya*, are respected and studied by very rigid adherents of the Vedas, who are taught, however, to reject so much as disagrees with, and to treasure up what is consonant to, their scriptures. *In Canadi's doctrine, in the Sanc'hya, and in the Yoga, that part which is inconsistent with the Vedas is to be rejected by those who strictly adhere to revelation. In Jaimini's doctrine, and in Vyasas* [the Vedanta], *there is nothing whatever at variance with Scripture.*" — *Trans. Royal As. Soc.*, vol. i. part i. p. 19.

*that which is created cannot possess life; therefore all life is the Creator or Brahm; God is the soul of the world.** *This is the substance of the Vedanta philosophy.* Not only is God thus declared to be the soul of the world, but the writer of the above work affirms that *the world itself is God — God expanding himself in an infinite variety of forms. All things, past, present, and to come; all that is in the earth, sky, &c., of every class and description; all this is Brahm, who is the cause of all things, and the things themselves.*" I can scarcely, however, suppose that Mr. Ward has thus misrepresented the fundamental tenet of the Hindu religion, and supported this misrepresentation by mistranslation, from mere ignorance; because in the very Sanscrit works which he had evidently read, and also in his conversations with Hindus, he must have become acquainted with the universal prevalence of the doctrine of Maya, or of the non-existence in reality of this universe, of matter, and of distinct substances, though in fact such illusive appearances are manifested by the supreme Being. But this opinion is alone sufficient to disprove the material system which Mr. Ward has adopted in his work, and to which he has made bend the clearest authorities that directly contradict it, and which so fully evince that the Hindus have from time immemorial denied the real existence of matter, and have always believed that the sole *ens* is one supreme, indivisible, and all-pervading Spirit.

Had not, however, Mr. Ward presented materialism as the fundamental tenet of the Hindu religion, and of the Vedanta school of philosophy; but merely represented it as the system which necessarily resulted from the language employed to describe the creation and existence of this universe, he would have been perfectly correct: for, though the Hindus affirm and believe that *spirit* alone exists, still, in

* The whole of this sentence is most grossly mistranslated, as nothing in the original justifies it in the slightest manner. But as Mr. Ward has mixed up with the original in his translation, some commentary with which I am not acquainted, or probably the verbal explanations of his Pandit, I cannot so ascertain the precise passage, which perhaps was intended, as to admit of my quoting it. It will be however observed, that, in the passages here cited from the *Vedanta Sar*, the translation is obviously inconsistent; as the writer is made to express a belief in both unity and duality at the same time. But the Hindus deny the existence of duality, and reduce all to unity.

either treating or speaking of the illusive appearances which men, until enlightened by divine knowledge, consider to be real entities, they are, in words at least, decidedly materialists. The origin even ascribed to this universe is an unquestionable creation *ex nihilo*; for the elementary atoms, the three qualities, and *ahankar* are invariably described as having originated in consequence of the volition of the supreme Being to manifest himself. In the subsequent process, also, of the agitation and combination of these elements, from which this universe and all that it contains animated and inanimated are supposed to have been formed, it is obvious that a substance perfectly distinct from the divine essence, must have had an actual existence. In the Purans, therefore, except in such passages as treat of the soul, divine knowledge, and the real nature of God, and in all other works in which the creation of the universe and subsequent circumstances are discussed, the language employed most clearly admits the existence of matter. Whence this discordancy has arisen would be a curious subject of enquiry, were there any data by which it could be determined; but it at least betrays that the Hindu religion, as it has existed from remote times, must have been formed from two systems held in equal veneration, so that neither of them admitted of being rejected: for, had the spiritual system been alone received, it is evident that there could have been no popular mythology; and, had that been abandoned, religion would have become nothing more than a system of materialism.

The strict union, therefore, of these two incongruous systems, gives to the Hindu religion, when attentively examined, a very inconsistent appearance; nor have any attempts been made to reconcile together the *virtual admission* and the *express denial* of the existence of matter, which occur in the sacred books of the Hindus, and in the writings of the Vedantikas. In perusing, however, such works, it should be remembered that the essential tenet of this religion is that of final beatitude; and that, as this depends entirely on the spiritual system, such expressions and descriptions as imply materialism ought not to be understood in a literal sense and as contradictory of that system, but as merely proceeding from imperfect notions of the real nature of spirit and matter: for the Hindus are firmly of opinion that a material form is indispensable for action, and they have been thus led to suppose that the Supreme Being could not have effected the manifestation of the universe by mere volition; and that, as he was himself devoid of form and quality, it was necessary that his power should become efficacious by the assumption of a material existence. For this purpose, therefore, the Supreme Being invested the three qualities, which had originated from his own essence, with substantial forms, and hence sprang into being Brahma, Vishnu, and Shiva, or the creative, preservative, and destructive energies of the one self-existent God. But, even for effecting this, it is deemed requisite that the Supreme Being should have momentarily assumed a corporeal form; as in the *Naradiya* Puran, it is said:—" The primeval male multiplied himself into three persons, for the purpose of creation, preservation, and destruction. Three forms were thus produced from the essence of the supreme Being, which received different names according to the power exercised by each. But though he is thus known under the appellation of Brahma as the creator, of Vishnu as the preserver, and of Shiva as the destroyer, of this universe; he is still but one and the same, incorporeal, immortal, eternal, unchangeable, devoid of passion and quality; and his sacred name is *Parabrahm*."*

In the mythology, however, of the Hindus, the peculiar character ascribed to each of these divine hypostases is not attempted to be either preserved or illustrated. For Brahma, though named the *creator*, is not represented as such, but merely as the *pater magnus* (*pitamaha*) of all animated beings; since, in all accounts of the cosmogony, the formation of this universe is attributed to other causes. Nor does Shiva ever appear as the *destroyer*, and it is but obscurely intimated that he occasions the destruction of all things at the end of each *kalpa*. The *avatars*, however, of Vishnu might be considered as indications of his being the *preserver*; were it not that these manifestations of such a character are merely occasional and solicited, not spontaneous; and, at other times, he exerts not the constant watchfulness of a superintending providence. Of such a power, indeed, the very conception is unknown,

* Naradiya Puran, chap. 3.

and even incomprehensible, to the Hindus, who are firm believers in fate and predestination. In whatever manner this universe may have been created and life given to animated beings, laws were at the first imposed upon nature from which it never will deviate until all things become annihilated. To these laws Brahma, Vishnu, and Shiva are equally subject as the meanest reptile; and they can, therefore, act merely to that extent within which their powers were originally circumscribed. Nor are these great; for, though they may give to a certain degree new modifications to that illusion which assumes the form of matter, they can neither increase, diminish, nor annihilate it. But, as a belief in absolute fate seems inconsistent with that power over his own actions of which man is sensible, the Hindus, as it has been above observed, believe that the states of future being, to which they are subject, depend on the manner in which they shall conduct themselves in the present life; and, consequently, in the case of misfortune, their remark is not that it has been predestinated; but that it is the consequence of sin committed in a former birth. At the beginning of time, however, the whole series of these transmigrations was predestined; but whether absolutely, or merely conditionally, so as to admit of their being influenced, or their termination being accelerated, by the acts of man, is a question, which, as far as I am aware, has not been agitated by Indian metaphysicians or theologists: but all the religious observances and ascetic practices of the Hindus evince a firm belief in the latter opinion.

The Hindus at the same time believe that the apparent laws of nature might be interrupted by the power which holy men, and men unholy, and even women, particularly chaste wives, possessed of dooming by their curse any individual, with whom they were offended, to suffer such a metamorphosis, and for such a period, as they thought proper. But, after the curse had been once pronounced, it could not be recalled, and all that could then be done was for the curser to alleviate it as far as circumstances would admit. Thus by the curse of Shiva was Brahma deprived of temples and worship; Shiva himself was deprived of his share of sacrifices by the curse of Daksha; Vishnu's *avatars* were the consequence of his being cursed by Bhrigu; and the thousand eyes of

Indra were substituted, as an alleviation of a curse pronounced by Gautama, for other unseemly marks of the saint's displeasure. In short, the whole Hindu mythology rests principally on the effects produced by such curses; and on the devotional means adopted for procuring liberation from their effects. Another deviation from the laws of nature is supposed to have proceeded from individuals propitiating some one of the principal deities by devotional acts and penances of the most inconceivable nature, until the deity invoked at length granted them the boons which they wished for. As, however, the favours desired were, in general, supernatural power and exemption from death by all known means, the individuals who obtained them always converted them to the worst purposes, and, in consequence, either Vishnu or Shiva were obliged to redress such grievances by destroying the individuals who made so bad a use of the boons which had been bestowed upon them. But these means of effecting a change in the usual course of nature ceased at the end of Dwapar Yug; and in the present age, or Kali Yug, the possession of such powers or the exercise of such penances for the propitiation of a deity have been altogether unknown.

From the preceding remarks it will perhaps appear that the Hindus, admitting three divine hypostases and several inferior deities, have still always maintained the unity of God; and that, though they neither erect temples nor address any external worship to him, they nevertheless believe that he ought to be adored mentally and with devout abstraction. But it is, at the same time, undeniable that the Hindus are at this day divided into three great sects; the *Vaishnavas*, who reject the worship of Shiva and adore Vishnu as the Supreme Being; the *Shaivas*, who direct their devotion to Shiva under this character, and deny that Vishnu is an object deserving of worship; and the *Smartas*, who deem that both these gods are equally entitled to adoration, though most of them appear to consider Shiva as the deity to whom their devotion ought to be peculiarly addressed.* In the Vedas, how-

* It is singular that Mr. Colebrooke, Mr. Ward, and other writers in Bengal, take no notice of the sect of Smartas, though it is the prevalent one *under this name* in the Konkan, and in the whole of the Peninsula. Mr. Colebrooke, even, in a note in As. Res., p. 279.,

ever, in several of the Upanishads, in three of the Purans, the Brahmanda, Kurma, and Vaiu, and in the Institutes of Menu, Brahma appears to be the same as the Supreme Being. A very mistaken opinion, therefore, seems to prevail with respect to these sects; for Professor Creuzer has remarked: — "The Indian religion goes back to such remote antiquity, that its origin admits not of being ascertained by history; yet some general indications have been preserved even until our day, which evince that it has existed at different periods in three different states or systems. The oldest system is that which is involved in the obscurity of antiquity, and which was revealed by Brahma, the creator of the universe: this Brahma (who, according to the Indian doctrine, is the first and supreme person of the triad, God the Father), the first incarnate god and teacher, did men, many thousand years ago, adore in the purest and most pious manner, and with the holy innocence of simple hearts, offering him no bloody sacrifices, but only their first fruits, the milk of domestic animals, &c. But such a religion could not last on this wicked earth; it must decay, and be so utterly destroyed that not a trace remains of those ancient temples in which Brahma once was worshipped. . . . . About a thousand years after this primeval system

---

remarks that "*Shancara Acharya*, the celebrated commentator on the Veda, contended for the attributes of Shiva, and founded or confirmed the sect of Shaivas, who worship *Maha Deva* as the *Supreme Being, and deny the independent existence of Vishnu and other deities.*" The last two points, however, are not the distinguishing characteristics of the two sects of Vaishnava and Shaiva; but the rejection of the worship of either of these gods; and Shankara Acharya, though selecting Shiva as the peculiar object of devotion, denied not that adoration was equally due to Vishnu. So far, however, from exalting either of these deities to the place of the one God, the incessant endeavours of Shankara Acharya were directed to the restoring correct notions respecting the unity of God and his divine nature, and the whole of his writings, consequently, breathe nothing but the purest and sublimest theism.

I may observe, that the first Brahman with whom I commenced Sanscrit was a native of the Konkan, and a Smarta. He was willing to read with me any profane work, but declined to assist in the perusal of the Purans or any other sacred book. The one, Marayan Shastri, who now attends me, is a native of the Carnatic, and is not only a Smarta, but also a follower and a great admirer of Shankara Acharya. On showing him the sectarian marks in plate 2. of Moor's Pantheon, he immediately recognised the three horizontal lines with the circlet in the centre, as being the distinguishing mark of the Smartas, though this sect is also omitted by Major Moor.

had originated, religious wars ensued. Then appeared Shiva, the second incarnation, and brought with him the Lingam, the symbol of life and death. The ancient, pure, simple, and tranquil festivals must now cede the place to new orgies; religious enthusiasm hurried into the wildest ceremonies, and bloody sacrifices fell on the altars of the terrific Kali. The temples of Brahma were overthrown; but it is still known from the sacred writings of the temples of Sheringham, that Brahma had formerly there temples, altars, and images, as well as Shiva. Love and life, anger and death, were the characteristics of these new deities and of their worship. Next followed Vishnu, the third incarnation, who attempered the wild fire of Shivaism. Vishnu gave a milder form to the worship of the Lingam, purified it from its grossness, and softened its savageness by spiritualising it. . . . . But the sect of Shiva was not destroyed by the followers of Vishnu; and the two sects remained generally at peace with each other, and admitted of a common reformation, which was effected by Buddha, who appeared as the ninth incarnation, Vishnu, about thirty-six years after that of Krishna. The latter had attempted to overturn the worship of the Lingam, but had not succeeded. Buddhism, though it coincided in substance with the primeval system, set itself against that which had been the fundamental tenet of the catholic church during all the three periods, during which the predominance of the priesthood had prevailed; and abolished the restrictions of caste, and called persons from all classes to perform the functions of the priesthood. . . . . During this sundering of the old and new systems of Brahmanism and Buddhism, were composed the eighteen Purans by Vyasa, who was born 1600 years before Christ; and thus the sects which at the present day prevail in Hindustan are those of Shiva, Vishnu, and Buddha."* Mr. Patterson, also, has observed: — "The first founders of the Hindu religion do not appear to have had the intention of bewildering their followers with metaphysical definitions, their description of the Deity was confined to those attributes which the wonders of the creation so loudly attest: his almighty power to create; his providence to pre-

* Symbolik und Mythologie, vol. i. p. 568, et seq.

serve; and his power to annihilate or change what he has created. In fact, no idea of the Deity can be formed beyond this; it is simple, but it forces conviction on the mind. This simplicity, however, was destroyed, when they attempted to describe these attributes to the eye by hieroglyphics: perhaps letters had not been then invented; in which case they could have no other mode of instruction than by signs and emblematical figures. . . . . But the introduction of images soon led the mass of mankind to consider these personified attributes as real distinct personages; and as one error brings with it many in its train, men separated into sects, each selecting one of the triad as the particular object of their devotion, in preference to and exclusive of the others; the followers of Vishnu and Shiva invented each new symbols to ascribe to their respective divinity the attribute of creation.* This contention for preeminence ended in the total suppression of the worship of Brahma, and the temporary submission of the sect of Vishnu to the superiority of Shiva. But this did not last long; the two rival sects raised crusades against each other. Hordes of armed *fanatics*, under the titles of *Sannyasis* and *Vairagis*, enlisted themselves as champions of their respective faiths, the former devoted their lives in support of the superiority of Shiva, and the latter were no less zealous for the rights of Vishnu. Alternate victory and defeat marked the progress of a religious war, which for ages continued to harass the earth and inflame mankind against each other." †

But of such crusades and wars having ever occurred not the slightest indication is to be found in either the traditions or the sacred books of the Hindus. The worship, indeed, of Brahma has ceased; but the cause which produced this change in the Hindu religion is totally unknown. The great mass, also, of the Hindus are Smartas, though all who are so do not adopt this name‡; that is, they consider both

* This is incorrect, as the point of distinction which is contended for is, that either Vishnu or Shiva is the supreme being who produced the other.

† Asiatic Researches, vol. viii. p. 44—45.

‡ The Brahmans of the Deccan, for instance, and of Guzerat call themselves Shaivas; but they are in reality Smartas, as they do not reject the worship of Vishnu, though they consider it of less importance than that of Shiva. The same is the case with many of the Brahmans in other parts in India, who call themselves Vaishnavas, but consider Shiva as

Vishnu and Shiva to be equally entitled to adoration, though some of them identify either Vishnu or Shiva with the Supreme Being,—opinions which are clearly inculcated in several of the Purans. But, though in some of these works Vishnu is represented to be in some degree inferior to Shiva, still the latter himself is frequently introduced in the *Shaiva* Purans as enjoining the necessity of worshipping Vishnu, and explaining the mysterious nature of his incarnations; and in the same manner, though, in the *Vaishnava* Purans, the supremacy is ascribed to Vishnu, still the fullest justice is done to the divinity of Shiva: but the *Vaishnava* refuses all adoration to Shiva, in the same manner as the *Shaiva* denies Vishnu to be a proper object of worship. The *exclusive* votaries, therefore, of either of these deities are, comparatively speaking with respect to the population, by no means numerous in India; and the *Sannyasis* and *Vairagis*, who have in modern times occasionally acted in the manner stated by Mr. Patterson, are, according to all accounts, sects of very recent origin. To me, therefore, it appears that, according to the original principles of the Hindu religion, Brahma, Vishnu, and Shiva were considered to be equally entitled to the same reverence, to the same adoration, and to the same sacred honours; as they were each produced in the same ineffable manner from the essence of the Supreme Being. But, as the contemplation and worship of an invisible and untypified deity became too difficult for human faculties, the first professors of the Hindu religion began to identify with the one God some one of the divine hypostases, who were no doubt represented by visible symbols or images; and hence solely originated that preeminence which is ascribed to either Brahma, Vishnu, or Shiva, in their sacred books, and to one or other of the two latter by the Hindus of the present day. But such attribution of supremacy was not intended to deprive the other two divine hypostases of that adoration to which they were entitled; for the former preeminence and worship of Brahma are attested by these very books, a circumstance which strongly proves that they have suffered no new

---

entitled to adoration. The *real* Vaishnavas and Shaivas also have peculiar sectarian marks, which are never used by the others.

modelling or interpolation; and, whatever cause may have occasioned his being deprived of divine honours, it in no manner affected the opinions entertained with respect to the relative dignity of Vishnu and Shiva.

It must also be observed that to the votaries of each of these three gods are promised four degrees of beatitude, namely, cohabitation (inhabiting the same heaven), approximation, assimilation, and identification, independent of that final beatitude which consists in becoming identified with the essence of the Supreme Being. For in the Skanda Puran occurs this passage: —

Shiva, addressing Vishnu. — "Hear, O Vishnu! with faith, while, for the benefit of the world, I explain to thee the different degrees of beatitude; for these are various, but consist principally * of four kinds, viz., *Salokya* (cohabitation), *Samipya* (approximation), *Sarupya* (assimilation), and *Sayujya* (identification) the termination of pleasure and pain. Then becomes the soul unaffected by changes, being no longer subject to the effects of good and evil; and, being released from the delusions of duality, it reassumes its real essence. Then, liberated from all bonds and identified with Brahma, shall the soul enjoy bliss beyond all thought and expression; but other kinds of beatitude exempt not from the misery attendant on future births, as it is alone by successive degrees of celestial happiness that the soul acquires such purity as to admit of its identification with the Supreme Being. Thus, O lotos-eyed! there are various kinds of beatitude; for some souls attain assimilation to Shankara, some to Vishnu, and some to Brahma; for Brahma, Vishnu, and Mahesha were originally united in one essence, and from one essence were they derived. Other souls obtain approximation to Shankara, or to Vishnu, or to Brahma; and others abide in the same heaven with Shankara, Vishnu, or Brahma. Thus, according to its purity, and according to the wish by which its devotion has been directed, does the soul obtain different degrees of beatitude; but when the wish is fixed on becoming identified with the Supreme Being, and divine knowledge has been duly

* There are seven heavens appointed for the reception of souls according to the degrees of purity which they have acquired; the second lowest of which is the heaven of Indra, and the highest that of Brahma; but *Varkuntha* the abode of Vishnu, and *Kailasa* that of Shiva, are considered to be distinct from these heavens.

acquired, then is identification obtained, and the soul for ever released from the bonds of delusion."*

In this passage Shiva is considered to be the supreme Being, and, as he is the speaker, he is naturally made to restrict *Sayujya* to identification with himself; or, in other words, to use this term as signifying final beatitude. † But in other Purans *Sayujya* is predicated of both Brahma and Vishnu, and the terms employed for final beatitude, that is identification with the supreme Being, and not with one of the divine hypostases ‡, are *kaivalyam*, *moksha*, or *jivan-mukti*. It cannot, therefore, be doubted but that at one time an equality in divine power and honours was ascribed to Brahma, Vishnu, and Shiva; and, though but faint traces of the veneration, in which Brahma was originally held, occur in the Purans, still in these works the equality, or rather identity of Vishnu and Shiva are expressly and unequivocally inculcated. In proof of this, I quote the following two short passages, though many others to the same effect might be produced; for in the Naradiya Puran Vishnu thus speaks:—"But who can declare the greatness of him who assumes the form of the Lingam? for that form represents both Hara and Hari; since there is no difference between them, and he who thinks there is commits a sin. Both Hari and Shankara are gods without beginning or end, and none but sinful men sunk in ignorance make a distinction between them."§ And in the Padma Puran Shiva thus speaks:—"He who thus worships Vishnu in fact worships me, and whoever thinks otherwise shall be condemned to hell: for Vishnu Shiva, Shiva Vishnu, are but one form, though existing separately."||

* Skanda Puran, Suta Sanhita, 36th chapter.

† In the Lahyadri Khand, however, of the Skanda Puran, it is said:—"Brahma sprang from the right side of Shiva, Vishnu from the left, and Rudra from his middle. Whoever, therefore, meditates on Shiva will obtain the Sayujya of Rudra." (Chap. 38.) But here occurs that difficulty of distinguishing Rudra from Shiva, which I have pointed out in p. 172.; for as Shiva is here considered as the supreme Being, the writer should have said, *whoever meditates on Rudra and not on Shiva.*

‡ To which last alone the term Sayujya is properly applied.

§ Naradiya Puran, chapter 6th. In a stanza following shortly after it is said:—"The man who makes a distinction between Vishnu, Shiva, and Brahma, shall experience the torments of hell as long as the moon and stars shall endure."

|| Padma Puran, Uttara Khand, chapter entitled, *Ekadashi jagarana mahima.*

With respect to the other deities worshipped by the Hindus, Mr. Ward has affirmed that "this energy [of God] is said to have created the universe, and therefore this, as displayed in the grandest of the forms it assumes, is the object of worship. Hence the gods, the heavens collectively, the sun and moon, as well as the stars, the sea, mighty rivers, and extraordinary appearances in nature, receive the adoration of the Hindus. This energy itself has been personified and worshipped, not only in the form of Bhagavati, but as it is equally manifested in creation, in the government of the world, and in the work of destruction, in Brahma, Vishnu, and Shiva. The universe being full of the divine majesty, a deity has been consecrated as the regent of every element; and, to complete the mass of folly, the Brahman and devout mendicant, sharing more largely of the indwelling deity, have received the adoration of the multitude."* But Mr. Ward must here evidently employ the term *adoration* in some other than its usual meaning: for, in the second volume of his work, the only deities to whom he states that temples are erected in Bengal are Vishnu, Shiva, Durga, and Kali; and the only other deities besides these, as it appears from his first volume, to whom images are dedicated and any kind of worship is addressed are Brahma, Sarasvati, Lakshmi, Indra, Agni, Vaiu, Varuna, Yama, Ganesha, Skanda, Kamadeva, Surya, Soma, and the other five planets, and certain forms of Vishnu, Shiva, and Parvati. It is hence obvious that, if *adoration* and *worship* be synonymous terms, his general remarks are inconsistent with his particular statements; and it is the latter alone, consequently, which will be found to be correct.† If, however, there is nothing incongruous in the ideas thus beautifully expressed by Milton, why should the Hindus be blamed for supposing that angelic beings exist every where?

——"Nor think, though men were none,
That heaven would want spectators, God want praise:
Millions of spiritual creatures walk the earth
Unseen, both when we wake, and when we sleep;

* Ward's View of the Hindus, vol. i. p. 18.

† But even of those deities the Hindus consider five only to be principal objects of worship; viz. Vishnu, Shiva, Devi, Surya (the sun), and Ganesha.

All these with ceaseless praise His works behold
Both day and night: how often from the steep
Of echoing hill or thicket have we heard
Celestial voices to the midnight air,
Sole, or responsive each to other's note,
Singing their great Creator! Oft in bands,
While they keep watch, or nightly rounding walk,
With heavenly touch of instrumental sounds
In still harmonic number join'd, their songs
Divide the night, and lift our thoughts to heaven."

But to these "spiritual creatures" the Hindus address neither *dulia* nor *hyperdulia*, far less *latria;* and neither the veneration, therefore, with which they regard a sacred river or mountain, or other holy place*; nor even that reverence, sometimes amounting to prostration, with which they honour a personage deemed sacred, can be in the slightest degree considered as the same kind of adoration with which they approach the Deity.

There seems, consequently, to be much indistinctness, if not inconsistency, in the view which Mr. Colebrooke, in his Essay on the Vedas, has taken of the Hindu religion; for, he remarks that in them Indra or the firmament, fire, the sun, the moon, water, air, the spirits, the atmosphere, and the earth, are the objects most frequently addressed; and that every line is replete with allusions to mythology, and to the Indian notions of the divine nature and of celestial spirits. Not, however, he adds in a note, a mythology which avowedly exalts deified

* Did the Christians *adore* Jerusalem? when,

"Al gran piacer che quella prima vista
Dolcemente spirò nell' altrui petto,
Alta contrizion successe, mista
Di timoroso e reverente affetto.
Osano appena d' innalzar la vista
Ver la città, di Cristo albergo eletto,
Dove morì, dove sepolto fue,
Dove poi rivestì le membra sue.

"Sommessi accenti, e tacite parole,
Rotti singulti, e flebile sospiri
Della gente ch' in un s' allegra e duole,
Fan che per l' aria un mormorio s' aggiri."

Ger. Lib., canto iii. § v.—vi.

heroes (as in the Puranas); but one which personifies the elements and planets, and which peoples heaven and the world below with various orders of beings. "I observe, however," he continues, "in many places, the groundwork of legends, which are familiar in mythological poems; such, for example, as the demon Vritra slain by Indra, who is thence named *Vritrahan;* but I do not remark any thing that corresponds with the favourite legends of these sects, which worship either the *Lingam*, or *Shakti*, or else Rama or Krishna. *I except some detached portions, the genuineness of which appears doubtful;* as will be shown towards the close of this essay." But, instead of considering the allusions to the popular mythology, which occur in the Vedas, as being the *groundwork* of subsequent legends, would it not be much more consonant with reason and probability to conclude that these allusions actually referred to well known legends? For, otherwise, it will be evident that they must have been altogether unintelligible, expressed as they were with so much brevity, and, in fact, merely mentioned in that cursory manner, which is usual in adverting to circumstances perfectly notorious. In which case it would also appear most likely that the legends had been previously collected, and rendered accessible to every one by having been recorded in those very works which are still extant under the name of Purans; for it is quite impossible to discover in the Purans a single circumstance which has the remotest semblance to the deification of heroes, and such a notion is totally unknown to the Hindus. But it is obviously from the influence of so erroneous an opinion that Mr. Colebrooke has been led to remark, in the same essay, "that the antiquity of some of the Puranas now extant is more than questionable; and the authenticity of any one in particular does not appear to be as yet sufficiently established;" and to express doubt respecting the genuineness of several portions of the Vedas and Upanishads. If, however, citation and commentation be valid grounds, as Mr. Colebrooke very justly argues, for maintaining the authenticity of the Vedas, the former of these reasons applies even more forcibly to the Purans, as quotations from them, or allusions to circumstances contained in them, pervade all Sanscrit literature; and, though they have not been equally authenticated by commentaries, still the very

Puran, the Bhagawat, which Mr. Colebrooke is inclined to think was composed only six hundred years ago, has been commented by two or three individuals, and the Vishnu Puran, with the Kashi Khand of the Skanda Puran has likewise been commented. But that the Avatars of Vishnu are alluded to in the Vedas seems indubitable from this verse, quoted by Mr. Colebrooke himself: —" *Thrice did Vishnu step, and at three strides traversed the universe; happily was his foot placed on this dusty earth:*" *—which so unquestionably relates to the *Vaman Avatar.* Not the slightest difference, therefore, appears to exist between the descriptions of the Hindu religion given in the Vedas and in the Purans, except that in the first allusions only are made to circumstances which are detailed at greater or lesser length in the latter. The objects of worship †, however, and the theological doctrines, are in both precisely the same; and it may, consequently, be reasonably concluded that, so far from the Purans being spurious and of recent composition, they are, in fact, of equal antiquity with the Vedas; since the Vedas themselves must evidently be unintelligible, were it not for the explanations contained in the Purans.

The deities, consequently, which have been worshipped by the Hindus from the remotest times, are the three divine hypostases and their female energies; certain forms, in which Vishnu, Shiva, and Devi have manifested themselves; and impersonifications of the firmament, the air, fire, water, and the earth. The sun and the sacred fire have also been deemed peculiarly entitled to adoration; but the moon and the other planets are considered only as inferior objects of worship. Nor to these deities have there been added, during a course of three thousand years, any deified heroes, or any other gods, supposing that they are not mentioned in the Vedas, which point is not yet ascertained, than Ganesha, Yama, Skanda, Kama, and the Ashwinau ‡: for all the other angelic beings receive no divine honours, nor are they in any manner worshipped by the great mass of Hindus; though

* Asiatic Researches, vol. v. p. 359.

† I must except the Lingam, the worship of which does not appear to be mentioned in either the Vedas or the Upanishads.

‡ I have, however, observed in the Rig Veda the names of Yama and the Ashwinau; and of the Upanishads, composing the Atharva Shiras, one is entitled *Ganapati Upanishad.*

sacred rites are, on certain occasions, addressed by the Brahmans to the angels, and to the regents of the eight quarters collectively, and also to some others of these spiritual creatures.

There is, at the same time, a peculiarity in the Hindu religion that is not sufficiently adverted to; which is, that the performance of all religious ceremonies and duties has been confided to one single class; and that the great mass of the people are not required to evince their faith by any external worship of God at stated times. * The sacrifices, the processions, the orgies, and even the meeting together for devotional purposes, by which other religions have been distinguished, are all totally unknown to the Hindus. The view, therefore, given of this religion by Mr. Ward is radically erroneous, because he seems never to have attempted to distinguish between the religious duties of the priest and those of the layman; and in judging, consequently, of its merits and demerits, he has employed a criterion which is obviously inapplicable; for he remarks: — "The reader will perceive that, in all these religious ceremonies, not a particle is found to interest or amend the heart; no family Bible, profitable for doctrine, for reproof, for instruction in righteousness, that men may be thoroughly furnished with all good works; no domestic worship; no pious assembly, where the village preacher —

> "Attempts each art, reproves each dull delay,
> Allures to brighter worlds, and leads the way;"

no standard of morals to repress the vicious; no moral education, by which the principles of virtue and religion may be implanted in the youthful mind. Here every thing that assumes the appearance of religion ends (if you could forget its impurity) in an unmeaning ceremony, and leaves the heart cold as death to every moral principle." † Of this passage the correctness must depend entirely upon what is considered to be morality; for it must be admitted that the youth of

* But no individual of the three inferior castes can obtain final beatitude until he has been born a Brahman; and thus rendered capable of perusing the Vedas, and performing all those other acts of devotion which he was not allowed to practise in his former births, but the performance of which is indispensable for purifying the soul.

† Ward's View of the Hindus, vol. i. p. 83.

India are not educated in that moral and religious manner which a Christian missionary would no doubt prescribe. But if filial love and respect, fraternal affection, kindness to every animated being, the detestation of every dishonest act, adherence to truth, and, in short, all that can form the mind to rectitude, be admitted to constitute morality, such are the lessons which are carefully taught to every Hindu child. Nor are even the minor morals neglected; so that in propriety and decorum of manners the Hindu will, in general, be found to surpass the European, child.

The polytheism, also, which prevails in India does not prevent the parents and the spiritual teacher from inculcating into the minds of the young those general principles which result from the belief in one God, since that, in fact, is the real faith of the Hindu. Whether, therefore, the *God* and *Lord*, to whom the reverence and fear of the child are directed, is Vishnu or Shiva, is perfectly immaterial; since it is equally taught that there is a supreme Being, who punishes the wicked and rewards the good, and whose favour and mercy can be obtained solely by virtue and piety. Although, also, it cannot be denied that there are not a few censurable legends in the sacred books of the Hindus, still those selected for the instruction of youth are never liable to objection, as they always contain the purest principles of morality, and exalted notions of the Deity; though the Christian world would, of course, disapprove of some of the observances and tenets which the Hindu children are necessarily taught, as constituting the religion of their fathers.

It will hence, perhaps, appear that, in the Hindu religion, monotheism and polytheism are so intimately blended together*, both in their

* Cudworth contends that the same was the case with the other ancient systems of polytheism, for he remarks: — " Wherefore a god, in general, according to the sense of the Pagan theists, may be thus defined: *an understanding being superior to men, not originally derived from senseless matter, and looked upon as an object for men's religious worship.* But this general notion of the word *god* is again restrained and limited by differences in the division of it. For such a god as this may be either αγεννητος, *ingenerate* or *unproduced*, and consequently self-existent; or else γεννητος, *generated* or *produced*, and dependent on some higher being as its *cause*. In the former sense the intelligent Pagans, as we have declared, acknowledged only *one God*, who was, therefore, called by them ὁ Θεος κατ' εξοχην. According to that of Thales in Laertius, Πρεσβυτερον των οντων ὁ Θεος, αγεννητον γαρ· *God is the oldest of*

sacred books, which were most likely composed more than 3000 years ago, and in the daily thoughts of the Hindus of the present day, as to render it probable that neither of these two systems preceded the other, but that they were both actually coeval in origin. The polytheism, however, which now prevails in India is evidently not a complete system; for, though perfectly homogeneous, and free from every appearance of foreign innovation, it still exhibits a want of connection in several of its parts, and presents but few and faint indications of the causes which originally produced its peculiar form. It cannot, also, but excite surprise, that a distinct class of priests, who restricted to themselves the cultivation of all learning, should never have thought it requisite to remedy this incompleteness, or even to reduce to uniformity the variant circumstances which occur in their sacred books. For they content themselves with observing that, in whatever number of different manners a legend may be related, they are all equally true; because the events did actually take place exactly as they are described, but at different periods, and in distinct renovations of this universe: since it is the belief of the Hindus that this universe has been destroyed and renovated 18,000 times; and that the same personages appear, though occasionally under different names, and nearly the same circumstances happen during each period of its duration. In this system of polytheism, however, it is impossible to discover the slightest indication of recent invention or foreign innovation; because, though in it a few *lacunæ* are perceptible, the perfect concordancy with which the existent parts harmonise with each other is so undeniable, as to leave no reasonable doubt that the Hindu religion is, at the present day, in precisely the same state in which it existed more than three thousand years ago.

But this religion evidently comprises two perfectly distinct systems,

---

things, because he is unproduced, and the only thing that is so; but in the latter they admitted of *many gods*, many understanding beings, which, though *generated* or *produced*, yet were superior to men, and looked upon as objects for their religious worship. And thus the Pagan theists were both *polytheists* and *monotheists* in different senses, as they acknowledged both *many gods* and *one God;* that is, *many inferior deities* subordinate to *one supreme.*" — *Intellectual System*, book i. chap. iv. sect. 14.

and in forming, therefore, any opinion respecting it, the theological doctrines ought always to be carefully distinguished from the polytheistic tenets, in which the Hindus at the same time believe: for the unity of God, and the identity of the human soul with the divine essence, are considered to be truths of too sacred and mysterious a nature to admit of their being discussed, except upon particular occasions and with the utmost reverence. They, consequently, do not appear to exert much, if any, influence on the great mass of the Hindus; and hence the adoration and fear of God under some one of his supposed forms, a belief in the immateriality and immortality of the soul, and in a future state of reward and punishment, and the practice of those acts of devotion by which beatitude is to be obtained, are the fundamental doctrines of his religion, by which a Hindu is more or less guided and actuated during the whole course of his life. But, as he is likewise instructed that identification with one supreme self-existent God, distinct from the deities which he is in the habit of worshipping, is the sole means by which he can be liberated from the miseries of this life, and from liability to future states of being, it must necessarily follow that every Hindu, who is in the least acquainted with the principles of his religion, must in reality acknowledge and worship God in unity. Men, however, are born with different capacities, and it is therefore necessary (as the Brahmans maintain) that religious instruction should be adapted to the powers of comprehension of each individual; and hence a succession of heavens, a gradation of deities, and even their sensible representation by images, are all considered to be lawful means for exciting and promoting piety and devotion. The man who might be incapable of comprehending the existence and divine nature of an invisible and immaterial Being, might easily understand the *avatars* of Vishnu; and, from being made sensible of the superhuman powers manifested in them, might be led to raise his ideas still higher, and to form correct notions of Deity. Placed at the bottom of a flight of steps, no person can at once spring to the top, but must ascend gradually from step to step; and it is in the same manner that the feeble powers of man can only by intermediate helps, as successive gradations of instruction and new births, attain the knowledge of the real nature of God. But such means being requisite for dispelling the ignorance of created beings, and for enlightening them with divine knowledge, affects not the unity of God ; and all these apparently diverging paths, which the worship of different deities presents, lead but to one and the same object.

CHAP. VII.

THE THEOGONY OF THE HINDUS : — THE SUPREME BEING.

For the explanation of the opinion which the Hindus entertain respecting the Supreme Being, I shall avail myself of these very correct remarks of Dr. Taylor : — " From this brief statement," as he observes, " of the fundamental doctrine maintained by the followers of the Vedanta, I think we may infer that their philosophy is founded on the contemplation of one infinite Being, existing under two states or modifications. The first state is that of a pure, simple, abstract essence, immovable and quiescent; the second state is that of a Being displaying motion, or active qualities. * . . . The fundamental principle of the Vedanta philosophy is, that the universe is one simple, unextended, indivisible Being, who is destitute of all qualities and attributes, but who is denominated the true, the living, the happy, to distinguish him from visible but illusory and unreal appearances. It is evident that no description can be given of this Being: hence, in answering enquiries, the Vedantikas sometimes say that he is nothing; which must be understood merely to intimate a negation of sensible qualities, figure, extension, &c., and also of mental affections, passion, &c. Whilst this Being remains in a state of rest, there is no visible world, or sensitive existences; but when, at the impulse of desire, motion is excited in him, all the variety of appearances and sensations which form this universe are displayed. The first condition of this Being is called *nirgun*, or without quality; the second condition is that of *sagun*, or with quality. † The question, how does desire or volition arise in this simple

* Prabod'h Chandrodaya, p. 111.

† Here, however, a difficulty arises; for in a note to this play, p. 8., Dr. Taylor remarks, — " During this sleep of Maya, the Deity perceives a variety of phenomena, and is under the influence of passion, — a state incompatible with pure intellect, which, like crystal, is clear and without any diversity of appearance : hence, while the world exists, God is in a state different from that of simple being or intellect; and the question is, how will he again return

Being? forms the subject of many disputes; but I believe that even the subtlety of Hindu metaphysics has not yet furnished a satisfactory reply." *

But this opinion respecting the nature of a Supreme Being is not confined to the followers of the Vedanta; for every Hindu of the least information is more or less acquainted with it. Mr. Ward, therefore, correctly observes, — "It is true, indeed, that the Hindus believe in the unity of God. *One Brahm without a second* is a phrase very commonly used by them when conversing on subjects relating to the nature of God. They believe, also, that God is almighty, allwise, omnipresent, omniscient, &c.; and they frequently speak of him as embracing in his government the happiness of the good, and the punishment of the bad: yet they have no idea of God's performing any act, either of creation or providence, except through the gods."† But it is evident that such a Being can be only the object of devout meditation; and that the representing him by images, or the honouring him by the institution of sacred rites and the erection of temples, must be perfectly incompatible with every conceivable notion of an all-pervading, immaterial, and incorporeal Spirit. It is difficult, therefore, to understand what Mr. Ward intended by this remark: — "It is a painful reflection, that not a single Hindu temple, dedicated to the one God, is to be found in all Hindusthan; nor is any act of worship, in any form, addressed by this people to God."‡ For would the heinousness of idolatry be in the slightest degree lessened, in consequence of the idolatrous worship being addressed to the one God?

In this statement, however, Mr. Ward is incorrect: because the Hindus, on ceasing to adore an invisible and untypified Deity, did from remote times invest either Brahma, Vishnu, or Shiva, with the character

to this condition?" But from all that I have heard and read on the subject, I am led to conclude that there must be here some mistake: for, though the manifestation of this universe continued after it had been willed by the Supreme Being, yet in him the volition immediately ceasing, he then returned to his original state; and thus he is invariably described as quiescent, and without form, quality, or affection of any kind.

* Prabod'h Chandrodaya, p. 107.

† Ward's View of the Hindus, vol. i. p. 1.

‡ Ibid.

and attributes of the one God; and, even at this day, the *Smarta* in worshipping Shiva or Vishnu, the *Vaishnava* in directing his devotion to Vishnu, and the *Shaiva* in glorifying Shiva, address not their adoration to one of the divine hypostases, but to him whom they deem to be the Supreme Being. But in thus transferring the character of the supreme God to one of the divine hypostases, this hypostasis necessarily became the producer of the other two. Such a mode, however, of originating the triad being directly contrary to the tenet of this religion, which holds that the supreme God is perfectly distinct from the three beings whom he has produced; the sacred writers endeavour to obviate this contradiction by establishing a difference between Hiranyagarbha and the four-faced Brahma, between Narayana and Vishnu, and between Shiva and Rudra or Mahesha; the former name being applied to each in the character of the Supreme Being, and the latter in that of a divine hypostasis. But the distinction is so badly maintained during the course of a Upanishad or a Puran, that it becomes, in general, quite impossible to perceive any difference in the two characters intended. Hence, as the term THEOGONY can properly apply only to the triad and their female energies (the other deities and angels being the descendants of the sons or grandsons and grandaughters of Brahma, according to the usual manner of mortal generation), the Supreme Being and the divine hypostases are necessarily always mentioned together in the sacred books of the Hindus; and it would seem, therefore, that the belief in one God, and in the impossibility of his rendering his power manifest except through the intervention of other celestial beings, were coexistent and fundamental tenets of this religion from its very first origin.

The apparent discordancy, therefore, which occurs in the descriptions of these three principal gods, in consequence of the character and attributes of each being ascribed collectively to either Brahma, Vishnu, or Shiva, proceeds from each of them being in such cases considered, not as a divine hypostasis, but as the Supreme Being himself. Another opinion, however, of the Hindus, respecting the exercise of the power of God, is not so intelligible: for they impersonify his energy under a female form, which they consider as the actual agent in producing the illusive appearances of which this universe consists; and that, as similar female energies were requisite for rendering the powers of the three divine hypostases effective, the energy of the Supreme Being, in order to originate them, multiplied herself into three female forms, which were respectively denominated Saraswati, Lakshmi, and Parvati.

But the following extracts will best explain this subject:—

The Kaivalya Upanishad.

Ashwalayana, having approached Brahma, thus addressed him:— "O lord! instruct me in the knowledge of God, that most excellent and hidden truth, which is sought for by both good and bad men; and by which sin being destroyed, the enlightened man obtains identification with the most excellent Being." *Pitamaha replied:*—"By faith, piety, meditation, and devout abstraction, is immortality obtained, and not by works, or progeny, or wealth, or ascetic practices. Those whose minds are illumined with divine knowledge, and who have, by devout abstraction, become acquainted with the real nature of things, are released from liability to death, and become identified with the immortal essence of the Supreme Being. To obtain, therefore, this knowledge, let the aspirant remain seated on a properly selected spot, immovable, and in an erect posture, having the complete command of his passions, and being obedient to the instructions of his spiritual teacher, with his heart pure and free from all affections; and thus let him meditate intensely on that inconceivable, imperceptible, eternal, happy, placid, and immortal form, the source of divine knowledge; that form which is without beginning, or middle, or end; which enjoys eternal blessedness, and is deserving of all admiration. Whether it be considered as Shiva, the supreme Lord, the three-eyed, the black-necked, the destroyer [or as any other of the principal deities], he who meditates upon it will acquire divine knowledge, the dispeller of the illusive darkness in which he is involved; and he will then become convinced that that form is Brahma, and Shiva, and Indra, unchangeable, and of itself supreme; that it is Vishnu, and the vital breath, and time, and fire, and the moon; that it is all which is, or was, or will be until all eternity. He who knows this truth becomes liberated from mortality, and there is no other way. All that exists is *spirit*; and not until the soul perceives that there is nothing but *spirit*, will it obtain identification with the Supreme Being. Having, however, made the soul the under piece of wood, and the mystic word *Om* the upper, by the exercise of their friction* will scepticism be destroyed, and replaced by true knowledge. Then will it be known that He causes by his delusion all things to assume a material appearance; and that in this life, as in a dream, man finds delight in eating, drinking, and other enjoyments; but soon as he awakes they yield no longer pleasure: for the joys and pleasures of this life are as unreal as dreams; and as these occur not in the time of profound repose, so do they disappear to him who, by devout abstraction, has been enabled to awake from the sleep of illusion. Thus, in the three states of dreaming, profound abstraction, and awakening to the full consciousness of its own nature, does the soul sport, until it attain identification with that blessed, intelligent, indivisible, and universal essence; from which proceeded the vital breath, the mind, the senses, the ether, air, fire, water, and the earth, and all that it contains. When, therefore, awakening from the deceptive dreams of illusion, thou art enlightened by divine knowledge, then wilt thou learn that the supreme and eternal Spirit is the sole and universal shrine, and that thou thyself art that Spirit; and thus, being convinced that *I am Brahm*, thou wilt be released from the bonds of illusion. Then wilt thou know that I alone am the object of enjoyment, the enjoyer and the joy, always happy, the primeval source of existence; that by me all things were created, are preserved, and shall finally be destroyed; and that no other god than I exists: for I am less than the least, and greater than the greatest, universal and wonderful; I am the ancient of days, the primeval male, the supreme Lord, possessed of a refulgent and felicitous form. Without hands or feet, my power is beyond conception; without eyes I see; and without ears I hear. I know the nature of all forms, but nothing exists

* This alludes to the friction of two pieces of a particular wood, by which fire for sacred purposes is produced.

that knows my real essence; for I am incomprehensible. I am the Vedas, and the divine knowledge which they contain. Virtue and vice affect not me, nor am I subject to life and death; nor for me exist the earth, water, fire, air, and ether. By thus learning the nature of that Spirit which is supreme, mysterious, wonderful, undivided, adualistic, omnipresent, without entity or nonentity, absorbed in bliss, immaculate and omnipotent, divine knowledge, which destroys the sea of illusion, will be acquired, and the advantage which will result from its acquisition will be final beatitude."

From the Naradiya Puran.

Narada said: —"Narayana, imperishable, eternal, omnipresent, devoid of affections, by whom all things movable and immovable are pervaded, having at the origin of creation invested himself with three qualities and assumed three forms, rendered by his effulgence this universe manifest. Then, for the purposes of creating, did he produce Brahma from his right side; of destroying, Rudra from his middle; and of preserving, Vishnu from his left side: and the Supreme Being having thus, at the beginning of time, assumed three forms, is sometimes called Brahma, sometimes Vishnu, and sometimes Shiva. Of that God the *Shakti* (energy), the imperceptible cause of the manifestation of this universe, is celebrated as possessed of two twofold natures, entity and nonentity, knowledge and ignorance. Whenever, by separation from Narayana, she manifests this universe, then is ignorance produced, and various pains are the consequence; but when it is known that there is nothing but one essence, then is knowledge acquired and illusion destroyed. Thus the *Maya** of the Supreme Being, when separated from him, is the cause which gives apparent reality to this universe, and to all the anxieties and sufferings to which mortality is doomed; but when she remains unseparated from him, then is she the cause of this world's ceasing to be. All things movable and immovable exist only as the effects of *Maya*; and when, therefore, her power is with-

* This word is synonymous with *Shakti*.

drawn, they sink into non-existence. But it is ignorance alone which enables *Maya* to impress the mind with a sense of individuality; for as soon as that is dispelled, it is known that severalty exists not, and that there is nothing but one undivided whole: for as this whole is pervaded by Narayana, he and Maya must necessarily subsist together as fire in the brand.

" This *Shakti* is sometimes named *Uma*, sometimes *Lakshmi*, or *Saraswati*, or *Ambika*, or *Durga*, or *Bhadra-Kali*, or *Chandi*, or *Maheshwari*, or *Kaumari*, or *Vaishnavi*, or *Indrani*; sometimes *Brahmi*, or Knowledge, or Ignorance, or Maya, and by holy sages she is named *Prakriti*. It is this *Shakti*, which is the efficient cause of this universe, and visibly or invisibly pervades and dwells in all things. *Purusha*, *Prakriti*, and *Kala** are the threefold causes of creation, preservation and destruction. Their complete union is the form of *Parabrahm;* and, when disunited, a God receives his name from each: for he who creates, is called Brahma; who preserves, Vishnu; and who destroys, Shiva. *Parabrahm*, however, is a Spirit supreme, enjoying bliss ineffable, immaculate, eternal, devoid of qualities, and exempt from illusion; but, as he once subjected himself to the consciousness of individuality, fools suppose to be corporeal and divisible that all-pervading, undivided, and glorious essence." — Chapter 3.

From the Lainga Puran.

Suta addressed the Sages: — " Shiva, the mighty Lord and God, is the supreme and self-existent Spirit; and, though invisible, by his divine power has a wonderful work been manifested; but he is one devoid of senses, immortal, immovable, imperishable, eternal, actuated by no will except his own, without beginning or end, the body of all things, but himself incorporeal, the always existent Parabrahm. . . . . At the time of creation this God issued from the mundane egg in a corporeal form resplendent as the sun; and then sprang from his left side Vishnu, the adored by men and gods, and Lakshmi; and from his right

* The active and passive powers of Nature and Time.

side Brahma and Sarasvati. From that egg did he produce these worlds into the day of existence, but at the stated time will he reduce them into the dark night of annihilation; and then, desirous of manifesting himself, will the supreme Lord create again the universe. Manifestation, therefore, and disappearance, are the accidents peculiar to this universe: for, when the three qualities are equally united together, then all things are invisible; but, when opposition and predominance take place between them, then entities become evident. As in sesamuin oil, and in milk butter, exist though unperceived, thus the universe exhibits the effects of the mutation and interchange of the three qualities; and thus Maheshwara at one time diffuses the dark night of nonentity, and at another causes to shine the bright day of existence. As soon as he wills creation, then are produced from his divine essence three gods, the lords of this universe, eternal, profoundly mysterious, in reality spiritual though in appearance corporeal; and thus, as there are three Vedas, three qualities, three worlds, and three fires, so are there three gods who depend upon and assist each other, and, together mutually subsisting and acting, are never for a moment disunited. Shiva is the supreme God; Vishnu also is supremely eminent; and Brahma, being united to the quality of impurity, is the creator of all things. At the beginning of time, by the will of Ishwara, the cause of entity and nonentity, the three qualities becoming disproportionately combined, visibility was produced from invisibility, and the powers of Vishnu and Brahma for framing and preserving this universe were originated. Thus there is but one Supreme Being, though assuming three forms, whose divine nature is wonderful and incomprehensible." —Part I. chapter 68.

From the Skanda Puran.

Suta addressed the Sages. — "I will explain to you the profoundly mysterious essence of all the *Shastras,* with which, O Brahmans! having become acquainted, never again will man be subject to mortality: for the truth of most importance to be known is the real nature of the supreme Spirit but when it is so difficult to understand the nature of our own souls, how much more unattainable must it be for our littleness to comprehend the mightiness of divine spirits. Rudra, however, and Vishnu, and Brahma sometimes render themselves manifest; but knowledge convinces us that these are merely three forms of one Supreme Being, who is not, in reality, an object visible to our senses. Through his favour alone it is, that by the manifestation of other gods we are enabled to comprehend his essence; and, after having with steadfast faith meditated profoundly on this mysterious truth, to obtain identification with the supreme Spirit. As, therefore, those three forms are his efficient agents, let us always with delight devoutly meditate on the celestial figures of Rudra, Vishnu, and Brahma; who, when they proceeded from his essence, were not subjected to the accidents of this life: for it is in consequence of Maya that the human soul ceases to be identical with the supreme soul, and man becomes liable to virtue and vice; to anger, hate, and other passions; to birth and death, and all the miseries of this mortal state: but Brahma, Vishnu, and Rudra are exempt from all accidents and qualities peculiar to man. Yet are not these three gods equal to Shiva [the Supreme Being], and whoever considers them as such shall visit the regions of hell; for Vishnu, Brahma, and the other gods, acknowledge the supremacy of Shiva, who can alone grant liberation from all the terrors of existence. Let those, therefore, who wish for final beatitude, continually meditate on the real nature of Shiva; since the powers of Brahma, Vishnu, and the other gods, operate only in connection with the illusive appearances produced by Maya: but it is reality, and not unreality, that ought to be the object of devout meditation; and, consequently, as neither Vishnu nor Brahma can effect emancipation from the influence of these unreal appearances, it is solely by acquiring a knowledge of the true essence of that supreme and universal God in whom all power and divinity is centred, that final beatitude can be obtained."—*Suta Sanhita*, the Part entitled *Yadgna-veibhava*, chap. 6.

It is not, however, in separate Purans only that preeminence is ascribed to either of these gods, or even to Brahma; but this distinction also occurs in the very same Puran: for, as far as I have observed, there are but five Purans in which the supremacy is uniformly given to one deity; namely, the Lainga and Shiva, in which Shiva is identified with the Supreme Being; the Vishnu and the Bhagavat, in which this honour is assigned to Vishnu; and the Brahma Vaivarta, in which Krishna is represented as the Supreme Being, and his beloved mistress Radha as his *Shakti* or energy: but in no Puran have I remarked any circumstance or injunction which virtually or expressly sanctions the rejection of the worship of either Vishnu or Shiva, as practised by the exclusive votaries of these gods. Nor, even with respect to Brahma, is the cessation of his divine honours in any manner authorised by any passages which occur in the sacred books of the Hindus; for the legend respecting his being deprived of them by the curse of Shiva does not specify the Kalpa in which this event happened, nor the length of time during which the effects of this curse were to operate. The speculations, consequently, in which the literati of Europe have indulged with respect to Brahmaism, Vishnuism, and Shivaism, are completely at variance with the opinions of the Hindus of the present day, and with all that is contained in their sacred books, as the following extracts will sufficiently evince: —

From the Padma Puran.

Shiva, addressing Parvati. — "Now will I explain to you, O lovely daughter of Himawan, the divine nature of *Narayana.** Narayana is eternal, immutable; the sacrificer of all that ought to be sacrificed, the hearer of all that ought to be heard, the creator of all that ought to be created; the primeval male, who appeared with a thousand heads and a thousand eyes: he it was who rendered manifest these worlds; and who is all that has been, is, or shall be. He, Wasudeva, is the always existing Hiranyagarbha and the Sun, the supreme Lord of this universe, exempt from illusion, the supreme and indivisible Spirit. . . . . That God was the first by whom the Vedas were delivered, and who is their sole end and object. His divine power is of a two-

* Here follow various explanations of the name Narayana; amongst others occurs the signification given in the Institutes of Menu, which is the one generally received.

fold nature; for in his sport he creates and he destroys, and, though his spiritual essence is invisible, he sometimes manifests himself in a corporeal form. He is the Lord and enjoyer of sacrifice, the sacrificer and the victim; for, when he assumed the form of Virat, then did he [as Hiranyagarbha] perform with himself an expiatory sacrifice for the three worlds; and from that sacrifice have been derived all other sacrificial and lustratory ceremonies. From the body, also, of that divine victim were formed all things movable and immovable; his countenance became the splendour of day, his lower extremities the earth, his mind the moon, his eyes the sun, his mouth fire, his head the heavens, and his vital breath the air. Thus all things were produced from Vishnu, and hence is Vishnu named the universal form; and, as he has created it, thus also in his sport will he devour the universe, and again create it from his own essence, like the web produced by the spider."*

Shiva, addressing Rama. — "That eternal, imperishable, incorporeal, and supreme God, Shiva, though exempt from quality, yet, being desirous of creation, assumed the three qualities, and then separated from his spiritual essence three hypostases. From his right side proceeded Brahma, from his left Vishnu, and from his back Rudra; and thus did that God produce three sons. Scarcely were they born, when they thus enquired: — 'O Lord! who art thou? and who are we?' Shiva replied: — 'You are my sons; and I am your father, who have generated you for beneficial purposes, in a mysterious and ineffable manner.' The sons said: — 'O Lord! inform us what quâlity shall we each assume? and until what period shall we be subjected to its

* Uttara Khand, the chapter entitled *Mantrartha*.

In the sixth volume of the Journal Asiatique, p. 8., M. Burnouf, in consequence of the defectiveness of the manuscript at his disposal, has inaccurately stated that this Puran consists of two Khands only. But it contains six: viz. the *Adi* or Swarga, *Bhumi*, *Brahma*, *Patala*, *Shrishti*, and *Uttara*; and, with exception of the Skanda, is by far the longest of all the Purans. Can *le traité, ou plutôt l'éloge, de la plante sacrée du lotus*, mentioned by M. Langlès as forming part of the contents of this Puran, be the *Pushkara Mahatmiam*, or the legend respecting the celebrated temple and lake of *Pushkara* (now Pokur) near Ajmere, which occurs in the Shrishti Khand; and which place received that name in consequence of Brahma having once dropped, by accident, from heaven, upon that spot, a *pushkara*, or lotos?

influence?' Shiva replied: —'As long as the universe endures, so long shall your existence last; and, during that period, let each of you assume one of the three qualities, — Vishnu that of purity, Brahma that of impurity, and Rudra that of darkness.'" *

From the Kurma Puran.

Vishnu, in the form of the Kurma, addressing the Sages, and having explained the formation of the mundane egg, thus continues: — "In order to give completeness to this work, the Supreme Being, under the form of *Brahma*, having entered the egg, caused it to attain maturity; and hence, from having been the first corporeal form, is Brahma named the primeval male; and he, also, is the original cause of all things. . . . Thus have I explained to you, O Brahmans! the mysterious formation of that egg, and you will hence perceive that it was the first form under which the Supreme Being manifested himself; the next was that of *Hiranyagarbha*, who issued from that golden egg; then, for the purpose of delivering the Vedas and creating the universe, he united himself to the quality of impurity, and appeared as the four-faced Brahma; to preserve, likewise, these worlds, he has combined himself with the quality of purity, and assumed the form of Vishnu; and at the end of time will that Supreme Being, uniting himself to the quality of darkness, under the character of Rudra, destroy this universe. Thus there is but one omnipotent God, who, though devoid of affection and quality, yet invests himself with the three qualities, and appears under three forms, for the purposes of creation, preservation, and destruction. At first he manifested himself as *Hiranyagarbha*, always existing, the first God, unproduced, eternal, of nature incomprehensible; *Brahma*, the Lord of created beings, and hence named *Prajapati;* the greatest amongst the gods, and hence called *Mahadeva;* the supreme Lord, and hence denominated *Parameshwara*. But why should I enter into a long description of this God, when this universe is a manifestation of his divine essence; and,

* Patala Khand, the chapter entitled *Bhasmotpatti widhanam.*

though appearing under different forms and names, he still remains the one sole, self-existent, and supreme God?" — Part I. chapter 4.

The Kurma, addressing the Sages. — " All was one tremendous ocean, in which Narayana, with a thousand heads and a thousand eyes, reposing on Shesha, slumbered profoundly; and while thus immersed in mysterious sleep, the thought of creation arose in his mind. Instant then, in divine and wondrous sport, a lotos sprang from his pure navel, expanding to the distance of a hundred yojans, refulgent as the young sun, blooming with sacred petals and filaments, and diffusing celestial fragrance; and from this lotos, after a long time had elapsed, was produced Brahma. Bewildered by illusion, he immediately approached the universal Lord, and, awakening him with his hand, thus addressed him in gentle accents: — ' In this tremendous, unpeopled, and darkness-involved ocean, why, O Lord! dost thou repose, solitary and alone?' Vishnu, smiling, replied in a voice loud as the clashing of clouds: — ' O excellent being! Know that I am Narayana, the one God, the Lord of all things; and behold in me the creator of the universe, and the great father of all animated beings: but who art thou?' Brahma replied: — ' I am Dhata, Vidhata, Swayambhu, Brahma, the origin of the Vedas.' On hearing these words, Vishnu, by means mysterious, entered the body of Brahma, and within it beheld comprised the three worlds, with angels, demons, and men: and, having then issued from his mouth, Vishnu thus addressed Brahma: — ' Now, O Lord! enter within me, and behold there also the three worlds.' Having heard this agreeable speech, Brahma immediately entered within Vishnu, and there viewed with wonder this universe, and all that it contains. But, while he wandered, contemplating it, Vishnu closed the gates *, and Brahma could find no exit except through the stem of the lotos, from which he had been produced; and then, seated on its flower, he thus addressed Vishnu, in a voice loud as the clashing of clouds: — ' What, O Lord! hast thou, desirous of victory, now done? but I am the sole Omnipotent Being; there is no other than me, and no one therefore can overcome

* The five orifices of the body; viz. the mouth, the nostrils, the eyes, the ears, and the anus.

me.' To pacify him, Vishnu thus replied in gentle words:— 'O Brahma! it was not through malice that I closed the gates, but merely through sport; for who can oppose Pitamaha, the God of gods? but since thou hast been produced by me, thou shalt be considered as my son, and shalt be named the *Lotos-born.*' Brahma replied:— 'There is but one God, the supreme Lord of all things; how then can there be two, and Narayana and Brahma be each that Lord?' Vishnu then said:— 'Who can acknowledge the supremacy of Brahma, when I alone am without beginning and end, and the sole Supreme Being? Therefore, O Brahma! seek protection from me.' Pitamaha with anger thus replied:— 'O Lord! I know myself to be supreme, imperishable, the creator of the universe, the most excellent recipient; and no where can there be found any other supreme God than me. Dispel, therefore, thy slumber, and know thyself.' Having heard these angry words, Vishnu thus spoke:— 'O Brahma! why art thou thus deceived by illusion; and perceivest not the real truth, that I alone am the supreme Lord?'

"To appease this contention, then appeared Shiva, the one God, with an eye in his forehead, adorned with matted locks, holding a trident, and refulgent as the sun. On beholding whom Brahma, bewildered by illusion, thus addressed Vishnu:— 'O Janardana! who is that dark-coloured being, holding a trident, having three eyes, and diffusing such effulgence?' Vishnu, having heard these words, looked to that bright lustre which irradiated the pure waters, and recognising Shiva, thus replied to Brahma:— 'That is the great God of gods, shining in his own refulgence, eternal, without beginning or end, devoid of thought, the supreme Lord of the universe, Shankara, Shambu, Ishana, the sole and universal Spirit. He it is who creates, preserves, and destroys; and who, though his essence is one and undivided, yet produced thee from it, and gave to thee the Vedas; and who likewise originated me, and gave me various names.' The mind of Brahma being thus enlightened by the words of Vishnu, they both sought the protection of their father Shiva, and with clasped hands addressed him in words of praise."— Part I. chapter 9.

The accounts, also, of the origin of the three principal goddesses are equally discordant; as it will sufficiently appear from the following quotations: —

From the Varaha Puran.

Brahma having come to Kailasa, Shiva thus addressed him: — "Say quickly, O Brahma! what has now induced thee to come here?" Brahma replied, — "There is a mighty *Asura*, named Andhaka, by whom all the angels having been distressed, they came to me to implore protection; and I have hastened hither to inform you of their complaints." Having thus spoken, Brahma looked at Shiva, and he in thought summoned Narayana. Instantly Vishnu stood between them; and the three gods viewing each other with delight, from their three refulgent glances sprang into being a virgin of celestial loveliness, of hue cerulean like the petals of a blue lotos, and adorned with gems, who bashfully bowed before Brahma, Vishnu, and Shiva. They said, — "Who art thou? O lovely one! and why hast thou now appeared? and why art thou distinguished by the three several colours of black, white, and red?" She replied, — "From your glances was I produced; but do you not know your own omnipotent energies?" Brahma then praised her, and bestowed on her this blessing: — "Thou shalt be named the goddess of the three times *, the preserver of the universe; and under various other appellations shalt thou be worshipped, as thou shalt be the cause of accomplishing the desires of thy votaries. But, O goddess! divide thyself into three forms, according to the colours by which thou art distinguished." On hearing these words, she divided herself into three forms of a white, a red, and a black colour. The white was Saraswati, of a lovely felicitous form, the source of wisdom, and the co-operator with Brahma in creation; the red was Lakshmi, the beloved of Vishnu, who with him preserves the universe: the black was Parvati, endowed with many qualities, and the energy of Shiva. †

* The morning, noon, and evening.

† The first chapter of the legend entitled *Tri-Shakti-mahatmye.*

From the Markandeya Puran.

The Rajah said, — " Acquaint me, O lord! with the true form and nature of that goddess, whose achievements you have just communicated to me." * *The Sage replied,* — " O rajah! this is a mysterious and ineffable subject; but, on account of thy piety, I will in some measure explain it to thee. Know, then, that the origin of all things is Maha Lakshmi, who visibly or invisibly pervades and dwells in all that is: and her form is resplendent as molten gold, diffusing refulgence around; while her four hands display a citron, a mace, a shield, and a goblet. Separating from herself the quality of darkness, she gave origin to a form black as night, with dreadful tusks and large eyes, four-armed, and holding a sword, a goblet, a head, and a shield, and adorned with a necklace of skulls; which is distinguished by the names of Maha Kali, Ekavira, Kala Rattri, and other similar appellations. Then, from the quality of purity residing in her own essence, she produced a lovely form, lustrous as the moon, holding a rosary, a lotos, a *vina*, and a book; which is known under the names of Maha Vani, Bharati, Vak, Saraswati, &c. Soon as they were formed, thus did Maha Lakshmi address Maha Kali and Saraswati: — 'Let us from our own forms produce twin deities.' Having thus spoken, Maha Lakshmi generated a male and female; the former named Brahma, and the latter Padma, Kamila, or Lakshmi: in the same manner Maha Kali produced Shiva and Saraswati; and Saraswati likewise generated Gauri and Vishnu. † Maha Lakshmi then gave in marriage Saraswati to Brahma, Gauri to Shiva, and Lakshmi to Vishnu; and, shortly after, Brahma and Saraswati produced the mundane egg, which

* In the *Devi Mahatmiam*, an analysis of which is contained in the fourth volume of the Journal Asiatique: but M. Burnouf, not having the rest of this Puran, has been misled by the equivocal term *Devi*, and has, in consequence, erroneously ascribed this legend to Parvati. The first words, however, of the chapter which immediately follows it are these: — " The Rishi said, 'I have thus related to you, O raja! the most excellent legend, entitled the *Devi Mahatmiam*; and it is in this manner that the GODDESS deludes the world, and thus through ignorance does the *Maya of Vishnu* continually operate.' "

† Of this passage, in order to render it perfectly intelligible, I have merely given the substance.

was broken by Shiva and Gauri; and the universe therein formed is preserved by Vishnu and Lakshmi."*

From the Lainga Puran.

Desirous of effecting the creation, Brahma performed a long and severe course of devotion; but still did not in any degree succeed in accomplishing his wish. Hence, for a long period, did he suffer vexation and anger, till at length tear-drops flowed from his eyes, inflamed with passion; and from these sprang into being ghosts and goblins. On beholding his elder-born in such loathsome and dreadful forms, Brahma fainted away; and from the breath which he then expired from his mouth appeared Rudra, half male and half female, and resplendent as the young sun. Then Rudra dividing himself, the male half he multiplied into eleven forms, and the female half became Uma; from whom were produced Lakshmi, Durga, and Saraswati. — Part I. chap. 38. †

The preceding quotations will, no doubt, evince the total erroneousness of the opinion which has been hitherto entertained respecting the Hindu triad; and which has been even sanctioned by Mr. Wilson, in his Sanscrit Dictionary, giving this as an explanation of the term Trimurti, — *the united form of Brahma, Vishnu, and Shiva, or the Hindu triad.* But such a notion is perfectly unknown to the Hindus, and, though the expression *eko deva trimurti,* one God but three forms, occurs repeatedly in the Upanishads and Purans; still by the one God is invariably intended the Supreme Being, from whose essence proceeded, in an ineffable manner, the three divine hypostases. ‡ It is

* The chapter entitled *Devimahatmel weikritekam.*

† For another account of the production of Saraswati and Lakshmi, contained in this Puran, see p. 201.

‡ With respect to the figures, which have been supposed to represent the *trimurti* in the sense to which I object, I have not been able to obtain any information. But in neither the passages descriptive of the forms of the Hindu deities which are contained in the Matsya and Agni Purans, nor in any other Sanscrit work on this subject, is there any mention of such a figure.

in this respect that the Indian triad differs so radically from the Christian Trinity; for a *Trinity in unity* is a conception altogether unintelligible to the Hindus, who, indeed, ascribe to the Supreme Being the power of multiplying himself into as many forms as he pleases; but each of these forms, they maintain, has a distinct and independent existence. In the present state, however, of the Hindu religion, in which either Vishnu or Shiva is considered as the *one God*, a greater apparent similarity exists between this triad and the Trinity when peculiar functions are ascribed to each of its divine persons: for, supposing Shiva to be the Supreme Being, he would thus represent the Father; Vishnu would become the Son, the Saviour and Preserver; and Brahma would resemble the Holy Ghost, by whom the creation was effected. But it seems that in all systems of religion, except the Christian and Mohammedan, it has been a universal and invariable tenet, that the Supreme Being does not exercise his power directly, but always through the intervention of subordinate spirits: and a similar belief appears to prevail in many of the religious opinions of the Christians, particularly of the Roman Catholics; since, according to these, a character is ascribed to God the Father, which differs not materially from that attributed to *Parabrahm* by the Hindus. *

It will also be observed that, in the Hindu religion, though the triad of gods has hitherto alone attracted notice, yet the triad of goddesses is equally remarkable. But I find it impossible to form any satisfactory opinion respecting the principles or process of reasoning from which so singular a tenet could have originated. It seems, however, to flow necessarily from that persuasion which men entertained, that action was inconsistent with the felicity of the Supreme Being; and

* The following remarks of Hume, in his account of the reign of Henry the Eighth, will probably recur to the recollection of the reader: — "The devotion to him (Thomas à Becket) had quite effaced in that place the adoration of the Deity; nay, even that of the Virgin. At God's altar, for instance, there were offered in one year three pounds, two shillings, and sixpence; at the Virgin's, sixty-three pounds, five shillings, and sixpence; at St. Thomas's, eight hundred and thirty-two pounds, twelve shillings, and threepence. But next year the disproportion was still greater: *there was not a penny offered at God's altar*; the Virgin's gained only four pounds, one shilling, and eightpence; but St. Thomas had got for his share nine hundred and fifty-four pounds, six shillings and threepence." — *History of England*, vol. iv. p. 181.

that, consequently, an intermediate agent was requisite for giving effect to his power. Still the difficulty recurs, why this agent should have been impersonified under a female form, and energy attributed to that sex which has been universally considered as a passive recipient. But in popular mythology neither Saraswati nor Lakshmi appears to be considered of much consequence; as Parvati or Devi, under her several forms, has become the great object of worship. The particular characters, however, and attributes of these goddesses will be explained in a following chapter.

CHAP. VIII.

THE COSMOGONY OF THE HINDUS.

If the illusive appearances, of which this universe is supposed to consist, are merely effects produced by *Maya* (or the impersonified energy of the Supreme Being), and if their continuing manifest depends on *Maya*'s exerting an independent power; it must necessarily follow that no other agents can be required for the organisation, the preservation, and destruction of this universe. With this spiritual system, therefore, a material generation of the world would seem to be perfectly incompatible; and yet in the Vedas, the Upanishads, and the Purans, the manner in which the process of creation is described most incontestably admits the existence of matter and of individuated substances. In the two preceding chapters, however, I have endeavoured to explain as clearly as possible the nature of what may be termed the Hindu theology; and in perusing the following remarks and quotations, it will be remembered that, though the system described in them is decidedly material, still the Hindus firmly believe that there is in reality no other entity than one sole, self-existent, eternal, and indivisible Spirit.

It will also be observed, that the formation and economy of this universe depend not on the three divine hypostases; and that the peculiar attributes ascribed to Brahma, Vishnu, and Shiva are never exemplified by their actions; for in all the sacred books of the Hindus it is the Supreme Being who is uniformly represented as being the primary cause of creation, and the sole originator of the elementary atoms and qualities, from the reciprocal action and combination of which all things were produced. But the Hindus, at the same time, conceive that these elements and qualities could not of themselves have so combined together as to give form and arrangement to this universe;

and that a superior power was therefore requisite for producing this effect. Power, however, as they maintain, can be exerted solely by a corporeal being; and hence the only variance that occurs in the accounts of the cosmogony proceeds from the character of the *primeval male* being ascribed to either Brahma, Vishnu, or Shiva. The energy, also, of the male is supposed to be inoperative, until it is excited into action by the passive qualities of the female: for Mr. Paterson has correctly remarked that the Hindus assert that the dissolution and destruction of bodies were not real with respect to matter, which was indestructible in itself, although its modifications were in a constant succession of mutation; that the power which continually operates these changes must necessarily unite in itself the attributes of creation and apparent destruction; that this power and matter are two distinct and coexistent principles in nature; the one agent, the other patient; the one male, the other female; and that creation was the mystic effect of the union of these two principles.* The principles are named *Purusha* and *Prakriti;* but their influence in effecting creation is restricted to the producing and maturing the celebrated mundane egg, in which the exemplars of this universe and all that it contains, were first formed and elaborated. This subject, however, will be best explained by the following quotations: —

From the Padma Puran.

Suta thus addressed the Sages: — " The universe and all created things having been annihilated, there existed nothing except him who is named Brahm, the sole cause of manifestation, self-existent, eternal, devoid of passion and quality, immaculate, enjoying ineffable felicity, the adored by those who desire beatitude, omniscient, supreme, and all-pervading. That Being, knowing that the time of creation had arrived, effected a change in his own essence, whence proceeded *Prakriti*, intellect, and the three qualities of purity, impurity, and darkness. From the three qualities agitated by *Prakriti* were produced the five elementary atoms; and, in the same manner, from intellect was generated *ahankar* (consciousness of individual existence);

* Asiatic Researches, vol. viii. p. 53.

and from these atoms combining with the three qualities, and undergoing the requisite permutations, were originated the five senses,—hearing, sight, touch, smell, and taste,— with their respective organs, and also ether, fire, air, water, and earth. Such, O sages! were the original elements of things; but, though each of them had distinct powers, yet until they were duly combined together it was impossible to produce this universe and animated beings; and therefore it was requisite to adopt other means than fortuitous chance, for giving them appropriate combination and symmetrical arrangement. For this purpose Purusha and Prakriti gave origin to an egg, in which these elements were enclosed; and this floating like a bubble on the abyss of waters, under the influence of the Supreme Being, gradually increased in size until it acquired maturity; and then the Supreme Being without beginning or end issued from it, for the purpose of creation, in a visible and corporeal form as Vishnu." — *Swarga Khand,* chap. 2.

From the Brahma Vaivarta Puran.

*Krishna, addressing Radha.** — "Listen, O goddess! and I will explain to thee the mysterious and difficultly comprehended nature of *supporting* and *being supported.* For behold, O lovely one! this universe, and thou wilt perceive that all things depend on their possessing the property of *supporting* and *being supported:* since the blossom supports the fruit, and the branch supports both; the trunk supports the branch; the root, the trunk; the earth, the root; Shesha, the earth; the tortoise, Shesha; the air, the tortoise; I support the air; and thou, essence of my essence, supportest me. In thee I subsist as thou art Shakti, Prakriti, the supreme goddess, the aggregate and source of all things. Thy body is the supporter of the three qualities; and thy soul am I, of myself inoperative, but with thee active. From man proceeds seed, and from seed progeny; and thus from Prakriti,

* In this Puran Krishna is represented as the Supreme Being, and Radha as his energy; and though this opinion is not prevalent among the Hindus, yet the following description of Purusha and Prakriti correspond exactly with what is found on the same subject in other Sanscrit works.

operated upon by me, are generated all things. Withoutthe soul, where is the body? and, without the body, where is the soul? and, without us, how could existence have a beginning? There is not any distinction, O Radha! between us two, who are the seeds of this universe: for, where the soul is, there is the body; nor are they disjoined, but coexist, as whiteness in milk, burning in fire, smell in earth, and coldness in water; and in the same manner do I exist in thee, and thou in me. Without me thou art lifeless, and inactive am I without thee. Without thee, O lovely one! I am certainly not sufficient to produce creation; for, without clay, how can the potter make a vessel? and without gold, how can the goldsmith prepare an ornament?" —*Krishna-jamna Khand,* chap. 6.

From the Skanda Puran.

Skanda thus replied to Agastya: — "Of depth mysterious is the question which thou hast now asked; but I will explain to thee the subject in the same manner as Shiva formerly communicated it to Parvati, the mother of the universe. 'At the time when all things,' then, said Shiva, 'movable and immovable were annihilated, a universal darkness reigned; and neither sun, nor moon, nor stars, nor planets, existed; nor day, nor night, nor ether, fire, air, water, and earth. Nature remained unanimated, and the heaven was devoid of radiance; and sight, hearing, smell, taste, and touch were become powerless. In midst of this darkness, impenetrable to a needle's point, Brahm, the sole-existing essence, immaterial, indescribable, devoid of dimensions, infinite, imperishable, reposed. That Being not subject to action or passion, exempt from qualities, without beginning and end, omnipotent, omnipresent, becoming apprehensive, said *Brahm is;* and, displeased with his solitariness, a wish for duality arising in his mind, he, though devoid of form, in sport imagined a form; and instant was produced from his own essence one possessed of all divinity, the universal form, the universal cause, the universal object of sacrifice and adoration, immaculate, and resplendent in beauty; and then Brahm became again invisible. That form, O my beloved! am I, whom sages name the lord of priority and posteriority; and from mine was thy immortal body framed. Thee wise men name Pradhan, Prakriti, Maya, the most excellent possessor of the three qualities, the universal mother, and the cause of all mutations.'" Skanda added, "Hence that god, Shiva, from having been the primeval male, is named Purusha, and his energy Prakriti." — *Kashi Khand*, Part I. chap. 26.

From the Vaiu Puran.

Suta thus addressed the Sages: — "The invisible and eternal cause of all things, the source of entity and nonentity, men acquainted with truth name Prakriti or Pradhan; and him who is devoid of senses, self-existent, immovable, imperishable, eternal, self-sufficing, the invisible and wonderful body of all things, they name Parabrahm. That incomprehensible Being, without beginning or end, devoid of form and quality, first appeared corporeally as Brahma; for until then his divine essence remained immersed in profound darkness, and the three qualities had not yet originated; but when the time for creation arrived, then, by the will of the Supreme Being, these qualities becoming operative from the quality of purity residing in Prakriti, was intellect produced, and from intellect sprang mind and understanding. God, also, desirous of creation, gave rise to the elementary atoms, in order that this universe might consist of different forms and properties. . . . . Thus were formed the seven primary causes of things, viz., intellect, consciousness, and the five elementary atoms; but these, disunited and uncombined, were unable to produce this world and animated beings. The supreme Spirit, therefore, caused Purusha and Prakriti to produce an egg, into which these elements entered; and this for a long time floated like a bubble on the wide abyss of waters, until, by the divine will, it acquired maturity: for that egg did the supreme Spirit, who is named Brahm, vivify; and, having assumed a corporeal form, issue from it as Brahma, who, being the first man, is hence named the primeval male. Hence sprang into existence Hiranyagarbha, Brahma adorned with four countenances, the original creator of all things." *

* In my copy of this Puran, neither the divisions nor the chapters are titled or numbered; but this quotation will be found near the commencement.

The being who thus issued from the mundane egg under a corporeal form, with a thousand heads and a thousand eyes is also named *Viraj*, or *Virat Purusha*. With respect to whom Mr. Colebrooke has remarked, — "The notion of Viraj dividing his own substance into male and female occurs in more than one Puran; so does that of an incestuous marriage and intercourse of the first Menu with his daughter Shatarupa; and the commentators on the Upanishad understand the legend to be alluded to in this place, But the Institutes ascribed to Menu, make Viraj to be the issue of such a separation of persons, and Menu himself to be his offspring. There is, indeed, as the reader may observe from the passages cited in the present essay, much disagreement and consequent confusion in the gradations of persons interposed by Hindu theology between the Supreme Being and the created world."* In no Puran, however, have I observed Shatarupa to be described as the daughter of Menu; nor have I perceived any discordancy in the account of the formation of the mundane egg, which is so uniformly given in all Sanscrit works: for Viraj is, in fact, the Supreme Being under a corporeal form, as the *primeval male*; and in the same manner as that character is ascribed to Brahma, Vishnu, or Shiva, so does each of them respectively become Viraj. But it is particularly as a personification of the universe, the manifested form of the one supreme and invisible God, that Viraj is considered; and its different parts are therefore described as being nothing more than the different members of Viraj. His character, however, and the primary process of creation, will be fully understood from the following extract: —

From the Bhagavat.

Brahma, addressing Narada. — "When the time for creation arrived the lord of *Maya*, having spontaneously conceived the desire of multiplying himself, assumed time and action as his own nature. Then in time, by the will of the Supreme Being, was intellect produced from his divine essence, invested with the three qualities; and, from intellect, consciousness. From the predominance, also, of one of the three quali-

* Asiatic Researches, vol. viii. p. 426.

ties proceed matter and the capacity of action and of knowledge; and from these qualities, united with intellect and consciousness, originate three powers: for the predominance of the quality of darkness produces material energy; of impurity, active energy; and of purity, intellectual energy. From the material energy, likewise, and the five elementary atoms produced from it, originated, first, the ether, the essential element of which is sound; from the ether, a change taking place, proceeded air, possessing the property of touch; from air, a change taking place, sprang luminousness, the property of which is sight; from luminousness, a change taking place, was produced water, having the property of taste; and from water, a change taking place, originated earth, possessing the property of smell. In the same manner, from the active energy proceeded the ten organs * and the vital breath; and from the intellectual energy the ten gods, who preside over the five senses, and their organs, viz. *Dish*, *Vata*, *Arka*, *Pracheta*, *Ashwinau*, *Vahni*, *Chandra*, *Upendra*, *Mitra*, and *Ka*; and also understanding. But unless all these various elements had been combined, creation could not have taken place; and, therefore, they were collected together in one vast egg by the power of God, who thus gave origin to existence and non-existence.

"In that egg, floating on the abyss of primeval waters, did the Supreme Being dwell for a thousand Yugs; and having at length vivified the inanimate elements, he, dividing that egg, issued forth as the primeval male, with a thousand heads and a thousand countenances. Of the body and limbs of this male wise men believe that this universe is formed; the upper part of his body constituting the seven superior worlds, and the lower part the seven inferior worlds: for *Burlok* is situated in his feet, *Buwarlok* in his navel, *Swarlok* in his heart, *Maherlok* in his breast, *Janalok* in his neck, *Tapalok* in his eyes, *Satyalok* in his head, *Atalam* in his hips, *Vitalam* in his thighs, *Sutalam* in his knees, *Talatam* in his legs, *Mahatalam* in his ancles, in the upper part of his feet *Resatalam*, and in the soles *Patalam*. His voice is fire, his mouth the source of the Vedas and sacred hymns, his

* They are here enumerated, viz. the five organs of the senses, the voice, the hands, the feet, the virile organ of generation, and the anus.

tongue the origin of taste, his breath of air, his nostrils of smell, his eyes of sight, his ears of audibility, his body the substance of all things, and his skin the cause of tangibility. The hairs of his body are trees and plants, of his head the clouds, of his beard lightning, and his nails are rocks: his arms the origin of the protectors of those who observe the divine ordinances; for from his mouth was produced the Brahman, from his arms the Kshattrya, from his breast the Vaishya, and from his feet the Shudra. His step traverses the three worlds, and his feet are the asylum of devout men, who seek for beatitude; his seed water; his virile organ the source of generation; his back and posterior parts injustice, shedding of blood, deeds of darkness, hell, and damnation; his veins the rivers; his bones the mountains; his belly the source of existence and non-existence; and his heart of intellect. His divine spirit is the origin of virtue, truth, and knowledge; of myself, and Shiva, and thy elder brothers; of the Suras and Asuras, mankind, birds, beasts, serpents, and reptiles; of the Gandharvas, Apsaras, Yakshas, Bhutas, Uragas, the Pitaras, Siddhas, Vidhiadharas, Charanas, and all animated beings in air or water; and of all inanimate things in heaven or on earth, as trees and plants, the sun, planets, stars, thunder, and lightning.

"Thus the primeval male, who is all that is, or was, or shall be, of whose essence this universe consists, compressed into a small space his infinite form, and appeared as Viraj, diffusing, like the sun, splendour around. From a lotos, also, sprung from his navel, did I derive my existence; but I could then find nothing for sacrifice, except the members of that primeval male: and with these, therefore, I prepared the holy grass, the altar, the oblations, and the victim; and offered up as a propitiatory sacrifice that god, under the form of Viraj, who thus became the primeval victim. This is the same visible and invisible victim, which has been at stated times sacrificed by the gods, by thy brothers the Rajapatis, by the Manus, by holy sages, and by the Asuras; that Narayana, who, himself devoid of quality, illusively assumed the three qualities for the purpose of manifesting this universe, and who displays a threefold power; for when united to me he creates, to Vishnu he preserves, and to Shiva he destroys. Thus have I, my dear son, answered thy enquiries, because there is no other cause, nor ever will be, of entity and nonentity, than Narayana, the sole, self-existent God." — Skand II. chap. 5 and 6.

In the last quotation it will be observed, that the different parts of the universe are described as situated in different parts of the undivided form of Viraj: but in the Vedas, and in the quotation from the Padma Puran inserted in page 204., the formation of the universe is ascribed to the immolation of Viraj, from whose dismembered limbs its *apparently* component parts were formed. The same circumstance, also, seems to be implied in the following passage of the Bhagavat; for the author, having in the preceding book described the primeval sacrifice, which, of course, took place with the freewill and consent of the Supreme Being, under the form of Viraj, may have thought it unnecessary to advert to it again: —

" The Supreme Being, having dwelt for myriads of years within the mundane egg, at length issued forth as Viraj; and, for the purpose of framing this universe and all that belongs to this system, divided himself, of his own freewill, into a variety of parts. Now listen, while I enumerate the different shrines which were occupied by portions of his divine substance. His mouth and the effulgence of his countenance became speech and Agni; his tongue and palate, taste and Varuna; his nostrils, smell and the Ashwinau: his eyes, sight and the sun; his skin, touch and Vaiu; his ears, hearing and space; the hair of his body, trees, and plants, and irritability; his virile organ, the cause of generation; and his seed, the pleasure of sexual intercourse; his posterior parts, natural evacuation and Mitra; his hands, the power of action and Indra; his feet, the power of motion and Vishnu; his mind, imagination and Chandra; his soul, understanding and Brihaspati; his consciousness, self-sufficiency and self-confidence; his purity, intellect and knowledge; his head, the heaven; his feet, the earth; and his navel, the interambient ether. Those, therefore, in whom the quality of purity predominates, inhabit heaven, the symbol of Vishnu; those endued with impurity abide on the earth, the symbol of Brahma; and those under the influence of the quality of darkness people the interambient ether, the symbol of Rudra. From the divine words, also, repeated by his mouth, was produced the Brahman, who is thence the chief of the four castes and the preceptor of men; from his protecting arms the Kshattrya, who is therefore the protector of the other castes; from his breast the seat of life, the Vaishya, and hence his duty is to provide the necessaries of life; and, from his feet, the Shudra, whose duty is to obey the other three castes." — Skand III. chap. 6.

But in the Institutes of Menu it is said, chap. i. verses 12, 13. — "In that egg the great power sat inactive a whole year of the creation, at the close of which, by his thought alone, he caused the egg to divide itself, and from its two divisions he formed the heaven above and the earth beneath; in the midst he placed the subtle ether, the eight regions, and the permanent receptacle of waters." A similar account occurs in the Purans; as, for instance, in the following passage in the Matsya Purǎn:—" Narayana, the self-existent, being desirous of creating, from his own divine substance, a multiform universe, first created the abyss of waters, and placed in it an excellent seed, which became, in the course of myriads of years, an immense golden egg, refulgent as a thousand suns. Into this egg the self-existent of himself entered, and, having pervaded it with his divine power, at length divided it, and issued forth as the primeval male. He then formed, from the two parts of the shell of this egg, the heaven and the earth; from the white, the ether; and from the yolk, Meru, the chief of mountains."

Such are the accounts given of the primary formation of this universe, and its duration is thus calculated:—4,320,000 years of mortals form an age of the gods, which period is divided into four ages of mortals: viz., the Krita or Satya Yug, consisting of 1,728,000 years; the Treta, of 1,296,000; the Dwapara, of 864,000; and the Kali, of 432,000. One thousand such ages of the gods constitute a *kalpa*, which thus consists of 432,000,000 years of mortals: a kalpa forms a day of Brahma; and, his night * being of the same duration, his year

* The night of Brahma, though it endures for the same period, is not named a kalpa, because time and its divisions have not then existence: but, in fact, the year of Brahma consists of a period equivalent to 720 kalpas.

Sir

will consequently consist of thirty-one billion one hundred and four thousand million years of mortals; and the life of Brahma endures for one hundred of such years; at the termination of which inconceivable period takes place the *Prakriti Pralaya*, or the complete destruction of the universe, which reduces all things to nonentity: but previously to this total annihilation, a disorganisation of the universe takes place at the end of each kalpa, in consequence of Brahma going to sleep during the night of his day; and this is named a *Naimittika Pralaya*. The nature, however, of these Pralayas * will be best understood from the following passages: —

From the Bhagavat.

Shuka, addressing Parikshit. — "Hear, O king! while I explain the kinds of destruction to which this universe is subject. A thousand

---

Sir W. Jones has, therefore, correctly remarked, — "The aggregate of their four ages they call a divine age; and believe that, in every thousand such ages, or in every day of Brahma, fourteen Menus are successively invested by him with the sovereignty of the earth: each Menu, they suppose, transmits his empire to his sons and grandsons during a period of seventy-one divine ages; and such a period they name a *manwantara*: but, since fourteen multiplied by seventy-one are not quite a thousand, we must conclude that six divine ages are allowed for intervals between the *manwantaras*, or for the twilight of Brahma's day. Thirty such days, or *kalpas*, constitute, in their opinion, a month of Brahma; twelve such months, one of his years; and an hundred such years, his age; of which age they assert that fifty years have elapsed. We are now, then (in A. D. 1788), according to the Hindus, in the first day, or *kalpa*, of the first month of the fifty-first year of Brahma's age, and in the twenty-eighth divine age of the seventh manwantara; of which divine age the three first human ages have passed, and four thousand eight hundred and eighty-eight of the fourth." — *Sir W. Jones's Works*, vol. i. p. 285.

* It requires, however, to be remarked, that the *Pralaya* is of three kinds: viz. according to the general opinion, *nitya*, or daily, that is, when man falls into sound sleep at night; *naimittika*, occasioned by Brahma's sinking into repose at the end of each kalpa; and *prakritika*, when all things are reduced to nonentity. But, according to the account contained in the Vaiu and Brahma Purans, the *nitya* is omitted, and the third is named *atyantika*, or final beatitude, proceeding from identification with the Supreme Spirit. In the seventh chapter, however, of the first part of the Vishnu Puran, it is said that the *naimittika*, *prakritika*, *atyantika*, and *nitya*, are the four kinds of *pralaya* to which created things are subject. The *naimittika* takes place when Brahma slumbers; the *prakritika* when this universe returns to its original nature; *atyantika* proceeds from divine knowledge, and consequent identification with the supreme Spirit; and *nitya* is the extinction of life, like the extinction of a lamp, in sleep at night.

maha yugs * form a day of Brahma and are named a kalpa, during which period fourteen Manus are successively the lords of this world. At the termination of a kalpa the night of Brahma takes place, when the three worlds are destroyed; and this destruction is named the *Naimittika Pralaya.* Then the creator, having resumed all things into his divine essence, reposes on his serpent couch. But when the two halves † of Brahma's life are expired, then will take place the *Prakritika Pralaya,* and intellect, consciousness, the five elements, and the whole of this system will be annihilated. Rain shall pour upon this earth for a hundred years, and for want of food famished men and animals shall devour each other, and mankind shall thus gradually perish. The sun with terrific beams shall drink up the sea and the waters of the earth, and by fire aided by a violent wind shall a universal conflagration reduce the world to vacuum. Above, below, on every side, the glowing rays of the sun and fire shall burn up this universe like a ball of cow-dung, and for more than a hundred years shall a strong wind involve the sky in smoky darkness. Then from a multitude of variegated clouds shall pour, for a hundred years, with tremendous sounds, torrents of rain, until that vacuum becomes a vast abyss of waters; then earth and its property of smell shall be devoured by water; water and its property of taste by luminousness [fire]; luminousness and its property of sight by wind [air]; air and its property of touch by the ether; and the ether and the five elements absorbed in the quality of darkness. In the same manner the organs, faculties, and gods, produced from the active and intellectual energies, shall be absorbed in the qualities of impurity and purity. Intellect shall devour consciousness; and Prakriti, intellect; and the three qualities and Prakriti shall be absorbed in the Supreme Spirit. Time shall cease, and nothing exist except him who is without beginning or end, invisible, incorporeal, and the sole eternal cause." — Skand XII. chap. 4.

* A *maha yug* is the aggregate of the four yugs.

† Though the term *parardha* is applied to the two divisions of Brahma's life, it does not properly signify half; but is the name of the utmost term in notation known to the Hindus, which extends to eighteen places only; and consequently a *parardha* is equal to one hundred thousand billions. (See Dr. John Taylor's Translation of the Lilaw-ati, part i. chap. 1.)

From the Mtsya Puran.

Vishnu, in the form of a fish, addresses Satyavrata Manu. — "O son of Ravi! the Satya Yug consisted of four thousand divine years*, and the twilights at its commencement and conclusion of the same number of hundreds. During this period Justice † [in the form of a bull] stood on four feet, and Injustice on one, and men adhered to virtue, religion, and their respective duties. Brahmans were assiduous in the observance of the divine precepts, kings duly attended to the proper discharge of their legal functions, Vaishyas pursued agriculture, and Shudras practised obedience. Then purity, truth, and virtue flourished, and this age received its name from the pure and virtuous conduct of mankind. The Treta Yug and its twilights consisted of three thousand six hundred divine years, and during it Justice stood on three feet and Injustice on two; then truth and virtue were diminished by one third, and the ambition of belonging to a higher caste began to introduce confusion among the castes, and impaired the strict observance of religious rites and duties. The Dwapar Yug and its twilights consisted of two thousand four hundred divine years, and during it Justice stood

---

The duration of Brahma's life, therefore, is two hundred thousand billions of years; but this computation does not agree with the one deduced from a calculation of kalpas given in a preceding page. The cause, however, of this difference cannot be ascertained, because it is no where mentioned of what kind of years the *parardha*, as applied to Brahma's life, consists.

* A year of the gods consists of 360 years of mortals.

† The Sanscrit term *dharma* is not adequately translated by the word *justice:* nor is there any single word in English which would properly convey its meaning; for it implies the correct performance of such civil, moral, and religious duties, as are prescribed by the Hindu religion to each individual, according to his caste and situation in life.

The origin of this impersonification is thus related in the Varaha Puran: — "As Brahma was reflecting on the manner in which the beings whom he had created might be preserved, a form in the shape of a white bull issued from his right side; and Brahma thus addressed it: — 'Do thou protect my creatures, O excellent one! for which purpose thou shalt stand in the Krita Yug on four feet; in the Treta on three, in the Dwapar on two, and in the Kali on one. Thy four feet shall be celebrated as wealth, observance of the institutions of caste, acts of devotion, and virtue; thy three horns as the three vedas; and thy two heads as the beginning and end of Om.' "

on two feet and Injustice on three: then the minds of men were intent on riches, and deeds of impurity prevailed; offspring was produced from unlawful connections, the wickedness of the Kali Yug commenced, and virtue and religious observances were disregarded. To the Dwapar succeeded the Kali Yug, which, with its twilights, lasted for one thousand two hundred divine years; and during it Justice stood on one foot and Injustice on four: then through lust deeds of darkness became general, and purity, truth, virtue, devotion, and religion no longer existed; selfishness dissevered the bonds of affection; Brahmans performed the acts of Shudras, and the duties incumbent on each caste were contemned, and ignorance and misery prevailed.*

"Thus one thousand of these four yugs with their twilights completed a day of Brahma, and then the Supreme Being, beholding that this universe was ripe for destruction, appeared as Hara for the purpose of effecting it. Instant from his eye proceeded a flame which spread a universal conflagration, while mighty tempests raged and horrid clouds poured down torrents of rain. Narayana, also, infusing himself into the sun; dried up the sea, the rivers, and the waters of the earth. At that time the most excellent of males attracted into his own essence the immortals, all corporeal forms, the five elements, the vital breath, and the organs of the five senses, which last found a place in his tongue, ears, eyes, nostrils, and skin. The divine Maya which gave apparent form to this universe was annihilated, and mind, intellect, and soul were absorbed into the most excellent spirit of Narayana. But, when the universe had thus been reduced to ashes, the Supreme Being poured down torrents of rain from the sky, and the vacuum became one mighty ocean of water, resembling milk; and, except that ocean, all entity had become non-existent. The sun, the wind, the ether, the sea, and all things corporeal and incorporeal, were absorbed into his divine essence; and, the universe being consumed, the eternal and omnipotent God, having assumed an ancient form, reposed myste-

* It is to be remarked that, in describing the duration of these *yugs*, the past tense is here used; which necessarily implies that, at least, one destruction and renovation of the universe was supposed to have taken place previously to that deluge from which Satyavrata was preserved.

riously for myriads of ages upon the surface of that ocean. But no one is capable of knowing whether that being was then visible or invisible, or what the holy name of that person was; or what the cause of his mysterious slumber. Nor can any one tell how long he thus reposed until he conceived the thought of acting; for no one saw him, no one approached him, and none can penetrate the mystery of his real essence." *

From the Vaiu Puran.

Suta, addressing the Sages.—" At the end of one thousand *maha yugs*, and fourteen *manwantaras* takes place the universal conflagration. Then the immortals, the *pitara*, the divine sages, the *Manus*, and those who have observed the duties prescribed for the four castes and the four orders repair to *Maharlok*, where those of least virtue remain; but such as more distinguished for their religious purity proceed, according to the degrees of it, either to *Janalok*, or *Tapalok*, or *Satyalok*. † When arrived in the last of these heavens, the blessed spirits become in form the same as Brahma, and along with him enjoy eternal happiness; nor are they again subject to mortal birth: but those who have remained in the other heavens, according to the nature and degree of the sins committed by them which are still unexpiated, again assume, on the renovation of the universe, the corporeal forms of gods, of demons, of Brahmans, Kshattryas, Vaishyas, and Shudras, of beasts and birds, or of serpents and reptiles. These will continue to inhabit the three worlds for one thousand *maha yugs*, and then will the universe be again destroyed, and the vacuum filled up by one mighty ocean. Thus, during a night of Brahma, for one thousand *maha yugs* shall the three worlds be submerged in water, and a universal darkness reign. Then shall Brahma again desire to create, and for that purpose shall he

* The second and third chapters of the legend entitled *Padmodbhava Pradurbhawa*.

† It is to be observed that, in the *Naimittika Pralaya*, or occasional destruction of the universe, these four superior heavens remain unaffected, and that the other ten worlds are merely covered by the deluge; but all animated and inanimated things are consumed by the general conflagration.

The *Satyalok* is the residence of Brahma, and it is, therefore, sometimes named *Brahmalok*.

become manifest as the primeval male, with a thousand heads, a thousand eyes, a thousand arms, and a thousand feet, and with a form resplendent as burnished gold." *

At the primary creation of this universe, and at its reorganisation after those periodical destructions, the process by which all things animate and inanimate were produced is described in precisely the same manner. In the latter case, however, the four superior worlds remain unaffected, and the ten lower worlds are merely overwhelmed by a deluge, but not disorganised: but by what means the vast abyss of waters disappears on the renovation of the universe I have no where found explained; though it is generally supposed that it is dried up by the sun, in the same manner as the waters were when the *Naimittika Pralaya* commenced. In order, however, to give a satisfactory account of this latter stage of the cosmogony, I must be allowed to produce a rather long quotation.

From the Bhagawat.

Maitreya, addressing Vidura. — " Krita, Treta, Dwapar, and Kali are the names of the four yugs, which, with the twilights at the commencement and close of each, consist of 12,000 divine years, and are respectively composed of 4,000, 3,000, 2,000, and 1,000 divine years, and each of their two twilights consist of the same number of hundreds of divine years. In the same proportion, the bull of justice is during them gradually deprived of his feet, and that of injustice acquires them. One thousand of these four yugs added together is named a day of Brahma, and then his night takes place, in which he slumbers for the same space of time; and, at the conclusion of this night, will creation again take place, and the fourteen Manus will again successively, each for one *Manwantara*, rule over the three worlds during one day of the lord. Thus are the different races of immortals, divine sages, kings, men, and all other created things renewed in each day of Brahma; and in each does the omnipotent Vishnu, assuming different forms, protect the

* The above quotation is not translated literally, but merely the substance of the original given. It will be found near the commencement of this Puran, and is sufficiently indicated by the first sentence.

universe: but soon as each day expires, the Supreme Being surrounding himself with darkness remains in tranquillity and in the gloom of night; the three worlds unirradiated by sun or moon disappear; and, while the universal conflagration rages, the immortals, divine sages, and others, oppressed by the heat, hasten from Maharlok to Janalok. At length, the seas being augmented and their waves agitated by strong winds, the three worlds are overwhelmed by a vast mass of waters; and, in the midst of this ocean, Vishnu reclining on Ananta with closed eyes reposes in mysterious slumber, while the inhabitants of Janalok unite in his praise and adoration. A hundred years, composed of three hundred and sixty such days and nights, comprise the life of Brahma; the former half of which has expired, and the latter has now commenced. Of that former half, the first kalpa was named Brahma, because the knowledge of Brahm was then first revealed in the Vedas; and the second was called Padma on account of the lotos which sprang from the navel of Vishnu, and gave origin to the creator of the universe. Of the latter half, the first and present kalpa is named Varaha, because in it Hari assumed the form of a boar (*varaha*).

"Now attend to me while I explain to thee the manner in which Brahma, desirous of creation, proceeded to form this universal system. First, he produced Tama, Andha-Tamisram, Maha-Tamisram, Moha, and Maha-Moha.* But, displeased with so sinful a production, he meditated with a pure mind, and then created Sanaka, Sananda, Sanatana, and Sanatkumara, who devoted themselves to contemplation and holy abstraction. To them Brahma said,—'Produce progeny, my sons!' But they, anxious for beatitude, complied not, and attached themselves to the service of Vishnu. Observing his order contemned, Brahma waxed wroth; but, as he hastened to repress his anger, there instantly sprang from the middle of his forehead a black-coloured youth, the offspring of his wrath. This first-born of the gods wept and said,—'O Dhata! confer on me different names, and appoint different places for my abode.' Having heard these words, the lotos-born replied,—

* The commentators are not agreed with respect to the meaning of these words; but they imply spiritual darkness, and all the evil passions which necessarily result from such a state of the mind.

'Weep not, for I will comply with thy request: and, since thou hast from apprehension wept like a child, created beings shall call thee Rudra *; and thou shalt dwell in the mental faculties, the five vital breaths, the ether, fire, water, the earth, the sun, the moon, in ascetic practices, and in sacrifice. By various other names, also, shalt thou be honoured; therefore be satisfied, and with these wives create a numerous offspring.' The black-coloured lord, having been thus ordered, created beings similar to his own essential nature. But when Brahma beheld innumerable troops of Rudras about to devour the universe, he became alarmed and said,—'O best of gods! enough. Create no more such beings, capable of consuming the universe with myself by the flaming glances of their eyes: but depart to the forest, and there devote thyself to holy meditation; for by such devout abstraction did the lord at first become creator.' On hearing these words, Rudra obeyed, and sought a secluded forest.

"Brahma then by meditation gave origin to ten sons, for the purpose of filling the three worlds with created beings; Marichi, Atri, Angiras, Pulastya, Pulaha, Kratu, Bhrigu, Vasishta, Daksha, and Narada. † Narada was produced from his haunch, Daksha from his thumb, Vasishta from his breath, Bhrigu from his skin, Kratu from his hand, Pulaha from his navel, Pulastya from his ear, Angiras from his face, Atri from his eye, and Marichi from his mind. From his breast was generated Justice, and from his back Injustice, from which last originated Death. From his heart sprang *Kama* (love); from his brow, Anger; from his lip, Lust; from his mouth, *Vacha* (speech); and, from his shadow, Kardama.

"For his daughter Vacha (Saraswati), as we have heard, whose beauty captivated his mind, Brahma was inflamed with unlawful love; but his daughter, observing her father's impious passions caused Marichi and the other divine sages to recall him to recollection by these words:—'No one ever before contracted such a love, nor shall any one hereafter

* A *weeper*; from *rud* to weep.

† Amongst the Prajapatis are also sometimes included Kardama and Ruchi, who both sprang from Brahma; Kardama from his shadow, but I have nowhere met with the manner in which Ruchi was produced.

do so; nor do thou, O lord! seek connection with the offspring of thy own body. The more illustrious a person may be, the more ought he to exercise self-control; and that justice, therefore, which sprang from the lustre of thy own soul, ought to be observed by thee.' Hearing these words, Brahma became ashamed, and relinquished his love for his daughter.

"Brahma then perceiving that the universe could not be by these means replenished with created beings, changed by divine power his form into a body of two distinct natures, and then dividing it the male half became Manu, the son of the self-existent, and the female half Shatarupa, who became his queen; and from them the increase of mankind proceeded. For Manu begot on Shatarupa five children, two sons, Priavrata and Uttanapada, and three daughters, Akuti, Dewahuti, and Prasuti; Akuti they give in marriage to Ruchi, Dewahuti to Kardama, and Prasuti to Daksha. Soon as created, Manu with his wife, bowing themselves before Brahma, thus with clasped hands addressed him:—'Thou, O lord! art the sole father and supporter of all the beings whom thou hast created, how, therefore, should we not be the most obedient of creatures? Praise be to thee, then! deign to instruct us in the acts which we ought to perform here in order to ensure beatitude in a future life.' Brahma replied:—'I am pleased with you, since you have with sincere minds expressed the wish, order us; for those sons, who with humble and unenvious minds as far as in their power revere his orders, alone duly honour their parent. Do thou, therefore, O king! beget on her a virtuous offspring; rule over the earth; and by thy sacrifices propitiate Vishnu: and as thou, obedient to me, protectest mankind, so shall he, the preserver, be pleased with thee; for of those who despise that lord, and propitiate not his favour, the exertions shall ever be fruitless.' Manu then said,—'O destroyer of sin! obedient to thy orders I shall ever remain: but, O lord! appoint a place of abode for me and mankind; for the earth, the residence of immortal souls, is submerged beneath that mighty mass of water, and to uplift it must require a vast effort.'

"Parameshti, then, beholding the earth sunk amidst the waters, long meditated on the means by which it might be replaced in its former situation. 'Whose divine aid,' he thought, 'shall I implore to upraise from the deep abyss that earth which I formerly created? That lord, from whose heart I sprang, can alone effect this mighty work.' As Brahma thus resolved, suddenly from his nostrils sprang a young boar, no larger than the thumb; but, as he viewed it, in an instant it wonderfully increased to the size of a mighty elephant. The Rishis *, Prajapatis, Rumaras, and Manu, beholding the boar-like form in astonishment, thus in their minds conjectured:—'What can be this delusive form of a boar, since, in reality, it must be of a divine nature? How wonderful that it should spring from Brahma's nostrils no larger than the top of the thumb, and, in an instant, become equal to a mighty mountain! Can it be that mighty lord, on whom we meditate with minds devout?' While thus they thought, that lord, who was the primeval victim, emitted a sound loud as thunder, and, as the eight regions re-echoed the sound, Brahma and his sons were delighted; for they hence knew the lord, and, their anxiety being dissipated, the pure inhabitants of Janalok, Tapalok, and Satyalok united in addressing to him their holy praise. Pleased with these praises, the wondrous boar displayed himself like a vast mountain, with tail erect, mane waving, his bristles sharp as lances, and hoofs striking the sky, and snuffing, in imitation of a boar, to discover the earth. Then he of the terrible tusk, with terror-divested eyes regarding those who were adoring him, like a sportive elephant dived into the abyss of waters; and the waters being divided, as if a thunderbolt, vast as a mountain, had fallen precipitately into them, resounded like the thunder; and, raising in pain its wide billows, the abyss profound exclaimed,—'Save me, O lord of sacrifice!' Thus, subduing the waters with his sharp hoofs, he reached their utmost extremity, and saw lying there the earth, which he had originally intended for the abode of souls. Having then

* The seven Rishis were originally Marichi, Atri, Angiras, Pulastya, Pulaha, Kratu, and Vasishta, who are generally supposed to have sprung from the mind of Brahma. But, as in each manwantara different saints are exalted to this dignity, the names of those who enjoyed it during the manwantara of the sixth Manu, Chakshusa, viz. Atri, Vasishta, Kashyapa, Gautama, Bharadwaja, Vishwamitra, and Jamadagni, are in most common use at the present day; and the same circumstance explains the variance respecting the names of these Rishis which occurs in Sanscrit works.

slain the demon Hiranyaksha, he uplifted it on his tusks from the dark abyss, and Brahma and his sons extolled his wondrous power." — Book III. chap. 13.

After the lower worlds had been thus restored to their former position, and the waters of the deluge had been dried up, Manu and Shatarupa descended from the higher heavens into this earth, and founded the first kingdom in *Brahmavarta*, or the tract of country which extends between the Ganges and Jumna, the capital of which is supposed to have been the present Betoor, on the Ganges, at a short distance to the north of Caunpoor. The first Manu had two sons, Priavrata and Uttanapada, the former of whom succeeded to his father, and divided the world into seven dwipas, viz. Jambu, Plaksha, Kusha, Krouncha, Shaka, Pushkara, and Shalma; over which he appointed seven of his sons to reign, the others having embraced a religious life.* These dwipas are described as vast islands, Plaksha being surrounded by a sea of sugar-cane juice; Kusha by one of clarified butter; Krouncha by one of sour curds; Shaka by a sea of milk; Pushkara by one of sweet water; Shalmala by one of spirituous liquors; and Jambu dwipa alone by a sea of salt waters. Of the first six of these dwipas a general description is contained in the Purans; but none of them are ever the scene of any of the numerous legends which occur in those works. The Hindus, indeed, consider that all communication between Jambu and the other dwipas has ceased from the remotest times, and that it is of the events which happened in the former only that any memorials have been preserved.† But, though some references may occur to other parts of Jambu dwipa, the scene of Puranic descriptions and legends is restricted almost entirely to India in its greatest extent.‡

* For an account of the descendants of Priavrata and Uttanapada, and the genealogies of the other royal races of India, I beg to refer to Ward's View of the Hindus, vol. iii. chap. 1.

† From what sources Lieutenant-Colonel Wilford derived his fanciful system of Hindu geography I know not; but most assuredly he could not find, with the exception of proper names, the slightest grounds for it in the Purans. It is, indeed, difficult to determine whether the Puranic description of the system of the universe, or the attempt to reduce its extravagances to rationality is the most absurd.

‡ It may be proper, however, to observe that Jambu dwipa is divided into nine distinct

The Hindus, therefore, suppose that the four quarters of the world known to Europeans are comprised in Jambu dwipa; and, consequently, that ships have traversed the sea of salt waters, by which it is surrounded, in every direction, without discovering the other dwipas, is no proof, in their opinion, that these do not actually exist, but merely that the ships have not been able to penetrate to them.

From Manu and Shatarupa are all mankind descended; but celestial beings were the children of Kashyapa, the son of Marichi, who derived his origin from the mind of Brahma: for to Kashyapa were given in marriage thirteen daughters of Daksha; of whom *Aditi* produced the gods, *Diti* the *Daityas*, *Danu* the *Danavas;* and the other wives also produced separate classes of beings distinct from mortals. * But it would be uninteresting to enter into any account of the progeny of the *Rishis*, the *Prajapatis*, and their children, as detailed at great length in the Purans; it seems sufficient to observe that in them the origin, not only of all classes of beings, but even of qualities and properties, of virtues and vices, and of all inanimate things, is ascribed to the usual process of generation; and that for this purpose the children of the *Rishis* and *Prajapatis*, corporeal or allegorical, are described as intermarrying together, and producing farther progeny; because an acquaintance with these genealogies is not necessary for understanding the Hindu mythology, in which the only actors, besides these *Rishis*, *Prajapatis*, and a few of their holy descendants, are the divine hypostases, the gods, the *Manus*, the *Daityas*, *Danavas*, and *Rakshasas*, the last of whom were also descended from a wife of Kashyapa.

Such is the account which occurs, with scarcely any variation, in all the Purans, of the cosmogony and the stated destructions and renovations of the universe. It is hence obviously impossible to reconcile to this account the legend of Satyavrata; because he is uniformly represented as being the seventh Manu; and it is universally admitted that a

---

countries; viz. Ilavrata, Bhadrashwa, Hiranmaya, Hari, Ketumala, Kimpurusha, Kuru, and Bharata; and that India is comprised within the last of these divisions.

* I have nowhere found a complete enumeration of the names of these wives of Kashyapa or of their children; but it is to be remarked that amongst them is included *Ira* or *Ila*, the earth, which produced all kinds of trees, plants, creepers, and herbage.

deluge does not take place until after the expiration of the sovereignty of fourteen Manus. It is also remarkable that, though allusions occur in, I believe, all the Purans to the Matsya Avatar, no detailed relation of this event is to be found in any of them *, except the Matsya, the Agni, and the Bhagawat: and in this last work a material contradiction with respect to it has taken place; for in it Satyavrata is correctly enumerated as the seventh Manu; and yet, at the end of the eighth skand, it is said: — "There was, at the termination of the last kalpa, a Naimittika Pralaya (or occasional deluge), and the worlds were overwhelmed by the ocean. Then, as Brahma, slumbering, reposed upon the waters, the Vedas flowed from his mouth, and were purloined by the Asura Hayagriva. No sooner, however, did the lord Hari perceive this act, than, assuming the form of a small fish, he appeared to a pious king, named Satyavrata, who was then performing his devotions in the river Kritumala, — he who was the son of Vivaswat, and is also named Shraddhadeva, and who obtained in this kalpa the dignity of Manu, through the favour of Hari." †

In the Matsya Puran this legend is thus related.—*Suta, addressing the Sages:* — "Formerly, there was a king named Manu, distinguished by every virtue; who, having resigned his kingdom to his son, withdrew to a certain spot, and there, indifferent to pain and pleasure, performed

* On the contrary, Vaivaswat, or Satyavrata, is stated in them to have been the ancestor of the *Surya Vamsha*, and no deluge is interposed between him and his immediate successor Ikshwaku. As, however, he was the son of Surya and his wife Sangnia, I have nowhere found it explained how he became a terrestrial sovereign; but it seems clear that he must have reigned, at least, over the whole of India, and not over the southern peninsula only, as intimated in the Bhagawat.

† For a translation of the rest of this passage of the Bhagawat, see Sir W. Jones's Works, vol. i. p. 238., or Asiatic Researches, vol. i. p. 230. It must, however, be observed that Sir W. Jones has, in order to accommodate this legend to the Mosaic account of the deluge, translated one material passage in a manner which is not authorised by the original. His version is thus: —" Then shalt thou take all medicinal herbs, all the variety of seeds; and accompanied by seven saints, *encircled by pairs of all brute animals*, thou shalt enter the spacious ark," &c. The words here printed in Italics are intended as a translation of the Sanscrit ones, सर्वसत्वोपवृंहित: which signify, *replete with all virtuous qualities;* an epithet here obviously applied to Satyavrata, as this compound adjective can be in construction with no other word in the sentence than the preceding त्वं. The Sanscrit word नौ, also, does not signify an *ark*, but a *boat* or a *ship*.

the severest devotional penance for a hundred thousand years. At length Brahma appeared to him and said, — ' Choose whatever boon thy mind desires.' The king, bowing to Brahma, thus replied, — ' From thee one most excellent boon I crave; and wish that, when the *pralaya* takes place, I may be preserved from that destruction in which all things movable and immovable shall be involved.' — ' So be it,' Brahma replied, and then disappeared; and the angels rained on the king from heaven a shower of flowers.

" Sometime after, as near his hermitage he was offering water to the *Manes*, a small fish came into his hands along with the water; and the compassionate king, in order to preserve it, placed it in a small vessel. But in one night it increased sixteen inches in size, and exclaimed, — ' Save me! save me!' The king then successively threw it in a jar, a well, a lake, and a river; but, in each night, the fish grew larger, and entreated a more roomy place of abode. At length the king threw it into the sea, when it immediately occupied with its bulk the whole ocean. Manu then alarmed exclaimed, — ' What god art thou? or canst thou be any other than Vasudeva, whose form has thus expanded to such immensity? I know thee now; but why hast thou thus pained me, by assuming the form of a fish, O Keshava? Praise be to thee, O Vishnu, lord of the universe!' The lord replied, — ' Excellent! excellent! Thou hast discovered the truth, O sinless one! Know that in a short time this earth shall be submerged in water, and that this ship has been prepared by all the gods for thy preservation. When, therefore, the deluge takes place, enter this ship, and take with thee all kinds of seeds, and of animals that are produced from heat, from eggs, or from the womb; and fasten it to this horn of mine. Thus shalt thou be preserved, and, after the deluge has ceased, shalt thou become, on the renovation of the world, the progenitor of all beings; and thus shall a holy devotee, steadfast in ascetic practices, and completely conversant in divine knowledge, become at the beginning of the Krita Yug the lord of a manwantara.' Having thus spoken, the lord disappeared, and Manu continued his devotions to Vasudeva until the deluge took place, as foretold by Vishnu; and then Janardana appeared in the form of a horned fish; and while the ship into which Manu had entered was attached to its horn, Vishnu, under the form of this fish, in answer to the questions of Manu, revealed unto him the Matsya Puran." But in the relation of the genealogy of the *Surya Vamsha*, which occurs in this Puran *, no notice is taken of the deluge; and it is, on the contrary, distinctly stated, that Kashyapa was the son of Marichi, Vivaswat the son of Kashyapa, Vaivaswat Manu, or Satyavrata, the son of Vivaswat, and that the latter had ten sons, without any interruption taking place in this filiation.

It would hence seem probable that, according to the primitive mythology of the Hindus, the object of the Matsya Avatar was merely the recovery of the Vedas from the Asura Hayagriva †, and that the legend respecting the preservation of Satyavrata must have been subsequently invented: for the calculation of time is uniformly the same in all Sanscrit works, and even in the Matsya, Agni, and Bhagawat Purans; and, consequently, as Satyavrata is unquestionably the seventh Manu, he could not have been preserved from a deluge; and it is equally clear that since each kalpa contains fourteen *manwantaras*, the seventh Manu could not have existed at the end of a kalpa, as expressly stated in the Bhagawat, and sufficiently intimated in the Matsya. The legend, however, is curious, in consequence of its resemblance to the Mosaic, Chaldean, and Grecian accounts of a virtuous individual having been preserved from a deluge, in which all the rest of mankind perished. But, before an inference is drawn from these remarks that this legend must have been derived from a foreign source, it would be necessary to point out the manner in which the Hindus could have received it from any other people. Could, indeed, implicit credit be given to the fragments of Berosus which have been preserved, and were my hypothesis that the Brahmans were originally Babylonians admitted, the reception of this legend, at whatever time invented, by the Hindus, would be at once explained. But if this hypothesis be rejected, it will obviously become impossible to evince that the Hindus have borrowed any part of their mythology: because it seems highly

* In the chapter entitled *Budha sangamana*.

† It is so related, without any mention of Satyavrata, in the Uttara Khand of the Padma Puran.

probable that the Brahmans were established in India at least 1200 years before Christ, and that their religious system was then completely formed; and it is undeniable that there are no indications in history which show that, subsequently to that date, any such communication took place between Babylonia, Syria, Greece, and India, as could have effected the introduction into the latter country of any innovations in its mythological legends and established religion.

CHAP. IX.

VISHNU. — BUDDHA.

Of the three divine hypostases, the character of Vishnu alone remains at the present day, in all essential circumstances, precisely the same as it seems to have been represented on the first institution of the Hindu religion. The only alteration which has occurred in it is the ascription to him, by the Vaishnavas, of the attributes and qualities of the Supreme Being, while the Shaivas consider him to be, in a certain degree, inferior to Shiva. But in every other respect the utmost uniformity prevails in the Purans; nor have I observed in them the slightest variation in the accounts given of his peculiar characteristics, and of the particular events in which his divine power has been manifested: for Vishnu is invariably described as an impersonification of the quality of purity, and as, therefore, exempt from those imperfections to which Brahma and Shiva are necessarily subject, in consequence of their having been formed from the qualities of impurity and darkness. * This difference in the characters of the three divine hypostases is well illustrated in the following legend, which occurs in the Bhagawat †: —

Shuka, addressing Parikshit. — " O king! once, when the holy sages were performing a course of sacrifice, on the banks of the Saraswati, a dispute arose amongst them respecting which of the three gods was the greatest; and, in consequence, they sent Bhrigu, the son of

* In the Varaha Puran, at the commencement of the Rudra-gita, Shiva is introduced thus speaking to the gods and Agastya Muni: — " That deity to whom you offer sacrifice, and by whom this universe was produced, is Narayana the supreme god and universal form. That almighty lord created three kinds of spirits; and hence, from the qualities of purity and impurity combined, was produced from the lotos of his navel the lotos-seated Brahma; from the union of the qualities of impurity and darkness was I created; and from the quality of purity was formed Hari, who thus became the most excellent of the gods." But Shiva concludes this speech with these emphatic words: — " But whoever makes a distinction between us three commits a sin, on account of which his future state shall be miserable."

† In the second part of the tenth skand, chap. 89.

Brahma, to ascertain this point. He accordingly proceeded to the heaven of Brahma, and, desirous of discovering the truth, entered his assembly without paying him the usual honours. Incensed at this disrespect, Brahma glowed with anger; but recollecting that it was caused by his own son, he assuaged with the water of patience the fire of wrath which had arisen in his mind. Bhrigu then proceeded to Kailasa; and when Maheshwara gladly hastened to embrace him as a brother he did not accept the offered embrace, but turned away. Enraged at such improper conduct, the god, seizing his trident, prepared to kill the divine sage; but Parvati fell at his feet, and by her words appeased the anger of her lord. Bhrigu next went to Vaikunta, and struck with his foot the breast of Vishnu, as he lay slumbering on the lap of Lakshmi. The lord, immediately arising, descended from his couch, and, respectfully bowing to Bhrigu, thus addressed him:—'Welcome to thee, O Brahman! be seated for a little, and deign to excuse the fault which I have committed through ignorance *, and the hurt which your very tender feet must have received.' Having thus spoken, he rubbed the feet of Bhrigu with his own hands, and then added,—'To-day am I a highly honoured vessel; since thou, O lord! hast imprinted upon my breast the dust of thy feet, which dispels all sin.' When Vishnu ceased speaking, Bhrigu was so affected by these benevolent words that he was unable to reply, and he therefore departed in silence, while tears of devout emotion rushed from his eyes. Having then returned to the banks of the Saraswati, he related to the holy sages all that had occurred, and their doubts were immediately dispelled; for they then firmly believed that Vishnu was the greatest of the three gods, because he was exempt from impatience and passion." †

* In not having been prepared to receive Bhrigu in a proper manner.

† The same legend occurs at the conclusion of the Uttara Khand of the Padma Puran; but the circumstances that took place in Kailasa and Brahmalok are related differently. In its commencement, also, it is said, the holy sages, in considering the true nature of the gods, differed in opinion respecting the one which was the greatest and most deserving of worship. Some contended that it was Rudra, others that it was Brahma, others that it was Vishnu, and others that it was Surya. But Swayambhuva Manu remarked, that the god in whom purity alone resided was more worthy of adoration than one in whom that quality was mingled with the qualities of either impurity or darkness.

But his avatars form the distinguishing characteristic of Vishnu, and that these are alluded to in both the Vedas and the Upanishads is, I believe, undeniable: for, though Shiva has also appeared under several characters for the destruction of Asuras, he never was born from a mortal womb; and the avatars ascribed to Brahma by Polier are mere fictions, as they are not to be found in the Purans, or in any other Sanscrit work. Respecting, however, the incarnations of Vishnu, some variances occur in the Purans; but in the Bhagawat and Garura the number of them is stated to have been twenty-two. On this subject I may quote the following passage from the Garura: —

Suta, addressing the Sages. — "There is but one god, Narayana, the lord of lords, the Supreme Spirit, who, though subject to neither birth nor death, has on different occasions assumed different forms for the protection of the universe. For the unborn first appeared under the forms of the four Kumaras, and devoted himself to a life, hard to be endured, of ascetic celibacy. In his second avatar he, under the figure of a boar, upraised the earth from the deep abyss of waters. In his third he became the divine sage Mahidasa *, and excelled in acts of devotion. In his fourth he took the forms of the eremites Nara and Narayana, celebrated for their uninterrupted devotion. In his fifth he delivered, as Kapila, the Sankhya philosophy, by means of which truth is so undoubtedly ascertained. In the sixth he became, in reward of the conjugal virtues of Anasuya, under the name of Dattatreya, the son of Atri, and instructed Alarka, Prahrad, and others, in divine knowledge. In the seventh he became the son of Ruchi, under the name of Yadgna, and protected the universe during the manwantara of Sway-

* Neither in the Bhagawat nor Garura is the name of this avatar specified; and the commentators on the Bhagawat are not agreed with respect to the personage intended, some considering him to be Narada, and others Mahidasa; with respect to whom, I find in Moor's Hindu Pantheon, p. 78., the following extract from Mr. Colebrooke's Essay on the Vedas, which, however, is not contained in my copy of the eighth volume of the Asiatic Researches: — "A portion of the Veda is ascribed to Mahidasa, an incarnation of Narayana, proceeding from Visala son of Abja. A commentator on the Veda says that, on the sudden appearance of this deity at a solemn celebration, the whole assembly of gods and priests fainted; but at the intercession of Brahma they were revived, and, after making their obeisance, they were instructed in holy science. This avatara was called Mahidasa, because these venerable personages (Mahin) declared themselves his slaves (dasa)."

ambhu. In the eighth he was born the son of Nabhi, and performed, in a remarkable manner, all the observances prescribed to the four classes (ashrama). In the ninth he appeared, at the entreaties of the holy sages, as Prithu, and milked from the earth * all kinds of fruit, grain, and herbage required for the support of men and animals. In the tenth he assumed the form of a fish, and preserved Vaivaswat Manu from the deluge which took place at the end of the manwantara of Chakshusha. In the eleventh he supported the world, as a tortoise, on his back, while the sea of milk was churned by the Suras and Asuras. In the twelfth he then issued from that sea as Dhanwantari, bearing a goblet filled with the beverage of immortality. In the thirteenth he assumed the female form of Mohini, in order to deceive the Asuras, and deprive them of that beverage. In the fourteenth, under the figure of a man-lion, he tore in pieces with his nails the mighty Asura Hiranyakashipu. In the fifteenth he came, as a dwarf, to the sacrifice of Bali; and, having obtained from him as much ground as he could traverse in three steps, these steps extended over the three worlds. In the sixteenth he was born as Parashu Rama; and, beholding the injustice and oppression of kings, he slew in anger twenty-one generations of the royal race, and rendered the earth devoid of Kshattryas. In the seventeenth he became the son of Parashara and Satyavati; and, observing the little understanding of men, he, as Vyasa, divided the Vedas into separate portions. In the eighteenth he was born as Rama Chandra, the son of Dasharata, for the destruction of the enemy of the gods. In the nineteenth and twentieth he became incarnate in the race of Vrishni, as Bala Rama and Krishna, for the purpose of relieving the earth from the weight of impious men. In the twilight, also, preceding the Kali Yug shall Vishnu be born in Kikata, as Buddha, the son of Ajita, for the purpose of deluding the enemies of the gods; and in the twilight at its termination shall he appear as Kalki, for the destruction of mankind. Such are a few of the incarnations of Vishnu, but his avatars are innumerable." †

* Until then the earth had refused to produce any thing: but Prithu caused her to be vexed by ploughs in every direction; when she assumed the form of a cow, and entreated his compassion, promising to be productive in future.

† Garura Puran, chap. 1.

Vishnu is also considered to be the protector; and it is to him, therefore, that in all cases of difficulty and distress the gods are represented as applying for protection; and even Brahma and Shiva are described as recommending the gods, under such circumstances, to have recourse to Vishnu, since he alone could accomplish their wishes. But, as I have before observed, these interpositions of his divine power are not only thus solicited, but they also are the unavoidable consequences resulting from the curse of Bhrigu. As this legend is curious, I quote it from the Matsya Puran:—

"The Asuras having been repeatedly defeated by the Suras, and deprived of all share in sacrifices, were meditating to withdraw from the unavailing contest, when Shukra, their spiritual preceptor, determined to propitiate Shiva by a severe *tapas**, and to procure from him a charm by means of which the Asuras might obtain victory over the Suras. Shukra having departed for this purpose, the Asuras began thus deliberating amongst themselves:—'As our preceptor has laid aside his arms, and assumed the barken dress and the black skin † of an ascetic, how shall we be able to conquer the Suras in battle? Let us, therefore, with our arms seek refuge with the mother of Kavya ‡, and endure this distress until our preceptor, Shukra, having finished his *tapas*, shall return to us; and then let us, bracing on our armour, engage in combat with the Suras.' Having thus resolved, they, alarmed, hastened to the mother of Kavya, who, taking them under her protection, thus spoke:—'Fear not, fear not; but remain near me, and no danger shall approach you.' The Suras, beholding the Asuras thus received under the safeguard of the mother of Kavya, were proceeding to attack them, when the goddess, perceiving the Asuras encompassed by the Suras, in anger thus addressed Indra,—'If thou desist not, I will deprive thee of the sovereignty of heaven.' And Indra,

* A *tapas* is the propitiating of one of the principal deities by a course of severe penance; such as in the hot season standing amid five fires, *i. e.* fires on the four sides, and the sun above; and in the cold season standing up to the neck in water, living on dry leaves or on air, &c. &c. The *tapas* is also performed for other purposes, and the advantage derived from it is always superhuman power.

† The skin, or rather hide, used for a seat.

‡ A name of Shukra, the son of Bhrigu.

alarmed at her angry words, and dreading her magic power, was yielding to her desire, when Vishnu appeared among the immortal bands, and said to him, — 'Yield not, for I will assist thee.' On observing Indra protected by Vishnu, the goddess thus angrily spoke: — 'Now let the contending foes behold how the power of my devotion shall subdue both Indra and Vishnu.' Thus finding themselves likely to be overcome, they asked each other, — 'How shall we liberate ourselves from this difficulty?' And Indra said, — 'Hasten, O Vishnu! to conquer before she has finished her invocations, or we shall be defeated.' Then Vishnu, considering the detriment that must be incurred by the gods should the mother of Kavya bring her incantations to a successful conclusion, deemed that the slaying of a woman under such circumstances was allowable, and immediately seizing his disc smote off her head with it. But, on beholding so horrid a deed as the murder of a woman and the death of his wife, Bhrigu was violently incensed, and thus cursed Vishnu: — 'Since thou hast knowingly committed so impious an act as the murder of a woman, thou shalt be seven times * born amongst men;' and then added, as a mitigation of the curse, 'but each birth shall be for the advantage of the world, and for the restoration of justice.' Having thus spoken, Bhrigu took up the head of his wife, and, bringing it to the body, thus said, — 'This goddess, O Vishnu! whom thou slewest, will I now restore to life.' Having thus spoken, he adjusted the head to the body, and said, — 'Become again alive;' and instantly the mother of Kavya, restored to life, arose as if from a deep slumber." †

But the distinct character of Vishnu, as one of the divine hypostases, has been so long confounded with the ascription to him of the qualities and attributes of the Supreme Being, that it is now impossible to find any specific account of the precise nature of that character.

* In the Lainga Puran, however, it is said that Vishnu suffered the misery of ten incarnations in consequence of the curse of Bhrigu; and this is the generally received opinion.

† Matsya Puran, the chapter entitled *Somawamsho yadur-Varnanum-prasangena deshavatara Varnanam*.

This legend is also related in almost the same words in the Shrishti Khand of the Padma Puran.

For, in the Padma Puran, even Shiva, in conversing with Parvati, is represented as thus introducing the description of Vishnu's avatars, and of the benefits resulting from his worship:—"I will acquaint thee, O mountain-born! with the real essence and form of Vishnu. Know, then, that he is in truth Narayana, the Supreme Spirit, and Parabrahm, without beginning or end, omniscient and omnipresent; eternal, unchangeable, and supremely happy. He is Shiva, Hiranyagarbha, and Surya: he is more excellent than all the gods, and even than me myself. But it is impossible for either me, or Brahma, or the gods, to declare the greatness of Vasudeva, the originator and lord of this universe."*

In the Varaha Puran, however, occurs this passage.—*The hermit Mahatapa thus addressed the king Prajapala:*—"O king! the supreme god Narayana, having conceived the thought of creating this universe, considered also that it was necessary that it should be protected after it was created; 'but, as it is impossible for an incorporeal being to exert action, let me produce from my own essence a corporeal being, by means of whom I may protect the world.' Having thus reflected, the preexisting Narayana created from his own substance an ungenerated and divine form; on whom, as he was entering the system of this universe, he bestowed these blessings:—'Be thou the framer of all things, O Vishnu! be thou always the protector of the three worlds, and the adored of all men; be thou omniscient and almighty; and do thou at all times accomplish the wishes of Brahma and the gods.' The Supreme Being having thus spoken resumed his essential nature. Vishnu, then, as he meditated on the purposes for which he had been produced, sank into a mysterious slumber; and, as in his sleep he imagined the production of various beings under different forms, a lotos sprang from his navel. In the centre of this lotos appeared Brahma; and Vishnu, beholding the production of his body, was delighted.†

* See Padma Puran, the chapter entitled *Sudershana-Mahatmiam;* but I have quoted only a few verses, and these not in their regular order. Similar descriptions also of Vishnu, by Shiva, occur in other Purans.

† The power of creating conferred by Vishnu on Brahma, which is mentioned in other Purans, is here omitted, though clearly implied from Brahma being subsequently described as the creator.

This Vishnu, also, in every yug, assumes different forms for the protection of the Suras and the destruction of the Asuras; but never must it be said, with want of understanding, that, on this account, he is a mere man: for whoever with faith meditates on the divine nature of Vishnu, his sins shall be destroyed, and he shall obtain beatitude." The production, likewise, of Rudra from Brahma is afterwards related in nearly the same manner as in other Purans. This account of the origin of the three divine hypostases is the one generally received, and it is found in both the *Shaiva* and *Vaishnava* Purans. The *Vaishnavas*, however, contend that Narayana and Vishnu are one and the same god; and the *Smartas* and *Shaivas* maintain that Rudra was merely a form of Shiva, and not that god himself. But this cannot be admitted, because not only all the names of Shiva are applied to Rudra, but it is distinctly stated in several Purans that Brahma bestowed as a boon on Rudra the eight forms by which Shiva is peculiarly characterised; viz. the five elements — ether, fire, air, water, and earth, — the sun, the moon, and a sacrificer.

It also deserves remark, that, though *Narayana* is a name in general restricted to Vishnu, still it is sometimes applied to both Brahma and Shiva. This circumstance, and also not drawing a distinction between their characters, when each is represented as the Supreme Being, or as a divine hypostasis only, have occasioned much inconsistency and confusion in the accounts hitherto published of these three gods. Sir William Jones, for instance, in the argument to his hymn to Narayana, says that the third and fourth stanzas are taken from the Institutes of Menu; and yet in them he identifies Narayana with Vishnu: but in that work Brahma is unquestionably represented as Narayana. Still more singularly does Mr. Colebrooke, in his Essay on the Vedas, describe Brahma as sacrificing himself; for he states that the primeval sacrifice of Narayana was an allegorical immolation of Brahma*: but the primeval victim is, I believe, invariably considered to have been Vishnu, under the character of Viraj.† Yet

* Asiatic Researches, vol. viii. p. 393.

† See ante, p. 221. Of all the names of Vishnu, also, none is of more frequent occurrence than *Yadgna-purusha*, or the *Victim-man*, in allusion to his being the first victim under

it seems evident that the difference of opinion with respect to which of the triad the name of Narayana was originally applied to, proceeds from its being generally admitted that it was under this form that the Supreme Being first manifested himself; and, therefore, when his attributes are ascribed to Brahma, Vishnu, or Shiva, each of them necessarily becomes Narayana. * On the primitive institution, however, of the Hindu religion, this name appears to have properly belonged to Brahma; but, as his preeminence decreased, it was probably transferred to Vishnu, to whom, at the present day, it is exclusively applied, both by *Vaishnavas*, *Shaivas*, and *Smartas*. †

Of Vishnu's ten principal avatars so much has been already written, and with sufficient correctness, that I shall confine myself to a few remarks with respect to his ninth incarnation. ‡

BUDDHA.

It seems to be generally admitted, that the only satisfactory mode of conducting any investigation consists in carefully collecting facts, and then deducing conclusions from these facts. But in researches into Hindu mythology a very different method has been pursued: for it has

---

the form of Viraj, or the primeval male. *Yadgna-krit* is, likewise, a name of Vishnu; which epithet must evidently, in this instance, be translated, *he who was made a victim*; though the term *krit*, in composition, may have either a present, past, or future signification.

* But a difficulty here occurs: for the form under which the one god first manifested himself was unquestionably the being who issued from the mundane egg; and that this being was Brahma is expressly stated in several Purans, and also in the Institutes of Menu. But in these works he is likewise represented as having immediately afterwards, for no conceivable purpose, assumed the form of Narayana. This confusion seems to have arisen from not having drawn a distinction between the primary creation, and the period which elapses between the stated destructions and renovations of the universe, during which the god who reposes on the abyss of waters is invariably denominated Narayana: but this Narayana is also universally represented as being the reorganiser of the new universe by means of Brahma, who springs from a lotos produced from his navel. In fact, it is impossible to reduce the Hindu accounts of the first process of the cosmogony to one clear and consistent description.

† See also the Upanishad contained in Appendix C.

‡ But in Appendix C I have inserted a pretty full account of them taken from the Agni Puran.

been found more convenient to construct systems on a few imperfect and isolated particulars, the bearings even of which to each other have never yet been sufficiently explained, than to ascertain the real opinions on the subject, which are sanctioned by the sacred books of the Hindus. In no instance, however, has this propensity to prefer imagination to the labour of research been more singularly exemplified, than in the speculations which have been published respecting Buddha and his religion; because, from the simple coincidence of names, it has been at once concluded that the ninth incarnation of Vishnu, and the alleged founder of Buddhism, were one and the same person.

A late writer has even observed, that "the doctrines he (Buddha) taught were, according to the Purans of the Brahmans, only a series of mischievous delusion. But, though such is their present doctrine, and though the mythological history of the Brahmans is adapted to this theory, its origin is probably modern. It does not correspond with the doctrines in their ancient books, nor with the inscriptions which time has thrown up to expose their inconsistency." * With respect to the last part of this remark, it is merely necessary to peruse the inscription found at Buddha Gaya, and translated by Mr. Wilkins †, to perceive immediately that the epithets therein contained are applied to Vishnu, and not to Buddha, precisely in the same manner as in the invocations to his other forms which frequently occur in Sanscrit works. But, were this not the case, it cannot be admitted that an inscription dated A. D. 1063 is proof sufficient to determine that Buddha was one of the gods who were originally, and in remote antiquity, worshipped by the Hindus.

The account, also, given of the ninth incarnation of Vishnu is substantially the same in the Purans and other Hindu works, and in the traditionary legends respecting it, which have been preserved to the present day. What, therefore, ought to excite surprise is, not that so little notice is taken of this appearance of Vishnu in these books, but that the Brahmans have admitted it into their mythology as one of his

* Transactions of the Bombay Literary Society, vol. iii. p. 529.

† Asiatic Researches, vol. i. p. 284.

incarnations*; because, in the Bhagawat, the work at present held in most esteem by the great majority of Hindus, it is expressly declared that the appearance of Buddha was for the purpose of deluding the enemies of the gods, and of effecting their destruction by leading them into the rejection of the Hindu religion, and into the profession of heretical opinions. On this point four passages only occur in the Bhagawat, which are as follows:—"Then, at the commencement of the Kali Yug, will Vishnu become incarnate in Kikata, under the name of Buddha, the son of Jina, for the purpose of deluding the enemies of the gods." †—"The Undiscernible Being, having assumed a mortal form, preached heretical doctrines in the three cities founded by Maya (and in Kashi), for the purpose of destroying, by deluding them, the enemies of the gods, steadfast in the religion prescribed by the Vedas." ‡—"Praise be to the pure Buddha, the deluder of the Daityas and Danawas."—"By his words, as Buddha, Vishnu deludes the heretics." § It is precisely in the same manner that this avatar is alluded to in most of the Purans, as it is in the Skanda alone that any detailed account of it occurs. ‖

* It must be recollected, however, that the piety of the inhabitants of the *three cities* and of Kashi is supposed to have been insincere, and this appearance of devotion to have been merely assumed in order to effect an unjust purpose.

† Bhagawat, book i. chap. 3. stanza 24.

‡ Ibid., book ii. chap. 7. stanza 37. The words are,—देवद्विषां निगम वर्त्मनि निष्टितानां पूर्भिर्मयेन विहिताभिर दृश्यमूर्त्तिर्लोकानघ्नतां मतिविमोह मातप्रलोभं वेषं विधायबहुभाष्यत आपधर्म्यं ॥ But it became necessary to insert a gloss in the translation, in order to convey the meaning. For part of the stanza refers to Vishnu's appearance in a former age in the city of the Tripura Asuras, and part to his incarnation as Buddha.

§ Skand 10. part 1. chap. 39. the first hemistich of the 22d stanza. Skand 11. chap. 4. stanza 22. the words are, वादैर्विमो हय यज्ञकृतोतदहान्

‖ The following account, however, contained in the sixteenth chapter of the Agni Puran, is not only somewhat more detailed, but also, in some degree, different from other accounts of this incarnation:—"*Agni, addressing Vasishta.*—Listen, while I now relate the avatar of Buddha. Formerly the Suras, having been conquered in battle by the Asuras, sought the protection of Vishnu; and he, who always defends those that make him their refuge, assumed the delusive form of Buddha, and was born the son of Jina. Under this form he deceived the Asuras, and induced them to renounce the religion of the Vedas,

This legend is, however, related in a more detailed manner in the Kashi Khand of the Skanda Puran, and in the Ganesha Upa-Puran *, in which the appearance of Buddha is described merely as a manifestation, and not as an incarnation, of Vishnu ; for this account states, that Divodasa, a king of the solar race, finding Kashi unoccupied, took possession of it, and there established the religion of the Vedas on so firm a basis, and rendered his people so virtuous, pious, and happy, that the gods became alarmed lest they should lose their supremacy. As usual, therefore, they had recourse to both Vishnu and Shiva to liberate them from their anxieties ; but both at first declared that it would be unrighteous to deprive so virtuous a prince of his kingdom. At length Shiva, grieved at having been so long banished from his favourite place of residence †, consented to accomplish the wishes of the deities. This, however, it was impossible to effect, as long as Divodasa and his subjects remained steadfast in their religion; and it consequently became necessary to lead them into error. For this purpose, Devi, the twelve suns, and Ganesha, were employed unsuccessfully, until, at last, Vishnu appeared as Buddha, and effected their apostasy.

Nothing, therefore, can be more consistent than the Brahminical accounts of the two appearances of Vishnu for the purpose of disseminating heretical doctrines: for in both instances, at Tripura and at Kashi, the king and his people had become the enemies of the gods, in consequence of their extreme piety and virtue, which threatened to deprive Indra and the immortals of heaven. No means, consequently, remained for preventing this dispossession, but by rendering the king and his people the voluntary instruments of their own downfall. This consideration alone will, *a priori*, explain the doctrines which it was

---

and thus enabled the Suras to conquer their enemies. Since that time, heresy, the rejection of the Vedas, and Buddhism, began to prevail; and during the Kali Yug shall prideful men be eager to embrace this damnable heresy."

* The passage respecting Vishnu's appearance as Buddha, will be found in the fifty-eighth chapter of the Kashi Khand, and in the thirty-ninth chapter of the Krira Khand of the Ganesha Upa-Puranam.

† Divodasa had obtained as a boon from Brahma, that none of the deities should remain in his kingdom, or exercise any power in it.

requisite for Buddha to propagate, in order to render Divodasa and his subjects apostates from the religion of the Vedas. Accordingly, as related in the Kashi Khand of the Skanda Puran, and in Ganesha Upa-Puran, his doctrines were, as correctly stated by Mr. Erskine, "that no credit is due to the Vedas or Shastras; that it is useless to worship the images of gods; that sacrifices (and the killing) of animals are cruel and sinful; that there is no transmigration; but that, at death, the five elements in the body dissolve, never to reunite; that pleasure is the object of life, and all acts of abstinence, worship, and charity, unprofitable; that the body is man's real god, and should alone be attended to; that agreeable food, fine clothes, and handsome women form the grand felicity of man." * To which may be added, that this world is without beginning, and owes its existence to neither creator nor cause; and that neither Brahma, Vishnu, Rudra, nor any other god, ever existed.

It must be hence obvious, that whether the Brahminical Buddha be an incarnation according to the *Vaishnavas*, or a manifestation of Vishnu according to the *Shaivas*, his appearance was merely for a local and temporary purpose; and it is equally obvious that the heretical doctrines, to which he was obliged to have recourse, in order to render Divodasa the voluntary cause of his own downfall, were not topics on which any Brahminical writer would think himself at liberty to enlarge. But to such very adequate reasons may be justly ascribed the very slight notice which is taken of this incarnation in Sanscrit works; and, consequently, this circumstance affords no grounds for supposing that the Brahmans ever entertained a different opinion on the subject. On the contrary, there exists not a single authentic memorial which will support these remarks of Mr. Erskine: — "In them (the doctrines of ancient Hindu books and inscriptions) the Hindu Buddha of older times is a being of very different estimation from the Buddha they now acknowledge. He is not a false teacher and impostor; he is great, kind, and merciful; the chief of the gods, adorned with every attribute of wisdom and benevolence, and worthy to receive all praise and worship." † For, according

* Transactions of the Bombay Literary Society, part iii. p. 532.

† Ibid., p. 529.

to the *Shaivas*, this appearance of Buddha being merely a manifestation of Vishnu, the appearance ceased as soon as the object for which it was assumed was effected; and in this character every Hindu has always considered Buddha to have been a false teacher and impostor; nor is there, I believe, a single Puran or other work, wherein the *Vaishnava* tenets prevail, in which any detailed account of the birth and subsequent actions of Buddha, the son of Jina, can be found.

From the above short summary, also, of the doctrines ascribed to the Brahminical Buddha, it seems evident that these do not any farther correspond with the accounts of Buddhism which have been hitherto published, than in the rejection of the Vedas, and of the religion founded upon them. If, therefore, there is no similarity in these doctrines, and if there are no detailed accounts of the ninth incarnation of Vishnu, which might be compared with the incidents in the life of Buddha which are believed by the Buddhists, it must necessarily follow that there are no data whatever which will justify an identification of these two personages. A mere supposition that coincidences in the accounts given of these two Buddhas may have formerly existed, but have since been misrepresented or expunged in Sanscrit works, is much too futile a ground on which to admit the correctness of any argument. But on a point for the determination of which there is no historical evidence, tradition ought not to be entirely disregarded; and it may, therefore, be observed, that in the western parts of India it is the general opinion, among well informed natives, that Buddha was born, as related in the Bhagawat, in Kikata, the son of Jina; and that, after having effected the apostasy of Divodasa, having been prevailed upon by the Brahmans and holy men to terminate the propagation of his heretical doctrines, he immediately disappeared in a deep well at Gaya; and that he left behind him no writings nor disciples. They further maintain that no Buddhists were known in India, until their sect was established by Gautama; in support of which opinion they refer to the following legend, which is transcribed from the Shiva Puran.

Suta thus began: — " Hear, O Rishi! a most excellent and sin-destroying narrative, which I will relate as I heard it with other Rishis from Vyasa. Formerly there was a famous Rishi, named Gautama, and his virtuous wife was named Ahalya: with her he performed, during a thousand years, a rigorous *tapas* in the southern country, near the mountain Brahmadri. At this time a drought had desolated the country, and neither moisture nor rain had the earth experienced for a hundred years; water there was not; and ascetics, men, birds, and beasts, died every where. On beholding this lamentable state, Gautama, having reflected, performed for six months the severest mortifications in honour of Varuna; at the termination of which the god appeared to him and thus said:—'I am propitiated by thee, O holy devotee! demand whatever boon thou wishest, and I will grant it.' Gautama then requested rain; but Varuna replied,—'How can I transgress the divine command? Ask some other boon which it may be in my power to bestow upon thee.' On hearing this, Gautama said,—'O god! if thou art pleased with me, and willing to grant me a favour, I will request that which thou canst easily perform: cause then to appear a hermitage which shall surpass all others in beauty, and shaded from the sun by fragrant and fruit-bearing trees, where men and women by holy meditation shall be liberated from pain, sorrow, and anxiety; and also, as thou art the lord of water, let it enjoy a perennial fountain.' Varuna replied, 'So be it;' and then causing a pit to be filled with water, he thus said,—'This water shall remain unexhausted, and thy name shall become celebrated by this reservoir becoming a place of pilgrimage.' Having thus spoken, Varuna disappeared. In this manner did Gautama obtain water with which he performed in due manner the daily ceremonies: he sowed, also, rice for holy offerings, and watered it from this inexhaustible fountain; and grain of various kinds, trees, flowers, and fruits adorned his hermitage. Thus the grove of Gautama became the loveliest on the terrestrial orb; and there resorted ascetics, birds, and beasts, to live in happiness; and there, likewise, holy men fixed their abode with their sons and disciples. In this grove none knew sorrow, and gladness alone prevailed; but listen to what afterwards happened.

"On one day Gautama had sen this disciples to bring water; but when they approached the fountain, some Brahman women who were there prevented them, and scoffingly called out,—'We are the wives of holy anchorets; after we have filled our pitchers, you may then draw water.' The disciples returned, and mentioned this circumstance to the wife of Gautama; and Ahalya, having consoled them, proceeded herself to the fountain, and having drawn water, brought it to her husband. Thus she did daily; and the other Brahman women not only scoffed her, but at length went, and thus each falsely addressed her husband: — 'My lord! Ahalya daily taunts me and the other Brahman women, and I have no other resource than thee. Violence, falsehood, deceit, foolishness, covetousness, and inconsiderateness, are the innate vices of women; and, alas! of what avail will holy meditation be to me, if I suffer every day the reproaches of Ahalya?' Each husband, having heard these words, revolved them in his mind, and thought that they could not be true, and that they would be guilty of ingratitude if they noticed them. But their wicked wives every day reproached them for not affording them redress; and at length one day, as they were passing through the grove, they overheard their wives making the same complaints to Gautama, and therefore believed that what they had said was true. The devotees, having then assembled together, began to consult respecting the manner in which they might resent this injury, so that their revenge might not appear to proceed from them; and after deliberation determined on invoking the assistance of Ganesha. They then propitiated him with offerings of durwa, lotoses, and rice; of vermilion, sandal wood, and incense; of rice milk, cakes, and sweetmeats; and with prostrations, prayers, and burnt-offerings. Well pleased, the god appeared and thus spoke, — 'I am propitiated: say, what boon do you desire?' They replied, — 'If thou art willing to grant us a favour, contrive to remove Gautama from his hermitage; for, if we adopt any means for that purpose, we shall expose ourselves to censure.' Ganesha answered, — 'To injure or destroy a man who is free from blame is not just; and to return evil for good will be productive of sorrow, and not of benefit: whoever performs holy meditation will obtain the happiest result; but the injuring of another will destroy the advantages which would be derived from it. Gautama has given you gold, and you wish to return glass; but that which is right ought to be performed.' Having heard these words, the devotees, from mental delusion, thus replied, — 'O lord! we entreat thee to do what we have requested, as we desire no other favour.' Ganesha then said, — 'Good cannot produce evil, nor evil good: from its very essence evil must produce misery, and good happiness. Gautama will enjoy happiness from his holy meditation; but sorrow alone can result from your present wish. But you are deluded by female fascination, and you cannot, therefore, discriminate between good and evil. I will, however, comply with your request; though you will undoubtedly hereafter regret having made it.' Having thus spoken, Ganesha disappeared.

"Gautama, unacquainted with the evil intentions of the devotees, joyfully performed each day the sacred ceremonies: but one day, being in a field of rice and barley, Ganapati, having assumed the form of an extremely debilitated cow, appeared there trembling, and scarcely able to move, and began to eat the rice and barley. Observing this, the compassionate Gautama lifted a stalk of grass and struck the cow with it, in order to drive her away; but scarcely was she touched with the stalk when she dropped on the ground, and immediately died, while all the devotees beheld what passed with looks of distress. The holy men and their lovely wives then exclaimed, — 'O Gautama! what hast thou done?' Gautama, also, in amazement, thus addressed Ahalya: — 'What an accident! how can I have incurred the anger of the gods? what shall I do? where shall I go? thus involved in the guilt of the murder of a cow.' The devotees at the same time thus reproached him: — 'Alas! O holy Rishi! of what avail has been thy knowledge? Alas! of what avail thy burnt-offering and thy strict performance of every ceremony?' In the same manner their wives thus reproached the wife of Gautama: — 'Alas! Ahalya, of what avail have been thy wisdom, and the universal respect shown to thee? Alas! of what avail thy virtue and piety?' Thus they reviled Gautama and his wife, and then exclaimed to each other, — 'Let us not look on the face of this slayer of a cow: whoever looks on his countenance will become equally guilty; and whoever approaches his hermitage, that man's offerings neither will fire nor the manes receive.' Thus reviling Gautama, they all threw stones at him. Gautama then exclaimed, — 'Alas! alas! what shall I do? I swear, O holy men! that I will depart from this place.' Having thus spoken, he removed to a distant spot, and there erected a hermitage: but as long as this sin, falsely imputed to him, remained unexpiated, he could perform no holy ceremony, and his wife continued exposed to the insults of the other Brahman women; and thus Gautama suffered the greatest misery. At length, after a short time, Gautama assembled the holy men, and thus addressed them: — 'Have compassion on me, and acquaint me with the ceremonies by which my sin may be expiated; for without instruction no good act can be effected.' The Brahmans then consulted together, respecting the penance which ought to be prescribed, while Gautama stood at a distance in an humble posture; and after deliberation they thus said: — 'Sin can never be expiated except by suitable purification: for this purpose, therefore, do thou circumambulate the whole earth, and on returning here, circumambulate a hundred times the mountain of Brahma, and thus thou wilt be purified; or make ablutions in the Ganges, and on its banks having made ten millions of earthen lingams, worship the god whose symbol is the lingam, and then perambulate the sacred mountain and bathe in the hundred holy pools. By these means thy sin will be expiated.' Having heard these words, Gautama first circumambulated the holy mountain; and afterwards, as directed, formed the earthen lingams in order that he might be restored to his pristine purity. He then, with Ahalya, and his disciples, worshipped Shiva with the holiest rites, and most intense devotion. At length the lord of the mountain-born goddess descended from the summit of Kailasa and thus addressed him: — 'Say, what boon dost thou desire?' On beholding that form divine, a sight of which is so difficult to be obtained, Gautama was filled with delight, and having reverenced the mighty god with laudatory strains, requested that he would liberate him from the guilt that he had incurred. Shiva replied: — 'Happy art thou, O mighty Rishi! and the fruit of all thy pious acts hast thou obtained, for thou art free from sin. Thou hast been deceived by these wicked men, for even the three worlds become purified by thy presence. How then canst thou be polluted by an act committed by these evil-minded men, and who will suffer for it hereafter?' Shankara then explained to him all their wickedness and ingratitude, and Gautama listened with astonishment; and, after Shankara had ceased speaking, he thus said:—'These Brahmans have done me the greatest favour, for if it had not been for their act I should not have enjoyed the felicity of beholding thee, O lord!' Pleased with these words, Shiva again expressed his satisfaction with the piety and devotion of Gautama, and desired him to ask a boon. Gautama replied that all he entreated was, that the Ganga might there appear, in order that he might purify himself in it; with this request Shiva complied, and the consequence was the establishment of the sacred place of pilgrimage at Trimbucka on the Godavery."*

But Gautama, according to tradition, was so offended with the conduct of the Brahmans on this occasion, that he determined to separate from their communion, and to establish a new religion. If, therefore, the miraculous part of this legend be rejected, nothing can seem more probable than that Gautama, having experienced some unjust treatment from the Brahmans, should thus attempt to revenge himself. Nor is it necessary to suppose that this Gautama was one of the seven Rishis who sprang into existence at the volition of Brahma at the creation of this universe; for he may have been merely a learned Brahman, and not improbably the very same person who founded the Nyaya school philosophy. †

To this supposition an objection may arise from the list of the first thirty-three patriarchs of the religion of Buddha, which M. Abel Remusat has thus characterised:—"Je pense donc qu'on ne verra

* Shiva Puran, part i., the legend respecting Trimbucka; but the chapters are not numbered in my copy of this Puran.

In the Varaha Puran, however, it is said that Gautama, on becoming acquainted with the deceit of the Brahmans, imprecated, as a curse on them, that they might become outcasts from the ordinances of the Vedas; and that, in consequence, these Brahmans, on being born again in the Kali Yug, all became heretics. It is also related, that the boon which Gautama obtained from Shiva was a lock of his hair (containing, of course, a portion of the water of the Ganges), and that when he struck the dead cow with it, it was not only restored to life, but a river also gushed out from the spot where it was lying, which was, in consequence, name Godavari.

† It certainly seems much more probable that in India a Brahman should be the founder of a new sect, than that it should owe its origin to the son of a king. Gautama, however, is not included amongst either the seven original Rishis or the ten Prajapatis, but his origin is generally ascribed to Brahma.

pas sans intérêt une liste de trente-trois personnages que les Bouddhistes nomment illustres, et par lesquels, suivant ces sectaires, la doctrine secrète a été transmise successivement depuis Bouddha lui-même jusqu'à une époque posterieure à celle ou les livres sacrés qui lui sont attribués furent traduits en Chinois (A. D. 418). L'importance de ce document pour la chronologie et pour l'histoire pourra être développée ailleurs, il suffit en ce moment de le présenter sous une forme abrégée. S'il eût été connu plutôt, on eût peut-être émis moins d'idées hasardées sur l'antiquité des diverses opinions Bouddhiques, et en particulier sur l'origine de la hiérarchie des Grands Lamas." * But before any argument can be founded on this list, it must be satisfactorily proved that it was formed from authentic materials, and that it is not a mere imaginary account of a succession of patriarchs, invented long after the time of Gautama: for, as M. Abel Remusat himself admits that "celui-ci dans l'ordre des divinités incarnés vient immediatement après Bouddha," on what grounds are the ten intervening patriarchs inserted in this list? and what were the reasons, according to the Buddhists, which rendered it necessary for the divinity to become incarnate in this eleventh patriarch alone? Nothing hitherto published tends in the slightest degree to explain these circumstances, or to prove that Buddha ever established a sect, or that the doctrines ascribed to him were transmitted through a regular succession of patriarchs to Gautama.

But a writer in the seventh number of the Calcutta Oriental Magazine, after examining a variety of dates given by different authors, very justly observes: — "Besides these dates †, which, for the greater

* Journal des Savans, Janvier, 1821, p. 8.

† These dates are as follows: —

Abul Fazl	B. C. 1366	Bailli	B. C. 1031
Couplet from Chinese historians	1036	Sir W. Jones	1027
De Guignes, ditto	1027	M. Klaproth	1027
Georgi	959	M. Remusat	970
The Burmese	546	The Peguers	638
The Siamese	544	A Chinese writer, cited by M. Klaproth	688
The Cingalese	619		

Mr. Erskine, also, in the third volume of the Transactions of the Bombay Literary Society, after fully examining this point, has very justly concluded: — "Upon the whole,

part, agree as nearly as could be well expected, and which certainly point to the existence of a Buddha, between ten and twelve centuries anterior to the Christian era, there is an equally extensive and consistent series, which bears testimony to the existence of a similar personage, a Buddha, or revival of that legislator, in a more recent period (between B. C. 688 and 544). . . . . At the same time nothing further is known of any such prior legislator; for all the legends which have been gathered by Klaproth, Pallas, and Remusat, from the Chinese, Thibetan, and Mongol writers, are referable to the latter Buddha, and relate uniformly to the Buddha named Sakya Sinha, the same with Gautama."

This question, therefore, arises, whether the general belief amongst different people of the existence of a prior Buddha is sufficient to prove his reality as a historic personage? or whether this belief may not be merely the result of some dogmas of the Buddhist religion, and the actual existence of this Buddha altogether imaginary? The same question applies still more strongly to the Brahminical Buddha; because unless all the other twenty-one incarnations of Vishnu are admitted to be historic events, there can be no reason whatever for ascribing such importance to his ninth principal incarnation alone. No authentic memorial, however, can, I believe, be produced, which will satisfactorily attest the historic existence of these two Buddhas; while, on the contrary, the historic existence of Gautama, and his institution of the Buddhist religion, seem to be substantiated by every proof which the case admits of.

From these remarks it will perhaps be apparent that the speculations respecting Buddha and his religion, in which some writers have indulged, are purely European, and that they are not in the slightest degree sanctioned by the writings of either the Brahmans or the Buddhists; for, according to the former, Vishnu was incarnated as the son of

---

until some proof is discovered of the existence of a Bouddhist religion older than Gautama, or existing more than 540 years before Christ, I should be disposed to adopt that era as the origin of the sect, and to suppose the religion of the Brahmans to be older, and that of the Jains more modern than that date."

Jina, or appeared for the purpose of effecting a local and particular object by the propagation of doctrines in direct opposition to the Hindu religion; and, according to the latter, Buddha became incarnate as the son of Sudhodana, for the purpose of reforming mankind, and restoring Buddhism to its original purity. The latter deny that Gautama established their religion, and ascribe its origin to the remotest antiquity; while the Brahmans have invariably considered the ninth incarnation of Vishnu, as exhibiting the power of that god who could so effectually delude the minds of men as to induce them to apostatise from the pure and holy religion prescribed by the Vedas. The singular incorrectness, therefore, of these remarks of M. Guigniaut must be evident; but they are quoted in order to show on what insufficient grounds the literati of Europe adopt opinions respecting Hindu mythology:—"Peut-être, aussi, serait-il plus sage de s'en tenir à des faits généraux, et de tâcher de combiner ces indications précieuses en elles-mêmes avec celles que nous donnent vaguement les Brahmanes; au moins jusqu'à ce qu'il nous soit permis de percer, à l'aide de nouvelles recherches, tout ce qui concerne Bouddha. Ils le reconnaissent, ils avouent même une partie de la réforme mise sur son compte, celle qui touche la religion, proprement dite, et le dogme comme le culte; leur doctrine est sa doctrine, et il n' y a qu'un pas de la philosophie Védant au Bouddhaisme."* One step from the purest spiritualism to the grossest materialism! and the doctrine of the Brahmans the same as the doctrines of the Buddhists! But it is equally incorrect to affirm that the Brahmans acknowledge Buddha: if by Buddha is intended a mere man, the founder of a new religion, for in such a character they never have acknowledged him; and it still remains to be proved that the son of Jina and the prior Buddha of the Buddhists are one and the same person, before any arguments can be justly founded on such an identification.

It has also been hitherto overlooked that the appearance of Vishnu as Buddha is merely a repetition of a similar incident which occurred in the Krita Yug, when, as intimated in the passage above

* Religions de l'Antiquité, tom. i. p. 300.

quoted from the Bhagawat, "the Undiscernible Being, having assumed a mortal form, preached heretical doctrines in the three cities founded by Maya." * This legend is thus related at length in the Shiva Puran:—

"Three Asuras, in consequence of a boon granted by Brahma, obtained the construction of three cities,—one of gold, situated in heaven; another of silver, in mid-air; and the third of iron, on the earth; and became so powerful as to occasion the utmost distress to the gods. The gods, therefore, as usual, repaired to Brahma, and communicated their grievances to him. Pitamaha having heard related the distress occasioned by the Tripura † Asuras, replied,—'They have grown powerful through me, and consequently it would not be proper that their death should proceed from me. Virtue and piety also flourish in their cities; but entreat Shiva and he will accomplish this affair.' The immortals accordingly proceeded to the abode of Shiva, and implored his assistance. Shiva answered,—'That chief of the Asuras promotes virtue; and it is not allowable to kill a virtuous being. As long, therefore, as he continues virtuous, he cannot be slain by me: but repair to Vishnu, and represent your wishes to him.' The gods, in consequence, hastened to Vishnu, and acquainted him with their griefs; but he replied,—'This is undoubtedly a true saying, that where justice and piety flourish there distress shall no more take place than darkness occur when the sun shines.' Having heard these words, the gods were afflicted, and thus, with desponding countenances, addressed Vishnu:—'What then shall we do? or where shall we dwell? or how shall justice or piety exist, if these Asuras be allowed to live? Either consign us to an untimely fate, or imagine means for effecting their destruction.' Vishnu, beholding them thus affected, was moved with compassion, and reflected in what manner he might accomplish their wishes; and then said,—'Propitiate Maheshwara with sacrifice, and he will destroy the Tripura Asuras and thus protect the three worlds.' The immortals having heard the words of Achuta, were delighted, and hastened to perform sacrifice to Shiva.

* This is the divine architect of the Asuras, as Vishwakarma is of the Suras.

† Tripura in Sanscrit signifies three cities.

"Vishnu then thus reflected: — 'How shall I, through the favour of Parameshwara, effect the wishes of the gods by destroying these mighty Asuras; for undoubtedly the destruction of virtuous beings is an improper act, and both the chiefs and the inhabitants of the three cities are distinguished by their virtue? They are also safe from death, since they adore Shiva and worship the lingam, and are thus liberated from all sin and its consequences. But, if their piety and devotion could be interrupted, then might they be instantly destroyed. Since, therefore, they cannot be destroyed as long as they adhere to the precepts of the Veda and to the worship of Shiva, let me, for the protection and benefit of the gods, induce these Asuras to forsake the religious observances to which they are at present so much devoted.'

"Vishnu, having thus determined, formed for this purpose, from his own substance, a man capable of deluding the Tripura Asuras, dressed in dirty garments, with his head shaved, bearing in his hands a pot and a besom, walking step by step, incessantly applying the end of his garment to his mouth, and saying, — 'This alone is the true faith.' This being, then, joining his hands, and making an obeisance to Hari, thus said, — 'Command what I shall do.' The lord replied, — 'Listen, while I inform thee for what purpose thou hast been created; for, as thou hast been formed from my substance, it is proper that thou shouldest do whatever I desire; and thou shalt, in consequence, be hereafter worshipped as myself. Publish, therefore, these sixteen hundred thousand delusive couplets, in direct contradiction of the Vedas and other sacred books, and destructive of castes and orders, in order that the Tripura Asuras may be induced to apostatise from the pure doctrines of the Vedas, and that they may thus obtain hell instead of heaven. In order, also, to spread amongst them these heretical opinions, I will inspire thee with such power as to render that which is desirable undesirable, and that which is holy unholy, and to give to that which is evil the appearance of excellence.' Having thus spoken, Hari himself instructed Mayi * in the heretical doctrines which

* This is the name of the being formed from the substance of Vishnu, and therefore considered the same as Vishnu himself.

he was to publish; and then said,—'Now hasten to Tripura, and effect the apostasy of their inhabitants; after which, proceed to Marwar, and there remain the chief of thy sect, until the Kali Yug commences; and then thy doctrines shall acquire splendour, and thy disciples and followers shall become numerous.'

"The *shaved-head*, that he might perform the orders of Vishnu, then formed a number of disciples, and also four *shaved-heads* like himself, to whom he gave in charge the four heretical books which were to supersede the four Vedas, all dressed in dirty clothes, with cloths applied to their mouths, holding in their hands a pot and a besom, and speaking little, but saying,—'By this faith alone can true knowledge be obtained.' Thus accompanied, Mayi entered the city, and fixed his abode in a grove therein situated; and soon, by his deceptive arts, widely diffused his delusive doctrines. All who came to his abode were induced to accept initiation; and there many were led by his fame to resort. Soon as this had been effected, Narada entered the city, and having become initiated by Mayi repaired to the king, and informed him that the teacher of a new sect, distinguished by piety, had there established himself. Having received this information, the king determined that, since Narada had been initiated in the new sect, he would also become initiated; and he accordingly proceeded to Mayi, whom having saluted he thus addressed,—'Let me be initiated by thee, O pure and holy sage!' Mayi, having removed the cloth from his mouth, replied,—'If thou wilt give thyself and thy subjects up to me; not otherwise.' The king, hearing these words, consented, and immediately he and all the inhabitants of Tripura were initiated in the new doctrines. Then were abolished the duties prescribed to women, funeral obsequies, the adoration of Shiva, sacrifice to Vishnu, bathing at stated times, the presenting of gifts, and other pious acts; the worship of the lingam, the observances of castes and orders, and all the other ordinances of the Vedas. Thus were the three cities deprived of their prosperity, by being led into the adoption of heretical doctrines, and the renunciation of the true religion, by the delusion of Hari. Vishnu, then, with the gods, proceeded to entreat Shiva to destroy these Asuras; and, having addressed him as usual, in a long litany of praises, Shiva embraced Vishnu, and thus replied: — 'Since the piety and virtue of the Tripura Asuras have been destroyed by the powerful delusion of Vishnu, now can the wishes of the gods be accomplished, and I will therefore immediately effect the destruction of their enemies.'" *

It will not, however, be contended, I may suppose, that this legend is founded on a historical event; and yet it rests on precisely the same authority as that on which Buddha, the ninth incarnation of Vishnu, has been converted into a historical personage. The character, also, under which both Mayi and Buddha appeared, is exactly the same; and, according to the firm belief of the Hindus, they were both employed to effect apostasy from the Hindu religion. The singular inaccuracy, therefore, of these remarks of M. Guigniaut must be evident: — "Bouddha joue évidemment plusieurs rôles dans la religion des Hindous; et soit par ses caractères intrinsiques, soit par ses attributs extérieurs, il se rattache à la fois aux trois systèmes dans lesquels cette religion nous a paru se diviser: les rapports avec Siva sont manifestes; il tient à Dherma, roi de justice, et partage son nom; car la vérité et la justice, la science et la vertu, sont inseparables: aussi son image est-elle placée entre les symboles et les dieux du Sivaisme dans les plus anciens temples de l'Inde, et lui-même, nous l'avons vu plus haut faire alliance avec Siva, trop faible pour resister seul à ses ennemis. D'un autre côté il complète la serie des incarnations passées de

* Shiva Puran, the commencement of the legend of the Tripura Asuras. This legend is related in nearly the same words in the Lainga Puran, part i. chap. 71. But the account given in the Bhagawat, skand vii. chap. 10., of Vishnu's appearance in Tripura, is so different that it may be proper to insert the material part of it: — "The gods having entreated the protection of Shiva, he told them not to be afraid, and seizing his bow discharged arrows at the cities; and his fiery shafts fell on them like beams from the sun. Whomsoever they touched he fell dead; but Maya lifting him up threw him into a well of amrit, and he was thus restored to life. But Vishnu, perceiving that Shiva was in consequence cast down and dispirited, immediately imagined a means of ensuring success. For which purpose he assumed the form of a cow, and caused Brahma to take the shape of a calf, and the two entered the city at noon-day, and drank up the well of amrit." This account is singularly puerile, and is not only contrary to the usual style of the Purans, but also inconsistent with the passage before quoted from the Bhagawat, in which it is intimated that Vishnu prepared the destruction of the inhabitants of Tripura in precisely the same manner as it is related in the legend which I have quoted from the Shiva Puran.

Vichnou; il continue Crichna comme dieu miséricordieux, gardien des hommes, ancre du salut, chargé de preparer la terre au jour terrible ou paraitra son juge. Dans le Brahmaisme c'est une planète, mais c'est aussi un *Mouni*, un fils de *Richi*, un *Richi* même, peut-être; et l'on entrevoit je ne sçais quelle correspondence entre les Bouddhas et les Menous qui président également aux périodes successives du monde; d'ailleurs, Bouddha fils de la lune est visiblement l'analogue et comme le pendant nécessaire de Vaivaswata fils du soleil. *. . . . . *Bouddha, Maya, Brahm, voilà toute la religion des Brahmanes*, ou dans son germe, ou, par un retour plus naturel qu'on ne pourrait le croire au premier abord, dans son plus haut développement." † But Buddha is universally considered by the Hindus to have been (partially, indeed) the *subverter*, and not the *reformer*, of the Hindu religion, and, consequently, *il ne joue aucun rôle* in the Hindu mythology: for the incarnation of Vishnu as Buddha is merely slightly alluded to in Sanscrit works, and it is a subject which attracts no attention whatever at the present day. But M. Guigniaut himself observes: — " Chose singulière, mais qui n'est pas sans exemples dans les annales des peuples! Bouddha naquit parmi les Hindous; son nom n'a pas cessé d'être révéré de cette pieuse nation; long-temps ses adorateurs veçurent paisibles, respectés même, entre les sectes nombreuses qui repartagent le pays; et cependant, depuis plusieurs siècles, *Bouddha ne jouit d'aucun culte dans l'Inde; ses temples ses idoles y sont renversés ou abandonnés, une ténébreuse horreur, une ignorance feinte ou réelle, une haine non moins violente qu'irréfléchie, règnent chez les Brahmanes, sur tout ce qui concerne sa doctrine*." ‡ It is, however, obviously impossible to reconcile the passage in Italic with the preceding assertion that Buddha has not ceased to be revered by this pious nation. This confusion of ideas necessarily proceeds from not having formed a correct notion of the character of Buddha: for, as long as he is merely considered as an incarnation of Vishnu, he is held to be an object of reverence; not, however, as Buddha, but as that deity himself. But the Hindus have never acknowledged him under any other character,

* Religions de l'Antiquité, vol. i. p. 294. † Ibid. p. 296. ‡ Ibid. p. 296.

and, consequently, all else that has been written concerning him is totally foreign from the Hindu religion. *

If, however, the ninth incarnation of Vishnu be so clearly a mythological fable, it must necessarily follow that, as it cannot therefore receive a place in history, the identification of Buddha the son of Jina with the prior Buddha of the Buddhists, can afford no valid argument in favour of the antiquity of Buddhism. I cannot, consequently, assent to the justness of the following remarks of Professor Heeren: — "We are certainly unable to illustrate historically the origin of the sects (in India), or to specify the probable period when this took place. The sects of Shiva and Vishnu are at present the most prevalent, but they are not the only ones; for there is that of Ganesha, and several others. From its internal nature, and its objects of worship, it seems highly probable that the sect of Shiva, whose votaries adore the lingam, is the most ancient; and perhaps even it is the oldest religion of the Hindus. On the contrary, the worshippers of Vishnu under the form of Krishna, are indebted to a reformation for their origin, the object of which was to refine the grossness of the then existing religious system. But the sect of Krishna is so intimately connected with those epic poems of the Hindus, the principal subject of which is this incarnation of Vishnu, that this system of belief may be very justly called a poetical religion. The attempt made by Jones to fix the period of the first appearance of this sect at 1200 years before the birth of Christ, and that of Buddhism about two hundred years later, rests on very weak grounds. What we know with certainty respecting Buddha is merely that he also was the founder of a sect which must have once predominated in a great part of India, the doctrines and system of belief of the votaries of which were in direct opposition to the religion of the Brahmans; so that a deadly hatred

* I may add that mistakes seem also to have arisen from its not having been recollected that the Amara Kosh was written by a Buddhist; and that consequently the names or epithets therein contained are such as are applied to Buddha by his own sectaries only, and never by the Hindus.

Though it may seem trivial, it may perhaps deserve remark, that the name of the regent of the planet Mercury in Sanscrit is spelled *Budha* बुध, and that of the founder of Buddhism *Buddha* बुद्ध; and that in Hindu mythology they are represented as perfectly distinct personages.

sprang up between them, which terminated in the expulsion of the Buddhists from India. But the many important historical problems respecting this sect which remain to be solved must be obvious. It is not the period only when it originated which is doubtful; yet that this sect must be very ancient is evinced by the oldest cave-temples being dedicated to Buddha. *But another stronger proof arises from the Buddhists being mentioned* (at least once, as far as we yet know) *in the Ramayan*, along with atheists, *i. e.* the opponents of the Brahmans; for those who deny the doctrine of the Vedas are considered to be all of the same stamp. It is hence clear, *that when the Ramayan was composed the Buddhists not only existed, but were deemed the adversaries of the Brahmans.* With respect to the connection that there may be between the doctrines of the Buddhists and of the Brahmans, and to the history of the persecution and expulsion from India of the former, these points still remain involved in darkness." *

This opinion, however, of Professor Heeren seems to be principally founded on a wrong reading, or a mistranslation of a verse contained in the printed edition of the Ramayan †; but I will venture to assert, without the fear of contradiction, that the term Buddhist does not occur even once throughout the whole of that poem. At the same time, were this not the case, such a circumstance would prove only the recentness of the period in which the Ramayan was composed, and not the antiquity of Buddhism; for there are clearly no grounds, either mythological, traditional, or historical, for placing the origin of this sect at an earlier period than that of Gautama, or about 540 years before Christ. It is rather singular, however, that Professor Heeren should refer, in support of his opinion, to these remarks of Mr. Colebrooke: —

* Ideen ueber die Politik, &c. vol. viii. p. 127. 4th edit.

† I have not the Serampore edition of the first two books of the Ramayan; but, in two MS. copies of this poem which I have consulted, there is not, throughout the whole of the conversation between Jabali and Rama, a single term used which signifies Buddhist, though the word *nastika*, or atheist, occurs several times. In the original, the words quoted by Professor Heeren (ibid., p. 129. note), *As a thief so is a Buddhist*, are यथा हि चोरः तथार्थलुब्धस्त था गतं नास्तिकमल्पबुद्धिं *As a thief, so one covetous of riches; and as both is he who has embraced atheism the consequence of little understanding.*

" According to the notions which I entertain of the real history of the Hindu religion, *the worship of Rama* and of Krishna by the Vaishnavas, and that of Mahadeva and Bhavani by the Shaivas and Shaktas, *have been introduced since the persecution of the Buddhas and Jainas.* The institutions of the Vedas are anterior to Buddha, whose theology seems to have been borrowed from the system of Kapila."* For it seems evident that the incarnation of Vishnu, as Rama Chandra, must have acquired a considerable degree of celebrity before an epic poem would have been composed on the subject; and that, if these incarnations are not mentioned in the Vedas, as stated by Mr. Colebrooke, there can be no sufficient grounds for ascribing an earlier date to the Ramayan than the origin of the sect which first considered Rama to have been an incarnate god. If, therefore, this poem be of comparatively recent composition, it must follow, that, though Buddhists were mentioned in it, this would be no proof of the antiquity which Professor Heeren ascribes to Buddhism. As, however, I differ entirely from Mr. Colebrooke in the notions which he has expressed respecting the real history of the Hindu religion, I do not contest the antiquity of the Ramayan; and I have therefore thought it necessary to point out so material a mistake as the one which has taken place in the printed edition of that poem.

* Asiatic Researches, vol. viii. p. 474.

CHAP. X.

BRAHMA. — FURTHER REMARKS ON THE HINDU RELIGION.

That, on the first institution of the Hindu religion, a certain degree of preeminence over the other two divine hypostases was ascribed to Brahma seems fully evinced by his name *; by his being universally acknowledged to have been the author of the Vedas; and by his name slightly modified having been employed to designate that priesthood who have always been the sole guardians and preceptors of the Hindu religion. Although, also, he is both in the Upanishads and Purans identified with the Supreme Being, still his character, as a divine hypostasis only, has been much more clearly preserved than that of either Vishnu or Shiva; for in the Institutes of Menu (as well as in several Purans) it is said: — "He, whom the mind alone can perceive, whose essence eludes the external organs, who has no visible parts, who exists from eternity, even He the soul of all beings, whom no being can comprehend, shone forth in person. He, having willed to produce various beings from his own divine substance, first with a thought created the waters, and placed in them a productive seed: that seed became an egg bright as gold, blazing like a luminary with a thousand beams; and in that egg He was born himself, in the form of Brahma, the great forefather of all spirits." † The peculiar epithet, however, of *creator*, by which Brahma is distinguished, is obviously misapplied, because no act of creation is ever ascribed to him; for the primary elements of things were first created by the Supreme Being, and also by his influence subsequently combined and arranged in the mundane egg. Brahma, therefore, is invariably represented as being only the producer or progenitor of all classes of animated beings; and of the trees, plants, and

* A derivative from Brahm, the Supreme Being.

† Institutes of Menu, translated by Sir W. Jones, chap. i. ver. 7, 8, 9.

herbage which adorn the earth, and which also the Hindus consider to be endued with life.

But this deity must have long ceased to be an object of popular worship, since he is never described in the Purans as exerting his divine power for the benefit and protection of men and gods; nor is there in them the slightest trace of such legends respecting him as have been invented in honour of Vishnu and Shiva. The name and attributes, indeed, of Brahma have been preserved; but, without recurring to the probable state of the Hindu religion at its origin, it would at the present day be difficult to discover that he was one of the gods of Hindu mythology, or to understand how he could ever have been invested with such a character.* But the cause which may have occasioned the cessation of his worship, and of the absence in the sacred books of the Hindus of all mention of any manifestation of his divine power†, must now remain unascertainable, as neither writings nor tradition afford any information on the subject. The abolition, however, of the worship of Brahma is at the present day generally attributed to the inevitable consequences resulting from the curse of Shiva; and this event is thus related in the Skanda Puran: —

'The lingam of Shiva, having in Daruwanam fallen on the ground in consequence of the curse of the holy sages‡, instantly increased in size until its base went far beyond the lowest profound and its head towered above the heavens; and Brahma, Vishnu, Indra, and all the gods, having hastened to behold this wonder, thus spoke to one another: — 'What can be its length and breadth? where can be situated its top and base?' Having thus considered, the gods said, — 'O Vishnu! do thou ascertain the base of this lingam, and O lotos-born, do thou discover its head, and let this be the place where you shall return to relate what you may have seen.' Having heard these

* It deserves notice that Sir W. Jones, in his Essay on the gods of Greece, Italy, and India, has almost entirely passed over Brahma; most probably because he could learn nothing respecting him.

† I ought to except that of bestowing boons of the greatest efficacy, as in this respect Brahma is generally the actor; but he always grants them so injudiciously that they never fail to produce the utmost distress to men and gods.

‡ See an account of this circumstance, post, p. 298.

words, Vishnu proceeded to Tartarus, and Brahma to heaven; but high as he ascended, Pitamaha could not perceive the head of that lingam, and he was therefore returning and had arrived at the top of Meru, when *Surabhi**, as she reclined under the shade of a *ketaki* tree†, saw him and thus spoke,—'Where hast thou gone, O Brahma! whence dost thou return? say, can I do any thing for you?' Brahma, smiling, replied,—'I have been sent by the gods to discover the head of this wonderful lingam which fills the three worlds, but I have not been able to reach it. What, therefore, shall I say to them when I return; for if I falsely assert that I have seen its top they will require witnesses to attest the truth of it? Do thou, then, with this *ketaki*, give testimony to what I shall declare.' *Surabhi* and the *ketaki* tree consented to act as Brahma desired; and he, having made this agreement, proceeded to where the angels had remained, and thus addressed them:—'O gods! I have seen the top of this lingam, which is spacious, pure, delightful, adorned with the leaves of the *ketaki*, and wonderful to behold, but without my assistance no one can see it.' On hearing these words the immortals were astonished, and Vishnu said,—'This is most surprising; for I have penetrated through all the lower worlds, and have not been able to discover its base: but most assuredly this lingam form of Mahadeva has neither beginning, nor middle, nor end; for it was through his divine will that you, O gods and holy sages! were produced, and also this universe with all that it contains, movable and immovable; and in this lingam of the lord is centred creation, preservation, and destruction.' Brahma then said,—'O Vishnu! why art thou surprised that I have seen the top, because thou hast not been able to reach the base of this lingam; but what proof dost thou require to convince thee that I have seen it?' Vishnu, smiling, replied,—'Explain, O Brahma! how thou couldst have seen the head in heaven while I could not discover the base in Tartarus; but if this be really the case, who are the witnesses to your having seen it?' Brahma quickly answered,—'The *ketaki* and *Surabhi*; these, O ye

* The celestial cow, from whose teats stream all things that the gods desire. The curse, however, pronounced on her mouth, applies to that of all cows.

† Pandanus odoratissim

gods ! will attest that I speak the truth.' The immortals then immediately sent for them ; and, when they arrived, *Surabhi* and the *ketaki* declared that Brahma had actually seen the top of the lingam. At this instant a voice was heard from heaven, saying, 'Know, O Suras ! that *Surabhi* and the *ketaki* have spoken falsely, for Brahma has not seen its top.' The immortals then imprecated this curse on *Surabhi*,—'Since thou hast with thy mouth uttered a falsehood, may thy mouth be henceforth deemed impure!' and on the *ketaki*,—'Though thou smellest sweetly, mayest thou be considered unworthy to be offered to Shiva!' After the gods had ceased speaking, the voice from heaven thus cursed Brahma:—'Since thou hast childishly and with weak understanding asserted a falsehood, let no one henceforth perform worship to thee.'"—*Kedar Khand*, chap. 6.*

The only other legend in which Brahma appears as an actor, or rather as a sufferer, is the one respecting his having been deprived of his fifth head; which circumstance is thus related in the Skanda Puran:—

"Once, formerly, when they were assembled on the top of Meru, the holy sages having saluted Brahma requested him to declare the true nature of the godhead; but the creator, influenced by the delusion of Mahesha and his mind obscured by spiritual darkness, asserted his own preeminence and thus replied:—'I am the womb of the universe, without beginning or end, and the sole and self-existent lord, and he who does not worship me shall never obtain beatitude.' On hearing these words Kratu, a form of Narayana†, smiled and said,—'Hadst thou not been misled by ignorance, thou wouldst not have made an assertion so contrary to truth: for I am the framer of the universe, the source of life, the unborn, eternal, and supreme Narayana; and, had I not willed it, creation would not have taken place.' Thus Vishnu and Brahma

* It is very remarkable that this curse is not mentioned in either the Lainga or Shiva Purans, or in any other, as far as I have observed; and if the *Prabhasa Mahatmyam* be a genuine portion of the Skanda Puran, it is therein said that this curse was pronounced by Savitri. The same is stated in the Padma Puran; and in the Brahma Vaivarta the cessation of Brahma's worship is ascribed to the curse of Narada.

† The seventh incarnation of Vishnu, mentioned ante, p. 242., *Yadgna* and *Kratu* being synonymous words in Sanscrit; but here the name is intended for Vishnu himself.

disputed; and, at length, having demanded proofs in support of each other's assertions, agreed to refer the point to the decision of the Vedas. The Vedas replied, — 'If, O ye gods of creation and preservation! you will accord in our decision, we will produce such proof as shall determine your doubts.' They answered, — 'Be you the proof which shall convince us of the real truth.' The Rig Veda said, — 'He who creates, preserves, and destroys is in truth Shiva alone.' The Yajur said, — 'He who is the real object of sacrificial rites and of mysterious contemplation is Hara.' The Sama said, — 'He through whom this universe moves and is illumined is Trimbaka.' The Atharvan said, — 'That god of gods by obtaining whose grace, through devotion, final beatitude can alone be attained is Shankara.'* Having heard these words, Vishnu and Brahma, still bewildered by the darkness of delusion, thus said: — 'How can the lord of goblins, the delighter in cemeteries, the naked devotee covered with ashes, haggard in appearance, wearing twisted locks ornamented with snakes, and mounted on a bull, be the Supreme Being?' The incorporeal *Prana*† then assuming a form thus said, — 'That is not the real form of Shiva; but, when united to his energy, he sometimes, under the figure of Rudra, delights himself in various illusive sports." But these words dispelled not the spiritual darkness of Vishnu and Brahma; when suddenly appeared between them a wondrous effulgence filling the heaven, and earth, and mid-air, in the midst of which they beheld a human form, vast, uncreated, of a dark hue, holding in his hands a trident and a rosary, and wearing a serpent for the Brahminical string; on seeing whom the fifth head of Brahma glowed with anger, and thus spoke: — 'I know thee well, O Chandrashekera! for from my forehead didst thou formerly spring, and because thou didst weep I called thee Rudra; hasten then to seek the refuge of my feet and I will protect thee, O my son!' At these proud words of Brahma, Shiva was incensed, and from his anger sprang into existence a terrific form‡, whom he thus addressed: — 'Chastise this lotos-born.' No sooner did Bhairava hear this order than he instantly,

* These last three names are appellations of Shiva.

† This is the Sanscrit name for the sacred and mysterious syllable OM.

‡ Hence named Bhairava.

with the nail of his left thumb, cut off the head of Brahma; that member which had committed the fault received punishment, and therefore of his fifth head was Brahma deprived. On beholding this event Vishnu propitiated Shankara with praises, and Brahma, also alarmed, addressed him with the humblest supplications." — *Kashi Khand*, chap. 30.

This legend, however, is related in so different a manner in the Padma Puran, that it may be proper to subjoin it: — " Above his four heads, Brahma had formerly a fifth; and hence he, from the impurity of his nature, became so arrogant as to think that he, and no other, had created all things, and that, besides himself, there was no other god, neither Shiva nor Vishnu. One of his mouths had delivered the Rig Veda, and the others the Yajur, Sama, and Atharvan, with the *Angas*, *Uphangas*, *Itihasas*, and all sacred learning; and from its having read, from its elevated situation, the Vedas, the fifth had acquired such a splendour that it could not be endured by either Suras or Asuras. Unable, therefore, to approach or behold it, they determined to apply for relief to Shiva; and having proceeded to his abode, they with praises supplicated his assistance. Being thus propitiated, Shiva granted their request, and proceeded with them to where Brahma remained inflated with pride. On seeing, therefore, Shiva enter, Brahma, involved in spiritual darkness, did not pay him the usual honours; and Shiva, beholding Pitamaha's fifth head inflicting distress on the universe by its effulgent beams, brighter than a thousand suns, approached him and said, — 'Ah! this head shines with too much splendour;' and immediately cut it off with the nail of his left thumb, with as much ease as a man cuts the stem of a plantain tree." — *Shrishti Khand*, chap. 14. *

* I add a third version of this legend from the 95th chapter of the Varaha Puran: — " In his third birth, Brahma, when he was born with five heads, created Rudra; and, having once placed him on his shoulder, the fifth head thus addressed Rudra: 'O youth! who excellest in might, protect the universe, and be celebrated in the three worlds under various appellations, and amongst others that of *Kapali* (the bearer of skulls).' On hearing the word *Kapali* Rudra was incensed, and immediately with the nail of his left thumb cut off the fifth head of Brahma."

In another khand, also, of the Skanda Puran this event is related in nearly the same manner as in the Padma; and as the legend relating to it not only contains an account of Brahma's being produced with five heads, but also several other curious circumstances, I transcribe the whole of it:—

"Formerly, all things movable and immovable having been destroyed, naught remained but one boundless ocean: nor fire, nor air, nor sun, nor atmosphere, nor stars, nor planets, nor light, nor earth, nor heaven, nor gods, nor demons, existed then, and all was involved in impenetrable darkness. One being alone, Maha Kala *, self-subsisting, then pervaded all space; who, becoming desirous of creation, churned his left arm with his right fore finger, when issued a bubble, which, increasing in size, became an egg resembling gold. This egg Maha Kala divided with his hand, and of the upper half formed the heavens, and of the lower half the earth; and in the centre of it appeared Brahma, with five heads and four arms, to whom Maha Kala thus said,—'Through my favour effect creation;' and, having thus spoken, disappeared. Brahma, having then considered in what manner he could accomplish this object, propitiated the lord Bhava by a severe *tapas*, and, in consequence, received from him the four Vedas, and was thus enabled to become the creator. But as Shiva had not revealed himself, Brahma continued his *tapas*, in order that he might behold that god. Shiva was propitiated, but still invisible thus said,—'O Brahma! choose whatever boon thou pleasest.' He then craved that Shiva would become his son; and Shiva replied,—'Propitiated by thy piety, I will become thy son under the form of Rudra: but, as thou hast craved a boon which ought not to have been asked, I shall on this account hereafter cut off one of thy heads; nevertheless, though thou shalt afterwards possess but four heads, yet as thou hast been formed by me, from my own substance, which is that of Brahm, shalt thou, in remembrance of this circumstance, be denominated in the three worlds by the name of Brahma, and also from my becoming thy son shalt thou be called Pitamaha (the great father).'

* A name of Shiva.

"Brahma, having thus obtained both a boon and a curse, proceeded, in order to effect creation, to sacrifice to that fire which had sprung from his own effulgence, and, from the heat, perspiration collected on his forehead; to wipe off which he raised his hand, in which was a billet of wood, and his forehead being slightly grazed with it, a drop of blood fell in the fire; from which, by the will of Shiva, sprang Rudra, of a dark hue, with five heads, ten arms, and fifteen eyes; with a serpent for the Brahminical string, bearing twisted locks, and the moon on his head, and clothed in the skin of a lion. Having beheld such a son produced to him, Brahma was delighted, and bestowed on him various appellations. Brahma, having then created the various classes of beings, they all adored him except Rudra, to whom Brahma said,—'Why dost thou not also adore me?' Rudra replied,—'I worship none other than that effulgence from which I sprang;' and, having thus spoken, he departed to where Shiva abided. But Brahma, from the impurity of his nature, became immersed in spiritual darkness, and thought that it was by his own power alone that he had effected creation, and that there was no other god equal to him. His fifth head, also, from having read the Vedas, which the other four heads had delivered, acquired a splendour which neither Suras nor Asuras could endure," &c.—*Avanti Khand*, chap. 2. (The rest of this legend is here related in almost the same words as it is in the passage of the Padma Puran above quoted.)

In consequence of these two events, it has become a favourite opinion that, although Brahmaism was the primitive religion of the Hindus, yet the worship of Brahma was at some remote period superseded by that of Shiva. Mr. Paterson has even remarked, that "the annihilation of the sect and worship of Brahma, as the *Ishwara* or supreme lord, is allegorically described in the Kashi Khand of the Skanda Puran, where the three powers are mentioned as contending for precedency. Vishnu, at last, acknowledges the superiority of Shiva; but Brahma, on account of his presumptuous obstinacy and pride, had one of his heads cut off by Shiva, and his *puja* (worship) abolished.

The intent of the fable is evidently to magnify the sect of Shiva above those of Brahma and Vishnu; and if, instead of the Devatas themselves (who are described as the actors in this allegorical drama), we substitute the contending sects, the fable will appear not destitute of foundation in historical fact." * The inaccuracies in the first part of this quotation will be evident, after a perusal of the passages which I have above translated from the Skanda Puran; and Mr. Paterson assigns no sufficient reason in support of his proposed removal of the scene of these legends from heaven to earth. It deserves remark, also, that it is Vishnu and Brahma alone, who are in several Purans represented as contending for supremacy; and that in these cases Shiva is not present, but appears either personally, or at first under the form of the lingam, for the purpose of deciding the dispute. These legends therefore, as related in the Purans, afford no grounds whatever for supposing that Brahmaism and Shivaism existed in India at distinct periods, and that the former was abolished in consequence of holy wars which had taken place between the sectaries of Brahma and Shiva.

But the notions of M. Guigniaut respecting the Hindu religion are so extraordinary that they require, notwithstanding their length, to be transcribed; for he remarks,— " Cette cause destructive avec laquelle le dieu conservateur est dans un perpétuel combat, que peut-elle être sinon le principe même de toute corruption, de tout mal physique, et par une transition si naturelle, de tout mal moral, Siva-Roudra, le dieu destructeur? *Ici éclate une opposition aussi frappante que diverse et complexe, non seulement entre les deux divinités, mais entre les deux cultes; tellement qu'on est tenté d'y voir la lutte de deux religions ennemies qui se rencontrent, se heurtent, se froissent, grandissent et se développent dans le cours même de leurs débats;* et, après des longs déchiremens, finissent par s'amalgamer l'une avec l'autre, sans pourtant se confondre, et s'unissent sans cesser jamais d'être distinctes. Ceci demande quelques éclaircissemens. Le Sivaisme a, dans sa simplicité pleine de grandeur, quelque chose de singulièrement barbare, qui dénote une haute antiquité; d'ailleurs, *ses formes générales ont manifestement servi de types aux*

* Asiatic Researches, vol. viii. p. 49.

créations successives des autres systèmes et de toute la mythologie des Hindous. Il en est comme le corps, mais un corps vivant, animé ; et tel a été son empire sur l'imagination des peuples, que le culte de Mahadeva et de Bhavani, de l'Hermaphrodite et du lingam, est jusqu'ici resté dominant. * . . . . . Il est peut-être plus difficile d'expliquer les singuliers rapports qu'une foule de traditions concourent à établir entre Brahma et Siva. Ici encore Brahma est inférieur et subordonné; et, en effet, les deux sectes rivales s'accordent à le presenter comme un simple ministre des deux grands dieux qu'elles revêtent à des titres differéns, comme l'intermediaire entre ces dieux supérieurs et les divinités inférieurs qu'elles reconnaissent également l'une et l'autre; enfin, comme le chef et le gouverneur des mondes, mais sous leur empire et sous leur autorité suprème. *Cependant, quoiqu'il soit question cà et là des luttes de Vichnou avec Brahma, quoiqu'on nous montre Siva et Vichnou s'unissant tous deux pour châtier leur frère infidèle, les combats* † *de Brahma et de Siva paraissent bien plus anciens, plus caractérisés;* et l'on ne peut se défendre d'y chercher un sens curieux ou profond. ‡ . . . . . . Suffit-il, pour rendre compte de ces fables, d'alléguer des mystères cosmogoniques ou physiques, les combats des élémens et des puissances de la nature? l'essence même du rôle de Brahma qui, une fois la création consommée, doit nécessairement céder la place aux deux autres dieux, l'un chargé de la conserver en y entretenant les principes de vie, en y ramenant les équilibres des forces, l'autre de la renouveller en y détruisant et y reproduisant sans cesse les formes? ou bien faut-il avoir recours à des conjectures historiques, et chercher encore une fois dans les guerres des sectes religieuses ou dans les dissensions des castes, la raison de la prétendue abolition du culte de Brahma et de la disparition totale de ses temples?" §

* Religions de l'Antiquité, tom. i. p. 214.

† Brahma is in no Sanscrit work described as having ever been engaged in battle, or in the slightest degree acquainted with the use of arms. In his figures, also, he is represented holding in his four hands a manuscript book containing a portion of the Vedas, a pot for holding water, a rosary, and a sacrificial spoon.

‡ Religions de l'Antiquité, tom. i. p. 239.

§ Ibid. p. 240. These remarks belong to M. Guigniaut, for they are not to be found in the original work of Professor Creuzer. M. Guigniaut has, however, translated correctly the fol-

I am, however, obliged to observe that these remarks and speculations are completely refuted by the sacred books of the Hindus, by the whole of Sanscrit literature, by the traditional opinions which have been preserved until the present day amongst the Hindus, and by the actual state of their mythology and religion: for the dogma of the two principles of good and evil is totally unknown to the Hindus, and no where is there to be found the slightest trace of any combats for supremacy between Vishnu and Shiva. It seems, also, to be entirely overlooked that this religion is indisputably founded on the Vedas, and that the rites and ceremonies now practised by all the orthodox sects are precisely such as are prescribed in those books; and that no alteration whatever has taken place in them, except the institution of a few festivals and devout observances which have been from time to time adopted. But even these have been made to conform most scrupulously to the precepts of the Vedas; for the mode of worship and the offerings presented to the particular deity are such only as have been deemed holy from time immemorial.* If, therefore, Brahmaism, Vishnuism, and Shivaism differ from each other, as some writers suppose, and if there ever existed any sects which professed merely one

---

lowing passage of the original:— "Cette première doctrine (de Brahma) avait subsisté mille ans environ, quand commencèrent les guerres religieuses. Alors parut Siva, la seconde incarnation, apportant le lingam, image de la vie et de la mort. Les fêtes simples et pures de l'antique Brahmaisme font place au sauvage délire des orgies, et de sanglans sacrifices souillent les autels de l'affreuse culte. Les traces même du culte de Brahma furent effacées; l'amour et la vie, la colère et la mort, voilà les élémens dont se compose le nouveau dieu, aussibien que son culte."—Ibid., p. 141.

* I allude not, of course, to the worship of Bhadri Kali, or to any of the sects which are said to have originated from the Tantras; because in this part of India they are so little known that I have not been able to obtain any information respecting them.

Sir W. Jones also has observed in a note to the Institutes of Menu,— "The learned Hindus are unanimously of opinion, that many laws enacted by Menu, their oldest reputed legislator, were confined to the three first ages of the world, and have no force in the present age, in which a few of them are certainly obsolete." Amongst these specified is the sacrifice of a bull, of a man, and of a horse; but this prohibition is understood to extend in the present age to the sacrifice of all animals. The ceasing, however, to observe certain rites and ceremonies is no proof of any change having taken place in the essential principles of that religion, to which such rites and ceremonies at one time belonged.

of these systems of belief; it is self-evident that, as Brahma is the unquestionable author of the Vedas, and as according to this conjecture Brahmaism was the first of these systems, the followers of Shiva and Vishnu could not have possibly continued to belong to the Hindu religion, but must have become equally heretics with the Buddhists. But at the present day divine honours have ceased to be paid to Brahma; the great body of Hindus believe that both Shiva and Vishnu ought to be worshipped, though some ascribe a certain degree of preeminence to the one and some to the other; and, even among the comparatively few exclusive votaries of Shiva and Vishnu, no difference exists in their rites and ceremonies, but merely in the object of worship.

The Vedas, Upanishads, and Purans still continue to be acknowledged by the *Shaiva*, the *Vaishnava*, and the *Smarta*, to be the sole authorities on which his religion is founded; nor is there either writing or tradition which in the slightest degree explains the causes which have occasioned the cessation of the worship of Brahma, or the ascription of the attributes of the Supreme Being to either Vishnu or Shiva: but that the adoration of the one God must have ceased, or been transferred to one of the divine hypostases, at a very remote period, is clearly evinced by the Upanishads, which are universally admitted to contain the theological doctrines of the Vedas; for in some of these Brahma appears as the Supreme Being, in others Vishnu, and in others Shiva. The cessation, therefore, of Brahma's worship appears to have taken place during the interval that may have elapsed between the composition, or extraction from the Vedas, of the Upanishads, and the compilation of the Purans: for in these last works no mention occurs of either rites or ceremonies, or festivals, or temples*, or holy places, being dedicated to Brahma; nor in them is there recorded a single legend to attest and magnify his divine power. But, had Brahma's worship been abolished by force, and after sanguinary battles between his sectaries and those of Shiva, it must seem highly improbable that no notice of such events, or at least allusions to them, should occur in the Purans: nor have I observed in them the slightest appearance of

* Except at Pushkara, now Pokur, near Ajmere.

allegory, nor any circumstances which could be tortured, by the most expert allegorist, into the remotest semblance of religious wars between the supposed sectaries of Brahmaism, Vishnuism, and Shivaism.

Some singular misapprehension, also, seems to prevail with respect to the character and worship of Shiva; for it is *assumed* that as this god is represented as the avenger and destroyer, he must consequently delight in being honoured by bloody sacrifices and barbarous orgies. But the images which may perhaps have been at one time erected to Shiva under different characters, and the worship addressed to them, have been long superseded by the symbol of the lingam: and Mr. Ward has correctly remarked that "under different names several images of Shiva are described in the Shastras; but none of these images are made at present, nor is any public worship offered to them."* Mr. Ward has farther, with equal justness, observed: — "Images of Shiva under the form of Maha Kala are not made in Bengal; but a pan of water, or an *anadi* lingam, is substituted, before which bloody sacrifices are offered, and other ceremonies performed, in the month *Chaitra* at the new moon. *Only a few persons perform this worship.* Except before this image, bloody sacrifices are never offered to Shiva, who is himself called (by the *Vaishnavas* of course) a *Vaishnava*, i. e. a worshipper of Vishnu, before whose image no animals are slain, and whose disciples profess never to eat animal food."† The offerings, also, presented to the lingam consist solely of leaves, flowers, fruits, grains, preparations of milk, sweetmeats, incense, and perfumes.

But, as far as I can learn, the worship of the lingam is not mentioned in the Vedas, nor is it even alluded to in any of the Upanishads which I have read; and consequently, as Shivaism has, since at least the compilation of the Purans, consisted entirely in this worship, it necessarily follows that it could not have been the most ancient form of the Hindu religion, and the type of all its subsequent forms. I must, however, confess myself ignorant of what M. Guigniaut intends by *le culte de Mahadeva, et de Bhavani, et de l'Hermaphrodite.* I am equally at a loss to discover the faintest resemblance to their religion, as it is

* Ward's View of the Hindus, vol. i. p. 18.

† Ibid., p. 17.

described by either the Hindus themselves or in their sacred books, in the following passage:—"Le Sivaisme repose principalement sur la personification des forces de la nature, considérées ou comme génératrices et productrices, ou comme destructrices et régénératrices, et ainsi à l'infini. C'est une vue déja haute et vaste de la marche du monde, et de la succession constante que nous présentent ses innombrables phénomènes. Les agens de ces grands opérations de la nature, dans lesquels l'idée de cause et celle de substance commencent à poindre obscurément, ce sont, pour généraliser les formes diverses sous lesquelles ils se produisent, la chaleur et l'humidité; deux principes préexistens, dont le soleil et la lune offrent aux yeux les types primitifs. .... C'est au sein de la nuit qui se consomma l'union féconde des deux principes, alors que tout d'un coup parut le lingam apportant la lumière, alors que la première hermaphrodite lança dans l'espace et les astres et tous les corps de la nature, et les animaux, et les hommes, alors que les germes des êtres se développèrent, pour la première fois dans l'immense *yoni*, qui depuis reconcilie et les reproduit incessamment. Voilà les croyances fondamentales et les objets dominans de ce culte antique (Sivaisme); le lingam en est le mystère par excellence, et déja il nous offre, sous une image grossière en apparence, une sorte de cosmogonie ou de création primitive des choses, au-delà de laquelle nous entrevoyons l'unité, comme le principe des principes."*

But never was there a religious system so abhorrent from symbols † and allegories as the Hindu; and it would therefore be impossible to justify the preceding remarks by a single passage from any Sanscrit work. On the contrary, the fundamental principles of this religion are, that an invisible and immaterial being cannot manifest himself or exert his power except under a corporeal form, and that the energies of the male must remain inoperative until rendered active by a union with the passive qualities of the female. Hence, on willing creation, the Supreme Being necessarily, in order to effect that object, first gave existence to a male and a female, which are known under the names of

* Religions de l'Antiquité, tom. i.

† The only ones which I have been able to discover are, the lingam, symbolical of Shiva and Purusha; and the yoni, symbolical of Devi and Prakriti.

Purusha and *Prakriti*, and which alone are considered to be the original agents in the formation of this universe.* Although, also, the Hindus believe that production is merely an antecedent to destruction, and destruction an antecedent to production, still they consider that these changes proceed from a fixed law impressed upon nature by the Supreme Being, and not from the operation of any intermediate agents. Neither the lingam, therefore, nor the yoni have ever been supposed by the Hindus to be symbolical of the productive and destructive powers of nature; nor is such a conjecture in the slightest degree sanctioned by any thing which is contained in the Purans.

The metaphysical hypothesis, likewise, of M. F. von Schlegel, respecting the different states in which the Hindu religion has existed since its first institution, is equally imaginary, and equally contrary to the actual belief of the Hindus, and to the uniform account of this religion which is contained in their sacred books. For he observes that "the most important epochs of Indian, and in general of Oriental, philosophy and religion are the following:—First, the system of emanation, which finally degenerated into astrological superstition and fanatical materialism; then, the doctrine of the two principles, which system of dualism became at a later period changed into pantheism."† With regard to the first three of these epochs, M. von Schlegel expresses the same opinions respecting Brahmaism, Shivaism, and Vishnuism, which I have just controverted; but I do not clearly understand his illustration of the fourth epoch, nor do his own notions on this point seem to have been sufficiently distinct and determined.‡ This uncertainty

* It must likewise be observed, that all males, whether gods or men, are considered to be merely forms of *Purusha*, and all females, whether goddesses or women, to be merely forms of *Prakriti*; and that *Purusha* and *Prakriti* are themselves in reality corporeal manifestations of the essence of the undiscernible Supreme Being. Thus the severalty and diversity which apparently prevail in the universe are clearly and consistently reduced into that unity which is, as M. Guigniaut justly remarks, *le principe des principes*.

† Ueber die Sprache und Weisheit der Indier, p. 152.

‡ So much so that he has been obliged to hazard this very improbable conjecture:—"As no doubt can remain, after a perusal of the Bhagawat Gita, that the Sankhya system is altogether pantheistic, it must be concluded that *the author has throughout misunderstood it, or that he has violently compelled it to conform to his own manner of thinking* (*oder nach seiner eignen denkart gewaltsam umgedeutet*)."—Ibid., p. 147.

appears to have been occasioned by the doctrines inculcated in the Bhagawat Gita, and by M. Schlegel not clearly perceiving the difference that exists between the Sankhya * and Vedanta systems of philosophy, or which is the same thing, between the material and spiritual systems of pantheism. But that a belief in emanation, if by this term is meant a positive separation of the human from the supreme soul, never prevailed among the Hindus is indisputably attested by every passage in the Vedas, the Upanishads, and Purans, which relate to the real nature of the soul and of God; while, on the contrary, every such passage equally proves that spiritual pantheism is the sole doctrine which is inculcated in these works; and that the fundamental principle of the Hindu religion is, that nothing actually exists except one self-subsisting, all-pervading, and indivisible Spirit. It is, therefore, evidently impossible that a belief in the doctrine of two principles, or in a material pantheism, could have ever prevailed among the Hindus.

I am, at the same time, aware that, in controverting these opinions respecting the relative antiquity of the principal sects which prevail in India, I am opposed by the high authority of Mr. Colebrooke; who has remarked: — "According to the hypothesis which I then hinted, the earliest Indian sect, of which we have at present any distinct knowledge, is that of the followers of the practical Vedas, who worshipped the sun, fire, and the elements; and who believed the efficacy of sacrifices, for the accomplishment of present and future purposes. It may be supposed that the refined doctrine of the *Vedantis*, or followers of the

* The Bhagawat Gita is composed entirely according to the Sankhya system of philosophy, and the mistakes which have arisen from not adverting to this circumstance are not peculiar to M. Schlegel. But there is no inconsistency in its having been written by Vyasa, the reputed founder of the Vedanta system, because the Vedantas admit that *material* pantheism has an *apparent* existence; and they only contend that it does not exist *in reality*, but is merely an illusive appearance produced by Maya. It must also be recollected that the Ramayan and Mahabharat, as well as the sacred books of the Hindus, have always been, and still are, first read under the tuition of a preceptor, who has thus an opportunity of putting an orthodox construction on opinions which might otherwise appear to be heterodox: and this is particularly the case with the Sankhya system; for, as it is supposed to have been revealed by Vishnu himself under the form of Kapila, it cannot be rejected; and it is therefore made to conform to what the Vedantikas maintain to be the true doctrines of the Vedas.

theological and argumentative parts of the Vedas, is of later date; and it does not seem improbable that the sects of Jina and of Buddha are still more modern. But I apprehend that the *Vaishnavas*, meaning particularly the worshippers of Rama and Krishna, may be subsequent to these sects, and that the *Shaivas* are also of more recent date."* But Mr. Colebrooke's notions respecting the Hindu religion rest on two assumptions; the one that the incarnations of Vishnu are not mentioned in the Vedas, and the other that Rama and Krishna are deified men: neither of which have been supported by the requisite proof, nor do they appear to be susceptible of it; for I am assured that the incarnations of Vishnu are noticed in the Vedas, and the deification of men is a mere gratuitous supposition which is unsupported by any evidence whatever. What is still more remarkable is, that Mr. Colebrooke has thus qualified his own hypothesis:—"In explanation of a remark contained in a former essay, I take this occasion of adding that the mere mention of Rama or of Krishna in a passage of the Vedas, without any indication of particular reverence, would not authorise a presumption against the genuineness of that passage, on my hypothesis; nor, admitting its authenticity, furnish an argument against that system.

"I suppose both heroes to have been known characters in ancient fabulous history; but conjecture that, on the same basis, new fables have been constructed elevating these personages to the rank of gods. On this supposition, the simple mention of them in genuine portions of the Vedas, particularly in that part of it which is entitled *Brahmana*, would not appear surprising. Accordingly, Krishna, son of Devaki, is actually named in the *Chandogya Upanishad*."†

But I must confess that I do not understand this reasoning; for, if the occurrence of the names of Vishnu's incarnations in the Vedas does not prove that the legends respecting them must have existed when

* Asiatic Researches, vol. ix. p. 293. The hypothetical manner in which these remarks are here offered contrasts singularly with the positive tone in which the same opinions were expressed in the Asiatic Researches, vol. viii. p. 292. Has this proceeded from Mr. Colebrooke having begun to entertain doubts respecting the soundness of his hypothesis?

† Asiatic Researches, vol. ix. p. 293. note. The *son of Devaki* is also mentioned in the Upanishad quoted in Appendix C, in which he is identified with Narayana.

those books were composed, I know not by what other evidence this circumstance can be established. Mr. Colebrooke, however, quotes a passage from the Vedas, in which these words occur; *he* (the lord of creation) *saw this earth, and upheld it, assuming the form of a boar;* which he prefaces with this remark, — "The present extract was recommended for selection by its allusion to a mythological notion which apparently gave origin to the story of the *Varaha-avatara.*" * But would it not be much more reasonable to conclude that this concise and otherwise unintelligible allusion referred to some well known legend, than to suppose that the legend was subsequently founded on so dark and enigmatical a hint? On what grounds, also, is it assumed that the Hindus ever considered Rama and Krishna to be mere men? for, most assuredly, such a notion cannot be supported by a single passage that is to be found in any Sanscrit work; and the very authorities, on the contrary, from which alone their existence is known, uniformly attest that they were incarnate portions of the second divine hypostasis.

This point is of the last importance in forming a correct opinion respecting the Hindu religion: for, if the incarnations of Vishnu be not mentioned in the Vedas, and if the acknowledging of Rama and Krishna to be incarnate portions of the Deity be of recent date, it must inevitably follow that the long-established notion, that this religion is founded on the Vedas, must be totally erroneous. Nor does Mr. Colebrooke conceal that this is the conclusion to which his consideration of the subject has led him; for he remarks, — "Most of what is taught in the Vedas is now obsolete; and, in its stead, new orders of religious devotees have been instituted, and new forms of religious ceremonies have been established. Rituals founded on the Purans, and observances borrowed from a worse source, the Tantras, have, in a great measure, antiquated the institutions of the Vedas." † But it will, I think, be admitted that nothing but an attentive perusal of all the Vedas, and an intimate acquaintance with the principles of all the sects in India, could justify so sweeping a conclusion as this; and that the

* Asiatic Researches, vol. viii. p. 436. † Ibid., p. 474.

information on the subject which has been hitherto collected is much too defective, to allow of any accurate judgment being formed with respect to the differences that may have taken place in the state of the Hindu religion as it existed when the Vedas were composed, and that in which it still prevails at the present day.* The above-quoted remark, however, seems to have been made by Mr. Colebrooke without due consideration; for in another part of the same essay he says, — "Citations from the Indian scripture occur in every branch of literature studied by orthodox Hindus. In all these branches of Indian literature, while perusing or consulting the works of various authors, I have found perpetual references to the Vedas, and have frequently verified the quotations." It, therefore, remains to reconcile these statements, which I believe to be perfectly accurate, with the assertion that *most of what is taught in the Vedas is now obsolete;* for it is impossible to understand how doctrines, which are thus continually referred to as an authority from which there is no appeal, can have become antiquated.

It is also remarkable that M. von Schlegel, in order to give consistency to his view of the four epochs of the Hindu philosophy and religion, has been obliged to omit all notice of that singular opinion, according to which every orthodox Hindu believes that this universe, with all that it contains, has no real existence, but is composed solely of illusive appearances produced by *Maya*, or the energy of the Supreme Being. Nor does Mr. Colebrooke, in forming his notions respecting the real history of the Hindu religion, seem to have taken this circumstance into consideration. Whether, however, this doctrine may be mentioned in the Vedas or not, I am not aware; but that it is the principal subject of the Upanishads is undeniable; and, consequently, the principles of the Vedanta system, if not the system itself, must be of as ancient a date as those works. As, therefore, the belief in Maya, in there being no entity except one self-subsisting Spirit, and in final

* The most indispensable of all labours for deciding this question, that of comparing the Vedas with the Purans, in order to ascertain whether and how far they disagree, has not yet been performed, or even attempted; and the assumption, therefore, that such a disagreement exists, is, as yet, *vox, et præterea nihil.*

beatitude, consisting in identification with that Spirit, is equally entertained by the *Shaiva*, the *Vaishnava*, and the *Smarta*; and as this belief is inculcated in the Upanishads, and most probably in the Vedas; it will be obvious that the fundamental principles of these sects must be the same, and that there are no sufficient grounds for supposing that these principles are in the slightest degree inconsistent with such as prevailed on the first institution of the Hindu religion. It appears clear, also, from the extracts from the Vedas given by Mr. Colebrooke, that, at the period when these works were composed, the adoration of the one God had long ceased, and had been superseded by the worship of the very same deities who form at the present day the popular mythology of the Hindus. Is it not, therefore, most probable that at this very period existed also the sects of *Vaishnavas* and *Shaivas*? for, if they did not, how happens it that in some of the Upanishads the attributes of the Supreme Being are ascribed to Vishnu, and in others to Shiva? The only real alteration, consequently, which has evidently taken place in the primitive religion of the Hindus, and this seems to be as old as the Vedas, is the ceasing to adore by outward forms the one God, and the substituting in his place one of the divine hypostases. Subsequently, also, to the composition of those works, the worship of Brahma has almost entirely disappeared: but this circumstance has in no manner affected the fundamental principles of this religion; nor have these undergone any change by the transferring of the divine honours paid to Shiva from his representation under a human figure to the symbol of the lingam *; and it is self-evident that the *Vaishnava* sect must have existed before the minor sects, which adopt the incarnations of Vishnu under the forms of Rama and Krishna as their principal objects of devotion, could have originated. The more, therefore, that this subject is elucidated, not by crude and groundless hypotheses but by an attentive examination of Sanscrit works, the more conclusively, I am convinced, will it appear that the Hindu religion, in all essen-

* The very first act of the ritual prescribed for the worship of the lingam is to meditate on that god who has five heads, three eyes, and ten arms, and thus to fix in the mind the real form of Shiva.

tial respects, is in precisely the same state at the present day, as that in which it prevailed at the period when the Vedas were composed. †

† Rites and ceremonies are obviously mere accessaries to every religious system; and to found, therefore, any argument on some of those prescribed in the Vedas having become antiquated, and others having been subsequently instituted, with respect to the changes which may have taken place in the essential principles of the Hindu religion, is a mode of reasoning so obviously erroneous, that any remark respecting it must be unnecessary: for no person will, I suppose, deny that the belief and religious observances of the Roman Catholic, the Lutheran, the Episcopalian, and the Presbyterian are all equally founded on the Scriptures, or on their reputed traditional interpretation.

CHAP. XI.

SHIVA.

THE worship of Brahma, and the legends respecting him which may have at one time existed, have merely disappeared; but Shiva is represented under two characters so perfectly distinct, and yet so intimately blended together, that it becomes extremely difficult to determine whether both belonged to the early religion * of the Hindus, or whether one of them is not of much later invention. These characters cannot be better explained than by the following two passages which occur in the very same book of the Bhagawat: — At a certain solemn sacrifice performed in heaven, when Daksha entered, all the deities rose and saluted him, except Shiva. "Daksha observing Shiva sitting apart, and not enduring his want of respect, thus addressed the assembly, his eyes burning with anger: — 'Hear, all ye gods, what I now speak, impelled by truth and not by ignorance or hatred. That despiser of fame, who is devoid of shame, a deviater from the right path, and a contemner of all virtuous observances, having obtained my consent, took before priests and fire the hand of my daughter, excellent as Savitri, in marriage. But though that monkey-eyed has married my fawn-eyed daughter, yet he rises not to salute me, nor does he address me with proper compliments: and even despising the spotless maiden, treats her as if she were the child of some low-born man; for he wanders about, surrounded by ghosts and goblins, inebriated, naked, with dishevelled hair, covered with the ashes of a funeral-pile, ornamented with human skulls and bones, and sometimes laughing, sometimes weeping. Nor does aught appertain to him, either good or auspicious, except his name (Shiva); and yet, at the desire of Brahma, I gave my

* By this expression I mean the Hindu religion as it existed at the time when the Vedas were composed, for it had then evidently deviated considerably from its primitive nature.

tender and virtuous daughter to this delighter in inebriated men, this lord of ghosts and demons, whose hardened heart is dead to all affection, and whose soul is formed of naught but darkness." * But when Virabhadra has destroyed this sacrifice, and killed Daksha, and the gods, being unable to withstand his attack, hasten to Kailasa to entreat the protection of Shiva, it is in this very different manner in which he is then addressed by Brahma:—"I know that thou, O lord! art the eternal Brahm, that seed which, being received into the womb of thy *Shakti*, produced this universe; that thou, united with thy Shakti, dost in sport create this universe from thy own substance, like the web of the spider; that thou dost protect it; and that thou wilt finally devour it. I know that thou, being the distributer of justice, didst destroy the sacrifice of Daksha, on account of his improper conduct, in order that Brahmans and the other inhabitants of this world might place their faith on thee, and might continue steadfast in the observance of virtue and piety: for it is thou who bestowest on men the fruits of their good and evil actions; and who rewardest the virtuous with the bliss of heaven, and condemnest the wicked to the torments of hell," &c. †

It is under this latter character that Shiva is principally considered by the *Smartas*, who pay little attention to those legends which seem to have been invented at the same time that the worship of the lingam was instituted, in order to attest and magnify the efficacy of that new mode of devotion. But it is these legends which now form the mythological history of this god; and as I have, perhaps, sufficiently explained the divine nature of Shiva, when he is considered simply as the Supreme Being, I shall confine the following quotations to such passages as illustrate his popular character. ‡

* Skand iv. chap. 2. After uttering these words, Daksha also imprecated, as a curse on Shiva, that he might henceforth be deprived of his share of all sacrifices; and Shiva, on learning this circumstance, in revenge condemned Daksha, by his curse, to have his human head replaced by that of a goat, to mortal birth, and to ignorance of divine knowledge. It was in consequence of the first of these curses, that after Daksha was restored to life a goat's head was substituted in the place of his own, which had fallen into the sacrificial fire and been consumed.

† Skand iv. chap. 6.

‡ As, however, so little has been hitherto published respecting Shiva, I have inserted in Appendix D some extracts illustrative of his character.

From the Vamana Puran.

Pulastya, addressing Narada. — "Formerly, when staying on the mountain Mandara, Devi, oppressed with the violent heat, thus said to Maheshwara: — 'O Isha! the heat increases in violence, hast thou no house to which we might repair, and there abide protected from the wind, the heat, and the cold?' Shankara replied, — 'I am, O lovely one! without a shelter, a constant wanderer in forests.' Having thus spoken, Shankara with Sati remained during the hot season under the shade of trees; and when it was passed, the rainy season with its dark clouds succeeded. On beholding which, Sati said to Shiva,—'Heart-agitating winds blow, O Maheshwara! and rushing torrents roar; the lightning flashes amidst the black clouds, and the peacock calls to its mate; rain falls from the clouds, and the heron and crane hasten to the water which they love; and, shaken by the storm, the flowers of the trees strew the ground; alarmed by the thunder the swans hastily quit their native lakes, as ascetics forsake their families and all the attachments of life; the herds of animals, emitting glad cries, gambol and sport, delighted with the gloomy clouds; the rivers rush with such rapidity that their brightness has become turbid; the sky is involved in dark clouds; the lakes are overspread with the leaves of the lotos; and the streams appear like milk. In such a season, difficult to be endured, O Shankara! let me entreat thee to build a house on Kailasa, where I may abide with thee in comfort.' Shiva replied, — 'O my beloved! I have no riches for the erection of a house; nor am I possessed of aught else than an elephant's skin for a garment, and serpents for my ornaments?' The soul of Shiva, Mridani, having heard these harsh words, seemingly true but devoid of truth, was alarmed, and looking on the ground she thus, with bashfulness and anger, said, — 'Then say, O Shambu! how can we pass in comfort the rainy season under the shade of trees?' Shiva replied, — 'With our bodies covered with a cloud, O lovely one! shall the rainy season pass without any rain falling on thy tender frame.' Having thus spoken Hara stopped a cloud, and with the daughter of Daksha fixed his abode within it; and hence has he been since celebrated in heaven under the name of *Jimuta-ketu*, i. e., *he whose banner is a cloud.*

"Thus the three-eyed god resided in a cloud until the rains were past, and the sultry season had arrived to delight the world. Then the dark clouds forsook the sky; the herons and cranes the banks of lakes; the crows their nests; the deer lost their horns, and the rivers their turbidness; the lotoses opened their blossoms; plants and creepers were covered with flowers; the herds of cattle lowed with gladness, and holy men were delighted; the ponds were adorned with lotoses, the heaven with stars; the rivers and lakes shone with water, the hearts of holy men with purity, the regions of the earth with brightness, clear as the lustre of the cloudless moon. Then, also, Shiva and Sati returned to the mountain Mandara, and there joyfully passed their time. It was at the conclusion of this sultry season that Daksha made preparations for a great sacrifice, to which he invited all the immortals and holy sages, with their wives, and all his daughters and sons-in-law, except Shiva and Sati."

Narada said,—"Why were not the lord of the world Maheshwara, and the eldest and most excellent of his daughters, invited to this sacrifice by Daksha?" Pulastya replied,—"Daksha did not invite them, on account of Shiva being a *kapali*."* Narada enquired,—"How did the supreme god, the bearer of the trident, the three-eyed, become a kapali?" Pulastya answered,—"Listen, while I relate an ancient and

* This word merely signifies a religious mendicant, who carries a human skull for an alms-dish. The existence of this sect at the present day seems doubtful; but its tenets will be understood from the following speeches of a Kapalika, introduced as one of the characters in the *Prabodh Chandrodaya*, translated by Dr. J. Taylor:—

"My necklace and ornaments are of human bones; I dwell among the ashes of the dead, and eat my food in human skulls. I look with eyes brightened with the antimony of *Yog*, and I believe that the parts of the world are reciprocally different, but that the whole is not different from God."

"O Digamber! hearken to our rites: after fasting we drink liquor out of the skulls of Brahmans; our sacrificial fires are fed with the brains and lungs of men mixed up with their flesh, and human victims covered with the fresh blood gushing from the terrible wound in their throats, are the offerings by which we appease the terrible god."

"I contemplate the lord of Bhavani, the powerful god, who creates, preserves, and destroys the fourteen worlds; whose glory is both revealed in the Vedas and displayed in his works."—Pages 38, 39.

celebrated story, which was first revealed by Brahma. Formerly, when all things movable and immovable had been destroyed and naught remained but one vast ocean, while universal darkness reigned, that lord, who is incomprehensible and subject to neither birth nor death, reposed in slumber on the abyss of waters for a thousand divine years. But when his night had passed, desirous of creating the three worlds, the skilled in the Vedas, investing himself with the quality of impurity, assumed a corporeal form with five heads. Then, also, was produced from the quality of darkness another form with three eyes and twisted locks, and bearing a rosary and a trident. Brahma next created *ahankar**, which immediately pervaded the nature of both gods; and, under its influence, Rudra thus said to Pitamaha, — 'Say, O lord! how camest thou here, and by whom wert thou created?' Brahma replied, 'And whence art thou?' and instantly caused the new-made sky to reverberate with a wondrous sound like the tinkling of a vast *vina*.† Shambu was thus subdued, and stood with a countenance downcast and humbled, like the moon in an eclipse; and the fifth head of Brahma thus addressed him, rendered dark with anger in consequence of his defeat: — 'I know thee well, thou form of darkness! with three eyes, clothed with the four quarters of heaven (i. e. naked), mounted on a bull, the destroyer of this universe.' On hearing these words Shankara became incensed with anger, and while he viewed the head with terrible glances of his world-consuming eye, his five heads, from his wrath, grew white, red, golden, black, and yellow, and fearful to behold. But Brahma, on observing these heads, glowing like the sun, thus said, — 'Why dost thou agitate thyself and attempt to appear powerful? for, if I chose, I could this instant make thy heads become like bubbles of water.' This heard, Shiva, inflamed with anger, cut off with the nail of his left hand the head of Brahma, which had uttered such fierce and boasting words; but, when he would have thrown it on the

* This word properly signifies consciousness of individual existence, and seems adequately expressed in German by *die icheit*. But it also implies self-sufficiency, and the pride necessarily resulting from it.

† The correct transcription of this stanza in my MS. seems questionable; but, as there given, it evidently admits of no other interpretation than the one above.

ground, it would not, nor ever shall it, fall from his hand. Then Brahma, also enraged, created a man mighty in strength, four-armed, clad in armour, and holding a bow and arrow, a javelin and a sword, with a large quiver at his side; to whom Brahma said,—'Hasten and slay this evil-minded bearer of the trident; for how can he, who is burdened with sin, attempt to resist?' On hearing these words, Shankara, rendered powerless by the sin which he had committed, fled to Badarikashramam."—Chap. 1, 2.

Pulastya continued:—"In this manner, O Narada! did Shiva become a *kapali* *, and for this and other reasons Daksha did not invite his daughter and him to the sacrifice. At this time Jaya, the daughter of Gautama, paid a visit to Sati; who, on observing her arrive alone, said,—'Why have not Vijaya, Jayanti, and Aparajita come with thee?' Jaya replied,—'They are all gone with their mothers and husbands to the sacrifice, and my father Gautama and mother are also gone there; but I am come to see thee, and to enquire why thou and Maheshwara are not repairing to that festival of heaven, to which all the immortals and holy sages have been invited.' On hearing these words, Sati, as if struck with a thunderbolt, fell to the ground and expired with anger †; and, when she beheld Sati lying dead, Jaya, oppressed with grief, gave vent to her tears and loudly bewailed her loss. No sooner did Shiva hear the sound of lamentation than he exclaimed,—'Ah! what can this mean?' and hastened to where Jaya was; and there beholding Sati stretched lifeless on the ground, like some tender plant cut down by the axe, he asked Jaya the cause of this sad event. She replied,—'On being informed that all the immortals and her sisters had been invited to the sacrifice, and no invitation having been received by her, she died through inward grief.' On hearing these words, Shiva was

* One of Shiva's names is *Kapala-bhrit*, i. e., the bearer of a human skull; as he is obliged, as a penance, to carry always the skull of Brahma. But the particular sanctity of Kashi is, at the same time, ascribed to that being the place that Shiva was enabled to relieve himself from Brahma's fifth head, and from the continual pursuit of the being who had been produced from the sin of *Brahmanicide;* and hence Kashi is called Avimukta, according to a passage in the Sanatkumara Khand of the Skanda Puran.

† The death of Sati is related differently in other Purans; but I defer giving the generally received account until Chapter XIII.

enraged with anger; and, while his body glowed with the flame of his wrath, from his hair sprang a numerous band, at whose head was Virabhadra, whom Shiva ordered to hasten and destroy Daksha and his sacrifice." — Chap. 4.

Narada said,—" For what reason was Kama* consumed by Shiva?" Pulastya replied, — " When Sati the daughter of Daksha had departed to the abode of Yama†, Khandarpa of the flowery bow observed Shankara reflecting on the destruction of Daksha's sacrifice, and wounded him with the arrow of madness. Then Hara, maddened by the shaft of Kama, began to traverse woods and rivers while his thoughts were fondly fixed on Sati, nor, like a wounded elephant, could he obtain the least repose. Once Shankara threw himself into the Kalindi river, but the waters were scorched and changed into blackness; and ever since its dark stream, though holy, flows through the forest like the string

* With regard to Kama, the god of love, it may be sufficient to transcribe the following stanzas from Sir W. Jones's ode to this god: —

" 'Know'st thou not me?' — Celestial sounds I hear!
'Know'st thou not me?' — Ah! spare a mortal ear!
'Behold!' My swimming eyes entranced I raise;
But, oh! they shrink before the excessive blaze.
Yes, son of Maya! yes, I know
Thy bloomy shafts and cany bow,
Cheeks with youthful glory beaming,
Locks in braids ethereal streaming;
Thy scaly standard, thy mysterious arms,
And all thy pains, and all thy charms.

" He bends the luscious cane, and twists the string
With bees, how sweet! but, ah! how keen their sting!
He with five flow'rets tips thy ruthless darts,
Which through five senses pierce enraptured hearts:
Strong *Chumpa*, rich in odorous gold;
Warm *Amer*, nursed in heavenly mould;
Dry *Nagkeser*, in silver smiling;
Hot *Kiticum*, our sense beguiling;
And last, to kindle fierce the scorching flame,
Love shaft, which gods bright *Bela* name.

† This is a common expression for *died*; but it is here inapplicable, as death is never predicated of Sati.

that binds a maiden's hair. Thus Shiva roamed over mountain and forest, grove and plain, hill and valley, rich in streams and lakes and all that affords delight, and yet could find no rest; and, ever as he thought on the lovely daughter of Daksha, he sometimes laughed and sometimes wept. Even did sleep for a moment seal his eyes, he saw in his slumbers his beloved Sati and would thus address her: — 'O pitiless! stay: why dost thou forsake me who am blameless? for, enamoured of thee, I am through thy absence consumed with the fire of love. O Sati! though thou wert justly angry, yet bear not anger, O lovely one! to me, who prostrate myself at thy feet; and deign to speak to me, in whose thoughts thou art continually present. Fondly do I dwell on all thy former words of love; and shouldst thou now render them untrue, and me desert, how can I survive? Who does not pity him whom he beholds lamenting, and canst thou, O pitiless! refrain from compassionating thy lord? Come, then; come, then, O lovely one! and enfold me in thy embrace; for otherwise, O my beloved! the fire of love, with which I consume, can never be extinguished.' Thus did Shiva lament during his slumber; and, when he awoke, he again filled the forest with the low sad moanings of his heartfelt grief." * . . .

"Then Hara, wounded by the arrows of Kama, wandered into a deep forest, named *Daruvanam*, where holy sages and their wives resided. The sages, on beholding Shiva, saluted him with bended heads, and he, wearied, said to them, — 'Give me alms.' Thus he went begging round the different hermitages; and, wherever he came, the minds of the sages' wives, on seeing him, became disturbed and agitated with the pain of love, and all commenced to follow him. But when the sages saw their holy dwellings thus deserted, they exclaimed, — '*May the lingam of this*

* This description, it will be no doubt admitted, is very different from this account given by Wilford: — "Mahadeva then took up the body of his beloved *Sali* (Sati) on his shoulders, and went seven times round the world. Here I shall remark that when any accident happens to the gods, they generally set off at full speed, going seven times round the world, howling all the way most wofully." — *As. Res.*, vol. vii. p. 477. With regard to the latter part of this quotation, no such custom is ascribed to the gods in any Sanscrit work with which I am acquainted; nor have I ever heard it mentioned in conversation with natives.

*man * fall to the ground!"* That instant the lingam of Shiva fell to the ground; and the god immediately disappeared. The lingam, then, as it fell, penetrated through the lower worlds, and increased in height until its top towered above the heavens; the earth quaked, and all things movable and immovable were agitated. On perceiving which Brahma hastened to the sea of milk, and said to Vishnu, — 'Say, why does the universe thus tremble?' Hari replied, — 'On account of the falling of Shiva's lingam, in consequence of the curse of the holy and divine sages.' On hearing of this most wonderful event, Brahma said,— 'Let us go and behold this lingam.' The two gods then repaired to Daruvanam; and, on beholding it without beginning or end, Vishnu mounted the king of birds and descended into the lower regions in order to ascertain its base; and, for the purpose of discovering its top, Brahma in a lotos car ascended the heavens: but they returned from their search wearied and disappointed, and together approaching the lingam, with due reverence and praises, entreated Shiva to resume his lingam. Thus propitiated, that god appeared in his own form and said,—'If gods and men will worship my lingam, I will resume it; but not otherwise.'* To this proposal Vishnu, Brahma, and the gods assented; and Brahma divided its worshippers into four sects, the principal one of those, that which simply worships Shiva under the symbol of the lingam; the second, that of Pashupati‡; the third, of Mahakala; and the fourth, the Kapali; and revealed from his own mouth the ordinances by which this worship was to be regulated. Brahma and the gods then departed, and Shiva, having resumed the lingam, was also leaving the spot, when he beheld Kama at a distance; and, incensed with anger on remembering the pains which he had endured, looked at

* Shiva was disguised; and the sages, therefore, did not know him.

† In the *Nagar Khand* of the Skanda Puran, it is said that Shiva, afflicted for the loss of Sati, thus replied: — "O gods! it was in consequence of the grief which I suffer in being separated from Sati that I cast away this lingam, apparently fallen through the curse of the sages; but, had I not willed it, who is there in the three worlds that could have deprived me of it? why then should I resume it?"

‡ These are names of Shiva under different characters: and the lingam, of course, becomes, in such cases, the symbol of Shiva under that particular character.

him with his world-consuming eye and reduced him to ashes." * — Chap. 6.

The resumption, however, of the lingam by Shiva is related differently in the Shiva Puran; and, as this account explains the reason of the particular form under which that symbol is represented, I subjoin it.

"On falling in consequence of the sages' curse, the lingam became like fire, and caused a conflagration wherever it penetrated; the three worlds were distressed, and as neither gods nor sages could find rest, they hastened for protection to Brahma. Having heard them relate all that had happened, Brahma replied:—'After having committed knowingly a reprehensible act, why say that it was done unknowingly? for who that is adverse to Shiva shall enjoy happiness, and yet when he came as a guest at noonday you received him not with due honours. But every one shall reap the fruit of his good or bad actions, and the lingam therefore shall not cease to distress the three worlds until it is resumed by that god. Do ye, therefore, adopt such means as you think best for restoring tranquillity to the universe.' The gods said,—'But, O lord! what means ought we to adopt?' Brahma replied,—'Propitiate by adoration the mountain-born goddess, and she will then assume the form of the *yoni* and receive this lingam, by which means alone it can be rendered innocuous. Should you thus obtain her favourable assistance, then form a vessel of the eight kinds of leaves, place in it boiled rice and sacred plants; and having filled it with holy water, consecrate the whole with the proper prayers and invocations; and with this water, repeating at the same time suitable prayers, sprinkle the lingam. After, also, Parvati shall have under the form of the yoni received the lingam, do you erect and consecrate the form of a lingam

* This account of Kama's being reduced to ashes by Shiva differs entirely from the one given in other Purans; and on which Sir W. Jones's hymn to Durga is founded. For the generally received account is, that the gods, finding that they could not relieve themselves from the distress occasioned by an Asura, named Taraka, except through the assistance of a son of Shiva; and that Shiva, after the death of Sati, was perfectly insensible to love; entreated Kama to wound him with one of his arrows just as Parvati appeared. Kama effected this object, and Shiva became instantly enamoured of Parvati; but, angry at Kama for his having ventured to direct his arrows at him, he reduced him to ashes.

in the yoni; and, by worshipping it with offerings of flowers, perfumes, and such things, by kindling lamps before it, and by singing and music, propitiate Maheshwara, and thus will the forgiveness and favour of that god be undoubtedly obtained.' Having heard these words, the gods and sages hastened to implore the protection of Shiva and the assistance of Parvati, as directed by Brahma; and these deities having been propitiated, Parvati, under the form of the yoni, received the lingam and thus appeased its consuming fire; and in commemoration of this event was instituted the worship of the lingam." *

But in the Padma Puran the origin of the particular form under which this symbol is represented is ascribed to the effects of a curse imprecated on Shiva by Bhrigu; for it is therein said that, when Bhrigu was sent to ascertain the preeminence of the three gods, as mentioned in p. 240., on arriving at Kailasa he thus addressed Shiva's doorkeeper: — " 'Quickly inform Shankara that I, the Brahman Bhrigu, am come to see him.' But the doorkeeper said, — 'Stop, stop, if thou wishest to preserve thy life; for my lord cannot be approached at present, as he is engaged in amorous dalliance with Devi.' The divine sage, being thus denied access, waited some time at the gate of Shiva's abode, and at length incensed with anger imprecated this curse: — 'Since thou, O Shankara! hast thus treated me with contempt, in consequence of thy preferring the embraces of Parvati, your forms shall on that account become the lingam in the yoni.' "† Though not here specified, it is generally understood that it was in consequence of this curse that Shiva was deprived of his lingam in the Daruvanam, and that Parvati assumed the form of the yoni, in order to receive and render it innocuous.

But in the Shiva, as well as in other Purans, the origin of the worship of the lingam is related differently, and I therefore add this account, as it occurs in the Lainga Puran.

Brahma, addressing the angels.—" When I sprang into existence, I beheld the mighty Narayana reposing on the abyss of waters; and, being under the influence of delusion, awakened him with my hand and thus addressed him, — 'Who art thou that thus slumberest on this terrible

* Shiva Puranam, part i., the chapter entitled *Linga-vidhanam.*

† Padma Puran, Uttara Khand, last chapter.

ocean?' Hari awoke, and, dispelling sleep from his lotos eyes, looked upon me, and then arising said,—'Welcome, welcome, O Pitamaha! my dear son!' On hearing the first of gods smiling thus speak, I, confined within the bonds of the quality of impurity, replied, —'Why dost thou say, my dear son? for know me to be the eternal god, the universal spirit, the creator, preserver, and destroyer of the three worlds.' But he immediately answered, —'Hear the truth, O four-faced! and learn that it is I who am the creator, the preserver, and the destroyer, how canst thou thus forget Narayana the self-existent and eternal Brahm? but thou committest no fault, for thy error proceeds from the delusion of Maya.' Hence arose between us a terrible combat amidst the waters of the deluge, when, to appease the contest and recall us to our senses, appeared a lingam blazing like a thousand suns. Bewildered by its radiant beams, Hari thus said to me, lost in amazement, —'I will proceed downwards in order to ascertain the termination of this wondrous column of fire, do thou, O lord! proceed upwards and seek for its top.' Having thus spoken, he assumed the form of a boar, and I that of a swan, and we both prosecuted our search for four thousand years; but being unable to ascertain its terminations, we then returned back wearied and disappointed. Thus still under the influence of delusion, we prostrated ourselves before the lingam, and were reflecting on what it could be, when we heard a voice saying, *om, om, om,*— and shortly after appeared Shiva in the midst of that column of fire." In commemoration of this event, therefore, was the worship of the lingam instituted.

* Lainga Puranam, chapter 16th.

These are the only accounts of the origin of this worship which occur in the Puranas, and I therefore leave the reader to form his own opinion on this statement of Mr. Ward:—"There are several stories in the Purans respecting the origin of the lingam worship, three of which I had translated, and actually inserted in this work, leaving out as much as possible of their offensive parts; but, in correcting the proofs, they appeared too gross, even when refined as much as possible, to meet the public eye." (vol. i. p. 15.) Mr. Ward takes every opportunity of objecting indecency and obscenity to the Hindu mythology; but, after a most attentive examination of the subject, I have not been able to discover, unless calling a spade a spade be considered a sufficient ground, the slightest foundation for such an objection in either the Purans, Upa-Purans, Ramayanam, or Mahabharat; and, with regard to other Sanscrit works, I agree entirely in the justness of this opinion expressed by Mr. Wil-

Sir W. Jones, in alluding to the lingam, has remarked that he supposes Bhavani to be Venus herself, Venus presiding over generation, and on that account exhibited sometimes of both sexes, and sometimes under figures which had the form of a *conical marble; for the reason of which figure we are left* (says Tacitus) *in the dark.* The reason appears too clearly in the temples and paintings of Hindustan, where it never seems to have entered the heads of the legislators or people, that any thing natural could be offensively obscene. * But the lingam is formed of stone, and consists of a base three or four feet high, the top of which is surrounded with a raised rim; and in the middle is slightly excavated, and raised on a level with the rim, the figure of a yoni (pudendum muliebre), from the centre of which rises a smooth round stone slightly conical towards the top, of a foot and a half in height, and about three inches diameter at the base. Major Moor has, therefore very justly observed:—"It is some comparative and negative praise to the Hindus, that the emblems under which they exhibit the elements and operations of nature, are not externally indecorous. Unlike the abominable realities of Egypt and Greece, we see the phallic emblem in the Hindu

---

son in a note to his translation of the *Magha Duta*, p. 78.:—"I have, indeed, in this place concentrated, and in part omitted, two verses of the original, as offensive to our notions of the decorum of composition. I cannot admit, however, that Hindu literature, speaking generally, is more liable to the reproach of indecency than that of Europe: nothing can be found in their serious works half so licentious as are many passages in the writings of Ovid, Catullus, Propertius, and even the elegant Flaccus. To descend to modern times, Ariosto and Boccacio amongst the Italians, Brantome, Crebillon, Voltaire, La Fontaine, and the writers of many recent philosophical novels amongst the French, furnish us with more than parallels for the most indelicate of the Hindu writers. With respect to ourselves, not to go back to the days in which '*obscenity was wit*,' we have little reason to reproach the Hindus with want of delicacy, when we find the exceptionable, though elegant, poetry of Little generally circulated and avowedly admired. We should also recollect the circumstances of Indian society, before we condemn their authors for the ungarbled expressions which we conceive to trespass upon the boundaries of decorum. *These authors write to men only, they never think of a woman as a reader.*"

* Asiatic Researches, vol. i. p. 254.

The words of Tacitus (Hist. lib. ii. c. 4.), in describing the Paphian Venus, are:—"Simulacrum deæ non effigie humana: continuus orbis latiore initio tenuem in ambitum, metæ modo exsurgens, et ratio in obscuro." But this is clearly a description of the lingam, and consequently there is nothing in the Hindu mythology which tends in the least to explain why such a symbol was consecrated to Venus.

Pantheon without offence; and know not, until the information be extorted, that we are contemplating a symbol whose prototype is indelicate. The plates of my book may be turned and examined, over and over, and the uninformed observer will not be aware that in several of them he has viewed the typical representation of the generative organs or powers of humanity." From the very nature, also, of this symbol, it will be evident that it was never intended to be carried in the processions consecrated to Shiva; and *Abraham Roger*, nearly two hundred years ago, has in consequence correctly stated,—"Mais quand on fait la procession par les villes avec l'idole Eswara, ce qui arrive en certains temps, on ne le porte pas sous la figure de lingam, mais sous la figure d'homme: la raison est, comme le Bramine témoignoit, pour ce que les hommes ont plus de plaisir et de contentement en la veuë d'une figure humaine que dans la veuë du lingam, en laquelle figure il est dans son pagode." *

The precise nature, however, of the form under which the phallus of the ancients was represented, is not explained by either Herodotus or Diodorus Siculus; and some doubt, therefore, seems to exist respecting it. For Lilius Gyraldus remarks:—"Phallus Priapus vocatur, et veretrum significat; quare, cum Herodotus ait in sacris Dionysii fuisse phallos, Priapos intelligimus, hoc est, veretra quæ e collo propendebant. Diodorus in sacris Ægyptiacis pudendum Osiridis phallum vocavit, et in ejus rei memoriam cubitales statuæ factæ eodem nomine dicebantur, quæ præcinente tibia circumferebantur. . . . . Alii phallos esse dicunt ligna longa, quæ in summo pudenda haberent." † But Mr. Payne Knight has stated:—"In Egypt, nevertheless, and all over Asia, the mystic and symbolical worship appears to have been of immemorial antiquity. The women of the former country carried images of Osiris in their sacred processions, with a movable phallus of disproportionate magnitude, the reason for which Herodotus does not think proper to relate, because it belonged to the mystic religion. Diodorus Siculus, however, who lived in a more communicative age, informs us that it signified the generative attribute, and Plutarch that

* La Porte Ouverte, p. 157.

† Lilii Gyraldi Opera, tom. i. p. 282.

the Egyptian statues of Osiris had the phallus to signify his procreative and prolific power; the extension of which through the three elements of air, earth and water, they expressed by another kind of statue, which was occasionally carried in procession, having a triple symbol of the same attribute. The Greeks usually represented the phallus alone, as a distinct symbol, the meaning of which seems to have been among the last discoveries revealed to the initiated." * This last opinion, however, seems extremely questionable; but, were it admitted, it seems indisputable that the phallus was always formed in such a manner as to leave no doubt with respect to the object which it represented, and that in religious processions it was always attached to a human figure. † It hence appears evident that the phallus bore no similarity to the lingam, and that, though the causes which may originally have produced the worship of these objects may have been the same in Egypt and India, still the symbols adopted for their representation, and the adoration paid to them, by the Egyptians and the Hindus, differed most materially.

As the lingam, also, is never carried in procession, and as its worship is not celebrated by orgies and bacchanalian rites, it will be equally obvious that the following passages of the Cohortatio ad Gentes of Clemens Alexandrinus are totally inapplicable to the Hindus: — "Extinguish the fire, O hierophant! be ashamed of thy own torches, O torch-bearer! the light betrays thy Iacchus: permit, if thou wish them to be reverenced, thy mysteries to be concealed by night, and thy orgies to be covered with darkness; fire does not dissimulate, but exposes and punishes all that is subjected to its power. These, therefore, are the mysteries of atheistical men; atheists, I call them justly, because, ignorant of the true God, they unblushingly worship an infant who was torn in pieces by the Titans, and a lamenting woman, and those parts of the body which modesty forbids us to name." ‡ — "The games

* An Enquiry into the Symbolical Language, &c., part i. sect. 23.

† Lucian, in his Tract de Syria Dea, expressly says: — Φαλλους Ἑλληνες Διονυσῳ εγειρουσι· επι των και τοιον δε τι φερουσι, ανδρας μικρους εκ ξυλῳ πεποιημενους, μεγαλα αιδοια εχοντας. καλεονται δε ταδε νευροσπαστα. εστι δε και τοδε εν τῳ ἱρῳ. εν δεξιᾳ του νηου καθηται σμικρος ανηρ χαλκεος, εχων αιδοιον μεγα.

‡ Besides the phallus, Clemens Alexandrinus mentions, Κτεις γυναικειος, ὁ εστιν, ευφημως

and phalli consecrated to Bacchus, not only corrupt manners, but are considered shameful and disgraceful by all the world."—"In commemoration of that event * was this mystery instituted, and phalli erected in every city in honour of Dionusos; so that Heraclitus even says *that misfortune would ensue, if processions were not made, and hymns sung, and pudenda shamelessly worshipped, in honour of Dionusos.* This then is the Hades and the Dionusos, in whose honour men become agitated with bacchanalian madness and fury; not so much, in my opinion, on account of natural inebriation, as in consequence of the reprehensible ceremonies which were first instituted in commemoration of that abominable turpitude."

To place this point, however, beyond doubt, it is merely necessary to transcribe from the Lainga Puran the ritual prescribed for the worship of the lingam; which is as follows:—Having bathed in the prescribed manner, enter the place of worship; and, having performed three suppressions of the breath †, meditate on that god who has three eyes, five heads, ten arms, and is of the colour of pure crystal, arrayed in costly garments, and adorned with all kinds of ornaments: and having thus fixed in thy mind the real form of Maheshwara, proceed to worship him with the proper prayers and hymns. First, sprinkle the place and utensils of worship with a bunch of *darbha* dipped in perfumed water, repeating at the same time the sacred word *om*, and arrange all the utensils and other things required in the prescribed order; then in due manner, and repeating the proper invocations,

---

και μυσταως ειπειν, μοριον γυναικειον. But the *yoni* by itself has never been to the Hindus a general object of worship; though it is said that there is a sect in India which adores this emblem in the same manner as the Smartas and Shaivas worship the lingam. Nothing, however, relating to this sect occurs in the Puran, nor have I been able to obtain any information respecting it; and I am, therefore, inclined to consider much that has been written respecting it to be extremely apocryphal.

* The event described admits not of translation or transcription, but nothing so abominable occurs in any Sanscrit legend.

† *Pranayama*, which Mr. Colebrooke thus describes:—"Closing the left nostril with the two longest fingers of the right hand, the worshipper draws breath through the right nostril, and then closing that nostril likewise with his thumb, holds his breath; he then raises both fingers off the left nostril, and emits the breath which he had suppressed."—*As. Res.*, vol. v. p. 348.

prayers, and hymns, preceded by the sacred word *om*, prepare thy offerings. For the padiam*, these should consist of ushiram †, sandal, and similar sweet-smelling woods; for the achamanam ‡, of mace, camphor, bdellium, and agallochum, ground together; and, for the arghya §, of the tops of kusha grass, prepared grains of rice, barley, sesamum, clarified butter, pieces of money, ashes, and flowers. At the same time, also, must be worshipped Nandi ‖ and his wife, the daughter of Marut. Having then with due rites prepared a seat, invoke with the prescribed prayers the presence of Parameshwara, and present to him the *padiam*, *achamanam* and *arghya*. Next bathe the lingam with perfumed water, the five products of the cow, clarified butter, honey, the juice of the sugar-cane, and lastly pour over it a pot of pure water, consecrated by the requisite prayers. Having thus purified it, adorn it with clean garments and a sacrificial string, and then offer flowers, perfumes, frankincense, lamps, fruits, and different kinds of prepared eatables, and ornaments. Thus worship the lingam with the prescribed offerings, invocations, prayers, and hymns, and by circumambulating it and by prostrating thyself before Shiva, represented under this symbol. ⸸

* Water for the ablution of the feet rendered fragrant by these means. The water is not here specified, as it is implied in the word padiam.

† The root of the Andropogon muricatus.

‡ Water for rinsing the mouth.

§ A particular kind of oblation, which consists of different articles in the worship of different deities. Here the pieces of money are unusual, and ashes (made from dried cow-dung) are sacred to Shiva only.

‖ The principal attendant of Shiva, and supposed to be a portion of that god, who granted a son as a boon to a holy ascetic named Shilada, and also consented that he would be born as that son.

⸸ Lainga Puranam, part i. chapter 25. I have here considerably abridged the original, but nothing material is omitted, as the invocations, prayers, and hymns are not inserted at length, but merely referred to by their titles. At the present day the whole of this ritual is not observed, nor is this worship performed in that costly manner which is recommended in the Purans. But the worship of all the deities consists of sixteen essential requisites: — 1. *asanam*, the preparing a seat for the god; 2. *asahanam*, the invoking his presence; 3. *padiam*; 4. *achamanam*; 5. *arghya*; 6. bathing the image; 7. clothing it; 8. investing it with a sacrificial string; offerings of, 9. perfumes; 10. flowers; 11. incense; 12. lamps; 13. naivedya, i. e. offerings consisting of fruits and prepared eatables; 14. betel leaf; 15. prayers, &c.; 16. circumambulation. The more of these acts that are performed the more complete is the worship; but at present it in general consists of nothing more than

The legends, however, respecting the origin of the worship of the lingam given above, cannot satisfy the philosophical enquirer; and the real cause, therefore, which produced the adoration of so singular an object might appear to be a curious subject of speculation. But, though in the Purans there are copious descriptions of the high importance of this worship, and of the spiritual advantages to be derived from it, still these works contain not the slightest indication from which any just conclusion could be formed, with respect to either the period when it was first introduced, or the motives which may have occasioned the substitution of this symbol for the image of Shiva. Yet it seems probable that this change had not been effected at the time when the Vedas were composed, and that the earliest record of this worship which has been preserved is contained in the Purans. But, as in those sacred books there is not the least appearance of its being either mystical or symbolical, it must be evident that if it originated in such causes they have long ceased to exist; and consequently that the speculations on this subject, in which the literati of Europe have indulged, are totally incompatible with the simple principles, as far as they are known, on which this worship is founded. For, in fact, both in the Purans and by the Hindus of the present day, the lingam is held to be merely a visible type of an invisible deity; and nothing whatever belongs to its worship, or to the terms in which this is mentioned, which has the slightest tendency to lead the thoughts, from the contemplation of the god, to an undue consideration of the object by which he is typified.

But it is impossible to understand by what process of reasoning the founders of the Hindu religion were induced to place Shiva among the divine hypostases; for they supposed, at the same time, that dissolution and death proceeded from the fixed laws of nature, and that

---

presenting some of the prescribed offerings, and muttering a short prayer or two while the lingam is circumambulated: the rest of the acts being performed by the officiating priest.

It ought to be added, that this worship need not be performed at a temple, but in any properly purified place; and that it is most efficacious when performed on the bank of some holy river, before a lingam formed *pro hac vice* of clay, which, on the worship being terminated, is thrown into the sacred stream.

his power was not called into exertion until after the termination of twelve millions of years. During the whole, therefore, of this inconceivable period, what functions could be ascribed to this god consistent with his character of destroyer? This difficulty, however, seems to have been very soon obviated by investing him with the attributes of the Supreme Being, and even in the Purans it is under this character that he is generally represented. As, therefore, the attributes which are, according to the Hindus, peculiar to the one god are immovability and inaction, Shiva is described as being principally engaged in devout meditation, and as exerting his divine power through the means either of Devi (or his energy personified) or of certain forms which he creates for the occasion, such as Bhairava and Virabhadra. In Hindu mythology, consequently, there are only three legends, the destruction of the Tripura Asuras, and of the Asuras Andhaka, and Jalandhara, in which Shiva appears as the actor, unconnected with any reference to the worship of the lingam. But, on the introduction of this worship, not a lingam seems to have been erected without its foundation having been ascribed to some miraculous appearance of Shiva *; and hence have originated a multiplicity of legends in the highest degree puerile, and every one erring against the just principle, —

> Nec deus intersit, nisi dignus vindice nodus
> Inciderit.

For in the Shiva Puran, Suta thus speaks; " Innumerable are the lingams which are adored, as the type of Shiva, in heaven, earth, and

* Mr. Ward has stated, in his work on the Hindus, vol. i. p. 17. : — " Besides the clay image of the lingam, there are two kinds of black stone lingams: these are set up in the Hindu temples. The first is called Swayambhu, the self-existent; or *Anadi*, that which has no beginning: the second they call Vana lingam; because Vana, a king, first instituted the worship of this image. These stones are brought from the neighbourhood of the river Gandaki." This passage is singularly incorrect, for the Swayambhu or Anadi lingams are supposed, as the epithet imports, to be self-existent and unmade, and wherever miraculously revealed and fixed the temple was erected over them, and not they in the temple. Nor is there any mention to be found any where of such a king as Vana; but a certain stone of the shape of a hen's egg, though of a greater size, is found in the Narmada, not Gandaki, river, which is named Bana, and is held sacred to Shiva, in the same manner as the Shalagrama is to Vishnu. In the Shiva Puran, indeed, it is said that all the stones in the Narmada are forms of Shiva; but the Bana alone is employed for the construction of lingams.

Tartarus; but where some of these are erected, there Shiva for the good of the three worlds appeared, and consequently whoever visits and worships them acquires more complete remission of sins and a greater degree of holiness. Even of these, however, the number is unascertainable, but I will mention the twelve which are on earth considered the most sacred, and which are distinguished by the names of *Jyolisha* lingams. They are in Saurashtra Somanatha, and in Shri Sheila Mallikarjuna; in Ujain Mahakala, and on the Narmada Omkar; Kedar on the side of Himavan, and Bhima Shankara in Kamarupa; Vishwesha in Kashi, and Trimbakam on the Godaveri; Vaidyanatha in Chitabhumi, and Nagesha in Darukavanam; Rameshweram at the Setubandha, and Ghushmesham in Shivalaya. Each of these lingams, also, has an inferior one dependent upon it, which are named Andakesha, Bhrigukaccha, Dugdhesha, Kardamesha, Bhutesha, Bhimeshwara, Sharanyeshwara, Siddeshwara, Vaidyanatheshwara, Bhuteshwara, Guptesha, and Viaghreshwara. Besides these there are many other principal lingams, the worship of which insures the remission of sins and final beatitude."*

As a specimen of the legends attached to the most celebrated lingams, I extract the following from the Shiva Puran:—"A Rakshasa, named Bhima, the son of Kumbakarna, having obtained invincible

* I spare the reader a further catalogue of names; but I have inserted the above, though I can identify only a few of the places, because I conceive that one of the most effectual means of illustrating the ancient geography of India, is the ascertaining of the exact situation of its most celebrated temples. Somnath is well known to be a town near the southern extremity of the Guzerat peninsula; Mallikarjuna is, I believe, situated near the junction of the Krishna and Bheema rivers: Omkar, or Omkar Mandatta, is situated near Mundessoor in Malwa; Kamarupa is to the east of Bengal, and was formerly an independent state, but now forms part of Assam; Vaidyanatha is in the Bengal provinces, district of Birbhoom; Rameshwaram, or Ramisseram, is in the southern Carnatic, and is supposed to mark the spot where Rama formed a mound (Setu) from the continent to Ceylon; Ujain (Ougein) Kedar, Kashi or Benares, and Trimback do not require notice; but I have not been able to ascertain where Nagesha and Ghushmesham may have been situated. The *upa lingams*, or dependent ones, are given above in the same order as the *Jyolisha* lingams; but I can learn nothing respecting them, though it would appear that they must have been situated at no very great distance from the latter. It is to be remarked, that the names of several of Shiva's temples in different parts of India, now better known and more celebrated, are not specified in the Shiva Puran.

might as a boon from Brahma, commenced exerting his newly acquired power by attacking the king of Kamarupa. Him he conquered, and having seized his riches and kingdom, he placed him in chains in a solitary prison. This king was eminently pious, and, notwithstanding his confinement, continued daily to make clay lingams, and to worship Shiva with all the prescribed rites and ceremonies. Meanwhile the Rakshasa continued his conquests, and every where abolished the religious observances and worship enjoined by the Vedas; and the immortals, also, were reduced by his power to great distress. At length the gods hastened to implore the protection of Shiva, and to obtain his favour by the worship of clay lingams; and Shambu, being thus propitiated, assured them that he would effect the destruction of the Rakshasa through the medium of the king of Kamarupa, who was his devoted worshipper. At this time the king was engaged in profound meditation before a lingam, when one of the guards went and informed the Rakshasa that the king was performing some improper ceremonies in order to injure him. On hearing this, the Rakshasa, enraged, seized his sword and hastened to the king, whom he thus addressed:— 'Speak the truth, and tell me who it is that thou worshippest, and I will not slay thee, but otherwise I will instantly put thee to death.' The king having considered, placed his firm reliance in the protection of Shiva, and replied undauntedly,—'In truth I worship Shankara: do then what thou pleasest.' The Rakshasa said,—'What can Shankara do to me? for I know him well, and that he once was obliged to become the servant of my uncle (Ravana); and thou, trusting in his power, didst endeavour to conquer me, but defeat was the consequence. Until, however, thou showest me thy lord and convincest me of his might, I shall not believe in his divinity.' The king replied,—'Vile as I am, what power have I over that god? but, mighty as he is, I know that he never will forsake me.' The Rakshasa said,—'How can that delighter in *ganja** and inebriation, that wandering mendicant, protect his worshippers? let but thy lord appear, and I will immediately engage in battle with him!' Having thus spoken, he ordered

* An intoxicating drug prepared from the hemp plant.

the attendance of his army, and then, reviling the king, the mighty Rakshasa, while he smote the lingam with his sword, thus, laughing, said, — 'Now behold the power of thy lord.' But scarce had the sword touched the lingam than Hara instantly issued from it, exclaiming, — 'Behold! I am Ishwara, who appears for the protection of his worshipper, on whom he always bestows safety and happiness; and now learn to dread my might.' On having thus spoken, Shiva engaged in combat with the Rakshasa, and, after fighting with him for some time, at length with the fire of his third eye reduced him and all his army to ashes; and in commemoration of this event was the spot where it occurred rendered sacred, and the lingam, under the name of Bhimashankara, an object of pilgrimage and worship until all succeeding ages." *

On perusing this legend, it will immediately occur that it is a mere imitation of the fourth *avatar* of Vishnu, the concluding part of the account of which is thus given in the Padma Puran: —" Hiranyakashipu having ordered his son Pralhada to be put to death on account of his devotion to Vishnu, and all means employed for this purpose having proved ineffectual, the king of the Daityas was astonished, and with gentleness addressed his son: — 'Where is that Vishnu whose pre-eminence thou hast declared before me, and who, as thou sayest, was called Vishnu because he pervades all things, and consequently, being omnipresent, he must also be the Supreme Being? Show to me a proof of the divine power and qualities which thou ascribest to him, and I will acknowledge the divinity of Vishnu; or let him conquer in battle me, who have obtained the boon of being unslayable by any existing thing.' Pralhada astonished replied, — 'Narayana, the eternal, omnipotent, omnipresent, and supreme Spirit dwells in heaven, and man cannot obtain the view of his divine form through anger and hatred, but, though unseen, he is present in all things.' Having heard these words, Hiranyakashipu was incensed with anger, and, reviling his son, said, — 'Why dost thou thus with endless boasts exalt the power of Vishnu?' and then, striking a pillar of his royal hall, thus continued:

* This and the preceding quotation will be found in the Shiva Puran, in the legend entitled *Jyolisha-linga Mahatmyam*.

'If Vishnu pervades all things let him appear in this pillar, or I will this moment put thee to death.' This said, he struck the pillar with his sword, and instantly from it burst a loud and dreadful sound, while Vishnu issued forth under a fearful form, half man and half lion." *

But as the avatars of Vishnu are unquestionably an essential part of the Hindu religion, since they are noticed in the Vedas, Upanishads, and Purans, and as the miraculous appearances of Shiva, on which the sanctity of various lingams is founded, are not generally acknowledged by the Hindus, and are mentioned only in the Shanka and Shiva Purans, it must necessarily follow that the fourth avatar of Vishnu is the original from which the above legend of Bhima Shankara has been merely copied. The introduction, however, of a new mode of worship is always, as experience has shown, supported by miracles; and it may therefore be concluded that the legends respecting the *Jyolisha* lingams, at least, are as ancient as the first institution of the worship of the lingam. In which case it will be evident that the transferring by the *Shaivas* to Shiva of the peculiar attribute of Vishnu, that of preservation, and their founding various miracles on such transfer, are convincing proofs that Vishnuism must have existed before the present form of Shivaism; and that, in inventing these miracles, the *Shaivas* have wished to ascribe to the god of their particular adoration similar manifestations of divine power to those by which Vishnu was supposed to be peculiarly distinguished. This opinion, therefore, of M. Guigniaut, —" Le Sivaisme a, dans sa simplicité pleine de grandeur, quelque chose de singulièrement barbare, qui dénote une haute antiquité; d'ailleurs, ses formes générales ont manifestement servi des types aux créations successives des autres systèmes et de toute la mythologie des Hindous †,"—is clearly unfounded; for there is nothing whatever barbarous in the worship of the lingam ‡, and this worship seems indisputably to

* The battle between the man-lion and the Daityas, with the final destruction of Hiranyakashipu by Vishnu under this form, is related at considerable length; but I omit this account, as it is well known.

† Religions de l'Antiquité, tom. i. p. 214.

‡ M. Guigniaut, indeed, states (ibid., p. 148.): — " Sur la mont Merou aussi, à la nouvelle lune, étaient célébrées, en l'honneur de Siva, les fêtes du phallus, où l'on portait

have been instituted after the Vedas and Upanishads were composed; and, consequently, after the Hindu religion had acquired that form, which has been preserved since that time, in every essential respect unchanged, until the present day.

The following opinion, also, presents so strange a misrepresentation of the essential principles of the Hindu religion, that it requires remark: for M. Guigniaut observes, — "La lingam dans l'yoni, l'hermaphrodite réunissant les deux sexes, enfin Mahadeva et Bhavani, Iswara et Isi, représentant, dans le culte populaire de Siva, le Grand Etre, auteur de toutes choses, et la forme ou mère universelle, dont l'union donna naissance à la trimourti, ces premiers symboles de la religion Hindoue, &c."* But in p. 211, I have pointed out that the term *trimurti* is never applied to a *triune* junction of Brahma, Vishnu, and Shiva, and their origin is never ascribed to the union of Shiva and Bhavani, as it will be sufficiently evident from the different accounts of the theogony given in Chapter VII. Nor, though the form of the lingam is symbolical of these deities, is its worship intended to be addressed to both of them, but only to Shiva. It is a material mistake, therefore, to suppose that Mahadeva and Bhavani are ever adored conjointly: for they are always considered as distinct deities; and, as such, temples are erected to each, and to each are distinct rites, ceremonies, and festivals consecrated. But *l'hermaphrodite primitif* is a character entirely unknown to me; for Rudra is the only deity who is said, in several Purans, to have been produced both male and female: but, as the sexes were immediately separated, he, of course, remained male only. Nor is Brahma ever supposed to have been a hermaphrodite, though he produced from his own substance both Manu and his wife Shatarupa.† The wonderful

solennellement cette image sacrée; là aussi, dans des orgies délirantes, ses adorateurs mus d'un enthousiasme sauvage, semblaient céder eux mêmes au pouvoir qui emporte la nature d'un mouvement irresistible, et la vivifie comme un feu dévorant." But this statement is in direct contradiction to the present practices of the Hindus, and not a trace of such festivals and orgies can be discovered in the Purans, or in any other Sanscrit work.

* Religions de l'Antiquité, tom. i. p. 176.

† I am aware that there exists a hermaphroditic image named *Ardhanareshwara*; but I cannot learn that it is ever worshipped, nor do any legends respecting its origin occur in the Purans. Mr. Ward, indeed, gives one which he says is taken from the Lainga Puran;

absurdity, therefore, of the following conclusions of Mr. Faber must be self-evident:—"From these legends," he remarks, "we may collect, in a manner which cannot be easily misunderstood, that the hermaphroditic unity of Brahma, or the Supreme Being, whom the meditative Hindu identifies with himself, is an imaginary androgynous conjunction of Adam and Eve *, the universal parents of the human race; and, consequently, that the divine unity, venerated by the pagans, and described by them as partaking of both sexes, a unity which has so often been mistaken for the real divine unity of the true God, is produced solely by the fabled amalgamation of the great father and great mother."† The divine unity of the Brahmans, indeed, is certainly not the same as that of the Christians; but the unification is still more complete, for they resolve all apparent realities into one, sole, self-existent God, without sex, or form, or quality.

Even, however, in the worship of the lingam, it is evident that the adoration is addressed to Shiva, as the Supreme Being; but I have nowhere found the slightest explanation of the causes which have occasioned his being considered in the very contemptuous character in which he is so frequently represented. Nor does this character occur in the *Vaishnava* Purans alone, but even in the *Shaiva*; for in the Skanda, Shiva himself, under the disguise of a Brahman, is described as thus addressing the female friends who were attending Parvati, while she was performing *tapas*, in order to obtain Shiva as a husband:—"Parvati must be foolish, and unable to distinguish between what is advantageous and disadvantageous, since she thus practises a severe *tapas* in order to obtain Rudra, a wandering mendicant, without riches, a bearer of a human skull, a delighter in cemeteries, ornamented with human bones and serpents, covered with ashes, and with no garments but an

---

but it is not contained in two copies of this Puran which I possess. All the accounts, also, given by Mr. Ward, have evidently not the slightest relation to the theogony and cosmogony, or to Shiva as the Supreme Being.

* I take this opportunity of observing that neither in any Sanscrit work, nor in conversation with Hindus, have I ever found Manu and Shatarupa denominated *Adima* and *Iva*.

† Origin of Pagan Idolatry, vol. iii. p. 67.

elephant's skin, riding on a bull, and always accompanied by ghosts and goblins. How then can such customs be suited to a tender maid; or what has Rudra in common with beauty and loveliness? If, therefore, friends, you wish to preserve her from death, dissuade her from her present resolution, and prevail upon her to employ her *tapas* for the purpose of obtaining a more desirable god, such as Indra, or Varuna, or Kubera." Even when he afterwards appears to Parvati in his proper form, it is described as in a manner not in the least more divine; for he then showed himself with two arms, one head, with matted locks, covered with ashes, clothed in an elephant's skin, and wearing serpents as ornaments. But I have not as yet met with any thing which explains the reason why a character so incompatible with divinity is ascribed to Shiva; and I must, therefore, leave this point to be elucidated by farther research.

CHAP. XII.

SARASVATI. — SAVITRI. — GAYATRI. — LAKSHMI.

The energy of Brahma, personified as a female, is in general distinguished by the name of Sarasvati; but in, I believe, every Puran she is also called either Savitri or Gayatri. But so little occurs in the sacred books of the Hindus respecting these deities, that it is difficult to determine whether they are one and the same goddess, or distinct personages. In the following extract, however, these names are considered to be synonymous, and to designate but one divinity: — *

From the Matsya Puran.

"Brahma next formed from his own immaculate substance a female, who is celebrated under the names of Shatarupa, Savitri, Sarasvati, Gayatri, and Brahmani. Then, beholding his daughter, born from his own body, Brahma became wounded with the arrows of love, and exclaimed, 'How surpassing lovely she is!' But Shatarupa turned to the right side from his gaze, and, as Brahma wished to look after her, a second head appeared; and thus, as she passed, in order to avoid his amorous glances, to his left and his rear, two other heads successively manifested themselves. At length she sprang into the sky, and, as Brahma was anxious to gaze after her, a fifth head was immediately formed. Then Brahma thus called to his daughter, — 'Let us generate all kinds of animated beings, men, Suras, and Asuras.' On hearing these words she descended, and, Brahma having espoused her, they withdrew into a secluded spot, and there indulged in the delights of love, for one hundred divine years; at the expiration of which period was

* It is the same in the following passage of the Garura Puran: — "*Hari, addressing Rudra.* — Gayatri is the supreme goddess, the giver of bliss and final beatitude; and whoever repeats, at morning, noon, and evening, the prayer so called, the prescribed number of times, shall be absolved from all his sins. But let him add to it this invocation: 'Praise be to thee, O Gayatri! praise be to thee, praise, O Savitri! O Sarasvati!'" &c.

born Manu, who is also called Swayambhuva and Viraj. Brahma is the principal of all the gods, and Gayatri was formed from his body; both in reality incorporeal, but assuming a corporeal form, and hence is even copulation predicated of them. Wherever Virinchi is, there is the goddess Sarasvati; wherever Bharati is, there is Prajapati; and as the shadow is inseparable from its object, so does Savitri never leave the side of Brahma." — Chap. 3, 4.

In the following singular legend, however, Savitri and Gayatri are clearly distinct personages, and no mention is made of Sarasvati: —

*From the Skanda Puran.**

Ishwara, addressing Devi.—" Listen, O Devi! and I will relate to thee how Savitri forsook Brahma, and how he in consequence espoused Gayatri. The Vedas have declared the great advantages which are derived from sacrifice, by which the gods are delighted, and therefore bestow rain upon the earth; and by rain is produced seed, and from seed vegetation and life. To ensure, therefore, the verdure and vitality of the three worlds, I perform sacrifice, and in imitation of me, innumerable sacrifices are performed by gods and men. For the same purpose Brahma and his wife Savitri, the immortals and holy sages, repaired to Pushkara; but, when all preparations had been made with due rites and ceremonies for performing the sacrifice, Savitri, detained by some household affairs, was not in attendance. A priest accordingly went to call her, but she said to him,—'I have not yet completed my dress, nor arranged several affairs! Lakshmi, also, and Bhawani, and Gunga, and Swaha, and Indrani, and the wives of the other gods and of the holy sages, have not yet arrived, and how, therefore, can I enter the assembly alone?' The priest returned, and thus addressed Brahma: — 'Savitri is engaged, and will not come; but without a wife what advan-

* This legend is given at much greater length in the Shrishti Khand of the Padma Puran, and also in the Nagar Khand of the Skanda Puran, under the title of Pushkara Mahatmyam, and it is alluded to in several other of the Purans. But even the account of it given above I have found it necessary to abridge considerably.

tage can be derived from these rites?' The god, incensed at the conduct of Savitri, thus spoke to Indra :—' Hasten, and in obedience to my order bring me a wife from wherever you can find one.' Indra proceeded accordingly, and as he passed hastily along, he observed a milkmaid, young, beautiful, with a smiling countenance, and carrying a jar filled with butter. He immediately seized her, and brought her to the assembly, when Brahma thus spoke :—' O gods and holy sages ! if it seem good unto you I will espouse this Gayatri, and she shall become the mother of the Vedas, and the cause of holy purity to the three worlds.' This said, Brahma was united to Gayatri with due rites and ceremonies, and she was then led into the bower of the bride, and there arrayed in silken garments, and adorned with the costliest ornaments.

" At this time Savitri, accompanied by the wives of Vishnu and Rudra, of the other gods, and of the holy sages, and by numerous attendants, bearing various kinds of flowers, fruits, spices, perfumes, and comfits, proceeded unsent for to the place of sacrifice. On seeing her approach, Indra was alarmed, and Brahma feared what she might say unto him ; Vishnu and Rudra became anxious, and all the assembly was filled with apprehension. She entered, and, on beholding in the bride's bower the milkmaid, resplendent as the sun with gorgeous garments and celestial ornaments, and the priests engaged in performance of the sacred rites, the goddess incensed with anger thus addressed Pitamaha:—' O Brahma, how hast thou conceived so sinful an intention as to reject me, who am thy wedded wife? Hast thou no sense of shame, that, thus influenced by love, thou committest so reprehensible an act? Thou art called the great father of gods and holy sages, and yet thou here publicly actest in a manner which must excite the derision of the three worlds. But how can I now show my face ; or, deserted by my husband, call myself a wife ?' Brahma replied,—' The officiating priests informed me that the time for the sacrifice was passing away, and that it could not be profitably performed unless my wife were present. I therefore ordered one to be procured as quickly as possible; and Indra having brought that Gayatri, Vishnu and Rudra gave her in marriage to me. Forgive, therefore, O most excellent one ! this one act, and I will never again offend thee.' On hearing these words, Savitri exclaimed :—'By the power which I have acquired from the performance of *tapas*, may Brahma never be worshipped in temple or sacred place, except on one day in each year, in the month of *Kartika!* and, Indra! since thou didst bring that milkmaid to Brahma, thou shalt be bound in chains by thy enemies, and confined in a strange country, and thy city and station shall be occupied by thy enemies.' Savitri then addressing Vishnu thus continued :—'Since thou gavest her in marriage to Brahma, shalt thou, in consequence of Bhrigu's curse, be born amongst men, and shalt endure the agony of having thy wife ravished from thee by thy enemy, and long, also, shalt thou wander the humble keeper of cattle.' Then turning to Rudra, she added,—'By the curse of the holy sages shalt thou be deprived of thy manhood.' She next imprecated this curse on Agni (the fire):—'Mayest thou be a devourer of all things, clean and unclean!' and this on the officiating priests and Brahmans:—'Henceforward shall ye perform sacrifices solely from a desire of obtaining the usual gifts, and from covetousness alone shall ye attend temples and holy places; satisfied alone shall ye be with the food of others, and dissatisfied with that of your own houses; and in quest of riches shall ye unduly perform holy rites and ceremonies.' Having imprecated these curses, Savitri left the assembly, and was accompanied to a short distance by Lakshmi and the other goddesses, when they all declared their intention of proceeding no farther, and of returning. On hearing this, Savitri was incensed, and thus addressed them :—'Since you now forsake me, mayest thou, O Lakshmi!*, never remain stationary in one place, and mayest thou always abide with the vile, the inconstant, the contemptible, the sinful, the cruel, the foolish, and the barbarian! and, Indrani, when Indra incurs the guilt of Brahmanicide by slaying Twashta's son, then shall Nahusha acquire his kingdom, and, desirous of seeing thee, shall exclaim,—"Am I not Indra? and why then does not the young and lovely Indrani wait upon me? but if I do not obtain her I will slay all the gods:" and thou, on learning his wishes, shalt

* It must be recollected that Lakshmi is the goddess of riches and prosperity, or, in one word, fortune.

remain in thy house, immersed in grief and borne down by the weight of my curse.' Savitri then imprecated this curse on all the wives of the gods collectively: — 'May you all remain barren, and never enjoy the pleasure of having children!' and Gauri, included in this curse, was tormented day and night by that terrible word *barren*. Then, standing on the outside of her husband's place of sacrifice, Savitri wept aloud, and Vishnu hastened to appease her grief and anger; but all his persuasions were in vain, as she would not return to the assembly, but departed to *Prabhasa Kshetra*.

"On Savitri's departure, Gayatri thus addressed the assembly: — 'Listen, O ye immortals and sages! while, standing beside my husband, I bestow upon you boons which shall alleviate the curses of Savitri. For all pious men who worship Brahma shall obtain wealth, progeny, conjugal felicity, prosperity, happiness, and finally identification with him. If, also, Indra be chained by his enemies, he shall be released by his son, and afterwards reign over heaven in security and peace. Vishnu, likewise, shall recover his wife and destroy his enemies, and shall acquire high renown in the three worlds; and the lingam of Rudra shall become an object of universal worship. Nor shall any sin attach to you, O Brahmans! for receiving gifts; because you shall become gods of this earth, and offerings of all kinds shall be presented to you as such, and not as officiaters at holy rites and ceremonies.' Gayatri then addressing Lakshmi thus continued: — 'Never shall thy presence be despised, but by all shalt thou be received with pleasure; and whoever is countenanced by thee shall enjoy happiness, but misery shall be the lot of him who is deserted by thee; and, Indrani, though Nahusha shall desire to see thee, he shall, before his wish is accomplished, be changed into a serpent by the curse of Agastya.' She then consoled all the wives of the gods, and assured them that, though the curse of barrenness could not be removed, yet that they should experience on that account neither regret nor sorrow."* — *Prabhasa Mahatmyam*, chapter entitled *Savitri Mahatmyam*.

* In the Padma Puran it is farther stated that, as the sacrifice was drawing to its termination, Brahma requested Vishnu to prevail upon Savitri to return; and that Vishnu, accompanied by Lakshmi, having proceeded to where she was staying, they at length per-

In the following legend, however, Gayatri not only appears as the energy of Brahma, but the names also of both Lakshmi and Parvati are ascribed to her: —

From the Varaha Puran.

" The gods having implored the assistance of Brahma, in order to effect the destruction of an Asura named Vettra, Brahma was considering the means by which their wishes might be accomplished; when from his cogitation was produced an unborn virgin, arrayed in white garments and resplendent with ornaments, and displaying in her eight hands a conch, a disc, a mace, a noose, a cimeter, a bell, a bow and arrow, with a replenished quiver at her side. This goddess immediately hastened with the speed of the wind to attack the Asura, and slew him after a long and protracted combat. On Vettrasura being slain, celestial music resounded, and the gods prostrating themselves before her, with praises thus adored her:—'Victory be unto thee, O Gayatri! O Mahamaya! Praise be to thee, O mother of the Vedas, the adored by all beings! Praise be to thee, O dweller in the three worlds, the three Vedas, and the three fires! Praise be unto thee, O Maheshwari, bearer of the trident, with three eyes and a dreadful countenance! Praise be to thee, O Devi, O Sarasvati! Praise be to thee, O Kamala, with eyes like the lotos! thou art the pervader and lord of all things, eternal, unchangeable, and the source of all divine knowledge: praise, then

---

suaded her to return with them to the assembly. On entering which, Brahma thus addressed her: — " O goddess, this Gayatri was my helpmate at a time when thou wert absent, but say what shall I now do with her?" While her lord thus spoke, Savitri hung down her head bashfully and looked not up; and, at the suggestion of Brahma, Gayatri cast herself at her feet. But Savitri raised her, and, embracing her, consoled her with these words: — " A wife ought to obey the wishes and orders of her husband; for that wife who reproaches her husband, who is complaining and quarrelsome, and, instead of being his life, deprives him by her conduct of length of years, shall, when she dies, most assuredly go to hell. Considering this, the virtuous wife will do nothing displeasing to her husband; and, therefore, let us both remain attached to Brahma." " So be it," replied Gayatri; " thy orders will I always obey, and esteem thy friendship precious as my life. Thy daughter am I, O goddess! then deign to protect me." In this manner was a complete reconciliation effected between them, and the milkmaid secured in the participation of divinity.

be unto thee, O supreme goddess! from whom alone created beings can derive real advantage.' "—Chap. 28.

In this Puran, however, it is evident that Sarasvati, Savitri, and Gayatri are considered to be names of but one and the same goddess. For, in the commencement of it, Narada thus speaks to Priyavrata:—" I lately visited Shweta Dwipa, where, on the banks of a lake covered with lotoses, I beheld a lovely female, whom I thus addressed:—'*Say, O beauteous one! who art thou, and what is thy employment here?*' She looked at me with half-opened eyes, but remained silent; and I perceived that by the look of that maiden I was deprived of all sacred learning and divine knowledge. Then was I seized with astonishment, and, deeply afflicted, sought in my thoughts her protection; until at length I beheld three male forms situated in her body,—one in her breast, one in her heart, and one in the umbilical region, and each resplendent as the twelve suns; but, while I gazed, these three male forms were changed into three female ones, and at last there remained but the single maiden whom I had at first seen. Lost in amazement, I beseeched her to inform me what this might mean; and she then said,—'*I am the mother of the Vedas, and named Savitri. Dost thou not know me, O Narada! who alone could deprive thee of thy divine knowledge?*' She here ceased, when I asked her who the three male forms were, and she replied,—'*He whom you saw situated in my breast is the Rig Veda under the form of Narayana; in my heart the Yajur, under the form of my father Brahma; and in my umbilical region the Sama, under the form of Rudra. These, O Narada! are the three Vedas, and the three gods; and if thou bathest in that lake of the Vedas, thou wilt recover thy sacred learning and divine knowledge.*' Having thus spoken she disappeared, and I, having bathed in that lake, found that her words were true."

In popular mythology, however, the goddess is always called Sarasvati; and she is considered to preside over speech, learning, and eloquence. Such attributes, therefore, preclude the exercise of her divine power in that miraculous manner on which all Hindu legends are founded; and, in consequence, her name scarcely ever appears in the Purans, nor are any actions ascribed to her which have become the theme of story sacred or profane. In her popular character she is the daughter and wife of Brahma *; but in the theological part of the Hindu religion, she is one of the three female divine hypostases formed from the energy of the Supreme Being. Hence, as his attributes are ascribed to each of the male divine hypostases, the energy of each equally becomes the *parashakti* or supreme energy; and, consequently, the attributing of the names of the other two goddesses to Gayatri or Sarasvati, in the preceding quotation, is in strict conformity to the opinion entertained by the Hindus on this subject. The precise character, however, which may have been ascribed to this goddess on the first institution of the Hindu religion, or the subsequent modifications which may have taken place in it, cannot now be ascertained; but at the present day Sarasvati is considered to be a deity of very secondary importance, to whom neither images † nor temples are erected, and to whom one day's festival only in each year is consecrated.

LAKSHMI.

In the Vishnu, Garura, Lainga, and Padma Purans, Lakshmi or Shri is said to have been born the daughter of the divine sage Bhrigu, the son of Marichi who sprang from the mind of Brahma, and to have obtained Vishnu for her husband. But she is more generally considered to be the female energy of that god, and therefore to be exempt from birth. The history and character, however, of this goddess will be best understood from the following extract: —

From the Vishnu Puran.

Maitraya, addressing Parashara. — "If, O lord! Shri were formerly produced from the sea of milk when it was churned by the gods,

* Mr. Ward does not mention on what authority he makes Sarasvati the wife of Vishnu, and such a statement is contrary to all that I have either heard or read.

† Major Moor, in his Pantheon, p. 129., remarks: — "Images of Sarasvati are seldom seen: I have not one among my images; nor do I immediately recollect having ever seen one."

why is she also called the daughter of Bhrigu?' Parashara replied: — 'O excellent Brahman! in truth, Shri is inseparable from Vishnu, for wherever Vishnu is, there also is Shri. She is speech and he the meaning; she is morality and he theology; she is understanding and he intellect: Vishnu is joy and Lakshmi enjoyment; he is the sacrificer and she the victim; Vishnu is the creator and Shri the creatrix; he is Shankara and she Gauri*; he is the sun and she its splendour; he is the moon and she its radiance; Govinda is the ocean and Kamala the tide; he is the day and she the night. But why should I uselessly prolong this enumeration? for all that is *masculine* is Vishnu, and all that is *feminine* is Lakshmi.

"But listen, O Maitraya! while I answer the question which thou hast asked me. As Durvasa, an incarnate portion of Shiva, was once traversing the earth, he saw a celestial garland in the hand of a Vidiadhari†, formed from a tree of paradise, the flowers of which exhale such divine fragrance as to inebriate the senses. The lovely Vidiadhari, on being requested, respectfully gave this garland to Durvasa; who placing it on his head yielded to its influence, and wandered about as one inebriated. At length he met Indra, accompanied by the immortals, to whom he gave the fated garland; and Indra thoughtlessly placed it on the head of his elephant, where it shone like Ganga on the summit of Kailasa; but, the eyes of the elephant being darkened by the garland, it seized it with its trunk and cast it on the ground. On beholding which Durvasa became angry and thus addressed Indra: — 'O Vasava! since thou art rendered by pride so stupid as to despise a garland given by me, and which was the abode of Shri; may Shri abandon the three worlds‡, and mayest thou, by the loss of thy prosperity, learn how to honor my gifts!' Scarce had Indra heard these words when he dismounted from his elephant, and, prostrating himself before Durvasa, besough this favour; butDurvasa replied,—'Pity dwells not in my heart.

* In the same manner Vishnu and Lakshmi are identified with all the other gods and goddesses.

† The Vidiadharas form an inferior class of immortals.

‡ It will be recollected that Shri is the goddess of fortune and prosperity; and in consequence of this curse, Shri immediately withdrew her influence, and concealed herself in the sea of milk.

nor do I grant forgiveness. Other sages, O Indra! have pardoned thee, but Durvasa pardons not. Gautama and others, having experienced thy haughty disdain, were compassionate to thee, but Durvasa is inexorable. Well may he tremble who offends me, and casting his eyes on the ground fear to look me in the face, for I will never forgive an insult, however earnestly and submissively the offender may supplicate.' Having thus spoken, Durvasa departed, and Indra, remounting his elephant, returned to Amaravati.

"In this manner, O Maitraya! were Indra and the three worlds deprived of Shri; and the earth no longer produced plants, flowers, and fruits. Holy men no longer performed sacrifice, or devoted themselves to an ascetic life, and men ceased to bestow gifts and to observe the divine ordinances. Virtue and piety gave place to covetousness and the indulgence of the passions; and all manly and generous qualities disappeared. [At length the gods, unable to support this distress, proceeded as usual to represent the circumstances to Brahma, who directs them to apply to Vishnu, and then conducts them to the sea of milk, where, after having been duly propitiated by praises, Vishnu appears and thus speaks.] 'I will, O gods! increase your splendour, and instruct you in the manner by which the effect of Durvasa's curse may be removed. For this purpose do ye, along with the Asuras, bring all kinds of medicinal plants, and throw them into the sea of milk; then, employing Mandara for the churn-staff and Vasuki for the rope, churn that sea, and by this means will ye recover Shri, and also acquire other inestimable advantages.'* On hearing these words, the Suras hastened and made an agreement with the Asuras; and then, together, brought and threw into the sea of milk various plants. They next

* Some mistake seems to have taken place in this Puran, for the object of churning the sea of milk is here said to have been the obtaining of the beverage of immortality. But this is clearly inconsistent with what precedes and follows this part of the account; and it is at the same time in contradiction to the manner in which this legend is related in several other Purans, where it is said that the recovery of Shri was on this occasion the only object contemplated by the gods.

But there are, also, two other causes assigned for this event; the one that the gods were desirous of obtaining a beverage which might insure them immortality, for they were not created immortal; and the other that they might obtain a new moon, the former one having lost its splendour in consequence of its having been cursed by Daksha.

wound Vasuki round Mandara, and the Asuras taking hold of the head, and the Suras of the tail, commenced churning the sea of milk, while Vishnu, in the form of a tortoise, supported it on his back. From this agitation were produced,—1. Surabhi, adored by the gods; 2. Varuni, with eyes sparkling with wine; 3. The tree Parijata, diffusing a celestial fragrance; 4. The Apsaras, resplendent in youth and loveliness; 5. The moon, which Shiva placed on his head; 6. Dhanvantari, arrayed in white garments, and bearing a goblet of amrit. Then appeared Shri, seated on a lotos, and refulgent as the rising sun; on beholding whom the gods and divine sages addressed her in laudatory strains; the Gandharvas sang, and the Apsaras danced before her; the Ganga and other sacred streams formed a bath for her; and Vishvakarma presented her with costly garments and ornaments. Shri, having then bathed and adorned herself, proceeded in presence of all the gods, and placed herself on the breast of Hari. Thus was Shri restored to the three worlds, and Indra, having regained his prosperity, reigned over heaven in happiness.*

"In this manner, O Maitraya! was Shri produced from the sea of milk, though she had first appeared under a corporeal form as the daughter of Bhrigu; and in the same manner, whenever her lord shall become incarnate on earth, whether as a dwarf, as Parasurama, as Rama Chandra, as Krishna, or in other forms, will she accompany him; for Lakshmi partakes of the substance of Vishnu, and as he assumes mortality or divinity, so does she equally become a mortal or a goddess."

As Vishnu always acts personally, no opportunity occurs for his energy manifesting her divine power by miraculous interpositions; and, consequently, no legends relating to Lakshmi occur in Hindu mythology. But, as I have observed in page 210., this goddess is also worshipped under the name of Maha Lakshmi †, and under this character are

* For Indra's address to Lakshmi on this occasion, see ante, p. 54.

† The *Devi* in plates 30, 31. and 33. of Moor's Pantheon, and whenever she is represented with four hands only, and with elephants pouring water over her, is *Maha Lakshmi* and not *Parvati*.

ascribed to her the different actions which are related in the *Devi-mahatmyam*, and which are more usually attributed to Parvati. There is, also, a celebrated temple consecrated to Maha Lakshmi in Karavira or Kollapoor; but this character of the energy of Vishnu does not appear to be generally known or recognised among the Hindus.

CHAP. XIII.

PARVATI, OR DEVI.

In the same manner as the energy of Vishnu assumed corporeality, and was born the daughter of Bhrigu, in order that she might be united to her lord in due form; so, for the same purpose, did the energy of Shiva become the daughter of Daksha, under the name of Sati: for it is said in the Kurma Puran, that, when Brahma was angry with the sons whom he had first created for adopting an ascetic life, a form half male and half female was produced from that anger; to whom Brahma said, "Divide thyself," and then disappeared. The male half became Rudra, and the female, at the command of Brahma, became the daughter of Daksha under the name of Sati, and was given in marriage to Rudra; and, when she subsequently gave up her life on being treated with disrespect by her father, she was born a second time the daughter of *Himavan* and *Mena*, and named Parvati. These last circumstances have been touched upon in Chapter XI., and the following extracts will fully explain them:—

From the Padma Puran.

Pulastya, addressing Bhishma.—"Formerly, O Bhishma! Daksha prepared a sacrifice at Gungadwara, to which came all the immortals and divine sages. At this festival celestial viands abounded, the consecrated place of sacrifice extended for several yojanas; numerous altars were erected; the sacred rites and ceremonies were duly performed by Vasishta, Angiras, Vrihaspati, and Narada; and Vishnu protected the sacrifice. But Sati thus addressed her father *:—'My

* It must be understood that Shiva was not present; and the attendance of Sati is thus explained in the Bhagavat:—"Sati, observing that all the immortals, the divine sages, and her sisters with their husbands, were hastening along the sky to the high festival of Daksha, thus addressed Shiva:—'O Vama! my father and thy father-in-law has prepared a great sacrifice to which all the gods are proceeding; should it, therefore, seem good unto thee, let us

lord! all the immortals, the divine sages, and my sisters with their husbands, adorned in the costliest manner, have honoured this festival with their presence; and I observe that not a single one has been uninvited except my husband. But, unless he attend, empty will be all these rites, and productive of no advantage. Say, then, has it been through forgetfulness that thou didst not invite my lord?' On hearing these words, Daksha with parental affection placed his youthful daughter, who showed such fondness for her husband, in his lap, and thus replied:—'Listen, my darling! while I explain the reason why thy husband has not been invited. It is because that he is the bearer of a human skull, a delighter in cemeteries, accompanied by ghosts and goblins, naked or merely clothed with a tiger's or elephant's skin, covered with ashes, wearing a necklace of human skulls, ornamented with serpents, always wandering about as a mendicant, sometimes dancing and sometimes singing, and neglecting all divine ordinances. Such evil practices, my darling! render thy husband the shame of the three worlds, and unworthy to be admitted at a sacrifice where Brahma, Vishṇu, and all the immortals and divine sages are present.' He ceased, and Sati, incensed by his words, with anger-inflamed eyes thus spoke:—'That god is the lord of the universe, from whom all things and beings have received their rank and station, and whose supreme excellence no tongue is able to declare; and, though delighting in cemeteries, covered with ashes, and adorned with human bones and

---

also repair there. For why should not a daughter, on hearing of festivity in her father's house, hasten to participate in it; and, since friends and relations visit each other uninvited, why should not I, though uninvited, proceed to the abode of him to whom I owe my being?' Shiva, smiling, replied:—'Thou speakest truly, O lovely one! but where enmity exists an uninvited guest will meet with an unwelcome reception; and, therefore, since Daksha is my enemy, shouldst thou attend his sacrifice he will not, on account of thy relation to me, honour thee as his daughter; and thou wilt be so overcome by the disrespect shown to thee as to seek a refuge in death.' He ceased with thoughts intent on the approaching death of his beloved; and Sati, alarmed, but still desirous to see her relations, twice passed the threshold of her home and twice reentered, while tears of fond affection gushed from her eyes as she, trembling, hesitated. At length the foolishness of the female disposition prevailed, and, her heart agitated with grief and anger, she left her husband in order to proceed to her father's house."—Skand IV. chapter 4.

serpents, he is the creator, the provider, and the preserver. It was alone through the favour of Rudra that Indra obtained heaven; through the will, also, of Rudra, Brahma creates; and, were it not for Rudra, how could Vishnu have the power to preserve? If, therefore, I have derived might from my devotion, and if I be beloved by Rudra, since thou hast despised him, this sacrifice shall be undoubtedly destroyed.' Having thus spoken, Sati fixed her mind in profound abstraction, and by her own splendour consumed her body, while all the immortals exclaimed in astonishment,—'How wonderful!' On being informed of this event, Shiva, much afflicted, collected myriads of ghosts, goblins, and demons, and hastened to Daksha's place of sacrifice; which he completely destroyed, after having vanquished all the immortals that opposed him."—*Shrishti Khand*, chap. 5.

*From the Brahma Vaivarta Puran.**

"That daughter, who has been born unto thee, O Shailendra! is *Ishwari*, *Prakriti*, the origin and mother of this universe, the adored by all the gods. For the protection of the immortals has she manifested herself in different kalpas, and dispersed and destroyed innumerable hosts of Asuras. Formerly, also, was she born the daughter of Daksha, who married her with the prescribed rites to the bearer of the trident. But unfortunately, at a festival given by Brahma, a dispute took place between Shiva and Daksha, and enmity was the consequence. When, therefore, Daksha shortly afterwards prepared a sacrifice, he did not invite Shiva, nor assign him any portion of it. On observing which, Sati reviled her father, and with an agitated heart left the assembly and hastened to her mother. To her she, skilled in the future, foretold the defeat of Daksha, and the destruction of his sacrifice; the flight of the immortals before the victorious army of Shankara, and her own approaching death. She then in deep affliction proceeded to the banks of the celestial Ganga, and there, having worshipped Shankara, and having fixed her thoughts on his lotos feet,

* In my copy of this Puran, it does not appear who the speaker is in this passage; but it would seem to be Narada, addressing the king of mountains, Himavan, after the birth of Parvati.

forsook her body. On beholding which the Suras exclaimed:—'Ah! ah!' and the troops of Shiva immediately attacked and destroyed the sacrifice of Daksha.

"On hearing of this event, Shiva fainted from grief; then, having recovered, he hastened to the banks of the river of heaven; where he beheld lying the body of his beloved Sati, arrayed in white garments, holding a rosary in her hand, and glowing with a splendour bright as burnished gold. No sooner did he perceive the lifeless form of his spouse, than, through grief for her loss, his senses forsook him; but reviving, he thus, while gazing on her beauteous countenance, with tears and mournful accents spoke:—'Arise, arise, O my beloved Sati! I am Shankara, thy lord, look therefore at me who have approached thee. With thee I am almighty, the framer of all things, and the giver of every bliss; but without thee, my energy! I am like a corpse, powerless and incapable of action: how then, my beloved! canst thou forsake me? With smiles and glances of thy eyes say something sweet as *amrit*, and with the rain of thy gentle words sprinkle my heart, which is scorched with grief. Formerly when thou sawest me from a distance thou wouldst greet me with the fondest accents, why then to-day art thou angry, and wilt not speak to me, though thus lamenting? O lord of my soul! arise. O mother of the universe! arise. Dost thou not see me here weeping? O beauteous one! thou canst not have expired. Then, O my faithful spouse! why dost thou not to-day honour me as usual? and why dost thou thus, inobedient to my voice, infringe thy marriage vow?' Having thus spoken, he raised the lifeless body, and, in the anguish of separation, pressing it to his bosom, embraced it and kissed it again and again. Lip to lip and breast to breast, Shankara clasped the corpse of his beloved; then, after frequent faintings, he hastily arose, and, closely pressing Sati to his bosom, rushed forward maddened with grief; and, like one deprived of his senses, the preceptor of the universe thus wandered over the seven Dwipas, until exhausted by fatigue and anguish he sank down in a swoon at the foot of a banyan tree."*—*Krishna-jamma Khand*, chap. 43.

* As the reader may not wish to leave Shiva in such a situation, I subjoin what follows. On beholding Shiva in this state the gods were astonished, and accompanied by

'Sati soon obtained another birth in the womb of the wife of Himavan; and Shiva, collecting the ashes and bones from her funeral pile, made a necklace of the bones, and covered his body with the ashes, and thus preserved them as fond memorials of his beloved. Soon was Sati born, the daughter of Mena, excelling, in beauty and every virtuous quality, all created beings, and grew up in her mountain home like the young moon, increasing to its full splendour. But she was still a girl when she heard a voice from heaven, saying, 'Perform a severe course of austere devotion, in order to obtain Shiva for a husband, as he cannot otherwise be obtained.' On hearing this, Parvati, proud of her youth, smiled disdainfully, and thus thought,— 'Will he, who bears the bones and ashes that belonged to me in a former birth, not accept me when he beholds me thus young and lovely? Will he, who, on account of the grief he felt for my having formerly consumed myself, wandered over the world, not accept me

---

Vishnu and Brahma hastened to the spot where he was lying; when Vishnu placing the head of the fainted Shiva in his bosom wept aloud, and then reviving him thus spoke:— "O Shiva! recover thy senses, and listen to what I now say. All things in this universe are interchangeable into each other, as they proceed from the effects produced by the union of Maya with the three qualities; and from the same cause originate pleasure and pain. Grief, fear, pain, and misfortune occur; but they pass away, and are replaced by joy, confidence, pleasure, and good fortune. Resume thy spirits, therefore, O Shankara! for thou wilt certainly regain Sati, since Shiva and Sati are as inseparable as coldness from water, heat from fire, smell from earth, or radiance from the sun." On hearing these words Shiva faintly opened his eyes bedewed with tears, and thus said:—"O form of splendour! who art thou, and who are these that accompany thee? what is thy name, and what are their names? and say who am I, and where have my attendants gone? where, also, art thou and are these going? and where am I, and whither proceeding?" On hearing these words Hari wept, and his tears uniting with those which Shiva was shedding, formed a lake, which hence became a celebrated place of pilgrimage. Vishnu then again addressed Shiva, and by a speech, much too long to be transcribed, succeeded in tranquillising him. Shiva also replies in a long speech. As he ceased speaking, Shiva, delighted, beheld before him Sati seated in a gem-adorned car, and accompanied by numerous attendants, arrayed in costly garments and resplendent with ornaments, while her placid countenance was irradiated with a gentle smile. The anguish of separation ceased, and joy filled his soul while Sati thus addressed him:—"Be firm, O Mahadeva, lord of my soul! for, in whatever state of being I may exist, I shall never be separated from my lord; and now have I been born the daughter of Himavan, in order to become again thy wife; therefore no longer grieve on account of our separation." Having with these words consoled Shiva, Sati disappeared.

for his spouse, when redolent of life? And how can disjunction exist between those who have been predestined from their first being to be husband and wife?' Thus confident in her youth, her loveliness, and numerous attractions, and persuaded that, on the first mention of her name, Shiva would be anxious to espouse her, Parvati did not seek to gain him by the performance of austere devotion, but night and day gave herself up unweariedly to joyous sport amidst her damsels." * — *Ibid.*, chap. 38.

As Parvati, this goddess is the constant companion of Shiva; and no independent actions are ascribed to her. In the Purans, these deities are in general represented as either engaged in amorous dalliance, or, rather a singular change, as seated on Mount Kailasa, and discussing the abstrusest topics of Hindu theology: —

> ——— "And reasoning high
> Of providence, foreknowledge, will, and fate,
> Fixed fate, free-will, fore-knowledge absolute.
> Of good and evil much they argue, then
> Of misery and final happiness."

Occasionally, however, a quarrel takes place between them, as when Shiva reproached Parvati with the blackness of her colour; which so incensed her that she left him, and, repairing to a deep forest, there performed a severe course of austere devotion, until Brahma at length granted her, as a boon, that her colour should become white; and from this circumstance she was named *Gauri*, or white.

This goddess, however, also acts independently; and then she is celebrated principally under the characters of Devi, Durga †, or

* Parvati, however, found her hopes disappointed, and was obliged to perform a severe *tapas* before she obtained a reunion with Shiva. But the legend relating to this circumstance, which occurs in, I believe, all the Purans, is much too long to be extracted; and it is, also, sufficiently explained in Sir W. Jones's hymn to Durga; which, however, should have been entitled to *Parvati* and not to *Durga*.

† In the Kashi Khand of the Skanda Puran, it is said that Devi was named Durga on account of having slain an Asura called Durga. The long and short *a* in Sanscrit mark the feminine and masculine genders, for they are represented by distinct characters.

Katyayini, and of Kali: with regard to which, the following extracts will afford sufficient information: —

From the Vamana Puran.

Pulastya, addressing Narada. — "The gods, having been defeated by Mahisha Asura, forsook their abodes and hastened, with Brahma at their head, to implore the protection of Vishnu. Shankara was also present; and, when the immortals had related their grievances, Vishnu, and at his command, Shankara, Brahma, and all the gods, emitted such flames of anger from their eyes and countenance, that a mountain of effulgence was formed; from which became manifest *Katyayini*, refulgent as a thousand suns, with three eyes, hair black as night, and eighteen arms.* To her Shiva gave a trident, Vishnu a disc, Varuna a conch, Agni a dart, Vaiu a bow, Surya a quiver and arrows, Indra a thunder-bolt, Yama an iron rod, Kubera a mace, Brahma a rosary and a water-pot, Kala a sword and shield, Vishvakarma a battle-axe and other weapons, Himavan a lion, and the other gods various arms and ornaments. Being thus armed, and having been adored by all the gods, Katyayini proceeded to the Vindhya mountain. There two Asuras, Chanda and Munda, saw her, and immediately hastened to their king, and informed him that a most lovely goddess had singly fixed her abode on the mountain Vindhya. On hearing the high encomiums with which Chunda and Munda described the beauty of this goddess, Mahishasura determined to obtain possession of her, and ordered his army to be collected and to march to the vicinity of the mountain. There, also, he entered a lofty pavilion, and then sent the son of Maya to summon the goddess to his presence. Dundabhi accordingly proceeded towards her, and thus, at a short distance, addressed her, — 'I am, O virgin! a messenger sent to thee by the chief of the Asuras.' Katyayini replied, — 'Approach! approach! and dismiss thy fear, and truly deliver the message which thou bringest.' Encouraged by these words, Dundabhi answered, — 'Thus says Mahisha, the king of the

* In the original there is an account of the particular beauties of the different parts of her body, and of the deities from which each of them was derived.

Asuras, — *The gods wander upon earth, helpless and powerless, as the three worlds have been conquered by me. It is I who am Indra, and Rudra, and Surya, the sole lord of the universe; and there is no other god than me. In battle am I unconquerable; and by my victorious arms have I acquired possession of every desirable thing that the world contains. But on thy account, O lovely virgin! have I now approached this mountain; hasten, therefore, to pay due obedience to the lord of the universe, for thou art worthy of becoming his spouse.'* Durga Katyayini replied, — 'It is true that the mighty Asura Mahisha has subdued the three worlds, and I also am ready to obey him; but there is a custom, long established in my family, which requires that each daughter of my house should be conquered in battle by her wooer before she can be united to him in marriage, from which I cannot deviate. Before, therefore, I can become the spouse of thy king, he must vanquish me in combat.' Dundabhi having heard these words, returned to Mahisha, and acquainted him with the determination of the goddess; and he immediately ordered his army to advance. On observing which, the gods exclaimed to Durga, — 'Bind on thy armour.' But she said, — 'I will not, for what necessity is there for armour, when none but these vile Asuras stand before me?' Vishnu, however, presented her with armour, and entreated her to defend herself with it against the weapons of her enemies; especially as, in consequence of a boon granted by Shiva, Mahisha had been rendered invulnerable.

"When Devi perceived the elephants, horse, foot, and cars composing the army of the Asuras approach, she strung her bow and rained on them a ceaseless shower of arrows. Many of the enemies of the gods she slew with her shafts; others with her sword; and with her various weapons scattered havoc amongst their ranks, as brandishing its mane her lion bore her onwards.* Thus Katyayini destroyed countless numbers of the boldest Asuras, and on beholding the battle ground strewed with their corses, she seized a vina and damaru, and laughing began to play. Wherever she moved, drawing music from

* I have omitted the account which is contained in the original of Durga's achievements in this battle.

her instruments, ghosts and goblins shouting danced; and her lion in sport tossed about the bodies of the slain. But Mahisha, on viewing the destruction of his army, hastened to engage the goddess; and Katyayini equally eager for the combat, urged on her lion. Then commenced a terrible battle, in which the summits of the mountain were rent beneath their feet, earth and ocean trembled, and the clouds were scattered. But in vain did Durga employ her various weapons, as the art of Mahisha rendered them innocuous; even when she had bound with the noose given to her by Varuna his horns, his muzzle, and hoofs, he escaped from the bonds*; and when she hurled a thunderbolt at him he shrank into such a diminutive shape that it passed him harmless. At length Durga dismounted from her lion and sprang upon the back of Mahisha, and with her tender feet so smote his head that he fell senseless on the ground, when she immediately cut off his head with her sword, while all the host of the Asuras exclaimed, 'Ah! ah!'" — *Vamana Puran*, the legend entitled *Devi-Mahatmyam.*†

From the Lainga Puran.

Suta thus spoke: — "Formerly a female Asura named Daruka had through devotion obtained such power, that she consumed like fire the gods and Brahmans. But, as she was attended by a numerous host of female Asuras, Vishnu and all the gods were afraid to engage in battle with her, lest they should incur the sin of *feminicide.* They in consequence proceeded to Shiva, and with laudatory strains entreated his assistance; and he then regarding Devi, thus addressed her: — 'Let me request, O lovely one! that thou wouldst now for

* Mahisha Asura is here represented under the figure of a buffalo, which is the signification of the word *mahisha.*

† It requires to be observed that Mr. Ward has given a most confused account of Durga, in consequence of his supposing that the *Devi-Mahatmyam* contained in the Markandeya Puran related to this form of Parvati. But in that legend a number of distinct actions, which are in general held to have been performed by this goddess under different characters, are collected together, and the whole ascribed, not to her, but to the energy of Vishnu, under the character of *Mahamaya* or *Maha Lakshmi.*

the benefit of the universe effect the destruction of this Daruka.' Having heard these words, Parvati created from her own substance a maiden of black colour, with matted locks, with an eye in her forehead, bearing in her hands a trident and a skull, of aspect terrible to behold, and arrayed in celestial garments and adorned with all kinds of ornaments. On beholding this terrific form of darkness, the gods retreated in alarm. Parvati then created innumerable ghosts, goblins, and demons, and, attended by these, Kali in obedience to her order attacked and destroyed Daruka, and removed the distress of the world." — Part II. Chap. 100.*

Other legends, also, are ascribed to Devi, and from her different achievements she receives different names; but under all these characters she is still considered to be but one and the same goddess — the personified energy of Shiva.† The following extract, however, will best explain her real nature: —

From the Skanda Puran.

Vasishta, addressing the king Mandhata. — "Formerly two Asuras, named Chanda and Munda, became, through a boon granted to them by the divine mothers, so powerful as to subdue the three worlds. The gods in consequence implored the assistance of Devi, who, being propitiated, appeared to them under the character of Chandi, and said that she could not accomplish their wishes until she had obtained by devotion the favour of Shiva, who could alone relieve the three worlds

* This legend concludes in the following singular manner: — "Shiva also appeared as an infant in a cemetery surrounded by ghosts, and on beholding him Kali took him up, and caressing him gave him her breast. He sucked the nectareous fluid; but becoming angry, in order to divert and pacify him, Kali, clasping him to her bosom, danced with her attendant goblins and demons amongst the dead until he was pleased and delighted; while Vishnu, Brahma, Indra, and all the gods, bowing themselves, praised with laudatory strains the god of gods, Parvati and Kali."

† As, however, Shiva is also considered to be the Supreme Being, Devi likewise becomes the supreme energy; and it is under this character that she is described in the Upanishad contained in Appendix E.

from the distress occasioned by Chanda and Munda. Having thus spoken, Chandika repaired to a secluded spot and there commenced a severe *tapas* in order to propitiate Shiva, during which she was waited upon by the divine mothers.* At length Shiva appeared to her under the form of a vast lingam, and concealed within it thus spoke: — 'O Chandi! what is it that thou desirest to obtain by this *tapas?*' She replied, — 'Reveal thyself, and I will then inform thee.' Shiva then manifested himself, and Chandi with the divine mothers praised him with laudatory strains. She ceased, and Shiva said, — 'O goddess! thou art celebrated in the three worlds as *Parashakti* (the energy of the Supreme Being); wherever thou art there am I, and wherever I am there is Chandika. There is no difference between us, for I am Shiva and, thou art my energy, and the energy of Shiva pervades all things movable and immovable. Then say, O Maheshani! what shall I do to please thee; for whatever *Parashakti* wishes, that shall be accomplished.' Chandi replied,—'O god of gods! formerly I slew Chanda and Munda in battle, but they have been born again as mighty Asuras; and, having become powerful through a boon, have oppressed the three worlds; and it is, therefore, in order to be enabled to effect their destruction that I have now sought thy protection.' Shiva said, — 'Behold, O Chandika, and ye divine mothers! I will slay these Asuras Chanda and Munda, who have filled the three worlds with alarm.' Having thus spoken, he directed Maheshani to hasten to them and challenge them to engage in combat with him. On hearing this, Chandi said, — 'O Shankara! I will proceed with the divine mothers, assuming the guise of messengers, to these Asuras, and deliver to them thy message.' Chandi accordingly proceeded to them, and, having been introduced into their presence, thus spoke with a smiling countenance: — 'I am Chandika the messenger of Mahesha; listen, therefore, to what he says. — *There is no one in the three worlds who dares to engage you two in battle; but hasten to Shri Mala and I will fight with you, and undoubtedly liberate by your deaths the universe from fear and distress.*' On hearing these words, Chanda replied, — 'Who is this

* Thus far I have merely given the substance of the original.

Mahesha that now with so little understanding defies me to battle, and who has ever heard of him? But the mighty Munda shall march with an army to Shri Mala, and having slain him in combat shall return victorious.' Having received this answer, Chandi departed, and hastened to communicate it to Shiva." — *Skanda Puran, Mala Khand*, the legend entitled *Chandisha-Mahatmyam.**

But Devi is at the present day principally distinguished by a sanguinary character and worship, that are clearly inconsistent with the indisputable principles of the Hindu religion; which condemn bloody sacrifices, and the use of flesh and spirituous liquors. † Such, however, appear to have been the offerings presented to this goddess from remote times; for although in the Purans they are not distinctly prescribed, still such allusions to them occur as leave no doubt that, when those works were composed, the worship of Devi must have differed materially from that of the other deities. It is, nevertheless, remarkable, that, at the conclusion of the *Shristi Khand* of the Padma Puran, a very detailed account of this worship is given, and yet no mention is made in it of meat-offerings or libations of wine; and that, as far as I have observed, oblations of this kind are not expressly noticed in any of the Purans, except in the following passage of the Markandeya ‡:—

* In this legend Chanda and Munda are slain by Shiva; but in a former birth, as intimated in it, they had been destroyed by Devi, whence she derived her name of *Chandi.*

† In the Kashi Khand of the Skanda Puran occurs this stanza: — "From ancient times this verse has been sung by those who were acquainted with the divine nature of Shiva: — *Where flesh is, how can there be devotion to Shiva? Where spirituous liquors are, how can there be the worship of Shiva? Shankara stands far off from those who are addicted to flesh and spirituous liquors.*"

‡ The Brahmans say that the worship of Devi is of two kinds; the one *pure*, in which the offerings are the same as those presented to the other deities; and the other *impure*, in which blood, flesh, and spirituous liquors are offered, but at the last they maintain that Brahmans never officiate.

In his Essay on the Vedas (As. Res. vol. viii. p. 423.) Mr. Colebrooke remarks: — "It may be hence inferred, or conjectured at least, that human sacrifices were not authorised by the Veda itself; but were either then abrogated, and an emblematical ceremony substituted in their place, or they must have been introduced in later times, *on the authority of certain Purans or Tantras, fabricated by persons, who, in this as in other matters, established many unjustifiable practices on the foundation of emblems and allegories which they misunder-*

"Maha Lakshmi is the supreme mistress of the three qualities, and visibly or invisibly pervades all things; she displays in her four hands a citron, a mace, a shield, and a goblet, and, refulgent as burnished gold, fills all space with her splendour. From her substance she separated the quality of darkness, and gave it the form of a female black as collyrium, with large eyes, terrible tusks, a slender waist, and bearing in her hands a cimiter, a cup, a head, and a shield, and adorned with human and serpent heads. This form of darkness then thus spoke to Maha Lakshmi:—'Praise be to thee, O mother! assign to me names and functions.' Maha Lakshmi replied:—'I give to thee as names *Mahabhaya*, *Mahakali*, *Mahamari*, hunger, thirst, sleep, night, *Ekavira*, *Kalarattri*, and *Chandika*, these shall be thy names, and from them thou wilt know what functions thou hast to perform.' . . . . This goddess* worship by offering the *argha*, *padyam*, *achamanam*, ornaments, perfumes, flowers, incense, lamps, prepared eatables of various kinds, *blood, flesh, spirituous liquors*, saffron, sandal, camphor, and betel leaf. On her left, also, worship Mahisha with his head cut off, who in consequence of being slain by that goddess obtained beatitude; and on the right, the lion which is her vehicle. Thus adore Chandika, by the prescribed prayers and hymns, and with due rites and ceremonies, and thou wilt finally obtain identification with her.'"—The chapter entitled *Devi-mahatyme weikritikam*.

With regard to the character of the goddess to whom such impure offerings are presented, it will be sufficiently understood from what has preceded, and from the following speech of Vishnu to Rudra contained

---

stood." But this observation is totally inapplicable to the eighteen Purans; for in not one of them is the sacrifice of either man or animal enjoined, nor are any rites or ceremonies prescribed but what are perfectly consistent with all that is yet known of the Vedas. In the Purans, however, the advantages derivable from sacrifice are often alluded to.

* She is here also described with eighteen hands, in which she holds a rosary, a lotos, an arrow, a sword, a thunderbolt, a mace, a disc, a trident, a battle-axe, a conch, a bell, a noose, a lance, an iron rod, a shield, a bow, a goblet, and a cup. It is to be observed that the same deity may be represented with more or fewer arms, the *maximum* and *minimum* only being fixed.

in the Garura Puran:—"On the ninth of each half month invoke Durga with these words:—*Hrim, protect me, O Durga! O chief of the divine mothers! giver of blessings, accept these various offerings of flesh and my prayers.* On the third, also, of Margashirsha commence the worship of Durga before her image having eighteen hands, and holding in them a mace, a bell, a looking-glass, an iron rod, a bow, a banner, a small drum, a battle-axe, a noose, a lance, a club, a trident, a disc, a shield, an *ankush*, a dart, a thunderbolt, and a skull*; and address to her the following hymn:—'Om, praise be to thee, O Bhagawati, Chamunda! dweller in cemeteries, bearer of a skull, borne on a car drawn by ghosts, Kalarattri, large-mouthed, many-armed, sounding thy bell and drum, laughing terribly, gnashing thy horrid teeth loudly, clothed in an elephant's skin, with a body full of flesh and blood, and a tremendous tongue. Praise be to thee, O Kali! with terrific tusks and fear-inspiring eyes flashing like lightning, with a countenance dark with frowns, bearing the moon on thy matted locks, and on thy neck a string of skulls; *Hram, Hram,* O destroyer of difficulties! quickly accomplish this business! O delighter in flesh and blood! be propitious, be propitious, and enter this place! Enter, enter; tread, tread; dance, dance; why delayest thou to enter? O wearer of human heads and skulls! seize, seize; tear, tear; consume, consume; slay, slay! *Hrum, Hrum,* destroy, destroy; pierce, pierce with thy trident; kill, kill with thy thunderbolt; smite, smite with thy rod; cut off, cut off with thy disc; fell, fell with thy mace; strike, strike with thy axe! come, come, O Maheshwari! come, O Kamarini! come, O Varahi! come, O Aindri! come, O Chamunda! come, O Kapalini! come, O Mahakali! come, O frequenter of Kailasa! enter, enter this place, O thou who executest the wrath of Rudra, and causest the destruction of the Asuras!'" But this sanguinary character and worship are peculiar to Devi, and nothing of the kind belongs to the other rites and ceremonies of the Hindu religion, or to the attributes which the Hindus ascribe to their other deities.

* There is in the Purans a great discordancy with respect to the different things which Devi holds in her hands. In the Skanda, for instance, they are thus enumerated: an iron rod, a small drum, a bell, a trident, a hatchet, an arrow, a noose, a lance, a cimeter, a lotos, a disc, a conch, a mace, a club, a water-pot, a banner, a sword, and a shield.

It requires to be remarked, that, although the name *Bhavani* occurs not unfrequently as synonymous to either Parvati or Devi, I have never met with it employed as descriptive of a distinct character of this goddess. These observations, therefore, of Sir W. Jones, rest on no grounds:—"Bhawani now demands our attention; and in this character I suppose the wife of Mahadeva to be as well the Juno Cinxia or Lucina of the Romans as Venus herself: not the Idalian queen of laughter and jollity, who, with her nymphs and graces, was the beautiful child of imagination, and answers to the Indian Rembha with her celestial train of *Apsaras* or damsels of paradise; but Venus Urania, so luxuriantly painted by Lucretius, and so properly invoked by him at the opening of a poem on nature; Venus presiding over generation."* The hymn, also, addressed by Sir W. Jones to Bhavani is altogether inconsistent with Hindu mythology; and it seems obvious that he has mistakingly ascribed to Bhavani the attributes which are peculiar to Lakshmi. In no account, however, of the cosmogony is either the primary impulse to creation or the formation of the universe referred in any manner to the agency of any one of the energies of the three divine hypostases †; and, consequently, the following stanza is obviously contrary to the opinions entertained by the Hindus on the subject:—

"Mother of gods, rich nature's queen,
Thy genial fire emblazed the bursting scene;
For, on the expanded blossom sitting, ‡
With sun-beams knitting
That mystic veil for ever unremoved,
Thou badest the softly kindling flame
Pervade this peopled frame,
And smiles, with blushes tinged, the work approved."

---

* Asiatic Researches, vol. i. p. 254. But in p. 47. of this work I have pointed out several coincidences in the characters ascribed to Lakshmi, to Venus Urania, and to the Egyptian goddess Athor.

† In the spiritual system there is, properly speaking, no cosmogony; for in it all seeming realities are considered to me merely illusive appearances produced by Maya.

‡ Parvati is never represented as seated on a lotos; but Lakshmi when she issued from the sea of milk, appeared seated on one.

CHAP. XIV.

SURYA (THE SUN). — GANESHA.

I CAN discover no grounds for this fanciful remark of Sir W. Jones: — "It is probable that the triple divinity of the Hindus was originally no more than a personification of the sun, whom they call *treyitenu* *, or *three-bodied*, in his triple capacity of producing forms by his genial heat, preserving them by his light, or destroying them by the concentrated force of his igneous matter." For, though Surya is considered to be the same as the Supreme Being, he is never identified with Brahma, Vishnu, or Shiva, as a distinct personage.† If, however, as it seems highly probable, the sun was in remote antiquity an object of popular worship amongst the Hindus, its adoration appears to have assumed, at the time when the Vedas were composed, a mysterious nature, and to have become restricted to the Brahmans. But Mr. Ward has justly remarked, — "The Brahmans consider Surya as one of the greatest of the gods, because in glory he resembles the one Brahm, who is called *tejomaya*, or the glorious. In the Vedas, also, this god is much noticed: the celebrated invocation called the *Gayatri*, and many of the forms of meditation, prayer, and praise, used in the daily ceremonies of the Brahmans, are addressed to him." ‡

Nothing, indeed, can more clearly evince the preeminence over all the other deities, which must have been at one time ascribed to the sun, than the singular degree of importance, sanctity, and power which

* This word is thus explained by Mr. Wilson in his dictionary: — "The Sun: *trayi* the three Vedas and *tanu* diffusion; celebrated through the three sacred books, or because the Sama Veda, and portions of the other Vedas, are said to have proceeded from the sun."

† I may, also, point out another mistake of Sir W. Jones with respect to this deity; for he has stated that "Surya is believed to have descended *frequently* from his car in a human shape, and to have left a race on earth, who are equally renowned in the Indian stories with the Heliadai of Greece." But neither in the Purans, nor in any other Sanscrit work, as far as I am aware, are such avatars ascribed to Surya, and the *human* ancestor of the *Suryawamsha*, or solar race, was Vaiwaswat Manu.

‡ Ward's View of the Hindus, vol. i. p. 50.

is ascribed to the Gayatri: for, in the Skanda Puran it is said, "Superior to all learning is the difficultly obtained invocation, named Gayatri, preceded by the mystic syllable; nothing in the Vedas is more excellent than the Gayatri; no invocation is equal to the Gayatri, as no city is equal to Kashi; the Gayatri is the mother of the Vedas and of Brahmans; from repeating it man is saved (*gayantam trayate*), and hence is it celebrated under the name of Gayatri. By the power of the Gayatri the Kshatriya Vishwamitra, from being a Rajarshi, became a Brahmarshi, and even obtained such power as to be able to create a new world. What is there, indeed, that cannot be effected by the Gayatri? for the Gayatri is Vishnu, Brahma, and Shiva, and the three Vedas." But all that this celebrated verse, divested of the glosses of commentators, contains, is simply *Om, Bhur, Bhuvah, Swah, Tat*, let us meditate on the excellence of the Sun, of the god Bharga†, may he excite our understandings; om, praise be to Surya, the flame of heaven!* "This," adds the Lainga Puran, from which it is taken‡, "is the radical invocation, and is addressed to that great spirit, the Sun." In the Rig Veda the Gayatri is as follows: — "*Tat*, let us meditate on the excellence of the Sun, of the god Bharga; may he excite our understandings." §

It will hence be obvious, that from the mere words of this verse, so highly revered, no other conclusion can be drawn than that it is simply an invocation to the sun, and neither the commentators nor the Brahmans are agreed with respect to whether the sun ought to be considered as the Supreme Being, or only as a type of his divinity. Nor

* These last four words signify literally, earth, sky, heaven, *that*. With respect to the last, Mr. Colebrooke, in his Essay on the Vedas, observes: — "The pronoun (*tad*), thus emphatically used, is understood to intend the Supreme Being, according to the doctrine of the Vedanta. In his remarks on the Gayatri, however (As. Res. vol. v.), he considers it to denote truth, and to refer to the Satyaloka, or seventh heaven.

† This is a name of the sun.

‡ Part II. chapter 122.

§ As the original text of this celebrated verse has never, I believe, been published, I transcribe it from the Rig Veda. तत्सवितुर्वरेण्यं भर्गोदेवस्य धीमहि ॥ धियोनाः प्रचोदयात्. Which words will evidently admit of no other literal translation than that which I have given above.

am I sufficiently acquainted with the Vedas to admit of my stating if the sun be ever in them addressed as the one God; but this character is unquestionably ascribed to Surya in the Upanishads, and in several passages of the Purans, as it will appear from the following quotations: —

*The Surya Narayan Upanishad.**

" In reciting this Upanishad, let the reciter place his thoughts on *Surya*, seated upon a red lotos of a golden hue, with four arms; two of his hands holding lotoses, and of the other two, one as if granting a boon, and the other protection, borne in a car drawn by seven horses, and as Shri Narayana the director of the wheel of time.

" *Om Bhu, om Bhuvah, om Suvah, om Mahar, om Janah, om Tapah, om Satyam, Tat,* let us meditate on the excellence of the Sun, of the god Bharga; may he excite our understandings, and dispel their darkness! The Sun is the soul of the world; from the Sun proceed existence and non-existence; from sacrifice to the Sun proceeds rain, the cause of sustenance. Praise, therefore, be to thee, O Aditya! who art manifestly Brahma, Vishnu, Rudra, and all the gods; who art manifestly the Rig, the Yajur, the Sama, and Atharvan Vedas, and all sacred verse. From the Sun proceed life, the earth, the sky, and space; and that Sun, which irradiates the universe, is the heart, the mind, the understanding, the intellect, consciousness, the vital breaths, the senses, and their organs. That Sun consists essentially of bliss, knowledge, and intuition. Praise, then, be to thee, O Mitra! save us from death! Praise be to thee, O illuminator and benefactor of this universe! Thy eye, O Sun! pervadeth all; may, therefore, thy all-provident eye protect us! We acknowledge thee, O Sun! to be the one God, and we meditate on thy countless rays; enlighten, therefore, O Sun! our understandings. The Sun is in the west and the east, the north and the south; may that Sun, who is every where present, bestow upon us length of days! *Om,* this one syllable is Brahm, Ghrani is two

* This Upanishad, which forms part of the *Athava Shiras* Upanishad, is prefaced in the same manner as the hymns in the Vedas, by stating that Brahma is the *Rishi* and Aditya the *Devata*, and by specifying the rhythm, &c.

syllables, Surya is also two syllables, and Aditya consists of three; and thus *Om Grani Surya Aditya* is the eight-syllabled invocation, which whoever repeats, he becomes in reality a Brahman.* He, likewise, who seated opposite to the Sun repeats it, is liberated from fear and sickness; misfortune ceases; and unlawful meats, drinks, intercourse, and connections become pure and lawful. Whoever in the morning repeats that invocation, which ought never to be communicated to another, he becomes prosperous, and obtains every temporal and spiritual advantage; and whoever repeats it continually at morning, noon, and night, he obtains the fruit of a hundred sacrifices, and passes over the dreadful sea of mortality."

From the Brahma Puran.

"As Narada was passing, he observed Nitra † performing a *tapas*, and wondering to what god this *tapas* could be offered, he thus addressed him: — 'Thou art the object of adoration in the sacred books, and of gods and virtuous men; thou art unborn, eternal, the most excellent of all things: from thee proceed the past, present, and future, and all beings worship thee. Say, then, who is the god that thou worshippest, for I know him not.' Mitra replied: — 'I will unfold to thee a most mysterious and eternal truth. The god whom I worship is that universal Spirit which pervades all things; himself material, he ‡ assumes the three qualities, and manifests himself as Purusha and Prakriti; incorporeal, he yet dwells in all bodies, but is not affected by their actions; within me, within thee, and within others he resides, the witness of every thing, but himself unseen and incomprehensible: he is the universal head, the universal eye, the universal arm, the universal foot; he alone pervades all bodies (*Kshetra*), and hence is he called *Kshetradgna;* he assumes a corporeal form, and hence is named *Purusha;* and as the universe is but his visible manifestation,

* That is, acquainted with the real nature of Brahm, or the one God.

† One of the twelve suns; but here addressed by Narada as the sole Sun.

‡ The pronoun refers to the Sun, as it will appear at the conclusion of this passage. The beginning, also, of this narration thus commences. — Brahma addressing the holy sages: "I will explain unto you the deeply mysterious nature of the sun," &c.

he is known as the universal substance. From multiform entities he is named the universal form, but still unity alone can be predicated of him, for all things are created from his essence; yet unity and diversity proceed from him, as various fires kindled from one fire may burn in different places; and as a thousand lamps may be lighted from one lamp, so does his effulgence manifest itself in Brahma and the other gods. His unity is the destruction of the universe, and his diversity its existence*; all things movable and immovable are finite, but he is infinite, eternal, and all-pervading; know him to be the originator of Brahma, the author of entity and nonentity; no one is superior to him, and he is adored by all who love virtue and desire beatitude. Being convinced of these truths, I worship Surya; by devotion to whom alone can final beatitude be obtained; and hence is the Sun worshipped as the Supreme Spirit by gods, holy sages, and pious men.' . . . . Brahma thus continued his address to the holy sages:—'The Sun is the root of the three worlds, and from him proceeded this universe, Suras, Asuras, and men; Rudra, Vishnu, Brahma, Indra, and all the dwellers in heaven. Surya is the mighty effulgence which is universally diffused, the universal spirit, the universal lord, the creator, the God of gods. From the Sun, in the beginning of time, proceeded existence and nonexistence, and on identification with him depends final beatitude.'"—*Brahma Puran*, the chapter entitled *Aditya-Mahatmya warnana*, and the commencement of the following one.

To the same purpose Mr. Colebrooke quotes the following passage from a commentary of Yadgnavalkia:—"The concluding prayer is subjoined to teach the various manifestations of that light which is the Sun himself. It is Brahm, the supreme soul. The Sun (says Yadgnavalkia) is Brahm: this is a sacred truth revealed in the sacred Upanishads, and in various *shakas* of the Vedas. So the Bhavishya Puran, speaking of the Sun. Because there is none greater than he, nor has been, nor will be, therefore he is celebrated as the SUPREME SOUL in all

* That is, when all things are identified with the Supreme Being, the universe ceases to exist, as its existence depends entirely on his manifesting himself under various forms.

the Vedas." * In another place: — "That which is the Sun, and thus called light, or effulgent power, is adorable, and must be worshipped by them who dread successive births and deaths, and who eagerly desire beatitude. The being, who may be seen in the solar orb, must be contemplated by the understanding, to obtain exemption from successive births and deaths, and from various pains." †

The Sun, also, is supposed to have assumed, for more effectually diffusing his genial power over the universe, twelve forms; and hence, as every form of a deity is believed to possess a distinct and independent existence, have originated the twelve suns which are so often alluded to in Sanscrit works. Their names are thus given in the Brahma Puran: — "The first form of the Sun is named *Indra*, the lord of the gods, and the destroyer of their enemies; the second *Dhata*, the creator of all things; the third *Parjanya*, residing in the clouds, and showering rain on the earth from its beams; the fourth *Twashta*, who dwells in all corporeal forms; the fifth *Pusha*, who gives nutriment to all beings; the sixth *Aryama*, who brings sacrifices to a successful conclusion; the seventh derives his name from almsgiving, and delights mendicants with gifts; the eighth is called *Vivasvan*, who ensures good digestion; the ninth *Vishnu*, who constantly manifests himself for the destruction of the enemies of the gods; the tenth *Amshuman*, who preserves the vital organs in a sound state; the eleventh *Varuna*, who, residing in the waters, vivifies the universe; and the twelfth *Mitra*, who dwells in the orb of the moon for the benefit of the three worlds. These are the twelve splendours of the Sun, the Supreme Spirit, which through them pervades the universe, and irradiates the inmost souls of men." ‡

* Asiatic Researches, vol. v. p. 352.

† Ibid., p. 351. It must be recollected, that exemption from future states of being is acquired only by identification with the Supreme Spirit.

‡ This passage occurs in the beginning of the chapter before quoted.

In a passage, however, following shortly after, it is said that the common names of the twelve suns are Aditya, Savita, Surya, Mihira, Arka, Prabhakara, Martanda, Bhaskara, Bhanu, Chittrabhanu, Divakara, and Ravi; and that the twelve sacred names are those given above, viz. Vishnu, Dhata, Bhaga, Pusha, Mitra, Indra, Varuna, Aryama, Vivasvan, Amshuman, Twashta, and Parjanya. But the Sun has, altogether, one thousand names or epithets.

It will hence be evident, that in the Hindu religion Surya appears under two perfectly distinct characters, the one as the Supreme Being, and the other as an inferior deity, the regent of the solar orb. It is, however, under this last character that he is generally considered; and his subjecting himself to birth and assumption of corporeality is thus related in the Brahma Puran: — *The holy Sages said,* — "O lord! thou hast first informed us that the Sun is without form or quality, and always existing, and now thou sayest that he was born the son of Kashyapa; a great doubt, therefore, has occurred to us how such an orb of mighty splendour, darting its fiery beams, could be subject to birth." Brahma replied *, — "Aditi, beholding her sons vanquished by the Daityas and Danavas, deprived of the sovereignty of the three worlds, and perishing from hunger in consequence of being deprived of their shares of sacrifices, commenced a severe *tapas* to the Sun, and kneeling on the ground adored him with many a laudatory strain. At length, after a long period had elapsed, that god, being propitiated, manifested himself. Then Adita beheld within a well a wondrous splendour, and on the ground around her a heavenly radiance, difficult to be gazed upon; and, agitated with fear, she thus spoke: — 'Through thy favour, O god of the universe! I now reverently behold thee; but be pleased to permit me to see thee in a visible form, O Divakara!' Surya then revealed himself in a form refulgent as burnished gold, and beholding Aditi prostrated before him, he thus said: — 'Choose whatever boon thou desirest.' Aditi bowing her head, and paining the ground with her knees, thus replied, — 'In compassion to my sons, O god! deign to permit a portion of thy divine nature to be born from my womb, in order that he may destroy their enemies, and restore them to the sovereignty of the three worlds, and to a participation in sacrifices.' Surya replied, — 'I will comply with thy wishes, and be born thy son;' and then disappeared. Thus did Aditi finish her *tapas*, having obtained all she wished; and, shortly after, a beam of the Sun descended into the womb of the mother of the gods. In order, therefore, that she might conceive this son in all purity, during the hundred

* I have omitted the first part of the answer.

divine years allotted for her gestation, she performed daily the severest penances and devotional acts. On beholding which, Kashyapa became somewhat angry, and thus addressed her: — 'Why dost thou, by these daily practices, kill the fœtus in thy womb?' She replied, — 'In order that the fœtus may become a being superior to all others, and the death of the Asuras;' and in consequence of her displeasure at her husband's words, the child was immediately born, blazing like the sun. On beholding this splendour of Surya, Kashyapa adored him with laudatory strains; and, as he was thus engaged, an incorporeal voice thus spoke from heaven: — 'Because thou saidst to thy wife, '*killed* will this *fœtus* be by thee' (*Marita-andam*), he shall be named *Martanda*, and he shall destroy the Asuras, and restore the Suras to the sovereignty of the three worlds, and participation in sacrifices.' The gods having heard this celestial voice were delighted, and Indra challenged the Daityas and Danavas to battle. They came, and a terrible combat ensued; in which Martanda appeared, and with his blazing beams reduced the enemies of the gods to ashes. Thus restored to their sovereignty, the gods, after praising Martanda, resumed their different powers, and Martanda also proceeded to exercise the dominion which was assigned to him." —*Brahma Puran*, the chapter entitled *Martandaya janma-lambana.*

Before quitting the account of this deity, it seems proper to advert to the following statement of Mr. Colebrooke in his Essay on the Vedas: — The seventh chapter [of the tenth book of the *Sanhita* of the Rig Veda] opens with a hymn, in which Surya, surnamed Savitri, *the wife of moon*, is made the speaker." But I strongly suspect that Mr. Colebrooke has not here adverted to the form of a word which is evidently a *patronymic**, and that he has, in consequence, converted the *daughter* into the *father*. At least, the commentator Sayancharya intimates most distinctly, that it was not the *Sun*, but his daughter, who was given in marriage to the *Moon;* and says, — "She was the daughter

* In the text of this Veda the name of the person given in marriage to the Moon is Suryā in the feminine gender, and not Suryă in the masculine, the form in which it always occurs when applied to the Sun. It is to be remarked, that in the Sanscrit alphabet there are distinct characters for the short and long *a*.

of the *Sun*, but called the daughter of *Prajapati*, on account of the affection which he bore to her.* In the text, also, of this hymn it is explicitly said that *Savita* (*the sun*) *gave Surya to her husband.* † It seems evident, therefore, that from neither the text nor the commentary of the two passages quoted by Mr. Colebrooke, are there any grounds for supposing that in the Hindu religion the female sex was ever ascribed to the *Sun*; and, on the contrary, in numerous passages of the Rig Veda, and I hence conclude of the other Vedas, the Sun invariably appears under the masculine gender. Had, also, such an opinion ever prevailed, some traces of it might be justly expected to be found in the Upanishads and Purans, but in these works not the slightest allusion to it occurs. ‡ This mistake, however, is of the utmost importance, because it tends to confound the *Sun*, in consequence of an appellation resting on an erroneous supposition §, with *Savitri*, the female energy of Brahma. (See ante, Chapter XII.)

GANESHA.

I have before observed, that the five deities held principally in veneration by the Hindus, are Vishnu, Shiva, Devi, Surya, and Gane-

* These words occur in his commentary on the passage in the *Aitareya Brahmana* quoted in a note by Mr. Colebrooke. But in the commencement of his commentary on the hymn immediately preceding the one quoted from the *Sanhita* by Mr. Colebrooke, *Sayancharya* says, सूर्य्या स्वविवाहं स्तुतवती. In the first hymn *Surya celebrates her marriage*, which words can leave no doubt that the proper name here applies not to the Sun, but to his daughter.

† The words are सूर्यां यत्पत्येशं सत्ती मनसासविताददात्. Sayanacharya, however, understands *Savita* to be here intended for *Prajapati*, which is the name used in the Aitareya Brahmana. But most assuredly *Savita* can be nowhere found as one of the names of Brahma.

‡ According to the Purans, also, the Moon was not married to one wife only, but to twenty-seven wives, the daughters of Daksha.

§ In the translation of an extract from the Rig Veda, relating to the primeval sacrifice, given by Mr. Colebrooke in his Essay on the Vedas, occur these words: — "First was produced the *Gayatri* joined with fire; next the Sun (*Savitri*) attended by *Ushnih*." But in the text the name of the Sun is distinctly written *Savita*, and the crude nominative of this noun is scarcely ever used. It must also be carefully remarked, that this crude nominative is *Săvitrĭ*, and that the name of the female energy of Brahma is *Sāvitrī*, two words perfectly distinct. It is the last, however, which is given in the *Aitareya Brahmana* as a surname to Suryā the daughter of *Savita*, and which the commentator considers to be a patronymic regularly derived from the crude nominative *Săvitrĭ*.

sha*: but it is impossible to understand why the last has been so highly exalted; for he is a *derivative*, and not an *original*, god, and no legends attesting his divine power occur in the eighteen Purans. As applicable, however, to the present day, and perhaps to remoter times, this remark of Sir W. Jones is perfectly just: — "All sacrifices and religious ceremonies, all addresses even to superior gods, all serious compositions in writing, and all worldly affairs of moment, are begun by pious Hindus with an invocation of *Ganesha*." The accounts, also, of his production in the different Purans are variant, and it is, I believe, in the Padma alone that it is said that he was the son of Shiva and Parvati; as in several of the others he is described as either having been formed by Parvati†, who was desirous of having a son, or having been produced by her in a mysterious manner. In the following extract, however, his production is ascribed to Shiva only: —

From the Varaha Puran.

"The immortals and holy sages observing that, whether the actions which they or others commenced were good or bad, no difficulty occurred in accomplishing them, consulted together respecting the means by which obstacles might be opposed to the commission of bad actions, and determined to have recourse to Rudra. They accordingly proceeded to Kailasa, and thus with reverence addressed him: — 'O Mahadeva, god of gods, three-eyed, bearer of the trident, it is thou alone who canst create a being capable of opposing obstacles to the commission of improper acts.' On hearing these words, Shiva

* See also the Upanishad contained in Appendix F., in which Ganesha is identified with the Supreme Being.

† One day, when she was bathing, Parvati formed the oil, ointments, and impurity that came from her body into the figure of a man, to which she gave life by sprinkling it with the water of the Ganges. In the Matsya Puran it is said that this figure was formed with the head of an elephant; but in the Shiva it is related, that, after giving Ganesha life, Parvati placed him at the door to prevent intrusion while she finished bathing, and that, Shiva, having come there, on his wishing to enter a battle ensued between them. In which Shiva cut off the head of Ganesha; but, on Parvati explaining the mistake and lamenting the death of her son, he directed the first head that was to be found to be brought to him, which happened to be an elephant's, and this he fitted to the body of Ganesha, and resuscitated him.

looked at Parvati, and began to consider in what manner he could effect the wishes of the gods; and, as he was immersed in thought, from the splendour of his countenance sprang into existence a youth, shedding radiance around, endowed with the qualities of Shiva, and evidently another Rudra, and captivating by his beauty the female inhabitants of heaven. Uma regarded him, and when she saw him thus lovely, her natural disposition* was excited, and incensed with anger she uttered this curse: — 'Thou shalt not offend my sight with the form of a beautiful youth, therefore assume an elephant's head and a large belly, and thus may all thy beauties vanish!' . . . . Shiva thus spoke to his son: — 'Thy names shall be Ganesha, Vinayaka, Vighnaraja, the son of Shiva; thou shalt be the chief of the Vinayakas and Ganas; success and disappointment shall proceed from thee; and great shall be thy influence amongst the gods, and in sacrifices and all affairs. Therefore shalt thou be worshipped and invoked the first on all occasions, or otherwise the object and prayers of him who omits to do so, shall fail.'" — *Varaha Puran*, the chapter entitled *Vinayakotpatti*.

In the following passage, however, of the *Skanda Puran*, the birth of Ganapati is ascribed to Parvati only: — *Shiva, addressing Parvati.*— "Formerly during the twilight that intervened between the Dwapara and Kali Yugs, women, barbarians, Shudras, and other workers of sin, obtained entrance into heaven by visiting the celebrated temple of Someshwara.† Sacrifices, ascetic practices, charitable gifts, and all the other prescribed ordinances ceased, and men thronged only to the temple of Shiva. Hence old and young, the skilled in the Vedas and those ignorant of them, and even women and Shudras, ascended to heaven, until at length it became crowded to excess. Then Indra and the gods, afflicted at being thus overcome by men, sought the protection of Shiva, and thus with reverence addressed him: — 'O Shankara! by thy favour heaven is pervaded by men, and we are nearly

* Indignant at Shiva producing without her participation so perfect a son.

† The same as Somanath.

expelled from it. These mortals wander wherever they please, exclaiming, "I am the greatest; I am the greatest;" and Dharma Rajah, beholding the register of their good and evil deeds, remains silent, lost in astonishment. For the seven hells were most assuredly intended for their reception; but, having visited thy shrine, their sins have been remitted, and they have obtained a most excellent futurity.' Shiva replied, — 'Such was my promise to Soma, nor can it be infringed; and all men, therefore, who visit the temple of Someshwara must ascend to heaven. But supplicate Parvati, and she will contrive some means for extricating you from this distress.' The gods then kneeling before Parvati, with folded hands and bended heads, thus invoked her assistance with laudatory strains: — 'Praise be to thee, O supreme of goddesses, supporter of the universe! Praise be to thee, O lotos-eyed, resplendent as gold! Praise be to thee, O beloved of Shiva, who createst and destroyest! Praise be to thee, O mountain-born! Praise be to thee, O Kalarattri, O Durga, who pervadest the universe, and art the sole substance from which all female forms, whether mortal or immortal, originate! grant us thy aid, and save us from this fearful distress.' Having heard the supplication of Indra and the gods, thou, O goddess! wert moved with compassion, and, gently rubbing thy body, there was thence produced a wondrous being with four arms and the head of an elephant; when thou thus addressed the gods: — 'Desirous of your advantage have I created this being, who will occasion obstacles to men, and deluding them will deprive them of the wish to visit Somanatha, and thus shall they fall into hell.' This heard, the gods were delighted, and returned to their own abodes, relieved from all fear of mankind.

"The *Elephant-faced* then thus spoke to thee, O Devi: — 'Command, O lovely goddess! what I shall now do.' Thou didst reply, — 'Oppose obstacles to men's visiting Somanatha, and entice them to give up such a purpose by the allurements of wives, children, possessions, and wealth. But from those who propitiate thee by the following hymn, do thou remove all difficulties, and enable them to obtain the favour of Shiva by worshipping at his shrine of Somanatha: — *Om, I praise thee, O lord of difficulties! the beloved spouse of Siddhi and Bud-*

dhi; Ganapati, invincible, and the giver of victory, the opposer of obstacles to the success of men who do not worship thee! I praise thee, O Ganesha! the dreadful son of Uma, but firm and easily propitiated! O Vinayaka, I praise thee! O elephant-faced, who didst formerly protect the gods and accomplish their wishes, I praise thee!* Thus,' continued Parvati, 'shalt thou be praised and worshipped on the fourth of each half month; and whoever previously invokes the god Vinayaka, no difficulties shall impede the attainment of his purposed object, and a most beneficial result shall he derive from sacrifices, pilgrimages, and all other devotional acts.'" — *Skanda Puranam; Prabhasa Mahatmyam,* the chapter entitled, *Kapardi-Mahatmyam.*†

* *Knowledge* and *Understanding,* the two wives of Ganesha.

† *Prabhasa Kshettram* is the Sanscrit name of the temple of which Shiva, under the character of Somanatha (the moon's lord), is the deity. A lingam was here set up by Soma in commemoration of his having been relieved by Shiva from the effects of Daksha's curse; and hence originated this name, as Shiva then placed Soma on his head in order to cure him of the consumption, with which he was afflicted in consequence of that curse.

CHAP. XV.

INDRA AND THE INFERIOR DEITIES.

In power and divinity the deities who have been the subject of the preceding remarks are considered to be perfectly distinct from the three hundred and thirty-three millions of angelic beings who reside in *Swarga*, or the heaven of sensual pleasures. But, even amongst those *dwellers in heaven**, eleven alone, viz. *Indra* who is their king, *Varuna* the god of the ocean, *Vaiu* the god of the wind, *Agni* the god of fire, *yama* the monarch of the dead, *Kubera* the guardian of riches, *Kartikaya* or *Skanda* † the chief of the celestial armies, *Kama* god of love, the *Ashwinau* the physicians of heaven, *Surya* the sun (*Mitra* and *Varuna* two of the twelve suns are also often mentioned), and *Soma* the moon, are held to exercise distinct divine functions, and therefore entitled to worship.‡ With exception of *Yama* and the *Ashwinau* who were the children of Surya, *Kubera* the son of the *Rishi Pulastya*, *Skanda* the son of Shiva, *Soma* the son of *Atri*, and *Kama* who sprang from the mind of Brahma, all these angelic beings were the children of *Kashyapa* and *Aditi.*§ From Kashyapa, also, were born, by his wives, *Diti* and *Danu*, two other races named *Daityas* and *Danavas*, or collectively *Asuras*. But to the sons of Aditi was *Swarga* or Olympus assigned as a place of abode, and to the Asuras *Patalam* or Tarta-

* *Divaukasa* is a very common Sanscrit term for all these beings taken collectively.

† He, however, is generally represented as residing with and accompanying Shiva.

‡ I have omitted Nairrita, one of the guardians of the eight points of heaven, because he was not originally one of the angelic host, and the accounts of his first state are variant. But see Appendix, p. 417. These *dikpalas*, or guardians of the eight points, viz. Indra, Agni, Yama, Nairrita, Varuna, Vayu, Kubera, and Isha, being worshipped collectively, Nairrita is of course included, but I am not aware that any other divine honours are paid to him.

§ In the Purans, however, the production of Agni is related in a variety of manners; but what may be considered as his divine and primeval origin was from the mouth of Brahma.

rus.* The latter, however, could not understand the justice by which they were, though descended from the same father, deprived of a participation in the delights of heaven; and hence originated an enmity against the Suras (or sons of Aditi), and continual attempts on the part of the Asuras to acquire and to retain the possession of heaven.

The cause of this seemingly inequitable partition amongst brothers is thus explained in the Brahmanda Puran †:—" The Supreme Being assigned different kinds of bodies to the Devatas, Asuras, *Pitris*, and men, according to whichever of the three qualities, or the proportions of them, their souls were composed of. Hence, as the souls of the Asuras were derived from the quality of darkness, their bodies were deformed, and they received neither honour nor worship. But the souls of the Devatas having originated from the quality of purity, they were endowed with celestial forms, and became the objects of sacrifice and adoration." In the Padma Puran, also, Kashyapa thus accounts to Diti for the misfortunes of her sons, and by this reasoning, which seems far from satisfactory, endeavours to console her grief:— " In this transitory state of existence there is neither father, nor mother, nor brother, nor kindred, nor friends; for all these are merely illusions produced by Maya. Every one is his own father, and mother, and brother, and kindred. Since by practising piety and the prescribed ordonnances, he obtains peace and happiness; but if he be sinful, impious, and irreligious, he is condemned to many a cruel birth. The situation of every one proceeds from his actions; and he who seeks

* It must be recollected that, as observed by Mr. Payne Knight in his *Enquiry into the Symbolical Language, &c.*, Tartarus " was not part of the regions regularly allotted to the dead by the ancient Greek mythologists; but a distinct and separate world beyond chaos, as far from earth as earth from heaven." Mr. Knight here quotes this verse from Homer,

Τοσσον ενερθ' αιδεω, οσον ουρανος εστ' απο γαιας.

This description, omitting the chaos, is perfectly applicable to the *Patalam* of the Hindus.

† It may be remarked that I have never yet quoted this Puran; but I have found it not adapted for such a purpose, because it consists of three parts: the first of which is principally occupied with a description of the earth and the planetary system; the second contains a very detailed account of Parasu Rama; and the third is the *Adhyatma Ramayanam*, descriptive of the exploits of Rama Chandra, which is generally circulated as a distinct work.

enmity will find enemies, as he who cultivates friendship will acquire friends. Such as is the seed which the husbandman sows, such will be the fruit that he will reap. Thus thy sons having forsaken virtue and devotion have incurred the necessary consequences of their actions; and on account of their sins have they fallen from a high estate." It will hence be evident that there is not the most distant similitude between the Suras and Asuras of the Hindu mythology, and

> " The infernal serpent, he it was whose guile,
> Stirr'd up with envy and revenge, deceived
> The mother of mankind, what time his pride
> Had cast him out from heaven, with all his host
> Of rebel angels; by whose aid, aspiring
> To set himself in glory above his peers,
> He trusted to have equall'd the Most High,
> If he opposed; and, with ambitious aim,
> Against the throne and monarchy of God
> Raised impious war and battle proud,
> With vain attempt. Him the Almighty Power
> Hurl'd headlong flaming from the ethereal sky,
> With hideous ruin and combustion, down
> To bottomless perdition, there to dwell
> In adamantine chains and penal fire,
> Who durst defy the Omnipotent to arms."

For the enmity of the Suras and Asuras originated in consequence of the future lot assigned to each by Brahma*; and there is no character in the Hindu religion which in the slightest degree resembles that of Satan.†

Almost all the legends concerning Indra and the inferior deities, which occur in the Purans, relate to the continual contests which take

* In the Markandeya Puran, it is said, — " Such was the progeny of Kashyapa, severally formed from the qualities of purity and darkness; and Brahma, the creator, appointed the Devatas to be the enjoyers of sacrifice and the lords of the three worlds; on which account the Daityas and Danavas waged war against them; and, being victorious, expelled them from heaven." It is singular that the Asuras are almost always conquerors in the first instance, and that the Suras are only able to overcome them by obtaining the assistance of Vishnu or Shiva.

† That a belief, however, in the existence of the devil is altogether unconnected with the belief in a state of future punishment, is fully evinced by the religions of Greece and India.

place between them and the Asuras in consequence of that enmity. I therefore subjoin the following rather long extract, as it is sufficiently illustrative of the nature of these wars in heaven : —

From the Skanda Puran.

" The Daityas and Danavas, having been deprived of the beverage of immortality by Vishnu under the delusive form of Mohini, were enraged, and immediately seized their arms : and Bali, the mighty son of Virochina, mounting his chariot, led on his troops to attack the Suras; myriads of Asuras of various forms, and some mounted on buffaloes, some on lions, some on tigers, some on vultures, others on peacocks, swans, or crows, others on mules or camels, and many on horses, elephants, or carts, and all armed with various weapons. But the thousand chiefs of Bali proceeded along in chariots, shouting, and eager for combat; and, while innumerable warriors overspread the battle-ground, in the air floated umbrellas and chowries, flags and banners. The Suras, also, having drank the *amrit* with delight, armed themselves, and, mounting their chariots, hastened to oppose the Asuras. Indra, brandishing a thunderbolt, advanced, mounted on the elephant Airavati, the Sun also proceeded in a car, the Moon on an antelope, Yama on a buffalo, Shiva on a bull, and the other deities on such conveyances as pleased them.* Desirous of victory, but dreading the fear-inspiring looks and terrible power of the Asuras, Indra and all the gods bowed themselves before Vishnu and implored his protection. Then joined the two contending hosts, and a horrid tumult arose; showers of arrows fell, and the clash of weapons far resounded; no blows were struck in vain, and dead and dying strewed the battle field. Broken was the army of the Asuras, and loud shouted the Suras, while the sound of their musical instruments filled the three worlds.

" Bali, beholding his army defeated, arose, and mounting his chariot, resplendent as the sun, hastened, with fresh troops, to restore

* The Moon is generally described as borne in a car drawn by an antelope; the car of the Sun has only one wheel, and is drawn by seven green horses: Agni mounts a ram, Varuna a fish, Vayu an antelope, Kubera is borne in a chariot, and Nairrita carried in a palanquin by ghosts.

the battle. Then single combats took place: Indra encountered Bali the chief of the Asuras; Yama, Namucha; Nairrita and Varuna, Kumba and Nikumba; Kubera, Sudamshtra; and other Suras, other Asuras. But Ketu and Rahu having engaged, no sooner had the gods beheld the latter's dreadful head, than they all fled; and thus did the head of Rahu insure victory to the Daityas and Danavas. Again did the Suras form their line and advance with Soma (the moon) at their head; and the Asuras, placing Rahu in front, marched forward to meet them. Then Rahu rushed forward to devour Soma, who, terrified, sprang into heaven, and sought the protection of Shiva*; but the gods again and again attacked the Asuras, desirous of victory. On both sides, struck by various weapons, numbers fell, and gore bedewed the battle-ground; and broken cars, with fallen flags and banners, heads, headless corses, horses, and elephants, bestrewed the field. Ghosts, goblins, and demons, rejoicing, sported amongst the slain, and drank the warm blood and devoured the palpitating flesh. Long fought Indra and Bali, till at last Indra, with a hundred thunderbolts, cut off the hundred arms of Bali, and the chief of the Daityas fell from his resplendent car. Then Vrishaparva, beholding his prince thus fallen, rushed forward, and covered Indra with a shower of arrows; and between them arose a terrible combat, until Indra at length slew Vrishaparva.

" Vrishaparva being thus slain, and Bali vanquished, Indra carried havock with his thunderbolts wherever he moved; and Yama, Vaiu, Varuna, Kubera, Nairrita, Agni, and Isha added to the slaughter. But the mighty Asura well skilled in arms, Kalanemi, mounted on a lion, advanced with myriads of valiant Asuras, all mounted on lions. On beholding this fear-inspiring army, Indra and all the gods were seized with terror, and thus thought, — 'What shall we do, and how shall we conquer so numerous and powerful an army as this?' As they were thus lost in doubt, Narada appeared, and having reminded Indra of the might which Kalanemi had acquired by *tapas*, informed him that it would be impossible to conquer him without the assistance

* In the original here follows a long account of the proper manner of worshipping Shiva.

of Vishnu. Enlightened by this advice, Indra and the gods invoked by devout meditation the aid of Hari; and the holder of the Chakra being propitiated, appeared in the air mounted on Garura. On beholding that god, Kalanemi was inflamed with anger, and thus laughing addressed him: —' Say who art thou of a black hue, youthful, of an excellent form and strength like a maddened elephant, and displaying in thy hand that resplendent disc?' The lord replied,— 'Hither am I come to battle in order to accomplish the wishes of the gods; therefore, stand firm, for this day will I undoubtedly consume thee.' Then arose a terrible combat between Vishnu borne on Garura and Kalanemi mounted on a winged lion; but Mukunda, as if in sport, at length struck with his hand Kalanemi so forcibly that he instantly fell senseless. Soon reviving he opened his eyes, and, beholding Vishnu before him, thus spoke:—' I am unable to contend in battle with thee, and in this world I have no longer hope. Those Asuras, also, who have been slain, will, according to the word of Brahma, attain an immortal abode, and like the gods enjoy various delights in the heaven of Indra; but after a stated time must they again be subject to birth. But he, O lord, who falls by thy hand on the battle-field, shall never again know the pains of birth; and, therefore, grant that I may now obtain final beatitude.' With these words Kalanemi expired, and disappeared. Their chief thus slain, Indra carried havock through the troops of Kalanemi, until Narada appeared, and thus addressed him: —' Innumerable Asuras have fallen, and the rest are seized with fear, why, therefore, dost thou still urge on their slaughter? Knowest thou not that these valiant Daityas are Brahmans, and that the slayers of them will incur the guilt of *Brahmanicide?*' This heard, Indra ceased the pursuit, and returned with the gods, delighted with victory, to Amaravati; and on account of Indra's success there was great rejoicing in heaven. Conchs, trumpets, kettle-drums, and various instruments resounded, the Gandharvas sang, the Apsaras danced, and the Siddhas, Charanas, and Guhyakas recited laudatory strains.

" During this war Shukra had retired with his disciples to Manasottara, and thither the Asuras hastened to inform him of their defeat, and the great loss which they had sustained. Their words the son of

Bhrigu heard with anger, and immediately proceeded to where the Asuras lay dead, and by the science of resuscitation, restored them all to life. Bali also arose, and thus spoke to Bhargava: — 'Why hast thou thus resuscitated me, and what use have I for life, since I have been overcome by Indra, and lost is my fame for valour?' But Shukra consoled him; and, according to their preceptor's advice, Bali and the Asuras returned to Patalam." — *Kedar Khand*, chapter 14.

"At this time his messengers acquainted Bali, residing in Patalam, with Indra's having slain Vritra; and he, being incensed with anger, consulted Shukra with respect to the means by which Indra might be overcome. Shukra replied, — 'Perform a sacrifice for the purpose of conquering the universe; for without sacrifice no object can be accomplished.' In obedience to this counsel, Bali prepared a costly sacrifice, at which Shukra officiated; and, as Bali presented his offerings to the sacred fire, he obtained from it a wondrous car drawn by four white horses, with a banner displaying a lion, and divine armour and weapons. The holy rites being finished, Bali assembled a numerous army of Asuras, and mounting his fire-given car ascended with it to heaven, and laid siege to Amaravati. The gods beholding their city besieged were alarmed, and thus addressed their preceptor: — 'What shall we now do, since such a powerful army of valiant Asuras, all skilled in war and eager for battle, thus surrounds us?' Brihaspati replied, — 'The Asuras have been all rendered invincible by a *tapas* enjoined by the son of Bhrigu.' On hearing these words the gods were overcome with fear, and the mind of Indra was agitated, as he found himself again exposed to shame and reproach. At length he asked Brihaspati what resource there was in their present distress. The preceptor of the gods replied, — 'Forsake Amaravati, assume other forms, and proceed to somewhere else.' The gods obeyed, and leaving Amaravati, Indra became a peacock, Yama a crow, Kubera a lizard, Agni a pigeon, Isha a daw, Nairrita a parrot, Varuna a partridge, and Vaiu a dove, and hastened to the hermitage of Kashyapa, to whom they related their misfortune. On hearing this relation Kashyapa immediately desired his wife Aditi to perform speedily a severe *tapas*, to obtain that Vishnu might be pleased to become her son, in order to effect the restoration of the Suras to heaven. * Meanwhile the Asuras, ignorant that the gods had left it, continued the siege of Amaravati; until becoming acquainted with the circumstance, they entered the city, and found it empty. Then was Bali with great rejoicing inaugurated as king of heaven, and with the Daityas and Danavas enjoyed all the delights of Swarga, over which he reigned supreme." — *Ibid*, chapters 17, 18.

It would, however, be contrary to the object of this work, were I to enter into any detailed account of the adventures of Indra and the inferior deities which are related in the Purans; for such circumstances tend not in the least to explain the principles of the Hindu religion. But the extracts from the Vedas given by Mr. Colebrooke sufficiently evince that, at the time when those sacred books were composed, the host of heaven presented precisely the same appearance as it does in the Purans, and in the popular mythology of the present day. It is also said in the Rig Veda that Indra and the Devas were the children of Aditi, the daughter of Daksha; and even Mr. Colebrooke has made this admission. "I observe in many places (of the Vedas) the *groundwork of legends*, which are familiar in mythological poems; such, for example, as the demon *Vritra* slain by Indra, who is thence named *Vritrahan*." The slightest perusal, however, of the Vedas must demonstrate how totally improbable it is that the Puranic legends could be founded on any passages contained in them; for these legends are merely alluded to, in a manner so very concise and enigmatical, as to be perfectly unintelligible without the assistance of a commentary or of oral instruction. In either of which cases it seems indisputable that the legend must have previously existed in a circumstantial form; or otherwise neither the commentator nor the preceptor could have possibly had it in his power to explain that which could not in consequence admit of illustration. If, for instance, the history of *Vritra*

* This was the cause of the *Vamana Avatar* of Vishnu; in which, under the form of a dwarf, having obtained from Bali as much ground as he could traverse in three steps, he in two strides comprised the universe, and thus obliged Bali with his Asuras to quit heaven, but allowed them to return to Patalam.

and his having been slain by Indra, had not been well known, the epithet *Vritrahan*, which is all, I believe, that occurs in the Vedas*, could not evidently have conveyed any information whatever on the subject.

But Mr. Colebrooke is no doubt correct in considering the mythology of the Vedas to be " one which personifies the elements and planets, and which peoples heaven and the world below with various orders of beings." The Vedas, however, are not yet sufficiently known to admit of its being determined whether in them Indra and the inferior deities ever appear merely as the elements or planets of which they are impersonifications; but that such must have been the origin of the veneration paid to them seems sufficiently proved by such names as *Vaiu*, *Agni*, *Surya*, and *Soma* being even at this day the most common terms in India for the *wind*, *fire*, the *sun*, and the *moon*. But to the elements and planets have been added a few other deities, and various classes † of celestial beings whose divinity must have originated in some other cause, which it would now, perhaps, be impossible to ascertain.

* Or expressions similar to it, denoting that Vritra was slain by Indra, but without entering into any detailed account of the circumstances connected with his death, which are related at length in the Purans.

† These deities and classes, however, are, I believe, all mentioned in the Vedas.

CHAP. XVI.

ON THE AFFINITY BETWEEN ANCIENT AND HINDU MYTHOLOGY.

In the preceding pages I have endeavoured to ascertain the precise nature of the information respecting ancient mythology which is still available, and to explain the principles of the Hindu religion; and the reader will now be enabled to judge how far any identity or similarity exists between these two systems: but, as he may expect me to state the opinion which I have myself formed from these Researches, I may observe that they have led me to draw a conclusion very different from that which is thus stated by Mr. Faber: — "The fact is, that the various theological systems of the Gentiles agree, not only in what is *obvious* and *natural*, but in what is *arbitrary* and *circumstantial*. There is such a singular and minute and regular accordance between them, both in *fanciful speculations* and in *artificial observances*, that no person, who takes the pains of thoroughly investigating the subject, can avoid being fully persuaded that they must all have sprung from some common origin." * It is equally inconsistent with the result of these Researches to admit, as this common origin, that "the demon-gods of Paganism were the mortals who lived during the golden age; and since there was a golden age, both immediately after the creation and immediately after the deluge, it will plainly follow that those demon-gods were the members of the Adamitic family in the one instance, and the members of the Noatic family in the other. . . . . . Yet, if we examine the legendary histories of the chief deities worshipped by the Gentiles, we shall almost invariably find them replete with allusions to the creation and paradise on one hand, and to the deluge and the ark on the other." † On the contrary, the Mosaic account of the creation is a cosmogony *sui generis* ‡, and bears not the remotest resemblance to

* Origin of Pagan Idolatry, vol. i. p. 59.

† Ibid., p. 10, 11.

‡ Consequently its authenticity cannot be invalidated by this dissimilitude, but must depend entirely on the book of Genesis being of divine origin.

the cosmogony of any other religious system, except that of the Mohammedan, which is copied from it. For it would be utterly impossible to find in any other description of the first process of creation such circumstances as God having employed six days to effect it; the formation of the first man from the dust of the earth, and of the first woman from one of his ribs; the planting of the garden of Eden, and the prohibition to eat the fruit of the tree of knowledge; the temptation of Eve by the serpent, the eating of the forbidden fruit by Adam and Eve, and their expulsion from paradise; and the murder of Abel by Cain. Although, also, the tradition of a deluge seems to have been generally prevalent in antiquity, still no legendary histories are founded upon it, nor are there the slightest allusions to an ark in the mythology of any ancient people. Nor in any can there be discovered the slightest trace of the person who was preserved from this deluge, having had three sons only *, and of his having divided the earth among them and their respective descendants.

I concur, therefore, entirely in the justness of these remarks of Mr. Faber: — "The Israelites were neither so universally celebrated, nor was their commonwealth of so ancient an origin, compared with that of many other nations, as to warrant the belief that mythologists flocked from every quarter of the globe to derive wisdom from the books of Moses. In fact, the very same idolatry which has subsisted even to the present day was established, substantially at least, both in Egypt and Palestine, *previously* to the Exodus of the Children of Israel: and so intimately, in every region, is the prevailing idolatry combined with some hypothesis respecting *the* creation, and with some account of *the* deluge; or rather, I should say, so evidently is Pagan idolatry *built* upon traditions of *the* creation and *the* † deluge, that where the former is found, there we may rest assured that the latter must have

* In the Hindu mythology the first Manu had only two sons, to the eldest of whom he left the empire of the earth; and Vaivaswata Manu had ten sons, among whom he divided the world: and the formation of mankind, after the deluge of the Greeks, from the stones thrown by Deucalion and Pyrrha, is too well known to require remark.

† The definite article should be changed into the indefinite: *a* creation, *a* deluge; and this remark would be then correct as far as it relates to creation; but I am not aware of any mythological legends having been built upon traditions of a deluge.

prevailed. Hence it is manifest, that the Canaanites and the Egyptians cannot have borrowed their theories from Moses; and, if they did not, how strangely improbable is it, that the remote and ancient nations of the Hindus, the Chinese, and the Scythians should have been indebted to him?" *

It will be observed that, in the present as well as in the former work, I have maintained a hypothesis which in some respects assimilates to that of Mr. Faber; and that, although I do not derive all the nations of the earth from Shem, Ham, and Japhet, I still think that Babylonia was the original seat of the Sanscrit language and of Sanscrit literature. I have farther contended that, as Asia Minor was most probably peopled from Babylonia, the emigrants must have introduced into the former country the language and institutions of their parent land, and that these were thence communicated to Thracia, Greece, Etruria, and Latium by the Pelasgi. So far, therefore, as it relates only to the mythology of the Greeks and Romans, for with respect to that of the Thracians no satisfactory information has been preserved, the correctness of these remarks of Sir W. Jones seems indisputable:— "We cannot," he observes, "justly conclude, by arguments preceding the proof of facts, that one idolatrous people must have borrowed their deities, rites, and tenets from another, since gods of all shapes and dimensions may be framed by the boundless powers of imagination, or by the frauds and follies of men, in countries never connected; but when features of resemblance, too strong to have been accidental, are observable in different systems of polytheism, without fancy or prejudice to colour them and improve the likeness, we can scarce help believing that some connection has immemorially † subsisted between the several nations who have adopted them. It is my design, in this essay, to point out such a resemblance between the popular worship of the old Greeks and Italians, and that of the Hindus." ‡ But I dissent entirely from the opinion of Sir W. Jones as expressed in this remark:

* Origin of Pagan Idolatry, vol. i. p. 201.

† It would have been more correct, had Sir W. Jones, instead of *immemorially*, said, *must have, at some remote though unknown period, subsisted.*

‡ Asiatic Researches, vol. i. p. 221.

—"The Scythian and Hyperborean doctrines and mythology may also be traced in every part of these eastern regions; nor can we doubt that Wod, or Oden, whose religion, as the northern historians admit, was introduced into Scandinavia by a foreign race, was the same with Buddha, whose rites were probably imported into India nearly at the same time, though received much later by the Chinese, who soften his name into Fo." *

It is this strange manner of adducing, in support of a position, arguments drawn from the real or supposed institutions of people, Scandinavians, Greeks, Indians, and Chinese, who differ from each other in geographical situation, language, customs, and religion, which has cast so much ridicule on antiquarian researches.† But this error necessarily proceeds from the assumption that the first eleven chapters of Genesis give an authentic account of the creation and of the earlier ages of the world, which renders it necessary to insult common sense, and to disregard the plainest principles of evidence and reasoning, in order to prove that all the races of mankind and all systems of polytheism were derived from one and the same origin. It is, however, undeniable that the Old Testament contains an account of no other people than the descendants of Abraham; and to connect, therefore, the posterity of Shem, Ham, and Japhet with the nations which occupied the different countries of this world when they first became known to profane tradition and history, it is evident that no data whatever exist. To construct, consequently, systems on vague conjectures and mere gratuitous assumptions can never tend to rectify error, or to increase real knowledge. But it will, no doubt, be admitted, that the evincing, on sufficient grounds, that an unquestionable similarity exists between the religious systems of any two people must materially contribute to illustrate the origin and affinity of nations; and such alone are the coincidences between ancient and Hindu mythology which I now proceed to point out.

* Asiatic Researches, vol. i. p. 425.

† In referring to the contents of Mr. Faber's work, I observe that the second chapter of the first volume contains the Hindu, Egyptian, Iranian, Chinese, Burman, Cingalese, Gothic or Scythic, Greek, Roman, Druidical, and Mexican statement of the doctrine of a succession of similar worlds.

It will, I think, be admitted that, when a similarity exists between two systems, the one of which is consistent and complete, and the other incongruous and imperfect, it must have been from the former that the latter proceeded, unless it can be shown that they were both derived from some one common origin; but it seems indisputable that, as far as any information is afforded by tradition and history, the mythology of no people has been preserved in so perfect a state as that of the Hindus. In contrasting, therefore, the accounts of the cosmogony given by Grecian and Hindu writers their similarity becomes unquestionable; and the deficiencies of the one are so satisfactorily supplied by the more ample details of the other, as to leave no reasonable doubt that the opinions respecting the creation, which prevailed in Greece, were derived from that country in which the Hindu religion first originated. For, in both these systems, chaos*, darkness, and water are supposed to have existed previously to the formation of the universe; and, although the Grecian mythological account has most similarity to the secondary creation of the Hindus, still the memory of the primary creation from the mundane egg has been clearly and unequivocally preserved in the Orphic doctrines, and in the verses of Aristophanes. But such opinions, particularly the last, are of an arbitrary nature, and not of that obvious and natural kind which might occur to different people placed under similar circumstances; and amongst the Greeks, therefore, as their antiquity is not so remote as that of the Hindus, these opinions must be considered to have been derivative, and not original.

But Mr. Payne Knight has observed that "the similitude of these allegorical and symbolical fictions with each other, in every part of the

* It is difficult to understand in what sense this term was used; but it seems to have denoted a state in which the elements of things existed previously to their being employed in the formation of the universe: and in this sense chaos would aptly denote the state in which the elements of things remained, according to the Hindu cosmogony, until they were enclosed in the mundane egg; or, more correctly perhaps, the state of things attendant on one of the periodical destructions of the universe. The two primitive principles, also, considered requisite for creation, whether ether and chaos, light and darkness, or heaven and earth, are immediately recognised in the more obvious and correct primary causes of generation of the Hindus, — the *Purusha* and *Prakriti*, or primeval male and female.

world, is no proof of their having been derived, any more than the primitive notions which they signify, from any other people; for, as the organs of sense and the principles of intellect are the same in all mankind, they would all naturally form similar ideas from similar objects, and employ similar signs to express them, so long as natural and not conventional signs were used. Wolves, lions, and panthers are equally beasts of prey in all countries, and would naturally be employed as symbols of destruction wherever they were known. . . . The characteristic qualities of the egg, the serpent, the goat, &c., are no less obvious."* The mundane egg, however, was not originally a symbol, even if it subsequently became such, but a thing which was supposed to have actually existed: and Mr. Knight himself remarks "that it was carried in procession at the celebration of the mysteries; for which reason Plutarch, in the passage above cited, declines entering into a more particular disquisition concerning its nature, the Platonic interlocutor, in the dialogue, observing that, *though a small question, it comprehended a very great one concerning the generation of the world itself, known to those who understood the Orphic and sacred language; the egg being consecrated, in the Bacchic mysteries, as the* IMAGE OF THAT WHICH GENERATED AND CONTAINED ALL THINGS IN ITSELF."† But these last words most formally contradict Mr. Knight's opinion as expressed in the sentence immediately preceding: Bacchus "is said to have sprung from the egg of night, because the egg was the ancient symbol of organic matter in its inert state."‡ In the Hindu religion, also, all is positive, and symbols are, therefore, totally unknown in it; and, consequently, to

* An Inquiry into the Symbolical Language, &c., part ix. sect. 230.

† Ibid., part i. sect. 24.

‡ Does not also the very term *symbol* suppose the preexistence of the object of which the symbol was the emblem: and is it not more natural to conclude that, as in this instance, the egg borne in the mysteries was a symbol or memorial of the mundane egg from which Bacchus was thought to have sprung; rather than that its consecration had originated in a philosophical opinion respecting inert matter, and the properties of the egg? For the existence of a popular religion, on whatever principles this may have been founded, previous to the invention of the mysteries, is undeniable; nor have any data been preserved, from which a probable opinion could be formed with respect to the process of reasoning which led to the supposition, that the enclosure of the elements of things within an egg was requisite for effecting the formation of the universe.

it all that has been written with respect to the symbolical meaning of eggs, serpents, bulls, &c., is perfectly inapplicable; and it may hence be justly concluded, that it must be equally so to Grecian mythology in its earliest state. The difference of opinion, at the same time, which seems to have prevailed in Greece, respecting the being who issued from the mundane egg, is of no importance; because, whatever character may have been there ascribed to him, he is unquestionably the *primeval male* of the Hindu religion. For, whether he be considered as Phanes or Eros, his divine nature and his being the framer of this universe were circumstances that were universally admitted.

" An ancient notion (observes Mr. Faber) has very generally prevailed in the East and the West, that there have been four successive ages, symbolised by the four metals of gold, silver, brass, and iron, during which mankind gradually degenerated from a state of peace and holiness to one of violence and wickedness." But Mr. Bryant, after examining this point, very justly observes, — " We have here seen four divisions of times, in some of which the poet has endeavoured to make a distinction*, though no material difference subsists." It is in the Hindu mythology alone that the gradual corruption of mankind in these successive ages is clearly defined. But even this system is evidently imperfect, because the periodical destruction of the universe does not take place at the termination of each kali yug, or fourth age; and the transition, therefore, from an age of such guilt and impurity, to one of innocence and purity, without any previous convulsion of nature, seems to indicate that this could not have been the original opinion. The Purans, also, all concur in placing the appearance of Kalki, the tenth incarnation of Vishnu, for the destruction of the world, at the end of the current kali yug; and yet in several of these works it is as uniformly stated, or at least intimated, that the present is the first cycle of the four yugs of the Varaha Kalpa, and not the thousandth; at the termination of which last only the destruction of the universe takes place. But, notwithstanding this inconsistency, the opinion respecting these four ages is so intimately connected with the religious

* As in the silver, brazen, and the heroic of Hesiod. See Bryant's Anal. of Anc. Myth. vol. iv. p. 209. et seq.

system of the Hindus, and particularly with their division of time; and, on the contrary, it appears, in the mythology of the Greeks, so isolated and so like a poetic fiction; that it may be reasonably concluded that the latter derived from the former an opinion, which certainly is not of that obvious and natural kind which might have been adopted by two people, without any communication having subsisted between them.

The destruction and renovation of the universe, also, appears to have been an opinion generally prevalent in antiquity; and that it differed in no respect from the same doctrine which has been immemorially entertained by the Hindus will be evident from these words of Seneca: — " Ut ignis diversis locis ortus cito miscet incendium, flammis coire properantibus, sic momento redundantia pluribus locis maria se committent. Nec ea semper licentia undis erit, sed peracto exitio generis humani, exstinctisque pariter feris, in quarum homines ingenia transierant, iterum aquas terra sorbebit, natura pelagus stare, aut intra terminos suos furere coget: et rejectus e nostris sedibus, in sua secreta pelletur oceanus : et antiquus ordo revocabitur. Omne ex integro animal generabitur, dabiturque terris homo inscius scelerum, et melioribus auspiciis natus. Sed illis quoque innocentia non durabit, nisi dum novi sunt. Cito nequitia subrepit." * But the destruction and renovation of the universe was not merely a philosophical opinion, for Brucker remarks, — " According to the testimony of Plutarch, Clemens Alexandrinus, and Proclus, Orpheus held that this universe would be consumed, and that from this conflagration would arise a new world. Which dogma prevailed amongst almost all the people of antiquity, particularly those of the East and the North, and was adopted by Orpheus from his own Thracians and the Egyptians." Nor does the ascription of eternity to this universe, which was the general opinion of antiquity, detract from the identity of this doctrine as it was

* Seneca, Natural. Quæst. lib. iii. chap. 30. In the 28th chapter he had said, — " Per centena millia quibusdam locis æstus excurrit innoxius, et ordinem servat. Ad mensuram enim crescit, iterumque decrescit. At illo tempore solutis legibus sine modo fertur. Qua ratione, inquis? Eadem, qua conflagratio futura est. Utrumque fit, cum deo visum ordiri meliora, vetera finiri. Aqua et ignis terrenis dominantur; ex his ortus, et ex his interitus est."

adopted amongst both the Greeks and the Hindus: because, if the universe is, according to the belief of the latter, to endure for two hundred thousand billions of years, eternity may be very justly predicated of it; or, at least, it becomes almost impossible to conceive that it is not eternal.

It is, however, more difficult to form a satisfactory opinion with respect to whether or not the origin of the triads of antiquity ought to be ascribed to that country in which the Hindu religion originated. For Mr. Payne Knight contends that "the triform division of the attributes or modes of action of one First Cause seems to have been the first departure from simple theism, and the foundation of religious mythology in every part of the earth. To trace its origin to patriarchal traditions, or seek for it in the philosophy of any particular people, will only lead to frivolous conjecture, or to fraud and forgery, which have been abundantly employed upon this subject. Nor have repeated detection and exposure either damped the ardour, or abashed the effrontery, of those who still find them convenient to support their theories and opinions. Its real source is in the human mind itself, whose feeble and inadequate attempts to form an idea of one universal First Cause would naturally end in generalising and classing the particular ideas derived from the senses, and thus forming distinct, though indefinite, notions of certain attributes or modes of actions, of which the generic divisions are universally three,—such as goodness, wisdom, and power*; creation, preservation, and destruction; potential, instrumental, and efficient, &c. &c. Hence almost every nation of the world, that has deviated from the rude simplicity of primitive theism, has had its trinity in unity." † But it may be affirmed, without the fear of contradiction, that the notion of a *trinity in unity* is not only beyond the comprehension of human reason, and, therefore, such a one as could never have originated amongst the earlier races of mankind; but that not a trace of such a dogma can be found in any philosophical or

* Is it at all probable that divinity would be ascribed to any being who was supposed to possess one only, and not all, of these attributes?

† An Inquiry into the Sym. Lan. &c., part ix. sect. 229. Is not, however, the last assertion much too unqualified; and ought it not to be confined to the people descended from, or influenced by, that race who originally spoke the Sanscrit language?

religious system, except the Christian. In the Hindu religion it most assuredly does not exist; and even with regard to the triad of Plato, Brucker has observed, " But Plato, although he also mentions three principles, yet represents them under a perfectly different character [from that ascribed to the divine hypostases in the Christian religion]; for he does not consider them as a trinity subsisting in the divine essence, but merely as principles by which the formation of this universe may be explained.* But are these to be considered as attributes only of God, or not? To decide with certainty on a point which is involved in so much obscurity is impossible; but, judging from what has been already said with respect to ideas and the soul of the world, it appears probable that these principles, according to Plato, were not mere abstract notions, but that two of these principles were actual emanations from the infinite nature of God; *in reality distinct from God, but, on account of the source and origin from which they were derived, held to be, in a certain sense, one with him.*"†

But there seems to have been an essential difference between the triads of antiquity and the triad of the Hindu religion; because in the former, contrary to the opinion entertained respecting this point in the latter, the Supreme Being himself was considered to have been one of the divine hypostases. This apparent difference, however, may probably proceed from the very imperfect state in which the accounts of the religious systems of antiquity have been transmitted to latter ages; and the ancients, therefore, may have in reality believed that the Supreme Being was perfectly distinct from the three hypostases which had proceeded in an ineffable manner from his divine essence. It is, at least, unquestionable, that in Greek and Roman authors there is a frequent reference to some divine power superior to Jupiter, Neptune, and Pluto. Unfortunately the Orphic doctrine on this point has been so imperfectly preserved as to afford little assistance in its elucidation. But it appears sufficiently evident from the summary of these

* Brucker's words are, — " Sed, de principiis rerum genitarum sollicitus, rationem Dei et animam mundi, ad hunc ipsum mundum suo modo retulit, et ideas divinas materiæ impressas et animam ei inditam statuit."

† Historia Critica Philosophiæ, vol. i. p. 705.

doctrines given by Brucker, supported by the authorities which he has quoted, that the mundane egg was distinct from the one God; and, consequently, that, if the three heads of the being which issued from it are to be considered as divine hypostases, they also must necessarily have been distinct from the Supreme Being. For Brucker says,— "According to the Orphic theogony, on the egg being broken, a monstrous animal, in the form of a dragon, issued from it, which had joined to its own head that of a lion, and, in the middle of these two, another which had the countenance of a god. The former were called Hercules and Chronos, and the latter Phanes."* In another place he observes,— "It will be evident, from what we are about to say respecting the Orphic cosmogony, that Phanes, Uranus, and Chronos, cannot be identified with the Supreme Being. All, therefore, that Timotheus has written inaptly with respect to there being in God, according to the Orphic doctrines, a trinity of persons or divine natures, namely, counsel, light, and life, may be excused in a Greek sciolist, but ought not to be adopted by wise and learned men."† If, however, the dragon form and two of the heads be rejected, it seems obvious that the Phanes of Orpheus is absolutely identical with Viraj, or the primeval male of the Hindu religion‡; and it would, therefore, remain uncertain whether Orpheus admitted a triad or not: but Cudworth concludes his remarks on this point with these words of Timotheus:— Ὁ δε αυτος Ορφευς, εν τῃ αυτου βιβλῳ, συνεταξεν, ὁτι δια των αυτων τριων ονοματων μιας θεοτητος τα παντα εγενετο, και αυτος εστι τα παντα. *And the same Orpheus, in his book, declared that all things were made by one Godhead in three names, and that this God is all things.*§ When, also, the prevalence of the belief in a triad is considered, it may be justly concluded that this opinion was adopted by Orpheus; and that, adverting to the

* Historia Critica Philosophiæ, vol. i. p. 394.

† Ibid., 391.

‡ It is remarkable, also, that the meaning of *Viraj*, which is derived from a root signifying *to shine*, corresponds in this instance precisely with the meaning ascribed by Lactantius (De Div. Inst. lib. i. cap. 5.) to Phanes. For he says,— "Eundem etiam Φανητα nominat; id est apparentem, quia, cum adhuc nihil esset (visibile), primus ex infinito apparuerit." This is exactly the Hindu opinion, that the first manifested appearance was that of the Supreme Being under the form of the primeval male.

§ Intellectual System, book i. chap. iv. sect. 17.

general tenour of his doctrines, it is most probable that, according to them, the three hypostases were supposed to exist distinct from, and not united with, the divine essence of the Supreme Being.

If, therefore, a general belief in a triad of divine beings distinct from the one God has prevailed in antiquity; and if, as Cudworth thought, "it cannot well be conceived how such a trinity of divine hypostases* should be first discovered merely by human wit and reason;" it would necessarily follow that this opinion must have originated amongst some one people, by whom it was communicated to other nations. But it is in the Hindu religion alone that this dogma appears clear, consistent, and intelligible; and from it, therefore, it would seem most probable that the Egyptians, Greeks, and Romans derived so singular an opinion. Nor, supposing it to rest on a direct revelation from heaven, would this conclusion be invalidated; because there are no grounds, not even in the Old Testament, for believing that the revelations of God have never been communicated to any other people than the Hebrews. But to this supposition there is one strong objection: for I have before observed, that these divine hypostases, even in the Hindu religion, are altogether unnecessary for the formation, preservation, or destruction of the universe, since its existence and duration depend entirely on the original *fiat* of the Supreme Being; nor does more importance appear to have been ascribed to these hypostases in any other ancient philosophical or religious system. But this very circumstance must be a strong proof that no two people would, of themselves and without communication, have imagined the existence of such a triad; as it seems to have originated rather in some metaphysical notion, than in the contemplation of certain divine powers which were supposed to be actually exercised by these hypostases.

That the transmigration of souls was another of the Orphic doctrines, Brucker considers to be indisputable; though, from the want of such memorials respecting them as are free from suspicion, it is not possible to explain the precise nature of the opinions on that point

* Cudworth, of course, endeavours to prove that this was a *trinity in unity.*

which Orpheus may have entertained. But this dogma was adopted by Pythagoras; and its accordance with that of the Hindu religion is sufficiently evinced by these verses of Ovid: —

> "Omnia mutantur; nihil interit. Errat, et illinc
> Huc venit, hinc illuc, et quoslibet occupat artus
> Spiritus; eque feris humana in corpora transit,
> Inque feras noster; nec tempore deperit ullo.
> Utque novis fragilis signatur cera figuris,
> Nec manet ut fuerat, nec formas servat easdem,
> Sed tamen ipsa eadem est: animam sic semper eandem
> Esse, sed in varias doces migrare formas."
>
> *Metam.*, lib. xv. v. 165—172.

But I doubt much whether Brucker is correct in supposing that Orpheus held that the soul was an *emanation* from God, and that it must, therefore, necessarily exist until it becomes so purified as to admit of absorption in God, that fount from which it originally emanated. For, if emanation means an actual separation of the human from the supreme soul, so constant a discerption of the divine essence seems to be so impious a supposition, that it could never have been entertained by men who were impressed with the slightest sense of religion.* Indivisibility, also, is one of those attributes which are obviously indispensable for completing the notion of an All-perfect Being. Speculations, however, on the nature of God and of the soul, are so unadapted to the limited powers of human reason, that, on its being once assumed that the soul and the divine essence were of the same

* The Mohammedan Sufis, however, would certainly seem to entertain a similar opinion; and Sir W. Jones has, therefore, justly remarked: — "The modern Sufis, who profess a belief in the Koran, suppose, with great sublimity both of thought and of diction, an *express contract on the day of eternity without beginning*, between the assemblage of CREATED SPIRITS AND THE SUPREME SOUL FROM WHICH THEY WERE DETACHED," &c. On so abstruse a subject, however, it is difficult to ascertain the precise meaning of the figurative and poetic language employed by the Sufis, and to deduce from it accurate conclusions with respect to the opinions which they really entertain. But I have not yet been able to discover in Sanscrit literature any trace of the mysticism which Sir W. Jones ascribes to the Hindus. On the contrary, the identity of the human soul with the divine essence of the Supreme Being, and the possibility of man becoming sensible of this truth, are, amongst them, religious dogmas inculcated in plain and express terms, and not by allegories or figurative language.

nature, it must have become impossible to explain satisfactorily how they became disjoined, and how the soul became subject to all the pains and miseries inseparable from its union with matter. Thus, to guard against impiety, the Hindus firmly believe at the present day, and have believed from remote antiquity, in an evident absurdity; for they virtually maintain that the soul is *separated* and *not separated* from the divine essence, of which it is itself a part: and it is, therefore, possible that Orpheus and his disciples may have adopted the doctrine of emanation, without being aware that it led to notions altogether incompatible with the divine nature of God. Admitting this, however, to have been the case, the slight difference of opinion with respect to the origin of the soul would not detract from the identity which exists between the Hindu and Orphic doctrine, so far as it relates to the soul being in some ineffable manner a portion of the divine essence, to its being apparently separated from it, and to its being condemned to various transmigrations before it can be restored to its real nature.

I have before stated that, as far as I can ascertain, the worship of the lingam is not mentioned in the Vedas; but these sacred books have not yet been sufficiently examined to admit of its being conclusively determined that no allusion to this worship occurs in them. If, however, the Brahmanical religion be not indigenous to India, but introduced into it by a Brahmanical colony, it would appear most probable that this worship must have been known to the Brahmans previously to their emigration.* For, unless it be supposed that the adoration of so singular an object is one of those obvious and natural notions which would spontaneously occur to all the earlier races of mankind, it becomes evidently impossible to account for its existence in two countries so widely separated as India and Egypt; since the manner in which it could have been communicated from the latter to

* This supposition involves no contradiction: for the worship of the lingam might have been known to, and partially practised by, the Brahmans previously to their emigration into India; and yet it might not have acquired general celebrity until after the Vedas were composed. It would hence only follow, that this worship does not rest on the same authority as that on which all the other Hindu institutions are founded.

the former is evidently inexplicable.* That, also, both in the Hindu and Egyptian religions, the origin of this worship was ascribed to the same cause, seems unquestionable from this passage of Diodorus Siculus, which expresses the general opinion of antiquity:—"They say that the members of Osiris which were found, were, in this manner, honoured with sepulture; but that this virile member, having been thrown into the river by Typhon, could not be discovered. Isis, however, did not on this account the less cause it to be reverenced with divine honours; for she directed its image to be erected in temples, and prescribed its worship, so that the sacrifices and mysteries instituted in honour of *this god* became the most celebrated and the most venerated. Hence, when the Greeks received the rites and orgies of Dionusos from Egypt, this member was held in honour in the festivals and mysteries of that god, and (its image) was named Phallus." †

That this legend differs materially from the one respecting Shiva having been deprived of his manhood by the curse of the holy sages in the *Daruvanam* forest is obvious: but, if all the accessories of the two legends be rejected on account of their improbability, there will

* I may presume that no argument will be founded on the fabulous exploits of Osiris and Sesostris; and with respect to the conquest of India by Dionusos, or Bacchus, Strabo observes:—Και τα περι Ἡρακλεους δε, και Διονυσου, Μεγασθενης μεν μετ᾽ ολιγων πιστα ἡγειται· των δ᾽ αλλων οἱ πλειους, ὡν εστι και Ερατοσθενης, απιστα, και μυθωδη, καθαπερ και τα παρα τοις Ἑλλησιν. Ὁ μεν γαρ εν ταις Βακχαις ταις Ευριπιδου Διονυσος τοιαυτα νεανιευεται.

Λιπων δε Λυδων τας πολυχρυσους γυας,
Φρυγων τε, Περσων θ᾽ ἡλιοβλητους πλακας,
Βακτρια τε τειχη, την τε δυσχειμον χθονα
Μηδων, επελθων Αραβιαν τ᾽ ευδαιμονα,
Ασιαν τε πασαν. Lib. xv. p. 687.

In another place Strabo says:—Ἡ δε επι Ινδους στρατεια Διονυσου, και Ἡρακλεους, ὑστερογενη την μυθοποιιαν εμφαινει.—Lib. xi. p. 505.

† Diod. Sic. lib. i. chap. 22.

Herodotus also says:—Την δε αλλην αναγουσι ὁρτην τῳ Διονυσῳ οἱ Αιγυπτιοι, πλην χορων, κατα ταὐτα σχεδον παντα Ἑλλησι· αντι δε φαλλων, αλλα σφι εστι εξευρημενα ὁσον τε πηχυαια αγαλματα νευροσπαστα, τα περιφορεουσι κατα κωμας γυναικες, νευον το αιδοιον, ου πολλῳ τεῳ ελασσον εον του αλλου σωματος. προηγεεται δε αυλος· αἱ δε ἑπονται αειδουσαι τον Διονυσον. . . . Εγω μεν νυν φημι Μελαμποδα γενομενον ανδρα σοφον, μαντικην τε ἑωυτῳ συστησαι, και πυθομενον απ᾽ Αιγυπτου, αλλα τε πολλα εσηγησασθαι Ἑλλησι, και τα περι τον Διονυσον, ολιγα αυτων παραλλαξαντα.—Lib. ii. chap. 48, 49.

still remain the simple fact, that the phallus and the lingam were originally intended to represent nothing else than the virile members of Osiris and Shiva. This remark, therefore, of Mr. Payne Knight evidently rests on no grounds whatever: — "The Greeks usually represented the phallus alone as a distinct symbol, the meaning of which seems to have been among the last discoveries revealed to the initiated. It was the same, in emblematical writing, as the Orphic epithet παγγενετωρ, *universal generator*, in which sense it is still employed by the Hindus." * But most assuredly the Hindus ascribe no symbolical or mystic meaning to the lingam; and, unless the very improbable supposition that the worship of Osiris and Dionusos was founded on mere metaphysical notions and abstractions be adopted, it must seem most probable that the phallus, also, must have been the simple type of some object which was supposed to have previously existed. In which case the identity of the origin of the worship of the lingam and the phallus cannot be disputed; and it therefore merely remains to determine whether it is most likely that it was introduced into India by the Egyptians †, or that the Egyptians derived it from that people among whom the Hindu religion originated, and who, as I conceive, at first dwelt in Babylonia.

This conclusion, therefore, cannot be invalidated by either the difference of form under which the prototype was represented by the Brahmans, the Egyptians, and Greeks; nor by the still greater dissimilarity which appears to have existed in the manner in which they worshipped it. For it is most probable that, on account of its simplicity, the Brahmanical ritual may have originally prevailed in Egypt;

* An Inquiry into the Symb. Lang., &c., part i. sect. 23.

This is also the explanation given by Diodorus Siculus in these words: — Το δε μοριον του σωματος, το της γενεσεως αιτιον, τιμασθαι προσηκοντως, ὡς αν ὑπαρχον αρχεγονον της των ζωων φυσεως. Καθολου δε το αιδοιον ουκ Αιγυπτιους μονον, αλλα και των αλλων ουκ ολιγους καθιερωκεναι κατα τας τελετας, ὡς αιτιον της των ζωων γενεσεως. — Lib. i. chap. 88.

If this, however, were one of the secrets which were revealed only in the mysteries, how did it become so generally known, and how did authors venture to divulge it so explicitly?

† The whole structure of the Hindu religion must clearly evince the improbability of its having been introduced by Brahmans, who, like the philosophers of Greece, may have travelled into Egypt for instruction.

and that it only gradually degenerated into those scandalous orgies by which the festivals of Dionusos, in Greece, were disgraced. Not a trace, however, of such orgies can be discovered in the Hindu religion; and the speculations on this subject, therefore, in which some of the German literati have indulged, would excite surprise, were it not that one of their own countrymen has ascribed to the Germans the dominion of the air. But to find such a passage as the following, in a grave and celebrated review of a northern metropolis, is really astonishing:—"It is an indisputable fact, that the worship of Osiris, distinguished by the same attributes and emblems*, has continued in India, from the earliest ages to this day, under the appellation of Ishwara. *This*, we think, *may be completely proved* by a comparative survey of both, before, as patron of the vine, he assumed in Europe a new character. Osiris was adored in Egypt, and Bacchus in Greece, under the emblem of the phallus. It is under the same emblem that *he* is still venerated in Hindustan; and Phalla is one of the names of Ishwara in the dictionary of Amara Sinha.† The bull was sacred to him in Egypt. . . . In India, the bull is the animal on which he always appears mounted: hence one of his Sanscrit names, *Vrishadwaja*, signifying whose ensign is a bull. Plutarch informs us, that *Nilum patrem ac servatorem suæ regionis, ac defluxum Osiridis nominant.* The Ganges, *in like manner*‡, is fabled by the Hindus to flow from the tresses of Ishwara; hence another of his names, *Gangadhara,* the supporter of the Ganges. . . . The attendants of Ishwara resemble, in their frantic demeanour, the furious bacchants of the god of Naxos. Many tribes of imaginary beings compose his train: the Pramatha, whose name denotes intoxication; and the Jacchi, from whom he derives the appellation of Jacches§,

* Compare the figures of Osiris and Shiva which have been published in several collections of plates, and it must appear inconceivable how any writer could hazard such an assertion as this. It is by such obvious and consequently useless exaggeration and misstatement, that antiquarian researches are rendered so ridiculous.

† Another misstatement, open to detection by a mere reference to the Amara Kosha.

‡ Plutarch does not explain in what manner the Nile was considered to be *defluxus Osiridis*.

§ No such words exist in Sanscrit; but, in Bengal, the Sanscrit compound letter *Ksha* is pronounced *ka*; and I therefore suspect that these Jacchi ought to be *Yaksha*; but these are the attendants of Kubera, and not of Shiva.

or Lord of the Jacchi, corrupted into Jacchus by his western votaries. It is remarkable that many of the appellations by which the Greeks distinguish Bacchus, are also used by the Hindus ; but, instead of applying them to Baghesha * himself, the latter refer them to his son, whilst both nations have their legends to account for them. Thus, the Greeks named Bacchus, *Dimeter*, having two mothers ; the Hindus call Skanda, the son of Baghesha, *Dwimatri*, with the same signification. † *Pyrigenes*, born from fire, and its equivalent, in Sanscrit, *Agnija*, are respectively Greek and Indian appellatives of Bacchus and of Skanda. The title of Thriambus, we are told by Diodorus, was assumed by the Greek deity in his triumph after the conquest of India. Try-ambo, in like manner, is one of the most common appellations of the Indian Bacchus, but we are not aware of its signification." ‡

I have quoted the above long passage, because it exhibits a complete specimen of the erroneous opinions which have been expressed on this subject, and because the writer has thus complacently concluded, — " We believe we have done more than was requisite to prove the identity of the Egyptian, Grecian, and Indian divinity : for our readers will remark, that our proofs do not rest, in this instance, on analogy of *sounds*, which may undoubtedly be fortuitous ; but on that analogy, combined with the unity of the *attributes* denoted by those names, which it is impossible should be accidental." With regard, however, to the identity of Ishwara and Osiris, I have, in the second chapter of this work, endeavoured to evince that it is highly probable ; but I have not been able to discover, in the accounts of Osiris and Dionusos or Bacchus which have been preserved, the slightest resem-

* The writer had said before, — " The most ancient worship of which any trace is left in Hindustan, is that of Osiris or Bacchus, whose Indian names are Ishwara or Baghesha." But there is no such word in Sanscrit as *Baghesha* or *Vagesha ;* and, most unquestionably, Shiva has no such name or epithet.

† Never : but they call him *Shanmatura*, *six*-mothered, in consequence of his being suckled by the Krittika, or *six* pleiades ; from which circumstance, also, originated his six heads, and another of his epithets, *Shadanana*, six-countenanced.

‡ Edinburgh Review, vol. xvii. p. 316.

The last sentence contains so singular a mistake and confession, as would even render questionable the writer's acquaintance with Sanscrit. For the Sanscrit word intended is evidently Try-ambaka (pronounced Trimbaka), a very common appellation of Shiva, which signifies nothing more than *three-eyed.*

blance between these deities. It is also indisputable that Dionusos does not appear amongst the gods of Olympus, which have been celebrated by Homer; and Hesiod uses these remarkable words:—

> Καδμειη, δ' αρα οἱ Σεμελη τεκε φαιδιμον υἱον,
> Μιχθεισ' εν φιλοτητι, Διωνυσον πολυγηθεα,
> Αθανατον θνητη· νυν δ' αμφοτεροι θεοι εισιν. Θεογ., v. 940.*

Even Herodotus says,—Επειτεν δε χρονου πολλου διεξελθοντος, επυθοντο εκ της Αιγυπτου απικομενα τα ουνοματα των θεων των αλλων, Διονυσου δε ὑστερον πολλῳ επυθοντο.† But though that historian affirms that Dionusos is the Greek name of Osiris, he no where explains the reasons which induced him to consider that such dissimilar appellations were merely names, in two different languages, for one and the same god; nor does he specify any other characteristics than the phallus, from which it might be justly concluded that these deities were identical. The long account, also, of Dionusos, given by Diodorus Siculus, is equally unsatisfactory, and fully justifies these words, with which he has prefaced it:—Των δε παλαιων μυθογραφων και ποιητων περι Διονυσου γεγραφοτων αλληλοις ασυμφωνα, και πολλους και τερατωδεις λογους καταβεβλημενων, δυσχερες εστι περι της γενεσεως του θεου τουτου και των πραξεων ειπειν.‡ And Cicero says,—"Dionysos multos habemus: primum e Jove et Proserpina natum; secundum Nilo, qui Nysam dicitur interemisse; tertium, Caprio patre, eumque regem Asiæ præfuisse dicunt, cui Sabazia sunt instituta: quartum, Jove et Luna, cui sacra Orphica putantur confici; quintum, Niso natum et Thyone, a quo Trieterides constitutæ putantur."§ But, judging from the paintings of Osiris which have been preserved to the present day, it would seem unquestionable that, in Egypt, this god must have been

* These words of Apollodorus, lib. iii. c. 5, are equally remarkable:—Δειξας δε (Διονυσος) Θηβαιοις ὁτι θεος εστιν, ἡκεν εις Αργος· κἀκει παλιν ου τιμωντων αυτον, εξεμηνε τας γυναικας. . . . . Ὡς δε, μαθοντες αυτον θεον, ανθρωποι ετιμων· ὁ δε, αναγαγων εξ ᾁδου την μητερα, και προσαγορευσας Θυωνην, μετ' αυτης εις ουρανον ανηλθεν.

† Lib. ii. c. 52.

‡ Bib. Hist., lib. iii. cap. 62.

§ De Nat. Deor., lib. iii. cap. 58.

To these, however, should be added the Dionusos supposed to be the son of Jupiter and Ceres, and the more popular one, the son of Jupiter and Semele.

always represented under one and the same character; and, consequently, had Dionusos been originally identical with Osiris, it becomes impossible to understand how such an extraordinary difference of opinion with respect to his parentage and actions, as I have just pointed out, could have existed among the Greeks. *

If, however, the alleged identity of Osiris and Dionusos rests on no sufficient grounds, it will necessarily follow that the identity which it has been attempted to establish between Dionusos and Shiva must be equally fallacious. Professor Creuzer has endeavoured to prove that the worship of Dionusos was communicated from India, through Ethiopia and Egypt, to Greece †; but it is unnecessary to quote his arguments in support of this opinion, because they are founded on the

* Banier also remarks, — "On les divisoit en grands dieux, *Dii majorum gentium*, ou dieux du conseil, *Dii consuentes* ou *consulentes*; et en dieux des moindres nations, *minorum gentium*. Les premiers étoient les grands dieux, reconnus partout, surtout dans la Grece, et dans l'Italie. Les seconds étoient ceux qui avoient été ajoutés et associés aux anciens; et ils étoient particuliers à certains peuples. . . . . Les Grecs reconnoissoient douze de ces grands dieux, dont Ennius nous a conservé les noms : —

> "Juno, Vesta, Minerva, Ceres, Diana, Venus, Mars,
> Mercurius, Jovis, Neptunus, Vulcanus, Apollo."
>
> *La Mythologie*, &c., tom. i. p. 128.

But amongst these twelve great gods, it will be observed that Bacchus is not included.

† See Symbolik und Mythologik, vol. iii. p. 117. et seq.

I may, however, transcribe the following equally extraordinary remarks of Mr. Faber: — "Such being the case, the name of Dionus clearly leads us to identify him (Bacchus) with the Hindu *Deo Naush;* though the legend of that personage does not at present coincide so minutely with the classical and Egyptian accounts of Bacchus and Osiris, as it appears to have done at the time when Arrian flourished. Still, however, he is described as similarly subduing and civilising the whole world. Descending, according to the Purans, from the elevated plains of Little Bokhara, the arkite and paradisiacal Meru of Brahminical theology, he invaded with a numerous army the countries of Samarcand, Balkh, and Cabul, then inhabited by the Sacas and Sacasenas, the Saxons of our western part of the globe. Afterwards he conquered Iran, Egypt, and Ethiopia; and then, proceeding through Europe, he conquered the British Isles, the favourite abode of the god Lunus. Next he advanced into the northern parts of Europe and Siberia; and at length, having made himself master of China, all the countries which lie to the south of it, and the whole of Hindustan, he returned to the high plains of Meru, through the pass of Hardwar. These fabulous conquests of *Deo Naush* are evidently the same as those of Dionusus and Osiris, and they certainly relate to the same events!" — *Origin of Pagan Idolatry*, vol. ii. p. 272.

I must, however, observe that nothing so absurd as the above statement can be found in the Purans.

often-cited passages of ancient authors with respect to the identity of Osiris and Dionusos, and principally on the groundless statements of Polier and Wilford: for never is the king *Nahusha* designated *Deva Nahusha* in Sanscrit books; nor are there any conquests ascribed to him in the Purans. A material link, at the same time, in this identification is deficient; because, previously to its being adopted, it might have occurred to Professor Creuzer and other writers, that it was first indispensable to prove the *divinity* of Nahusha, and, also, that he was considered by the Hindus to be one and the same god as Shiva: for the impossibility of adducing such proof would at once have shown the very futile basis on which this hypothesis rested. But I may presume that the account of Shiva which I have given in the preceding pages will sufficiently evince that, with exception of the lingam and phallus, there is not the slightest resemblance between the characteristics, attributes, and worship of Shiva, and those of Dionusos: and from the consecration, therefore, of that symbol to both these gods, their identity cannot be justly inferred; since there is no improbability in the general opinion of antiquity, that the Greeks received this symbol from Egypt, and then, according to more than one writer, ascribed it, with its concomitant festivals and orgies, to the son of Jupiter and Semele. The Hindu religion, also, had most probably assumed its present form before the age of Homer, and, consequently, previously to the institution of the worship of Dionusos in Greece: for Mr. Payne Knight remarks,—"As there is no mention of any of the mystic deities, nor of any of the rites with which they were worshipped, in any of the genuine parts, either of the Iliad or Odyssey; nor any trace of the symbolical style in any of the works of art described in them, nor of allegory or enigma in the fables that adorn them; we may fairly presume that both the rites of initiation, and the worship of Bacchus, are of a later period, and were not generally known to the Greeks till after the composition of those poems." *

* An Inquiry into the Symb. Lang. &c., part i. sect. 22.

In section 20. Mr. Knight had also remarked: — "According to Herodotus, the name Dionysus or Bacchus, with the various obscene and extravagant rites that distinguished his worship, was communicated to the Greeks by Melampus, who appears to have flourished about four generations before the Trojan war, and who is said to have received his knowledge of

There is, however, one character ascribed to Dionusos, under which he might be identified with either Brahma or Narayana, or even Shiva, as he is also supposed, though not commonly, to have issued from the mundane egg: for Mr. Faber oberves:—"Though the Greeks so far corrupted his (Bacchus's) real history, as to represent him as one of the younger gods, yet the Orphic poet tells us that he was the first-born, and that, under the name of Dionusos, he was the first who came forth to the light of day from the floating egg within which he had been enclosed. He was then the oldest of all the divinities." * But it does not appear clearly from the Orphic poet that Phanes and Dionusos were one and the same personage; and, on the contrary, he expressly says,—

Διος και Περσεφονειης,
Αρρητοις λεκτροισι τεκνωθεις, αμβροτε δαιμον.

It is true that, in another hymn, he says,

Κρυφιον Διος ερνος.
Πρωτογον' ηρικεπαιε, θεων πατερ ηδε και υιε.

But what reliance can be placed on such an authority as this, which makes the same being *the father and the son of the gods?* If, however, Phanes and Dionusos were identified in the mysteries, as Plutarch affirms, this circumstance does not seem to have made any alteration

---

the subject from Cadmus and the Phœnicians, who settled in Bœotia. *The whole history, however, of this Phœnician colony is extremely questionable;* and we shall show in the sequel that the name Cadmus was probably a corruption of a mystic title of the Deity."

* Origin of Pagan Idolatry, vol. ii. p. 270.

Mr. Payne Knight also states:—"In this universal character, he (Bacchus) is celebrated by the Greek poets under the title of love or attraction, the first principle of animation, the father of gods and men, and the regulator and disposer of all things. He is said to *pervade the universe with the motion of his wings, bringing pure light; and thence to be called the splendid, the self-illumined, the ruling Priapus,*—light being considered, in this primitive philosophy, as the great nutritive principle of all things. Wings are attributed to him as the emblems of spontaneous motion; and HE IS SAID TO HAVE SPRUNG FROM THE EGG OF NIGHT, because the egg was the ancient symbol of organic matter in its inert state."—*An Inquiry into the Symb. Lang.*, part i. sect. 24.

in the character which was usually ascribed to Dionusos; and his production, therefore, from the mundane egg, must be considered to have been merely the application to him of some traditionary opinion which related to a more ancient deity.

The preceding coincidences, though of a general nature, will perhaps evince that there is an actual identity, or, at least, a remarkable similarity, in several essential points, between ancient and Hindu mythology. But, to the derivation of Grecian from Hindu mythology, two difficulties may be objected. The first that occurs is, there having been, among the Greeks, no distinct class intrusted with the priesthood. For the separation of the priesthood from the rest of the people, in India, Persia, Babylonia, Palestine, and Egypt, would seem to evince that, had Greece received its mythology from Asia, or even from Egypt, so important an accessary of all religious systems would have been also adopted. That the contrary, however, was the case, is undeniable; for, even in the time of Homer, sacrifices and other religious rites were performed by princes, and not by priests. To explain this remarkable circumstance, no sufficient reason occurs; because, had a portion of the priesthood of their native country not accompanied the Pelasgi in their migrations, still this class ought to have existed in Phrygia and other parts of Asia Minor: but, according to the Iliad, priests were equally unknown to the Trojans as to the Greeks. This difficulty, therefore, must be considered as one of those anomalies that do not admit of explanation, which too often occur in antiquarian researches; and it only remains to determine whether or not it is of so much weight as to overbalance the evidence, resulting from numerous coincidences, which attests that the similarity observable between the Hindu and Grecian mythology could not have existed unless the latter had been actually derived from the former.

Another difficulty arises from the opinion which is so well expressed in these verses of the Prometheus Vinctus of Æschylus:—

> "Thou dost thy message proudly, in high terms,
> Becoming well the servant of such lords.
> Your youthful power is new; yet vainly deem ye
> Your high-raised towers impregnable to pain.

Have I not seen two tyrants of the sky
Sink from their glorious state? And I shall see
A third, this present lord, with sudden ruin
Dishonourably fall. What! seem I now
To dread, to tremble at these new-raised gods?
That never shall their force extort from me." *

For the dethronement and expulsion from heaven of Cœlus by Saturn, and of Saturn by Jupiter, are circumstances which would seem to indicate that the Grecian mythology must have been derived from some other origin than the Hindu religion. Homer, indeed, ascribes the generation of the gods to Oceanus and Tethys†; but, in the following verses, he alludes to the deposition of Saturn:—

" For, lo! I haste to those remote abodes,
Where the great parents (sacred source of gods!),
Ocean and Tethys, their old empire keep
On the last limits of the land and deep:
In their kind arms my tender years were pass'd.
What time old Saturn, from Olympus cast,
Of upper heaven to Jove resign'd the reign,
Whelm'd under the huge mass of earth and main."

To such mutations, however, in the government of heaven, nothing similar occurs in Hindu mythology: for, though it is said in the Purans that in each Kalpa a new Indra presides over Swarga, or Olympus, and that whoever performs a hundred sacrifices of horses will obtain that dignity, yet I have not observed in those works any legend which describes Indra as having been deprived of his celestial sovereignty.‡ But, as the fables respecting Cœlus and Saturn are so incompatible with the notions which even the rudest men have entertained of a Supreme Being, and as they are not recognised in the Orphic doctrines, it seems extremely questionable that these fables formed part of the primitive mythology of the Greeks.

* Verse 953—961. of the original. I have availed myself of Dr. Potter's translation, except in one word.

† Ωκεανον τε, θεων γενεσιν, και μητερα Τηθυν. — Il. Ξ. v. 101.

‡ When Nahusha was chosen by the gods to supply the place of Indra, the latter had voluntarily withdrawn from heaven in order to expiate the sin of *Brahmanicide*, which he had incurred by slaying the Asura Vritra.

But, from the preceding chapter, the striking similarity which exists between the wars of Jupiter and the gods of Olympus with the Titans *, and those of Indra and the gods of Swarga with the Asuras, will be obvious. Nor would it, perhaps, be carrying the coincidence too far, to find a resemblance between the march of Bali from Patalam or Tartarus, to Swarga or Olympus, and the consequent flight of Indra and the other gods under the forms of different animals, and these verses of Ovid:—

> " Bella canit Superûm; falsoque in honore Gigantas
> Ponit, et extenuat magnorum facta Deorum:
> Emissumque ima de sede Typhoea terræ
> Cœlitibus fecisse metum; cunctosque dedisse
> Terga fugæ, donec fessos Ægyptia tellus
> Ceperit, et septem discretus in ostia Nilus.
> Huc quoque terrigenam venisse Typhoea narrat,
> Et se mentitis Superos celasse figuris.
> Duxque gregis, dixit, fit Jupiter; unde recurvis
> Nunc quoque formatus Libys est cum cornibus Ammon.
> Delius in corvo, proles Semeleïa capro,
> Fele soror Phœbi, nivea Saturnia vacca,
> Pisce Venus latuit, Cyllenius ibidis alis."
>
> *Metamor.*, lib. v. v. 319—331.

To pass, however, from coincidences of so general a nature, it must be acknowledged that it is much more difficult to determine satisfactorily whether or not any identity exists between the respective deities of Hindu and Grecian mythology; because, even in the time of Homer and Hesiod, the attributes of the Grecian deities had become so effaced or incongruous, that it is almost impossible to ascertain the peculiar character and functions which were, no doubt, originally ascribed to each of them. It may, therefore, be doubted whether

* In words passing from one language into another, it is difficult to determine which of the cases of the noun would be adopted. But there appears an unquestionable identity between the accusative case of the Sanscrit noun *Daity-am*, and the nominative of the Greek one Τιταν, and the identity is still more striking in the genitive cases plural *Daityānām*, Τιτανων.

The Titans are generally said to have been the children of Cœlus and Tellus; but Diodorus Siculus, in speaking of the gods of the Atlantes and Cretans, says that their mother was named *Titæa*, who was afterwards denominated Tellus, and the name of the mother of the *Daityas* was *Diti*.

Jupiter, Neptune, and Pluto ought to be considered as a proper triad; for they appear not under that spiritual character which is so essential to the conception of a divine hypostasis formed from the essence of the Supreme Being.* Possibly, however, other attributes may have been ascribed to them in the primitive state of the Grecian mythology; but if so, these have been long consigned to oblivion, and it is hence impossible to discover any resemblance between these three gods and Brahma, Vishnu, and Shiva, as divine hypostases. Jupiter, also, is the only one of them who was generally invoked by both the Greeks and Romans as the one God; under which character, however, he seems, from several circumstances, to bear a marked resemblance to Shiva. For the account given by Pausanias of the statue mentioned in the note below seems deserving of attention, because it is such a traditionary story as might have been easily preserved by the priests of the temple. This statue that writer describes as having had two eyes in their natural places, and one in the forehead, and as having originally belonged to Priam. His conjecture, however, respecting the intention of the carver in giving this wooden image three eyes, is evi-

* Cudworth, however, remarks, — "That these three, Jupiter, Neptune, and Pluto, were not three really distinct substantial beings, but only so many several names for one Supreme God (according to the true and natural theology of the Pagans), is thus plainly declared by Pausanias in his Corinthiacs; he there expounding the meaning of a certain statue of Jupiter with *three* eyes (called the Country Jupiter of the Trojans) in this manner:— *Τρεις δε οφθαλμους εχειν επι τῳ δε αν τις τεκμαιροιτο αυτον· Δια γαρ εν ουρανῳ βασιλευειν, οὑτος μεν λογος κοινος παντων εστιν ανθρωπων. Ὁν δε αρχειν φασιν ὑπο γης, εστιν επος των Ὁμηρου Δια ονομαζον και τουτον.*

Ζευς τε καταχθονιος, και επαινη Περσεφονεια.

Αισχυλος δε ὁ Ευφοριωνος καλει Δια και τον εν θαλασσῃ· τρισιν ουν ὁρωντα εποιησεν οφθαλμοις ὁστις δη ουν ὁ ποιησας, ἁτε εν ταις τρισι ταις λεγομεναις ληξεσιν αρχοντα τον αυτον τουτον θεον. Now that this statue of Jupiter *was made to have three eyes, one may guess this to have been the reason; because, first, the common speech of all men make* Jupiter *to reign in the heaven: again, he that is said to rule under the earth is, in a certain verse of Homer, called Zeus or Jupiter too; namely, the infernal or subterraneous Jupiter, together with Proserpina: and, lastly, Æschylus, the son of Euphorion, calls that god, who is the king of the sea, also Jupiter. Wherefore this statuary made Jupiter with three eyes, to signify that it is one and the same god which ruleth in those three several parts of the world, the heaven, the sea, and the earth.* Whether Pausanias was in the right or no, as to his conjecture concerning this three-eyed statue of Jupiter, it is evident that himself and other ancient Pagans acknowledged Jupiter, Neptune, and Pluto to be but three several names and partial considerations of one and the same God who ruleth over the whole world." — *Intellectual System*, book i. chap. iv. sect. 32.

dently, a fanciful or philosophical, but not a traditionary, explanation of the real cause; and this, consequently, may have been forgotten, though the statue itself preserved the remembrance of Jupiter having been, in remote times, thus represented. But three eyes form one of the distinguishing characteristics of Shiva, and these are considered by the Hindus to be the sun, moon, and fire. Lilius Gyraldus also observes, "*Lapis*, qui et ab aliquibus *Lapideus Jupiter*, apud Romanos sanctissimum jusjurandum: Gellius. M. Cicero in Fam. ad Trebatium in septima, *Jovem Lapidem jurare.* Apuleius de Deo. Socr. *Quid igitur jurabo, per Jovem Lapidem?* .... Consueverunt quoque Athenienses, ut Aristoteles in Repub. Atheniens. et Philochorus prodiderunt, ad lapidem quendam juramenta facere. Demosthenes in oratione in Cononem, και προς λιθον αγοντες, και εξορκουντες, id est, *ad lapidem agentes, et ejurantes.*" Is it, therefore, too forced a supposition to conclude that these sacred stones had been at one time consecrated to Jupiter, in the same manner as the lingam to Shiva; and that their sanctity had been immemorially preserved, though its real cause had long ceased to be remembered? *

But it is between *Jupiter*, as the ruler of Olympus, and the other Grecian deities subject to his authority, and *Indra* with his heavenly host the dwellers in Swarga, that the resemblance appears most remarkable. For the qualities pride and lust, which are particularly ascribed to Jupiter, are those also by which Indra is peculiarly characterised; and as Jupiter is θεων ὑπατος, so is Indra *Surapati* (*angelorum dominus*). Jupiter was, also, called in Latin *Diespiter*, and Indra is named *diwaspati* (*diei dominus*): the former was denominated pluvius Jupiter, and ομβριος Ζευς; while the latter presides over and dispenses

* That this supposition is highly probable is evinced by the mention, which occurs in ancient writers, of sacred stones, without any sufficient reason being assigned for their sanctity. But it is at once satisfactorily explained by supposing them to have been originally lingams, the proper worship of which had been by some means superseded, though they still continued to be venerated. It is at the same time very remarkable that the description of the statue of the god Heliogabalus, as it existed in Phœnicia in A. D. 218, is precisely the same as that of a lingam without a base; for Herodian thus describes it: — Αγαλμα μεν ουν, ὥσπερ παρ' Ἑλλησιν η Ῥωμαιοις ουδεν ἑστηκε χειροποιητον, θεου φερον εικονα· λιθος δε τις εστι μεγιστος, κατωθεν περιφερης, ληγων εις οξυτητα. κωνοειδες αυτῳ σχημα, μελαινα τε ἡ χροια. — Lib. v. cap. 3.

rain: and both are distinguished by being armed with the thunderbolt. But what renders this similarity still more striking is, that the term *Zeus**, for which so many strange etymologies have been proposed, supposing it to have been originally written with the digamma, is evidently identical with one of the epithets of Indra, namely, *dewesha*, (*deorum dominus*) †; and the irregular genitive case *Dios* is clearly the genitive of the first word of this compound Sanscrit term, *dewasya*. *Zen* (Ζην), however, may have been derived from *isham*, the accusative case of *isha*, a name of Shiva.

If the functions, also, ascribed to the other Grecian deities be only considered, *Neptune* would become the same as *Varuna* the god of the ocean, and *Pluto* as *Yama* the sovereign of the dead. But I have not been able to discover any Sanscrit term which resembles either Poseidon or Neptune, though a common epithet of Varuna is *Pashi*, from the noose which he carries, and this word might perhaps have formed the first part of *Poseidon*. It is singular, however, that *Adhas* in Sanscrit, and *Hades* in Greek, equally signify the regions below the earth, and that from Hades Pluto derived one of his names. *Orcus*, likewise, is equally a name of the lower regions and of Pluto, and, in its accusative case, it bears a strong resemblance to the Sanscrit *uragam*, a snake; from the abode of which reptiles in the lower regions these are called, in the Sanscrit, *uraga-sthanam*.

Another Sanscrit word, *arah*, gen. *arasya*, which signifies the planet Mars, is obviously identical with the Greek *Ares*, *Areos*, the name of the god Mars; nor, when the appearance and astrological character of this planet are considered, can its conversion into the god of war by the Greeks be deemed improbable.‡ Mr. Whish, however,

* Mr. Payne Knight, in his Analysis of the Greek Alphabet, p. 32., observes:—"When a consonant aspirate follows a mute, as in the Z, Ξ, and Ψ, the preceding vowel, or rather the syllable taken collectively, must necessarily be long; for though the Δ or ΤΣ, the Γ or ΚΣ, and the Β or ΠΣ are each signified by one character, they never completely coalesce in sound. But, as it is well known, Ζευ; was also written Δσευς; and Phurnut. de Nat. Deor. c. 2. even says,—Παρα τισι δε και Δευς λεγεται (ὁ Ζευς)."—*See Knight's Inquiry into Symb. Lang.*, part i. sect. 4. and note.

† This epithet is also indiscriminately applied to Brahma, Vishnu, and Shiva.

‡ Dupuis remarks:—"En suivant ces raisons d'analogie, on aperçoit tout de suite, pourquoi la planète de Mars, qui est d'un rouge presque couleur de sang, a été réputée

in a very curious Memoir, contained in the Transactions of the Madras Literary Society, has endeavoured to prove that the Hindus derived the names of the planets from the Greeks. But the term *arah*, in Sanscrit, also signifies *brass*, and *a shoemaker's awl or knife*; and it is, therefore, very improbable that such meanings would have been given to it, had the word not existed in the language before it was introduced into it by a foreigner. It is likewise remarkable that, with the exception of Heli, clearly a Sanscrit word, the names of the other five planets, and of the twelve signs of the zodiac, given by Mr. Whish, are most probably Greek and not Sanscrit; and it might hence be concluded that Yavanacharya had adopted the two Sanscrit words *Arah* and *Heli* on account of their similarity to the Greek ones.*

Γη μεν εστιν ή Ἡρα, καθαπερ ειρηται, says Eusebius, quoting Plutarch †, and *Ira* is one of the Sanscrit names for the earth. But, unless this explanation be admitted, it would be in vain to attempt identifying Juno ‡ with any of the Hindu goddesses. *Ceres*, however, both in name and attributes, is identifiable with *Shri* or *Lakshmi*; for, in the vernacular dialects of India, nothing is more common than interposing the short *a* between two conjoined consonants of a Sanscrit word; and supposing the accusative case to be pronounced *Sharim*, as the Latins had no such sound as *sh*, the identity of *Sharim* and *Cerem* can scarcely

---

sinistre et de dangereuse influence par les astrologues, et pourquoi le dieu Mars a eu sous son domaine la guerre sanglante et les combats meurtriers. Si sa couleur lui a fait assigner la fonction cruelle de verser le sang, son voisinage du soleil, dont il reçoit de si près la chaleur, le remplit de l'ardeur bouillante, qu'allume la colère, et qui provoque les combats et le carnage." A little farther on Dupuis quotes the opinion of the ancients on this point, given by Porphyry, as preserved by Eusebius: — "*Quant à Mars, à qui ils [les anciens] donnoient les qualités ignées et brûlantes, ils le crurent fait pour provoquer les guerres, et pour répandre le sang.*" — *Origine des Cultes*, tom. i. p. 141.

* My ignorance of astronomy, and unacquaintance with the works referred to by Mr. Whish, prevent my forming any opinion with respect to the correctness of the argument which he has maintained with so much ingenuity. But I have before observed, that, whatever innovations may have been admitted by the cultivators of astronomy in India, these were restricted entirely to that science, and in no manner affected the Sanscrit language, literature, or religion.

† Præp. Evang., lib. iii. cap. 1.

‡ Varro, also, De Ling. Lat., lib. 4., says, — "Quod Jovis Juno conjux, et is cœlum hæc terra."

be questioned. The Greek name *Demeter* seems, also, allowing for the suppression of the digamma, to be the same as the Sanscrit *Dewamatr;* an appellation applied to *Shri,* when she appears as the energy of Vishnu, and one of the eight heavenly mothers. *Minerva,* likewise, under her warlike character, seems identifiable with *Devi,* nor is the origin of these two goddesses altogether dissimilar, though in the one mythology she is described as springing from the head of Jupiter alone, and in the other as appearing from the effulgence emitted from the glances of all the gods. Nor would it perhaps be an unfounded etymology to suppose that her Greek name, *Athene,* was derived from *Ishani,* an appellation of Devi. In her character, however, of the goddess of genius and science, she closely resembles Sarasvati.

For *Hephaistos* or *Vulcan,* and the inferior deity *Æolus,* I can find no corresponding names in Hindu mythology; but the functions assigned to them and to *Agni* and *Vaiu* are clearly the same. It is, however, impossible to identify Mercury and Venus, either in name or attributes, with any Hindu deity. With regard to *Vesta,* Mr. Payne Knight observes; — " Vesta, whose symbol was fire, was held to be, equally with Ceres, a personification of the earth, or rather of the genial heat which pervades it, to which its productive powers were supposed to be owing; wherefore her temple at Rome was of a circular form, having the sacred fire in the centre, but no statue." * But he quotes the following line from the Fasti of Ovid: —

> " Nec tu aliud Vestam quam vivam intellige flammam;

in which character this goddess would correspond, according to the Hindu mythology, with *Swaha* the spouse of Agni.† In Hesiod, however, in the poems ascribed to Homer, and in Apollodorus, the sun and moon are represented as distinct deities from Apollo and Diana; but in this case the regents of those great luminaries would have held no place among

* Inquiry into the Symb. Lang., &c., part ii. sect. 42.

† But Natalis Comes, quoting Posidonius, observes, p. 897.; — " Nam cum Vesta, Saturni filia, prima domos exstruere invenisset, intra domos ubique pingebatur, quo et domos servaret, et custos esset habitantium;" and it is therefore remarkable that, in Sanscrit, *Vastu* not only signifies the site or foundation of a house, but that, in the Brahmanical ritual, there is a particular form of worship prescribed under the name of *Vastu-puja,* or the worship of Vastu.

the gods of Olympus, which must seem highly improbable. That, indeed, some strange confusion has taken place in the attributes ascribed to these two deities appears very evident; but, considering the general structure of the two mythologies, it may perhaps be justly concluded that *Apollo* * and *Diana* were originally the same as *Surya* and *Soma,* with the exception of the Greeks having represented the moon under the female sex.

It will hence, perhaps, appear that, even with respect to the twelve great deities of Greece and Rome, there is such a striking similarity in names, functions, or attributes, between them and the deities of the mythology which still prevails in India, as to leave no doubt but that the religious systems of these countries were derived from one and the same origin. But too little is known of the gods of the Thracians, to admit of its being determined whether the mythology of that people was also originally of a similar nature. As Orpheus, however, was a Thracian, and as the Orphic doctrines, on several essential points, are identical with those which have been entertained from time immemorial by the Hindus, it may, perhaps, be justly concluded that the primitive religion of the Thracians differed not from that of the Hindus. Its having subsequently assumed that simple form among the Thracians which is described by Herodotus and other writers, and among the Germans which is described by Cæsar and Tacitus, seems to have been a necessary consequence of that barbarous state in which the Thracians, though increasing in numbers, and occupying new countries, lived for so many ages. It is useless, therefore, to attempt to discover any coincidences between their rude idolatry and the more perfect mythology of the Hindus; and, most assuredly not the slightest similarity exists between the latter and the still more barbarous system of belief which is exhibited in the Eddas.

But it is certainly a very remarkable circumstance, that an acquaintance with the seven days of the week, so familiar from remote

* It seems, also, more probable that Apollo derived his epithet of *Grynæus* from *Ghrini,* one of the Sanscrit names of the sun, than from a town or sacred grove in Asia Minor; and it may not appear unlikely that another of his epithets, *Carnæus,* is likewise derived from *Kirana,* a synonyme, in Sanscrit, for *Surya,* or the sun.

antiquity to the people who originally spoke the Sanscrit language, though unknown to the Greeks and Romans, should have been preserved among the Germans. It is true, indeed, that among them the days received their names from their principal deities, and not merely from the planets, which, in Hindu mythology, are considered only as celestial beings of an inferior description. But, though religion must have existed before astronomy, still the transferring by the Germans of the names of their deities to the seven planets and the days of the week, in order to effect so singular a division of time, proves not that this was of indigenous invention : for Delambre has observed ; — "Il en est de même des jours de la semaine et de leurs noms planétaires, comme au zodiaque, il leur faut une origine commune." This transfer, at the same time, explains the difference which exists between the Teutonic and Sanscrit names of the days, among which the only one that can be identified is *Woden*, which bears a great similarity to *Buddham*, the accusative case of *Buddha*, the regent, according to the Hindus, of the planet Mercury.* There seems, also, to be no doubt but that the Germans selected the names of the same planets to designate the days of the week, which have been immemorially used for the same purpose by the Hindus; and that, in both Germany and India, their consecutive order was the day of the Sun, the Moon, Mars, Mercury, Jupiter, Venus, and Saturn. With the exception, however, of this remarkable circumstance, I have been unable to discover any other coincidence between the religious systems of the Hindus and of the Teutonic people.†

* The strange mistakes into which several writers have been led by identifying the regent of this planet with Buddha, a perfectly distinct personage (see ante, p. 267.), will be sufficiently exemplified by these remarks of Mr. Faber : — "As the Goths and Saxons, then, emigrated from the Indian Caucasus, and as the Scaldic traditions of their descendants positively declare the worship of their god Woden to have been brought into Europe by a colony of Asæ or Asiatics, it seems impossible not to conclude that Woden was the identical divinity whom their ancestors had venerated while yet occupying their original settlements in the East. But that divinity was certainly Buddha ; for Buddha has ever been the god of the Chusas of Mount Meru. We are compelled, therefore, to believe, even *à priori*, that Buddha and Woden are the same deity, and, consequently, that the theology of the Gothic and Sanscrit tribes was a modification of Buddhism." — *Origin of Pagan Idolatry*, vol. ii. p. 354.

† On what grounds Sir W. Jones made this assertion (Works, vol. i. p. 123.) I cannot

It will be observed that, in the preceding pages, I have not adverted to the ancient religion of Persia; but no account of it previous to Zardusht has been preserved, though some Mohammedan writers, on very questionable authority, state it to have been Sabaism. The questions, therefore, to be determined are, whether the Zoroaster of the Greeks and the Zardusht of the Parsees are the same person; and, if not, whether the Magian religion existed previously to its being established by the latter. For, if the doctrines peculiar to this religion were not known before the time of Darius Hystaspes, it is perfectly obvious that they are of much too recent a date, to admit of their being employed with propriety in the illustration of other more ancient religious systems. But Bryant has observed; — "This learned man (Hyde) supposes all these personages, the Mede, the Medo-Persic, the Proconnesian, the Bactrian, the Pamphylian, &c., to have been one and the same. This is very wonderful, as they are by history apparently different. He, moreover, adds, that, however people may differ about the origin of this person, yet all are unanimous about the time when he lived. To see that these could not all be the same person, we need only to cast our eye back upon the evidence which has been collected above; and it will be equally certain that they could not be all of the the same era." *

L'Abbé Foucher, also, who adopts the hypothesis of there having been two Zoroasters, remarks; — "Je ne m'étonnerois pas qu'on mît Zoroastre au rang des auteurs apocryphes, s'il avoit vécu long-temps avant la guerre de Troie, et qu'il eût été contemporain de Ninus; car, comme Pline le remarque très-bien, par quel prodige ses ouvrages seroient-ils venus jusqu'à nous, au travers de tant de révolutions, sans qu'on voie une succession non interrompue de disciples intéressés à

---

imagine: — "For," he remarks, "I confidently assume that the Goths and the Hindus originally gave the same appellations to the stars and planets, adored the same false deities, performed the same bloody sacrifices, and professed the same notions of rewards and punishments." I can only say that I have been unable to discover this identity, or even the slightest resemblance between the Brahmanical and Scandinavian rituals and religious systems.

* Analysis of Ancient Mythology, vol. ii. p. 392. 8vo ed.

les conserver. *Mirum hoc imprimis durasse memoriam artemque tam longo ævo, commentariis non intercidentibus, præterea nec claris nec continuis successionibus custoditam.* Mais si l'on reconnoît, avec ce judicieux écrivain, un dernier Zoroastre, contemporain du père de Xerxès, alors le prodige cesse. Je ne dirai rien de l'ancien Zoroastre qui vivoit sous le règne de Cyaxare premier; s'il a laissé quelques mémoires, il n'est pas douteux qu'on ne les ait conservés avec soin. Mais je n'insiste avec Pline que sur le dernier Zoroastre, et je dis que non seulement il est vrai-semblable qu'il a laissé quelque chose par écrit, mais qu'il seroit contre toute vrai-semblance qu'il ne l'eût pas fait." * L'Abbé Foucher, however, places the death of the second Zoroaster in about the year 630 B. C., which would still render the Magian the most recent of ancient religions. It is at the same time undeniable that the peculiar and characteristic tenet of the religion established by the Zardusht of the Parsees is the doctrine of the two principles of good and evil; and yet Cudworth observes: — "However, from what hath been declared, we conceive it doth sufficiently appear, that this *ditheistic* doctrine of a good and evil god, asserted by Plutarch and the Manicheans, was never so universally received amongst the Pagans as the same Plutarch pretendeth. Which thing may be yet further evidenced from hence, because the Manicheans professed themselves not to have derived this opinion from the Pagans, nor to be a subdivision under them, or schism from them, but a quite different sect by themselves."† But had Pythagoras been instructed by the second Zoroaster, as l'Abbé Foucher supposes, or had his doctrines even been in existence at that time, it must seem highly improbable that no notice of them should occur in any ancient writer until Plutarch.

It will hence be evident, that the writers who have employed the Magian in illustration of other ancient religions, have neglected that most essential point, of first satisfactorily establishing its greater antiquity. For whether its invention be placed in the seventh or sixth

* Mémoires de l'Académie des Insc. tom. xxvii. p. 301.

† Intellectual System, book i. chap. iv. sect. 13. So little assistance, even on this point, had Cudworth derived from his great erudition, that he actually questions whether Zardusht had really taught such a doctrine.

century before the Christian era is quite immaterial, because its relative recentness would be equally evident; and that it cannot be placed earlier seems sufficiently proved. It becomes, therefore, unnecessary to enter into any discussion with respect to the authenticity of the writings ascribed to Zardusht *, or to whether any similarity exists between his religious system and that of the Hindus; for the latter had received its present form long before the other was invented.

The Chaldean cosmogony, also, of Berosus, appears in too questionable a shape to admit of any remarks being founded upon it, were it even less absurd and extravagant than it is: for Berosus lived about the time of Alexander the Great, or perhaps later; and even Bryant admits, — "There is a large extract from this author, taken from the Greek of Alexander Polyhistor, and transmitted to us by Eusebius, which contains an account of these first occurrences in the world. But it seems to be taken by a person *who was not well acquainted with the language in which it was supposed to be written*, and has made an irregular and partial extract, rather than a genuine translation. And as Berosus lived at a time when Babylon had been repeatedly conquered, and the inhabitants had received a mixture of many different nations, there is reason to think that the original records, of whatever nature they may have been, were much impaired, and that the natives, in the time of Berosus, did not perfectly understand them." † The existence, at the same time, of the books, which Berosus affirmed to have been preserved for 2,150,000 years ‡, is so improbable a circumstance as to deprive this writer of all credibility; and it may, therefore, be

* That the religion of Zardusht existed nearly in the same state as that in which the Parsees have preserved it to the present day, some centuries before the Christian era, I believe; but I as firmly believe that the Zendavesta is not only a spurious production of comparatively modern times, but that it is also in every respect totally unworthy of attention. For I concur entirely in the justness of this dilemma, proposed by Sir W. Jones to Anquetil du Perron: — "Ou Zoroastre n'avait pas le sens commun, ou il n'écrivit pas le livre que vous lui attribuez: s'il n'avait pas le sens commun, il fallait le laisser dans la foule, et dans l'obscurité; s'il n'écrivit pas ce livre, il était impudent de le publier sous son nom."

† Analysis of Ancient Mythology, vol. iv. p. 122.

‡ This number is taken from the Armenian edition of the Chronicon of Eusebius, but Syncellus has only 150,000 years. Either of these numbers, however, is absurdly extravagant.

justly concluded, that there are no grounds whatever for supposing that his cosmogony, supposing it to have been faithfully given by Polyhistor, exhibits a correct view of the opinions which were entertained on this subject by the ancient Babylonians.

There is, however, a remarkable peculiarity in the Hindu religion, of which but faint traces are discoverable in other ancient religions: for the legends upon which it is founded are supposed to describe events which took place, not only during a period which ended in the year 3102 B. C., after it had lasted for 3,888,000 years; but also in the anterior renovations of the universe, which are believed to occur at the expiration of 864,000,000 years of mortals. The extravagance of such numbers is self-evident; but the singularity of the conception, though it is impossible to understand in what process of reasoning it could have originated, requires attention, because upon it depend the whole system of Hindu mythology, and the apparent variances which are observable in it. For, though the renovation of the universe, according to the opinion of the Hindus, is correctly represented in these verses of Virgil,—

> "Ultima Cumæi venit jam carminis ætas;
> Magnus ab integro sæclorum nascitur ordo.
> Jam redit et Virgo, redeunt Saturnia regna;
> *Jam nova progenies cœlo* demittitur alto.*
> * * * * *
> Alter erit tum Tiphys, et altera quæ vehat Argo
> Delectos heroas: erunt etiam altera bella;
> Atque iterum ad Trojam magnus mittetur Achilles."

—yet a difference occasionally takes place in the names and actions of the deities and heroes, notwithstanding that they are still considered to be the same personages who thus successively reappear on each renovation. But the present age, or kali yug, of which 4930 years have expired, is considered to be so sunk in vice and impiety, as to render it unworthy to be distinguished by the illustrious deeds of either god, saint, or hero. It is thus in the past, removed to an inconceivable distance, that the Brahmans have placed all the circumstances relating to their religion which seem to rest on facts; and the impossibility, therefore, of reducing them to historical accuracy must be too obvious

* See ante, p. 228. l. 18.

to require remark. Nor is any attempt made in the Purans to connect these remote events with the occurrences of the kali yug, which last, indeed, appears to have been considered of too base a description to deserve the slightest notice: for the following verses of Ovid do not exaggerate the hideous picture of the present age which is given in Sanscrit works; and the Latin poet has altogether omitted the indifference and contempt shown to Brahmans and religion, the degeneracy of the Brahmans, and the confusion of castes and occupations, on which the Brahman writer dwells with so much indignation:—

> "Protinus irrumpit venæ pejoris in ævum
> Omne nefas: fugere pudor, verumque, fidesque;
> In quorum subiere locum fraudesque, dolique,
> Insidiæque, et vis, et amor sceleratus habendi.
> * * * * *
> Vivitur ex rapto. Non hospes ab hospite tutus,
> Non socer a genero; fratrum quoque gratia rara est.
> Imminet exitio vir conjugis, illa mariti:
> Lurida terribiles miscent aconita novercæ:
> Filius ante diem patrios inquirit in annos.
> Victa jacet pietas; et virgo cæde madentes
> Ultima cœlestum terras Astræa reliquit."
>
> *Metamorph.* l. i. v. 128. et seq.

I have thus pointed out such coincidences between ancient and Hindu mythology as, I think, will not be disputed. Having no hypothesis to maintain, I have contented myself with stating them in as few words as possible: nor have I considered it necessary to establish their identity or similarity by argument; far less to support this affinity by adducing questionable circumstances, the applicability of which no reasoning would satisfactorily evince. But it must be remembered, that the derivation of the Greek, Etruscan, Latin, and Thracian religious systems from the mythology which prevails in India at the present day, depends not solely on the remarks contained in the preceding pages, but that it is intimately connected with the philological arguments contained in my former work: for, if I have in that work rendered it highly probable that the Greek, Latin, and Teutonic languages were derived from Sanscrit, through the medium of the Pelasgic, it will, no doubt, be admitted that a less degree of evidence, than would otherwise be requisite, may suffice to evince that the

Pelasgi also received their religion from that people who originally spoke Sanscrit; and that they subsequently, in the course of their migrations, introduced it into Thracia, Greece, Etruria, and Latium. Whether or not the preceding pages contain such evidence, the reader must decide; but it will not, perhaps, be denied, that it at least shows how much more probable it is that the Grecian mythology was derived from Asia Minor than from Egypt: and in such case it appears clearly, from tradition and history, that there is no other people among whom it can be supposed to have originated, than that race of men who first spoke Sanscrit; since, even after the lapse of so many ages, such an unquestionable similarity between the Greek and Sanscrit languages, and the Greek and Sanscrit religious systems, is still discoverable.

APPENDIX A.

REMARKS ON THE PAPERS OF LIEUTENANT-COLONEL WILFORD CONTAINED IN THE ASIATIC RESEARCHES.

As Lieutenant-Colonel Wilford has been often quoted as an authority on the subject of Hindu Mythology, and as the view which he has given of it might therefore tend to render questionable many of the remarks and quotations contained in the preceding pages, it becomes necessary to ascertain the degree of credibility to which that writer is entitled. From the manner, however, in which he has produced the legends that he ascribes to Hindu Mythology, since he never quotes the chapter of the Puran from which they are said to have been taken, and often not even the name of the Puran, it becomes impossible to refute his misstatements by citing the original text: but, from my own examination of the Purans, I find myself fully authorised to affirm, that many of those legends are not contained in these works; and that the few which occur in them are, by Lieutenant-Colonel Wilford, so misrepresented and mixed up with irrelevant matter as to be scarcely recognisable. For my own part, I am convinced that he never could have read a single Puran from beginning to end, and that he always trusted to the extracts which were furnished to him by the natives in his employment; because, as his knowledge of the Sanscrit language is undoubted, it is impossible to attribute the manner in which he has translated more than one passage, when he could not have had any reason for interpolating the text, to any other cause than the unfaithfulness of the extract.

This statement, however, made by Lieutenant-Colonel Wilford, of the manner in which he conducted his researches, must alone evince how very improbable it was that their result could be either accurate or true. "Thus," says he, "when I began to study the Sanscrit language, I was obliged to wade with difficulty through ponderous volumes, generally without finding any thing valuable enough to reward me for my trouble; but, in the course of conversation, my pandit and other learned natives often mentioned most interesting legends, bearing an astonishing affinity with those of the western mythologists.

I consequently directed my pandit to make extracts from all the Purans and other books relative to my enquiries, and to arrange them under proper heads. . . . At the same time, *I amused myself with unfolding to him our ancient mythology, history, and geography*." * For it is surprising that the slightest acquaintance with the natives should not have satisfied Lieutenant-Colonel Wilford that not one of them was capable of executing such a task as this; and that it would in consequence inevitably lead the individual confided in to secure his employer's favour, by having recourse to invention and imposture. But, unless Lieutenant-Colonel Wilford himself had been under the influence of the strongest prejudice, it seems inconceivable how he could have received from his pandit the history of Noah and his sons, so identical with the Mosaic account, without his suspicion having been excited. Still more inconceivable must it be that Lieutenant-Colonel Wilford should, several years after, make these remarks:—"It [this history] is however mentioned, though in less explicit terms, IN MANY PURANS, and *the pandit took particular care in pointing out to me* several passages, which confirmed more or less this interesting legend." It is needless to remark on the groundlessness of this assertion; because Satyavrata, whom he indentifies with Noah in his Essay on Egypt, had nine sons †, and not three only.

But in this statement, or confession, Lieutenant-Colonel Wilford proceeds to remark: — "It is acknowledged that the three sons of Swayambhuva are incarnations of the *trimurti*, and they are declared, in general, in the Purans to have been created by the Deity to marry the daughters of the first man, Daksha, or Brahma in a human shape; Kardama, or Kapila, or Kabil (the name of Cain among Mussulmans), was Shiva, and the benevolent Ruchi was Vishnu; one of Ruchi's titles is Sharma, or Kama; Shiva is called Ha, or Ham in the objective case; Brahma, or Daksha, is declared to be Prajapati, nearly synonymous with Jyapati." Thus Noah is here identified with Swayambhuva Manu, who, according to Lieutenant-Colonel Wilford himself, in his Essay on the Chronology of the Hindus ‡, had *two sons only*. But the first *man* was this very Swayambhuva; and had the incarnations of *trimurti*, as here stated, been born his sons and espoused his daughters, they must have married their own sisters, an incestuous union expressly condemned by the Hindu law. In no Puran, however, is it said that Brahma, Vishnu, and Shiva became incarnate as Daksha,

* Asiatic Researches, vol. viii. p. 249.

† See Ward's View of the Hindus, vol. iii. p. 14. In the Bhagawat and other Purans, however, he is said to have had ten.

‡ And yet in this Essay Wilford identifies Swayambhuva with Adam, and Satyavrata with Noah. What reliance, therefore, can be placed on a writer who exhibits such a confusion of ideas in a paper which, as it must be supposed, must have been written with every attention, as it purports to explain the precise degree of credit which was due to his former essays?

Kardama, and Ruchi; and that writer must have a very superficial knowledge of the subject who identifies Kardama, who sprang from the shadow of Brahma, with Kaphila, who was really an incarnation of Vishnu, and not of Shiva. With regard, also, to the term Prajapati, common to both Brahma and Daksha, it is a compound Sanscrit word, *praja-pati,* which signifies *progeniei dominus,* and not the *venerable Japati.*

So unwilling, also, is Lieutenant-Colonel Wilford to give up a favourite hypothesis, that he even states: — " *My pandit's* voluminous extracts are still of great use to me, because *they always contain much truth; and the learned, therefore, have not been misled in their general conclusions from my Essay on Egypt.*" But I venture to affirm, without the fear of contradiction, that there is not a single passage in any one of the Purans which applies to Egypt; nor amongst the rivers enumerated in them have I ever observed the name *Nila,* which he identifies with the Nile. It is even self-evident, from the passage translated by Sir W. Jones, in the note annexed to this Essay, that the term *Nila* therein mentioned is used with several other of the epithets as synonymes of the well known river *Krishna* *; and Lieutenant-Colonel Wilford himself says, " In her character of Mahakali she has many other epithets, all implying different shades of black or dark azure; and in the Kalika Puran they are all ascribed to the river. They are *Kali, Nila, Asita, Shyama* or *Shyamala, Mechaca, Anjanabha, Krishna.*" To make, therefore, any comment on the perversity of judgment which transferred the *Krishna* from India to Egypt must be superfluous: but it requires to be remarked that the Puranic legends are confined entirely to India in its greatest extent; and that nothing contained in the Purans int he slightest degree warrants the geographical reveries in which Lieutenant-Colonel Wilford so much delighted. †

Lieutenant-Colonel Wilford farther states: — " My Essays on the Chronology of the Hindus and Mount Caucasus are almost entirely free from the forgeries which I have stated;" and yet in the first of these essays he asserts: — " The old continent is well described in the Purans, but more particularly the countries in which the Vedas were made public, and in which the doctrines they contain flourished for a long time. Accordingly, the *sacred isles* in the

* Sir W. Jones, however, here says, — " There are two of Mr. Wilford's extracts from the Furanas which deserve a verbal translation; and I therefore exhibit them word for word, with a full conviction of their genuineness and antiquity." But I have not met with the extract in question in any part of the Skanda Puran which I have perused; and the attributing of it to that Puran has a very suspicious appearance, for the reasons stated in the note (‡) p. 153.

† He might, for instance, have just as well attempted to fix the geographical position of *Vaikuntha* as of the *White Island* (*Shweta Dwipa*); since they are both the fabulous residences of Vishnu, and the one is as much of a reality as the other.

West, the countries bordering on the Nile, and, *last of all*, India, are better and more minutely described than any other country. *Atri*, called *Edris* and *Idris*, in the countries to the west of India, *carried the Vedas from the abode of the gods, on the summit of Meru*, first to the *sacred isle;* thence to the *banks of the Nile; and, lastly, to the borders of India.*" It can scarcely be necessary to observe that the Purans afford no foundation whatever for this statement; nor do they contain any account of the manner in which the Vedas were transmitted until they were arranged by Vyasa. The universal opinion, also, of the Hindus is, that Swayambhuva, the first man, inhabited the country named Brahmawarta, which is situated between the Ganges and the Jumna; and that it was he who received the Vedas from his father Brahma, and rendered them public.

In the Essay on Mount Caucasus occurs this singular passage: — "Kardameshwara is the destructive power united to a form of clay: Ishwara attempted to kill his brother Brahma, who, being immortal, was only maimed; but Ishwara, finding him afterwards in a mortal shape, in the character of Daksha, killed him as he was performing a sacrifice. Kardameshwara is then obviously the Cain of Scripture; and of course Capila is his son Enoch. The Mussulmans seem to have borrowed from the Hindus the appellation of *Kapila* or *Kabil*, which they give to Cain, *who* is sometimes called Kapileshwara in the Purans, *being an incarnation of Mahadeva:* Enoch was an incarnation of Vishnu, and is always called Capila-muni. Kapileshwara was a Muni also; hence he is sometimes called, though improperly, Kapila-muni; *which inaccuracy has occasioned some confusion in the Purans.*" But, in the eighth volume of the Asiatic Researches, Lieutenant-Colonel Wilford makes Kardama and Kapila to be the same personage, and an incarnation of Shiva; and here Kapila is represented as the son of Kardama, and an incarnation of Vishnu. To elicit accuracy from such contradictions as these is evidently impracticable: but these passages clearly show that he was not aware that such a word as *Kardameshwara* does not mean an *individual*, but a lingam erected by Kardama in honour of Shiva.* Nor is it said in any one of the Purans that Daksha was an incarnation of Brahma; but, on the contrary, that he sprang from the thumb of Brahma. This identifi-

* *Kapileshwara* would be equally a lingam erected by Kapila: but I do not immediately recollect whether, among the multitude of lingams mentioned in the Purans, particularly the Skanda, these two lingams are enumerated or not, though it is most probable; as there is not a distinguished personage in Hindu legendary lore who is not represented as having erected, on some occasion or other, a lingam in honour of Shiva; and as having received, as a boon from the god, that it should become celebrated under the name of the erecter.

Since writing the above note I have found the ***Kapileshwara lingam*** mentioned in the Prabhasa Kshetra Khand of the Skanda Puran.

cation, however, of Shiva and Brahma with Cain and Abel, absurd as it must appear, is even devoid of the requisite connection; because in their mortal forms Daksha ought to have been killed by Kardama, who, according to Lieutenant-Colonel Wilford, was the incarnation of Shiva: but he has not ventured to assert a circumstance, which would not only have been contradicted by the Purans, but would also be obviously incompatible with the pacific character ascribed to *Rishis* and *Munis*, who curse but do not fight.

In this same Essay occurs this passage, which is so frequently quoted or referred to by Mr. Faber in his work on *Pagan Idolatry*: — "During the flood Brahma, or the creating power, was asleep at the bottom of the abyss*; the generative power of nature, both male and female, was reduced to the simplest elements, the lingam and the yoni; the latter assumed the shape of the hull of a ship, since typified by the *Argha*, whilst the lingam became the mast. In this manner they were wafted over the deep under the protection of Vishnu.† When the waters had retired, the female power of nature appeared immediately in the character of *Kapoteshwari*, or the dove; and she was joined by her consort in the shape of *Kapoteshwara*." Unfortunately, however, for Lieutenant-Colonel Wilford's identification of the *Argha* with the ark of Noah and the Argo of the Greeks, Mr. Wilson has observed in the notes to his translation of the Megha Duta (page 7.): — "Mr. Wilford states that Argha in Sanscrit means a boat, whence he deduces the ship Argo, &c.; and whence, with Mr. Bryant's assistance, we may deduce the ark of Scripture: the Sanscrit word, however, has not been found in any of the vocabularies of the language with the import Mr. Wilford has assigned to it." ‡ But the slightest acquaintance with the Purans would have prevented Lieutenant-Colonel Wilford from adopting or imagining a fiction so contrary to the modes of thinking of the Hindus as is contained in the preceding passage: because in no Puran is there any account of what becomes of Shiva and Parvati during the period of the *pralaya*, or flood §; but it is universally believed that they are in no manner affected by it. It follows, therefore, that the alleged appearance, on the retiring of the waters, of

* On the contrary Brahma remains in his own heaven, to which the flood does not extend.

† In the eighth volume, however, of the Asiatic Researches (p. 273.), Wilford says, — "It is their (the Hindus') opinion, I DO NOT KNOW ON WHAT AUTHORITY, that at the time of the flood the two principles of generation assumed the shape of a *boat* with its mast, in order to preserve mankind."

‡ In the Amara Kosha *Argha* is explained as signifying *price, a mode of worship*. The latter, however, should rather be an *offering*; and the vessel in which it is presented (and this is what Wilford intends) is invariably named *Argha-patram*.

§ I have observed only one passage in the Varaha Puran, from which it appears that Kailasa is supposed to remain unapproachable by the flood.

Shiva and Parvati as doves is unsupported by any Sanscrit authority; nor is there any mention of a dove in any account which is given of the preservation of Satyavrata.*

In his fifth Essay, on the Sacred Isles in the West, Lieutenant-Colonel Wilford states: — "It appears that, long before Christ, a renovation of the universe was expected all over the world, with a saviour, a king of peace and justice. This expectation is frequently mentioned in the Purans. The earth is often complaining that she is ready to sink back into Patalam, under the accumulated load of the iniquities of mankind: the gods also complain of the oppression of the giants. Vishnu comforts the earth, his consort, and the gods, assuring them that a saviour would come to redress their grievances, and put an end to the tyranny of the Daityas, or demons; that for this purpose he would be incarnated in the house of a shepherd, and brought up amongst shepherds. . . . At that time the Emperor of India, uneasy at these prophecies, which he conceived portended his ruin and the loss of his empire, sent emissaries to enquire whether such a child was really born, in order to destroy him; and this happened exactly in the 3101st year of the kali yug, which was the first year of the Christian era. *This traditionary account is known all over India, and is equally known among the learned and the ignorant: but the Hindus fancy that these old prophecies were fulfilled in the person of Krishna. . . . The Hindus having once fixed the accomplishment of these prophecies to a period greatly anterior to the Christian era, every thing in their books was either framed or new-modelled accordingly, and particularly in the Purans.*" † These passages must evince how totally incapable the writer was of forming a correct judgment on any subject of antiquarian or historical research: for he admits that the universal belief of the Hindus applies these alleged prophecies to *Krishna;* and yet Lieutenant-Colonel Wilford, a native of Germany, attempts, on no grounds whatever, to prove that they were originally applied to *Shalivahana*, and only transferred to *Krishna* in order to give to the Hindu religion a greater antiquity than that of

* Wilford himself, at the same time, gives, in As. Res. (vol. iv. p. 362.), this correct account of the origin of the name Kapoteshwara (more accurately, Kapotésha): — "Mahadeva, having visited the country of Purushottama in Orissa, was surprised to find it overspread with long grass, and without inhabitants. He resolved to destroy this long grass [and to render the place habitable], and for this purpose, assuming the diminutive shape of a dove, commenced the performance of a severe *tapas;* his consort Parvati also transformed herself into a bird of the same species; and from that time they were known to mankind and worshipped under the names of Kapotesha and Kapoteshi, or Isha and Ishi, in the shape of a dove." This account is taken from the *Purushottama Mahatmyam*, said to be a portion of the Skanda Puran: but I have always understood that *Kusha-sthali*, the spot where this *tapas* was performed, was the same place as that on which *Dwaraka* was afterwards built; and that, consequently, it was in Guzerat and not in Orissa.

† Asiatic Researches, vol. x. p. 7. et seq.

the Christian religion. Nor is there the slightest reason for restricting these alleged prophecies to Krishna; because in the Purans all the incarnations of Vishnu, and even the manifestations of Shiva, are preceded by the complaints of the gods against the overpowering violence of the Daityas, and assurances to them on the part of those deities of safety and protection. In the Brahmanda Puran, for instance, occurs this passage: — *Shiva, addressing Parvati.* — "The Earth, sunk under the oppression of Ravana and other wicked beings, having assumed the form of a cow, and accompanied by the gods and holy sages, hastened to Brahma, to whom she weeping related all her sufferings. Brahma having reflected for a moment, proceeded with the celestial host to the sea of milk, and implored with laudatory strains the protection of Vishnu. [Vishnu appears, and Brahma having stated the cause of his coming, he replied: —] 'Kashyapa having formerly propitiated me by *tapas*, and requested as a boon that I would become his son, I granted it; and, as he and his wife now reign in Ayodhya as Desharata and Kaushilya, I will be born their son; and Lakshmi, also, shall be born the daughter of Janaka. Thus, accompanied by her, will I accomplish your wishes by the destruction of Ravana, and the restoration of the Earth to peace and happiness.' " *

But the history of Shalivahana is NOT *known all over India, nor equally known among the learned and ignorant.* On the contrary, scarcely any account of him can be obtained, and never did any Hindu consider him to be an incarnate god. Lieutenant-Colonel Wilford, indeed, states, "that the defeat of Vicramaditya took place, according to the *Kumarika Khand* [of the Skanda Puran], in the first year of the Christian era, when Shalivahana was in his fifth year." But in my copy of this *Khand* I can find nothing relating to either Vicramaditya or Shalivahana. † This point, however, is of the utmost consequence; because,

* Brahmanda Puranam, Uttara Khand, also entitled Adhyatma Ramayanam, chap. 2.

† Wilford expressly refers to the following passage, descriptive of events which are to take place in the *kali yug*, which, as it is the only one that I can find that has the least resemblance to what he states, I transcribe, with its context: — ततस्त्रिषुसहस्त्रेषुदशाधिकशत त्रय ‡ ॥ भविष्यंनंद राज्यंचचाणाक्यो यान् हनिष्यति ॥ शुक्लतीर्थसर्वपाप निर्मुक्तिं योभिलिप्स्यति ॥ ततस्त्रिषुविंशन्याचाधिकेषुव ॥ भविष्यति मार्कादित्यं मार्कादिन्यं राज्यं सोथ प्रलिप्स्यते ॥ सिधिं प्रसादादुग्राणादीनां योह्याध्दारेष्यति ॥ ततः त्रिषु सहस्त्रेषु शतेनाप्यधिकेषुव ॥ शकोनामभ

‡ The त्रय in the first verse is clearly a mistake, as it does not occur in the following dates.

were these personages expressly and unequivocally mentioned in any Puran, this would prove that it must have been written after the Christian era, unless it could be clearly shown that the passage in which they were noticed was an interpolation; and how difficult it is to prove an interpolation satisfactorily needs no remark. In the two or three Purans, however, in which prophetic passages respecting the *kali yug* occur, these are so concise, and, consisting almost entirely of names and numbers, afford such a likelihood of errors in transcription, that no argument can be justly founded on them, with respect either to the persons who may be intended, or the periods when they lived; nor, consequently, with respect to the date when these Purans may have been composed.

But it is difficult to determine whether there is most absurdity or impiety in thus attempting to identify Shalivahana with Jesus Christ. Lieutenant-Colonel Wilford, however, repeatedly admits, what cannot be denied, that Shalivahana was a prince who actually existed, reigned in the Deccan, and gave rise to the era which is named after him; and it is impossible, therefore, that he could be, as Lieutenant-Colonel Wilford also contends, an imaginary person, and that the legend respecting him *was taken from the apocryphal Gospel of the infancy of Jesus, written in Greek in the third century.* In fact, throughout the whole of this Essay the confusion of ideas, and the perplexity and the inconsistency of the reasoning, are so obvious, as to evince most fully the futility of the hypothesis which the writer, by such fallacious means, so vainly attempts to support. At the same time, Lieutenant-Colonel Wilford seems to concur in the justness of this remark of Sir W. Jones, that the story of Krishna "must induce an opinion that the spurious gospels, which abounded in the first ages of Christianity, had been brought into India, and the wildest of them engrafted upon the old fable of Krishna." This fluctuation of opinion, consequently, must show of what little value any conclusion of Lieutenant-Colonel Wilford must be

---

विषश्च योतिदारिद्र हारकः ॥ ततस्त्रिषुसहस्त्रेषुषदशतेंरधिकेषुव ॥ मागधेहेमसदनादजन्यां प्रभविष्यति विष्णोरांशोधर्मपाताबुद्धः साक्षा न्स्वयं प्रभुः *In the year* 3010 *of the kali yug there will be the kingdom of Nauda, who will be slain by Chanakya; but the latter will obtain expiation of the sin by making a pilgrimage to the Shukla-tirtham. Then in the year* 3020 *there will be the kingdom of Markaditya, who, through the favour of powerful beings, will obtain the accomplishment of all his wishes. Then in the year* 3100 *there will be a dispeller of poverty named Shaka. Then in the year* 3600 *will be born, in a golden palace in Magadha, Buddha, the protector of piety, and an undoubted portion of Vishnu.* It is possible that in this passage Vicramaditya and Shalivahana may be intended; but were it to be received as authority, it would, by placing Buddha at so late a period in the *kali yug*, contradict every other account of Hindu chronology.

considered; and it is hence likewise evident, that he knowingly attempted to pervert the Puranic legends to the support of his own favourite but unfounded hypotheses.

That Lieutenant-Colonel Wilford, also, was perfectly aware that he was misrepresenting the scene of the Puranic legends, and transferring it to countries totally unknown to Sanscrit writers, is evident from various passages in his Essays. For instance, in one place, in the Essay on Egypt, he correctly states, that "on the northern Himalaya is the celebrated lake *Manasasaras* or *Manasasarovara*, near *Sumeru*, the abode of the gods;" and yet in another place he says, "The *Ajagara* Mountains, which run parallel to the eastern coasts of Africa, have at present the name of *Lupata*, or the *backbone of the world;* those of *Sitanta* are the range which lies west of the lake *Zambre* or *Zaire*, words not improbably corrupted from *Amara* and *Sura*. This *lake* of the gods is believed to be a vast reservoir, which, through invisible or hidden channels, supplies all the rivers of the country." Thus the lake *Manasasarovara*, so celebrated in Sanscrit writings, is transferred from Little Thibet to Africa; and yet Lieutenant-Colonel Wilford, in stating the nature of the forgeries imposed upon him by his pandit, hesitated not to affirm that *the learned have not been misled in their general conclusions from his Essay on Egypt.*"

But it would be tedious to pursue this subject farther; and the preceding remarks will, perhaps, have sufficiently evinced how little credit is due to the authority of Lieutenant-Colonel Wilford on any point relating to Hindu antiquities and mythology. No reader, also, is likely to be misled by such a passage as this:—"We come now to the *Hayasilas* or *Habashis*, who are mentioned, I am told, in the Purans, though but seldom; and their name is believed to have the following etymology: Charma (identified with Ham), having laughed at his father Satyavrata (Noah), who had by accident intoxicated himself with a fermented liquor *, was nicknamed *Hayasila*, or the laugher; and his descendants were called from him *Hayasilas* in Sanscrit." But some doubt may possibly exist with respect to several legends, which may seem to have a Puranic appearance; and I therefore select, as an example, the following passage from the Essay on Egypt:—"The metamorphosis of *Lunus* into *Luna* was occasionally mentioned in the preceding section; but the legend must now be told at more length. The god Soma, or Chandra, was traversing the earth with his favourite consort Rohini; and, arriving at the southern mountain Sahyadri, they unwarily entered

* Nothing can more decisively show the total want of reflection and judgment under which Lieutenant-Colonel Wilford pursued his researches, than this single circumstance; for he must have been well aware that intoxication is held in such abomination by the Hindus, that no Sanscrit writer would have ever described any distinguished and revered personage as intoxicated.

the forest of Gauri, where some men, having surprised Mahadeva caressing that goddess, had been formerly punished by a change of their sex; and the forest had retained the power of effecting the like change on all males who should enter it. Chandra, instantly becoming a female, was so afflicted and ashamed that she hastened *far to the west*, sending Rohini to her seat in the sky, and concealed herself in the mountain, afterwards called Somagiri, where she performed acts of the most rigorous devotion. Darkness then covered the world each night; the fruits of the earth were destroyed; and the universe was in such dismay, that the Devas, with Brahma at their head, implored the assistance of Mahadeva, who no sooner placed Chandra on his forehead than she became a male again; and hence he acquired the title of Chandrashekhara." This passage has either not the slightest foundation in any thing that occurs in the Purans, or it must have been written from some imperfect recollection or fictitious relation of the two following legends: —

From the Bhagavat.

Shuka, addressing Parikshit. — "At the end of a preceding kalpa there existed no other being than Narayana, from whose navel sprang a lotos, whence was produced the four-faced Swayambhuva. From the mind of the latter was born Marichi, and from him Kashyapa; to whom was born, by the daughter of Daksha, Surya Vivaswan. His wife was Sandgna, and their son Manu, named also Shrāddha Deva; to whom was born by his wife Shrăddha ten sons, viz. Ihshwaku, Nriga, Sharyati, Dishta, Dhrishta, Karushaka, Narishyanta, Prishadhra, Nabhaga, and Kavi. * But at first he was without a son; and therefore, in order to obtain one, performed a sacrifice to Mitra and Varuna. His wife Shraddha, however, being desirous of a daughter, entreated the officiating priest to accomplish her wish; and he, in consequence, performed the sacrifice in an undue manner. Hence was produced a virgin, named Ila; on beholding whom Manu, by no means pleased, thus addressed his preceptor: — 'My lord, how has this untoward event happened, and why have the prayers and invocations of Brahmans, so devout and skilled in the Vedas, produced an unhappy result so contrary to my expectation?' On hearing these words Vasishta, having perceived the error of the officiating priest, thus spoke to the son of Ravi: — 'This difficulty has originated in the undue performance of the sacrifice; but I will accomplish thy wish for an illustrious son.' Having thus determined,

* Most of these names vary in different Purans.

he gave virility to her who had been a female under the name of *Ila;* and thus Ila became a distinguished man, known under the appellation of *Sudyumna.*

"He, Sudyumna, one day, armed and bearing a bow and arrows, mounted on horseback, and, accompanied by several ministers, proceeded for the purpose of hunting towards the country of Sindhu. But having entered the Kumara-vanam, at the bottom of the mountain Meru, where Shiva had formerly dallied with Uma, Sudyumna instantly observed himself changed into a female, and his horse into a mare. The sex, also, of his attendants was changed; and they despondingly looked at each other." Parikshit here said, — "My lord, how and by whom did this place acquire this property? Explain to me the cause of its producing so joyless an effect." Shuka replied, — "The Rishis once came here to see Shiva, while he was in dalliance with Uma; and by their splendour dispelled the darkness in which they were concealed. On seeing them Ambika, greatly ashamed, arose from her husband's lap, and hastily adjusted her loosened garment; while the Rishis, perceiving the inopportuneness of their visit, immediately retired. But Shiva, to please his beloved, thus said: — 'May every male who enters this place become a female!' Hence happened this change of sex to Sudyumna *, who, accompanied by his attendants, continued to reside in the forests. There Buddha, beholding the love-inspiring damsel surrounded by females, became enamoured of her, and she also was captivated with the son of Soma; and from their union was born Pururava. † Thus, O king! did Sudyumna become a female: but when he recollected the honours of his race, he hastened to implore the aid of Vasishta; and the divine sage, compassionating his state, and desirous of restoring him to virility, had recourse to Shankara. That god being propitiated, and from his favour to Vasishta, thus spoke: — 'One month shall he be a man, and one month a woman.' In this manner was Sudyumna, through the kindness of his preceptor, restored to the male sex, and afterwards reigned over the world; but the people did not delight in him." ‡ — Skand IX. chap. 1.

* When Sudyumna again became a female, he was known by the former name of Ila; and hence the lunar race are said to have descended from Buddha and Ila.

† I cannot avoid adverting to this remark of Mr. Ward (vol. iii. p. 19.): - - "The account of the birth of Pururava is given in the Brahma Puran; but it is too extravagant and filthy for insertion." For all I can find in this Puran respecting it is contained in this stanza: — "Ila, an opportunity having been obtained by Buddha, was compressed by him; and from this union with Buddha, the son of Soma, was born Pururava." — See the first chapter, entitled *Surya-wamsha Anukirtinam.*

‡ The commentator thus explains the last expression: — "On account of his secluding himself each alternate month in his palace, in consequence of his being ashamed of then becoming a woman."

Dr. Hamilton, in his *Genealogies of the Hindus,* is strangely perplexed with this male and

From the Shiva Puran.

Suta, addressing the Sages. — "Daksha, having given in marriage twenty-seven of his daughters to Chandra, he bestowed his love entirely on one of them, named Rohini. The others, being grieved in consequence, sought the protection of their father, and acquainted him with the cause of their affliction. On hearing which, Daksha proceeded to Chandra, and thus expostulated with him: — 'Thou art a chief, descended from a noble line, and shouldst therefore equally cherish all who are dependent upon thee: but what has happened, has happened; take only care that thou dost not again act in the same manner.' Having thus spoken to his son-in-law Chandra, Daksha, expecting from this a happy result, returned to his abode. But Chandra, deluded by love, paid no attention to his words: for he who is born with a good disposition will act well; but, if born with a bad disposition, how can he acquire goodness! Thus Chandra, being of a violent disposition, attended not to the words of Daksha, but remained unalterably attached to Rohini. His other daughters, therefore, again complained to Daksha, who thus addressed Chandra: — 'Since thou hast disregarded my repeated expostulation, mayst thou be afflicted with gradual decay!' Scarce were these words uttered, when Chandra began to wane, and thus lamented: — 'What shall I do, and where shall I go, to obtain relief from this distress?' The celestial host also, and holy sages, on the waning of Chandra, became oppressed with grief, and hastened to implore the protection of Brahma. That god then said, — 'Alas! how often will Chandra thus commit wickedness? Now has he acted improperly towards Daksha; and hear what he formerly did. Having once entered the house of Brihaspati, he carried away his wife Tara, and then took refuge amongst the Asuras; on which account a mighty war was waged between them and the Suras, until I prevailed upon him to give her up. But as she was pregnant, Brihaspati said, — "I will not receive her back." Persuaded, however, by me, he consented to receive her again, provided that she was immediately delivered and declared who was the father of the child. This accordingly took place, and she named Soma.* Such

---

female character of Sudyumna; for he remarks, under the name Ila, — "Great difficulties exist with respect to this personage. . . . We may, perhaps, explain these difficulties by supposing, that Pururava and Sudyumna are two names for one person; and that Ila, after his birth, took her son's name." But it was Sudyumna and Ila who were the same person; and though he had, after being restored to the male sex, other sons, the line of the lunar race was carried on by Pururava, to whom he gave birth when a female.

* The child was named Buddha, and became the regent of the planet Mercury. In other Purans it is said that, after Tara's delivery, Brihaspati, in order to purify her, reduced her to ashes, and then restored her to life.

sins has Soma repeatedly committed; but why should I enumerate them? To relieve him, however, from his present distress, proceed with him to Prabhasa Kshetra, and there propitiate Shiva.' [The gods accordingly adopt this advice; and after Soma, with their assistance, had performed the requisite *tapas*, Shiva appears, and thus addresses him: —] 'Excellent! crave whatever boon thou most desirest.' Soma replied, — 'If thou, O lord! art propitiated by me, what other good can I desire? But, O Shankara! remove this disease which has consumed my body.' Shiva replied, — 'Thou shalt, O Chandra! in one half of the month daily decrease, and in the other half daily increase:' and thus Chandra, who had become inoorporeal, was by this boon restored to a corporeal form. In commemoration, also, of this event, were erected a temple and lingam, which became celebrated in the three worlds under the name of Someshwara." *

It may, also, not be uninteresting to the reader to compare what Lieutenant-Colonel Wilford, in his Essay on Egypt, has written with respect to *Nairrita*, *Pingaksha*, and *Lubdhaka*, with the following legend which occurs in the Kashi Khand of the Skanda Puran; for there is nothing relating to this subject in the Brahmanda Puran, as he states: — "In the midst of the Vindhya Forest, on the banks of the Nirvindhya, lived, within a Shabara's† abode, a powerful chief of his tribe, the lord of a small village, named Pingaksha; who was valiant, averse from deeds of cruelty, and the destroyer of highway robbers, and of tigers and other wild beasts. He obtained his livelihood by hunting, but exercised his vocation‡ with such mercy, that he killed no bird or beast that had trusted in him, or was asleep, or had come to drink water, or was pregnant, or was still young; and thus carefully attended in shedding blood to the observances prescribed to his caste. To men who were weary with travel he afforded repose, the hungry he relieved from hunger, the shoeless he supplied with shoes, and to the naked he gave garments of soft leather. Whenever travellers entered the rugged and lonesome paths of the forest, he robbed them not of their property, but insured them security; and hence his name became the terror of evil-doers throughout the Vindhyan district; while holy mendicants, on proceeding on a pilgrimage to some sacred spot, showered blessings on him. Thus the forest became like a city; and, as no one obstructed the roads, men passed fearlessly through it.

* In one copy of this Puran this passage occurs, in the forty-fourth chapter of the first part.

† This name, which denotes that class of men which in India resides in the forests and mountains, is taken from the commentator, who explains the Sanscrit word *pakwana*, co tained in the text, as signifying *the abode of a Shabara.*

‡ It is passing strange that Wilford should convert these *wild hunters of* the *woods* into *shepherds.*

"But on a certain time, his uncle having heard of a valuable caravan which was to pass through the forest, the vile hunter (*lubdhaka* *) of the woods, covetous of such a treasure, took post in a difficult and concealed part of the road. But Pingaksha, as a reward for his virtue, having gone out a hunting, happened to remain, during the night, near that place: for thus the Lord of the universe, in order that the world may enjoy happiness, prevents the imaginators of treachery against the lives of men from accomplishing their wicked designs. When night, therefore, was over, and day had dawned, Pingaksha heard a great tumult, and loud cries of 'Strike, my brave men! Despoil! Kill!' and also, 'Save us, O warriors! Kill us not, for we are travellers; but, if necessary, lead us away prisoners, and plunder us.' Depending upon the faith of Pingaksha, we pass and repass this road without fear: can he now be at a distance from this forest?' On hearing these words from a distance, Pingaksha hastened to the travellers, exclaiming, 'Fear not! fear not! Who is he that dares, while Pingaksha lives, to plunder travellers, dear to me as my own life?' This heard, his uncle Zaraksha, from the desire of riches, thus thought, — 'Pingaksha commits sin by contemning the observances of our race†, and by considering them to be vile and wicked; long, therefore, have I intended his death, and now will I kill him.' Having thus determined, the evil-minded one called out to his attendants, — 'Kill that man first, and then the travellers.' But Pingaksha, singly engaging them, fought retiring, and safely conducted the travellers to near his place of residence, while he thus reflected: — 'As long as my bow remains unbroken, and my arrows unexpended, it matters not that my body is pierced with shafts; for, should I be slain, I will obtain the favour of God.' Thus resolved, he gave up his life for the sake of others, and the travellers reached the village in safety; and Pingaksha, having died through such a pious intention, received a precious reward, for, his form being changed, he became Nairrita, and the regent of the south-west quarter." — *Skanda Puran, Kashi Khand*, chapter 12.

It deserves, likewise, to be remarked, that there is no such word as *păli* with the *a* short ‡ in the Sanscrit language; and that *palli* signifies a small

* *Lubdhaka* means merely a hunter, the occupation of the Shabaras. This man's name, as will appear hereafter, was Zaraksha. In the text there is a play upon the words *lubdhaka* and *lubdha*, covetous.

† One of which, and the most important in Zaraksha's opinion, was to plunder and not to protect travellers.

‡ *Pāli*, with the *a* long, is a Sanscrit word, and has a variety of meanings, but never denotes a proper name.

village.* From this last word, however, Lieutenant-Colonel Wilford, or his pandit, has invented the name of a people, whom the former thus describes: — "They are now considered as outcasts, yet are acknowledged to have possessed a dominion in ancient times from the Indus to the eastern limits of Bengal, and even as far as Siam. Their ancestors are described as a most ingenious people, virtuous, brave, and religious; attached to the worship of Mahadeva, under the symbol of the lingam or phallus; fond of commerce, arts, science, and using the Paisachi letters, which they invented. . . . The history of the Palis cannot fail to be interesting, especially as it will be found much connected with that of Europe."† For this statement, however, there is not even the shadow of any authority whatever; and yet Mr. Faber gravely remarks: — "Now the Pali were formerly lords of all India, though their chief settlements appear to have been on the high land to the north of it: and from this region they spread themselves at once into Siam, towards the east; into Italy and Ireland, towards the north-west, under the names of *Pelasgi* and *Phaili;* and into Egypt and Palestine, towards the south-west, under the appellation of *Philitim*, or *Philistim*, or *Royal Shepherds*. . . . I would not build upon words, independently of circumstantial evidence: but since the Pali may be alike traced in Siam, in Thibet, on the coast of the Erythrean Sea, in Phœnicia or Palestine, in Etruria and Ireland; and since in all those countries the Great Father has been known by appellations kindred to Dagon, it is impossible not to feel that this latter circumstance corroborates the former; while, at the same time, the former amply accounts for the latter."‡

Even when Lieutenant-Colonel Wilford refers to a Puran, with seeming accuracy, it will be found that his misstatements are equally gross. As an example, I select the following passage: — "This is also confirmed in the *Krishna-jamma Khand*, a section of the Brahma Vaivarta. Parvati having fled on account of some petty quarrel with her consort, Mahadeva, the world was in great distress, and the poor husband also. He searched for her in vain for a long time, when he went to Vishnu, and, unbosoming himself, begged he would assist in the search. Thus, Hari or Vishnu, and *Trinetra* or Shiva, with three eyes, travelled all over the world; but they found her not. They were then at the extremity of the world, and both wept for grief and sorrow. Their tears

* The name of the people who inhabited the *palli* was, as appears above, *Shabara*. In the Amara Kosha it is said that *Shabara*, Kirata, and Pulinda are the names of different kinds of barbarians; and the name *Bhilla* (*Bheel*) does not occur in it. As far, however, as I have observed, *Shabara* and *Kirata* are used as synonymous terms in the Purans and other Sanscrit works; and Bheel is now the only name in general use for this class of Indians.

† Wilford also places colonies of this newly discovered people in Arabia, Ethiopia, Egypt, Palestine, and Phœnicia.

‡ Origin of Pagan Idolatry, vol. iii. p. 586.

formed a large lake, called *Ashru-tirtha*, or the place of worship near the *tearful* lake. It is to the west of the *Asto-giri*, behind which the sun disappears, near the Akshaya-vata, or Indian fig-tree, incapable of decay."* A correct translation, however, of the passage of this Puran here referred to has been already given in p. 332. of these RESEARCHES, from which it will obviously appear that Lieutenant-Colonel Wilford's strange version of this legend has not the slightest pretensions to accuracy. In fact, the mountain, the tree, and the formation of the lake (for its name is not mentioned in this Puran), are the only circumstances which correspond with the original text. But in that translation I omitted, as superfluous, these words: — "Thus Shiva roamed, until he came to an imperishable fig-tree, in an uninhabited spot at the foot of the mountain Shatashringa, near the banks of the Ganges; and there seated, he wept long and violently, thus forming a beautiful and sacred pool."† It will, therefore, scarcely be believed, though the fact is obviously unquestionable, that it is from these two passages that Lieutenant-Colonel Wilford or his pandit manufactured this statement, which occurs in the Essay on Egypt: "*Rodana-sthan*, or the place of weeping, is the island in the Lake of *Marisha* or Mœris; concerning which we have the following Indian story in the *Vishwasara-pracasha*.‡ Peti-suca, who had a power of separating his soul from his body, voluntarily ascended to heaven; and his wife, Marisha, supposing him finally departed, retired to a wilderness, where she sat on a hillock, shedding tears so abundantly that they formed a lake round it, which was afterwards named *Ashru-tirtha*, or the *holy place of tears*.§ Its waters were black, or very dark azure; and the same colour is ascribed by Strabo to those of Mœris. . . . At length Marisha dying *pativrata*, or dutiful to her lord, joined him in *Vishnu-loca*, or Vishnu's heaven; and her son, having solemnised the obsequies of them both, raised a sumptuous temple, in which he placed a statue of Vishnu at the seat of his weeping mother, whence it acquired the appellation of *Rodana-sthan*. *They who make ablutions (says the Hindu writer) in the Lake of Ashru-tirtha are purified from their sins, and exempted from worldly affections, ascending after death to the heavenly Vishnu; and they who worship the deity at Rodana-sthan enjoy heavenly bliss, without being subject to any future transmigration*."||

* Asiatic Researches, vol. xi. p. 55.

† The name is not given; but Wilford may be correct in calling it *Rodana-sthan*, or perhaps *Rodana-tirtham* may have been its appellation.

‡ With this book I am not acquainted; but that there is an evident interpolation in the *Indian story* said to be taken from it cannot, I think, be doubted.

§ This is clearly apocryphal, because neither divinity nor sanctity is ascribed to Marisha; and no place could become a *tirtham* except through some deity or saint bestowing holiness upon it.

|| Asiatic Researches, vol. iii. p. 340.

In his Essay, also, on the Kings of Magadha, Lieutenant-Colonel Wilford states: "This is also confirmed in the sixty-third and last section of the Agni Purana, in which the expiation of Chanakya is placed 312 years before the first year of the reign of Shaka or Shalivahana, but not of his era. This places this famous expiation 310 or 312 years before Christ." * But my copy of this Puran contains nothing whatever relating to the dynasties which were to reign in the kali yug; and judging from the contents of this Puran, given by Sir W. Jones, it is clear that these subjects were not mentioned in his manuscript of it. Sir W. Jones also says that it consists of 353 short chapters, and not of 63 as above stated.† It hence seems most probable that this quotation, on which Lieutenant-Colonel Wilford lays so much stress, is spurious.

From the preceding remarks it will, perhaps, appear undeniable that Lieut.-Colonel Wilford, instead of usefully employing his knowledge of the Sanscrit language and Sanscrit literature in rendering public the actual contents of Sanscrit works, has preferred to amuse himself in interpolating and perverting them, in order to support hypotheses which have not even plausibility to recommend them. This circumstance, however, would not have been of much consequence had he, by correct quotation, afforded the means of detecting his misstatements: but, on the contrary, the manner in which he refers to the Purans, and other Sanscrit works, evinces either that he had no wish to save the reader that labour of which he himself complained ‡; or, what is far too probable, that writing from extracts, or from oral information, and not with the original text before him, he had it not in his power to render his quotations more specific. § Hence, even on the occasions when his statements are correct, the reader hesitates to give them entire credit; because he is not exactly informed of the authority on which they rest, and he thus has no means of verifying it. The evident mixing up, also, of the writer's own ideas with all that he adduces on alleged Sanscrit authority, and the obvious spirit of hypothesis by which he is actuated at all times and on all subjects which he discusses, might alone have been sufficient to prevent other authors from adopting the erroneous opinions of

* Asiatic Researches, vol. ix. p. 98.

† In my copy the chapters are not numbered throughout, but only as far as the 290th chapter.

‡ "When I began," he says (As. Res. vol. viii. p. 249.), "to study the Sanscrit language, I was obliged *to wade with difficulty through ponderous volumes*, generally without finding any thing valuable enough to reward me for my trouble."

§ All the Purans are divided into chapters, which are either numbered or titled; and the larger ones are also divided into Khands, Skands, or parts; so that the person who quotes them can have no excuse for not referring to them with sufficient accuracy. In some manuscripts, likewise, the stanzas are numbered: but this is seldom the case; and it is not, therefore, possible to render the quotation still more specific, by giving the number of the stanza quoted.

Lieutenant-Colonel Wilford: but, as this has not been the case, I have found it necessary, in justice to my own RESEARCHES, to enter into the preceding investigation, and to show, by a few examples*, that no dependence can be placed on any thing which he has written respecting the antiquities, the mythology, or the history of the Hindus.

* In these I have not adverted to Nahusha, whom Wilford converted into Dionusos, and respecting whom so much has been so erroneously written; because, with the exception of the very short legend relating to his having been chosen to supply the place of Indra, and his having been changed into a serpent by the curse of Agastya, nothing more than his name, as one of the kings of the lunar race, occurs in any of the Purans. The erroneousness, however, of the account which Wilford has given (As. Res. vol. iii. p. 410. et seq.) of the legend relating to Divodasa and Buddha will be sufficiently evinced by Appendix B.

APPENDIX B.

LEGEND OF DIVODASA AND BUDDHA, FROM THE SKANDA PURAN.

SKANDA *said* :—"Formerly in the *Padma Kalpa*, in the Manwantara of Swayambhuva Manu, such a drought prevailed for six years, that all living beings were severely distressed. Men were compelled to live like ascetics, and sought the banks of rivers or of the ocean; towns and villages became like deserts; the trees, towering to the skies, were dried up; and the cities were filled with eaters of flesh; kings and powerful men, like robbers, plundered the defenceless; and those who ought to have protected animals lived upon their flesh. The earth was without government; and the beneficial purposes for which creation was intended were rendered ineffective. On thus beholding the drooping state of the earth, the decay of living beings, the cessation of sacrifices, and the distress of those who used to be supported by them, the Creator was moved with compassion; and, having considered the means of relieving the universe from its sufferings, his thoughts were directed to a distinguished royal ascetic: for at that time a prince named Ripunjaya, of the lineage of Swayambhuva, was, with subdued passions and a devout mind, performing a *tapas* in Kashi; and to him, therefore, Brahma repaired, and, having duly saluted him, thus addressed him:—"O high-minded Ripunjaya! protector of the earth! protect the earth with its seas and mountains, and Vasuki, the king of the Nagas, shall give thee in marriage his lovely daughter Anangamohini. The inhabitants of heaven (*divo*), also, shall serve thee (*dasyanti*), and therefore shalt thou acquire the name of Divodasa; and by my favour, O king! shalt thou obtain divine power, and reign happily over the world.' This heard, Ripunjaya, having praised Brahma, thus replied,—'O Pitamaha! are there not other kings to rule over the people scattered over this earth, and why then address thyself to me?' Brahma answered,—'All other kings are wicked; and the gods will not shower rain upon the earth, unless thou acceptest its government.' Ripunjaya said,—'On one condition, O Brahma! will I obey thy order, and with thy assistance undertake to rule over the world.' Brahma said,—'Speak without reserve, and say what it is that thou wishest.' Ripunjaya answered,—'If, Ȯ Brahma! I am to be the lord of the earth, then let the gods remain in heaven, and let none reside upon the earth, in order that I may, without a rival, confer happiness on mankind.' 'So be it,' Brahma replied, and then directed all the gods to return to heaven. Brahma then repaired to the mountain Mandara, and performed a severe *tapas* to Shiva, until that god, being propitiated, appeared, and said,—'Demand whatever boon thou wishest.' Brahma replied, that the only boon which he requested was, that Shiva would withdraw for some time from Kashi, and reside upon the mountain Mandara, in order to give effect to the boon which he (Brahma) had granted to Divodasa. Shiva was of course obliged to comply, and to forsake his favourite city."—*Kashi Khand*, chap. 39.

Agastya said,—"My lord! be pleased to relate to me the manner in which the three-eyed god expelled Divodasa from Kashi, and returned thither from Mandara." Skanda replied,—"The gods having departed, the wise and illustrious Divodasa took possession, without a rival, of Varanasi, and there established the seat of his government; and, ruling with justice, increased the prosperity of his people. Like the Sun, with the glances of his eyes he withered the hearts of his enemies; but, like the Moon, his countenance gladdened the hearts of his friends. Like Indra, never in battle was his bow broken, and the armies of his foes fled before the clouds of his arrows. Like Dharma Raja, he was a discriminator between justice and injustice, the protector of the innocent, and the punisher of the guilty. Like Agni, he consumed his enemies like forests; and, like Pashi, he bound with cords the serpents who were evil-disposed to him. Like Nairrita, he favoured the virtuous; and like Vaiu, his beneficial influence pervaded the universe. Like Kubera, he bestowed riches on the good, and in battle he appeared destructive as Isha. In form he seemed one of the Ashwinaus; and to all the different deities he bore resemblance in various qualities and endowments. Thus did he render his kingdom like heaven, and his subjects happy as its celestial inhabitants.

"But when Divodasa had reigned for eight thousand years, the gods, becoming desirous of revenge, repaired to their preceptor Brishaspati, and thus consulted him:—'O divine sage! we gods shall suffer extreme distress, should this king obtain the beneficial result of his piety and of his numerous sacrifices; for he governs his people as if they were his own children, and his enemies he subdues with ease. He is endowed with all virtuous qualities, and so wise, that though he injures the gods they cannot avenge themselves. He and all the men in his palace are attached each to one wife, and all their wives are faithful to their lords. In the country of the king Divodasa there is no Brahman who is unlearned, no Kshatrya unskilled in arms, no Vaishya unaddicted to commerce, and no Shudra disobedient. The kingdom abounds with Brahmacharyas; and not a day passes but preceptors instruct their pupils in the Vedas. Householders sedulously perform the rites of hospitality, and all other prescribed duties; the dwellers in towns treat with respect the ascetics who have retired to forests; and all castes observe their peculiar customs, and adhere to their proper occupations. In this country no one is childless, no one without riches, and no one dies untimely. In it there are no cheats, nor robbers, nor murderers, nor buffoons, nor sellers of spirituous liquors; nor are there in it any heretics, but every where is heard the recitation of the Vedas and other sacred books; and every happy dwelling resounds with songs of gladness: but there the sweet sounds of the vina, the flute, and the mridunga are not heard, and unknown are the revellings of the wine-shop. In that flourishing kingdom there are no eaters of meat at sacrifices, no gamblers, no lenders of money, and no thieves. There the gods are duly worshipped, and holy ordinances strictly observed; there the children are dutiful to their parents; the wives revere their husbands, and are obedient to their wishes; the younger brothers reverence their elders; and servants wait at the feet of their masters with respectful assiduity. There the Brahmans, learned, pious, of subdued passions, addicted to holy meditation, and devoted to Shiva alone, punctually perform their daily rites and ceremonies, and day and night the flames of their sacrifices arise, accompanied by due prayers and invocations. The king also employs his treasures in the construction of wells, tanks, ponds, and gardens; and so reigns as to render all classes of his people contented and happy. But Bali, Banasura, Dadicha, and others who have opposed the gods, have been overcome; and why, therefore, should Divodasa alone be permitted to reap the benefit of his virtuous acts?' Brihaspati replied, — 'O dwellers in heaven! one of the four resources of peace and war must be adopted, for unless that king acts voluntarily he cannot be vanquished; and this is the one named dissension, for could disagreement be created between him and the gods of the earth (the Brahmans), many of whom are partial to us, his prosperity would cease in one moment.' * . . . .

" During this period Shiva also abided on Mount Mandara; but, separated from Kashi, he was consumed with grief. At length he thus lamenting spoke to Parvati: — 'Never, O daughter of Daksha! will the fire of affliction, which consumes me on account of my absence from Kashi, be assuaged, until I again clasp it in my embrace. Say, O thou whose counsel is as salutary as the healing plants that grow on the mountain Himavan! how shall this grief, which

* The gods, in consequence, attempt to carry this advice into effect, but prove unsuccessful.

daily increases, be alleviated? for otherwise must I, from its violent heat, forsake this form. O Kashi! when shall I again enjoy peace and gladness within thy walls, and lave my fevered limbs within thy cool streams?' Parvati replied:—'O thou who pervadest the universe, and in whom all things are contained, and who, by thy divine omnipotence, createst, preservest, and destroyest! how canst thou be afflicted by junction or by separation? In an instant, when thou withdrawest thy inspection, the universe sinks into annihilation; and, when reorganised through thy mercy, all things would perish, were it not for thy support. How then canst thou be afflicted? or how canst thou be consumed with heat, when the sun, moon, and fire are thy three eyes, and the holy stream sheds a lustre on thy head? I do not, therefore, understand why thou art obliged to remain absent from that city, in which thou so much delightest. Well pleased, Shiva drank the nectar of her words, while she thus sweetly praised Varanasi *, and then said:—'O my beloved! in consequence of a boon granted by Brahma to Divodasa, no other power can exist in Kashi as long as justice and virtue prevail in it. How then can he be deprived of Kashi, since he rules over his people with such virtue that piety alone flourishes in his kingdom?' The god here ended, and revolved in thought the means by which he might accomplish his wish; and then, regarding Devi, he summoned a band of Yoginis, whom he thus addressed:—'O Yoginis! hasten to my city of Kashi, where the king Divodasa has reigned too long: subvert his virtue, and thus effect his ruin.' Having heard this order, the Yoginis made their obeisance to Shiva, and departed to Kashi. . . .

"Hara, still abiding on Mount Mandara, thus again began to reflect:—'The Yoginis and the Sun have not yet returned; so difficult it is for me to obtain tidings respecting Kashi. Whom now shall I employ to relieve me from this consuming desire to revisit my Kashi; or is there one more skilled or wise than Brahma?' Having thus thought, he summoned Brahma; and, having received him with all due honour, thus addressed him:—'O lotos-born! I first sent the Yoginis and then the Sun to Kashi, but they have not yet returned; and nothing can alleviate the pain which oppresses me, in consequence of my absence from it. Nor is the feverish heat produced by my separation from my beloved city assuaged by the cool drops of amrit which the Moon sheds on my head. Therefore, O Brahma! do thou hasten to Kashi, and employ thy wisdom in order to procure me relief: for thou knowest the cause of my quitting it, and that I cannot there return until Divodasa is voluntarily induced to abandon it. But thou art able to effect this by thy deception, and to restore me to

* This long panegyric on the holy city, which is introduced so *mal-à-propos*, I have omitted.

that Kashi which I so long to revisit.' This heard, Brahma obeyed the order of Shiva, and, mounting his swan-drawn car, proceeded to Kashi; and there arriving, he assumed the form of an aged Brahman, and sought the king.* . . . .

"As Ganesha delayed to return from Kashi, Shiva thus addressed Vishnu:—'Do thou also proceed there; and delay not in executing my wish, as those have done whom I before sent.' Vishnu replied:—'To the best of my ability and understanding will I, O Shankara! accomplish thy wish;' and having thus spoken, and paid due obeisance to Shiva, Hara, accompanied by Lakshmi and Garura, proceeded to Kashi; a little to the north of which he formed, by his divine power, a pleasant abode, which was named Dharma-Kshetram; and there, attended by his lovely spouse, did the lord of Shri, the deluder of the three worlds, reside, under the form of Buddha†; while Lakshmi became a female recluse of that sect. Garura also appeared under the name of Panyakirti, as a pupil, with a book in his hand, and attentively listening to the delusive instructions of his preceptor‡; who, with a low, sweet, and affectionate voice, taught him various branches of natural and supernatural knowledge.

"He then thus spoke:—'The only person who is truly virtuous is the Buddhist; therefore submissively listen, for submission is the ornament of a pupil, while I explain to thee the doctrines of that faith. Know, then, that this universe is without beginning, and attained completion without either cause or creator; for of itself it became manifest, and of itself it will become annihilated. From Brahma to the vilest clod all things are confined within the bonds of matter; and it is false to assert that there is one universal and supreme spirit: for Brahma, Vishnu, Rudra, and the rest §, are names of mere corporeal beings like ourselves; and as we at a certain time shall perish, so shall they; and though their forms may differ from our own, still are they equally subject as we to growth and decay, and to the necessity of eating, sleeping, copulating, and fearing. Corporeality and form depend upon nature; and all things

* It is unnecessary to transcribe the conversation which takes place between the king and Brahma, as it contains nothing interesting. But the result was, that Brahma was so pleased with the piety of Divodasa, that he did not attempt to deprive him of Kashi, but remained in Kashi in an abode provided for him by the king, officiating at sacrifices, and teaching the Vedas.

On Brahma's not returning Shiva sends a selected band of his *ganas*, or attendants, and then Ganesha to Kashi, but with as little success.

† In the text the word is *Saugata*, which is here clearly used as a proper name, and not as denoting a *Buddhist*.

‡ That is, Vishnu as Buddha.

§ The other beings supposed to be gods.

assume those to which their material organisation disposes them: and, in the same manner, the pleasure which each individual experiences is peculiar to himself; for, however delightful to the thirsty man is a draught of water, the pleasure is his alone. Thousands of lovely forms adorn the earth, but, when required, one alone can at one time be enjoyed; for had we a hundred horses, we could mount but one at a time; and thus does this unification prove the individuality of all existent things. As, also, when sunk upon our couches in sound repose, we obtain a cessation from all cares and pains; thus in death, to which Brahma and the rest, as well as the meanest insect, are liable, shall we find a peaceful sleep: and, therefore, why fear death? But since death is undoubtedly common to all beings, ought we not to abstain from the shedding of blood? and therefore have learned men declared that such abstaining is the first of virtues; that we should cultivate a tenderness for life, and preserve as our own the life of another; and that the shedder of blood shall go to hell, but he who is pure from blood shall ascend to heaven. Gifts also are productive of many advantages to the giver, and are of different kinds; as giving charity to the poor, medicine to the sick, food to the hungry, clothes to the naked, instruction to the ignorant, and counsel to the witless. But, above all, acquire wealth, and worship at the twelve shrines, which are the five senses and their organs, mind, and understanding: for pleasure is the only heaven, and pain the only hell, and liberation from ignorance the sole beatitude; since it is from ignorance that the pains and miseries of this world originate. Sacrifices, therefore, are acts of folly; because their divine institution is not only unfounded in proof, but they also cause the shedding of the blood of animals. Are not, also, the slaying of animals, the ensanguining of the ground, the cutting down of trees, and the burning in sacrificial fires of clarified butter and other offerings, admirable means of obtaining beatitude?' Thus instructed, Punyakirti spread these doctrines through the city.

"Lakshmi, also, under the name of *Vidgnana Kaumadi*, inflamed the minds of the women of Kashi with the delusive precepts of the Buddhist faith, and thus taught them to place all happiness in sensual pleasures:—'Know, that those who affirm that real happiness consists solely in identification with God, the essence of bliss ineffable, speak falsely: for, as long as our bodies remain healthy and free from disease, we are happy; but, when oppressed with pain, where then is enjoyment? The body, therefore, is the only source of happiness; and, as it must decay, let us, before it becomes dust, enjoy the pleasures which it gives: for men are all the same, and vainly has the distinction of castes been imagined; since, in such a distinction, where is the good, or where the piety? Because is it not said that Daksha and Marichi were the sons of Brahma, and Kashyapa the son of Marichi? and yet Kashyapa married the thirteen daughters of his uncle Daksha, and thus mankind are said to have sprung from an unlawful union. How, also, can the four castes be proper, when they descend from one father, and must therefore be of the same nature? and, consequently, it must be considered that such a distinction is contrary to the truth, and that no difference whatever exists among men.' Such doctrines the women of the city heard from Vidgnana Kaumadi; and then, communicating them to their husbands, induced them by their blandishments to embrace the delusive faith of Buddha. Vidgnana Kaumadi also attracted the women by rendering the barren mothers, by curing the sick, by giving them charms to increase their beauty, and by other artifices; and by such means she accomplished the deception of all the women of Kashi. Punyakirti, also, diffused throughout the city the doctrines of Buddha; and thus the inhabitants of Kashi were led to forsake the holy religion of the Vedas.

"As these heretic doctrines obtained a prevalence in his kingdom, the power of Divodasa was gradually diminished, and he became grieved and dispirited. At length Vishnu, assuming the appearance of a Brahman, visited the king, and was received by him with all due courtesy and honour. The enquiries after health, and the other ceremonies of reception, being finished, then did Divodasa thus speak:— 'O Brahman! relieve me from the burden of reigning, for I am weary of it, and only desirous of withdrawing from all temporal cares. Say, then, what shall I do, or what means shall I adopt, for obtaining repose? Long have I enjoyed happiness, domestic and public; and by my power have I rendered my kingdom flourishing: the people have I protected as my own children; and daily have I gratified the Brahmans with gifts. But, were my life to be prolonged until the end of a kalpa, I can no longer derive any pleasure from these enjoyments, which have now lost their zest, as repeated banquets pall on the appetite. Be thou, therefore, my preceptor, and point out the means by which I may acquire that happiness which shall never decrease: for there is but one fault with which I can reproach myself, that of having treated the gods with contempt. But many who have, like me, opposed the gods have perished; nor could their virtue and piety preserve them. The Tripura Asuras, for instance, governed their people with justice, observed the ordinances of religion, and were particularly devoted to the worship of Shiva. But, notwithstanding, Shiva, employing the mountain Himalaya for his bow, Vasuke for the string, Vishnu for his arrow, and the earth for his chariot, the sun and moon for its wheels, the Vedas for its horses, the starry sphere for his banner, and the lofty tree of Paradise for its staff, Brahma for his charioteer, and the mysterious monosyllable for his whip, in sport reduced them to ashes. Bali, also, was deceived at a sacrifice by Vishnu, and, in consequence of granting three paces of ground, was compelled to return to Patalam. The chief of Brahmans, likewise, Dadicha, on account of the rancour borne to him by the gods, was induced to embrace a voluntary death, in order that they might form from his bones a weapon with which Indra might slay Vritra; nor could the devotion of Banasura to Shiva prevent Vishnu from lopping off all his thousand hands except two. Thus even the virtuous commit a fault, when they oppose the gods. Yet I fear not the gods; for do I not surpass them in the performance of those acts of devotion by which Indra and the others obtained divinity? But, satiated with the pleasures of this life, do thou, O Brahman! now instruct me in the means by which I may be relieved from all temporal solicitude, and may attain that beatitude for which I am so desirous.'

"Vishnu heard these words well pleased, and thus, under the form of a Brahman, replied:—'Excellent, excellent! O most wise king! true is all that thou hast spoken, and what occasion therefore canst thou have for instruction from me? since thou art already of subdued passions, and the pollution of thy sins has been cleansed by the pure waters of devout meditation; nor hast thou been affected by the heresy which has pervaded thy kingdom. But it appears to me that thou hast committed one great fault, in having compelled Mahadeva to dwell at a distance from Kashi; and I will, therefore, point out to you the manner by which this sin may be expiated: for, were one's sins numerous as the hairs of his body, they would all find remission were he, with mind devoted to Shiva, to consecrate a lingam to that god; and thus, O king! wilt thou expiate thy sin by such a consecration.' The king, with tears of delight, replied:—'O Brahman! what pleasure and consolation do thy words afford me, for blessed will be the future state of him who has propitiated Shiva; and such is the beatitude which I so long to enjoy.' The Brahman replied:—'Thy wish will be accomplished, if thou consecrate a lingam, and devoutly worship Shiva; for, that god being so propitiated, a celestial car shall arrive to waft thee to his abode.' He ended, and Divodasa delighted bestowed on him rich gifts, and accompanied his departure with all due courtesy and honour. *

"Divodasa, accordingly, arranges all the affairs of his kingdom, and, having inaugurated his son as his successor, withdraws to a temple of Shiva, and, having erected a lingam, devotes himself to the worship of that god. After some

* Vishnu, Lakshmi, and Garura then returned to Mandara. This legend occupies from the 43d to the 58th chapter of the *Kashi Khand* of the Skanda Puran.

time had thus elapsed, one day, as he was engaged in his devotions, a celestial car descended from heaven, accompanied by attendants, all of the same form as Shiva; who having thrown a celestial necklace on the neck of the king, his form immediately began to change, his forehead shone with a third eye, his neck became black, his hue white as pure crystal, his hair matted, and serpents adorned his ears and neck, while on his head a crescent sparkled. Thus transformed was he conducted to Kailasa; and thus did Divodasa, in reward of his virtue, piety, and devotion, ascend to heaven without having experienced death."

APPENDIX C.

THE TEN AVATARS OF VISHNU, FROM THE AGNI PURAN.

THE FISH.

Agni, addressing Vasishta. — "Listen, O divine sage! while I relate to thee the different forms which Hari has assumed, in order to punish the wicked and to protect the good. Previously to the conclusion of the last Kalpa, at the termination of which the universe was overwhelmed with a deluge, Vaivaswat Manu performed with much devotion a severe *tapas*. One day as he was presenting water to the *manes* in the river Kritamala, a small fish came into his clasped hands, which, as he was about to throw into the water, said: — 'Throw me not into it, O best of men! for I am there afraid of the larger fishes.' On hearing this Manu placed it in a jar; but the fish increased in size, and said, 'Give me more space.' The king then placed it in a small pond, but it still increasing in size and demanding more room, he threw it into a lake, and at length into the sea; where it in an instant expanded to the size of a hundred thousand *yojanas*. With astonishment Manu beheld this wondrous change, and then said: — 'Why, O lord! who art Vishnu, Narayana, hast thou thus deluded me?' The fish replied: — 'On the seventh day from this the universe will be submerged beneath the ocean; do thou, therefore, taking all kinds of seeds, and accompanied by the seven Rishis, enter into a boat which has been prepared for thee, and during the night of Brahma fasten it with a mighty snake to my horn.' Having thus spoken the fish disappeared, and on the day foretold, the sea commencing to exceed its bounds, Manu entered the boat; and instantly appeared a vast and horned fish, to whose horn he fastened the boat. Then Vishnu revealed to Manu the *Matsya Puran;* and afterwards slew the Asura Hayagriva, who had purloined the Vedas from Brahma.

THE TORTOISE.

"Formerly the Suras, having been vanquished in battle by the Asuras, proceeded to the sea of milk and implored the protection of Vishnu. The god replied:—'Let peace be made between you and the Asuras; and then, making the mountain Mandara the churn staff, and Vasuki the rope, together churn the sea of milk for the beverage of immortality, and I will take care that you, and not the Asuras, shall partake of it.' Vishnu having then effected a peace between them, the Asuras came to the sea of milk, and they began to churn it; the Suras grasping the tail of Vasuki, and the Asuras the head, from the poisonous breath of which the latter suffered extremely. Vishnu, also, that the earth might not from the incumbent weight sink into the abyss, assumed the form of a tortoise, and supported the mountain Mandara. While thus they churned the sea, the poison *halahala* flowed from Vasuki, which, being swallowed by Shiva, tinged his throat of a black colour. At length, from the agitation of this sea were produced *Varuni*, the tree *Parijat*, the gem *Kaustubha*, the Cow of abundance, the *Apsaras*, the goddess *Lakshmi*, who hastened to Hari, then *Dhanwantari*, the author of the *Ayur-Veda*, holding in his hand a goblet of *amrit*. The Asuras immediately seized and carried it away; but Vishnu, assuming the form of a lovely female, went amongst them, and so deluded them with her charms, that, in hopes of espousing her, they gave up the amrit, which Vishnu then distributed amongst the Suras. Rahu alone, assuming the form of the moon, partook of it; but being detected by the sun and moon, Vishnu cut off his head from his body; and in consequence of not obtaining the amrit, enmity has ever since existed between the Suras and Asuras.

THE VARAHA, VAMANA, AND PARASU RAMA.

"There was a chief of the Asuras, named Hiranyaksha, who vanquished the Suras and took possession of heaven: but the gods having had recourse to Vishnu, he assumed the form of a boar and slew Hiranyaksha.

"His brother Hiranyakashipu having also conquered the Suras, and deprived them of their shares of sacrifices, Vishnu became a man-lion, and, having slain him and a number of Asuras, restored the gods to heaven.

"Formerly, likewise, war having taken place between the Suras and Asuras, Bali was victorious, and expelled the former from heaven. They accordingly sought the protection of Vishnu, who, having assuaged their fears, became the son of Aditi and Kashyapa, in the form of a dwarf (Vamana). He then went to a sacrifice which Bali was performing; who, having heard him recite the Vedas, promised, notwithstanding the prohibition of his preceptor Shukra, to grant him whatever boon he wished. The dwarf replied,—'Give me as much ground as I can comprise within three steps; for this is all I wish.' Scarcely, however, had the water, confirmatory of the donation, touched his hands, than he was no longer a dwarf, but comprised with his steps earth, mid-air, and heaven. Thus Hari compelled Bali to return to the lower regions, and reinstated Indra and the immortals in heaven.

"Observing, subsequently, that the Kshatriyas oppressed the earth, Hari assumed a mortal form, in order to protect the gods, the Brahmans, and mankind; and was born the son of Renuka and Jamadagni, the son of Bhrigu. At this time there was a king named Kartavirya, who, through the favour of Dattatreya, had obtained a thousand arms, and who excelled in valour and every warlike quality. One day that he had gone to hunt, he was invited to refresh himself from his fatigue by Jamadagni, who sumptuously entertained him and his attendants by means of the cow *Shabala*, which granted all that was wished: the king, in consequence, requested that this cow should be given to him; but, on this being refused, Jamadagni was slain by the son of Kartavirya, and the king returned home. During this occurrence Rama had gone to the woods, and on his return having found his father slain, he on this account delivered the earth from twenty-one generations of Kshatryas. He then performed expiatory ceremonies at *Kurukshetra*, and, having bestowed the world on Kashyapa and the Brahmans, retired to the mountain Mahendra.

RAMA CHANDRA.

"For the destruction of Ravana and others, Hari, assuming four forms, was born the four sons of Dasharatha, the son of Raghu of the solar race. To obtain these sons, Dasharatha had performed a costly sacrifice, and from the sacred fire had received a goblet of *payasa;* which he having distributed amongst his wives, Kaushalya produced Rama; Kaikeya, Bharata; and Sumitra, Lakshmana and Shatrughna. Afterwards his father, at the request of Vishvamitra, sent Rama, accompanied by Lakshmana, to protect that sage's sacrificial ceremonies; and Rama with his arrows destroyed the Rakshasas who interrupted them. Then he, accompanied by Vishvamitra and his brother, proceeded to the sacrifice of the king of Mithila, in order to behold the wonderful bow; and there Vishvamitra having explained to him its history *, Rama in sport bent and broke the bow, and Janaka in consequence betrothed to him

* This was the bow of Shiva, which had been given to an ancestor of Janaka, and he employed it as a test in order to ascertain who was a proper husband for Sita: but none of the princes who came as suitors to her were capable of raising it from the ground, far less of bending it. I have read, but I do not immediately recollect in what Puran, that Narada had revealed to Janaka that Sita was in reality an incarnation of Lakshmi, and that he should discover the person under whose form Vishnu had become incarnate, and to whom alone Sita was to be espoused, by means of this bow, as Vishnu alone would be able to bend it.

his lovely daughter Sita, and his other daughter Urmild to Lakshmana. To celebrate these marriages Dasharatha was invited from Ayodhya, and on his arrival they were duly performed; and at the same time Bharata and Shatrughna espoused the two daughters of Kushadhwaja, the younger brother of Janaka: Rama then, with his preceptor, his parents, and his brothers, returned to Ayodhya, and on the way there overcame the son of Jamadagni.

" Soon after Dasharatha thus addressed Rama: — ' To-morrow morning I intend to inaugurate thee as the *young king;* therefore chastely pass this night with Sita in religious exercises.' Having heard his father's words, Rama informed his mother Kaushalya of them, and then addressed himself to the worship of the gods. Meanwhile the king gave the necessary orders for preparing all that was required for the approaching inauguration; but a female friend hastened and informed Kaikeya that the city was adorning for the inauguration of Rama, and added, — ' If Rama become king, it will undoubtedly be the death of thy son Bharata.' Having heard these insidious words, Kaikeya bestowed on her friend a jewel, and then said, — ' I see no contrivance by means of which Bharata might enjoy the kingdom.' Her friend replied, — ' Formerly, in a battle between the Suras and Asuras, thou didst preserve thy husband's life, and he did then promise to grant thee two boons: now demand that Rama shall be ordered to reside in forests for fourteen years, and that thy son Bharata be inaugurated as the young king.' This heard, Kaikeya said, — ' What thou hast advised shall be performed:' and then she proceeded to the chamber of anger, and threw herself on the ground. No sooner was Dasharatha informed of this circumstance, than he hastened to her, and said, — ' Why art thou thus angry and troubled in spirit? Tell me what thou wishest, and I will perform it.' Kaikeya replied, — ' Formerly thou didst promise to grant me two boons: now, therefore, order Rama to reside fourteen years in the forests, and let the preparations now making be employed in the inauguration of Bharata; and unless thou grantest me these boons, I will now drink poison and die.' On hearing these words, as if struck with a thunderbolt, the king fainting fell; but, recovering his senses, he said, — ' What has Rama done to thee, that thou now pronouncest his name in this manner? and why dost thou wish to involve me in misfortune, and in the blame which will attach to me for complying with thy wish? Thou canst not be my wife, but must be some fiend; nor Bharata be my son. But without Rama I cannot live a moment; and therefore, since it is thy wish, on my death, as a widow govern this kingdom.' This said, the king, faithful to his promise, called Rama, and told him that he must leave the kingdom, in consequence of the boons which Kaikeya had demanded. Rama immediately, after having paid due obedience to his father and Kaikeya, and having consoled his mother Kaushalya, departed from the city, accompanied by ministers and attendants. That night he passed on the banks of the Tamasa, and in the morning pursued his journey, while those who had attended him returned to the city. There all the people were weeping and lamenting his departure; and Dasharatha, oppressed with grief, repaired to the apartments of Kaushalya, where for some days he continued incessantly repeating, 'Oh! that I had died before I was obliged to give that order! O my youthful son! given by the sacrifice performed on the banks of the Sarayu, how can I live without thee! but soon shall grief for thy absence end a life so unhappily prolonged.' At length, exhausted by his lamentations, the king sank one night into what seemed repose; but in the morning, when the bards and minstrels had come to awaken him, Kaushalya perceived that he had expired. On this being known, the people wept aloud and cast reproaches on Kaikeya; and Vasishta and Bharata, with Shatrughna and the elders of the people, determined to proceed to Rama, and to entreat him to assume the government. They accordingly hastened to where he was residing, and informed him that his father had ascended to heaven, and hailed him as the king of Ayodhya. Rama, however, said that he must fulfil the promise of his father; and he therefore gave the kingdom to Bharata; but, at the latter's request, he gave to him his sandals, which, during Rama's absence, were duly reverenced by Bharata.

"Rama, after travelling through several forests, and visiting several holy sages, at length came to the Dandaka Forest on the banks of the Godavari. There the ogress Surpanakha, having come to devour him, was, on beholding his beauty, inflamed with love, and thus addressed him:—'Who art thou? and whence hast thou arrived? Be my husband, or I will devour thee.' On hearing these words, Lakshmaṇa, by desire of Rama, cut off her nose and ears; and she, with her blood streaming, fled to her husband Khara, and thus spoke:—'Without thy assistance, O Khara! I shall die; for I cannot live unless thou give me to drink the blood of Rama, Sita, and Lakshmana.' This heard, Khara with a mighty army of Rakshasas attacked Rama; but he with his arrows slew them all. Then Surpanakha proceeded to Lanka, and acquainted Ravana* with what had occurred, and added,—'I will not live, unless thou carriest away Sita, and givest me the blood of Rama and Lakshmana to drink.' She ended, and Ravana thus spoke to Marichi:—'Hasten to the Dandaka Forest, and, assuming the form of a golden deer, withdraw Lakshmana and Rama from Sita, that I may then carry her away; or otherwise death is thine.'

* She was his sister.

Marichi then reflected, — 'If I must die, it is better that I should be slain by Rama than by Ravana;' and accordingly proceeded to the forest, and there appeared as a golden deer. On beholding which, Sita requested Rama to procure it for her, who hastened after it and mortally wounded it with an arrow; but as Marichi was expiring he exclaimed, — 'O Sita! O Lakshmana!' On hearing these exclamations, Sita obliged Lakshmana to proceed to the assistance of Rama, when Ravana immediately appeared and carried her away; and on the way mortally wounded the vulture Jathayusha, who attempted to oppose him. Thus in safety Ravana reached Lanka, and placing Sita in an Ashoka grove, thus spoke: — 'Be my wife, or this Rakshasa shall devour thee.' Rama, having slain the deer, was surprised when Lakshmana joined him, and hastened with apprehension to his abode; and there, not finding Sita, he was deeply grieved, and lamented aloud, exclaiming, — 'Why hast thou forsaken me? and where art thou gone?' Lakshmana having consoled him, they proceeded in search of Sita; and on the way found Jathayusha, who informed them that she had been carried away by Ravana, and then expired.

"Then, proceeding onwards to the lake Pampa, Rama formed a friendship with Sugriva and Hanuman, and having slain Bali, Sugriva's brother but enemy, he instated him in the kingdom of Kishkindha; and Sugriva promised to assist him in recovering Sita. Until, therefore, all preparations were made, Rama resided on the mountain Malya; but, Sugriva not arriving at the time appointed, he became angry, and sent Lakshmana to ascertain the reason. Sugriva then hastened to Rama, and apologised for his delay; and, having collected a numerous host of Vanaras, he despatched them in all directions to obtain intelligence of Sita. To Hanuman, also, Rama gave his ring, and he proceeded with his division towards the south; and on the road met Sampati, who informed them that Sita was detained by Ravana in an Ashoka grove in Lanka.

"On receiving this information, Hanuman proceeded onwards until he arrived at the sea; on beholding which the Vanaras exclaimed, — 'How can we pass over this, and live?' But Hanuman, in order to preserve their lives, and to accomplish the desire of Rama, immediately leaped across into Lanka, though the sea was there one hundred yojanas wide. Through Lanka then Hanuman took his way, beholding the groves and palaces of Ravana and the other princes of the Rakshasas, until he came into the Ashoka grove, where he heard Ravana threatening Sita unless she became his wife. But soon as Ravana departed Hanuman appeared, and thus spoke: — 'There was a king Dasharatha, who had two sons, Rama and Lakshmana, who went to reside in the forests, accompanied by Sita the wife of Rama; but she was carried away by Ravana. Rama hastened in search of her; and, having on the road formed a friendship with Sugriva, I have been sent in quest of Sita; since, therefore, thou art Janaka the wife of Rama, receive this ring, which he gave me in order that thou mightst know me to be his messenger.' Sita took the ring, and viewing it, thus spoke, while tears bedewed her cheeks:—'If Rama lives, why comes he not to save me?' Hanuman replied,—'He knew not the spot where thou wert concealed, but soon as informed of it he will hasten to slay Ravana and to take thee away: therefore, grieve not, but give me a jewel as a token that I have seen thee.' She gave it to him, and said,—'Now exert thyself that my lord may quickly take me hence.' Hanuman replied,—'If thou wishest it, I will this instant conduct thee to Rama and Sugriva;' but Sita said,—'With none but Rama can I hence depart.' Hanuman, in consequence, left her: but, unwilling to quit Lanka until he had seen Ravana, he, in order to obtain this object, began to destroy one of the royal groves; and, on being opposed, he slew the keepers, the guards, and seven sons of ministers, until at length he was bound with a serpent arrow by Indrajit*, and brought before Ravana, who thus spoke:—'Who art thou?' Hanuman replied,—'The messenger of Rama, who, unless thou deliverest Sita up to him, will slay thee and destroy Lanka.' This heard, Ravana in his anger would have slain Hanuman; but, being dissuaded from doing so by his brother Vibishana, he ordered his tail to be set on fire. Then Hanuman immediately broke his bonds, and, bounding away, set Lanka in flames, and again leaped over the sea and rejoined the Vanaras. He then hastened to Rama, and, having acquainted him with all that had occurred, delivered to him Sita's jewel; and, on receiving and beholding it, Rama wept aloud from the anguish of separation. Sugriva consoled him; and they then proceeded to the sea-shore; where Vibishana came to meet him, as Ravana had treated him disrespectfully in consequence of his advising him to restore Sita to her lord. The sea, however, having through pride denied Rama a passage into Lanka, the Vanaras commenced constructing a mound for that purpose.

"Meanwhile Angada was sent by Rama as an ambassador to Ravana, to demand the restoration of Sita; but he would not consent; and Angada returning informed Rama that Ravana's thoughts were bent solely on war. Rama, therefore, passed over into Lanka; and after various battles, and a great slaughter of the Rakshasas, at length slew Ravana, and bestowed his kingdom on Vibishana. Sita having been then purified by the ordeal of fire, he received her again: and having thus slain the wicked, and protected the good, he returned

* Ravana's son.

to Ayodhya, where he was received by his brothers and the people with the greatest rejoicings and gratulations. Being then enthroned, he reigned over the kingdom for eleven thousand years, and at length returned to heaven.*

KRISHNA.

"In order to relieve the earth, oppressed by wickedness, Hari was conceived as the seventh son of Devaki; but being extracted from her womb, and conveyed into that of Rohini, he was known as her son, under the name of Bala-Rama; and afterwards he was born the eighth son of Devaki, and became celebrated under the appellation of Krishna. His parents, however, fearing the vengeance of Kansa, his father Vasudeva conveyed him to the couch of Yashoda while she was asleep, and thence removed her new-born daughter, whom he gave to Devaki. But Kansa, having heard the cries of the infant, hastened to her chamber, and seizing it, was about to dash it on the floor, when she prevented him. Enraged, he exclaimed,—'Has it not been predicted that thy eighth conception shall be the cause of my death?' and threw the infant to the ground. But it sprang on high, and said,—'Why, O Kansa! dash me on the floor? for he who shall slay thee has been born.' This said, it slew the guards, and disappeared.† Kansa also sent Putana and others to effect the destruction of the child of Devaki, who had been entrusted to Yashoda by Vasudeva, and brought up by her in Gokula, in order to protect him against the attempts of Kansa; and thus Krishna and Rama, in reality the guardians of the universe, gladly became the guardians of cattle amongst cowherds and milkmaids. Once

* The above is an abstract of the Ramayanam; and it will hence appear that the incidents are well adapted for a narrative poem, which would not be devoid of very considerable interest. Unfortunately, however, in the Ramayanam of Valmiki the narrative is every moment interrupted by the introduction of some legend or other; so that the work inevitably becomes unconnected, prolix, and tedious, and the reader loses all interest in it: but in the translations of this poem in the vernacular dialects this defect does not appear, as almost all these legends are omitted; and it is in this manner that it should be presented to the European public, and its legends reserved for a dictionary of Hindu mythology. No opinion respecting the merits and demerits of the Ramayanam ought to be formed from the Serampoor version of it, for never was a work more abominably translated; and though it has the appearance of a literal translation, it does not even deserve this name, because the meaning of the original is often mistaken, and very seldom is the appropriate English word made use of. The total want, therefore, in this version, of poetical beauty and elegance is not to be ascribed to the original.

† The infant was a form assumed by Durga, who is thus addressed in the following stanza of the original:—"O most revered Durga! womb of the gods! Ambika! Badrakali! avenger! goddess with many names! the man who repeats at morning, noon, and evening, thy sacred names, shall assuredly obtain all his wishes."

Yashoda, being angry, bound Krishna to a mortar*; but he, dragging it, passed between two trees, by which it was obstructed; and he pulled until the two trees fell: another time she tied him to a cart, but he broke it into pieces with a blow of his foot: then Putana offered him her breast, and he sucked until she fell down dead. When, also, he had become a youth, he conquered the serpent Kaliya, and expelled him from the pool of the Yamuna; and restored to peace the Talavanam by slaying the Asuras, Dhenuka under the form of an ass, Arishta under that of a bull, and Keshina under that of a horse. He abolished the festival of Indra; and when the lord of the sky, in consequence, poured down torrents of rain, he uplifted the mountain Goverdhana, and rendered these torrents innocuous. Being then sent for by Kansa, he proceeded to Mathura with his attached cowherds, amusing himself as he went by various incidents. First, he slew the royal washerman who had refused him the garments of Kansa, and clothed himself and Rama with them: he then gave wealth to the flower-woman who had voluntarily supplied him with garlands: he next rendered straight the crooked woman who had presented him with perfumed ointments: and, having afterwards slain Kubala at the gate, he entered the amphitheatre, and beheld Kansa, with his ministers, guards, and attendants. There, in a wrestling match, he slew Chanura and Mushtaka, and then slew Kansa the king of Mathura; after which he made Ugra Sena the king of the Yadavas. Two of Kansa's wives, however, were the daughters of Jarasandha, who acquainted their father with what had occurred; and he immediately besieged Mathura with a mighty army. But, though Krishna defeated him, he afterwards caused Dwaraka to be built, and chose that city for the place of his residence; where he dwelt with sixteen thousand and eight wives, the chief of whom were Rukmini and Satyabhama. Having also been instructed in learning by Sandipana, he restored to him his child who had disappeared, after having slain the Daitya Panchajanya and having been duly honoured by Yama. He likewise caused the death of Kala Yavana by means of Muchukunda.

"By Rukmini was born a son, named Pradyumna, whom the Daitya Shambara, on the sixth day after his birth, carried away and threw into the sea. He was swallowed by a fish; which, being taken by a fisherman, was given to Shambara, and, on its being opened, the infant was found within it. This infant Shambara gave to his wife Mayavati†, who recognised it to be her

* A large wooden mortar in which rice is cleaned, and which always forms part of the household utensils in India.

† On Kama's having been consumed by Shiva, that god predicted to his wife Rati that her husband would be afterwards born as the son of Krishna; and it was in expectation of this event that Rati had assumed a female form under the name of Mayavati.

husband Kama, and brought it up with much care and affection. When also Pradyumna was grown up, she thus spoke to him: — 'Thou art Kama, whom Shiva rendered without a body (*Ananga*), and whom Shambara carried away and threw into the sea; do thou, therefore, slay him.' Pradyumna in consequence slew Shambara, and then returned to his parents.

"Thus the one lord, as Krishna, lived happily in this world with Rukmini and his other wives, and begot a numerous race of sons.* He also assisted the Pandavas in their war with the Kauravas; and, by their means, relieved the earth from the weight of wicked men by which it was oppressed. But when the object of his incarnation was accomplished, then was the whole race of Yadavas destroyed, in consequence of the curse of the divine sages, by mutual slaughter; Balabhadra, the incarnate form of Ananta†, departed to heaven; and Hari, forsaking mortality, returned to Vaikuntha.

BUDDHA AND KALKI.

"The Suras, having been defeated in battle by the Asuras, sought the protection of Vishnu; who, in consequence, was born under the delusive form of Buddha, the son of Jina, by whom the Asuras were deceived; and, being induced to abandon the religion of the Vedas, lost all power as warriors. From that time has the faith of Buddha flourished; and many are the heretics who have forsaken the sacred ordinances of the Vedas.

"In the *Kali Yug*, thoughtless men shall begin to commit acts deserving of hell; and the destruction of castes shall be continued. Then shall virtue and religion disappear, and scarce a single school remain; and barbarians, under the forms of kings, externally arrayed in justice, but internally composed of injustice, shall devour the people. But at length shall Vishnu appear as Kalki, destroy the barbarians, and reestablish the pure customs and morals which depend on a due observance of the duties prescribed to castes and to the four classes: after which shall Hari return to heaven; and the *Satya Yug*, then returning, shall restore the world to purity, virtue, and piety."

---

* I here omit an abstract of the Mahabharat.

† At the commencement of this account of the avatar of Krishna, it will be observed, that Bala-Rama is said to be an incarnation of Vishnu, and here he is described as an incarnate form of Ananta; but both these opinions are current amongst the Hindus, who sometimes exclude Buddha from the ten avatars, and make the eighth and ninth to have been Bala-Rama and Krishna; and this is supported by more than one Puran.

THE NARAYANA UPANISHAD.*

The primeval male Narayana loves the beings that he has created. From Narayana were produced the vital breath, the mind, the senses and their organs, ether, fire, air, water, and earth. From Narayana were produced Brahma, Rudra, the Prajapatis, the twelve Suns, the Rudras, and the Vasavas; and from Narayana were produced the Vedas and all sacred learning. By Narayana are all things created, preserved, and destroyed, and again produced. Thus, Narayana is Rudra, Narayana is Brahma, Narayana is the twelve Suns, the Vasavas, and the Ashwinau; Narayana is all *Rishis;* Narayana is Kala (time), and all that is above or below, external or internal; Narayana is all that was and shall be, without parts, without affection, incomprehensible, unnameable, and immaculate. Narayana is the one god, and there is not a second: HE is certainly Vishnu, HE is certainly Vishnu. Let *om* be first said, then *nama*, and afterwards *Narayanaya*. *Om* is one syllable, *nama* is two syllables, and *Narayanaya* five syllables; thus, *om Narayanaya nama* is that eight-syllabled invocation, from the repetition of which are obtained long life, wealth, and progeny; and, finally, immortality, by participating in the bliss ineffable of god. The syllable *om* is composed of the letters *a*, *u*, and *m;* and he who repeats these letters thus joined together shall be delivered from the miseries of transitory existence. Hence *om Narayanaya nama* is that invocation, which whoever repeats, he shall ascend to Vaikuntha, he shall ascend to Vaikuntha. Of divine nature is the son of Devaki — of divine nature is Madhusudana; for Narayana, who dwelleth in all things, the uncaused cause of all that exists, is Parabrahm. *Om*, he who meditates on this portion of the *Atharva Shiras*† at night, the sins which he has committed during the day shall be remitted; if in the morning, all nocturnal sin shall be destroyed; and, if at mid-day, seated opposite to the sun, the five great sins and all lesser ones shall be forgiven to him; his virtue shall become equal to that acquired by a thorough knowledge and observance of the Vedas; and he shall obtain identification with Narayana.

* This Upanishad forms part of the *Atharva Shiras* Upanishad.

† The *Atharvas Shiras* Upanishad consists of five distinct Upanishads, which relate to the five principal deities, or the *five shrines* (*panchayatanani*), and are therefore entitled the Ganapati, Narayana. Rudra, Surya, and Devi Upanishads.

APPENDIX D.

EXTRACTS ILLUSTRATIVE OF THE CHARACTER OF SHIVA.

THE RUDRA UPANISHAD.*

THE gods proceeded to the celestial abode of Rudra, and enquired, "Who art thou?" He replied,—"I am the first and sole essence; I am and shall be, and there is not any thing which is distinct from me." Having thus spoken, he disappeared; *and then an unseen voice was heard saying,* — "I am he who causeth transitoriness, and yet endureth for ever; I am Brahm; I am the east and the west, the north and the south; I am space and *vacuum;* I am masculine, feminine, and neuter; I am Savitri, the Gayatri, and all sacred verse; I am the three fires; I am the most ancient, the most excellent, the most venerable, and the mightiest; I am the splendour of the four Vedas, and the mystic syllable; I am imperishable and mysterious, but the revealer of mysteries; I am all that is, and all space is pervaded by my essence." This heard, the gods meditated on Rudra, though unseen, and then with uplifted hands thus adored him: — "Praise be to thee, who art Brahma, Vishnu, and Maheshwara †! praise be to thee, who art Uma, Ganesha, and Skanda! praise be to thee, who art Indra and Agni! praise be to thee, who art the earth, the sky, and heaven! praise be to thee, who art the Mahar, Jana, Tapa, and Satya Loks! praise be to thee, who art earth, water, fire, air, and ether! praise be to thee, who art the sun and moon! praise be to thee, who art the stars and planets! praise be to thee, who art time, death, and Yama! praise be to thee, who art immortal, the past, the present, and the future! praise be to thee, who art all that is, the sole and universal essence! praise, praise be to thee, O Rudra, O Ishana, O Maheshwara, O Mahadeva, O lord, for thou art Parabrahm, the one and only god!

---

* From the *Atharva Shiras* Upanishad.

† That is, who hast manifested thyself under all these different forms.

THE ISHWARA GITA. *

CHAPTER I.

The sages thus addressed Suta:—"Thou hast, O lord! explained to us all that relates to the creation, and to the divisions and periods of time; and now be pleased to acquaint us with the true nature of Mahadeva, and instruct us in that divine knowledge by which final beatitude can alone be obtained. For thou, O Suta! hast derived this information from Krishna Devipayana, who was undoubtedly an incarnation of Vishnu." Suta replied,—"Vyasa once came to where the holy sages were performing a course of sacrifice; who, on observing him, received him with all due salutations and honour. Vyasa being then seated, and having made the usual complimentary enquiries, Suta, having respectfully bowed to his preceptor, thus addressed him:—'O sage deeply skilled in sacred learning! thou art capable of instructing these sages in that divine knowledge which gives final beatitude, and thus to relieve them from that anxious search after truth with which their minds are at present disquieted.' Vyasa gladly replied in these pleasure-giving words:—'I will acquaint you with what Mahadeva formerly said, in answer to questions proposed to him by Sanatkumara and other divine personages. Formerly Sanatkumara, his brothers Angiras, Bhrigu, Kanada, Kapila, Garga, Vamadeva, and Vasishta, having agreed together, performed, with devout and abstracted minds, a severe *tapas* at Badarikashramam. † At length Narayana, who is without beginning or end, appeared to them; and, after having been received with due salutations and praises, enquired what was the object of the *tapas*. The sages, delighted that he, who was in truth Narayana, had appeared to them, replied,—"O lord! thou knowest all mysteries, and therefore be pleased to resolve the doubts by which we are perplexed, and to inform us what is the cause of all that is; how all things thus continually revolve; what is this world, and why was it created; what is the soul, what is final beatitude, and what the real nature of Parabrahm." This heard, Narayana threw off the appearance of an ascetic, and manifested himself resplendent in his own glorious form; refulgent as molten

* From the *Kurma Puran.* I need scarcely observe that, as this passage abounds as usual in repetition, I have abridged it considerably; but I have omitted nothing except what is mentioned more than once. In my copy of this Puran there are no titles to the chapters, and I have not, therefore, thought it proper to add them.

† This is the place where Nara and Narayana, incarnations of Shiva and Vishnu, are supposed to abide, though invisibly, as it appears from this passage.

gold, and displaying in his hands the disc, the conch, the lotos, and the bow, sharuga. Nara, also, at this time appeared, and revealed his divine figure; and appeared as Mahadeva, with three eyes, and the moon adorning his head. On beholding the lord of the three worlds the sages were delighted, and thus devoutly adored Maheshwara: — "Victory be to thee, O Ishwara, Mahadeva, Shiva, lord of the Bhutas! victory be to thee, O Isha, the adored by pious ascetics! victory be to thee, O lord, the creator, preserver, and destroyer of this universe!" Shiva, having then embraced Vishnu, enquired what was the wish of the divine sages: Vishnu informed him, and, after they had been all duly seated, Shiva complied with their request.

CHAPTER II.

'*Ishwara thus began:* — "I will communicate to you the mysterious and everlasting knowledge of my real nature; which when created beings have once acquired, O learned and holy Brahmans! they will no longer be subject to the evils of transitory existence. Know, then that the soul * is of a pure and subtle nature, unaffected by external or internal objects; it is invisible, but manifests itself as Purusha, Prakriti, Maheshwara, and Time. Through it this universe is produced and annihilated; for it is the cause of *Maya*, which delusively displays an endless variety of apparently existing forms. But the soul itself neither creates nor is created; it is neither earth nor sea; fire nor air; nor hearing, touch, sight, smell, nor taste; it has neither feet, nor hands, nor other organs; it neither acts nor suffers, for it is neither Purusha nor Prakriti, nor Maya †: for, as the mind is distinct from the thoughts which arise in it, so is the supreme soul distinct from the illusive appearances which it generates; and as the shadow in water is separate from its object, so is the soul of each created being from that illusion which it contemplates; because, when released from liability to transmigration, the liberated soul becomes identified with that sole immutable, incorporeal, ineffably happy, and supreme spirit. It is, therefore, *Ahankar* alone which, united to the souls of men, induces them to think that they act or suffer, or that they experience pleasure or pain. It is *Ahankar* which is the root of that ignorance, which leads men to consider Purusha and Prakriti

* The more proper translation of this word would be *spirit*, as opposed to *matter*. I have, however, employed the usual word; but the reader must recollect the leading principle of Hindu philosophy, which is, that there is no other *ens* than one sole self-existent spirit, and that all seeming realities are mere illusive appearances.

† This may appear inconsistent; but here the simple and real nature of *spirit* only is spoken of, and it will be afterwards seen that it loses its simplicity before Maya or Purusha is generated.

to be the first causes, and to mistake the real nature of their souls. But, when they know that there is but one supreme soul, and that the soul of every man is of the same nature, immutable, passionless, and imperishable ; then they become liberated from pleasure and pain, from anger and hatred, and from sin and its retribution. Wise men, therefore, say that the supreme soul is adualistic, and that duality proceeds solely from Maya ; and, consequently, as the sky is not blackened by smoke, so is not the soul affected by the evil passions which arise in the mind ; but as crystal shines with its own lustre, so does the soul, exempt from Maya, retain its splendour unsullied. They also, who know that the soul from its essential nature is always the same, immaterial, and exempt from modification, perceive that this universe, though consisting, in appearance, of an endless variety of mutable forms, is in reality but a manifestation of the one self-existent and supreme spirit ; for, as when a red flower is placed within a pure crystal vase, the vase retains its purity, though it assumes a red colour ; thus does the soul, though invested with various forms, still remain unaffected and unchanged. The soul, therefore, is immaterial, pure, all-pervading, immutable, and eternal.

" Those, consequently, who desire final beatitude, ought to meditate continually on the real nature of the soul. For whoever, steadfast in faith, has by means of abstract contemplation become acquainted with it, he is completely liberated from the bonds of Maya ; and that knowledge affords the only real remedy for all the pains and miseries attendant on transitory existence. Since, soon as a man is enlightened with this knowledge, he becomes identified with the supreme spirit ; and, as rivers become one with the ocean, so does he, who knows what the soul really is, attain identification with the unity of god. Thus, to the enlightened there is neither transitoriness nor illusion ; as it is ignorance alone which deceives, for knowledge exhibits the truth undisguised and free from all fallacious appearances. The only certain means, however, of acquiring this knowledge is by an adherence to the *Sankhya* and *Yoga* doctrines, for they are the same ; but he who sedulously devotes himself to them will undoubtedly become acquainted with the real nature of the deity. He will then know that I alone am the supreme spirit, and that there is no other god ; that I am the universal soul, the universal form, the beginning and end of all things ; without eyes I see, and without ears I hear ; I am the Vedas, and all sacred learning relates to me. But this truth men cannot know as long as they are involved in illusion ; and, therefore, they ought to addict themselves to devout contemplation, in order that they may obtain identification with my essence : for then they will be liberated from all the effects of Maya, and will, in union with me, enjoy supreme and eternal happiness."

CHAPTER III.

'*Ishwara continued.* — "From the supreme spirit proceeded Purusha, Prakriti, and Time; and by them was produced this universe, the manifestation of the one god. For I am that spirit; and men skilled in the Vedas know that all things, animate and inanimate, of which this universe consists, are merely multitudinous forms which are assumed by that all-pervading spirit. From it, therefore, existing from all eternity, proceeded Purusha, Prakriti, and Time, which, consequently, are also without a beginning.* From Prakriti, the delusive cause of all apparent corporeal forms, were produced intellect and consciousness (*Ahankar*); and by the permutation and interchanging of these elements originate the twenty-five principles †, from which are produced this universe, and all that it contains. But it is *Ahankar* that gives rise to vitality, sensation, and the consciousness of pleasure and pain, and the other consequences which are attendant on birth. From the union, also, or disjunction of Prakriti and Time are caused the creation and annihilation of this universe; for Time effects all that it wishes; and hence is the eternal and supreme being known under the name of Time (*Kala*). Of all the organs, too, of sense and intellect, the best is the mind, which proceeds from *Ahankar*, *Ahankar* from intellect, intellect from the supreme being, who is in fact Purusha. It is that primeval male whose form constitutes this universe, and whose breath is the sky; and, though incorporeal, that male am I: for there is no other being than me; and he who acquires the knowledge of my divine nature obtains eternal happiness. Besides all things movable and immovable, there is nothing transitory; because, when united to Time I manifest myself, then do I create the world; and when I conceal myself, then do I destroy it. But its existence and non-existence are mere illusions; for I, the supreme spirit, am self-existent and eternal."

CHAPTER IV.

'*Ishwara continued.* — "I will now explain to you, O Brahmans! the greatness of the god of gods, the cause of all things; for, without devout meditation, the knowledge of my divine nature is not to be acquired by the bestowing of

* That is, *quoad* their being essentially of the same nature as the supreme spirit, they are without *beginning*, though under these forms *beginning* is, of course, predicable of them.

† These are Purusha, Prakriti, intellect, consciousness, the five elementary atoms, the mind, the five senses with their five organs, and the five elements, ether, air, fire, water, and earth. These principles, however, are differently enumerated in Chapter VII. of this quotation.

gifts, by ascetic practices, or by sacrifice. Within all things I dwell, and yet no one knows me, though I am every where present; and no one beholds me, though I am in the very object which he contemplates. That one god am I, who is invoked in the Vedas, to whom sacrifices are offered, and on whom ascetics meditate. I am the enjoyer of all oblations, and the granter of the benefits resulting from them. I am the universal form, and the universal spirit; and to those who are virtuous, pious, and devout, I give the most excellent reward of eternal happiness; even Shudras and the lower castes, if they worship me, shall in due time obtain final beatitude: never shall those perish, who devoutly adore me, for all their sins shall be remitted. Such was the promise made from the beginning to my votaries, and the fool who reviles them reviles the god of gods; but he who worships me, even if he with devout mind offers but leaves, flowers, and water, shall obtain my favour. I am the creator of the universe, the divulger of the Vedas, the protector of the virtuous, and the destroyer of the irreligious, exempt from mutability, the causer of transitory existence, and the support and guardian of all that is created; at one time assuming the form of Brahma, I create this universe; and at another, under the form of Rudra, I destroy it. Animating Purusha and Prakriti, I cause the world to exist, but I do not act myself; and the destruction occasioned by Time, though ascribed to Mahadeva, I actuate, but I cause it not. Such, however, as I really am, some behold me by means of works, some by devotion, some by meditation, and some by the acquisition of divine knowledge; but he who seeks this knowledge by adhering to thè practices of the *Yogi* is most acceptable to me. Thus have I explained my divine nature; and he, who understands that such is really my essential being, has acquired that knowledge which insures him eternal happiness."

CHAPTER V.

"*Vyasa said:*—'Having thus spoken, the supreme lord danced and displayed his divine nature. Then did the holy sages behold Isha, refulgent with ineffable splendour, dancing in the pure expanse of heaven, with a thousand heads and a thousand eyes, with matted locks, and his head adorned with the crescent; clothed in a tiger's skin, displaying in his mighty hands a trident and a lance, his neck encircled with a string of skulls; the sun, moon, and fire forming his three eyes; with horrid tusks; of hue like pure crystal, effulgent as a myriad of suns, and emitting beams of fire difficult to behold, and capable of consuming the universe. Thus, as the eternal and supreme lord, the framer and preserver of this world continued dancing; on a sudden the sages beheld Vishnu obtain unification with Ishwara. On thus viewing the unity of the divine nature of the two deities, the minds of the sages were enlightened; and then, with bended heads and clasped hands, having often repeated the mystic syllable, they thus with laudatory strains began: — "Thou art the sole god, the primeval male, the ancient of days, the lord of life; thee do we adore, who dwellest in every heart, and whom devout men through meditation know to be that pure, all-pervading, and divine essence which is the supreme and universal soul. It is thou who art the producer of this universe, and of all that it contains; who art less than the least, and greater than the greatest; who didst, under the form of Hiranyagarbha, create the three worlds and divulge the Vedas; and who bestowest on thy votaries a future state of endless bliss. Beholding thee thus amid the sky wheeling in the dance as revolves the wheel of time*, we recognise thy greatness, and seek the protection of thy feet. Thee do we adore, who art Brahma, Vishnu, Rudra, the sun, the fire, and who appearest under a multitude of forms, but art still the one god, incorporeal, imperishable, and eternal."

CHAPTER VI.

'Having heard these words of the divine sages, Ishwara, regarding them, thus spoke with a loud voice: — "There is but one creator, but one preserver, and but one destroyer; and that is I, who am the eternal and universal soul; the beginning, the middle, and the end of all things, and there is no other than I. All that ye behold, O Brahmans! is my form; and all the apparent differences that you observe in it are occasioned by me, through Maya. For, though exempt from Maya, I yet, at the beginning of creation, invest myself with it, and, agitating Purusha and Prakriti, by their union are produced the elements from which this universe is formed; and from my essence also proceed Brahma, Vishnu, the sun, and the other gods. According, likewise, to my *fiat*, Brahma creates, Narayana protects, and Rudra destroys; Agni (fire) serves domestic purposes, and consumes the oblations offered to the gods; Varuna resides in the waters and vivifies all things; Vaiu, pervading the exterior of all bodies, supports them; the moon produces medicinal plants which restore life to man; the sun illuminates all things by its effulgence; Indra nourishes the earth with rain; Yama rules over the dead; Kubera presides over riches; Ganesha obviates difficulties; Skanda commands the celestial

* The mutations and vicissitudes of this world are compared by Sanscrit authors to the revolutions of a potter's wheel.

armies; Marichi and the other Prajapatis produce various classes of beings; Lakshmi, the spouse of Narayana, bestows fortune and prosperity; Saraswati confers eloquence; Savitri* preserves men from hell; Parvati communicates divine knowledge; Shesha supports the fourteen worlds on his head; the Manus protect mankind; and in like manner are their allotted functions performed by the Adityas, the Vasavas, the Maruts, the Ashwinau, the Gandharvas, the Vidiadharas, the Siddhas, the Charanas, the Yakshas, the Pisachas, and the Rakshasas. Thus, also, according to my *fiat*, all things on earth, and below the earth, movable and immovable, exist and act according to their respective natures. In like manner Prakriti, ether, air, fire, water, earth, mind, and understanding, continually undergo their appointed changes; Maya incessantly presents an endless variety of illusive appearances; and the soul is always succeeding in divesting itself of illusion and in obtaining final beatitude. This universe, therefore, with all that it contains, is but a manifestation of my energy, and on me do its existence and non-existence solely depend; for I am the lord god, the supreme spirit existing in my own effulgence, and eternal; but no one, except myself, knows my real nature."

CHAPTER VII.

'*Ishwara continued.*—"Listen, O Brahmans! while I reveal unto you a mysterious truth, the knowledge of which will preserve men from the misery of future births. Though I am the sole self-existent god, incorporeal, and immutable, still do I assume various forms. Amongst the skilled in divine knowledge, therefore, I am Brahma; amongst those exempt from Maya, I am that ancient god Hari; amongst Yogis, Shambhu; amongst females, the mountain-born goddess; amongst the Adityas, Vishnu; amongst the Vasdevas, Vani; amongst the Rudras, Shankara; amongst birds, Garura; amongst elephants, Airavata; amongst warriors, Rama; amongst Rishis, Vasishta; amongst the gods, Indra; amongst artificers, Vishwakarma; amongst the Asuras, Prahlada; amongst Munis, Vyasa; amongst the Ganas, Ganesha; amongst heroes, Virabadhra; amongst Siddhas, Kapila; amongst mountains, Meru; amongst the stars, the Moon; amongst serpents, Shesha; amongst leaders of armies, Skanda; amongst the yugs, the Satya yug; amongst the Yakshas, Kubera; amongst the Prajapatis, Daksha; amongst the Rakshasas, Nairrita; amongst the Devipas, Pushkara; amongst animals, the lion; amongst instruments, the bow; amongst

* Here Savitri means the Gayatri.

the Vedas, the Sama; amongst invocations, the mystic syllable; amongst the Manus, Swayambhuva; amongst countries, Brahma-Varta; amongst temples, Kashi; among destructive causes, Maha-Kala; and among the different kinds of beatitude, *Moksha* (identification with the supreme being). Know, farther, that the souls which exist in a transitory state are named *Pashava* (living beings), and, as I am their lord, I am called *Pashupati**; as, also, I bind men in bonds from which none can release them except myself, I am likewise known under the appellation of *Mochaka* (liberator). Those bonds, the causes of pain and misery, are the twenty-four principles, by means of which Maya exerts its power; namely, mind, understanding, *Ahankar*, ether, air, fire, water, earth, the five senses and their organs, the anus, the organs of generation, the hands, the feet, the voice, and Prakriti — that invisible cause, without beginning, or middle, or end, the supporter of the three qualities of purity, impurity, and darkness, from which this universe originated. But that Prakriti is merely my energy, and I am, consequently, the bond, its framer, its binder, and the liberator of men from it."

CHAPTER VIII.

'*Ishwara continued.* — " In the beginning of time were produced Purusha and Prakriti, the elementary atoms, intellect, the organs of sense and intellect, and the five elements; and these principles were enclosed within a golden egg, from which sprang Brahma refulgent as a myriad of suns, who, through the power which I conferred on him, created all things. Men, therefore, who are deceived by illusion do not acknowledge me to be the universal father, but the wise know me to be such; and whoever acquires this knowledge is liberated from illusion. For I am Brahma the creator, the supreme lord that dwelleth in all things; that destroyeth what is destroyable, and beholdeth all that is visible; but the soul is indestructible, and attaineth a future state the most excellent. He, therefore, who becomes acquainted with the seven subtle principles and six elements of which my essence is composed, obtains a knowledge of the divine nature of Parabrahm. Know then that these principles are self-existence, immaculateness, blessedness, self-sufficingness, omniscience, omnipotence, and eternity; and the six elements are the five primary atoms and intellect. But, as the oil appears not until the sesamum has been pressed, so do these remain undisclosed until they are excited to operation by Prakriti; which is itself

* *Pashu* is the singular, and *Pashava* the plural. In the original there is a continued play on the words *Pashu* and *Pasha*, a bond, a noose, &c.

inoperative until it is united to me under the form of Purusha. Hence do wise men name Prakriti the divine womb, and me that invisible seed from which this universe, with all that it contains, has been produced. Those, however, who are enlightened know that before all things one god alone existed; and that, as this universe is merely the manifestation of his splendour, there is in reality, notwithstanding the variety which seemingly prevails, but one sole and all-pervading spirit."

CHAPTER IX.

'*The sages said,* — "Explain, O Mahadeva! how this universe can be a manifestation of that supreme being who is without parts, without materiality, and without transitoriness." Ishwara replied, — "Know, O Brahmans! that I am not the universe, and yet the universe is not distinct from me: for that Maya, which is without beginning or end, and which resideth in my essence, is the cause of all that it is; and, though itself invisible, it renders manifest those illusive appearances of which this universe consists. But I, the supreme being, existing in brightness and in bliss ineffable, am the cause of Maya; and therefore it is that enlightened men consider the universe to be a manifestation of my form. For, though unity and diversity be apparent, yet there is but one self-existent and all-pervading spirit, and that spirit am I; and it is my energy alone which presents to men the semblance of divisibility and indivisibility, of difference of sexes, and of the varied forms with which they are surrounded. But as the interwoven threads form one web, so is this universe one whole; and he who knows that this whole is in reality the one god, becomes liberated from illusion. When a man, therefore, knows that as light, wherever it appears, is still the same, so the soul, however apparently individuated, is still but one and the same, he is delivered from an ignorant belief in materiality, and obtains immortality and bliss ineffable by identification with the sole god: for, as the splendour of the sky is reflected within a pure golden vase, so from divine knowledge arises in the mind of the enlightened a pure and bright effulgence; and then he perceives that there is no other soul than his own, and that *that* is in reality the supreme soul. Thus, there is but one sole, self-existent, and all-pervading spirit; and, consequently, except that spirit, nothing exists either in appearance or reality."

CHAPTER X.

'*Ishwara continued.* — "The invisible state of god is not denoted by any external indication; but when he manifests himself, then is light an indication of his divine being. Divine knowledge, also, is another indication; for those who acquire it become acquainted with my real nature; and there is no other means by which I can be known. Ignorance, therefore, is that darkness of understanding which creates a belief in the existence of this Maya-produced universe; but knowledge is a pure brightness which dispels illusion and reveals the true nature of spirit. Those, consequently, who learn to behold unity in diversity; to believe in this essential truth, that there is one god alone, and no other; and to know that their own souls are that god, are liberated from the bonds of transitory existence, and obtain the most blessed of all states, identification with my essence: for I am that one god, without beginning, middle, or end; and whoever knows me, Ishwara, Mahadeva, to be that sole, supreme, and ineffably happy god, shall obtain final beatitude."

CHAPTER XI.

'*Ishwara continued.* — "I will now explain to thee, O Brahmans skilled in sacred learning! the different acts of *Yoga*, by means of which man may acquire divine knowledge, and may behold, clearly as the sun, the real nature of his own soul and of god; for the fire of *Yoga* quickly and entirely consumes sin, and enlightens the mind with the pure beams of truth. Of these acts the names and peculiar modes of performing are innumerable; but I will mention a few of the principal ones. — The *Yama yoga*, then, consists in *Ahimsa*, in adherence to truth, in not stealing, in chastity, and in non-acceptance of gifts. *Ahimsa*, wise men define to be the abstaining from hurting living beings in any manner; and there is no virtue of greater excellence than this; but the shedding of blood prescribed by the Vedas does not become *Ahimsa*.* The *Niyama yoga* consists in *Tapas*, reading the Vedas, contentment, purity †, and the worship of god. The *Asanam*, in the different postures in which the *Yogi* should sit. Another

* It is not necessary to add the explanations given of the other virtues.

† Purity is explained to be of two kinds, eternal and internal; the one effected by pure water, and the other by cleansing the mind from all sinful affections.

act of *Yoga* is the *Pranayamam*, the greater or less efficacy of which depends on the number of the suppressions of breath, and the manner in which they are performed by the devotee. The *Pratyahara* is the non-employment of the organs of sense and intellect. *Dharana* consists in fixing the mind on the lotos of the heart, the pineal gland, or some other internal object; *Dhyanam*, in concentrating the thoughts into meditation on god alone; and *Samadhi*, which is the most excellent of these acts, in contemplating, without the intervention of any object, sensible or intellectual, the supreme spirit. But the most effectual mode of obtaining divine knowledge is for the aspirant to select a pure spot on the bank of a river, in some holy place, or even in his own house, devoid of animals and men; and there, seated in a proper posture, with subdued passions, and his half-closed eyes fixed upon the tip of his nose, to meditate on that supreme being who dwelleth in his own soul; for by these means the delusion of Maya will be destroyed, and he will learn that there is nothing but one supreme spirit, and that his soul is that spirit.

"There are, however, other acts of devotion by which beatitude can be obtained. The *Pashupati yoga*, for instance, requires, that after purifying his mind with the water of knowledge, and fixing his thoughts upon me, the *Yogi* should rub over his body the ashes taken from a sacrificial fire, and then meditate on my glorious form; by which means he will be liberated from the bonds of illusion, and obtain identification with my essence. Another is *Brahmacharya*, which consists in resignation, purity, ascetic practices, self-restraint, adherence to truth, contentment, and faith; and whoever acquires these virtues, and has subdued his passions, approximates to me. Thus, of the many who obtain identification with my essence, some acquire it by knowledge, some by virtue, and some by acts of devotion. Of these last, the most acceptable to me is the abandonment of the world, the living on alms, and the non-acceptance of gifts. But I am also pleased with him who, devoid of self-sufficiency, pride, hatred, and other evil passions, is endowed with tenderness to living beings, compassion, friendliness, and such virtues; for he who is of a pure mind, who neither hopes nor fears, who is indifferent to praise and blame, who is content with what he has, whatever it may be, who desires nothing, who is steadfast in devotion to me, and who, in all that he does, remembers me, shall obtain a most excellent future state. Mental acts, however, are the most efficacious; and the *Sanyasi*, therefore, who gives up the advantages resulting from works, and, without hope or desire, seeks no other object than me, more speedily obtains his reward. But works, also, though of a corporeal nature, will be recompensed;

for he who propitiates me by any work, in order to be delivered from the miseries of transitory existence, shall attain the desired object; and thus shall every work be rewarded according to its nature. In the same manner, he who seeks to derive advantage from the worship of any other deity, and at the same time believes in the unity of god, shall be pardoned his sins, and shall receive a suitable recompense. But superior in efficacy to devotion to the other gods is the worship of my lingam; for why should not that lingam be eternally worshipped, which exists, as enlightened men know, in fire, in sacrifice, in earth, in water, in ether, in the sun, and in all things of which this universe consists. Fools, indeed, think it to be merely earth or stone; but wise men know it to be the same as that lingam which is situated in their own hearts. Thus, O Brahmans! is divine knowledge acquired, through which men become acquainted with the real nature of their souls; and having learned that nothing but spirit exists, and that I am the sole, self-existent, and all-pervading spirit, they are for ever released from the miseries of transitory existence, and obtain eternal felicity by identification with my essence.

"Vyasa said, — 'Ishwara, having thus spoken, addressed himself to Narayana, and said, — "I have thus, O Narayana! instructed these Brahmans in divine knowledge; and may my words prove profitable both to them and their pupils!" Then addressing the holy sages, he thus continued: — "I have now fully explained the different subjects respecting which your minds were perplexed with doubts; but know farther, that this Narayana and myself are one and the same, and that there is no difference between us. He is, like me, incorporeal, imperishable, and the supreme and universal soul. Those, however, who behold diversity in this universe, consider us to be distinct deities, naming him Vishnu, and me Maheshwara; but those who know that we are in essence one and the same shall not be again subject to birth. Therefore worship Vishnu like myself, for he is equally without beginning or end, immaterial, and the sole self-existent spirit; and those who consider me to be a god distinct from him shall sink into the deepest hell. Vishnu, consequently, must be adored and worshipped by all who wish to propitiate my favour by their devotion to me." Ishwara here ended; and, having embraced Vasudeva, disappeared.'"

THE LEGEND OF JALANDHARA.*

One day Narada came to see the Pandavas sunk in affliction, and was received by them with the usual marks of respect; then bowing to the divine sage, Yudhishtira thus spoke :—" My lord, on account of what actions have we fallen into this sea of affliction?" The sage replied,—" O sons of Pandu! cast aside your grief: in this universe of pleasures and pains, what being enjoys pleasure alone? Even to that god, who is free from all afflictions, the assumption of corporeal existence produces pain; none is exempt from pain; pain is inseparable from the state of transitory existence. The powerful Rahu swallows the body of the sun, that Rahu whose head was cut off for having drunk the water of immortality; and the valiant Jalandhara, after having compelled the bearer of *Sharnga* † to repose in the sea of milk, was slain by Shambhu."

Yudhishtira said,—" Who was the valiant Jalandhara, whose son, and whence did he derive his power? How was he vanquished by him whose standard is the bull? All this relate in detail, O divine sage!" The omniscient Narada then, with kindness, related the following legend: —

CHAPTER I.

The Birth of Jalandhara.

" Hear, O king! the whole of that divine tale, the destroyer of a sea of sins, and the wonderful war which took place between Isha and the son of the Sea. One day, to adore Girisha, proceeded Pakhashasena ‡, surrounded by the angels and Gandharwas, and attended by a troop of Apsaras all radiant with costliest gems. Narada with his vina, dancers, and musicians, also accompanied the chief of the deities to the abode of Shiva. When there arrived, they beheld Kailasa, the most sacred place for devotion, the ornament of the mountains of the earth, the complete bestower of satisfaction, purity, and fulfilment of all wishes. There the trees and rocks inspire contemplation, and the mountain is resplendent with loftiest trees, the blossoms of which, waving to the wind, shed lustre and perfume. There appear ponds clear as crystal, with steps leading to the pure and deep water, ornamented with gold, resembling lotoses supported on beryl stalks: in them the white lotos casts around a silvery splendour, while the red lotos is refulgent as the ruby. Thus beholding Kailasa, the holiest of

* From the commencement of the *Uttara Khand* of the Padma Puran.

† This is the name of the bow of Vishnu.

‡ Indra.

mountains, adorned with such excellent loveliness, the deities were filled with astonishment. Then descending from their celestial cars, Indra thus addressed Nandi the warder: —'O chief of Shiva's attendants, hear! quickly inform Ishwara, the chief of gods, that I am come attended by the deities for the purpose of amusing him with a dance.' On hearing these words, Nandi went and addressed Girisha: —"O lord! Purandara, the king of the deities, has come here for the purpose of dancing.' Shiva replied,—'Quickly bring the husband of Sachi.' Nandi then introduced him along with the other deities, and on beholding Girisha Indra paid him due adoration; the musicians then began sounding their instruments, and the dancers danced before Hara: so harmoniously played the instruments, and so well was the dance performed, that Purandara was filled with arrogance; so that when Ishwara delighted thus addressed him, —'O chief of angels! I am well pleased; ask whatever is most agreeable to thee,'—Indra proudly replied, in words breathing defiance, —'Give me, O lord! to be in battle a warrior like thyself.' Having obtained* this boon from Shambhu, Ishnu departed.

"Shakra having left the assembly, Girisha thus spoke,—'O my attendants! heard you not the haughty words of the king of deities?' Thus spoke Hara, inflamed with anger, and immediately stood before him a corporeal form of anger, black as darkness, who thus addressed Mrira,—'Give me thy similitude, and then what shall I do for thee, my lord?' The lord of Uma replied,—'Having incorporated thyself with the River of heaven, and formed a union with the Ocean, go and conquer Vasawa.' Having thus spoken, Shiva disappeared, and his attendants remained lost in astonishment.

"In obedience to the orders of Isha, the lovely River, in immortal youth, hastened from the skies to form a union with the Ocean; and the King of Rivers, on beholding her, with heaving billows expressed his joy. Then, O king! was effected the union of Ganga and the Sea; and having obtained the mighty River, Ocean delighted joined with her in amorous dalliance. From their embraces sprang a mighty son, at whose birth the earth trembled and wept, and the three worlds resounded; and Brahma, having broken the seal of meditation, and having perceived the universe lost in terror, mounted his hamsa, and, reflecting on this prodigy, proceeded to the Sea. On his arrival, Ocean received him with due honours, and then Brahma said,—'Why, O Sea! dost thou uselessly produce such loud and fearful sounds?' Ocean replied,—'It is not I, O chief of gods! but my mighty son, who thus roars: let the beholding

* This is according to the original; but, from subsequent events related in the legend, it would seem that the boon must have been refused.

of thee, so difficult to be obtained, be the protection of the child.' He then said to his lovely wife, —'Let thy son be shown:' and she, in obedience to her husband's orders, brought her son, and, having placed him in the lap of Brahma, bowed herself to his feet. When Brahma beheld the wonderful son of Ocean, he was filled with astonishment; and the child having taken hold of his beard, he was unable to liberate it from his grasp. But Ocean, smiling, approached and loosed it from the hand of his son. Brahma, admiring the strength of this infant, then said,—'From his holding so firmly, let him be named Jalandhara;' and further, with fondness bestowed, on him this boon:— 'This Jalandhara shall be unconquered by the gods, and shall, through my favour, enjoy the three worlds.' Having thus spoken, Brahma disappeared.

CHAPTER II.

The Enthroning of Jalandhara, and his Marriage with Vrinda.

"Arrived at boyhood, this boy, supported in the lap of the wind, flew over the ocean; and having brought the whelps of lions, placed them in a cage for his amusement. On earth lions and elephants were alone fit objects for his might; and hurling from the sky the mightiest wanderers of the air, he with his shouts filled heaven with affright; and having entered the ocean, and destroyed its inhabitants, fear of Ocean's son pervaded all the waters of the deep; and the Fire of the sea, perceiving the unusual state of the ocean, forsaking from dread his wonted abode, sought shelter in Himalaya. When boyhood was passed, and Ocean's son had become a youth, he one day thus addressed his father:— 'Give me, O father! a suitable and ample place for my residence.' Ocean having heard his son's words, replied,—'I will give thee the kingdom of Bhanu, difficult to be acquired.' At this time the preceptor of the Daityas entered, and Ocean received him with all due honours; and, having placed him on a seat resplendent with gold and gems, with folded hands thus addressed him:—'Propitious is thy visit: say what shall I do.' Shukra replied, —'Thy son shall through his might firmly enjoy the three worlds: do thou, therefore, recede from Jambudwipa, the sacred abode of holy men, and leave unwashed by thy waves an extent of country sufficient for the residence of Jalandhara. There, O Sea! give a kingdom to this youth, who shall be invincible.' Shukra having thus spoken, to please the son of Bhrigu, and from fondness of his son, the Sea sportively withdrew his waves, and exposed devoid of water a country extending three hundred yojanas in length, and a hundred in breadth, which became celebrated under the name of the Holy Jalandhara.

" The Ocean then calling Maya*, the mighty Asura, thus spoke to him :— 'Build a city for Jalandhara, to be the capital of his kingdom.' Having heard the words of Ocean, Maya built a city of gems. There palaces resplendent with sapphires cast around a lustre resembling the plumage of the dancing peacock reflected from the clouds. There houses of coral and ruby darted rays around like the sprouts of the mango surrounded by birds. There lofty edifices of gold glowed with a splendour more terrible than fire, which beholding, the peacocks avoided them in alarm. There halls of crystal arose, glistening like the foam of the agitated ocean. There the various trees, waving to the wind, shed such perfume around as infatuated the senses of the women. There, marked by the smoke of incense wafted by the wind, the sky became like the junction of Yamuna with the Ganga. There, wearied by their nightly course, the horses of the sun, stopping over the tops of the palaces, rested at mid-day. There at night the stars cast a radiance amongst the edifices, like a necklace of flowers on the neck of a lovely woman. There golden swings, hung with golden chains, shed such lustre on the ground as made it seem a portion of Meru. In this city did Ocean, assisted by Shukra and the Rivers, inaugurate his son to the sound of musical instruments. He then gave to him a thousand mahapadmas of fear-inspiring troops. Shukra also gave to Jalandhara, from affection, the powerful charm by which the dead are raised to life again; and instructed him in the skilful use of all the various arms. Having thus enthroned his son, Ocean, attended by the divine River, returned to his usual abode; and Jalandhara, with Shukra and a number of Brahmans, contemplated the divine city, ornamented with such resplendent edifices.

" At this time, while Jalandhara was ruling over the kingdom given to him by his father, there was an Apsara, named Swarna, who formerly had, through the favour of Krouncha, borne a daughter named Vrinda, beautiful, elegantly formed, and love-inspiring. This daughter she gave to Shukra at his request, in order that she might be united to Jalandhara, and the son of Ocean espoused her according to the custom of the Gandharvas; and both casting aside fickleness, attached themselves solely to each other, and faithfully observed the duties of marriage.

" One day as they were sitting together they observed Rahu, and enquired of the son of Bhrigu respecting the depriving him of his head, and Shukra related the whole story. Jalandhara, also, having obtained from Shukra the power of resuscitating the dead, remembered his uncle†, and waged war with the gods."

* The divine architect of the Asuras, as Vishwakarma is of the Suras.

† That is, the *Sea of Milk*, which is here considered to be a brother of Ocean.

CHAPTER III.

Jalandhara's sending an Embassy to Indra.

Yudhishtira said, — "Who was the uncle of the son of Ocean, and in what manner did he carry on war against the gods? Relate the whole to me, O Narada!" Narada replied, — "Listen, O valiant prince! Jalandhara's uncle was the Sea of Milk, which was churned by the Suras and Asuras for the obtainment of various precious things, which the gods seized and appropriated to themselves. On being made acquainted with this, the Asura Jalandhara determined on war; but first despatched Durwarana, having instructed him in what he was to say, on an embassy to the chief of deities. Durwarana, having mounted his chariot, proceeded along the sky until he came to the abode of Indra; and as he wished to enter he was prevented by the warders. He then said: — 'I am the ambassador of Jalandhara sent to Indra; do you go and acquaint him with my arrival.' Having heard these words the warders went, and, having made obeisance to Indra, thus addressed him: — 'O lord! an ambassador has arrived.' He replied, — 'Bring him.' The warders then taking the ambassador by the hand, presented him to Indra. Durwarana, having entered the assembly, beheld Indra surrounded by three hundred and thirty-three millions of deities, seated on golden thrones and cooled by celestial fans, and his thousand lotos eyes sparkling with the love inspired by Sachi. Durwarana beholding the chief of deities, with his preceptor, smiling made obeisance to him; and Indra, having ordered a seat to be given to the ambassador of Jalandhara, thus addressed him: — 'Whose ambassador art thou, and by what road hast thou come?' Durwarana replied, — 'I am the ambassador of Jalandhara, who is the lord of the universe; therefore listen to his commands from my mouth. When, with the mountain Mandara, thou didst churn my uncle, the Sea of Milk, thou didst rob him of inestimable treasures: quickly, therefore, restore the moon, the amrita, the elephant, the horse, the gem, the tree, and the rest; give all, and afterwards give Swarga. What is the use of the ornamented body of the peacock, since its cry is so disagreeable? Or why employ the amrita in reviving the dead young of the vulture? Or, having the Hamsa for a preceptor, what use is there for the prattle of the parrot? Or what advantage is derived from placing a crow in a golden cage? Do quickly, therefore, all that I bid you; and, if thou wishest to preserve thy life, obey the king of the universe.' Maghawa then smiling thus replied to Durwarana: —

'Hear, O ambassador! the cause of churning the Sea of Milk succinctly stated. Formerly the son of Himavan, named Menaka, my enemy, was sheltered in the bosom of that sea; and, even after by his fire, in the shape of a horse, he had burned the world, the wicked wretch was still received by that sea; and while under its protection, he daily gave its milk to the Danavas, the enemies of the gods. It was for these reasons, O Durwarana! that it was formerly punished by being agitated by the gods. Hearken! if my friendship be rejected, my enmity will be intolerable; for how can an earthen pitcher support the collision of harder substances? Should, therefore, Jalandhara advance with a numerous army to wage war with us, he will only meet with destruction.' Having thus spoken, Indra ceased and dismissed the ambassador, who returning to the son of the Sea related to him all that Indra had said.

CHAPTER IV.

The Battle of the Devas and Danavas.

"Jalandhara having heard from his ambassador the words of Mahendra, inflamed with anger, commanded his army to assemble; and the Daityas who inhabited the earth and the lower regions immediately obeyed his orders. He then marched forward, and the three worlds resounded with the tumult of his innumerable forces. His warriors, distinguished by the heads of horses, elephants, camels, cats, tigers, and lions, eyes glancing like lightning, snaky hair, and enormous bodies whence hair like cimeters arose, rushed on with shouts loud as the thunder of clashing clouds. One hundred thousand crores of Asuras delighting in battle, marshalled on chariots, elephants, horses, and foot, formed the radiant host, which, with all the artillery of war, spread over one hundred yojanas of space. Jalandhara then having mounted his chariot proceeded on, and having arrived at the mountain of Mandara, at mid-day there halted, and encamped with his army. On the second day, having arrived with his army at the mountain Meru, that throne of the gods, he halted on its dust-enveloped summits. The groves and gardens of Indra were then destroyed by the Asuras; and on the eastern summit were encamped the elephants, on the south the chariots, and on the north and west the horse and foot. Thus Jalandhara arranged his host, while kettle-drums and trumpets so loud resounded that their clamour reached the abode of Indra; the sky trembled, and the thunderbolt fell powerless from his hand. Having then ascertained the cause that shook the heaven with fear, he thus addressed his preceptor: — 'What shall we do? what resource, what means, what power have we to support a war against Jalandhara?' Vachaspati replied, — 'Hasten to seek protection at the feet of Vishnu, the dweller in Vaikuntha.' This said, Indra, attended by his preceptor and the gods, in the utmost haste proceeded to the abode of the foe of Kaitaba. On arriving there the warder Vijaya went and thus addressed Vasudeva: — 'Agitated by the fear of Jalandhara, all the deities have sought thy protection: but, O lord! do not slay in battle my brother on account of the gods; for though he is under the effect of a curse, through kindness for me let him not be considered as deserving of death.' On hearing these words, Vishnu, the protector of the world, having mounted Garura the chief of birds, quickly leaving Vaikuntha, proceeded to the deities, whom he beheld shorn of their splendour through fear of Jalandhara. Then all the deities saw Hari with four gem-adorned arms, and bearing in his hands a bow, a mace, a conch, and a lotos; and having adored him, Indra thus began: — 'O lord! heaven has been destroyed by Jalandhara, the son of Ocean.' Hari, in reply, assuaged the fear of the gods, and assured them of victory, and of the destruction of the Asura. Matuli having then brought his chariot, Indra ascended it, and brandishing the thunderbolt proceeded on in front of Vasudeva, having on his left hand the gods, and on his right the goddesses, while his son Jayanta moved on before him mounted on the celestial elephant. Dhata, Yama, Mitra, and Varuna were also there, radiant in splendour. Virabhadra, likewise, accompanied him; and Shambhu far renowned, of limbs imperfect, of subdued affections, holder of the bow named Pinaka, bearer of a skull, lord of men and of the universe, celebrated under the names of Sthanu, Bharga, Bhagawan, Rudra, and the remembered on the eleventh day of the month. The Winds with their refreshing touch, the revivers of the soul even when on the lips, were also there. The Sun, likewise, in its twelve forms proceeded along, and the Giver of Riches reposing in a palanquin borne by his servants, and Rudra mounted on a bull and holding a trident, and Æolous on a deer with a club in nis hand. The Gandharvas, the Charanas, the Yakshas, the Pisachas, the Urugas, and the Guhyakas, all armed, preceded the army, which proceeded on in countless numbers like the billows of the ocean; and in the midst of it advanced Hari, the lord of the universe.

"Thus the army of the gods, desirous of vanquishing the Asuras, arrived at Sumeru, and occupied its northern summit. On the southern, formed of gold, stood the resplendent and mighty host of Jalandhara. But the battle-ground selected was over Havrati Varsha, between the mountains Mandara and Meru;

and to that, as Shukra had declared that it would be productive of victory, the Asuras with joy proceeded; and there also repaired the Suras. Then resounded the warlike instruments of both armies; and the tumult of warriors shouting to each other arose. Then was there a terrible battle between the gods and the Daityas, and a conflict capable of producing the annihilation of the three worlds. During this awful contest consumption and the king of death afflicted the Asuras with diseases. Thus, seized with excruciating pains in the midst of the battle, some of the Danavas falling rolled convulsive on the ground, while others fled to the mountains, whence plucking herbs of medicinal power they were enabled to renew the combat with the servants of Yama. Again the battle raged, while streams of blood flowed from myriads mutually slain, and the sky was bestrewed with the bodies of Suras and Asuras, horses and elephants. Chariots encountered chariots, and the charioteers fell slain by sharp-pointed arrows; elephants enraged shocking against elephants overthrew each other; horses strayed without riders; heads, limbs, and members, lopped from their trunks, fell on all sides: meanwhile a Khechari *, full bosomed, delicately formed, and love-inspiring, would hasten to the battle-ground, and quickly withdraw a Daitya from amidst the slain, and then in gentle sport impress repeated kisses on his lips.

"At length Janardana enraged attacked Kalanemi; Yama, Durwarana; Chandra and Surya, Rahu; Vaishvanara, Ketu; Vrihaspati, Shukra; the Ashwinau, Angara and Purwaka; the son of Indra, Shamhrada; Kubera, Nihoda; Rudra, Nishumbha; the Vishvadevas, Jambha; Vayu, Yajnaroma; Vasava, Bali; and other deities engaged in single combat with the Daityas.

CHAPTER V.

The Death of Bali, and his Ascent into Heaven.

"The gods and Asuras having thus engaged in single combat with each other, Hari with his mace struck Kalanemi senseless, as he shot his arrows at him. The Moon smote with his sword at Rahu, but he, in avoiding the blow, ran at the Sun, and, having defeated him in the battle, attacked the Moon. The king of night smote with his sword Sainhikeya, but from the hardness of his body the sword was shivered; and the tormentor of the Moon struck him

* The Khecharis are celestial nymphs who choose the slain on a field of battle, like the Valkyrias of Scandinavian mythology; but they are mentioned only incidentally in Sanscrit poetry, and I have nowhere met with any account of them.

with his adamantine feet, and he fell senseless with pain on the battle-ground. Rahu then swallowed the Moon, but afterwards vomited him up, from which time the Moon has borne a fawn-coloured mark on its bosom; and having seized the celestial horse, conducted and presented it to Jalandhara. Durwarana smote down Yama. The son of Indra fell senseless in battle, struck with sharp arrows by Samhrada, who seizing and mounting the celestial elephant presented it to Jalandhara. Nihoda with his mace disabled Kubera. Rudra attacked with his trident Nishumbha, who distressed him with a shower of arrows, and, having bound the causer of death, conducted the destroyer of the universe a prisoner to Jalandhara.

" Terrible raged the combat between Indra and Bali, who shone refulgent like the sun. All the arrows of Shakra shivered on the body of Bali; but he, with superior strength, smote Indra on the breast with his axe. In fear Indra cried out, and Bali laughed; and as he laughed pearls dropped from his mouth. Observing this, and desirous of obtaining Bali's body, Indra ceased the combat, and burst forth in praise of Bali, powerful as the ocean. Bali then said:— 'O chief of gods! ask a boon.' Indra replied:—'O chief of Daityas! if thou art pleased with me, bestow on me thy body.' On hearing these words, Bali, alarmed and agitated, thus thought:—'To a battle-axe a necklace of flowers, and to an avaricious man riches, are of no use. The generous-minded bestow favours on malignant enemies; lofty mountains furnish with their rivers the insatiable ocean. Even at the point of death good ought to be done to those by whom it is caused, as the sandal tree sheds perfume on the axe by which it is cut. The body and riches are only deposits entrusted to us by fate; but the moon remains, though it at times disappears. The generous are the ornaments of the earth; and never do they refuse to favour. The soul alone is to be considered, though the body be destroyed.' And then he said,—'Take then the boon which thou hast requested.' This heard, Indra struck Bali with his axe, but the blow penetrated not his body. Shakra then recollecting his thunderbolt, hurled it at Bali; and his body, struck with the bolt, was scattered afar: one part fell on the mountain Katuka, a second on Tuhina, a third on Anga, a fourth on Devanadi, a fifth on Mandara, and a sixth on Vijayagaja. From the purity of his actions, the parts of his body became the germs of all the various gems. The bones scattered by the thunderbolt became that precious stone which from it derives its name; the eyes became sapphires and amethysts; the blood, rubies; the marrow, emeralds; the flesh, crystal; the tongue, coral; and the teeth, pearls. Thus, from the body of Bali were produced gems and precious stones; and in the same manner will virtuous men enjoy the reward of their virtue. No sooner had Prabhavati, the wife of Bali, heard that he had been slain by Indra, than she hastened to the battle field, with tear-streaming eyes and dishevelled hair. The full-bosomed Prabhavati, on beholding the scattered members of her mighty and beloved husband, thus lamented aloud: — 'O my husband! why, forsaking me, ast thou thus fruitlessly given up thy body? Why, O my beloved! hast thou, adorned with a divine form and celestial ornaments, encountered the conflict of war, and left me to endless grief, unconsoled by the embrace of thy dissevered corse?' The son of the Sea, hearing the lamentations of the spouse of Bali, was afflicted, and requested Shukra to restore him to life. Shukra replied, — 'How can I restore one to life who has voluntarily embraced death? nevertheless the word of power shall be spoken.' Shukra having then meditated for a moment, the pleasing sounds were produced from his mouth; and Bali, reanimated, ascended to heaven. Shukra then said to Prabhavati, — 'Give up thy life.' On hearing these words, Prabhavati forsook this life, and rejoined her husband in Paradise.

CHAPTER VI.

The Acts of Jalandhara, and his Victory over Vishnu.

"Jalandhara, enraged, then thus addressed the slayer of Daityas (Indra): — 'O vilest of warriors! by deceit alone hast thou slain Bali.' Having thus spoken, the son of the Sea covered Indra's charioteer, his standard, and his car, with a shower of arrows; and he of the hundred sacrifices, overwhelmed by his violence, sank senseless. Observing that Shukra had fallen, the son of Ocean, with glowing countenance and eyes inflamed, exclaimed aloud, — 'In mind, the son of a slave will be still a slave.' Quickly, however, did Indra, recovering from his trance, hurl a thunderbolt at Jalandhara; but the son of Ocean caught it with his mountain-crushing hand, and, leaping from his chariot, rushed forward to seize Devendra. Perceiving his approach, Maghava, forsaking his chariot, fled for protection to Hari. The son of Ocean, having thus obtained his wish, mounted the chariot of Indra, and, causing Matuli to act as his charioteer, drove here and there through the ranks of his army. Then, inflamed with anger, Vishnu, grasping his sword Nandaka, and urging forward Garura swift as thought, attacked the army of the Daityas; and, attended by the son of Kasyapa, Janardana overthrew with his furious blows thousands of cars, horses, and elephants; and, faithfully observing the fearful institutes of war, he caused to flow a river of blood, mingled with bones, brains, heads, limbs, and warlike weapons; and on his dreadful course attended bloodthirsty demons, and birds and beasts of prey. On beholding Vishnu thus destroying his army, by Jalandhara's orders the mighty Danavas surrounded Hari on all sides, and, like clouds, rained on him a torrent of arrows, thick as the motes in sunbeams, as sand on the shores, as bees on a lotos, as clouds on a mountain, as birds on mango trees, as wreaths of smoke in the sky; which completely concealed Vishnu and Garura from the view of the battle field. All the mighty chiefs of the Asuras, mounted on chariots, thus assailed with loud and fear-inspiring shouts the lord of Vaikuntha. But the foe of the Daityas, enraged, overthrew all the horrific-formed Asuras as easily as the wind scatters the leaves of a tree. Shailaroma then rushed forward to attack Vishnu, who pierced his body with arrows; and Shailaroma at the same time covered Hari with shafts: but Vishnu, quickly seizing his sword, smote off the head of Shailaroma, and then the headless corse seized Garura with its arms, while the head instantaneously replaced itself on the shoulders.* Arrested in the midst of the conflict, Hrishikesha gazed in astonishment at this reunion of the head with the body, while Garura alighted on the ground. But when he perceived the head of Shailaroma fixed again in its place, he swiftly bore Hari away from the Asura, whose life, in consequence of his having been wounded by Vishnu, quickly departed, and he fell lifeless on the field.

"Jalandhara then said to his charioteer Khadgaroma:—'Advance the car, O charioteer! unto the god Janardana.' Khadgaroma having obeyed his lord's command, the son of the Sea, on beholding Vishnu, thus addressed him:—'Fearlessly conquer me, O Vishnu! for I will not slay thee, O Madhawa!' Hearing these words, Narayana, with anger-inflamed eyes, covered him with death-giving arrows; and the son of the Sea at the same time overwhelmed Hari with his shafts. Overcome by his arrows, Garura fell senseless to the ground, and Janardana immediately in thought called to his aid the chariot which stood in Vaikuntha; and instantly the chariot, with harnessed horses, appeared. Hari then, adorned with a tiara, and bearing on his breast the celestial gem, having mounted his car and advanced against Jalandhara, he and the gods destroyed with their arrows the army of the Danava. Beholding his

* This is free from the ludicrous manner in which Ariosto has related a similar occurrence:—

Se gli spiccano il capo, Orrilo scende,
Nè cessa brancolar sin che lo trovi;
Ed or pe 'l crine, ed or pe 'l naso il prende,
Lo salda al collo, e non so con che chiovi.
Piglia 'l talor Grifone, e 'l braccio stende,
Nel fiume il getta, e non par ch anco giovi,
Che nuota Orrilo al fondo, come un pesce,
E col suo capo salvo a la ripa esce.

Canto 15. st. 71.

army thus reduced to a small number, Jalandhara said to Shukra, — ' My army has been destroyed by arrows: O lord! renowned for thy skill in charms, restore them to life! Let thy knowledge, O Brahman! now protect those who apply to thee for succour!' Bhargava replied, — ' Behold, O king! the power of a Brahman on the field of battle.' This said, he sprinkled water over them, and muttered the word of power; when instantly the Danavas, who had been slain by the arrows of the gods, reanimated, arose, and marshalled around the son of the Sea. Then Narayana thus addressed Vrihaspati: — ' It would be a shame if the army of the gods were not also restored to life by their preceptor.' Dhishna replied, — ' I will, O lord! immediately reanimate them by medicinal herbs.' This said, Vrihaspati proceeded to the mountain Drona, situated in the Sea of Milk, and there culled a quantity of plants, and by their power restored to life the gods, who immediately arose and prepared for battle.

" The son of Ocean, beholding the gods thus reanimated, said to Kavi, — ' O Shukra! how have these arisen from the dead, without the assistance of thy charm?' Shukra replied, — ' There is a mighty mountain, named Drona, situated in the Sea of Milk, on which grow plants by which the dead can be reanimated; and the preceptor of the gods, having brought thence a quantity of plants, and pronounced the requisite incantation, has restored to life the deities who were slain.' Having heard these words, Jalandhara entrusted his mighty army to the command of Shumbha, and hastened to the Sea of Milk, where having arrived, he entered it. He then beheld the resplendent abode and delightful residence of this Sea. There neither hot nor cold winds are felt, nor is darkness ever perceived. There loveliest damsels sing, and dance, and sport, bending under the weight of their swelling bosoms, taper-waisted, with teeth like pearls, and rolling eyes casting amorous glances, waving their bewitching arms in pleasing attitudes, and gracefully moving their feet to the sweet sound of music; while slave girls, with waving fans, diffuse coolness and odours around. Into this abode of delight did the son of Ocean enter; but agitated with anxiety on account of the war, he thus, after due obeisance, addressed the Sea of Milk: — ' O father! thou killest me by washing with thy waves the mountain Drona, which produces deceitful herbs.' The Sea replied, — ' My son, shall I not wash with my waves him who has sought my protection? for what virtuous man has ever rejected the suppliant?' Having heard his uncle's words, Jalandhara became inflamed with anger, and struck the mountain's base with such furious blows that Drona, terrified, appeared before him in a material form, and thus addressed him: — ' I am thy slave; grant security and protection to me thy suppliant! I will hasten,

O mighty warrior! if it be thy order, to the lower regions; and there will I remain as long as thou mayst think proper to govern this kingdom, and to prevent its plants from being taken away.' Having then seen the mountain Drona sink into the lower regions, Jalandhara returned to the field of battle; and when there arrived, seeing Indra advancing in a chariot, he laughed aloud, and said, — 'As long as thou mountest a car, so long shall I be thy destruction.' This said, the son of Ocean destroyed the army of the gods. When Vrihaspati beheld this havoc, he hastened to the Sea of Milk; but finding to his astonishment that the mountain Drona had disappeared, he quickly returned to the army of the gods, and called aloud, — 'Fly speedily, O ye gods! for Drona has disappeared.' On hearing the words, Jalandhara, laughing, cut off with his arrows the sacrificial cord and hair of the preceptor of the immortals, who fled in utmost speed for fear of his life.

"The gods, having been thus put to flight by Jalandhara, hastened for refuge to Janardana; and Hrishikesha and the chief of the Danavas rushed to the encounter of each other. Then began a terrible battle between Vishnu and Jalandhara; and long with equal violence they showered arrows at each other. At length the son of Ocean leaped from his car to vanquish Janardana, who covered him with arrows as he approached; but, undismayed, Jalandhara arrived, and, having seized Garura with one hand, and the car of Vishnu with the other, and whirled them round, he hurled them through the air with such force that the car lighted in the White Island, and Garura in Krounchdwipa. While whirled the chariot, Vishnu fell from it, and, enraged, rushed on the chief of the Daityas, exclaiming, — 'Stand, stand!' and, seeing him advance, the son of the Sea covered him with arrows. But Hari wounding him on the breast with a sharp javelin, he fell; and his charioteer was conducting him from the battle, when he said, — 'Oh! why am I thus disgraced?' The son of Ocean then renewed the combat, and fierce raged the battle between him and the enemy of the Daityas. At length Hari fell senseless under the arrows of Jalandhara, who through affection slew him not, but, beholding Govinda extended on the ground, mounted his chariot. Then Indira, the beloved of Vishnu, hastened weeping to the battle field, and thus addressed the son of Ocean: — 'Listen, O brother*! Vishnu has been vanquished by thee; but it is not proper, O mighty warrior! that thou shouldst slay the husband of thy sister.' On hearing these words, Jalandhara, from piety to his sister, liberated her lord, and then, bending at their feet, adored both Lakshmi and Vishnu.

* Lakshmi, being the daughter of his uncle, the Sea of Milk, was his cousin-german; and in India cousin-germans are in the habit of calling each other brothers and sisters.

Hari then said to Jalandhara, —'O chief of the Daityas! I am pleased with what thou hast done; say, what boon shall I confer on thee?' Jalandhara replied, — 'If thou be pleased, O Keshava! with my valour, remain with Lakshmi in the residence of my uncle.' 'So be it!' Vishnu replied; and then in thought calling Garura, who immediately appeared, he mounted him, accompanied by Lakshmi, and proceeded to the Sea of Milk; and there with his beloved the lord of the world continued to remain."

CHAPTER VII.

The happy Reign of Jalandhara.

Yudhishtira said, — "O Narada! relate what took place after Jalandhara had defeated the gods, and Vishnu had retired to his own abode." Narada replied, —"Jalandhara, having acquired heaven, and in a moment obtained the fruit of a hundred sacrifices of a horse, proceeded to take possession of Amaravita, abounding in gems, gold, costly raiment, celestial flowers, and sweetest odours. There rain, cold, and heat are unknown, and golden swings and pensile couches wave of their own accord. There, united together in pleasing fellowship, birds of variegated plumage join in sweetest melody. There, instruments of various kinds harmonious sound; and nymphs divine, of loveliest forms, in graceful measure move, or strains enrapturing breathe. In this paradise the son of Ocean fixed his regal seat, and inaugurated Shumbha, dear to him as his soul, as the *yuva raja* (heir apparent); and having subjected to his power the inhabitants of heaven, and having recovered the precious things which had been ravished from the Sea of Milk, he ruled over the three worlds in fame and glory. During his reign no one was born, or died, or grew old; no one bore enmity to another; and domestic duties were piously observed. No one was seen who was ugly, deformed, or wicked; every woman was gentle and obedient to her husband, and no one deviated from chastity. No woman was a widow, and no person was without riches; all were givers, and no one required a return; all were pious, and bestowed gifts on the Brahmans; and every house contained young, lovely, and accomplished women; milk, curds, and butter abounded; all was happiness; and imprisonment and execution never occurred, for murder, and violence, and debts were unknown. Thus the three worlds enjoyed happiness, and the name of the son of the Sea became like sugar in the mouths of their inhabitants."

CHAPTER VIII.

The Formation of the Disc called Sudarshana.

Yudhishtira said,—"O *Muni!* what was done by the gods after they were conquered by Jalandhara, and were deprived of heaven by him?" Narada replied:—"The gods, being expelled from heaven, and deprived of sacrifices and the beverage of immortality, repaired to the abode of Brahma, to whom, in laudatory strains, they paid due adoration. Then Brahma said,—'What do you wish that I should do?' The gods, in reply, related how they had been defeated by Jalandhara. Brahma, having meditated for a moment, proceeded with the deities to Kailasa; and, standing on the side of that mountain, in the name of the gods thus began to adore the dweller on Kailasa (Shiva):—'Praise be to thee, O Bhava! O Sarva! O Nilagriva! Praise be to thee, O lord of various forms!' When Shankara, chief of beings, heard these words, he directed Nandi to introduce the immortals; and Nandi immediately obeyed his command. On entering, the gods with astonishment beheld Shiva seated on a throne, and attended by myriads of devoted servants, all naked, deformed, curly-haired, with matted locks, and embrowned with dust; and Brahma, after due obeisance, thus spoke:—'O Shankara! forget the anger that thou hast conceived against Indra, and grant favour to those who supplicate thy protection.' Then Shankara laughed aloud, and exclaimed,—'Behold the situation of the dwellers in heaven!' But the omniscient and universal god, knowing the wish of Brahma and the subdued pride of Indra, with kindness thus proceeded:—'O Pitamaha! how can the enemies, who have not been conquered by Vishnu, be vanquished by me? Other weapons must be formed; for Jalandhara cannot be slain by those which have been hitherto employed: and in what manner can this be accomplished by the gods?' Brahma replied,—'O Shankara! thy own mighty power is alone sufficient.' On hearing these words, Shiva said,—'O Brahma! let us and the immortals dart forth the flame of anger; and from this let a weapon be formed.' In obedience to his directions, Brahma and the gods, glowing with anger, darted forth volumes of flame, to which Shankara united the consuming beams of his third eye. He then in thought summoned Hari; and, on his immediately appearing, thus addressed him:—'O Vishnu! while Jalandhara remained unslain by thee in battle, why hast thou, deserting the immortals, withdrawn to repose in the Sea of Milk?' Vishnu replied,—'Had I slain him, what would have become of my beloved Lakshmi? But do thou, O husband of Parvati! vanquish Jalandhara in battle.' Shankara then said, — 'At least contribute the flame of thy anger.' And as soon as the collected beams had been increased by the rays darted from the refulgence of Vishnu, Shiva exclaimed, — 'Now from these beams let a weapon be formed for my use.' On hearing these words, Visvakarma and the gods, beholding the glowing mass, were alarmed, and feared to touch it. Perceiving the deities thus motionless, and knowing their thoughts, Shankara, laughing and looking at them, said, — 'If this refulgence cannot be endured, in what manner can it be borne in the hand?' Shiva then placed his left heel on the glowing beams, as if he were crushing a bee buzzing on the ground; and dancing on them, while the gods rejoiced caused music to resound, he, by repeated rotations, reduced them to the form of a disc. Thus was produced the disc called *Sudarshana*, darting such fiery beams, that the gods in terror exclaimed, — 'Preserve us! — Preserve us!' Shankara having then given the unendurable weapon into the hands of Brahma, his beard was immediately scorched by its beams; and the lord of Uma, laughing, took it from him and concealed it under his arm. Such is the result of presenting a gift to a great blockhead."

CHAPTER IX.

Occurrences in Kailasa.

Narada continued. — "At this time I went and informed Jalandhara that Shambhu had promised to effect his destruction. Jalandhara then said to me, — 'O holy sage! what precious things are contained in the abode of the bearer of the trident? acquaint me with the whole, as war should not be unless there be booty.' I replied, — 'Shambhu is old, covered with ashes, his neck marked with the poison of serpents, mounted on a bull, bearing a beggar's dish in his hand, and with an elephant-headed and a six-headed son, and he has nothing valuable belonging to him except the lovely and full-bosomed daughter of the mountain. Inflamed with love and captivated by her beauty, Mahesha passes his days in sport and dalliance, or sings and dances to amuse her. She is named Parvati, and far excels in loveliness either Vrinda or the nymphs of heaven.' Having thus spoken, and excited the desire of Jalandhara, I disappeared.

"After this the son of the Sea despatched Rahu on an embassy to Kailasa, who arrived there in a moment; and on beholding the resplendent abode of Shambhu, he exclaimed to himself, — 'How wonderful is this place!' He then wished to enter, but was prevented by the warders, who demanded his business. Rahu replied, — 'I am the ambassador of Jalandhara; but the message of a mighty king is not addressed unto a doorkeeper.' Nandi, hearing these words, hastened and informed Shiva; and, having received his commands, introduced Rahu. Having entered, he beheld Shambhu, five-faced and ten-armed, his sacrificial cord formed of a snake, and his matted locks adorned with the moon, waited upon by vile and ugly servants, but attended by all the immortals, who, looking to the ambassador, desired him to speak. Rahu then began: — 'O lord! I am sent to thee by Jalandhara: hear his auspicious words from my mouth; and do thou, who art addicted to devotion, devoid of affection, an abandoner of works, who hast neither father nor mother, nor observest the duties of the householder, obey his commands. The mighty Jalandhara enjoys the dominion of the three worlds; do thou also become subject to him: why shouldst thou, old, libidinous, and the rider of a bull, refuse to obey him?' While Rahu thus spoke, the sons of Shiva, Ganesha and Skanda, were rubbing his body; and, disturbed by their hands, Vasuki fell to the ground, and immediately began to swallow the rat, Ganesha's vehicle, beginning with the tail. Gananayaka, on observing the snake about to swallow his courser, called out, — 'Loose! loose!' At this time Skanda's peacock began to scream in the shrillest manner; and the serpent frightened disgorged the rat, and hastened to replace himself on the neck of Shiva; where, violently respiring, he dimmed the brightness of the moon with his poisonous breath. Then came the beloved of Vishnu, dripping from her couch in the Milky Sea, and bearing a vase full with the beverage of immortality, with which she reanimated the head of Brahma that Shiva's hand eternally displays. The head, falling and rolling on the ground, exclaimed in boasting accents, while the spectators expressed to each other their astonishment, — 'I am the first — I am the most ancient of beings — I am the creator — I am the lord of all things.' At this moment, from the matted locks of Shiva sprang myriads of beings, three-faced, three-footed, seven-armed, and with yellow hair hanging in long and matted locks: on seeing whom, the head became mute as the dead. Having beheld these wonders, Rahu, in fear and astonishment, thus again addressed Mahesha: — 'O lord! through the strength of thy devotion and abstraction, affections touch not thee; why then dost thou sacrifice to feelings and passions? Thou receivest adoration from Brahma and all other deities; but who is the god whom thou adorest? Thou art the supreme god; why, therefore, dost thou collect the scraps of the beggar? But, O chief of devotees! since thou preferrest a state of pious mortification, yield up Gauri and thy two sons Ganesha and Skanda; and do thou, with a beggar's dish, wander from door to door.' Thus Rahu urged his request in many words; but Maheshwara returned no answer. Then Rahu, as Isha would not break silence, thus addressed Nandi: — 'Thou art a minister and a general, and canst therefore inform me what means this departure from all received usages; as it is not becoming that a prince, to whom an ambassador is sent, should preserve silence.' But Nandi replied not; and immediately, on a sign from Shiva, reconducted and dismissed Rahu, who hastened to Jalandhara and related to him all that had passed."

CHAPTER X.

The Defeat of the Danavas by Shiva's Troops.

Narada continued. — "The mighty Jalandhara, having heard the relation of his ambassador, immediately arrayed his army and marched forward. Then the tumult of his approaching forces resounded through the inmost recesses of Mandara; and wide was it spread by the echoes of Meru, while lions started from their dens; warlike instruments with their clangour, dear to the warrior, deafened the three worlds; and, as trod the mighty Danavas, the lofty mountains trembled, and the seas were agitated. The armour of warriors clashed as on they marched, borne on various vehicles; and the wheels of the war-chariots harsh grated along the ground: white umbrellas shaded the mighty host from the sun, and fans, formed of peacocks' feathers, prevented heat. From the innumerable elephants, cars, horse, and foot, arose clouds of dust, which spread over the sky like the blue lotos, or the dark billows of the heaving ocean. As thus proceeded his army, Jalandhara, full of anxiety, having placed on his shoulder a javelin adorned with gems, hastened to the mighty Vishnu reposing in the Sea of Milk, and thus addressed him: — 'Say, O lord! what shall I give to thee in order to obtain felicity?' Vishnu replied, — 'What is thy wish, O son of the Sea?' Jalandhara then said, — 'I am proceeding to battle; do thou, therefore, O Keshava, remain with Lakshmi in the Sea of Milk.' This said, he hastened to his father, and, having prostrated himself at his feet, thus said: — 'O father! permit me to go and vanquish Nilakantha in combat.' Ocean replied, — 'My son, leave the devotee alone, and enjoy the kingdom which I have given to thee. Sufficient glory hast thou acquired, as there is none equal to thee in the three worlds; and thy kingdom is as resplendent as Vaikuntha. Leave alone, therefore, my dear son, Shankara the beggarly devotee.' But the son of the Sea, disregarding his father's advice, proceeded to join his warriors; and as, clad in armour, he was hastening to battle, Vrinda thus addressed him: — 'My lord, war should not be waged by the chief of kings against a contemptible devotee. Subdue thy passion for Parvati, and behold me with impartiality: why shouldst thou desire Gauri? for in what is she superior to me? Is she not a devotee, a dweller in solitude, eternally attached to Sthanu, unimpassioned, barren, and a former of artificial sons? Narada has deceived thee; do thou, therefore, think no more of her, but enjoy me.' The son of Ocean replied, — 'Vrinda, as long as the form of Parvati remains unseen, my soul will not repose in peace: though she may be inferior in beauty to thee, and though Shankara should slay me, my thoughts must still dwell on Gauri.' Hearing her husband's words, Vrinda, smiling, ascended her palanquin, and returned to the capital of Jalandhara; and the son of Ocean, with his mighty army, marched forward to Kailasa.

"In the mean time Shankara, with his beloved, his sons, and attendants, had departed from Kailasa; and Jalandhara, having arrived there, took possession of it, and, having encamped his army, proceeded to view the delightful abode of Shiva. On beholding it sparkling with gems, and abounding in every excellence, the chief of the Daityas was filled with joy and astonishment, and thus addressed the son of Bhrigu: — 'Forsaking with his wife so charming an abode through dread of me, where, O Kavi! has Shankara retreated?' Bhargava replied, — 'Shambhu has retired to a mighty mountain, situated on the northern bank of the lake Manasa, difficult to be approached by any one but him.' Jalandhara then said, — 'I will vanquish Devesha, O Bhargava! do thou return to the city.' Having thus spoken, Jalandhara marched forward until he beheld the mighty mountain towering sixty thousand yojanas in height, and immediately surrounded it with his troops; while the tumult of his innumerable army and the clangour of instruments spread through the heaven and caused the mountain to tremble. On beholding this mighty host, Shiva placed Gauri, surrounded by her female companions, on the highest peak of the mountain, and having arrayed his myriads of armed attendants, he thus spoke to Nandi their chief: — 'The valiant Daitya Jalandhara must be slain by thee in battle. Go, therefore, accompanied by Mahakala and the other warriors, and perform my wish. Faint not, nor yield to despondency, but let rivalship animate thy courage until thou hast conquered my enemy.' Nandi, having received these commands, desired his charioteer to bring him his car, and, after due obeisance to Shiva, mounting it, proceeded against the Danavas, accompanied by Vinayaka and Skanda, whom their father had ordered to join his army for its protection. In the mean time the Daityas were ascending the mountain; but assailed by Nandi and his troops, and overpowered by their sharp weapons, some fell dead, and the rest retreated from the mountain, while clouds of dust ascended to the sky. But reinforced by their leader, the Daityas renewed the conflict, and long and terrible raged the battle between them and the immortals. At length all the elephants of the Danavas were slain, the cars shattered to pieces, and numerous warriors strewed the battle field. Far over the sky were spread gasping heads with dishevelled hair, countenances pallid with fear, and ghastly eyes; and the ground was covered with headless corses and streams of blood. Thus Shiva's troops overthrew the Danavas, and spread destruction among their ranks like the waters of the deluge."

CHAPTER XI.

Shiva's Proceeding to Battle.

Narada continued. — "Shumbha, on beholding the defeat of the Daityas by the troops led by Nandi, enraged advanced with other Danavas to the conflict. Then Shumbha attacked Nandi; Nishumbha, Mahakala the lord of destruction; Shailaroma, Pushpadanta; Kolahala, present in the battle in material form, Maliavan; Rahu, Skanda; Sarparoma, Kushmanda; Gargaroma, Dana; Jambha, Vinayaka; and Patalaketu, Bringi. In this manner was a terrible combat commenced between the Danavas and the troops of Shiva. Then Nandi and Shumbha showered arrows on each other thick as the leaves are strewn on Mandara when storms agitate its trees. At length Shumbha, throwing away his bow, rushed to the chariot of Nandi, and wounding him on the breast he fell senseless, like a mountain* struck by a thunderbolt. Nishumbha received a blow on the breast from Mahakala, but, advancing, he struck him on the head with his mace and felled him senseless to the ground; then seizing him by his feet and shouting aloud, he whirled him round, and with force immense hurled him far away. Shailaroma struck with his fist Pushpadanta on the face, but he with his mace struck the Daitya to the ground; which seeing, the valiant Giriketu attacked Pushpadanta, who smote off his head with his sword. But Giriketu seizing his sword and shield rushed on, when his head called out, — 'Where art thou going, having forsaken me in this direful conflict? art thou not ashamed to engage in combat having only a headless body?' Having thus spoken, the head sprang into its place, and Pushpadanta again with his sharp sword severed it from the shoulders. But it immediately

* The mountains had at first wings; but on account of the inconvenience which this occasioned Indra cut them off.

became a hundred heads with two hundred eyes, and rejoined the trunk. These also Pushpadanta lopped off, but Jwara advancing compelled him to retreat to the mountain. Kolahala and Maliawan contended for some time with arrows, but at length the Daitya seizing a mountain overwhelmed Maliawan with it. Kartikeya, covered with arrows by Rahu, hurled at him a javelin blazing with refulgent beams, which seeing, Rahu sprang into the air and seized it with his hands. Then, as he had no head, Skanda directed a javelin at his breast: but his mother hastened to the assistance of her son engaged in battle with the son of Shiva, who, not wishing to offend the River, withdrew on his peacock to the mountain. Vinayaka was overwhelmed with arrows by Jambha, and attacked him with his trunk and battle-axe; but Jambha at length hurling a javelin wounded Ganesha in the mouth, who, alarmed and smarting with pain, thus exclaimed on the battle field: — 'Oh, my mother! Oh, my father! Oh, my brother! Oh, my dear rat!'

"On hearing the lamentations of Ganesha, Parvati descended in haste from the peak, and approaching Shiva, thus addressed him: — 'The Daityas are slaying Ganesha, and Skanda has also fallen on the battle ground. Oh, Shiva! why dost thou amuse thyself here? quickly arm thyself, and hasten to the protection of thy sons.' This heard, Shiva directed Virabhadra to prepare his bull. Having then put on a tiara refulgent as the sun, having bound round his neck a string of a hundred bells, having placed mirrors in his ears, tinkling ornaments on his shoulders, and rings on his legs, and his various arms being placed on the bull, Parvati thus addressed him: — 'Oh, Hara! leave not me oppressed with anxiety respecting the battle, but conquer the Daityas without engaging in combat.' Shiva replied, — 'Remain in hope, O my beloved! and if an evil-minded Danava come here, do thou protect thyself.' Having thus spoken, and having assumed all his ornaments and arms, and mounted his bull, Rudra proceeded to the battle field attended by myriads of troops. On his left hand marched Virabhadra borne in a chariot drawn by lions, and on his right hand Manibhadra bearing a bow in a chariot drawn by horses. In this manner he descended from the lofty mountain, and all the Danavas shouted aloud on beholding Shiva mounted on a bull, and in louder shouts replied the troops of Shiva. Then Nandi, Mahakala, Skanda, Maliawan, Pushpadanta, and the others, who had been defeated in the former combat, hastened to join Shankara; and the two armies encountering each other, terrible and long raged the destructive conflict."

CHAPTER XII.

Jalandhara in the Form of Shiva proceeds to Parvati.

Narada continued. — "Jalandhara on hearing the increased tumult of the battle mounted his car, and said to his charioteer, — 'Drive on the car, that I may kill that devotee with matted locks, ornamented with bones and ashes, and mounted on a bull.' This said, and bending his bow, the car rapidly advanced, when Virabhadra with sharp arrows opposed his progress, and Manibhadra likewise showered arrows upon him, but he still pressed forward calling out, — 'Come, Mahadeva, if thou darest to stand against my arrows; to-day will I slay thee, O bearer of the matted locks!' Then the two hosts in conflict joining, car met car, horse encountered horse, elephant shocked against elephant, blood bedewed the ground, the mountain troops slew the Danavas, and lifeless corses, heads, limbs, and members, bestrewed the battle field. But Jalandhara, having looked in vain for Gauri, thought to himself, — 'If I remain here, how shall I behold her? let me now proceed to her abode, and on another day combat with Shambhu.' Having thus determined, he called a Daitya, and said to him, — 'O warrior! equal in valour to myself, assume my similitude, and conduct the war until I return.' Having thus spoken, he delivered his army into his charge, and gave him his car, arms, and ornaments. The son of the Sea then, accompanied only by Durwarana and unadorned, secretly withdrew from his army, and assuming the form of Hara, while Durwarana assumed that of Nandi, proceeded to the residence of Gauri. On beholding them Bhawani was astonished, but attended by her companions she hastened rejoiced to Shankara and asked him, — 'In what manner, my lord, hast thou conquered in battle, and why dost thou seem afflicted?' Having thus spoken she presented him with his different ornaments, and having taken off his upper garment, the heads of Skanda and Ganesha appeared under his arm. Bursting into tears she exclaimed, — 'Ah, Skanda! ah, Ganesha! ah, Rudra!' and her companions afflicted with grief joined in her lamentations. Nandi then said to Parvati, — 'Cherish him (Shiva); for Virabhadra, Manibhadra, and the other chiefs have been slain in the conflict, and the heads of Skanda and Ganesha having been found on the battle field have been brought to thee.' Thus speaking he threw them before her; and Parvati embracing the heads of her sons bedewed them with her tears, while she thus lamented: — 'O foe of Taraka, how hast thou been slain in combat by the son of Ocean, thou whom the gods appointed their leader when only three days old? How hast thou, who vanquished the mighty Taraka and rivalled Nilakantha in power, fallen on the battle field? O Ganesha, my son! chief of the Ganas, adored by holy men, by whom hast thou been vanquished? O my sons! ungladdened by the sight of your countenances how shall I hereafter enjoy peace or happiness?' Thus lamented Gauri when Shiva said to her,—'I am undoubtedly Rudra, and thou art Devi; Hara is still thine, do not therefore yield to fear and grief.' She replied,—'Has thy bull been also slain in battle by Jalandhara? But what shall I do to relieve thy frame fatigued with the contest?' The delusive Shiva, sighing, answered,—'Why, O my beloved! shouldst thou long lament in vain over thy slaughtered sons? repose with me on the nuptial couch, and let us forget sorrow and fatigue in pleasure.' Having heard these insidious words, Ambika replied,—'Thy request is improper at a time of anxiety and affliction; and, when the ceremonies of the dead are to be performed, wise men abstain from conjugal rites. How can I repress the pain and grief which are caused by the death of my sons? or how refrain from lamenting with tears and black garments their untimely loss?' The Daitya, inflamed by the beauty of Gauri, replied,—'The women who refuse to comply with the wishes of their husbands will undoubtedly fall into the deepest and most tremendous hell. O lovely goddess! I am devoid of troops, of sons, of abode, of every thing, and, having preserved my life alone, have come to seek consolation from thee: but if thou refuse I will enter a secret retreat and there lay aside my existence. Arise, therefore, Nandi, and let us first go and purify ourselves in a sacred stream, and do thou, my spouse, also, voluntarily resign thy being.' Ambika having heard these words, sighed, profoundly oppressed with grief and distress, and in the greatest agitation replied not; but, bewildered by that delusion which pervades the universe, remained silent, perplexed, and undecided."

CHAPTER XIII.

The Deceptions of Vishnu for carrying off Vrinda.

Yudhishtira said,—"O Brahman! what took place after the daughter of the mountain had been deluded by the false Mahesha?" Narada replied,—"At this time, I shook the breast of Hari as he reposed in the Sea of Milk, and tears immediately starting into his eyes, the god, astonished by this prodigy, uprose from his serpent couch, and gazed on me and Shesha. I then said to him, 'Why, O Govinda! dost thou not remember Gauri?' Keshava instantaneously in thought summoned the son of Vinata, whom, appearing in a moment, and standing before him with folded hands, he thus addressed: — 'O Garura! hasten to the battle field, and ascertain if Jalandhara has been slain by Hara, or if he is still engaged in combat with him, or, if not, where he may now be.' Having thus spoken, Vishnu gave to Garura the magic ball, which placed in the mouth exposes the delusions of enchantment, and causes invisibility; and he, having encircled his lord, immediately with wonderful swiftness flew along the sky. Quickly he reached the field where gods and Danavas contended in fierce and dreadful battle, but there he sought in vain for Jalandhara. Then swift he flew to the mighty mountain which crowns the northern bank of Manasha, and searched the abode of Gauri, but found not there the goddess; but as the foe of serpents was proceeding he heard a noise, and, having approached to it, beheld the false Mahesha. Immediately Garura placed the charm-dispelling ball in his mouth, and, having instantly known that he was Jalandhara and not Mahadeva, flew in speed to the Sea of Milk, and thus addressed the foe of Kaitabha: — 'O lord! the wicked Jalandhara in a deceitful form is now in converse with Uma. If thou, O Govinda! wish to war against him, do thou also attack him with delusion. For I have seen his kingdom and his capital, which surpass in every excellence all that can be found in the three worlds. There the people pass their time in singing, dancing, and music; there the women are more lovely than the nymphs of heaven; but the wife of Jalandhara appears among the other women like a swan among crows, and happy would be the man who should merely touch her lovely form. Do thou, therefore, O lord! carry away the wife of Jalandhara, and thus confer a favour on Shankara, and obtain pleasure for thyself.' Vishnu, having heard the words of Garura, and approving the stratagem, assumed the form of a Brahman, and arrayed himself in suitable habiliments, and, captivated by the description of Vrinda, was departing in this false form, when Shesha thus addressed him: — 'O Janardana! let me accompany thee: it is in beholding thy countenance alone that I enjoy happiness; and, if deprived of this, where shall I go? what shall I do?' Vishnu replied, — 'I will, disguised, carry away the wife of Jalandhara, to draw him from the battle, and to do a favour to Parvati. Come, let us go and obtain Vrinda, and hasten the death of her husband.' Having thus spoken, Vishnu with Shesha repaired to a wood near the capital of Jalandhara, and, having assumed matted locks and barken garments, erected a holy hermitage, surrounded by trees, which yielded every fruit that was wished; and his pupils were in human forms, lions, tigers, boars, bears, apes, and monkeys. To attract Vrinda to this wood, Vishnu affected her with a fever; and, as oppressed with heat she reposed, while celestial nymphs with lovely forms, breathing odours and glittering with ornaments, cooled her with fans, a fearful vision appeared to her. In her slumber she saw the dried-up head of Jalandhara, crushed, white with ashes, the eyes pecked out by vultures, the ears and nose cut off, and devoid of hair, and, believing it to be the sign of his death, she fainted away. Her damsels quickly sprinkled over her various perfumes, and recalled her to sense, and thus the night passed away. In the morning the bards and minstrels came to awaken the spouse of the king of Asuras with laudatory strains; but she bid them cease, and, having bestowed on them joy-giving presents, dismissed them. Then Vrinda summoned Brahmans, and related to them the vision which she had beheld. The Brahmans replied,—'O queen! horrible and fear-inspiring is thy dream, present, therefore, gifts to the Brahmans, cows, garments, jewels, elephants, and ornaments, that through them the terrible omen may be averted.' The Brahmans, being thus gratified, sprinkled holy water over the queen, and departed well pleased. But the charms of Hari were too powerful, and the fever of Vrinda so increased that she could find no repose in her palace; and therefore mounting a chariot drawn by mules, and attended by her companion Smaraduti, proceeded to the pleasant wood, abounding in trees and birds, fountains and flowers, where no fire but that of love could enter. Thinking on her husband, and on the time when she might again see him, Vrinda entered the forest to procure ease, attended by her companions, and drawn on by the charms of Vishnu. Gazing around she beheld the forest filled with lofty trees and large rocks, where wild beasts roamed, and the meeting summits of the trees spread darkness beneath; and palpitating with fear exclaimed to Smaraduti, who drove her car:—'O Smaraduti! quickly direct the car home.' She replied,—'My friend! I do not know in what direction to drive the car: the mules are tired, and the path is not to be found; but I will urge it on, trusting to fortune that we may arrive there, if we be not eaten up before we reach it.' Thus speaking, she drove the car rapidly on, until they came to a part of the forest so gloomy and impervious, that the winds blew not there, nor were the notes of birds heard, no streams watered it, nor did the light of heaven enter. On arriving there, the mules held their breath, the flag waved not, and the bells ceased to sound; and Vrinda said to her companion,—'O Smaraduti! where shall we go, how shall we avoid the lions and tigers? No house, no place of repose appears in this horrid forest.' Smaraduti replied,—'My friend, thou seest that in front high rocks oppose our progress, and the trees on all sides, and that the mules are too frightened to move.' On hearing these words, Vrinda was filled with such dread, that her necklace arose erect on her neck, and at this moment a fearful ogress appeared, three-legged, five-handed, seven-eyed, tiger-eared, lion-headed, and with long gory locks: on seeing whom, Vrinda and Smaraduti, filled with terror, covered their eyes with their hands, and trembled like the plantain tree. The merciless ogress, then calling out, 'I am come to eat you,' ran to the chariot, and reaching it overturned it with its harnessed mules, as easily as a tiger brings a deer to the ground, and Vrinda and Smaraduti fell from it as an Ashoca tree when its root is cut. The ogress then ate the mules, and seizing Vrinda with her lion grasp, thus spake,—'Thy husband has been slain in battle by Hara, why shouldst thou any longer fear him? Drink, therefore, wine, eat meat, listen to the words of the go-between, and adopt the custom of an ogress.'"

CHAPTER XIV.

Vrinda is deceived by Vishnu, and afterwards obtains Beatitude by voluntary Death.

Narada continued.—"At this time Narayana clothed in barken garments, with an attendant, appeared, bearing fruits in his hand. On seeing whom, Smaraduti called out to Vrinda, and they, hearing the sound, approached, and said, 'Dispel thy fear, for we are come to save thee; but why hast thou entered this fearful forest, haunted by destructive animals?' Having thus assuaged her fears, Madhava addressed the ogress:—'Loose instantly that tender and lovely female. Eh! eh! thou wicked fool, what didst thou intend to do? Thinkest thou that thou mayst make every thing thy prey? But quickly release that beauteous goddess.' The ogress angrily replied,—'If thou hast strength sufficient, do thou liberate her from my hand.' Scarce had she said these words, when flames of wrath, darting from the eyes of Madhava, consumed her to ashes, and Vrinda escaped from her lifeless grasp. She then, deceived by illusion, thus addressed the god of the world:—'Who art thou, O holy devotee! who hast thus compassionately rescued my life from grief, pain, and dishonour? yet since thy sweet words deprived the ogress of life, let me in thy hermitage perform the duty of contemplation and abstraction.' The hermit replied,—'I am the son of Bharadwaja, named Devasharma, and having relinquished all worldly enjoyments, I have fixed my abode in this forest, with many Brahman youths and disciples, and, since thou wishest to perform abstracted devotion at my residence, come, O queen! and let us proceed to it, as it is situated at a distance.' Having thus spoken, he left the spot where lay the ashes of the ogress, and proceeded on slowly, while Vrinda and Smaraduti followed him. There arrived, they beheld a wonderful spot, where the various birds melodiously warbled, ponds covered with lotoses shone like gold, streams flowed with milk, trees dropped honey, and heaps of heavenly sugar, savoury food, and ornaments were falling from the sky. There the Muni having placed himself on a refulgent seat, covered with a tiger's skin, Vrinda not yet recovered from her alarm, thus addressed him:—'O lord, save me! Save me, O holy devotee! It is not in abstraction, contemplation, silence, and prayer, that consists devotion, but in the protection of the distressed.' On hearing these words, that wicked being, the enthraller of all souls, threw his arms around the gem-adorned neck of Vrinda, and clasped her enrapturing form in his embrace, as the creeper entwines around the Ashoca, and said,—'Again, and again will I embrace thee, who so excellest in all loveliness; but come into a hall most curiously adorned.' Vrinda then accompanied him into the hall, and having been seated on a regal couch, the Muni changed himself into the perfect form of Jalandhara, the same height, the same eyes, the same hair, and in every thing the same appearance. When Vrinda thus beheld the complete similitude of her beloved husband, she said,—'O my dear lord! say, what dost thou wish that thy suppliant should do?' The false son of the Ocean replied,—'O goddess! long did Shambhu and I contend in battle, until at last he smote off my head with his disc: but, as it had been destined, the head rejoined the body, and I became reanimated, and remembering, my beloved, that thou wouldst be grieved by my absence in battle, I have hastened to thee, that we might forget all anxieties in mutual pleasure.' Vrinda deceived by these words, and yielding to her transport, closely embraced and kissed her lord; and Narayana delighted found her embraces and kisses sweeter than those of Lakshmi. Thus Vrinda, the pain of absence being departed, sportively joined in pleasing dalliance with Madhava, as the swan gambols with her mate in a lotos-covered pond, and for many days more beauteous than Tulasi enjoyed with him in that forest the pleasures of love. At length one day as they lay enclasped, Vrinda perceived the true form of Vishnu, and immediately loosing her arms from his neck thus spoke,—'Who art thou, who hast thus deceived me in the form of a hermit?' This heard, Hari with soothing words replied,—'Listen, O Vrinda! know that I am the beloved of Lakshmi. Thy husband has gone to conquer Hara, and to carry away Gauri; but I am Shiva and Shiva is I: there is no difference between us; and as Jalandhara has been slain in battle, now enjoy pleasure with me.' Vrinda then said,—'If thou, my husband, disregarding thy father's counsel, hast fallen battle, in retribution for having carried away the wife of another,

Ishwara shall also suffer the penalty of his actions. Since, therefore, O Hari! thou hast deceived me in the assumed form of a hermit, and thus usurped the rights of a husband, may thy wife be also ravished from thee by similar deception!' Being thus cursed by Vrinda, Hari instantly disappeared, and at the same moment the hermitage and all that surrounded it vanished at once. On observing this, Vrinda exclaimed,—'Behold the crooked wiles of Vishnu!' then sighing said,—'Having forsaken my kingdom and city, and having been deceived in this forest, where can I now go, O Smaraduti?' Smaraduti replied, —'My life and thine are one.' Having thus resolved, they proceeded to a spacious pond, and having performed ablution in its water, and Vrinda having purified herself from the polluting touch of Vishnu, they seated themselves on the bank of a lotos-strewed couch, and, abstracting their minds from all earthly objects, observed a rigorous fast. Then, descending from heaven, a band of celestial nymphs approached Vrinda, and thus addressed her:—'Come, and through the power of the Gandharvas ascend into heaven without forsaking thy body; know that thy husband has been slain by Shiva. Why then shouldst thou give up thy life, because thou hast been deceived by the husband of Lakshmi? Come, mount this chariot, serve Chandibhadra, and enjoy the pleasures of heaven.' The spouse of Ocean's son replied,—'The wife of the chief of immortals was carried away, and forsaken by her valiant lord, and the pleasures of heaven are not so dear to me as the beatitude which I seek.' Having thus spoken, she left the Apsaras; but they, attached to her by the bonds of affection, continued to visit her until, consumed by the fire of devout abstraction, she resigned her breath and obtained supreme beatitude, when they burst forth in her praises, and poured on her from heaven a shower of flowers. Smaraduti then having collected dry wood, and placed the body of Vrinda on it, set fire to the pile, and leaped into it; and the mother of Vrinda, Svarna, having gathered her ashes together, threw them into the river of heaven. Hence the forest in which Vrinda gave up her life has been since named *Vrindavana*, and it is situated near the mountain *Goverdhana*."

CHAPTER XV.

Jalandhara's Deception unsuccessful.

Yudhisthira said,—"O Muni! relate in detail all that further took place between Gauri and the false Shiva." Narada replied:—"Parvati remained some time agitated and perplexed: at length, unable to decide, she arose and went out, determined to proceed to the Ganga, and on its banks to enter into holy contemplation. The milk-white Gauri then went on until she saw the Ganga falling from the sky into the lake Manasa; and, having adored the celestial river, and bathed in its holy stream, she seated herself with her companions on its bank. She then addressed one of them named Jaya, and said, — 'Assume my form, and hasten to him, and ascertain whether he be Shiva or some other person. If he should embrace and kiss thee, be assured that it is an Asura who has come in the form of Shambhu; but if he should say any thing, either good or bad, of me, he is undoubtedly the bearer of Pinaka.' Having received these orders, Jaya proceeded with speed to the false Shiva, who, seeing her approach, and inflamed with love, supposing her to be Gauri, clasped her in his arms. * Jaya, convinced that he could not be Rudra, and resuming her own form, thus addressed him, — 'By Shiva possessing far other strength shalt thou be slain.' Having ascertained the truth, she then returned to Uma, and thus spoke, — 'O goddess! he is Jalandhara, and not Shambhu thy beloved.' On hearing these words Parvati, in alarm, concealed herself in the bosom of a lotos; and her companions, becoming bees, fluttered around it.

"In the mean time her guardians, learning that their queen had been deceived by Vishnu, and that she had disappeared in the forest, were alarmed, and hastened to the battle-field, where, with fear, they related the circumstance to Shumbha. No sooner did Shumbha hear their alarming words than he left the conflict with Shiva, and despatched in haste Chanda and Munda to seek Jalandhara; who, having arrived with the swiftness of Danavas at Manasottara, and there found Jalandhara under the form of Shiva, they thus addressed him: — 'Why, O mighty king! hast thou retired to this place, where thy enemies cannot see thee, nor thy friends receive thy support? Shumbha has been defeated, and thy army been slain by Rudra. Come, therefore, come and engage in battle; for thou canst not obtain Parvati. How can the wife of the five-faced be obtained by an Asura? or how can the sun be dimmed with darkness? Return therefore with speed, for thy wife has been carried away by the foe of Mura. Having heard this intelligence, fight valiantly, and vanquish Shiva in battle.' This heard, Jalandhara, his eyes red with anger, departed from the mountain, having thrown aside the form of Shiva; and as he proceeded along he assuaged the fear of Chanda and Munda. He then said to Durvarana: — 'See, O Durvarana! what Vishnu has now done, and how he has deceived

* But I must here use the words of Nonnus: — Θερμον ακοντιζων αυτοσσυτον αφρον ερωτων.

Vrinda under a delusive form.' Durvarana replied, —'O king! what a man enjoys or suffers proceeds from his own actions: thou didst attempt to ravish the wife of Shiva; and thy own wife has been ravished by Vishnu.' Touched by these words, Jalandhara thought for a moment, and then said, —'Say, whether shall I hasten to conquer Shiva, or Hari the assumer of two forms?' Durvarana replied, —'If thou conquer Shiva, thou wilt obtain all thy wishes, and may then easily vanquish Govinda. But now hasten and encourage the Danavas, of whom such numbers have been slain in battle; and engage in terrible combat with Shiva.' Having heard these words, Jalandhara proceeded to the battle field."

CHAPTER XVI.

The Battle between Shiva and Jalandhara.

Narada continued.—"On arriving at the battle field, Jalandhara beheld a fearful scene of carnage, over which progress was impeded by headless corses, dissevered heads, mangled flesh, and scattered brains. Grieved at the sight, and lamenting the death of many Danavas dear to him, Jalandhara looked around the field for Shiva, and saw him seated on a bull, ornamented with horrific snakes, his matted locks adorned with the crescent moon, and his eyes glowing like fire. Quickly then the son of Ocean mounting his chariot, said to Shumbha, —'Why was not this devotee slain by thee?' Shumbha replied,—'How could he be slain? It is impossible for us to vanquish that devotee.' Hearing these words, Jalandhara was filled with anger, and rushed on, accompanied by myriads of Danavas, to attack Hara; and, bending his ebony bow, and selecting sharp, strong, and iron-pointed arrows, the son of Ocean poured them as rain from the clouds on the lord of Parvati; and Shambhu with his shafts piercing the armour of Jalandhara, scattered it in pieces on the ground, and caused his shield to fall like a mountain to the earth. Then Shiva covered the body of Jalandhara with arrows, whence blood gushed in streams that overflowed the battle field. The Danavas, struck with fear, trembling fled; but Jalandhara, undismayed, called aloud to Shiva, —'Thou art an excellent archer; but I will this instant destroy thee, if thou fliest not, with my arrows.' This said, he covered the body of Shiva with arrows thick as birds in the sky, or trees on a mountain. Virabhadra perceiving Shambhu thus encompassed with arrows, in anger rushed against Jalandhara; but the son of Ocean destroyed with his shafts the bow, the quiver, the flag, the car, and the charioteer of Virabhadra; who, still advancing with a mace, Jalandhara felled him to the ground with a blow of his mace. Manibhadra beholding Virabhadra extended senseless, rushed forward, and, as he came on, the son of Ocean overwhelmed him with arrows. At this moment Virabhadra, recovering from his trance, joined Manibhadra, and they fell on Jalandhara like mountains falling from the sky. Virabhadra with his fist attacked the son of Ocean, and Manibhadra seizing him by the feet attempted to whirl him from his chariot; but the mighty Jalandhara, striking Manibhadra with his foot and Virabhadra with his fist, overthrew them on the ground. Then Nandi advanced with Shiva's troops, and Shumbha observing his approach, rushed forward with the Danavas; and the two hosts in mutual conflict joined.

[The description of this battle is omitted, as it is scarcely more than a repetition of what has occurred before.]

"Skanda was now proceeding to attack Jalandhara, when Shankara, fearing for his son, interposed, and a terrible battle took place between him and the son of Ocean. Then Jalandhara, enraged, having selected a ponderous and fearful arrow, directed it at the forehead of Shiva; but it was consumed by the beams of his eye. Hara then pierced with an arrow the breast of Ocean's son, and streams of blood gushed from the wound; while, like a mountain struck by a thunderbolt, Jalandhara fell, and loud lamentations arose from the army of the Daityas. Shiva, perceiving that Jalandhara was senseless, attacked the Danavas with his troops, and, as long as Jalandhara remained insensible, pursued them with destructive havoc. After a long time, having recovered from his trance, the son of Ocean beheld with terror his army scattered in flight over the battle ground, and immediately summoned in thought his mighty preceptor, who instantly appeared, and, having recovered Jalandhara, enquired what he wished him to do. Having paid due obeisance to his preceptor, Jalandhara replied:— 'Reanimate, O Kavi! all the Danavas who have been slain.' This said, he looked to the field of battle, and beheld it strewed for thousands of yojanas with the corses of Danavas. Then Kavi, with charms and incantations, restored them to life; as far as the place where Shiva displayed his matted locks and snaky ornaments, so far did Kavi, by words of power, reanimate the slaughtered Danavas. When Shiva saw the lifeless corses upstarting in various forms, he thought,—'Who is this that thus restores the dead to life?' And while he thus reflected he saw Shukra engaged in incantation; and, enraged, rushed with uplifted trident to slay him: but Kavi, laughing, said,—'I am a Brahman;

how then can he who is acquainted with all duties slay me? O Rudra! dost thou wish to incur again the guilt of Brahmanicide?' Hearing these words, Shankara, remembering his former action, and the head of Brahma, which he is doomed to hold continually, liberated Shukra, and said, — 'A Brahman certainly is not to be slain; but that Daitya, whom thou hast recovered, and who is my aversion, I will quickly slay, and afterwards I will kill him nine times more when he is born in mortal wombs.' Having thus spoken, a hideous and terrific female form sprang from his third eye, whom he ordered to punish Bhargava. She immediately ran to Kavi; and, on seeing her, he fell on the ground, and the Danavas, in terror, fled; but she, dragging him by the hair, clasped him to her naked body. Jalandhara seeing his preceptor thus abused and dragged about, discharged his arrows at the fiend, until she at length disappeared."

CHAPTER XVII.

The Death of Jalandhara.

Narada continued. — "Then Jalandhara exclaimed, — 'Now, guard thy life, O Shiva, for I will instantly destroy thee and thy troops, then Madhusudana, and afterwards dragging Brahma along, I will hurl him into the sea; and having thus vanquished you, I will be alone the supreme god.' Having thus spoken, he again arrayed his army, led on by all the mighty Danavas, who had been slain before, and advancing, encountered the troops of Shiva, commanded by Virabhadra. Then raged a long and terrible combat, and the loud tumult of war arose, as Pramathas and Danavas in conflict joined. At last the troops of Shiva, overpowered by the Daityas, fled to Meru, and they closing surrounded Shankara, who, urging on his bull and drawing his bow, slew innumerable Danavas with his arrows, and spread havoc through their ranks.

"At this time Jalandhara formed by magic skill a figure similar to that of Gauri; lovely, possessed of every excellence, and adorned with all kinds of ornaments; and then formed one like Jaya, and directed her to hasten to the battle field, and to deceive Shankara. She immediately proceeded to Shiva, and stood before him with dishevelled hair and weeping. Interrogated by Hara, she said, — 'Thy beloved goddess has been carried away from the mountain of Manasottara by the son of Ocean.' This heard, Shiva said, — 'O Jaya, mount my bull, and the Danavas shall not injure thee.' Then Jaya mounted the bull, and clasping Shankara with her arms said, — 'Let us hasten, for Parvati will not live without Hara.' Having learned the rape of Gauri, Shiva reflected on the wiles of the Daityas, and remained undecided whether he should leave the battle. At this moment he beheld the son of Ocean advancing amidst his army with his beloved Gauri in his chariot, exposed to the view of the Asuras, afflicted by the pain of absence, disconsolate, and exclaiming, — 'O my beloved lord! O Rudra!' Shambhu, thus deceived by the illusions of the Asura, thought that the form and the lamentations of Gauri were real, and stood lost in grief and perplexity, considering how she could have been carried away by his enemy. When the son of Ocean observed Shankara thus subdued by the delusion, he approached him and said, — 'O Smara! thou art despoiled of every thing, and hast lost thy chiefest ornament; for what can Ishwara be without Ambika? But lament not, Shiva, as I will restore to thee thy beloved, and will protect thee in battle.' Having thus spoken, he caused Gauri to descend from his chariot, and Hara at the same time urged forward his bull to the midst of the Danava's army, where Gauri was exclaiming, 'Save me, save me!' But, as Shiva was about to take hold of Gauri, Shumbha drew her back; and Hara enraged hurled his trident at him, but Shumbha avoided the weapon, and it struck Parvati. Weeping and repeating the name of Rudra, the delicate and lovely Gauri fell lifeless before Shiva; and, beholding the inanimate form of Parvati, overcome by grief and delusion, and exclaiming, 'O my beloved!' Shankara sunk senseless on the ground. Recovering then on the field of battle, the lord of Uma thus cursed Shumbha and the Daityas: —'Gauri shall still slay the chiefs of the Danavas;' and in another age, O Yudhishtira! Shumbha and the other Daityas were slain by Gauri in consequence of the curse of Maheshwara. Having cursed them, Shankara thus lamented aloud :—'Where, O my beloved! has thy spirit fled, and why hast thou forsaken me in the dangers of battle, and thus left me to the pain of absence? How canst thou again forsake me, as thou formerly didst when thou didst cast thyself into the sacrificial fire of Daksha, and wert the cause of his head being cut off? Arise, arise, O my beloved! and restore me to peace and joy.' At this time Brahma, perceiving Shiva overpowered by delusion, hastened from heaven, and thus addressed him absorbed in grief: —'O Mahadeva! thou hast overcome the illusions of father and mother, of wife and children, of pleasure and pain, of getting and being begotten; thou knowest illusions, for thou causest them to arise in varied forms, numerous as the beams of the sun or the waves of the sea, and none can acquire, except by abstracted meditation, a knowledge of thy true and essential form. How then, O lord! dost thou now yield to delusion? This is not thy beloved; overcome, therefore, the wiles which have been invented by this Jalandhara. Parvati has taken refuge in the bosom of a lotos; fight then valiantly and vanquish thy enemies.' Having heard the words of Brahma, Maheshwara was restored to the powers of perfect discrimination; and knowing the form to be that of a deceitful Danavi, he hurled at it a huge rock, by which myriads of Daityas were at the same time slain, and then mounted his bull inflamed with wrath.

" But Jalandhara quickly manifested another deception. For he caused the battle ground to appear like a country ornamented with mountains and forests, with pleasing groves and temples, where heavenly nymphs with song and dance enraptured the senses. Shiva was instantly deluded by the delightful scene, and remained motionless, charmed by the harmonious voices and sportive movements of the nymphs. On beholding him thus captivated, the son of Ocean laughed aloud, but the immortals, alarmed, thus addressed him: —' O Shambhu! art thou again deceived by the wiles of Jalandhara? Why dost thou not hurl at him that disc so wonderfully produced, and thus slay him in battle?' His recollection being thus recalled, Shiva, mounting his bull, hastened to battle Then awful appeared the blazing form of Hara, the creator and destroyer, as in wrath he moved along, and his third eye shot forth consuming beams; and Shumbha and the Daityas, terror-struck, trembling, fled for refuge to the deepest recesses of Patala. But Jalandhara, undismayed, stood unmoved on the battle ground, beholding with joy the true form of Hara thus manifestly revealed. Shiva then said, —' O son of Ocean! demand a boon; as I am pleased with thee, since thou hast fearless dared to gaze upon my form, the refulgence of which few can endure.' This heard, Jalandhara demanded supreme beatitude, as a boon, from Hara. Shiva replied, —' Enjoy a celestial body endowed with immortal powers; for, O ignorant one! how canst thou desire beatitude? Vrinda, thy beloved queen, though deceived by illusion, has, by becoming acquainted with the essence of the supreme being, obtained beatitude; but difficult is it in this world of existence to obtain final emancipation: demand, therefore, some other boon.' Jalandhara replied, —' O god! I will by some action obtain beatitude, and attain emancipation unslain by thee.' Shiva said, —' My abode is surpassing in excellence; and, if thou wishest to ascend there, engage in combat with me; and, when thou art slain by my arrows, thou wilt ascend into my abode.' Jalandhara replied, —' But I will, before that, attack thee.' Having thus spoken to each other, Shiva, bending his bow, covered with arrows the body of the son of Ocean, so that it shone like a mountain of iron glowing with fire; and Jalandhara showered arrows on Rudra, which cast a radiance over him like the beams of the sun. Long thus they fought. At length Shiva struck with his trident the Danava on his breast, when instantly sprang from his mouth a horrific fiend, named Jwara, in human form, but with a lion's head; on seeing whom, Rudra muttered words of power, and a terrible *Sharaba* immediately rushed forward and slew the fiend. Jalandhara then, thinking that Shankara was invincible as long as he remained mounted on his bull, advanced, and seizing it by the tail, and whirling it round, hurled it on the summit of Himavan; then, mounting his car and bending his bow, he rushed forward. But Shiva with his resistless arrows pierced the charioteer and horses, and shattered the car to pieces. Dismounted, but undismayed, Jalandhara advanced, and long and terrible the battle raged between the lord of Parvati and the son of Ocean; and, as under their feet the earth trembled, and the heaven resounded with the tumult, the gods and Danavas feared that the time of universal destruction had arrived. Then Jalandhara, being deprived of all his weapons, assumed a thousand dreadful arms, and strove to bind Shiva within his mighty hands; but Shankara with his cimeter lopped off that forest of arms. Yet still the son of Ocean continued to fight valiantly, until Shankara, being delighted, thus spoke:—'I am pleased with thy valour, O Jalandhara! demand a boon, however difficult it may be to be obtained.' Jalandhara replied,—'Grant me, O Rudra! thy state of immortality: but it is not proper that thou shouldst commit the disgrace of killing me on account of a female; let me therefore destroy myself.' Having thus spoken, a hand sprang up, with which he mortally wounded himself on the breast. Then Shiva, grasping the disc Sudarshana, refulgent as a thousand suns, smote off his head with such force that it fell on Himavan, and as it fell the earth trembled; and his lifeless corse for some time danced amidst the gore and carnage of the battle field. But quickly the head rejoined the trunk, and repeatedly did it regain its wonted place after having been dissevered by Shiva. Shankara then scattered the Daitya's marrow over the earth, from which circumstance it has received the name of Medini, and the blood flowed away in copious streams, and the flesh appeared like a huge mountain. On observing which, Shiva summoned in thought the Yoginis, who instantly appeared, and thus with folded hands addressed him:—'O Shiva! what shall we do?' He replied,—'Quickly, in obedience to my command, devour the flesh of that Daitya.' Then Brahmi, Maheshwari, Kaumari, Vaishnavi, Varahi, and Mahendri, with cruel looks, hastened to devour the flesh of Jalandhara. Shiva then said to them,—'Drink up the blood:' and they, delighted, immediately quaffed the gory stream, and danced with joy.

"After this, Shiva summoned in thought Bhavani and his bull, and they immediately came. Having quitted the form of a bee, and accompanied by her damsels, the beloved of Hara appeared, and again enjoyed his embraces."

APPENDIX E.

THE DEVI UPANISHAD.

All the gods approached Devi, and said, — "Who art thou?" Maha Devi replied, — "I am the visible form of Brahm: from me proceeded Purusha and Prakriti, the causes of this universe: I am space and *vacuum:* I am joy and grief: I am knowledge and ignorance: I am Brahma and Brahmini: I am the five primary atoms, the five elements, and all that is: I am the Vedas, and all sacred learning: I am born and unborn: I am all that is above and below: I range with the Rudras and the Vasavas, the Adityas, the Maruts, and the Vishvadevas: I support Mitra and Varuna, Indra, Agni, and the Ashwinau: I support Soma, Twashta, Pushau, Bhaga: I support Vishnu the omnipotent, and Brahma the creator. He, therefore, who knows my divine nature, obtains felicity." The gods said, — "Praise be to thee, O mighty and felicitous goddess! praise be to thee eternally; praise be to thee, O Durga! O Devi! the cause of all things, resplendent with glory, delighting in rewarding good works, and liberating him who seeks thy protection from the evils of transitory existence. We adore thee, O Kalfarattri! for thou art Vaishnavi the mother of the Vedas, Sarasvati, Aditi the daughter of Daksha, from whom we were produced, the pure and happy. We acknowledge thee to be Maha Lakshmi; and we meditate upon thee as the sole and universal energy (*Shakti*); enlighten, then, O goddess! our understandings." *

He who knows that goddess, who displays in her hands a noose, an *ankush*†, a bow and arrow, to be the supreme energy, the deluder of the universe, the source of prosperity and learning, passes over the sea of transitory existence. Praise, therefore, be to thee, O Baghavati! Protect us always,

* Here follows a *mantra*, or sacred invocation, which, being expressed in words bearing a symbolical and mystic meaning, I cannot interpret, as the original is not accompanied with a commentary. The use, however, of this mystic language is a curious circumstance; but I doubt much whether any Brahman would explain it.

† A kind of hook used for guiding an elephant.

O mother! who art the eight Vasavas, the eleven Rudras, the twelve Suns, the Vishvadevas, the Yatudharas, Asuras, Rakshasas, Pisachas, Yakshas, and Siddhas; who art the qualities of purity, impurity, and darkness; who art the form of Brahma, Vishnu, and Rudra; who art the gods, the prajapatis, and men; who art the planets, stars, and heaven. Thee do we continually adore, O Devi! for thou art the destroyer of sin, the giver of bliss and final beatitude; eternal, victorious, immaculate, felicitous, and the bestower of felicity and protection. For whoever meditates on the one syllable (*hri*), which is thy peculiar invocation, with a pure mind, shall be liberated from Maya; and, obtaining divine knowledge, he shall become a participator in the bliss ineffable of the one God. He, also, who wishes for eternal happiness, let him in the morning, fixing his thoughts on thy form, represented with four hands (two holding a noose and *ankush*, and two as if bestowing a boon and protection), with three eyes, and clothed in red garments, thus worship thee: — I adore thee, O Maha Devi! destroyer of fear, the deliverer from misery, the incarnate form of compassion; who art named incomprehensible, because neither Brahma nor the gods know thy real nature; who art without beginning or end, therefore called eternal, infinite, because none can ascertain thy extrémities; unborn, because no one is acquainted with thy birth; one and many, because, though one, thou pervadest all things. Thou art the meaning of words, the principal elements of invocations, and the essence of knowledge. I adore thee, O Durga, O Devi! the destroyer of the wicked, the supreme goddess; be thou my deliverer from the fearful sea of mortality! *

* This Upanishad concludes, as in the *Narayana*, with an enumeration of the advantages which will be derived from reciting and meditating upon it.

APPENDIX F.

THE GANAPATI UPANISHAD. *

PRAISE be to thee, O Ganapati! thou art manifestly the truth; thou art undoubtedly the creator, the preserver, and destroyer; thou art certainly Brahm, the eternal spirit. I speak what is right and true: preserve me, therefore, when speaking, when listening, when giving, when possessing, when teaching, when learning, when in the west, the east, the north, or the south, when above or below; continually protect me every where. Thou art in essence speech, intellect, and divine knowledge; thou art manifestly the adualistic and universal spirit, by which this universe was produced, is preserved, and shall be destroyed. By thee was this universe manifested; for thou art earth, water, fire, air, and ether; thou art the three qualities, the three kinds of bodies †, the three times, and the three energies; and on thee do *Yogis* continually meditate. Thou art Brahma, Vishnu, and Rudra; thou art Indra, Agni, Vaiu, Surya, and Soma. *Om, bhur, bhuv, swar, gam,* praise be to thee, O Ganapati! we acknowledge thy divinity, O Ekadanta! and meditate on thy countenance; enlighten, therefore, our understandings. He who continually meditates upon thy divine form, conceiving it to be with one tooth, with four hands (one holding a noose, one an *ankush,* another a tooth, and the other as if granting a boon), bearing a rat on thy banner, of a red hue, with a large belly, anointed with red perfumes, arrayed in red garments, worshipped with offerings of red flowers, abounding in compassion, the cause of this universe, imperishable, unproduced, and unaffected by creation ‡, becomes the most excellent of *Yogis.* Praise, therefore, be to thee,

* This Upanishad forms part of the *Atharva Shiras* Upanishad.

† Divine, human, and irrational.

‡ It is to be remarked that the Hindus consider God to be susceptible of two states of being; *without form or quality,* and *with form and quality:* and though the former is his real and essential nature, still, in meditating upon him, the weakness of the faculties of the human mind requires that he should always be invested with some material form on which the thoughts may be fixed. Hence it is, that in the Vedas and Upanishads a form is attributed to that *ens* which is described in them to be an immaterial and incorporeal spirit.

O Ganapati! the destroyer of difficulties, the son of Shiva, the granter of boons to thy votaries. Whoever meditates upon this picture of the *Atharva Shiras* never will be impeded by difficulties; his happiness will increase; he will be liberated from the five great sins, and all lesser ones; and he will acquire riches, the objects of his desires, virtue, and final beatitude. Except to a pupil, this portion of the *Atharva Shiras* must not be communicated to another; and whoever communicates it to one spiritually blind shall incur sin; but whoever meditates upon it shall attain his every wish. Whoever, also, on the fourth of each half-month, repeats it fasting, shall acquire eloquence and learning.

THE END.